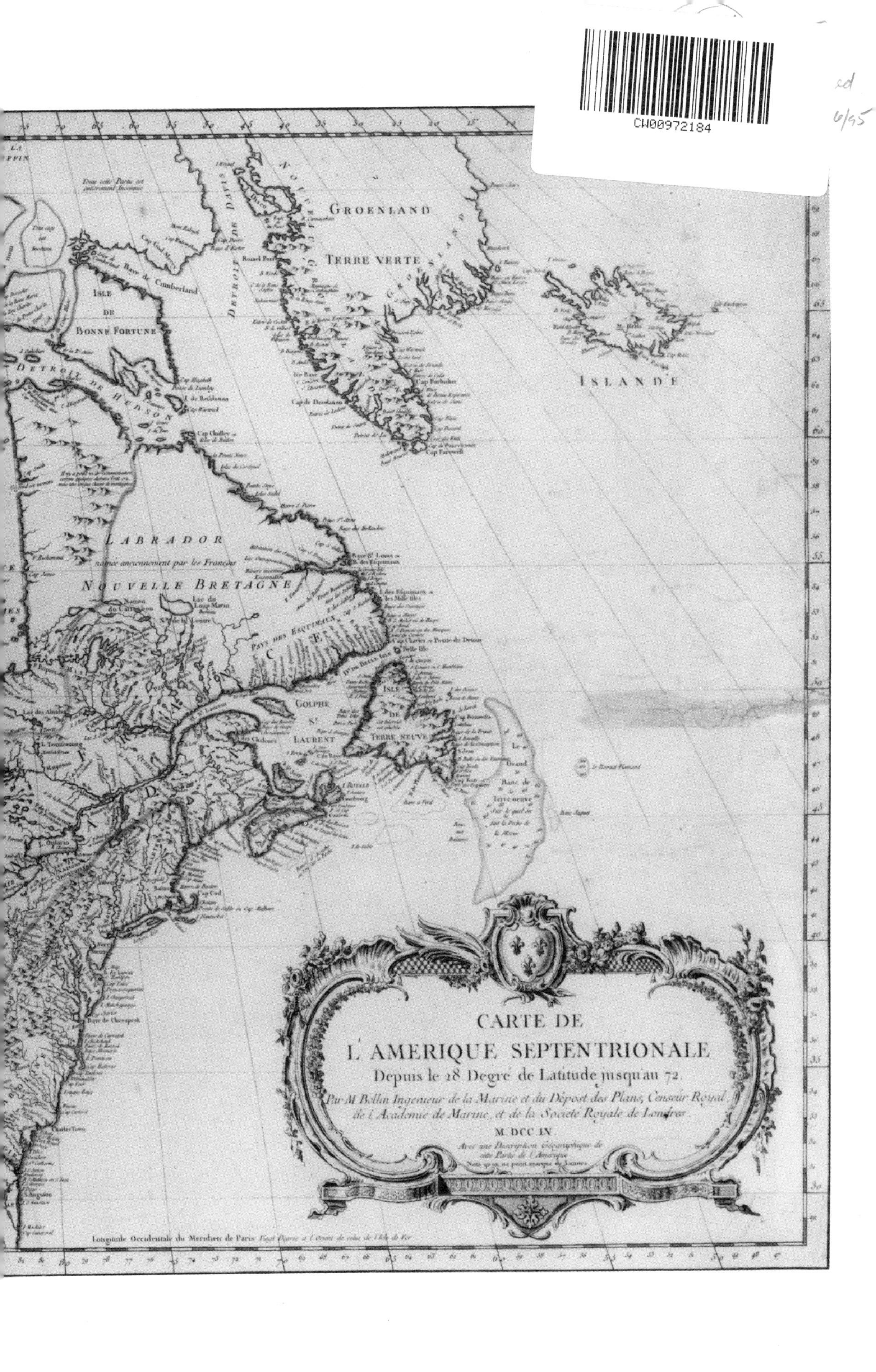
CARTE DE
L'AMERIQUE SEPTENTRIONALE
Depuis le 28 Degré de Latitude jusqu'au 72.
Par M. Bellin Ingenieur de la Marine et du Dépost des Plans, Censeur Royal
de l'Academie de Marine, et de la Societé Royale de Londres.
M.DCC.LV.
Avec une Description Géographique de
cette Partie de l'Amerique
Nota qu'on na point marqué de Limites
GROENLAND
TERRE VERTE
ISLANDE
DETROIT DE DAVIS
Baye de Cumberland
ISLE DE BONNE FORTUNE
DETROIT DE HUDSON
I. de Resolution
Cap Chidley
Cap de Desolation
Cap Farewell
LABRADOR
nommée anciennement par les François
NOUVELLE BRETAGNE
PAYS DES ESQUIMAUX
Lac du Loup Marin
Belle Isle
GOLPHE St. LAURENT
ISLE DE TERRE NEUVE
Le Grand Banc de Terre neuve sur le quel on fait la Peche de la Morue
Cap Cod
Baye de Chesapeak
Charles Town
Longitude Occidentale du Meridien de Paris

The Fur Trade Revisited

The Fur Trade Revisited

Selected Papers of the Sixth North American Fur Trade Conference, Mackinac Island, Michigan, 1991

Jennifer S. H. Brown, W. J. Eccles and Donald P. Heldman, Editors

Michigan State University Press
Mackinac State Historic Parks
East Lansing/Mackinac Island
1994

All Michigan State University Press books are produced on paper which meets the requirements of American National Standard of Information Sciences - Permanence of paper for printed materials ANSI Z39.48-1984

Michigan State University Press
East Lansing, Michigan 48823-5202

This project partially funded by MICHIGAN HUMANITIES COUNCIL

Printed in the United States of America

02 01 00 99 98 97 96 95 94 1 2 3 4 5 6 7 8 9

End sheets: "Carte De L'Amerique Septentrionale. . .MDCCLV," Bellin. Courtesy of the William L. Clements Library, University of Michigan, Ann Arbor, Michigan.

Cartography courtesy of the Center for Cartographic Research and Spacial Analysis, Michigan State University.

Library of Congress Cataloging-in-Publication Data

North American Fur Trade Conference (6th : 1991 : Mackinac Island, Mich.)
The fur trade revisited : selected papers of the sixth North American Fur Trade Conference, Mackinac Island, Michigan, 1991 / Jennifer S. H. Brown, W. J. Eccles, and Donald P. Heldman, editors.
p. cm.
Includes index.
ISBN 0-87013-348-9
1. Fur trade—North America—History—Congresses. I. Brown, Jennifer S. H., 1940- . II. Eccles, W. J. (William John) III. Heldman, Donald P. IV. Title.
HD9944.N6N67 1991
380.1'.456753'0971—dc20

94-11964
CIP

Contents

Part III
Becoming a Trader: Origins, Lives, and Survival

Part IV
The Fur Trade at Mackinac

Part V
Archaeology and Material Culture

Part VI
Into the Twentieth Century

Part VII
Fur Trade Literature and Interpretation: Issues and Problems

Illustrations

Foreword

Since 1958, the Mackinac Island State Park Commission has operated a professional, historic sites program at the Straits of Mackinac, restoring or reconstructing Fort Mackinac, Colonial Michilimackinac, and Historic Mill Creek. Archaeological, architectural and historical research have been cornerstones of the Commission's work. Commission staff have assembled extensive documentary and artifact resources, making them available as the basis for interpretive exhibits and programs. The Commission is committed to dissemination of research findings through an active publications program.

Commission sponsorship of the Sixth North American Fur Trade Conference was undertaken in this tradition. The 1991 conference offered the opportunity for scholars to gather at Mackinac Island to share current developments in the study of the fur trade with colleagues, museum staff, and the public. Publication of the selected papers will make the results of the conference available to a wider audience and will have immediate use in the development of accurate historic site and museum exhibits, programs, and live interpretation at our facilities and elsewhere.

The Fur Trade Conference project offers the rare opportunity for the results of scholarly research to be quickly assimilated into historical presentations for a large public audience. The Commission and its staff are grateful to Dennis M. Au for his work as project director, to each of the scholars who contributed, to the numerous donors who supported the project, to the staff of the Michigan State University Press who enthusiastically agreed to publish this volume, and to readers who will use these materials to continue the questioning, analysis, and discussion which furthers our understanding of the fur trade and those who lived by it.

Carl R. Nold
Director
Mackinac Island State Park Commission

Foreword

Preface

Outstanding, extraordinary, and superb are all adjectives that participants used to describe the Sixth North American Fur Trade Conference at Grand Hotel on Mackinac Island, Michigan on September 25-29, 1991. Its excitement, theme, and flavor all came to a crest at the Saturday evening banquet finale. The orchestra's playing and the audience's stirring singing of the American and Canadian national anthems left no doubt of the international focus which is the hallmark of these meetings.

Several gestures that night emphasized the heritage of the fur trade. In the fashion of the Beaver Club, the exclusive fraternity of the North West Company wintering partners, we raised glasses to the fur trade and remembered Marjorie Wilkins Campbell, Grace Lee Nute, and Robert Wheeler, colleagues in fur trade scholarship whose passing we mourned. When Hugh MacMillan asked registrants to recognize their fur trade ancestors, at least a third of the assembly rose. The symbolic handshake between Earl Boon of the new North West Company and Christopher Dafoe, representing *The Beaver* magazine and the Hudson's Bay Company, also brought to mind the historic rivalry of these companies and the cooperative spirit of scholarly inquiry that brought us together for discussions and socialization. As the orchestra played the old fur trade fiddle tunes such as "Whiskey Before Breakfast" and "Duck Dance," memories of the past bubbled through the audience.

Could there be more? Yes! We broke with tradition in selecting a featured speaker. No research paper this time. The speaker, Lily McAuley, from Churchill, Manitoba, proved a most fitting selection. A self-described "half-breed," she grew up on the traplines in the Canadian North. Articulate and expressive, Lily touched all in the audience. Lily's early life experience represented the heart and core of the fur trade: following seasonal "circles," learning to live off nature's resources, and mingling Native and European societies. We hope that the transcript of her address will focus the reader as it did the audience on the central fact that the fur trade is a particularly fascinating story of *people* interacting with nature and of exchanges between Native and European cultures.

Putting together a successful conference involves scores of individuals. We had the good fortune to build on the success of five previous meetings and especially on the preceding one at Montreal in 1985. Indeed, in the excitement of the Montreal gathering, Charles "Chuck" Hoover of the Historical Society of Saginaw County's (Michigan) Museum had envisioned Mackinac as the next site.

While Hoover initially explored the possibility of having the meeting in Michigan, credit must be given to the Mackinac Island State Park Commission and its director, David L. Pamperin, for the decision to host the conference on Mackinac Island. The Commission made a considerable commitment of staff and financial resources. Pamperin, and after June 1991, Acting Director David A. Armour, saw this commitment through to the successful symposium. Since January 1992, Director Carl R. Nold has backed the efforts to publish this volume.

The Park Commission and its staff recognized that Mackinac was an appropriate place for the meeting. For millennia Native people gathered here. In Indian lore and religion Mackinac had spiritual and cultural significance. Indians and Europeans paddled through the Straits on their way to and from Quebec and to other important destinations in the heart of North America ranging from Saskatchewan and Alberta to Illinois and Missouri. When the French expanded their quest for furs inland in the late seventeenth and early eighteenth centuries, they quickly recognized their trading posts west of Lakes Michigan and Superior depended on the establishment at Michilimackinac. Mackinac remained a major trade entrepôt until the 1830s under the French, British, and finally the American flag.

Today, Mackinac State Historic Parks carries on the legacy of the fur trade at its sites in Mackinaw City and on Mackinac Island. Initiated in 1959, the Parks' archaeological research at Michilimackinac, Mackinac Island, and Mill Creek is at the forefront of historical archaeology in North America. Recent initiatives in historical research have contributed significantly to the understanding of the fur trade and of the people who participated in it at Mackinac and throughout a large part of the continent. By sponsoring the Sixth North American Fur Trade Conference, Mackinac State Historic Parks provided a major opportunity for sharing new research and interpretations of the fur trade.

Central to the success of the conference was the Parks' staff who served as chairs. Curator of Archaeology, Donald P. Heldman, provided crucial intellectual guidance and direction in planning the meeting. His contacts in the anthropological community proved vital. Keith R. Widder, Curator of History, in turn attended to the details and protocol that make a conference work and did many of the necessary chores to bring this publication to completion. I depended on these gentlemen for much and not enough credit can be given to them.

Many other members of the Parks' staff helped with the conference, too. I must commend them all for the teamwork that made this meeting a success. I am especially grateful to Lana Cotton, Ron Crandell, Jim Evans, William H. Fritz, Dennis Havlena, Phil Porter, Mary Soper, Kay Stemkoski, and Larry Young. Members of the Parks' adjunct society, the Mackinac Associates, also lent a hand. Among the

Associates who volunteered were Kathy McVeigh, Lornie Porter, and Robert Raisch.

My work on this conference started with assembling an advisory council of scholars, people involved with past meetings, and key personnel at fur trade sites and heritage institutions. This committee provided guidance, acted as a sounding board for ideas, and served as a network for publicity, professional contacts, and institutional support. The eighteen people on this council were R.A. Bobiwash, formerly of the Native Canadian Centre of Toronto, Jennifer S.H. Brown, the University of Winnipeg, René Chartrand, Parks Canada (Ottawa), Robert Coutts, Parks Canada (Winnipeg), Christopher Dafoe, *The Beaver*, Rhoda R. Gilman, Minnesota Historical Society, Normand Gouger, *Archives nationales du Québec*, Donald P. Heldman, Mackinac State Historic Parks, Thomas L. Jones, Historical Society of Michigan, F.A. Ketterson, Jr., U.S. National Park Service (Omaha), Hugh MacMillan, Nor'Wester Partners, Toby Morantz, McGill University, H. Nicholas Muller III, State Historical Society of Wisconsin, David L. Pamperin, formerly of the Mackinac State Historic Parks, now of the State Historical Society of Wisconsin, James Schultz, Bureau of History, Michigan Department of State, Victoria Stewart, Lake St. Louis Historical Society (Montreal), James Thayer, Oregon Historical Society, and Wilcomb E. Washburn, Office of American Studies, Smithsonian Institution. They were a stellar group; a simple word of thanks is hardly adequate to express our gratitude for all of their efforts.

One advisory council member, however, deserves special recognition. Victoria Stewart of Montreal's Lake St. Louis Historical Society organized the previous conference, and we constantly drew on her experience.

The advisory council also provided suggestions and leads for fundraising. As a result several institutions made financial or substantive contributions. The previous conference sponsor, the Lake St. Louis Historical Society of Montreal donated seed money to get this meeting off the ground and pitched in to help with transportation. The Michigan Humanities Council awarded a matching grant to help fund the meeting and this volume. Mackinac Associates contributed with this book in mind. Lake Superior State University helped bring our banquet speaker, Lily McAuley, to Mackinac; and thanks to Donald Gerrie, who also provided transportation for some of our speakers. The Hudson's Bay Company continued its generous support of our historical endeavor, and the new North West Company was especially conspicuous in its backing. Revillon, the Fur Council of Canada, and the Fur Institute of Canada also contributed. The Bureau of Michigan History of the Michigan Department of State, Historical Society of Michigan, Minnesota Historical Society, Oregon Historical Society, and State Historical Society of Wisconsin provided valuable assistance. The Marquette Mission Park and Museum of Ojibwa Culture and Father Marquette Museum and National Memorial at St. Ignace and the Robert Stuart House on Mackinac Island all opened their facilities and lent their staffs. The wine at the banquet came courtesy of the Michigan Grape and Wine Industry Council. We appreciate the roles these patrons played!

Good speakers are essential to the success of a conference. Fortunately, we had an overwhelming response to our call for papers. Choosing from among the proposals was quite a task, but our paper selection committee proved equal to the job. They were a varied group with one thing in common, a deep interest in, and knowledge of, fur trade history. The five members were: Jennifer S.H. Brown, Professor of History, the University of Winnipeg; W.J. Eccles, Professor Emeritus of history, University of Toronto; Rhoda R. Gilman, Senior Research Fellow at the Minnesota Historical Society; Donald P. Heldman, Curator of Archaeology, Mackinac State Historic Parks; and Keith R. Widder, Curator of History, Mackinac State Historic Parks.

After the conference, three members of the committee, Brown, Eccles, and Heldman, took on the responsibility of editing this volume. On some matters pertaining to the fur trade in the western United States, they tapped the expertise of Professor Richard G. Beidleman, who, before retiring, taught at Colorado College. This was anything but a rubber stamp committee! All three are experienced scholars and editors in this area of history. They pored over the manuscripts checking sources, questioning conclusions, suggesting stylistic improvements, and working to make this volume of diverse papers polished and unified. This book's professional cast is in no small part the result of their efforts. We owe them a tremendous debt of gratitude.

The Michigan State University Press staff also played a central role in this publication. Right from our initial inquiry they expressed excitement and eagerly took on this book. Among their many staff members who worked on this publication, we owe special recognition to the Editor in Chief, Julie L. Loehr, who coordinated the editing and publishing, Ellen Link who did the copy editing, and cartographer Ellen White who drew most of the maps. They did a fine job!

In the early phase of this publication, the Rupert's Land Research Centre at the University of Winnipeg took an interest in this book and is supporting its production by distributing it as their annual membership publication. I must add additional words of appreciation to the authors who appear here and the other presenters. Their scholarship was the real substance of the conference. What is more, they and the session chairs responded like troopers to what must have seemed like dictatorial mandates to keep the conference sessions on schedule and to get their papers to me promptly.

Both the speakers and the audience were a mixed lot in their fields and backgrounds. Perhaps this was one of the reasons the meeting was such a success. A good example was the session on the late nineteenth- and early twentieth-century developments in the fur trade. Chaired by an activist Native North American, it featured a panel consisting of a historian looking at the economic shifts in the business, a librarian examining literary contributions, and a graduate student who focused on trends in Hudson's Bay Company public relations. These differences proved only superficial, and the papers inspired a lively exchange with anthropologists, Canadians, Americans, fur industry representatives, and avocationals adding their opinions. I had the distinct impression that everyone appreciated the fact that the conference was not limited to any one profession, nationality, or ethnic group and that it encouraged dialogue between an international scholarly community and the public. The sessions generated an enthusiasm which is very much in evidence in the papers which follow.

It is difficult to communicate the conference ambience through the articles alone, though. The elegance and impeccable service of the historic Grand Hotel made this meeting memorable. Grand is unlike any other hotel and its grandeur brought to mind John Jacob Astor and other nineteenth-century fur barons. The meeting had its pleasant surprises, too. On the first day, nearly thirty children of Indian descent came to hear presentations on the response of Native people to the fur trade. These youngsters were from the Michigan Indian Youth Traditional Values Conference directed by Robin Menefee. It was a positive experience and a hopeful sign of increased Native interest in fur trade history.

As a group, the conferees were a hearty lot. As they retraced the steps of the fur trade at Mackinac, cold and wet weather introduced them to some of the hardships endured by voyageurs centuries before. On the first day, a good number braved a driving rain for a guided tour of fur trade sites on Mackinac Island led by the Parks' Curator of Interpretation, Phil Porter.

The next evening a cold wind welcomed guests to a tour and reception at Fort Mackinac. The North West Company sponsored one of Grand Hotel's huge spreads of food and drink on the fort's parade ground, and we all partook with gusto. Afterwards, Dwight Teeple's "Four Winds Singers," a group composed of Chippewas, Ottawas, and Potawatomis from northern Michigan, treated us to a traditional drum social. This was an important moment, reminding all of the importance of the Indian facets of the fur trade. Gusty winds continued the next day. On the ferry ride to the program at Fort Michilimackinac those on the open top deck contended with waves and spray as the boat made its way through rough waters to the Parks' premier fur trade site. The hot coffee and mulled cider, and especially the chance for comradery in a warm building, attracted the crowd nearly as much as the reconstructions, animations, and exhibits on that blustery day.

In a demonstration of the extremes of climate here, sunshine graced our post-conference excursion to the museums at St. Ignace. Russell Magnaghi led this tour and Carol Hosler and Thomas Friggens hosted our people at the city and state sites. We had a poignant reminder that the voyageurs of the past had to contend with the vicissitudes of sea and weather as they negotiated the Straits of Mackinac. Chuck Hoover organized a large brigade of voyageur reenactors who intended to paddle their twenty-eight-foot north and thirty-two-foot Montreal canoes across the Straits to Mackinac Island. Driving rain and wind scuttled this plan. Our modern canoemen had one option unavailable to their predecessors—they hired a freight boat to bring them and their canoes over! In true voyageur fashion, they braved the elements for the duration of the conference in their primitive camp. Their costumed presence at the sessions and activities added a special charm and flavor. Nature did reward them with nearly calm seas to paddle back to the mainland.

The Fur Trade Conference was a gathering like no other. This was a group of diverse, serious, and spirited people bound together by their interest in this multifaceted topic. Mackinac was probably a once in a lifetime experience for most of those who attended. Today Mackinac is rather remote, and a good number of people had to make a considerable effort to come. Ironically, Mackinac was a relatively easier destination during fur trade days when it was the crossroads of well-traveled waterways! The conference was fertile ground for the exchange of information and the inspiring of new research, articles, and books on the fur trade. This was a reunion of old friends and a time for developing new relationships.

Personally, I cannot conceive of a more rewarding experience than being the manager of this conference and publication. I treasure the associations that grew. First, I must mention that remarkable lady, Lily McAuley. She is delightful, sincere, and full of spirit. We discovered we shared important things rooted in our common fur trade heritage—although mine is very distant. There was an instant bonding when we discovered we were both muskrat connoisseurs! Those without the fur trade in their blood are usually turned off by the mere mention of the animal's name—it is a delicacy you almost have to grow up with to appreciate! I wish Lily all the best.

I also value my association with the people on the editorial committee—Jennifer S.H. Brown, W.J. Eccles, and Donald P. Heldman. Working with these scholars over the past four years deepened my respect for these silver-penned masters of fur trade history.

I know better than anyone else that Keith R. Widder merits a large share of the credit for this volume and for the conference's success. As conference chair, he was a fine teammate during the meeting and through the publication process. Well organized, he was a tireless worker and attended to every detail. He had an uncanny knack of anticipating problems and the ability to resolve them before they became real trouble. What is more, he is an unfaltering friend who stood by me and carried the ball when I was incapacitated by an illness that struck me down during the production of this book. I owe him much, and I hope that readers recognize and appreciate his many contributions to this volume.

I trust all who were a part of this book are as proud of it as I am. No doubt it will be a valuable resource for many years to come. We all look forward with great anticipation to future meetings of the North American Fur Trade Conference.

Dennis M. Au
Project Director, Sixth North American Fur Trade Conference
Evansville, Indiana 18 November 1993

Introduction

The Sixth North American Fur Trade Conference, held on Mackinac Island, Michigan, 25-29 September 1991, demonstrated that fur trade studies continue to thrive in the 1990s. The field has a remarkable capacity to attract to each conference a broad range of scholars, students, and other enthusiasts who delight in the opportunity to come together in some locale made famous by the fur trade and to share their knowledge, experience, and common interests.

All the fur trade conferences held over the last twenty-five years have also generated more lasting legacies than the conversations of the meetings themselves—collected papers which have been published in a variety of forms. After the Mackinac gathering, our editorial committee of three, working in collaboration with the Mackinac State Historic Parks and with Dennis Au, our indefatigable conference manager, invited speakers to revise and submit the papers they delivered for publication. It gives the editors great pleasure to present this volume of selected papers from the Sixth North American Fur Trade Conference.

More than fifty presenters addressed the Mackinac gathering. They came from a wide variety of fields: history, anthropology, archaeology, geography, economics, and literature. Professors, graduate students, librarians, archivists, researchers with numerous national and state parks organizations, and other heritage groups were among the occupations represented. Their papers varied considerably in style, intent, focus, and depth of research. Some presenters will publish their material elsewhere or are still in the process of completing research; some had not generated a final written text or had produced a text too long to be published here.

We are grateful to all those speakers who submitted their papers for review, and we offer our thanks to all the authors who patiently put up with our editorial queries, requests, and revisions. As befits an interdisciplinary and transnational work such as this, we have been tolerant of different styles of referencing (while insisting on appropriate documentation). Authors have maintained the American or Canadian/British spelling styles of their choice, each article being internally consistent.

Twenty-eight essays appear in this book. Diverse in the breadth of their topics, regional or temporal coverage, and analytical approaches, they lend themselves more to thematic groupings rather than an overall chronological plan. Readers will find, however, that numerous papers are multifaceted, too rich in their content and range of implications to be easily categorized. The seven numbered parts of the book and their titles are only approximate guides to the broad content of each section.

One presentation defied classification into any one part and had the further distinction of being the highlight of the evening banquet attended by almost all the registrants. Lily McAuley in her talk, "Memories of a Trapper's Daughter," made fur trade life real and vivid. With feeling and humor, she brought to us all an appreciation of her experiences growing up on a trapline in the Cree country of northern Manitoba. She "stole the show," and it is only fitting to open this book by giving her the first word. We appreciate her efforts in checking over the taped transcript of her talk and in helping to select illustrations that convey some sense of the life and setting that she describes.

Part I focuses on the other side of the water—European economic intersections with the North American fur trade. Thomas Wien investigates "Exchange Patterns in the European Market for North American Furs and Skins, 1720-1760." He poses several intriguing questions and challenges ancient assumptions and conventional wisdom. His is a view of the fur trade from the consumers' side on the European continent. Specifically, he focuses on the question, "What happened to North American furs other than beaver once they reached France or Great Britain?" To answer that pregnant question, Wien examines the relation of the fur trade to each kingdom's internal economy and looks at what part these furs played in European export rivalry.

In his "British Capital in the Fur Trade: John Strettell and John Fraser," Harry W. Duckworth offers perspectives complementary to Wien's for the same century. He traces the complex network of mercantile arrangements established by the British to bring to market the furs trapped by Indian men, processed by their kinswomen, transported to Quebec by Canadians, and from there shipped to London for sale by merchant entrepreneurs.

In Part II, six papers examine the relations of Native peoples to the fur trade, the varied strategies employed in the trade, and some of their human and economic consequences in different regions and periods. Kathleen Pickering contributes a lively discussion of Lakota (Teton Sioux) economic dependence on the Euro-American fur trade and the resulting change in the Lakota mode of production from the mid-seventeenth century (when they occupied what is now Minnesota), through the nineteenth century, during which period they migrated west onto the Plains and into the Black Hills of South Dakota. She suggests that characterizations of the Lakota as self-sufficient horsemen and buffalo hunters need to be reassessed in light of their growing involvement in mercantile trade relations from the 1700s on.

Timothy K. Perttula details the impact of French and Spanish fur trading upon the Caddoan peoples of Louisiana and Texas between 1685 and 1800. Drawing upon archaeological data and documentary trade records from French

Louisiana, he concludes that the Caddoans did not begin to receive dependable supplies of trade goods from the French until after 1740.

The Native peoples of the Western Great Lakes were drawn into regular fur trade exchanges rather earlier. Dean L. Anderson analyzes records kept by a number of Montreal merchant families in the years 1715-1760, tracing the flow of European trade goods, notably cloth, into that region. Invoices of goods shipped to different posts offer evidence about contrasting trade patterns with different Native groups and, in turn, about their differing adaptations to trading opportunities.

Lynda Gullason shifts our focus to the Alberta fur trade sites of Fort George-Buckingham House in the 1790s. Her paper, "No less than 7 different nations," offers a case study of the problems of analyzing ethnicity, contact, and culture change through archaeological and documentary research, in a setting where woodland, plains, and parkland peoples all came to trade.

The paper by Royce Kurtz, "Looking at the Ledgers: Sauk and Mesquakie Trade Debts, 1820-1840," is a productive comparison of the credit records of George Davenport (1819-1830) and J.P. Eddy (1840-1841), traders in the Des Moines River region. Davenport's records demonstrate that the Native hunters of the 1820s pursued their winter trapping without much need of the trader's credit or supplies. The situation changed drastically, however, by 1840, due to Indian land sales, the rise of a cash economy, and accompanying changes in Sauk and Mesquakie needs and consumption patterns.

James L. Hansen concludes this section with a look at U.S. "Half-Breed" treaty rolls as sources on fur trade families of the upper Midwest from the 1820s to 1850s. He describes the detailed yet little used records available on the thousands of descendants of intermarriages between incoming traders and women of the Algonquian and Siouan peoples of the region.

Part III turns to the traders themselves, their origins, careers, outlooks, successes, and failures. Helen Hornbeck Tanner bravely undertakes to reconstruct the poorly documented life of Joseph La France, a peripatetic *coureur de bois* whose traces are found from the southern Midwest to Hudson Bay. His career demonstrates how an individual adapted to the French closing of the western posts in 1696-1715 and to changing political and market conditions, while also traveling and surviving among diverse Indian communities.

As La France began his career, another trading family was initiating five generations of involvement in the Great Lakes fur trade. Theresa M. Schenck traces the Cadottes on Lake Superior from the 1680s to 1850, drawing on records of the French trade and of the North West and American Fur companies. Through multi-generational marriage links with their Ojibwa associates, as well as their ties with Montreal, Schenck's ancestral kin were involved in almost every aspect of the fur business in the region.

Bruce M. White explores an often neglected side of the fur trade—its folklore. "The Fear of Pillaging: Economic Folktales of the Great Lakes Fur Trade" analyzes a common story motif in the documents—that of traders losing their goods to Indians. Whatever their (often uncertain) factual basis, the stories reflected both a folkloric genre and the traders' state of mind and notions of coping with danger; they also expressed and stabilized the strategies applied in risky situations.

Heather Devine's "Roots in the Mohawk Valley: Sir William Johnson's Legacy in the North West Company" returns to questions of trader origins. She traces the links of numerous Scottish Nor'Westers to Johnson's baronial estates in the Mohawk Valley before the American Revolution, where he presided over the Indian affairs of colonial New York. The social networks and cultural influences that these Scots brought from that context into Canada are visible, she argues, in their later lives and in the North West Company itself.

The final two articles of this section shift our focus westward to the Columbia River region. In "Faithful Service under Different Flags," William R. Swagerty and Dick A. Wilson present a socioeconomic profile of the personnel of the Hudson's Bay Company's Columbia Department and the American Fur Company's Upper Missouri Outfit, 1825-1835. Their quantitative comparisons of several hundred employees' length of service, compensation and debt levels, upward mobility, and ethnicity, and their correlations of these variables, provide strong bases for concluding that the contrasts between the firms were less sharp than has been assumed.

Bradford R. Cole offers a substantial reconsideration of the career of Nathaniel Wyeth, a Massachusetts merchant who tried his hand at fur trading from 1835 to 1837 and failed miserably. Noted as the builder of Fort Hall and a contributor to the American settlement of the Oregon country, Wyeth suffered, however, not only from competition and mishaps beyond his control but from troubles with employees and from overextending himself in a business of which he knew too little.

Since the conference was held in the historic ambience of Mackinac, it was a natural setting for presentations on the Mackinac area—four of which are gathered into Part IV. Peter Marshall offers a vivid and scholarly study of Benjamin Roberts, briefly the Commissary for Indian Affairs at Michilimackinac in 1767. The tribulations of this eminently forgettable character, dismissed and arrested for his mishandling of a cargo of rum, throw some light on the murkier side of the British establishment in North America at the time. The American Revolution was eventually to end that regime, posing new challenges to the interrelationships and loyalties of the multi-ethnic fur trade community as it relocated from Michilimackinac to Mackinac Island. Keith R. Widder examines this local fur trade society with a microscope, and does it very well.

By the 1820s, Mackinac Island was a nerve center for American Fur Company operations throughout the region. Looking in detail at the experiences of Henry H. Sibley, apprentice trader there from 1829 to 1834, Rhoda R. Gilman conveys a wealth of information about this future governor of Minnesota and about the surprisingly complex social and religious milieu in which Sibley found himself on the island.

In his paper, "Crucifixes and Medallions from Michilimackinac," Charles J. Rinehart investigates what we can learn from the study of these material objects so frequently associated with Fort Michilimackinac in the French period. He examines an enormous quantity of archaeological and documentary evidence to clarify the role of missions in that community and goes on to show how fur trading eventually superseded religious and other activities at Michilimackinac.

Part V turns its attention to fur trade material culture and archaeology beyond Mackinac. James R. Duncan carefully assesses gun fragments from a number of historic sites in the Mississippi Valley and southeastern United States. These data reveal that a hitherto unknown type of gun, made in England, was being traded widely in the region in the late eighteenth and early nineteenth centuries.

Douglas A. Birk in his "When Rivers Were Roads: Deciphering the Role of Canoe Portages in the Western Lake Superior Fur Trade," presents a study of the intricate and efficient networks of canoe trails and portages that Native traders had established before European contact. Portages were important landmarks and meeting places as well as crossing points between waterways, while overland trails were designed to minimize travel time in places where water routes were lengthy and arduous.

Finally, William J. Hunt Jr. provides a detailed review of documentary and archaeological evidence for the early years of Fort Union (1828-1836) on the upper Missouri River in North Dakota. National Park Service excavations and historical research in support of the fort's recent reconstruction have revealed the complexities of tracing the origins and early structural phases of this important trading center.

Part VI, "Into the Twentieth Century," presents three studies of aspects of the Hudson's Bay Company and the fur trade after 1870 when the old HBC territory of Rupert's Land became part of Canada. Henry C. Klassen looks at the commercial adaptations of the Hudson's Bay Company to an increasingly agricultural and urban society in southwestern Alberta. Fur trade posts in Calgary, Lethbridge, and elsewhere made sometimes rocky transitions into department stores, as the company reoriented its services and distribution of goods to new kinds of customers and a new regional economic order.

As the Hudson's Bay Company increasingly became a retail-oriented concern, at the same time it began to capitalize on its fur trade heritage in its public relations. Peter Geller examines how the company's magazine, *The Beaver*, contributed to this image building in the 1930s through the increasing use of professional photography with mass media appeal.

One of the Hudson's Bay Company's main rivals in the period produced a senior officer who made his own contributions to popular images of the fur trade north. The Swiss-born Thierry Mallet, who eventually became president of Revillon Frères, New York, became deeply attached to the northern wilderness on his inspection trips to Revillon's posts from 1908 to the 1920s. Gwyneth Hoyle offers a vivid view of Mallet's life and of his poetic prose writings which became classics among literary writings on the north.

Finally, Part VII assembles three papers which share a common thread in their concern with the interpretation and critical analysis of fur trade writings, both historical and literary. Michael Blanar in his "Long's *Voyages and Travels*: Fact and Fiction," provides a cautionary tale, a fine critical analysis of a supposedly primary source accepted for too long at face value. Blanar demonstrates convincingly that Long's book does not deserve the credence that many have given it since it first appeared in 1791.

I.S. MacLaren takes a new look at accounts of the Hudson's Bay Company's Arctic Expedition of 1836-1839. Peter Warren Dease's recently discovered journal of that trip offers perspectives widely different from those published by Governor George Simpson in his *Narrative of the Discoveries of the North Coast of America*. Like Blanar's, MacLaren's essay should oblige historians to stop repeating each other and instead examine critically the evidence in their sources, primary or secondary.

To conclude Part VII, Michael Payne reviews the directions taken by fur trade social history since Sylvia Van Kirk's review of the field at the Third Fur Trade Conference in 1978. He notes that this subject area has been largely taken over by public historians working at the behest of government heritage agencies such as Parks Canada, at sites such as Lower Fort Garry or York Factory. This trend has implications both good and bad: individual sites may become much better understood, but both their visitors and historians may be led to generalize about the fur trade from reconstructions that are anything but typical. No single site can do more than hint at the complexities hidden under the term "fur trade society" and at the variety of fur trades that have existed across North America.

Many original findings and stimulating ideas come together in these papers. At the same time, despite an information explosion in fur trade studies, we have no closure, no definitive overviews, no end of fresh questions. We hope that this collection of essays will encourage new thoughts and new lines of inquiry, and that it may challenge others to pursue in more depth issues and problems that could only be touched upon here. There is more than enough to do.

As a final note, we would like to express our thanks to Michigan State University Press, to the authors, to Keith Widder, Curator of History, Mackinac State Historic Parks, and to all the other parties who made the conference and this book possible; we second the acknowledgments expressed by Dennis Au in his Preface. We also take this opportunity to convey our special gratitude to Dennis Au himself. Conference registrants knew him as the one who kept everything running smoothly before and during the meetings. Only this committee fully knows how hard he labored in the many months since the conference, getting authors to submit their papers, telephoning us regularly to establish guidelines and deadlines, mailing papers and communications among us and to authors, cheerfully and patiently keeping track of the endless detail endemic in creating a multi-authored, edited volume, and all of this despite a severe illness followed by extended convalescence. It has been a real pleasure to work with him. If we had the ability to keep him and Lily McAuley supplied with muskrat tails for life, we would do so!

Jennifer S.H. Brown
W. J. Eccles
Donald P. Heldman
Editors

Memories of a Trapper's Daughter

Banquet Address of the Sixth North American Fur Trade Conference

Lily McAuley

This is a real pleasure. I can hardly believe that I'm here; in fact, I've had a terrible cold all week and I thought, "What if I lose my voice? What will I do?" The next thing that kept coming into my mind was, "What if I wake up and find that this is all a dream? I would be really disappointed." I was in contact with Linda Heard through the telephone several weeks ago, and we spoke for about half-an-hour. I don't know if you are like I am, when I hear a voice through the phone, I put a body and face to it. When I met Linda here, I was expecting to meet a lady who would be about five foot, eleven inches and about 180 pounds. Of course you can see that is not how it turned out. She is a very tiny lady—a very nice lady. She also said to me, "Lily, from the memories you shared with me, I expected to see, not you, but a woman about 106 years old."

The reason that I have such vivid memories is because I lived at such a place and time that was so isolated, time stood still. I feel sorry for the children of today that have memories that are not real. Little children that are growing up today in isolated areas have memories that are not real. The media has got to them. No matter where you go in the North, you can watch television and see things that you will not see until much later. Our memories are very, very clear because we actually lived them. There are a few memories, though, that are hand-me-down. There are memories that are first-person, and then there are those memories that are hand-me-down. My birth is a hand-me-down memory. My mama and my uncle and my father quite often told me about my birth. I was the only one of my mother's thirteen children to be born in the winter trapline. I'm told it was the coldest year on record, January 9, 1934. They tell me that my birthing house was very, very small and had no floor. For a window it had a forty-ounce whiskey bottle stuck between two logs. This is my husband here. Willie and I have a room here. It's the Eisenhower Suite. There is a four-poster bed there. The bed could be almost the size of the entire little building that I was born in. I'm certain it is much higher.

From these beginnings, things really worked out wonderfully for me. I've had many children. I've taken ten years off my life to have six children. They were all born and raised in Churchill [Manitoba]; they are all adult people now. And

Figure 1. Photograph of five Native girls in Island Lake, Manitoba District, c. 1927. "This is actually the way we dressed. Girls were never allowed to wear trousers. You'd be wearing layers of worsted wool stockings, then you'd have your moccasins and moccasin rubbers. You'd have quite a heavy wool dress, then a sweater, then you'd have a tuque—if you didn't have a tuque, then you'd have a kerchief." Photograph from the Rev. R. T. Chapin Collection, Western Canada Pictorial Index, The University of Winnipeg.

as you ladies know, having children is probably the hardest work you'll ever have to do. And just when the time came when I thought this is so hard, I would get a flashback of the place that my Mama birthed me; and if she could do it in that little shack with only a whiskey bottle stuck between two logs for a window, this is a piece of cake.

So I wanted to talk to you about where we were, who we were, and how we lived. After my birth, I was a first of many things for my Mama. I was the only one of her children to travel in a *tikanogan*. This is a cradle-board. First you are wrapped in a little blanket and then you have moss packed all around you. Then you are laced up very tightly. This is how we traveled when I was born, sixty-five miles from Cumberland House [Saskatchewan] and my Mama was very, very anxious for us to make it back to the settlement because there was a rumor that the Anglican minister was close by at another wintering camp. Mama didn't want him to get there before she had a chance to take me back to Cumberland House so that I could be done by the Catholic Church. It was almost a race as to who would get you. We traveled by dog team.

I don't know if you people have ever had the pleasure of seeing a plum pudding that is taken right out of the pot. A plum pudding, the way we used to have it, was done in a big cloth, tied up, and put in the kettle and boiled for five or six hours. The whole idea is that you keep the kettle boiling for the whole time so that the water is not sucked-up in the pudding. It is an amazing kind of pudding. None of us ever had a birthday cake. We always had a birthday pudding. The reason that I mention this plum pudding is another hand-me-down memory of Granny telling me that the day that my Mama arrived with this little baby in a moss bag, she said, "When your Mama put you on my lap and I unwrapped you, the steam rose off you as if you were a plum pudding." I can only imagine that I did not smell so sweet.

The way that we lived was that my Father was a trapper, a fire ranger, a conservation officer all in season later in his life, but all his life he was a trapper. As a matter of fact, he trapped 'til two weeks before he entered the hospital. The last thing he wanted to do was to enter the hospital. It was found that he had cancer, and he left this earth six years ago [1985]. I'm sure that my Dad is watching me right now. I'm sure that he is thinking that I have come a long way—and I certainly have.

The way that we lived, we were very fortunate that we were half-breed. I was telling Robin [Menefee], my new friend that I met who was running the Boy Scout Camp that for me where I grew up in northern Saskatchewan, to say that I am half-breed was not to put myself down, but rather to explain to anyone who wanted to listen that I was part Scottish and part Cree. To us the Metis were part French and part Indian and that was not what we were. Although I had one ancestor that was French, we always considered ourselves as half-breed. It was only about twenty years ago that our government legislated us all Metis. It's for easy identification purposes. So now we are known as Metis. When I tick off Metis on the census form I have the irresistible urge to add, "but I'm not part

Figure 2. This scene at Ponask Lake, c. 1927 was similar to Lily's winter home. "This is a winter cabin. It's like the cabin I was born in. It wouldn't have a wooden floor—very little light for windows. The one I was born in only had a 40 ounce whiskey bottle between two logs. When we would get to the winter cabin, we would chink them with the wetted moss—the moss would freeze." Photograph from the Rev. R. T. Chapin Collection, Western Canada Pictorial Index, The University of Winnipeg.

French!" Not that I have anything against the French, but that's not what I feel I am. Because we were half-breed, we were fortunate in that we did not have to be herded onto reservations when the treaties were signed. Because we were not part of the treaties, we continued to live more like the Indians than the Indians did.

My memories are sort of in a circle. We had the fall trapline, not too many memories about the fall trapline, it was more like an adjustment. Of course these places would be picked for whatever fur was in season at that time. Then we would move into the winter trapline; that area would be picked to make sure there was an abundance of big game, like moose. When I think of it now, the living was very easy. Even when we didn't have things like moose, we always had plenty of rabbits. My two older sisters, Flora and Muriel, always snared rabbits and my brother Daniel was always out getting partridge. We always had plenty of food. I don't know if you people are aware, but if you had a steady diet of rabbit, you could actually be malnourished. After a while your body craved some real meat. So quite often my Mother would awaken us about two or three o'clock in the morning to the aroma of fried moose meat and bannock because my Daddy would have come home during the night from a successful hunt. That is one of my most wonderful memories. That takes care of winter.

My greatest memory though is of the spring trapline. The spring trapline is where we had the most fun, where we had so much to eat, and when we knew that we had survived another winter and things were going to be great. There aren't too many teenagers here, but where you have junk food, we didn't know what junk food was. Our very special treat was muskrat tails. There is nothing on earth to compare with it. Dennis [Au] can vouch for that. It is just totally amazing. The other thing that we used to have is the spinal cord of sturgeon.

Our trapline in the spring was the Torch River. The number and size of the sturgeon in that river were unbelievable and what Mama would do, and it was always the women that would fish, Mama and her friend Isabelle would fish and if they couldn't lift the sturgeon into the canoe, they had to tow them into shore. Mama would cut the head right off them and the tail just right up to the spinal cord. Then she would wrap the spinal cord around her hand and pull. They could be up to six feet long. She would tie them in a knot and boil them for ten minutes and then give each of us one, and we would wear it around our neck like a necklace and we could chew it. It was like a white long rubber string with a salty membrane through the center. It was very chewy. You could skip with it, you could play tug-of-war with it. You could hit dogs with it. Then you could wash it in the river and then you could eat it. It would take you all day to eat it. And I'm still here! It was a very healthy thing.

Those of you who have read *Trader, Tripper, Trapper* by Syd Keighley,[1] know about the kind of traders I remember. During the spring breakup, the trippers and traders would literally race each other; you could see them coming as soon as the ice would break in the Torch River. They would be right there behind the ice break. Because of course, the first traders to hit your camp would be ones to get the prime pelts. In this one instance that I will never forget, the free trader Joe Angeleski came slightly ahead of the Hudson's Bay Company's clerks. He had this pound of butter in his hand, and he was doing his trade speech in broken English, with a Polish accent mixed with Cree. Of course in Swampy Cree the simplest thing you could think of to say was if you were going to be talking about butter, you could say *osawa peme,* which means the yellow lard. But we can't keep things that simple, we say *tootoosi poo pime,* which means the milk of the cow made into lard. And imagine this man trying to say this, and he said it will cost you two muskrats. As he said this, he stepped into the smooth mud which he thought was sand. He fell through this past his knee and fell face down into this mud. And without missing a beat, he came right up and continued to do his spiel.

I've heard white children say when going swimming, "The last one in is a rotten egg." Well we never did that. We always did Joe Angeleski. Before we could start swimming, we would look around for a stone that would resemble butter, and we would do our spiel and run into the lake and fall face down, and that was the only way we could start swimming. It really amuses me to think of how traditions begin. When I took my oldest daughter, who was then five years old to Cumberland House, I saw all these little children doing Joe Angeleski. I asked them why they did it. They said they didn't know, they have to do it. That's one of the memories.

When these trippers and traders would arrive, sometimes they wouldn't even take enough time to set up their tent. They would just unroll their wares on a canvas on the shore and then you would go and trade. Of course with our family, my Mama had many children already; she would only be able to afford what we call the "necessaries." So we didn't have anything extra. Although these people used to bring some things that were pretty amazing when you think of how they traveled. One of these amazing things brings me to my first encounter with an orange. When I say memory, this is a real memory. How many of you can remember the very first time you saw an orange?

To me it is the most awful thing, in the true sense of the word; I was in awe of this thing. When it happened there was one lady in our spring trapping camp that was childless. She had no children. In those days when you didn't have any children you raised someone else's child. But Ben's woman chose not to do this, and all the other women would talk about her. I think they all envied her. In thinking about it now, I realize she was childlike, probably a little bit backward. Whenever we visited there and she had candy, she would tantalize us with it, but when her husband was home, he would make her share. So this one day after the traders had left, I went to visit in her tent. She reached under her bed for a box and brought out the biggest berry I ever saw. I was totally amazed; and then she proceeded to skin it. There was no such word in my brain at the time for peel, but for skin; I've seen so many muskrats skinned. I got as close as I could to her, the musk, or smell of the big berry was overwhelming. She ate it.

Figure 3. Muskrat meat and skins on stretchers being smoked, Cumberland House Reserve, Saskatchewan. "This is a spring trap line but a very temporary camp. This is not how *we* lived. My Dad would build four logs up and then put the tent on top of that. The only similarity to how we lived in the spring line is the muskrats hanging up and also the drying rack in the foreground for drying muskrat flesh. Some of our neighbors in our spring camp would live in this fashion. We were never quite this rugged." Photographic Collection 1987/363-C-68/3 (N79/97), Hudson's Bay Company Archives, Provincial Archives of Manitoba.

At that point I couldn't stand it, I ran home and I started tugging at my Mama's apron and said, "Mama, Ben's woman had this big berry and she skinned it and she ate it." My Mama said, "Never mind my girl, that is just an orange." An orange," I thought, "that's pretty weird. Why would anyone name that big berry after the color of my friend Adelide's sweater?"

When I hear the song, "Summertime, and the Living is Easy," I think of the time that we'd be making our leisurely trip home to the settlement. We would have been in our fall trapline, our winter trapline, our spring trapline, and then we'd be heading back to Cumberland House. This is the time when we'd be stopping at Keyask Island, or Gull Island. This island would be half the size of this room. The gulls would have nests very close to each other. Sometimes when we'd arrive there and we'd see these little gulls swimming around, my Mama would look so sad and I didn't know why, because we'd have a lot of fun chasing these little gulls around the water. Of course, later I realized why she was sad; that meant that we'd have another year without tasting an egg. If there was no evidence of hatching eggs, my Daddy would check a few eggs. He would boil them to see if they were still okay. If they were still okay, not too old, he would set us to gather, saying, "If there is one egg, don't touch it; if there are two eggs, don't touch it; if there are three eggs, take one; if there are four eggs, take two. You must always leave two eggs. If you take too many, you will discourage the gull from coming there." So we'd have a big kettle of these eggs, and we would boil them right on the shore and then we'd have them with us in the canoe as we went on our merry way to Cumberland House. We would eat them until they literally came out of our ears. And that was a good year. It was the only time that you would ever eat eggs. That was a fond memory.

Another good memory was that spring was a very good time to eat ducks and geese. They would be coming from the south and they would be just rolling, they would be butter-balls. So my Mama wanted to make me a dress that didn't show dirt. She made me a dress that was the color of mud—nondescript, grayish, brown. She probably figured it wouldn't show dirt. But from eating those fat little geese and ducks, I'd be wiping my face, chin, and hands on my stomach, that earned me my second name, that was *tomatai*, "greasy belly."

When I was sixteen, I thought I had outlived the name, until I walked into a dance. Our dances were very much like the *ceilidh* they have in the Orkney Islands—impromptu Gaelic dances. I walked in and everybody was sitting around the outer edge of the room and my Uncle Joe Umpherville stopped the music and in Cree he said "There she enters, Greasy Belly." Needless to say, my ego went, phewt, just like that. The other fond memory I have is on the stop-over. We had one more stop-over and that was the area where we would meet other people and they would be tanning moose hides and other hides from the winter. It was always a show-off time. My Mama would be skimping and saving dried apples, raisins, and that type of thing, so that when we stopped off there where all these other people were coming together they would say, "Isn't it amazing that *Iskwäo*—meaning woman—still has so many provisions. Her man is such a good provider." To her, that was the best compliment that anyone could pay her. So what they would do is to pool all the left-over provisions, and we would have a feast.

The men would build these racks for the moose hide. The women would be in the back, scraping the hair off the moose hide. We children would be playing on the other side. All moose hides have tick holes. We were playing a form of Russian roulette, just ahead of the scrapers that were knocking the hair off. Well, all of a sudden Adelide's finger went flying—knocked right off by the scraper.

Some of the people we were with were real Indian and some were half-breed. The Indian women go through this and now I find out that other cultures do also. It is called keening—it is when a person dies, they have this terrible, terrible sort of crying, weeping sound, and the women started to do this for Adelide's finger. They believe that if you are not whole when you die, you cannot go beyond. We searched for Adelide's finger in this pile of moose hair. We never did find it, but that was the start of another tradition, because years later in the fall time when all the leaves were falling, we would pick up a little stick and we would say that this is Adelide's finger and throw it into a pile of leaves and say, "let's search for her finger." The kids continued to do this for years.

I want to thank Jennifer Brown for telling Dennis Au about me. And I wanted to thank Dennis for asking me to come here. It seems like an awful long time ago that he asked. At that time I was still with Canadian Parks Service and did not have an inkling that I would not be with them today. A few things happened to me last winter. Four days before Christmas, I was diagnosed as having breast cancer. On January 7th I had surgery. They thought they had it all. I was pretty excited about it. When I went to get my clean bill of health in April, they said they were sorry but it had reoccurred; so I went through twenty-nine radiation treatments. So for a wee girl that was born in a little trapper shack with only a whiskey bottle stuck between two logs, I've come a long way indeed because I've come right from there up to nuclear medicine, which is pretty amazing. I would be really foolish to miss this opportunity for those of you who believe in the Higher Power that the next time you make contact, I would ask you to please throw in a good word for me. I know that I am getting well. I know that I am going to survive, but I want it speeded up a wee bit. Having survived in a trapping life style, I can survive anything. Thank you very, very much.

NOTE

1. Sydney A. Keighley, *Trader, Tripper, Trapper: The Life of a Bay Man* (Winnipeg: Watson and Dwyer/Rupert's Land Research Centre, 1989).

Part I

Transatlantic Fur Trade Markets and Entrepreneurs

Exchange Patterns in the European Market for North American Furs and Skins, 1720-1760[1]

Thomas Wien

The contrast between the expansionistic Montréalers and their rivals to the north and south, who were much slower to establish posts in the interior, is one of the central themes of North American fur trade history. At no time was this asymmetry more apparent than in the later phases of the French régime. By the early 1750s, the Montréal canoe brigades supplied posts in a vast swath of Indian lands extending to the forks of the Saskatchewan in the northwest and the Sioux and the Illinois country in the southwest. Their English-speaking competitors, meanwhile, surveyed the Canadian traders from afar: a military expedition had halted the Anglo-American traders' advance into the Ohio country, and the Hudson's Bay Company's managers would wait another quarter-century before ordering the construction of inland pendants to their chain of posts on the bayshore.

Just how did Canadian merchants and traders maintain their delivery service to the Indian nations of the West against rivals with no or far fewer portages to make? Harold Innis first asked the question some sixty years ago. He answered it, essentially, with disbelief. Distance, he argued, was the Montréalers' Achilles heel; to move into the interior was to face rising transport costs and increasingly expensive military entanglements with the British and their native allies. Crisis-prone and overextended, the French fur-trading empire collapsed very much on schedule, in Innis's view, in 1760.[2]

The evidence that has accumulated since 1930 suggests, Innis to the contrary, that the Montréal trade was viable until well into the Seven Years' War. Not only did fur returns hold their own if not increase, but the *marchands-voyageurs* and *marchands-équipeurs* who prosecuted the trade tended to remain faithful to their calling, a sure sign that they found it worth their while.[3] By way of explanation, scholars have pointed to the advantages of exploiting a network of posts in the interior. Some have argued that French imperialism—and its complicated system of alliances with many of the nations of the Great Lakes region—brought commercial advantage and not just an additional burden of levies on the trade;[4] others have suggested that, in many cases, Indian consumers would pay a high price for goods that were delivered to them rather than taking their custom to the more distant competition.[5]

These arguments need not be contradictory and taken together, they may well identify the principal Canadian trade secrets.[6] But they are focused on North America; in neglecting the transatlantic phases of the trade cycle, they may also miss an additional source of advantages for the Montréalers. Before the nineteenth century, after all, most of the merchandise used in the North American fur trade came from Europe, and most of the furs received in return were consumed there.[7] It is conceivable that, compared to their competitors, the Canadians received their goods on particularly favourable terms and sold their peltry at particularly advantageous prices. In this way, European suppliers and buyers may have done their share to help Canadian traders and merchants bear the heavy burden of costs imposed on them in the North American theatre of the trade.

The European phases of the fur trade have received relatively little attention from historians. On the goods side of the ledger, only further research into the prices of merchandise imported by the Canadians and their rivals will permit us to conclude whether one or the other had a decisive advantage in this regard.[8] On the fur side, a few studies of the marketing of beaver, the mainstay of the trade, contradict the notion that France was a good place to sell furs. There is no doubt, for example, that the English were more successful than the French in clearing their home market of surplus beaver during the glut of the late seventeenth and early eighteenth centuries.[9] While by 1720, supply and demand for this hatter's fur had come into better balance in both markets, the Canadians were still at a disadvantage: now the French Indies Company used its monopoly of beaver exports from Canada to France to set a particularly low price for this kind of fur. It is true that the Montréalers recouped part of their losses by sending some of their beaver to New York, where the higher prices of the British system obtained, but this expedient was only partial consolation.[10] In the beaver trade, European marketing systems clearly favoured the British colonies and trading-factories.

There remained the other furs, the fine peltry and the hides that the Montréalers knew as *pelleteries* and *peaux*. The former ranged from fine marten and lynx pelts to such coarser furs as raccoon; the latter included the deer, elk, and moose skins, sometimes already "Indian drest," that were ultimately transformed into leather.[11] Together they represented slightly less than half of the value of Canadian fur exports.[12] These furs were important to Montréal merchants, not just on account of their value, but because they could be shipped to France on a free market; the official export monopoly and the low fixed price of the Compagnie des Indes extended only to beaver. We know very little about the European market or markets for furs of this type.[13] Did the French trading system supply a discrete group of buyers, French or European, who did not have access to English suppliers and who were thus likely to pay higher prices without complaint? Was there room in Europe for a special French premium on furs of this kind, a "special deal" that would help the Canadians compensate for their high costs? On the basis of an analysis of trade patterns and

Figure 1. *The Port of La Rochelle in the Eighteenth Century, seen from the Petite Rive.* Edouard Pinel, after Joseph Vernet. Courtesy of the Musée du Nouveau Monde, La Rochelle, France.

price behaviour, this paper answers these questions in the negative. It is with the contours of the European market that we begin.

What happened to North American furs other than beaver once they reached France or Britain? Did either kingdom keep its colonial peltry for itself, withholding it from the rest of Europe and preventing it from competing with the rival's shipments? Contemporaries leave the contrary impression. North American furs, they suggest, simply passed through England and France on their way to points beyond.[14] But in this they surely exaggerate. One need but count the Canada marten skins, usually known simply as *Canadas*, mentioned in Paris furriers' accounts,[15] or consider the place of black bear skins in the pantheon of English national symbols, to know that the respective domestic markets were by no means insignificant.

Customs statistics afford us a closer look at the relative importance of the home market. Pending further research in the original records, Murray Lawson's figures on English imports and exports of colonial fur in five scattered years are a suggestive starting point for the London side of the equation.[16] To put it mildly, they tend to confirm contemporaries' testimony: re-exports of fur sometimes exceed imports (table 1)! By contrast, during the same five years, the re-exportation rates at La Rochelle, the main French port for colonial fur,[17] are usually lower, sometimes markedly so.[18] Granted, the La Rochelle statistics present a particular problem. To a much greater extent than was the case in England, the French port's fur imports from North America arrived late in one year to be sold in the spring of the next. To avoid distortion, then, it makes sense to consider imports and re-exports of successive years. This has been done

TABLE 1. RATES OF RE-EXPORTATION OF SELECTED FURS FROM ENGLAND AND LA ROCHELLE.
(total number of skins in given years)

England	1720, 1725,	1730, 1739,	1750,	La Rochelle, same years				1736-40	1737-41	
type	imported	exported	rate[1]	type	imported	exported	rate[1]	imported	exported	rate[1]
marten	125,000	124,388	99.5	martre	159,329	78,566	49.3	94,557	60,941	64.5
cat (lynx)	18,851	18,569	98.5	loup-cervier	2,853	981	34.4	6,243	2,025	32.4
bear	14,944	14,263	95.4	ours	54,933	27,186	49.5	66,083	38,028	57.5
wolf	3,673	3,757	102.3	loup de bois	3,876	2,995	77.3	3,754	2,119	56.5
fox	66,827	64,762	96.9							
otter	21,954	21,929	99.9	pell. communes,						
raccoon	97,222	94,578	97.5	"du Canada"	200,975 lb	140,187 lb	69.8	150,362 lb	109,400 lb	72.8
wolverine	3,673	3,757	105.5							
deer		n.d.		chevreuil, cerf	142,786	42,519	29.8	300,247	38,575	12.8
elk (moose)		n.d.		orignal	4,814	2,363	49.1	2,736	2,108	77.1

[1] rate = $\frac{\text{exports}}{\text{imports}} \times 100$

sources: Lawson, Archives de la Chambre de Commerce et d'Industrie de La Rochelle (ACCLR) in the last three columns of table 1, which compare the total imports of the five years beginning in 1736 with the total re-exports of the five years beginning in 1737. The operation certainly changes the rates of re-exportation, but in the end attenuates but little the contrast between England and La Rochelle.

Should we conclude, then, that the French market absorbed a considerably higher proportion of furs reaching it from North America than did the English one? Nothing is less certain, for eighteenth-century customs figures promise more accuracy than they deliver. To begin with, it is likely that both series of imports are incomplete. We know, for example, that the Hudson's Bay Company failed to declare something close to a tenth of its beaver imports into England in order to lighten the burden of duties.[19] There is no reason to suppose that the honorable company—or colonial American merchants, for that matter—were any more patriotic when it came to declaring imports of other furs. Similar comparisons between the volume of the Compagnie des Indes' and La Rochelle's beaver receipts in years when no other ports were involved point to similar practices. Substantial in the early and mid-1720s, underenumeration declined to some 12 percent in the years 1750-1754.[20] The quality of the series thus seems to have improved with time, if the fate of beaver is any indication.[21] But if the Rochelais failed to count some imports, they were even more likely to miss part of the re-exports. This is so because furs slated for re-export usually entered the La Rochelle *entrepôt*, permitting them to leave the country in bond, free of all duties.[22] With no pecuniary interest in such articles, the tax-farmers' employees must have devoted little time to noting them down in their registers. Their English counterparts, by contrast, faced merchants who were very much interested in the totals they entered. The reason was simple: the customs authorities remitted ("drew back") more than half the import duties on North American furs that were re-exported.[23] Merchants thus had every reason to pad their figures and adjust upwards the volume of their shipments to the rest of Europe. For administrative reasons, then, it is likely that the La Rochelle figures underestimate re-exports and the English ones overestimate them. The contrast between the two countries was thus less marked than the statistics would lead us to believe.

This excursion into the shadowy domain of the customs-office permits us to draw one relatively solid conclusion: most (some three-quarters, perhaps more in the English case and less in the French) of the furs *stricto sensu* and some of the skins imported from North America did not remain in the two countries of importation. In terms of its importance to the trade, the principal exception to this generalization is deer skins. A large proportion of the skins of this sort shipped to La Rochelle from Canada and Louisiana was transformed in France into chamois leather (some of which would again leave the country in the form of sides of leather, breeches, and gloves).[24] Since Lawson did not include deer skins in his calculations, we cannot for the moment ascertain whether this product, thanks notably to the breeches-makers of Bristol, enjoyed the same exceptional status in England.

Tableau pour les Pelleteries venües du Canada en cette ville de La Rochelle en Décembre 1737, le prix courant d'icelles et leur montant en Total./

Parties N.os	Consignation	Ours Quantité	Ours Prix	Ours Montant	Oursons Quantité	Oursons Prix	Oursons Montant	Marmottes Quantité	Marmottes Prix	Marmottes Montant	Loutres Quantité	Loutres Prix	Loutres Montant
1	à Mr Pascaud	3700		22200	1200		3600	36600		64050	2700		14850
2		1600		9600	550		1650	10700		18725	534		2937
3		1765		10590	360		1080	7650		13387.10	445		2447.10
4		627		3762	83		249	6470		11322.10	300		1650
5		470		2820	200		600	4650		8137.10	240		1320
6		340		2040	82		246	3400		5950	316		1738
7		700		4200	320		960	3700		6475	108		594
8		550	à 6	3300	215	à 3	645	1810	à 35	3167.10	185	à 5.10	1017.10
9		490		2940	245		735	2550		4462.10	80		440
10		600		3600	200		600	1300		2275	148		814
11		500		3000	230		690	3920		6860	71		390.10
12		207		1242	56		168	1030		1802.10	337		1853.10
13		188		1128				1600		2800	118		649
14		212		1272	98		294	570		997.10	59		324.10
15		187		1122	138		414	3640		6370			
16		60		360	41		123	1460		2555	15		82.10
		12196		73176	4018		12054	91050		159337.10	5656		31108

Parties N.os	Pécans Quantité	Pécans Prix	Pécans Montant	Pichoux & Renards d. Virg. Quantité	Prix	Montant	Loups de bois Quantité	Prix	Montant	Loups-Cerviers Quantité	Prix	Montant	Montant Total en Nombre	Montant Total en Deniers
1	700		4200	2300		6900	400		1200	540		10800	48140 Pces	127800
2	163		978	1200		3600	88		264	30		600	14865 d.	38354
3	215		1290	720		2160	57		171	100		2000	11312 d.	33126
4	120		720	160		480	7		21	250		5000	8017 d.	23204.10
5	54		324	420		1260	18		54	3		60	6055 d.	14575.10
6	40		240	395		1185	20		60	6		120	4599 d.	11579
7	59		354	337		1011	12		36	17		340	5253 d.	13970
8	61	à 6	366	228	à 3	684	5	à 3	15	13	à 20	260	3067 d.	9455
9	20		120	215		645	24		72	33		660	3657 d.	10074.10
10	80		480	260		780				70		1400	2658 d.	9949
11	28		168	370		1110	16		48	17		340	5152 d.	12606.10
12	324		1944	10		30	2		6	200		4000	2166 d.	11046
13				227		681	29		87				2162 d.	5345
14	19		114	41		123	3		9	26		520	1028 d.	3654
15				84		252							4049 d.	8158
16	3		18	4		12							1583 d.	3150.10
	1886		11316	6971		20913	681		2043	1305		26100	123763 d.	336047.10

Suitte du même Tableau.

Reprise des parties N.os	Consignation	Carcajoux Quantité	Prix	Montant	Renards rouges Quantité	Prix	Montant	Renards croizés Quantité	Prix	Montant	Renards argentés Quantité	Prix	Montant
Comme dessus													
1		70		560	220		1210	10		300	6		180
2					255		1402.10						
3		3		24	257		1413.10						
4		18		144	100		550	6		180	5		150
5		1		8	18		99						
6					3		16.10						
7					30		165				51		1530
8			à 8			à 5.10			à 30			à 30	
9		4		32	64		352	10		300			
10					200		1100	250	à 25	6250	50		1500
11					6		33						
12		18		144	2		11	12	à 30	360			
13					32		176	55	à 30	1650	18		540
14		1		8	32		176	4	à 30	120			
15													
16					13		71.10						
		115		920	1232		6776	347		9160	130		3900

Reprise des parties N.os	Renards blancs Quantité	Prix	Montant	Visons Quantité	Prix	Montant	Martres ordinaires &c. Quantité	Prix	Montant	Martres Temiskaming Quantité	Prix	Montant	Reprise du Total en nombre	Reprise du Total en Deniers
Comme dessus													123763 d.	336047.10
1	11		110	470		705	8700		26100	500		2500	9987 d.	31665
2				255		382.10	2100		6300				2610 d.	8085
3				340		510	2370		7110				2970 d.	9057.10
4	4		40	50		75	850		2550				1033 d.	3689
5	2		20	62		93	1000		3000				1083 d.	3720
6				4		6	400		1200				407 d.	1222.10
7				18		27	638		1914				737 d.	3636
8		à 10		150	à 30	225		à 3			à 5		150 d.	225
9	3		30	68		102	1210		3630				1359 d.	4446
10				327		490.10	1100		3300				1927 d.	12640.10
11				15		22.10	325		975				346 d.	1030.10
12	11		110	19		28.10	500		1500	1600		8000	2162 d.	10153.10
13													105 d.	2366
14	1		10	34		51	414		1242				486 d.	1607
15														
16							28		84				41 d.	155.10
	32		320	1812		2718	19635		58905	2100		10500	149166 d.	429246.10

Recapitulation

N.o	Pièces	Montant	Total
N.o 1	48140 Pces / 9987 d.	127800 / 31665	58127 Pces pour £ 159465
N.o 2	14865 Pces / 2610 d.	38354 / 8085	17475 Pces p.r £ 46439
N.o 3	11312 Pces / 2970 d.	33126 / 9057.10	14282 Pces p.r £ 42183.10
N.o 4	8017 Pces / 1033 d.	23204.10 / 3689	9050 Pces p.r £ 26893.10
N.o 5	6055 Pces / 1083 d.	14575.10 / 3220	7138 Pces p.r £ 17795.10
N.o 6	4599 Pces / 407 d.	11579 / 1222.10	5006 Pces p.r £ 12801.10
N.o 7	5253 Pces / 737 d.	13970 / 3636	5990 Pces p.r £ 17606
N.o 8	3067 Pces / 150 d.	9455 / 225	3217 Pces p.r £ 9680
N.o 9	3657 Pces / 1359 d.	10074.10 / 4446	5016 Pces p.r £ 14520.10
N.o 10	2658 Pces / 1927 d.	9949 / 12640.10	4585 Pces p.r £ 22589.10
N.o 11	5152 Pces / 346 d.	12606.10 / 1030.10	5498 Pces p.r 13637
N.o 12	2166 Pces / 2162 d.	11046 / 10153.10	4328 Pces p.r £ 21199.10
N.o 13	2162 Pces / 105 d.	5345 / 2366	2267 Pces p.r £ 7711
N.o 14	1028 Pces / 486 d.	3654 / 1607	1514 Pces p.r £ 5261
N.o 15	4049 Pces	8158	4049 Pces pour £ 8158
N.o 16	1583 Pces / 41 d.	3150.10 / 155.10	1624 Pces pour £ 3306

Preuve de la Recapitulation

120285 Pces	332864.10
28881 d.	96382.10
149166 Pces	429246.10

Figure 2. "Table of furs arrived from Canada in this city of La Rochelle in December 1737": one of the rare detailed lists of La Rochelle fur imports. Courtesy of the Chambre de Commerce et d'Industrie, La Rochelle, France.

Be that as it may, one thing is clear: much North American fur found its way to other regions of Europe. It remains to be seen whether something akin to a unified European market had taken shape, or whether the two countries maintained relatively discrete commercial spheres of influence. The French consul in Hamburg, Champeaux, was well-placed to settle the issue. He left little doubt in the matter: "Much fur and peltry," he wrote in 1752,

> is consumed in the interior of Germany [and] in Poland. Part of it comes from the ports of France and is drawn from the colony of Canada; part is brought in by the English who obtain it from Hudson Bay or receive it from New England [...] We have no other real competitor in this trade except the English. Hence one should ensure, if possible, that Canada furnish a larger quantity, and that the English obtain [but] a small share of this trade.[25]

Generally speaking, the customs statistics confirm Champeaux's observations and point to a competitive European market. Figure 3 presents information from the middle of the period. It draws on two sources. Lawson's figures on the official value of English exports (including beaver) are presented here for 1739, the closest to the middle of the period of the five scattered years included in his statistical appendix. Since the La Rochelle records contain data for all but four years of the four decades under discussion, it is possible to compensate for the arbitrary fluctuations from one year to the next by presenting exports over a longer period, in this case the five years beginning in 1737 (1739 being the middle year). Since the two sources, whatever their other deficiencies, are not strictly comparable—one depicts shipments from a country, the other from a single port that was not the sole point of entry or egress—figure 3 presents percentage distributions rather than absolute values.[26]

If one considers that Holland redistributed much of the English fur it received in Germany and the Baltic, and that to French officials what I have labelled "Baltic" meant mostly northern Germany and Poland,[27] the patterns of trade are remarkably similar and bear out Champeaux's analysis. Southern Europe, to be sure, seemed to attract a greater proportion of furs from La Rochelle than from London, and the French had an understandable predilection for supplying their Swiss neighbours (and, presumably, Italy and other points beyond). All the same, despite these differences of emphasis, it would seem that many of the furs separated into French and English streams by the Indians of North America flowed together again in Central Europe.

All this, in addition to the signs that some North American fur reached France from England by way of the Dutch Republic or Flanders,[28] suggests that there *was* a unified market for a significant proportion of the peltry shipped to Europe from the continental colonies. That fact is, of course, significant in determining whether the Canadians could obtain their "special deal" in the form of a relatively high price for fur. Since demand for both "French" and "English" furs was determined in large measure in a single area of Europe, one would expect both La Rochelle and London prices to reflect conditions in that market, making

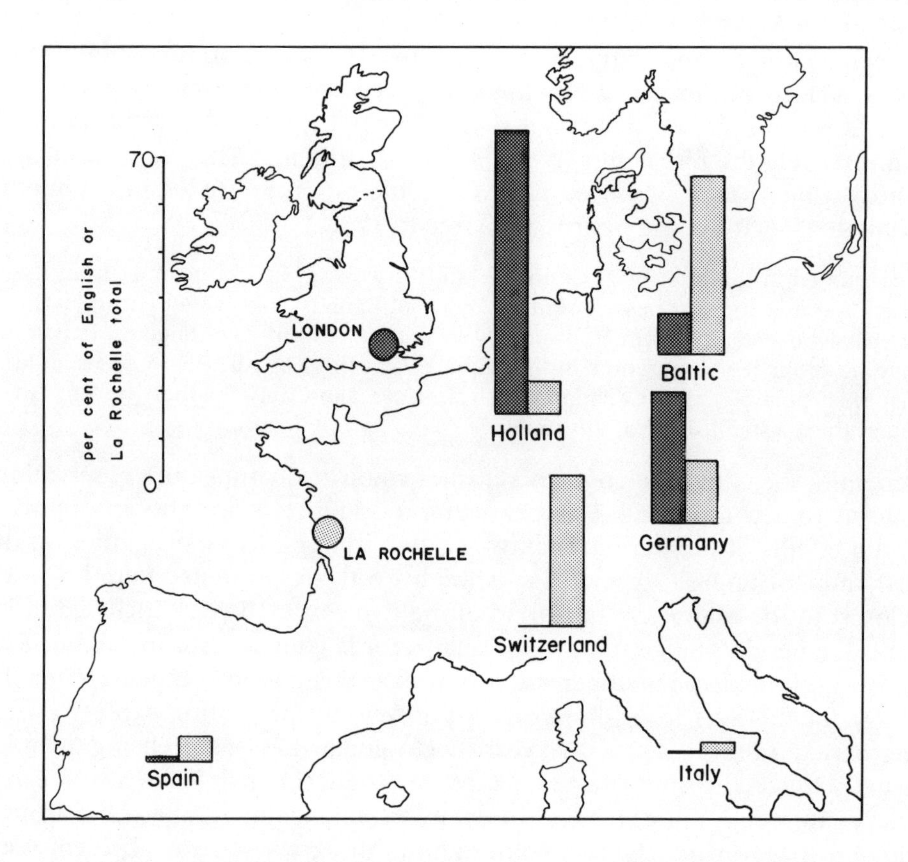

Figure 3. Distribution of English and Rochelais Fur Exports, ca. 1739. Sources: Lawson, ACCLR.

premium prices for French furs unlikely. That proposition, too, we can verify, but only after taking a methodological detour.

As no prices-current for North American furs seem to have survived for this period, a variety of series must fill the breach. All have their blemishes. As usual, the Hudson's Bay Company offers the most exact description of its dealings. The series extracted from its journals and sales books reflects the actual prices paid for prime furs at the company's annual fall sales (with the exception of moose ["elk"] skins, sold with the beaver in the spring).[29] Precision, then, is assured. Completeness, on the other hand, is not. From 1727, the journals refer the historian to the sales books, documents that the company seems to have kept only from 1737 onwards. Hence, a ten-year gap in the series. Of the other, shorter ones early and late in the period, only that of 1722-1723 can be filled by interpolation.[30]

For various reasons, the series describing transactions in the French commercial system do not offer us a similar front-row seat at the fur sales. Merchants routinely quoted prices to one another, of course, but only further research in the letters of the Rochelais to their Canadian correspondents will permit us to unearth the makings of a series. Fortunately, the archives of the La Rochelle

Figure 4. Quayside scene, London, 1750s, showing a customs officer at work, *Old Custom House Quay*, painted by Samuel Scott. Courtesy of the Board of Trustees of the Victoria & Albert Museum.

Chamber of Commerce contain an acceptable alternative. These statistics originated in a rather cumbersome administrative procedure. Each year the Bureau de la balance du commerce, charged with drawing up the country's trade balance, asked the customs bureaux (Bureaux des fermes) of the ports to tabulate the volume of external trade, commodity by commodity. It then sent copies of these lists back to the ports, ordering the local chamber of commerce to enter the average prices of each product.[31] In La Rochelle, customs officers usually listed four North American furs and three skins in their account of imports, in addition to coat and parchment beaver and a catch-all category labelled *pelleteries communes* or *pelleteries du Canada.*

The Chamber of Commerce prices do not enjoy the best of reputations. The clerks of the Chamber clearly had better things to do than to keep a close watch on price fluctuations from year to year. Their response to commercial reality, therefore, was often belated and sometimes inventive. If the Bordeaux Chamber's reading of coffee prices is indicative, the clerks reduced the amplitude of fluctuations, usually registered changes with a year's delay, and were not above entering a purely arbitrary price from time to time.[32] Fortunately, the La Rochelle clerks' performance in the case of North American furs is more encouraging. Comparison with a few spotty market quotations suggests that the Chamber of Commerce prices were slightly on the low side, at least as far as prime furs were concerned, and generally a year out of date. But they did reflect general trends.

Comparison with the third series of prices, pieced together from data in the account books and the post-mortem inventories of the Montréalers, bears out this conclusion. One would expect such detailed sources to yield an infinite variety of prices, depending on the whims of the evaluators of the estate, the quality of the furs, and so forth. But, as Louise Dechêne has shown, the Montréal *marchands-équipeurs* who outfitted the trading expeditions preferred to simplify matters.[33] Each fall, they met to determine a standard set of prices at which they would credit the *marchands-voyageurs* for their furs. That of 1746, used to evaluate the peltry in the estate of François Augé and Charlotte Lemire Marsolet,[34] serves as an example (table 2).

This *tarif de l'automne* or *prix des marchands-équipeurs*, as it was known, was a benchmark price for prime furs and those of inferior grades alike, the latter being credited as being worth a fraction of the former. In their deliberations, the merchants seem to have considered several factors: the average quality of the year's "crop" of a given type of fur; the quantity on hand that fall; the price of freight and insurance on the ocean voyage;[35] and, above all, market conditions at La Rochelle that spring and in previous years. By all accounts, they were wary of abrupt fluctuations and especially so of sudden price increases, for fear of being caught short by equally sudden declines. In sum, the Montréalers provided a cautious, delayed reading of La Rochelle market rates.[36]

Describing the *tarif* is one thing, but finding traces of it in the account books and the inventories is another.[37] Here the Canadians set all sorts of traps for the

Table 2. **Tarif** *for the year* ***1746.***

bears, large and middle-sized	4#		
bear cubs, idem		36s	
raccoons		22s	6d
bobcats (*pichoux du Sud*)		35s	
otters	3#	10s	
fishers	3#	10s	
martens		40s	
lynxes	10#		
wolves		40s	
wolverines	4#	10s	
mink		20s	
moose in the hair	9#		
elk in the hair	7#		
moose, dressed	3#		
elk, dressed	3#		
deer, dressed		22s	6d
deer in the hair, male		30s	
idem, female		25s	
red fox	3#		

researcher. In some cases, for example, inventory evaluators put aside the *tarif* and tailored their price to the average quality of the furs before them, sometimes informing us of this departure from established practice, sometimes not.[38] In their accounts, merchants often listed furs upon receipt in August, well before the *tarif* had been set, and added the fall's prices later. Others entered the prices of the previous year.[39] The historian is not always able to distinguish one from the other. The result of these difficulties, and of the penury of documents containing such information, is a mixture of lean years and fat so typical of the eighteenth century: certain years for which there appear to be three different prices are followed by several for which there are none.[40] All the same, the trend and some short-term fluctuations emerge in rough outline for most of the important furs.

Figure 5 presents results for seven types of fur sold by the Hudson's Bay Company which were also evaluated reasonably often in the Montréal sources and, in five cases, by the La Rochelle clerks as well. Together they account for a good fifth of the value of Canadian fur exports, beaver included. Several phenomena are worth noting. First, harmony prevails between Montréal and La Rochelle. Both sources convey the same message: with the exception of lynx, the prices of furs shipped to France rose very gradually from the beginning of monetary stability in 1726 until the end of the War of the Austrian Succession in 1748. Only in the interwar period lasting until the mid-1750s did a marked upward trend begin (Champeaux noted it as well).[41] The acute disruption to trade that was the Seven Years' War caused a slump in the very last years of the period.

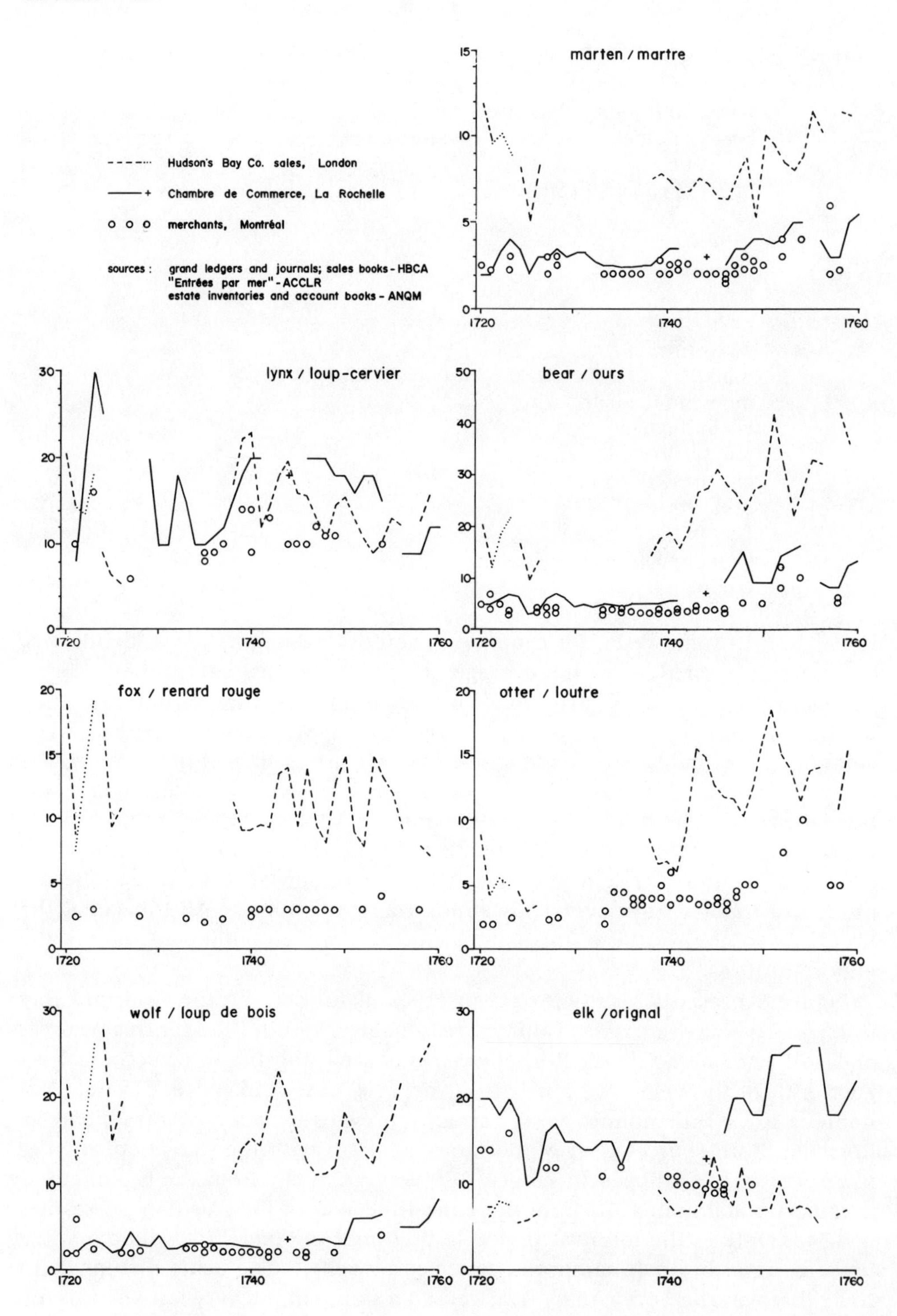

Figure 5. Prices of Selected Furs, 1720-1760 (*livres tournois* per skin).

Were the Hudson's Bay Company prices responding to the same forces? At first glance, the fluctuations in the London series, here converted into *livres tournois*,[42] bear little relation to those affecting sales across the channel or in Montréal. But then it would be unreasonable to expect complete fidelity. Consider, to begin with, the time lag between the fall Hudson's Bay sales and the spring La Rochelle ones, which placed readings from a single trading season in two calendar years. To this delay the La Rochelle clerks were wont to add another year. Consider also the effect of fluctuations in the exchange rate before 1727, and of the wars that disrupted commercial relations, notably in the latter half of the period. Finally, as Henry Sperling, the great export furrier, testified before a parliamentary committee in 1749, the London market for furs of a given type could become glutted when shipments from North America were particularly large, momentarily causing prices to fall.[43] La Rochelle must have faced the same problem from time to time. Some of these situations, when they were due to animal population cycles, for example, occurred in the same trading season and likely provoked parallel price movements on both sides of the channel. Others, reflecting particular developments in the area where Canadians traded, must have affected La Rochelle alone.

But enough qualifications: even if transmission was sometimes garbled or delayed, the curves in figure 5 suggest that prices in both trading-systems were responding to the same signal. The interwar high that is visible on most of the curves must have gratified Sperling, who made out its beginnings in 1749.[44] An earlier peak in otter and wolf prices departs from the La Rochelle experience, however, and merits further study. In some instances (marten, bear), on the other hand, the La Rochelle curve seems to echo earlier short-term price movements in London, much as one would expect in view of the slow response of the Rochelais clerks to market conditions. All three curves single out lynx as an exception to the general pattern by moving downward after 1740. Only in the case of elk (that is to say, moose) do the trend lines diverge, pointing, perhaps, to separate markets for skins of this type.[45]

Generally speaking, then, price movements, like the statistics concerning re-exports, encourage us to look beyond the two countries of importation to an as yet ill-defined market located farther to the east. Further research will permit us to trace its boundaries, both geographic and social, more precisely, and identify the instances where one or the other of the exporting countries occupied a niche of its own.

Even now, however, one thing seems certain: this market may not have been fully integrated, but it was sufficiently so not to accord especially favourable treatment to Canadian furs. A glance at the price-curves confirms this. In five cases out of seven, the Hudson's Bay Company prices converted from sterling into *livres tournois* are much higher than the La Rochelle ones. As we have seen, the Hudson's Bay series is composed of actual sale prices of prime peltry, while the Rochelais clerks, in compiling theirs, quoted something closer to an average price for all qualities of fur. But this technical explanation accounts for only part

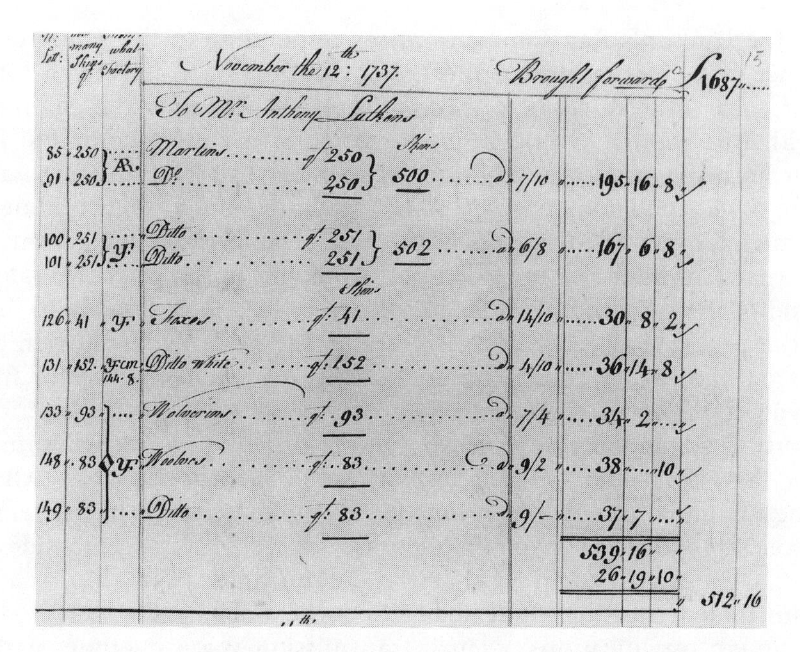

November the 12th: 1737. Brought forward £1687

To Mr. Anthony Luthens

Lot	No.	Ship	Furs	No.	Skins	Price	£ s d
85	250	A.	Martins	250	500	7/10	195 · 16 · 8
91	250	A.	Do.	250			
100	251	Y.	Ditto	251	502	6/8	167 · 6 · 8
101	251	Y.	Ditto	251			
126	41	Y.	Foxes	41		14/10	30 · 8 · 2
131	152	3 fcm 144·8	Ditto white	152		4/10	36 · 14 · 8
133	93	Y.	Wolverins	93		7/4	34 · 2
148	83	Y.	Woolves	83		9/2	38 · · 10
149	83	Y.	Ditto	83		9/-	37 · 7
							539 · 16
							26 · 19 · 10
							512 · 16

Figure 6. Page from the "Accompt Book of Sales" of the Hudson's Bay Company, showing a buyer and the furs he purchased at the November 1737 sale. Manuscript Collection A.48/1 fo. 15(N11172), Hudson's Bay Company Archives, Provincial Archives of Manitoba.

of the gap in prices. The remainder reflects a real difference in the average quality of the furs sold in the two ports. The Canadians, after all, purchased many of their furs from Indians living and hunting south of the Great Lakes, whose wares were of lower quality than most of those delivered to the Hudson Bay posts.[46] Of the "Canadian" furs listed here, only lynx came exclusively from the north and, appropriately enough, fetched roughly the same price on both sides of the Channel.[47] European buyers, then, compared for quality. Like the Indian suppliers of fur, they were comparison shoppers. As the market generally offered them the opportunity to compare North American peltry shipped through London and La Rochelle, it did not force them to pay a premium for the latter. There was no "special deal" in Europe for the Montréalers' furs.[48]

To return to our point of departure, it is clear that European buyers of fur did not pay a premium for Canadian furs, thereby bearing some of the cost of the Canadians' delivery service to the Naskapis, the Assiniboines, the Illinois and all the nations in between. An alternative source of fur from London gave them an excellent reason to refuse the Canadians such special treatment. European *sellers* of trade-goods imported into France and shipped to Canada may have been more generously inclined, or perhaps French manufacturers of such merchandise produced more cheaply than English ones. This other possible "special deal" will require further study. In the meantime, it is hoped that this brief excursion to Europe demonstrates the importance of studying the complete trade cycle. To understand even the North American phases of the fur trade, we must begin to see it whole.

Notes

1. While accepting full responsibility for the errors that remain, I would like to thank Hélène Bédard, Jennifer S.H. Brown, and W.J. Eccles for their comments on this paper. I am grateful also to Louis Lavallée for a reference to a post-mortem inventory containing fur prices, and to Hélène Lafortune and Normand Robert for hastening research in the notarial files by giving me access to print-outs from their Parchemin data base. The Université de Montréal and the Social Science and Humanities Research Council of Canada provided financial support in the form of a Canada Research Fellowship. Finally, I am indebted to the Hudson's Bay Company for permission to consult its archives.
2. H.A. Innis, *The Fur Trade in Canada* (1930; rev. ed., Toronto: University of Toronto Press, 1956), 84-145.
3. See the discussion in T. Wien, "Selling Beaver Skins in North America and Europe, 1720-1760: The Uses of Fur-Trade Imperialism," *Journal of the Canadian Historical Association* 1 (1990): 293-317. On the division of labor in the trade, see L. Dechêne, *Habitants et marchands de Montréal au XVIIe siècle* (Paris: Plon, 1974), 171-83.
4. E.R. Adair, "Anglo-French Rivalry in the Fur Trade during the Eighteenth Century" (1947), reprinted in *Canadian History before Confederation*, J.M. Bumsted, ed., (Georgetown: Irwin-Dorsey, 1972), 143-64; A. Rotstein, "Fur Trade and Empire: An Institutional Analysis," Ph.D. thesis, University of Toronto, 1967); and especially W.J. Eccles, "A Belated Review of Harold Adams Innis, The Fur Trade in Canada," *Canadian Historical Review* 60 (1979): 419-41; reprinted in his *Essays on New France* (Toronto: Oxford University Press, 1987), 61-78; W.J. Eccles, "The Fur Trade and Eighteenth-Century Imperialism," *William and Mary Quarterly* 40 (1983): 341-62; reprinted in *Essays*, 79-95.
5. See A.J. Ray and D.J. Freeman, *"Give Us Good Measure": An Economic Analysis of Relations between the Indians and the Hudson's Bay Company before 1763* (Toronto: University of Toronto Press, 1978); for an application to the Canadian trade, see Wien, "Selling Beaver Skins."
6. For an attempt at a synthesis of the two positions, see Richard White, *The Middle Ground. Indians, Empires, and Republics in the Great Lakes Region,1650-1815* (Cambridge: Cambridge University Press, 1991), 94-141.
7. On the importance of the American and Chinese markets in the late eighteenth and early nineteenth centuries, see John D. Haeger, *John Jacob Astor. Business and Finance in the Early Republic* (Detroit: Wayne State University Press, 1991), 65-93.
8. See Eccles's observations in "A Belated Review," 429-34.
9. Innis, *Fur Trade*, 64-83; E. E. Rich, "Russia and the Colonial Fur Trade," *Economic History Review* 7 (1954): 307-20; G. Frégault, "La Compagnie de la Colonie," reprinted in his *Le XVIIIe siècle canadien: études* (Montréal: Hartubise HMH, 1968), 242-88; D. Miquelon, *New France 1701-1744: "A Supplement to Europe"* (Toronto: McClelland and Stewart, 1987), 55-66; E. Mancke, *A Company of Businessmen: The Hudson's Bay Company and Long-Distance Trade, 1670-1730* (Winnipeg: Rupert's Land Research Centre, 1988), 22-41; Wien, "Selling Beaver Skins."

10. See Wien, "Selling Beaver Skins," 313.
11. The peltry is described in Dechêne, 147-50; cf. Wien, "Castor, peaux et pelleteries dans le commerce canadien des fourrures, 1720-1790," in *Le Castor Fait Tout: Selected Papers of the Fifth North American Fur Trade Conference*, B. Trigger, T. Morantz, and L. Dechêne, eds. (Montréal: Lake St. Louis Historical Society, 1987), 72-92.
12. *Peaux* and *pelleteries* could account for more than half of the value of official fur exports from Québec, but this predominance was usually illusory, as clandestine shipments of beaver to Albany and Oswego were not counted in the official totals.
13. In *Fur: A Study in English Mercantilism* (Toronto: University of Toronto Press, 1943), Murray Lawson provides useful statistics concerning the English fur trade of the period, but discusses mostly beaver and hats. J.G. Clark's brief analysis of La Rochelle's trade in peltry is marred by errors of arithmetic: *La Rochelle and the Atlantic Economy during the Eighteenth Century* (Baltimore: Johns Hopkins University Press, 1981), 167-68. On furs in ship-cargoes, see Miquelon, *Dugard of Rouen: French Trade to Canada and the West Indies, 1729-1770* (Montréal: McGill-Queen's University Press, 1978), 69-90.
14. Testimony of Henry Sperling, 1749, in "Report from the Committee Appointed to Inquire into the State and Condition of the Countries Adjoining to Hudson's Bay," Great Britain, *House of Commons Sessional Papers of the Eighteenth Century*, vol. 18 (Wilmington, Del.: Scholarly Resources, Inc., 1975), 245-48; Archives Nationales, Paris, Marine B7 381, Champeaux, "Du commerce des pelteries d'Amérique," 24 April 1752.
15. See, for example, Archives de Paris D4B6, 1/78, "Bilan de René Couraud," 1 July 1738.
16. Lawson, 87-97.
17. "Vous sçavez," noted a memorialist in 1748, "que La Rochelle fait seule le commerce et la vante des Pelleteries; c'est icy qu'elles abordent toutes et que les Etrangers se rendent pour en faire l'Emplette." Archives de la Chambre de Commerce et d'Industrie de La Rochelle, anciennes archives (ACCLR), 7178, "Mémoire à MM. les Directeurs et Sindics de la Chambre de Commerce de La Rochelle." During the 1730s and the early 1740s, R. Dugard and his associates imported Canadian furs into Rouen, and throughout the period Bayonne received shipments of skins. In wartime, ships from Canada were apt to seek refuge from the enemy all along the French Atlantic coastline.
18. ACCLR 9387-9424,"Entrées par mer" and 9447-9484, "Sorties." Since the customs officials tended to confuse deer (chevreuil) and wapiti (cerf) skins, the table combines the two.
19. Mancke, 34; Wien, "Selling Beaver Skins," 310 n.59.
20. Wien, "Selling Beaver Skins," 310 n.59.
21. Comparison with two lists of fur imports drawn up, apparently on the basis of merchants' invoices, in 1737 and 1752 confirms this impression. The first, which seems accurate because it corresponds very closely to the Québec export statistics, gives much higher totals than the La Rochelle customs clerks. In 1752, it is the latter who give the larger figures. See ACCLR, "Pelleteries de l'année 1752," and Wien, "Castor," 78-80.
22. ACCLR 7178, "Mémoire à MM. les Directeurs et Sindics" (1748); J. Savary des Bruslons, *Dictionnaire universel du commerce* (Paris, 1748), 2: 1050, s.v. "Entrepost."

23. The rates are listed in H. Crouch, *A Complete View of the British Customs*, vol. 1 (London, 1745), 219-24.
24. On this industry, see A. Benoist, "La vie économique à Niort du XVIe au XVIIIe siècle," in J. Combes, ed., *Histoire de Niort des origines à nos jours* (Poitiers: Projets Éditions, 1987), 182-89.
25. "Du commerce des pelteries." By "New England" Champeaux means all the British continental colonies. On the importance of the German and Polish markets, see ACCLR 7178, "Mémoire à MM. les Directeurs et Sindics" (1748).
26. The map is based on the same sources as table 1. "Spain" denotes the Rochelais "Espagne" and the English "Streights"; under "Baltic" are grouped, respectively, "Nord et villes hanséatiques," "Danemark," and "Suède" (the last an importer of marginal importance), and "East Country" and "Russia." "Germany" refers to "Lorraine et Allemagne" in one case and simply to "Germany" in the other. "Switzerland" does not appear in the English list, and is known as "Suisse et Genève" in the French one. I have added the value of furs sent to "Savoie et Piedmont," destinations to which the Genevans tended to re-export, to the Swiss total. Cf. A.-M. Piuz and L. Mottu-Weber, *L'économie genevoise, de la Réforme à la fin de l'Ancien Régime, 16e-18e siècles* (Genève: Georg, 1990), 532.
27. On the meaning of "Nord" in the Balance du commerce statistics, see P. Jeannin, "Les marchés du Nord dans le commerce français au XVIIIe siècle," in *Aires et structures du commerce français au 18e siècle*, P.Léon, ed. (Lyon: Centre d'histoire économique et sociale de la région lyonnaise, 1975), 47-74.
28. See, for example, Bibliothèque municipale de Rouen, fonds Montbret 849, "Objet général du commerce de la France avec l'Etranger en 1752."
29. Hudson's Bay Company Archives (HBCA), A/15/6-A/15/8, Grand Journals. The prices for the period beginning in 1737 are converted from the index numbers in A.J. Ray, "Buying and Selling Hudson's Bay Company Furs in the Eighteenth Century," in D. Cameron, ed., *Explorations in Canadian Economic History. Essays in Honour of Irene M. Spry* (Ottawa: University of Ottawa Press, 1985), 104, table 4, using base-year prices found in HBCA A/48/1, Fur Sales Books.
30. There is no detailed account of the London sales of 1722 and 1723 but, as was their habit, company bookkeepers evaluated the furs coming in from the Bay in "made beaver" and converted these into sterling by giving them an arbitrary value of two shillings and sixpence (HBCA A/15/6). In the fall sales, the furs invariably fetched a higher price. The following year, the clerks entered the difference under the heading "profit and loss." By dividing the made beaver evaluation plus the "profit" for each type of fur by the quantity received, one obtains an average price. As comparison with the actual sale prices of 1721 reveals, the result is on the low side, presumably because it includes "damaged and stage" furs while the sale prices refer to prime furs only.
31. It is the La Rochelle version of this list that contains the statistics used in table 1, *supra*. The Balance du commerce procedures are described in J. Tarrade, *Le commerce colonial de la France à la fin de l'Ancien Régime* (Paris: Presses universitaires de France, 1972), 718-26.
32. Ibid., 770-71.
33. Dechêne, *Habitants et marchands*, 148-50.
34. Archives nationales du Québec à Montréal (ANQM), not. J.-B. Adhémar, inventory, 10 April 1747. In table 2, (#), (s), and (d), respectively, denote *livres tournois, sols*, and *deniers*.

35. See Lamaletie to Guy, 1 January, 22 January, 21 March, 12 April, and 4 July 1745, Archives de l'Université de Montréal, Collection Baby, microfiche 5476.
36. The merchants of Détroit and Michilimakinac established similar price schedules.
37. The best collection of account books is that of the Société Historique de Montréal, available on microfilm: National Archives of Canada, reels M847-51, M858-59, M-869, M-1005. I scanned some 250 post-mortem inventories of *marchands-équipeurs, marchands-voyageurs*, military officers, and other persons bearing their surnames. They can be found in the files, all held by the ANQM, of the following notaries: J.-B. Adhémar, G. Barrette, J.-H. Bouron, N.-A. Guillet de Chaumont, L.-C. Danré de Blanzy, J. David, A. Foucher, C. de Gaudron de Chèvremont, F. Lepailleur, P. Mezières, P. Panet, C. Porlier, J.-C. Raimbault, P. Raimbault, R.-C. Chorel de Saint-Romain, F. Simonnet.
38. See, for example, ANQM, not. F. Simonnet, inventory, Joseph Durocher and Marie-Louise-Catherine Juillet, 30 May 1743.
39. See the practices used in Bibliothèque nationale du Québec, "Livre de comptes ou journal d'un marchand de Ville-Marie" (J.-A. Lemoine Monière, 1739-1751), microfilm copy in ANQM.
40. The Montréal account books yield only scattered quotations, most of them for the 1730s and 1740s. Post-mortem inventories of merchants' possessions are a most unsatisfactory substitute, as they were rarely drawn up during the busy commercial season of late summer and early fall. Yet this was the only time when the attics of most merchants' warehouses contained any furs to be inventoried.
41. "Du commerce des pelteries."
42. Pounds sterling were converted to *livres tournois* on the basis of the London on Paris exchange rate given in J. J. McCusker, *Money and Exchange in Europe and America* (Chapel Hill: University of North Carolina Press, 1978), 95-97.
43. "Report from the Committee. . . ," 246.
44. Ibid., 247.
45. La Rochelle's exports of moose skins went almost exclusively to Spain. There is as yet no information concerning the fate of "elk" skins imported into England, as Lawson limited his discussion to pelts sold to furriers or hatters, excluding those sold to the leather industry.
46. On the source of furs purchased by the Canadians in the early 1750s, see Conrad Heidenreich and Françoise Noël, "France Secures the Interior, 1740-1755," in *Historical Atlas of Canada*, R.C. Harris, ed. (Toronto: University of Toronto Press, 1987), 1: plate 40.
47. Canadian moose skins may have been of better quality than Hudson's Bay ones, which would explain the high La Rochelle price, but once again, the difference may just reflect the influence of the Spanish market alluded to above.
48. Only further research can tell us whether or not French *chamoiseurs* paid more than did their English counterparts for colonial deer skins, in the face of, say, strong domestic demand for breeches or gloves. The available evidence points in the opposite direction. See Miquelon, *New France*, 172 and R. White, *The Roots of Dependency* (Lincoln: University of Nebraska Press, 1985), 47-8. But in any case, deer skins do not a fur trade make. The relatively integrated character of the European market also meant, of course, that there was no "special deal" for furs passing through the English system either; as we have seen, prices tended to converge in the European market. Hence the Montréal merchants' tendency to

send few furs, but considerable amounts of beaver over the route linking the French and English price-systems that led, via Kahnawake or Oswego, to Albany and New York. Beaver, which fetched a lower price at Montréal owing to the influence of the Compagnie des Indes monopoly, made the operation worthwhile; there was no comparable price difference for furs.

British Capital in the Fur Trade: John Strettell and John Fraser

Harry W. Duckworth

Trade in Canada, after the Conquest in 1759-1760, took on the general form already worked out in the American colonies. Manufactured goods, mostly from Britain, were imported to serve the general needs of the white inhabitants and the special needs of the Indian trade, and commodities were sent back. The New World traders of the eighteenth century were not men of means, and the manufacturers and wholesalers in England who supplied them with goods were rarely in a position to advance those goods on long credits. Accordingly, a middleman was needed who could pay the manufacturers as the goods were delivered and send them on to his customers in America, and who was willing to tie up his own capital until the New World customer had sold the goods and remitted his payments. Those payments were sometimes in cash, but cash was scarce in the colonies; more often remittances came as commodities of the country--tobacco, indigo, grain, lumber, deer skins, furs, and so on, depending on which colony was involved and what was salable in London at the time.

In the economy of eighteenth-century Canada, furs and skins occupied a special role for all merchants, since they had a high ratio of value to bulk. As late as 1810, John Julius Angerstein, Chairman of Lloyd's, chose as an example of a particularly valuable property the cargo of a fur ship from Quebec, insured for £200,000.[1] Canadian traders who did not ship furs or other commodities themselves would pay their London debts with bills of exchange based on credits established by those who had.[2] Thus the middleman, to obtain his money, would have to arrange to sell the commodities he was consigned. The middleman who did all these things was the commission merchant, almost always located in London. His role in colonial business was critical, for it was he who provided the capital which allowed the business to develop, and exerted himself to find markets for the products which the colonies produced.

Most of the published information about the London commission merchants has come from historians of the trade of the American colonies.[3] Such correspondence as has survived for the Great Lakes fur trade, however, shows much the same kind of arrangements there.[4] The names of the London commission merchants who supported this and other business enterprise in Canada during the forty-odd years after the British Conquest, which had to pass before the colony began to accumulate capital of its own, are not at all well known, and practically no research seems to have been done on them. Thus, we lack information about a group of individuals very important in the development of business in Canada. There were not many: fewer than ten London firms were of any lasting importance to the Canada trade between 1760 and 1800. It is the purpose of this article is to outline the careers and indicate the influence of two of the more important, in that special subdivision of the Canada trade, the fur trade through Montreal. The individuals chosen, John Strettell and John Fraser, were major suppliers of the North West Company at different stages in its development--Strettell near its beginnings, Fraser during its maturity and decline—and their careers offer a mix of interesting similarities and contrasts.

John Strettell was the younger son of an Irish Quaker, Robert Strettell, who had set up as a brewer in London in the early years of the eighteenth century, was overwhelmed by the financial dislocations brought on by the South Sea Bubble, and later moved to Philadelphia, where he became successful. Young John, born in 1721, did not accompany the rest of the family to the New World, but was raised in business by his mother's eldest brother, the prosperous linen-draper John Owen, a stalwart member of the Quaker merchant community.[5] Little is known of the details of John Owen's business, but he had at least one important debtor, William Webb, in South Carolina,[6] and in view of his family connections he probably dealt with Pennsylvania as well. Introduction to business through John Owen was a double advantage to Strettell. Through the linen wholesale trade, an immensely profitable branch of the trade to America, he would have come in contact with several of the early merchant bankers, while connection with the Quaker merchants in particular ensured membership in a mutually helpful group of sound businessmen, who expected one another to conduct their affairs in an honest and conservative way.[7]

John Strettell first appears in a London Directory in 1753,[8] when he was already in his early thirties, but I have found no specific reference to his business until 1758. In that year the governing Council of the colony of Pennsylvania, of which Strettell's father was a member, created a Commission to manage the colony's relations with the Indians. John's brother Amos was one of the Indian Commissioners, and the order for half the goods required by the Commission to be used as Indian presents was sent to John Strettell. The business of supplying Indian trade goods to the Commissioners lasted until the outbreak of Pontiac's War in 1763; it was profitable in itself, and no doubt it gave Strettell valuable experience with manufacturers and wholesalers capable of supplying the special mix of goods suitable for the Indian trade.[9] Strettell's prominence in the Pennsylvania trade is suggested by the fact that when Benjamin Franklin was sent to London by the Philadelphia merchants in 1764, he carried with him, for expenses, a bill of exchange for £300 drawn on Strettell.[10]

How John Strettell became interested in Canada, after the Conquest of New France in 1759-1760 brought that colony and its population into the British

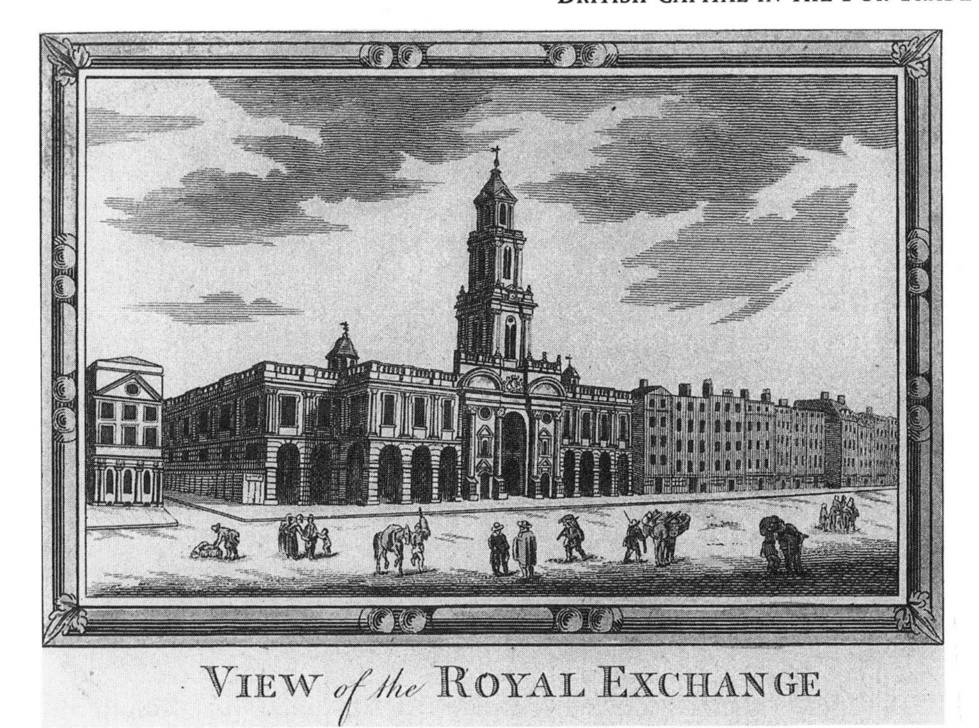

Figure 1. The Royal Exchange, taken from a tourist print of the mid-eighteenth century. Six days a week, between noon and 2 PM, the business world of London gathered here to make deals and exchange gossip. Lloyd's, the center of the shipping insurance trade, was located in rooms on the upper floor of this building. In the surrounding streets further business was transacted in the many coffee-houses—in the New York Coffee House just east of the Royal Exchange, most of the produce of the Canada fur trade was auctioned. Both John Strettell and John Fraser would have spent many hours under the arcades of the Royal Exchange. Courtesy of Harry W. Duckworth.

mercantile sphere, is not known. In January 1765 he declared that he held 154,456 *livres* in Canada paper money, for which, like his fellow merchants, he hoped to receive compensation under the terms of the treaty with France. This money Strettell must have acquired through trade with Canada, but relative to that held by other merchants the amount was small, suggesting that his entry into that trade was recent.[11] One of his early Canadian customers was Thomas Walker, whose name is generally known because of one celebrated event: the affair of Walker's Ear. How this incident blew up into a drawn-out political episode, in which the London merchants interested in Canada finally obtained the recall of General Murray, the first British Governor of Canada, is a long story, well known to Canadian historians. Little, however, has been published on Walker's business activities. A surviving Quebec Port Book for 1763-1764 records imports of large amounts of goods on various ships, consigned to Walker under the bale mark TW. The nature of these goods shows that most of them were intended for the fur trade.[12] One of Walker's fur trade customers was Hyacinthe Réaume at Detroit, whose debt was already old in 1768; Walker also supplied Réaume's son Charles. The Réaume debts to Walker were eventually pursued by the Montreal firm Todd & McGill as attorneys for John Strettell. This, and the fact that Todd & McGill, as Strettell's attorneys, seized Walker's goods in 1777 at Montreal, prove Walker's business link with Strettell.[13] Walker also had interests in the North West: it was reported to Hudson's Bay Company servants at York Factory in 1773 that Justice Walker was importing goods from Britain for the Grand Portage trade of Isaac Todd and his associates, a forerunner of the North West Company.[14] These goods, too, were doubtless supplied by Strettell.

Apart from his direct business dealings, Strettell was at the center of the lobbying effort of the London merchants, in the aftermath of the Walker affair, to see Governor Murray removed from office. It was Strettell, with another prominent Quaker linen merchant, Edward Wakefield, who presented the first memorial to the Lords of Trade within days of the arrival of the news of the Walker affair in London. After Wakefield's death, his place in the lobby with Strettell was taken by another Quaker merchant with interests in America, Robert Crafton.[15] The efforts of the London merchants led to Murray's recall to justify his government in 1766, and the next spring, though technically vindicated, he decided not to resume his command in Canada. Thus, Strettell and his associates got what they wanted. Murray's successor, Guy Carleton, had a more tolerant attitude to merchants, and saw the importance to Canada of furthering mercantile enterprise.

During the difficult period leading up to the revolution in America, John Strettell is occasionally glimpsed as a conciliatory force in London. He was one of the ten London merchants and firms trading to America who called for a general meeting of the American merchants in view of the political crisis in the colonies, at the end of 1774; that meeting appointed him, as one of three representatives from the merchants interested in "Quebeck," to a Committee charged with preparing a petition to Parliament. Three years later, he was an organizer of the subscription to relieve "the DISTRESSES of the AMERICAN PRISONERS, in Great-Britain and Ireland, by furnishing them with CLOATHING, or other NECESSARIES."[16] Strettell was in a delicate position in a time of high-running passions, having important mercantile interests and significant debts due from the colonies. It may have been because of the equivocal face he showed to the world that his application to export military stores (guns and powder for the fur trade) to Canada was denied by the Lords of Trade in the turbulent summer of 1776. This decision, potentially disastrous for Strettell, was circumvented when a re-application for the same goods was accepted from two other London merchants, one probably his cousin, a few days later.[17]

Strettell's business interests were widespread. In 1790 his executors claimed pre-1776 debts of about £15,000 due from the former colonies, most of it in Pennsylvania and the rest in New York.[18] He had customers at St. Thomas, West Indies, in 1782, and despatched a cargo of goods to Cape François, Haiti for the use of the Montreal Distilling Company in 1786.[19] It is probably also significant that John Brickwood, Strettell's clerk and successor in business, was appointed Agent for Bermuda in 1784; this office Brickwood held for the rest of his life.[20] It was in Canada, however, during the War in America, that John Strettell made his fortune. In 1784 he referred in a letter to "my Canada Friends, to whose favours I principally owe my present happy circumstances."[21]

Who were Strettell's Canada friends? Though fragmentary, the evidence is extensive enough to assemble a pretty complete picture. Thomas Walker, as already mentioned his first known customer, ended his Canadian career by making common cause with the Americans in 1775-76, and Strettell's representatives were forced to seize his remaining goods at Montreal soon after.[22] Though this experience was ultimately a poor one, Strettell did much better with his other Canadian correspondents. Most important were John Paterson and Isaac Todd.

John Paterson, a Lowland Scot, was established at Quebec by 1765, in partnership with a Highlander, Charles Grant.[23] It is likely that Paterson and Grant were first supplied by the London firm of Alexander, Robert, and William Grant, dissolved about 1768.[24] Documents show a business relationship between John Strettell and Paterson and Grant by 1770, and Strettell may have taken over the Grants' Canadian customers directly. John Strettell was supplying Paterson and Grant by 1770.[25] This partnership and its business successors were probably Strettell's most valuable customers, a point reinforced by the fact that Strettell left Paterson a legacy of £250. Paterson himself retired to London in 1778, leaving Charles Grant to continue at Quebec, and Grant soon added a very able young partner, John Blackwood, who was to become one of Quebec's more eminent businessmen. Blackwood remained an important customer of Strettell's London successors until after 1800.[26]

Although Paterson and Grant were mainly importers and wholesalers of English manufactured goods to the Canada retail trade, inevitably they also dealt in furs in order to remit value to London. Some of their customers were fur traders. In 1770, for instance, it was reported that "Paterson and Grant have made a wery great Hand at Temiskamingue this Year they made near 80 Packs."[27] Charles Paterson, who was involved in the proto-North West Company partnerships of the 1770s and was later an important fur trader at Michilimackinac, may well have been a relation of John Paterson, but information is lacking at present.[28]

Strettell's other favorite customer in Canada, Isaac Todd, was an Irishman who was involved in the fur trade beyond Grand Portage by the late 1760s; in 1770 his operations were first referred to as "la grande Compagnie de Nord Ouest." Todd sold his Grand Portage interests a couple of years later, but continued to supply his successors from Montreal. In 1776 he and a partner, James McGill, organized the firm of Todd and McGill there, importing goods directly from London; their supplier was John Strettell.[29] The long-lived firm of Todd and McGill was Strettell's most important customer at Montreal, and through them Strettell supplied such men as John Askin at Detroit and Andrew Todd at Michilimackinac. It was James McGill's share of the profit of this Montreal firm that ultimately made possible the foundation of McGill University. John Strettell evidently valued these correspondents, for his will included a bequest of £100 to Isaac Todd.

The aggressive and imaginative North West traders Benjamin and Joseph Frobisher also became Strettell's customers, probably in 1777. There are hints that Benjamin Frobisher's earlier partnership, the firm of Dobie and Frobisher, was obtaining goods from Edward Harrison, a Canadian customer of the London commission merchants Davis, Strachan and Co., around 1770.[30] Whether this arrangement survived the end of the Dobie and Frobisher partnership is unknown. Benjamin Frobisher went to England in the fall of 1776,[31] and such a trip would have had an important business purpose, very likely to settle a new London correspondent. In 1778 the Frobishers received goods from England on the *Hector*, the ship on which John Strettell sent his Canada goods in that year.[32] I believe that Benjamin Frobisher's visit to England in 1776-1777 settled an arrangement with Strettell to supply goods beginning in spring 1777. Strettell's business successors, Brickwood, Pattle and Co, were still supplying the Frobishers in 1786, and provided half the goods to the partnership of McTavish, Frobisher & Co. until 1791.[33]

John Porteous, a cousin of John Paterson's established at Montreal, was another of Strettell's customers, through whom the North West Company partnership of Holmes and Grant (consisting of Charles Grant's brother-in-law and cousin) received its goods.[34] After Porteous's sudden death in 1782, the supplying of Holmes and Grant was taken over by Charles Grant and John Blackwood, still using goods shipped by Strettell.[35]

It was the connections with John Paterson, Isaac Todd, the Frobishers, and their partners and customers that made John Strettell the most important source of capital for the famous North West Company. In the temporary North West Company of 1779, the sixteen-share partnership of Grand Portage traders included eight shares which John Strettell supported from London.[36] Even more significant, it would seem, was Strettell's role in the reorganized company of 1784. As W. S. Wallace pointed out long ago, the evidence of the Indian Trade licenses suggests that the North West Company of 1784 was created as a monopoly because certain powerful traders, Todd & McGill especially, withdrew from Grand Portage in that year and concentrated on the southwest trade through Michilimackinac and Detroit.[37] In light of the new insight—that John Strettell was supplying goods to most of the principals on both sides of the partition agreement which Wallace inferred—I would argue now that Strettell must have encouraged and may even have insisted on an arrangement that would prevent a head-to-head competition for furs among his own customers. In the sixteen-share North West Company of 1783, Strettell's customers again probably held eight of the shares.[38]

Figure 2 summarizes the range of connections which John Strettell, and his successor firms, enjoyed with the fur trade of the Great Lakes and the Northwest.[39] The extent of the business is impressive. Many of the best-known names

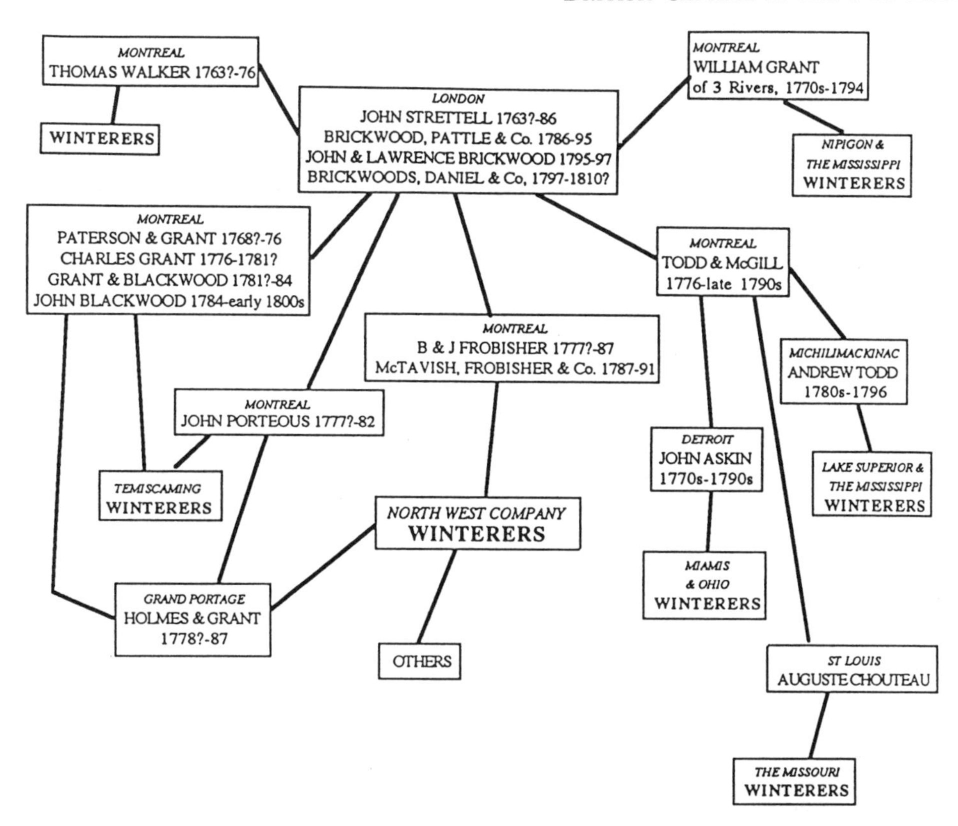

Figure 2. Fur trade supply lines involving John Strettell and his successor firms. Each box represents a firm or succession of firms or traders located at a particular place—London, Quebec, Montreal, or places in the Upper Country. The lines connecting the boxes represent the routes of flow of trade goods (outwards from London to the fur country) and furs (inwards from the fur country to London). Sources of information for this diagram are extensive; apart from references in the text, see relevant articles in the *Dictionary of Canadian Biography*.

in the fur trade appear on this diagram, and most of the more important fur-trading districts are represented. For the period around 1780, when the fur trade was starting to achieve a measure of vertical integration, no other London supplier could claim nearly so wide a series of connections.

Cautious in his private life as he was in his business, John Strettell stayed a bachelor until he was fifty-five. In 1776 he married his housekeeper, Mary Hayling, a Quaker from the Bristol community, and they had two sons—John, who died of whooping cough at the age of two, and Amos, born in 1782, who survived to inherit the fortune amassed by a father he had barely known.[40] Strettell's health began to fail in 1784, but there was time to transfer the business into new hands before he died two years later. The debts due to him in the New World were purchased by a new partnership of John Brickwood, Strettell's clerk of twenty-five years' service, and a returned East India Company servant with money in his pocket, Thomas Pattle.[41] Brickwood, Pattle and Company continued all the branches of Strettell's Canada business, though they lost the most important of their fur trade customers to Simon McTavish's new London firm in the early 1790s. With various reorganizations, John Brickwood's companies survived in the Canada trade till 1810, when the last one succumbed in the aftermath of the failure of Brickwood's merchant bank.[42]

John Strettell is an important figure who has been largely forgotten. John Fraser, the second subject of this paper, is a relatively familiar name because of his role in the London end of the North West Company's operations in the 1790s and after. He really appears out of nowhere in fur trade histories, though the responsibility he held and the skill with which he carried it out show that he was already a man of maturity and experience. Here, I shall limit myself to outlining the missing parts of his career. The problem of identification has been central, since the name was extremely common in Scotland. The crucial discovery, from which it could be shown that a number of scattered references all refer to the same John Fraser, is that he was the head of a small but recognized Fraser family, that of Achnagairn in Inverness-shire.[43] This finding, and others leading from it, allow the John Fraser who was established in London by the late 1760s, and who traded to Canada in the 1770s and early 1780s, to be identified with the man who ran the London firm of McTavish, Fraser and Company, supplying the North West Company in the 1790s and after.

How John Fraser began in business is not known, but his father was a merchant at Inverness, and John is found in the London Directories from 1769 onwards.[44] Access to capital would have been assured by the fact that George Ross of Pitkerrie, one of the most influential Scotsmen in London, was his cousin.[45] The full extent of Fraser's business concerns at this period is not known, but by 1776 he was shipping goods to Canada.[46] In the year 1781, one of Fraser's Montreal customers was the North West fur trader Simon McTavish,[47] whose family was itself of Fraser origin.

Business conditions in Canada during the period of the American Revolutionary War were badly overheated, and it was inevitable that a significant proportion of the Canadian merchants would eventually fail. John Strettell's customers avoided the worst, but John Fraser's correspondents were a different matter. In the spring of 1783 the Treasury in London instructed Governor Frederick Haldimand to move at once to recover Government moneys which had been advanced as credits, over several years, to a number of merchants in the colony. How these advances had come to be made is a story in itself, but in early 1783 the amount outstanding totaled about £130,000, of which over £70,000 was owed by the single firm of Shaw and Fraser. It is probable that Shaw and Fraser were John Fraser's biggest debtors in Canada. Governor Haldimand sued Shaw and Fraser in the Canadian courts in June of 1783, a judgment was quickly obtained and put into execution, and Shaw and Fraser went bankrupt. John Fraser had spent the summer in Canada, trying unsuccessfully to head off calamity; back in London, he followed them into bankruptcy the following January.[48]

Figure 3. John Fraser of Achnagairn (1741?-1824), London merchant and partner in the firm of McTavish, Fraser & Co., by his daughter, Justina Fraser. Probably painted around 1810 or 1815, when the subject was about seventy years old. In a private Scottish collection.

The experience must have been shattering--Fraser was in his early forties, married with a young daughter, at a stage when most merchants would expect to retire to ease and comfort, and now he would have to begin again. His cousin George Ross of Pitkerrie saved him from total ruin. A few months earlier, Fraser's ancestral property of Achnagairn had been mortgaged to Ross for £10,000, and this secured it from seizure. Ross also made some kind of arrangement with Fraser's creditors, which cost him so much money that Ross specifically mentioned his losses in his own will in 1786.[49] John Fraser himself spent much of the next four years in trips between London and Canada, painstakingly bringing legal actions against his debtors there, seizing property, reselling it, and gradually recouping his losses. Much if not all of this activity was performed by a new firm called Fraser and Young (apparently consisting of John Fraser and John Young, later to be prominent in Canada politics), which may have been set up specifically to handle the recovery of Fraser's Canada debts.[50] Fraser had completed his recovery by about 1788, and then probably settled down to a quiet life in London, like other businessmen sobered by bankruptcy but knowledgeable about the London community, writing insurance policies and brokering deals.

It may have come as a complete surprise to him when Simon McTavish approached him, probably in the winter of 1790-1791, with the proposal that Fraser become a partner in a new London firm of commission merchants, which would take over the supplying of goods to the North West Company. McTavish, Fraser & Company was to consist of three shares, two held by McTavish and one by Fraser; Fraser was to manage affairs in London while, at least for the time being, McTavish supervised matters in Montreal. The firm commenced business by selling the North West Company furs sent home in the fall of 1791, and shipped the North West Company's outfits in the spring of 1792. It acquired large premises, with a warehouse, counting house, and living quarters, at No. 2, Suffolk Lane, in the heart of the City's business district, and this was to remain the firm's address as long as the North West Company existed.[51]

The period of John Fraser's career beginning with the foundation of the commission firm of McTavish, Fraser & Co. is known to fur trade historians, and a full account of its dealings can be assembled from the McTavish letters in the Hudson's Bay Company Archives and elsewhere.[52] Briefly, the firm began by taking on several large Canadian customers, whom they attracted from other London commission merchants. By this they incurred resentment, and also soon found themselves overextended for the amount of capital they needed. John Fraser was worried about the cash flow problem by early 1793, and much of his activity in the next three years was devoted to solving it. The crisis passed, thanks to Fraser's good connections with sources of capital and to the firm's ability quickly to divest themselves of all of their Canadian customers except the North West Company itself. Thereafter, the business was stable and secure. In addition to his careful assembly of the North West Company's large outfits of each year,[53] his leasing or purchase of ships and hiring of captains to sail them,

Figure 4. Interior of the Royal Exchange, from a print dated 1807. The view shows the bustling activity under the arcades during "Exchange Time." Merchants interested in different branches of international trade gathered in different parts of the building. In this picture, note the Jewish merchant at the lower left, distinguished by his beard; the turbaned Turkish merchants meeting a bewigged Englishman at the lower right; and, at the foot of a pillar, a small boy, holding his father's hand, is introduced to the purposeful bustle of the London business world. Almost everyone is wearing a beaver hat. Courtesy of Harry W. Duckworth.

his marketing of the furs through the London auction houses, and his skillful management of cash and credit through the highly seasonal demands for both, Fraser was responsible for the management of McTavish's own share of the profits in London. These were invested in securities to some extent, while a steady income came from shipping insurance policies. Fraser's letters to McTavish reveal a genuine intimacy and friendly concern. The impression one draws from the correspondence is that the London firm could never have survived without the acumen, experience, and good financial connections which John Fraser brought to the partnership.

Fraser survived Simon McTavish by more than twenty years. He appears to have extricated much of his personal fortune from the complex affairs in which the North West Company was embroiled during the last years of its existence, and succeeded in getting for his son John a seat on the governing Committee set up to superintend the amalgamation of the North West and Hudson's Bay Companies in 1821. His eldest son James had a place in the East India Company Civil Service; his daughter Mary married the eldest son of another Fraser family, that of Belladrum, to her father's great pride; another son attended Cambridge University and became an Anglican priest.[54] John Fraser, the father, died at his ancestral property of Achnagairn in 1825, aged eighty-three. His will reveals that at the time of his death his son James was in business difficulties in India, which so far had cost the father some £6000.[55]

This article has been concerned with new information about the two most important London commission merchants serving the Canada fur trade of the late eighteenth century. The firms involved were durable, and like other businesses of the day were dependent for their success on the talents of single individuals. A man like John Strettell—cautious, scrupulous, but worldly-wise—could weave a personal fortune out of strands drawn from buying, selling, politicking, and the use of powerful friends and relations. Another, like John Fraser, could suffer financial misfortune in mid-career, yet survive with talents and experience which would serve another capitalist (in this case, Simon McTavish) in a way absolutely critical to the other's success. Strettell probably never set eyes on Canada, and Fraser was probably never west of Montreal, but the influence they had on Canadian business in general, and the fur trade in particular, was great and lasting, in the period when British capital was needed for all but the most modest enterprise within the colony. In the next generations, when colonial businessmen began to command capital of their own, men like Strettell and Fraser would largely be forgotten, and their careers and contributions would become a neglected facet of Canadian economic history.

Notes

1. C. Wright and C. E. Fayle, *A History of Lloyd's* (London: MacMillan & Co., 1928), 195.
2. Lawrence Ermatinger's correspondence illustrates the two methods of remitting payment to London, furs or bills of exchange, Ermatinger Letterbook, National Archives of Canada [hereafter NAC], MG19 A2 Ser. 1, 1 (Microfilm C-4556), pp. 81, 90, 95, *et cetera*.
3. See J. M. Price, "Capital and credit in the British-Chesapeake trade, 1750-1775" in *Of Mother Country and Plantations*, eds. V. B. Platt and D. C. Skaggs (Bowling Green, Ohio: Bowling Green State University Press, 1971), 7-36; J. M. Price, *Joshua Johnson's Letterbook 1771-1774. Letters from a merchant in London to his partners in Maryland* (London: London Record Society, 1979), especially the "Introduction"; F. N. Mason, *John Norton and Sons Merchants of London and Virginia*, 2nd ed. (Newton Abbot: David and Charles, 1968), especially the "Introduction" by S. M. Rosenblatt. Biographical data on sixty-seven London commission merchants who claimed debts in the United States after the Revolution are given by K. A. Kellock, "London Merchants and the pre-1776 American Debts," *Guildhall Studies in London History* (London: The Guildhall Library, 1974), 1: 109-49.
4. See letters from Phyn and Ellice of Schenectady to their London suppliers, Pigou and Booth and then John Blackburn, 1768-76, in Phyn and Ellice Letterbooks 1 to 3 (Buffalo and Erie County Historical Society, Buffalo, N.Y; microfilm at

NAC); and from Lawrence Ermatinger at Montreal to his London suppliers Benjamin Price, then Price and Morland, and then Davis, Strachan and Co., 1770-78, in Ermatinger Letterbook (note 2, above).

5. For Strettell's family connections, see J. J. Green, "The Quaker Family of Owen," *Journal of the Friends Historical Society* 1 (1903-1904): 28-39, 74-81, 111-16, especially 115; *Burke's Landed Gentry*, 18th ed., vol. 1 (London: Burke's Peerage Ltd., 1965), 654-5. The probate copies of John Owen's and John Strettell's wills are Public Record Office, London (PRO), PROB 11/835, Quire 48, and PROB 11/1145, Quire 452, respectively.
6. Philip M. Hamer, ed., *The Papers of Henry Laurens* (Columbia: University of South Carolina Press, 1968-), 1:10n.
7. For the Quaker merchants in general, see P. H. Emden, *Quakers in Commerce. A Record of Business Achievement* (London: Sampson Low, Marston and Co., 1939); A. Raistrick, *Quakers in Science and Industry* (New York: Augustus M. Kelly, 1968). Raistrick lists Strettell among a group of prominent Quaker merchants who cooperated in a scheme to help feed the poor of London, beginning in 1767 (229).
8. *Kent's Directory for the Year 1753*, 20th ed. (London: Henry Kent, 1753), lists "Strettell John, Mercht. at Mr. Merryweather's, Hatter, Lombard-street." William Merryweather, hatter, was the ground floor tenant of Lloyd's Coffee House in the early 1750s (Wright and Fayle, *History of Lloyd's*, 82). Strettell was still at Merryweather's in *Kent's* for 1754; at "Mr Darinbrook's, Nicholas-lane," in *Kent's* for 1755; at "Mr. Cooke's, Sise-lane," in various Directories between 1758 and 1763; at "Mr. Lynde's, Sise-lane," in *Kent's*, 1765; and from 1767 onward at his own premises: No. 1, Riche's-court, Lime-street. The lease of the Riche's-court house was taken over by Strettell's business successors in 1786. All citations of London Directories are to the collection in the Guildhall Library, London.
9. Historical Society of Pennsylvania (HSP), Philadelphia, Gratz Manuscript Collection, Indian Commissioners Correspondence and Accounts, dated between 1758 and 1764. I am grateful to Ellen Slack, Manuscripts and Archives Librarian to the Society, for locating and providing copies of these and other letters of John Strettell. For the Commissioners for Indian Affairs in Pennsylvania, see L. Mulkearn, ed., *George Mercer Papers Relating to the Ohio Company of Virginia* (Pittsburgh: University of Pittsburgh Press, 1954), 154, 626.
10. L. W. Labaree, ed., *The Papers of Benjamin Franklin*, vol. 11 (New Haven: Yale University Press, 1967), 427n.
11. For the list of London merchants holding Canada paper money, and the amounts, see the copy in NAC, MG 5 A 1, vol. 467, f. 66, pp. 195-98. The merchants swore to the amounts they held before William Stephenson, Lord Mayor of London, on 11, 12, and 16 January 1765; Strettell affirmed rather than swearing, no doubt because he was a Quaker. His holding was only 2 percent of the total of almost 7.6 million *livres* declared, making him the thirteenth largest holder; the five largest accounted for 54 percent between them.
12. For the story of Walker's Ear, see L. H. Thomas, *Dictionary of Canadian Biography* (*DCB*) (Toronto: University of Toronto Press, 1979), 4: 758-60. The references in the Quebec Port Book are NAC, RG4 A3 1, 27-32, 94-100, 113-26, 139-42; RG4 B28 28, gunpowder bond dated 20 May 1765 confirms that the TW bale mark was used by Thomas Walker.

13. Edgar Papers (photostats), NAC, MG19 A1 1, 168-9, 176-80, 738-42; Quebec *Gazette*, 15 May and 12 June 1777.
14. W. S. Wallace, ed., *Documents relating to the North West Company* (Toronto: Champlain Society, 1934), 41.
15. Strettell and Wakefield presented a memorial to the Lords of Trade, complaining about "several arbitrary proceedings and unconstitutional establishments at Quebec," on 22 April 1765 (*Journal of the Commissioners for Trade and Plantations, January 1764-December 1767* [London: HMSO, 1936], 167). What seems to be the actual (undated) memorial, signed by twenty-five London firms of commission merchants and warehousemen, is PRO, CO42 25, 241 (microfilm at NAC). For Edward Wakefield, of the firm of Wakefield, Willett & Pratt, see his death notice (*Gazetteer & New Daily Advertiser*, Saturday, 7 December 1765) and his will (PRO, PROB 11/914, Quire 813). Robert Crafton, hosier, of the firm of Crafton & Colson, signed various memorials concerned with American affairs, went bankrupt in 1778, and died in 1780 (*Gazetteer & New Daily Advertiser*, 16 October 1775; *Gentleman's Magazine [G. Mag.]* 1778, 191; London Burial Digest, Friends House, London). Letters from Strettell and Crafton concerned with the lobby against Governor Murray, dated Oct 3 1766 and Feb 26 1767, are in the Shelburne Papers (copies at NAC, MG23 A4 16, 85) and Hardwicke Papers (BL, Add. Ms. 31,195, 123; copy at NAC), respectively. During Thomas Walker's visit to London in 1765-66, Strettell was to open letters addressed to Walker in London in the latter's absence (Welles to Fowler Walker, 20 March 1766, in BL, Add. Ms. 31,915, 226 [copy at NAC]).
16. For the merchants' meeting, London *Daily Advertiser*, 23 December 1774, 12 January 1775; for the subscription for the American Prisoners, London *Gazetteer and New Daily Advertiser*, 26 December 1777 and following dates.
17. For the applications, see *Journal of the Commissioners for Trade and Plantations, 1776-1782* (London: HMSO, 1938), 35. That the re-application, by the London merchants Richard Pollard and John Bell, was for the same goods is indicated by the fact that they were to use the same vessel, the *Generous Friend*. The arrangement for Pollard and Bell to apply, and the acceptance of their application, were doubtless the result of some hasty behind-the-scenes lobbying once Strettell's original proposal had been turned down.
18. Kellock, 147.
19. Strettell to Vaux, 19 January 1782, in Vaux Papers, HSP; Samuel Birnie Letterbook, NAC, MG23, GIII, 8, p. 56.
20. L. M. Penson, *The Colonial Agents of the British West Indies* (London: University of London Press, 1924), 248, 254.
21. Strettell to Vaux, 30 July 1784, in HSP, Vaux Papers.
22. See note 13.
23. The earliest reference found so far to the firm of Paterson and Grant is in an account opened in May 1765 (NAC, MG19 A2 ser. 3, 63, no. 265). Other early references are in the Ermatinger Letterbook, 4, 79; in NAC, MG19 A2 ser. 3, 65, no. 276; and in the Quebec *Gazette*, 1 September 1768.
24. W. S. Wallace, "Strathspey in the Canadian Fur Trade," in *Essays in Canadian History Presented to George MacKinnon Wrong for His Eightieth Birthday*, ed. R. Flenley, ed. (Toronto: MacMillan and Co., 1939), 279-83.
25. Paterson and Grant drew a bill of exchange on Strettell in 1770 (Phyn and Ellice Letterbook, no. 1, 362), which shows that they were in correspondence with

him by that date. In 1774 Paterson and Grant represented Strettell and the London Grants in the sale of their joint property, the Montcalm House on the Ramparts of Quebec (Quebec *Gazette*, 18 August 1774). A letter from Paterson and Grant to Strettell was intercepted in fall 1775 and an extract made for Lord Shelburne (*Historical Manuscripts Commission, 14th Report, Appendix Part X* [London: HMSO, 1895], 395).

26. Paterson and Grant had wound up by the end of 1776, and John Paterson left Canada for England, probably for good, in 1778 (Quebec *Gazette*, 23 January 1777, 29 October 1778). His death notice called him "one of the oldest Merchants in the Canada trade" (London *Times*, 28 June 1806). For brief notices of Charles Grant see Wallace, *Documents*, 448, and "Strathspey in the Canadian Fur Trade," 283-84. For John Blackwood, see biography by J.P. Wallot in *DCB* (Toronto: University of Toronto Press, 1983), 5: 85-8.
27. Ermatinger Letterbook, 4.
28. For Charles Paterson, see Wallace, *Documents*, 491; other information is in the Ermatinger Letterbook, 2, 201.
29. For Isaac Todd, see biography by M. Momryk, *DCB* 5: 818-22. There are additional useful references to Todd's Grand Portage trade in the Ermatinger Letterbook, 18, 61, 201. The reference to "la grande Compagnie de Nord Ouest" [sic] is in Porteous to Todd, Detroit, 10 October 1770, copied into Phyn and Ellice Letterbook no. 1, 366. That John Strettell was the London supplier of Todd and McGill after 1776 is made clear by many items in the Edgar Papers, especially letters on pages 521-23, 717-18, and accounts of furs sold, submitted by Strettell, on pages 664-67, 733, 743-46, 808-15. Todd and McGill appear frequently in legal notices in the Quebec *Gazette* over the next twenty years, acting as attorney for Strettell or his business successors, Brickwood, Pattle, and Co.
30. Edgar Papers, 247-9, 262-4; Ermatinger Letterbook, 18; see also A. J. H. Richardson, "Edward Harrison," *DCB* 4:329-31.
31. Wallace, *Documents*, 58.
32. See advertisement by the Frobishers for a lost bale from aboard the *Hector*, Quebec *Gazette*, 7 September 1778. For Strettell's use of the *Hector* that year, *Journal of the Commissioners for Trade and Plantations from January 1776 to May 1782* (London: HMSO, 1938), 169; Edgar Papers, 694-97.
33. Joseph Frobisher Letterbook (McGill University, McLennan Library Department of Rare Books and Special Collections, CH132 S2), 3195, 3198, 3202-7, 3215, 3220-21, 3223-24; Simon McTavish Inward Correspondence, Provincial Archives of Manitoba (PAM), HBCA, F.3/1, 3-4, 10.
34. John Porteous received goods from Strettell in 1781 (NAC, MG19 A2 ser. 3, 68, no. 892, p. 35), and the Indian Trade Licences show Porteous acting in consort with others of Strettell's customers. The Montreal firm of Porteous and Sutherland was supplying the Grand Portage partnership of Holmes and Grant in 1778 (M. M. Quaife, ed., *The John Askin Papers*, vol. 1 [Detroit: Library Commission, 1928], 144), and Porteous usually signed Holmes and Grant's Trade Licences as security.
35. For Porteous's death from a fall from a horse, see John Paterson to Porteous, 2 October 1782, in Porteous Papers (Buffalo and Erie County Historical Society; microfilm at NAC), no. 63. John Blackwood supplied Holmes and Grant until 1788 (PAM, Hudson's Bay Company Archives [HBCA], F.3/1, 139v).

36. Of the sixteen shares in the temporary company of 1779 (Wallace, *Documents*, 66), the two shares each of Todd and McGill, the Frobishers, McGill and Paterson, and Holmes and Grant were certainly or probably supplied by Strettell; those of McTavish, Wadden, McBeath, and Oakes (seven in all) were almost certainly supplied by other London houses. The London supplier of John Ross' single share is unknown, and he may have obtained his goods in Montreal rather than importing them himself.
37. Wallace, *Documents*, 8-10.
38. Of the sixteen shares conjecturally listed by Innis (Wallace, *Documents*, 8), the Frobishers (3 shares), Robert Grant (2), Nicholas Montour (2) and William Holmes (1) were supplied directly or indirectly by Strettell. Those of McTavish (3), McBeath (2) and Small (2) were certainly supplied by others. The source of Peter Pond's goods (1 share) is unknown.
39. Apart from connections shown in figure 2, Strettell and his successors had Canadian non-fur trade customers. These included Jacob Jordan at Montreal and his protégé, the Montreal Distilling Company, 1785-1787 (Samuel Birnie Letterbook, NAC, MG23 GIII 8, passim); John Reed & Co. and John Bell, both at Montreal, in 1781 (NAC, MG19 A2 ser. 3, 68, no. 892, pp. 34, 43-4); William Grant of St. Roch, whose principal creditor, at his death in 1805 was Brickwood, Daniel & Co. (D. Roberts, "William Grant," *DCB* 5: 374); Thomas Aylwin at Quebec (J. Lafleur, "Thomas Aylwin," *DCB* 4: 37). Some of these connections may have lasted for many years, but the evidence is fragmentary. Richard Dobie was a customer of John Brickwood in 1788 (advertisement by Dobie & Badgley, Montreal *Gazette*, 2 October 1788); it is not clear whether this was a long-lived relationship.
40. For the marriage, see the slightly different notices in the London *Daily Advertiser* and the London *Gazetteer and New Daily Advertiser*, both of 19 June 1776; London Marriage Digest, Friends House. For the children, see *Burke's Landed Gentry* (as in note 5, above), and London Birth and Death Digests, Friends House. Strettell's widow, Mary, married secondly not John Walker, as *Burke's* states, but John Wathen, a banker: *Times*, 25 September 1787.
41. Strettell died at his house at Croydon on 20 July 1786 (Forbes to Vaux, 28 July 1786, in Vaux Papers, HSP; *Times*, 26 July 1786). For the new firm of Brickwood, Pattle, and Co., see Strettell to Vaux, 21 February 1786, in Vaux Papers, HSP; Birnie to Strettell and Brickwood, Pattle, and Co., copies in Birnie Letterbook, 60-61. For Thomas Pattle, see the Biographical Card Index, India Office Library and Records, London. Pattle was a director of the East India Company 1787-1795, returned to India in the Company's service in 1795, and died in London in 1818 (*Times*, 8 April 1785, 12 April 1792, 16 March 1795; *G. Mag*. 1787 part 1, 361; 1818 part 2, 376).
42. Brickwood, Pattle and Co. presumably dissolved when Thomas Pattle returned to India in 1795 (see previous note). Its successor, John and Lawrence Brickwood (Lawrence was John's brother), is noted from October 1795 to October 1797 (*Times*, 12 November 1795, 28 February 1797, 18 October 1797), and Brickwoods, Daniel & Co. first appears in October 1798 (*Times*, 6 October 1798). The latter firm signed a petition to the Board of Trade in 1806, praying for efforts to have reduced or removed the Russian tariffs on furs (G. C. Davidson, *The North West Company* [New York: Russell and Russell, 1967], 195n.). In 1809, John Brickwood was condemned by Parliament for slippery

dealings while serving as one of the Commissioners appointed, in 1795, to handle the cargoes of Dutch ships held in English ports during the war (*G. Mag.*, 1809 part 2, 753-54); perhaps as a result of this notoriety, Brickwood's bank went bankrupt the next year (London *Gazette*, 7 July 1810). He died in 1822; his will shows that he had retained much of his wealth (*G. Mag.*, 1822 part 1, 646; the will is PRO, PROB 11/1659, Quire 353).

43. See *G. Mag.* 1825 part 1, 652, death notice, "April 29. At Achnagairn, Co. Inverness, aged 83, John Fraser, esq. of that place, formerly of the house of McTavish, Fraser, and Co. of London." For the family of Achnagairn, see D. Warrand, *Some Fraser Pedigrees* (Inverness: Robert Carruthers & Sons, 1934), 19-21.
44. James Fraser, Bailie of Inverness, John's father, had leases of the salmon fishery on the River Beauly from the Commissioners for Forfeited Estates in the 1750s (Millar, *Forfeited Estates Papers* [Edinburgh: Scottish History Society, 1909] 57: 79, 90, 102-3, 106-8). "John Fraser & Comp. Merchts. No. 67 Basinghall-street" are listed in London Directories from 1769 to 1781; in 1782-1783 the firm was at No. 4, New-court, Swithin's-lane, a more central location. John Fraser is not mentioned in the Directories in 1784 or later, having gone bankrupt in January 1784 (see below).
45. For George Ross of Pitkerrie, see E. Haden-Guest in *The History of Parliament. The House of Commons 1754-1790*, vol. 3, eds. L. Namier and J. Brooke (London: HMSO, 1964), 378-9. Although Ross (born 1700) was certainly related to the family of Achnagairn, Warrand points out that the tradition that his mother was a cousin of John Fraser must be wrong, as she was clearly of an earlier generation, *Some Fraser Pedigrees*, 20. As agent for General Haldimand's regiment, Ross was in a good position to write Haldimand on behalf of Fraser's enterprises in Canada, and he did so several times (Haldimand Papers, BL, Add. Ms. 21,726, f. 161; 21,727, f. 194; 21,734, f. 508v; 21,735, ff. 40, v [microfilm at NAC]).
46. *Journal of the Commissioners for Trade and Plantations, 1776-1782*, 21-22; there are other references to Fraser's trade on pages 71 (where "Fraser" is mistranscribed "Turner"), 74, 169-70, 172, 232-33, 294-95, 386-87, 456.
47. NAC, MG19 A2 ser. 3, 68, no. 892, p. 37. Other customers of Fraser mentioned in this document of 1781, which lists goods damaged during shipping to Montreal in that year, and sold for the benefit of the underwriters, are John Grant, Thomas Fraser, Thomas Burn, and James McKenzie, all at Montreal (pp. 36-9, 44).
48. For the story of the merchants' debts and Haldimand's attempts to recover them, and for the especially exposed position of Shaw and Fraser, see A. R. M. Lower, "Credit and the Constitutional Act," *Can. Hist. Rev.* 6 (1925): 123-41. For John Fraser's financial difficulty and bankruptcy, see Ross to Haldimand, 25 March 1783, 9 January 1784, and Haldimand to Ross, 27 June 1783 (Haldimand Papers, BL, Add. Ms. 21,735, ff. 40, v, 334, v; 21,727, f. 194, respectively); Quebec *Gazette*, 5 June, 30 October 1783; and London *Gazette*, 10 January 1784.
49. Warrand, *Some Fraser Pedigrees*, 20, for the mortgage of Achnagairn. Ross to Haldimand, 9 January 1784 (note 48), and Ross's will, copy in PRO, PROB 11/1141, Quire 242, for the composition with the creditors.
50. For Fraser's movements, see passenger lists and legal notices in the Quebec *Gazette*, 7, 28 October 1784; 26 May, 27 June 1785; 9, 23 February, 15 June, 7, 28 September, 26 October 1786; and 5 June, 17 July, 30 October 1788. P. N.

Moogk, "John Young," *DCB* 5: 877, considered that the Fraser of the first firm of Fraser and Young was Simon Fraser, senior of Quebec, but John Fraser certainly appears as the firm's agent in advertisements in the Quebec *Gazette*, and the evident purpose of the firm was to recover debts due to John Fraser and Company of London.

51. The articles of partnership between Simon McTavish and John Fraser which formed the firm in 1790 or 1791 have not survived, but Fraser held a one-third share in all later renewals (Wallace, *Documents*, 97-98, 296, 298-300). McTavish, Fraser and Co. are listed at No. 2, Suffolk-lane, Cannon-street, in Kent's Directory for 1792, and continue there until the late 1820s. The firm took possession of the premises late in May 1792 (Fraser to McTavish, 16, 26/31 May 1792, PAM, HBCA, F.3/1, 61-2, 67v).
52. A valuable series of letters from Fraser to Simon McTavish, with dates in 1792 (3 letters), 1794 (10), 1795 (7), 1798 (4), 1799 (8), 1800 (7), and 1802 (3), is preserved as part of the McTavish Inward Correspondence, PAM, HBCA, F.3/1 and -2.
53. Invoices for what seems to be the entire North West Company outfit dispatched from London in spring 1798 survive in the Cameron Papers, PAM, HBCA, E.41/27. The goods, purchased from more than sixty suppliers, had a value, with commissions and charges, of well over £30,000. Most of the goods were shipped in early April, in exactly equal halves, in two vessels chartered for the purpose, and a small supplementary order was sent out in July.
54. John Fraser's wife was Jean Mackenzie (his mother was also a Mackenzie), but nothing is known of her family: Warrand, *Some Fraser Pedigrees*, 20. John Fraser, junior, was a member of the governing board of the Hudson's Bay Company after the amalgamation, but was replaced by Edward Ellice in 1824 (Wallace, *Documents*, 31). For James Fraser in the East India Company, see Biographical Card Index, India Office Library and Records. For Mary Fraser's marriage to James Fraser of Belladrum, see *Times*, 18 December 1799 and Fraser to McTavish, PAM, HBCA, F.3/1, 342-3. For Henry William Fraser, perpetual curate of Lindley, Yorks., see J. A. Venn, *Alumni Cantabrigienses* Pt. II, vol. 2 (Cambridge: Cambridge University Press, 1944), 569.
55. For John Fraser's death notice, see note 43. His will is PRO, PROB 11/1700, Quire 316.

Part II

Native People and Changing Trade Relations

Articulation of the Lakota Mode of Production and the Euro-American Fur Trade[1]

Kathleen Pickering

Scholars have debated the question of whether Indians generally were "dependent" upon the Euro-American fur trade or whether they retained options of economic independence until Reservation confinement. This debate has been complicated by different uses of the term "dependent." The everyday meaning of dependence as reliance on others may imply varying degrees of asymmetry in the relative power of trading partners. Dependency is also used in the theoretical sense of the outcome to small economies of being incorporated into the world system with the structural distortions that inevitably result, the expansion of a core country's economy implying the underdevelopment of peripheral economies (see, e.g., Kardulias 1990: 25-60; Swagerty 1988: 71-94; Krech 1988: 62-70; White 1983; Bishop 1984: 21-49).

Further difficulties have resulted from applying different scales of analysis to the question of dependence. Dependency theorists look at the macro-level of economic interaction, where it is difficult to argue that any one Indian group possessed the economic power of the expanding European empires. On the micro-level, by contrast, there are countless instances of Indian groups holding the upper hand in trade relations with agents of large trading companies who found themselves isolated and vulnerable.

It is difficult to quantify the notion of dependency. It is possible, however, to locate concrete changes in the micro-level organization of a particular Indian group by focusing on the articulation between their mode of production and that of the Euro-American mercantile fur trade. A society's mode of production describes the ways in which people produce their livelihood, including the materials and processes used and all the social relationships surrounding that production. The depth of penetration by the Euro-American mode of production may be measured through the nature and extent of transformations in an Indian group's mode of production during the course of their involvement with the fur trade (cf. Bishop 1984: 48-49).

Each Indian group had a different social structure, historic context, and fur trade experience. The Lakota, or Teton Sioux, experienced a long and gradual articulation with the Euro-American fur trade. Therefore, they provide a useful case for tracing the transformations in their mode of production and the implications of those changes for their economic self-determination.[2]

I. EARLY LAKOTA MODE OF PRODUCTION—BEFORE 1650

In the middle of the seventeenth century, the Lakota were located in south central Minnesota (Neill 1881: 9; Wedel 1974: 165-66; White 1978: 321; Jablow 1951: 3). The productive activities of men and women were complementary. Men primarily hunted and made weapons, while women focused on gathering wild food, preparing animal skins, and making clothing and household goods. Neither sex controlled the intensity, pace, direction, or distribution of the work of the other (Albers 1985: 117-19; Walker 1982: 63-64). The Lakota camped on the prairies in the summer to hunt buffalo, and on the more sheltered forest edge in the winter to hunt deer and be near ample firewood (Secoy 1953: 66-67; Walker 1982: 16-17; Neill 1881: 42). Women, young people, and dogs transported the camp to new locations, limiting the amount of food and goods that families could accumulate (Mishkin 1940: 19; Secoy 1953: 67, 87; Neill 1881: 42, 71; Jablow 1951: 10; Wissler 1914: 11-12).

Figure 1. Before acquisition of the horse, Lakota camps were transported to new locations by women with the help of dog travois. Painted by Kills Two. Courtesy of Hubert Alexander.

Kinship was the central institution for Lakota social relations. The *tiyospaye* or extended family group was the primary and relatively autonomous social unit (Hyde 1937: 30; Dorsey 1897: 218; Bamforth 1988: 104-5; Schusky 1986: 69; Neill 1881: 44; Walker 1982: 7-8, 24, 28; Wedel 1974: 166; Secoy 1953: 68; White 1978: 321). Several *tiyospayes* could join for ceremonies, hunting, or warfare. Groups of *tiyospayes* formed the seven Lakota divisions, such as the Oglala, Sicangu, or Hunkpapa (Schusky 1986: 68; Walker 1982: 6-7, 19, 28, 50). Every Lakota person was responsible for the welfare of all their relatives (Hassrick 1964: 201; DeMallie 1979: 233; Walker 1982: 63-64, 75, 94; Schusky 1986: 68; Albers 1985: 119-20). Social prestige was gained by acts of generosity toward others, not by accumulating property. Religious and ceremonial occasions centered around giving food and material goods to other members of the *tiyospaye* (Walker 1982: 40, 64-65; Deloria 1944: 40-44, 63-68; see O'Shea 1989: 58).

The Lakota were engaged in extensive intertribal trade long before the Euro-American fur trade (Wood 1980: 98, 103; Swagerty 1988: 75; Kardulias 1990: 40). Recognized kinship relations had to be established between trading partners, either constructively through ceremonial pipe smoking or physically through intertribal marriages (Blakeslee 1977: 81-82; Wood 1980: 99; Neill 1881: 94; Wedel 1974: 171; see O'Shea 1989: 62). The Dakota or Santee Sioux, neighboring to the east, were the Lakota's main trading and defense partner. These two groups spoke mutually intelligible dialects[3] and were constructive kin through a shared history, originally descending from the same council fire (Dorsey 1897: 221; Walker 1982: 11-12; Hyde 1937: 308).

There were two significant features of intertribal trade for the Lakota. First, each Lakota *tiyospaye* could produce all of its subsistence needs without engaging in trade. While tastes and custom favored access to corn and tobacco, the basic necessities of food, clothing, and shelter, and the tools to obtain and manufacture them, could all be directly produced and used within the *tiyospaye* (Epp 1988: 316; Holder 1970: 65, 123; Wood 1980: 103; Bamforth 1988: 6, 8). Second, trading partners had the social rights and responsibilities of kin relations. The value of a traded item was not reduced to equivalences in quantities and skills of labor. The social relations of exchange retained the human dimension of direct producers investing their goods with long-term human relationships (Blakeslee 1977: 94; Wood 1980: 100).

II. TRANSFORMATIONS WITH THE EURO-AMERICAN FUR TRADE

From 1650 to 1800, the Lakota gradually migrated from Minnesota across the Missouri River, with the Oglala reaching the Black Hills of South Dakota by 1775 (Hanson and Walters 1985: 3; Hyde 1937: 6-12; Secoy 1953: 67). Some historians attribute Lakota migration to competing groups like the Cree, Assiniboin, and Ojibwa obtaining more guns earlier from their direct contact with Hudson's Bay trading posts by the 1670s (Holzkamm 1983: 231; Roe 1955: 177; Secoy 1953: 67; Holder 1970: 18, 82). Others emphasize the southwest

Figure 2. Map of Lakota and Dakota migration, fur trading posts, agencies, and surrounding tribes, 1650 to 1880.

migration of buffalo during the same period (Bamforth 1988: 72; Epp 1988: 313-15; Reher and Frison 1980: 50-51).

Intertribal trade increased in volume and consistency with the introduction of European demand for furs and supply of horses, guns, ammunition, metal tools, blankets, and cloth. The Lakota had their first contact with guns and metal goods in the 1650s, but were not directly involved with the European fur trade at that time (Wedel 1974: 162-65; Secoy 1953: 65-66). French traders around the Great Lakes began supplying the Dakota with guns and trade goods by 1700, which the Dakota in turn traded with the Lakota (Walker 1982: 11-12; Hyde 1937: 308; Wood 1980: 100, 103; Holder 1970: 23, 65; Holzkamm 1983: 230-

31; Jablow 1951: 6, 38, 42, 53; White 1978: 322; Secoy 1953: 66-67; Hanson and Walters 1985: 3). This trade pattern intensified after the 1760s, when the Lakota began acquiring horses in large numbers from Indian groups to the southwest and north to trade with the Dakota for arms (Ewers 1968: 24-25; Ray 1974: 156; Wissler 1914: 5, 10-11; Hyde 1937: 8-9; Wood 1980: 100; Jablow 1951: 9-10, 14; Mishkin 1940: 10). Missouri River sedentary groups, like the Arikara, became major trading centers for horses, guns, and other European goods, as well as for their own corn and tobacco products (Hanson 1975: 102; Blakeslee 1977: 94; Ewers 1968: 20, 22; Wood and Thiessen 1985: 48; Swagerty 1988: 75; Jablow 1951: 12, 22-23, 27, 30, 45; Secoy 1953: 72; Wood 1980: 99-100, 103). Smallpox and cholera epidemics of 1772-1780 and 1837 severely reduced the trade involvement and power of the Missouri River groups, but were less devastating to the mobile and segmentary Lakota society (Wood and Thiessen 1985: 8, 73; White 1978: 325, 329; Ray 1974: 105-6; Hanson 1975: 105; Wood 1980: 107; Ewers 1968: 46; Swagerty 1988: 79; Secoy 1953: 74; O'Shea 1989: 62-63).

Once the Lakota relocated to the Plains, they traded buffalo robes, deer skins, and dried meat for basic trade goods, but were only marginally involved in the more lucrative beaver pelt trade (Hanson and Walters 1985: 4; Jablow 1951: 31; Secoy 1953: 72). By the 1840s, the market price for beaver pelts plummeted, while buffalo robes became the primary fur traded (Kardulias 1990: 35; Swagerty 1988: 73; Hanson and Walters 1985: 4, 15-16; Secoy 1953: 92). Fur-trading companies introduced steamboat transportation on the Missouri River in the 1830s, further enhancing the marketability of, and demand for, buffalo robes (Hanson and Walters 1985: 4; Swagerty 1988: 77; Secoy 1953: 75). Pierre Chouteau & Company built Ft. Pierre along the Missouri in 1832 as a depot for Lakota trade. The American Fur Company operated the Bordeaux Trading Post along the Ft. Laramie to Ft. Union transport route beginning in 1837, specifically for trade with the Sicangu Lakota. Traders with the American Fur Company and Sibille & Adams Company, as well as independent traders, regularly visited Oglala Lakota camps for trade (Hanson and Walters 1985: 4, 8, 13-15; Secoy 1953: 92-93). Initially, Euro-American traders involved with the Lakota participated in pipe ceremonies, or in some instances married Lakota women, to establish the social kinship ties necessary for trade (Wood and Thiessen 1985: 139; Blakeslee 1977: 82-85; Neill 1881: 20, 32; Hanson and Walters 1985: 9, 19; Swagerty 1988: 75, 82). By 1835, the Lakota had fairly constant and direct associations with non-Indian traders, and could produce enough buffalo robes to obtain quantities of both subsistence and 'luxury' or decorative trade goods.

Many transformations within the Lakota mode of production occurred between 1650 and 1880. The use of horses made buffalo hunting more certain and successful, particularly with metal arrowheads and spears. Greater amounts of camp goods, food, and larger tipi skins and poles could be transported by horses (Finnigan 1983: 18; Weist 1980: 257, 264; Reher 1983: 216; Hanson

1975: 96; Roe 1955: 14, 16; Hyde 1937: 11; Secoy 1953: 88; Mishkin 1940: 19; Jablow 1951: 11-12). With more meat available, larger aggregations of *tiyospayes* could be supported over longer periods of time. This higher population density, supported with ample guns, in turn made the Lakota a more forceful opponent against other tribes, like the Crow or Pawnee, competing for hunting territories (White 1978: 321; Bamforth 1988: 100-9, 126; Reher and Frison 1980: 45; Reher 1983: 220; Secoy 1953: 75-77, 88; Mishkin 1940: 20). Lakota women allocated more labor to preparing buffalo robes and dried meat for trade. This reduced the time women spent in other subsistence activities, such as making household utensils, preparing skins for clothing, or gathering food, and increased the categories of trade goods that were necessities (Klein 1980: 134; Weist 1980: 264; Holder 1970: 114, 123; Hanson and Walters 1985: 9; Swagerty 1988: 82; Jablow 1951: 14, 16-17, 20-21).

Tensions within Lakota social relations also began to appear. *Tiyospaye* members who possessed horses had greater economic opportunities to hunt individually for more buffalo robes to trade, to join in raids for additional horses, and to give more horses away to gather social prestige (Goldfrank 1943: 73; Klein 1980: 135; Bamforth 1988: 123; Mishkin 1940: 10-11). Members who initially lacked adequate horses to participate successfully in this new system of production were gradually identified as "poor," unable to engage in individual hunts, to accumulate robes for trade, or to reciprocate in gift-giving or meat distribution within the *tiyospaye* (Goldfrank 1943: 67, 77; Secoy 1953: 93; Kardulias 1990: 50-51; Wissler 1914: 17). Incidents of intragroup violence, often involving alcohol, physical coercion by *tiyospaye* officers, and factionalism within Lakota subdivisions between competing Lakota leaders increased in frequency from 1790 to 1860, as described in Lakota Winter Counts, traders' observations, and U.S. Indian Agent reports (Henning 1982: 60, 64; Klein 1983: 153-54; Denig 1961: 22, 32-33; Swagerty 1988: 81; Poole 1988: xxxi; Walker 1982: 21, 26, 29-31, 64, 76; Goldfrank 1943: 71-73, 79; Schusky 1986: 71-72, 75-76, 81).

The flourish of Lakota trade in buffalo robes was brief (Swagerty 1988: 80). The U.S. government became increasingly involved in the economic transactions of the Lakota. The U.S. government purchased Ft. Laramie in 1849, and Ft. Pierre in 1855, to be used as military installations. The army ordered an end to sale of breech-loading arms and ammunition to the Lakota and other groups in 1866. Political power in the region gradually moved from growing Lakota dominance in the 1790s to greater U.S. military presence after the Civil War. Under the Ft. Laramie Treaties of 1851 and 1868, the Lakota ceded lands in Nebraska and Wyoming in exchange for promises of annuity goods and rations (Hanson and Walters 1985: 14-18; Albers 1985: 116; Swagerty 1988: 76, 83; Poole 1988: xvi-xviii, 13). Even though the Lakota retained hunting rights in the ceded territory, those who exercised their hunting rights were characterized by the U.S. government as "hostile" and were subject to attack by Pawnee or Crow scouts for the U.S. (Poole 1988: xx-xxi, xxvii-xxix, 32, 50, 58). U.S. policy supported destruction of buffalo herds and containment of the Lakota within a defined territory to encourage their transition to agricultural production (Roe 1955: 65-66; Hyde 1937: 61; Poole 1988: 36). Indian agencies, such as Whetstone on the Missouri River and Red Cloud along the Platte, replaced fur-trading posts as the major source for trade goods, now in the form of treaty annuities and rations (Hanson and Walters 1985: 17-18; Poole 1988: xii-xiii, xxx, 45-46). By 1870, the fur trade with the Lakota was essentially over.

III. Implications of a New Mode of Production

The Euro-American fur trade did not simply result in the addition of a new trading partner to an old Lakota system of production and exchange. Rather, the articulation of the mercantile fur trade with Lakota economic activity resulted in the creation of new relationships surrounding production through the gradual introduction of new materials and tools for production that could only be obtained through trade. Because these transformations in Lakota society were gradual over the period from 1650 to 1870, it is tempting to assume that they were also insignificant in relation to Lakota economic self-determination. Highlighting particular changes in the Lakota mode of production during this period shows that, to the contrary, the transformations were vast and fundamental.

The internal Lakota social relations of production in the nineteenth century appeared to be unchanged. The Lakota maintained direct control over the land and buffalo resources they needed to produce subsistence and trade goods until

Figure 3. The use of horses made buffalo hunting more successful, particularly with metal arrowheads. Painted by Kills Two. Courtesy of Hubert Alexander.

the 1860s, and therefore were not 'free' laborers dependent on wage jobs for survival. The Lakota continued to control their labor processes, determining the amount of time allocated between production for immediate consumption and fur production for trade. In general, fur-trading companies relied on Indians as hunters and fur processors, and often lamented their limited and sporadic control over Indian labor when trying to get the most marketable furs (Wedel 1974: 162; Kardulias 1990: 36, 41-43; Swagerty 1988: 77; Jablow 1951: 25-26).

Nevertheless, important transformations in Lakota social relations of production had taken place. One major change was a gradual move from intertribal trading partners to direct trade with fur-trading companies. This was in part due to the gradual elimination and relocation of the surrounding tribes as the result of disease, warfare, and treaty cessions to the U.S. (Hanson 1975: 105; Neill 1881: 153; Wood 1980: 107; Denig 1961: 19). The relative power relations among the Lakota, other Plains tribes, and the U.S. government were in constant flux throughout this period. The U.S. government played an active role in reinforcing the transformation of Lakota society from independent subsistence to market exchange. Treaty provisions of annuities and rations for ceded land, coupled with the characterization of those who still procured their own food as "hostile," supported immediate submission to explicit domination by the U.S. system (Albers 1985: 116).

A change in the productive power of the Lakota relative to their Euro-American trading partners also occurred. With intertribal trade, the materials and processes of the Lakota and their trading partners were essentially equivalent. In contrast, the productive forces available to the Lakota were no match for the manufacturing and transport capacities of the Euro-American fur-trading companies and their suppliers. The only limit to a trading company's trade with the Lakota was market demand for buffalo products, since trade goods were available in ample supply. For the Lakota, however, human labor limited their potential production for fur trade below their potential demand for trade goods (Kardulias 1990: 28, 33; Hyde 1937: 61-62; Goldfrank 1943: 74; Roe 1955: 65-66, 190-92; White 1978: 330; Hanson and Walters 1985: 9). Different productive forces translated further into different market power. Although the Lakota were selective in the type and quality of trade goods they would accept, they had an insignificant influence on the demand or price for buffalo robes in the national or world market (Swagerty 1988: 77; Jablow 1951: 17; Kardulias 1990: 43).

Furthermore, the use-value orientation of Lakota robe production masked the extraction of surplus value by fur-trading companies. Robes were traded by the Lakota without regard to the market price of production. Anything produced after the immediate needs of the household was potential surplus for trade. Cost calculations of the hours of labor involved in preparing a robe or depreciation for land and natural resource depletion were not considered by the Lakota. These calculations were of fundamental importance to the fur-trading companies, however, who avoided the costs of hiring hunters and tanners by incorporating Lakota household production. The only limit to the amount of

Figure 4. With horses, greater amounts of camp goods and food could be transported, supporting a higher population density. Drawn by George Catlin, from *Souvenirs of the North American Indians* (London, 1850), 3: 129. Courtesy of Rare Books & Manuscripts Division, The New York Public Library, Astor, Lenox and Tilden Foundations.

profit that the fur-trading companies might extract from Lakota production was the amount of labor the Lakota needed to provide basic food, clothing, and shelter to their community (Hanson and Walters 1985: 17; Albers 1985: 116; Jablow 1951: 25-26; cf. Banaji 1977).

Finally, the institutional function of Lakota *tiyospayes* changed. Initially, kinship functioned both as an institution for material production and as an ideological institution of mutual support and long-term obligation (cf. Godelier 1978). In terms of material production, after extensive involvement in the Euro-American fur trade, *tiyospayes* were no longer independent units of production and consumption. During intertribal trade, it was possible for the Lakota to subsist without trade if necessary. Dogs, stone tools, skin clothing, and wooden utensils could all be produced within the labor processes of a Lakota *tiyospaye* for its own use. European trade goods transformed exchange from trading alternative subsistence surpluses to trading for actual tools and materials of production and subsistence. Horses, cloth, metal, and guns could only be obtained through production of furs as commodities for exchange (Holder 1970: 114, 123; Jablow 1951: 11; Kardulias 1990: 44; Denig 1961: 13-14). In turn, trading for more and more subsistence goods moved Lakota production toward buffalo hide and meat specialization (Jablow 1951: 17; Secoy 1953: 75; Kardulias 1990: 29-32).

Ideologically, there was also a change in the relations between trading partners from exchanges between direct producers to exchanges of fully commodified goods. In intertribal trade, partners conducted exchange within the social obligations of kinship. Direct producers interacted for goods and food that were initially made for their personal consumption (Blakeslee 1977: 94; Wood 1980:

100). Euro-American exchange, on the other hand, was based on simple commodity production, outside of human interaction. Exchange was no longer between direct human producers, like a buffalo hunter and a corn planter, but was between commodities, like a hide and a sack of flour. While trading companies conceded the need to establish constructive kin relations with the Lakota, compliance with the substance of those kin obligations gradually diminished.

With the destruction of buffalo resources and the appropriation of Lakota lands, dispossession of the Lakota from their means of subsistence was complete. Their self-sufficiency was uprooted as the U.S. began to enforce Reservation confinement (White 1978: 330; Hanson and Walters 1985: 18-19; Albers 1985: 116; Denig 1961: 25). It has been noted that Lakota land cessions of the 1860s are explained less by U.S. military might and more by Lakota hunger (Swagerty 1988: 72, 83).

This is not to say that the Lakota were merely passive players in a drama of predetermined outcome. They were actively making decisions which affected subsequent decisions by other Indian groups and the fur-trading companies. The Lakota chose to incorporate new materials for production that became available through intertribal and then Euro-American trade. The social relations surrounding this trade slowly shifted from the interaction of direct producers with constructive kin relations to the exchange of commodities producing profits for companies outside the obligations of kinship.

Whether the Lakota were "dependent" on the fur trading companies is difficult to assess. The articulation of Lakota economic activity with Euro-American trade produced gradual but substantial transformations to the Lakota mode of production, however. The kinship institution appeared the same, but changed in its function from a combination of organizing material production and providing ideological support for mutual welfare to primarily conceptual support for group survival within new economic institutions. The benefits of surplus value created by Lakota women in the production of buffalo robes were taken outside of the circle of kin relations to the accounts of trading companies without reciprocal obligations to the Lakota. Commodities demanded purchasing power, not personal relationships. Gradually, access to land and buffalo, to the extent they existed, was predominantly controlled by the U.S. government and its reservation agents, not by the *tiyospaye*. These transformations ultimately precluded other options for economic self-determination that had been available to the Lakota in earlier periods.

Notes

1. This paper is based upon work supported under a National Science Foundation Graduate Fellowship.
2. Some theorists have devoted their research to categorizing all human societies through history into a fixed number of modes of production, often organized in a hierarchical or evolutionary scale. While the Lakota may be characterized as

having a "primitive," "tribal," "kin-ordered," or "foraging" mode of production (Marx 1973: 471-96; Marx 1976: 32-35; Wolf 1982: 73-100; Southall 1988: 165-92), it is not the purpose of this paper to locate the Lakota within any particular developmental scheme. Rather, the mode of production analysis is used to measure change given the characteristics of Lakota social organization prior to Euro-American trade relations.

3. Dakota and Lakota are essentially the same except that when a Dakota speaker uses "d" in a word, a Lakota speaker would replace it with "l" (Poole 1988: 68). For example, the word "to sing" is dowan in Dakota and lowan in Lakota.

BIBLIOGRAPHY

Albers, Patricia C. 1985. "Autonomy and Dependency in the Lives of Dakota Women: A Study in Historical Change." *Review of Radical Political Economics* 17 (3): 109-34.

Bamforth, Douglas B. 1988. *Ecology and Human Organization on the Great Plains.* New York: Plenum Press.

Banaji, Jairus. 1977. "Modes of Production in a Materialist Conception of History." *Capital & Class* 3: 1-43.

Bishop, Charles A. 1984. "The First Century: Adaptive Changes among the Western James Bay Cree between the Early Seventeenth and Early Eighteenth Centuries." In *The Subarctic Fur Trade: Native Social and Economic Adaptations,* ed. Shepard Krech III. Vancouver: University of British Columbia Press.

Blakeslee, Donald J. 1977. "The Calumet Ceremony and the Origin of Fur Trade Rituals." *The Western Canadian Journal of Anthropology* 7: 78-89.

Deloria, Ella. 1944. *Speaking of Indians.* New York: Friendship Press.

DeMallie, Raymond J. 1979. "Change in American Indian Kinship Systems: The Dakota." In *Currents in Anthropology—Essays in Honor of Sol Tax,* ed. Robert Hinshaw. The Hague: Mouton Publishers.

Denig, Edwin Thompson. 1961. *Five Indian Tribes of the Upper Missouri.* Edited by John C. Ewers. Norman: University of Oklahoma Press.

Dorsey, James Owen. 1897. *Siouan Sociology.* 15th Annual Report of the Bureau of Ethnology 1893. Washington, D.C.: U.S. Government Printing Office.

Epp, Henry T. 1988. "Way of the Migrant Herds—Dual Dispersion Strategy Among Bison."*Plains Anthropologist* 33: 309-20.

Ewers, John C. 1968. *Indian Life on the Upper Missouri.* Norman: University of Oklahoma Press.

Finnigan, James T. 1983. "Tipi to Tipi Ring: Transformational Model." *Plains Anthropologist* 28 (102), Pt.2, Mem. 19: 17-28.

Godelier, Maurice. 1978. "Infrastructure, Societies, and History." *Current Anthropology* 19 (4): 763-68.

Goldfrank, Esther. 1943. "Historic Change and Social Character: A Study of the Teton Dakota." *American Anthropologist* 45: 67-83.

Hanson, Charles E., Jr., and Veronica Sue Walters. 1985. "The Early Fur Trade in Northwestern Nebraska." Reprint of *Nebraska History* 57(4): 1976.

Hanson, James A. 1975. *Metal Weapons, Tools, and Ornaments of the Teton Dakota Indians.* Lincoln: University of Nebraska Press.

Hassrick, Royal B. 1964. *The Sioux: Life and Customs of a Warrior Society.* Norman: University of Oklahoma Press.

Henning, Elizabeth R.P. 1982. "Western Dakota Winter Counts: An Analysis of the Effects of Westward Migration and Culture Change." *Plains Anthropologist* 27: 57-65.

Holder, Preston. 1970. *The Hoe and the Horse on the Plains*. Lincoln: University of Nebraska Press.

Holzkamm, Tim E. 1983. "Eastern Dakota Population Movements and the European Fur Trade: One More Time." *Plains Anthropologist* 28: 225-33.

Hyde, George E. 1937. *Red Cloud's Folks*. Norman: Oklahoma University Press.

Jablow, Joseph. 1951. *The Cheyenne in Plains Indian Trade Relations 1795-1840*. Monographs of the American Ethnological Society, vol. 19, ed. Marian W. Smith. New York: J.J. Augustin Publisher.

Kardulias, Nick P. 1990. "Fur Production as a Specialized Activity in a World System: Indians in the North American Fur Trade." *American Indian Culture and Research Journal* 14 (1): 25-60.

Klein, Alan. 1980. "Plains Economic Analysis: The Marxist Complement." In *Anthropology of the Great Plains*, eds.W. Raymond Wood and Margot Liberty. Lincoln: University of Nebraska Press.

______. 1983. "The Political-Economy of Gender: A 19th Century Plains Indian Case Study." In *The Hidden Half—Studies of Plains Indian Women*, eds. Patricia Albers and Beatrice Medicine. Lanham, Md.: University Press of America.

Krech, Shepard, III. 1988. "The Hudson's Bay Company and Dependence Among Subarctic Tribes before 1900." *Overcoming Economic Dependency*, Occasional Papers in Curriculum Series, Newberry Library, D'Arcy McNickle Center for the History of the American Indian, no. 9: 62-70.

Marx, Karl. 1973. *Grundrisse: Foundations of the Critique of Political Economy*. New York: Vintage Books.

______. 1976. "The German Ideology." In *Collected Works of Karl Marx and Friedrich Engels*, vol. 5. New York: International Publishers.

Mishkin, Bernard. 1940. *Rank and Warfare Among the Plains Indians*. Monographs of the American Ethnological Society, vol. 3. New York: J.J. Augustin Publisher.

Neill, Edward D. 1881. *Explorers and Pioneers of Minnesota*. Minneapolis: Minnesota Historical Society.

O'Shea, John M. 1989. "The Role of Wild Resources in Small-Scale Agricultural Systems: Tales from the Lakes and the Plains." In *Bad Year Economics*, eds. Paul Halstead and John M. O'Shea. Cambridge: Cambridge University Press.

Poole, D.C. 1988. *Among the Sioux of Dakota*, ed. Raymond DeMallie. St.Paul: Minnesota Historical Society Press.

Ray, Arthur T. 1974. *Indians in the Fur Trade*. Toronto: University of Toronto Press.

Reher, Charles. 1983. "Analysis of Spatial Structure in Stone Circle Sites." *Plains Anthropologist* 28 (102), Pt.2, Mem. 19: 193-222.

Reher, Charles A., and George C. Frison. 1980. "The Vore Site, 48CK302, A Stratified Buffalo Jump in the Wyoming Black Hills." *Plains Anthropologist* 25 (88), Pt.2, Mem. 16.

Roe, Frank Gilbert. 1955. *The Indian and the Horse*. Norman: University of Oklahoma Press.

Schusky, Ernest L. 1986. "The Evolution of Indian Leadership on the Great Plains, 1750-1950." *American Indian Quarterly* 10 (1): 65-82.

Secoy, Frank Raymond. 1953. *Changing Military Patterns on the Great Plains*. Monographs of the American Ethnological Society, ed. Esther S. Goldfrank. New York: J.J. Augustin Publisher.

Southall, Aidan. 1988. "On Mode of Production Theory: The Foraging Mode of Production and the Kinship Mode of Production." *Dialectical Anthropology* 12: 165-92.

Swagerty, William R. 1988. "Relations Between Northern Plains Indians and the American Fur Trade Company to 1867." *Overcoming Economic Dependency,* Occasional Papers in Curriculum Series, Newberry Library, D'Arcy McNickle Center for the History of the American Indian, no. 9: 71-94.

Walker, James R. 1982. *Lakota Society.* Edited by Raymond J. DeMallie. Lincoln: University of Nebraska Press.

Wedel, Margaret Mott. 1974. "Le Sueur and the Dakota Sioux." In *Upper Great Lakes Anthropology,* ed. Elden Johnson. St. Paul: Minnesota Historical Society.

Weist, Katherine M. 1980. "Plains Indian Women: An Assessment." In *Anthropology on the Great Plains,* eds. W. Raymond Wood and Margot Liberty. Lincoln: University of Nebraska Press.

White, Richard. 1983. *The Roots of Dependency.* Lincoln: University of Nebraska Press.

______. 1978. "The Winning of the West: The Expansion of the Western Sioux in the Eighteenth and Nineteenth Centuries." *The Journal of American History* 65 (2): 319-43.

Wissler, Clark. 1914. "The Influence of the Horse in the Development of Plains Culture." *American Anthropologist* 16: 1-25.

Wolf, Eric. 1982. *Europe and the People Without History.* Berkeley: University of California Press.

Wood, W. Raymond. 1980. "Plains Trade in Prehistoric and Protohistoric Intertribal Relations." In *Anthropology and the Great Plains,* eds. W. Raymond Wood and Margot Liberty. Lincoln: University of Nebraska Press.

Wood, W. Raymond, and Thomas D. Thiessen. 1985. *Early Fur Trade on the Northern Plains.* Norman: University of Oklahoma Press.

French and Spanish Colonial Trade Policies and the Fur Trade among the Caddoan Indians of the Trans-Mississippi South

Timothy K. Perttula

The participation of the Caddoan peoples of the Trans-Mississippi South in the European fur trade had lasting consequences for these aboriginal inhabitants of Texas and Louisiana (Usner 1985: 86). With the development of the fur and peltry trade, and a direct European presence in the Caddoan Area, European goods of considerable diversity became accessible to Caddoan peoples for the first time. The fur and peltry trade "provided the basis for the larger set of economic relationships which developed subsequently between the Caddoan [Indians] and both the French and Spanish" (Sabo 1987: 38).

These relationships were part of a broader interaction between Europeans and the Caddoan peoples because trade, and the fur trade specifically, was one of the key elements that structured the contact process (cf. Wilson and Rogers 1993). That interaction affected (1) the nature of male roles in Caddoan society; (2) the means to achieve social rank; (3) the authority structure and the composition of the traditional religious and political elite; and (4) the ceremonial and ideological significance of European trade goods, the use of traditional rituals and ceremonies, and the maintenance of symbols of political and religious legitimacy (Sabo 1987; Perttula 1993a; Wyckoff and Baugh 1980). Thus, the development of the fur trade after 1700 had far-reaching cultural ramifications for the Caddoan inhabitants of Texas and Louisiana.

The peltry, horse, gun, and salt trades carried on by the Caddoan peoples (Gregory 1973: 293-94) were part of an exchange network composed of European and aboriginal peoples that reflected basic political and economic alliances (Sabo 1987; Usner 1987). At times this relationship was part of a symbiotic association that ensured the European procurement of needed commodities such as salt, foodstuffs, and livestock from the Caddo, while at the same time the Caddo, now more mobile because of the adoption of the horse, were able to obtain access to products, materials, and new territories for advantageous trade opportunities in Texas and the Southern Plains (see Kniffen, et al. 1987: 63).

This symbiotic association contributed to their successful participation in the French fur trade, which became an important economic activity by the middle of the eighteenth century, and may have contributed to some significant reorientation in Caddoan economic pursuits on seasonal and long-term bases. The economic symbiosis between the Caddoan and European groups, although short-lived, was a key means of cultural interaction and change. These new economic opportunities led, however, to the Caddo becoming incorporated into a European-dominated trade and economic network (symbolized in part by the establishment of trading houses and factories). This was accompanied by social, political, and religious coercion (e.g., Kniffen, et al. 1987: 66) which affected Caddoan culture in a significant manner over a period of more than 150 years.

CULTURAL AND ENVIRONMENTAL SETTING

The Caddoan-speaking groups who lived in the Trans-Mississippi South are culturally affiliated with many of the Native American groups who lived in what is now the southeastern United States at the time of European contact. Archaeologically, they were one of the Late Prehistoric Mississippian societies who were present over much of the region after ca. 1000 (Milanich 1990).

These people were sedentary horticulturists with a complex social and political hierarchy centered around the construction and use of earthen mounds as temples, as burial tumuli, and for other ceremonial functions. The mound centers used by the Caddoan groups up to around 1700 were the "social and economic focal point of local polities" (Rogers in press: 5). Most of the people lived in "small social and economic groups around the center[s]" (Schambach and Early 1983: SW107), with the most important and largest centers and communities distributed along major streams such as the Red, Arkansas, Little, and Ouachita rivers. None of the Caddoan settlements were apparently ever fortified.

At the time of sustained contact with Europeans ca. 1685, it is estimated that the total Caddoan population was around 28,000 (Wood 1989: 82-84, table 1). It is likely that their population had been higher during the preceding 150 years, but had been much reduced following the introduction and diffusion of European diseases after ca. 1540 (Perttula 1992; 1993b).

The economy of the Caddoan peoples was based on the cultivation of maize, beans, and squash, as well as native cultigens (such as sunflower). By ca. 1100 to 1300, maize was probably the single most important food resource for Caddoan groups. The white-tailed deer was always the preferred source of meat and furs, although bison was commonly exploited by Caddoan groups in the Arkansas River Basin and the Ozark Highland of eastern Oklahoma. During de Soto's *entrada* in 1542, the Spaniards were offered bison hides as gifts by the *cacique* of *Tula*, in the Arkansas River basin (e.g., Schambach 1989), and "nearby to the north were many cattle" (Robertson 1933: 199). Similarly, although the Caddoan

Figure 1. Watercolor by Lino Sánchez y Tapia of Caddo Indians living in the Nacogdoches area, 1828. From the Collection of Gilcrease Museum, Tulsa.

peoples were sedentary horticulturists, they frequently traveled great distances on foot (50-100 km) to hunt deer and bison. In the 1690s, Spanish explorers frequently mentioned encountering Caddoan hunting parties west of the Trinity and Brazos rivers (Robbins 1991a; 1991b), and in fact, Hasinai Caddo guides for the Spanish were quite familiar with the area from northeast Texas to at least the San Antonio region (e.g., Johnson and McGraw 1991: 127).

The Caddoan peoples were loosely organized into affiliated kin-based groups, bands, or tribes referred to by European observers as the Hasinai, Kadohadacho, and Natchitoches confederacies. The Hasinai groups lived in the Neches and Angelina river valleys in eastern Texas, the Kadohadacho groups were on the Red River in the Great Bend area of southwest Arkansas, northwest Louisiana, and northeast Texas, while the Natchitoches-affiliated groups lived on the Red River in west-central Louisiana in the vicinity of the French post of Natchitoches, established in 1714 (Swanton 1942, figure 1; Tanner 1974). As of 1690, there were no permanent European settlements established anywhere in the Caddoan Area.

The Caddoan peoples were important political allies at various times with the European powers, particularly with the French and Americans, and remained a powerful social and political force on the Texas-Louisiana frontier through the early nineteenth century (Smith 1991). John Sibley, the American Indian agent for Louisiana, commented in a letter of 20 January 1810 that "the great Caddo Chief [Dehahuit]. . .is a man of more importance than Any other ten Chiefs on this side of the Mississippi within my Agency" (Garrett 1944: 389). Continued Anglo-American settlement, land cessions and purchases, disease outbreaks, and hunting pressure from immigrant Indians such as the Choctaw (e.g., Kinnaird and Kinnaird 1980: 358-60) led to severe encroachments on Caddoan lands and to their isolation within the Anglo-American community. The Kadohadacho were removed to Texas from Louisiana between 1835-1842, and then with the Hasinai groups to the Wichita Agency in western Oklahoma (Indian Territory) from Texas in 1859.

The Caddoan Area encompasses a large region of the mid-continental United States, including portions of the Trans-Mississippi South biome (Schambach 1982, figure 7-1) and surrounding areas centering on the Red River in the northeastern part of Texas, southwest Arkansas, eastern Oklahoma, and northwest Louisiana (Story, et al. 1990, figure 3). The region is not environmentally or ecologically homogenous, but consists of a broad band of hardwood and pine forests as well as small prairies, lying west of the Lower Mississippi Valley, east of the Great Plains, and north of the Gulf Coastal Prairies.

Caddoan groups lived mainly in the woodlands and along the alluvial valleys, but forayed into the nearby savannahs and tall-grass prairies to take advantage of the large-game animals (such as bison and pronghorn antelope) to be found there (e.g., Perttula 1990). Within the woodlands, the most significant faunal resources available to the Caddoan populations were deer (*Odocoileus virginiana*) and bear (*Ursus americanus*), followed by small game such as rabbit, squirrel, beaver,[1] and raccoon. Faunal assemblages from archaeological contexts in the Caddoan Area suggest that deer frequently accounted for 30 percent or more of the assemblage (by minimum numbers of individuals or MNI), and probably as much as 60 to 80 percent of the meat consumed. Prairie species, including bison (*Bison bison*), jackrabbit, and pronghorn (*Antilocapra americana*), could be exploited along the western edges of the Caddoan Area in prehistoric pre-horse periods.

In general, the deer biomass was relatively high, perhaps on the order of 10 to 80 deer per square mile (Flores 1984: 230 n.90), while bison and antelope occurred primarily in small herds. After about 1200, bison populations increased in the prairie-woodland border areas of the Trans-Mississippi South. In the Arkansas River basin of what is now eastern Oklahoma, for example, there was a four-fold increase in the relative abundance of bison in Caddoan faunal assemblages dating between 1200-1450 and after 1450 (Wyckoff 1980). Bison continued to be most common in historic times in the Arkansas Basin. In the eighteenth and nineteenth century, for example, Caddoan bison-hunting groups from the middle Red River area utilized this area, as well as the Ouachita Mountains and the prairies of north-central Texas, for the procurement of this faunal resource (e.g., Sibley 1832; Flores 1984).

Colonial Policies and The Fur Trade

Spanish colonial objectives in the Caddoan Area were to hold onto and expand their frontier settlements in Texas while attempting to persuade the Caddoan peoples to Christianity to "convert him, to civilize him, and to exploit him" (Bolton 1917: 45). To do so, a system of missions and presidios was established between 1690-1721 in what is now eastern Texas and western Louisiana. These missions lasted only a short time among the Caddoan groups (between 1690-1693, and 1716-1772), and they were a failure in several respects: (1) the lack of resettlement around the mission establishments, (2) few conversions of Caddoan peoples to Christianity (except in *articulo mortis*), and (3) the lack of participation by Caddoan peoples in the religious, social, and economic activities devised by the missionaries.

Given this situation, the self-sufficient nature of the Caddoan horticultural economy, and their strong religious and political hierarchy, as well as French trade encroachments, the Caddoan peoples had little to gain by resettling around the missions and converting to Christianity. With the French system of trade and presents (and the Spanish frontier policy to restrict trade during this period), the Caddoan peoples were able to acquire necessary and desired trade goods and supplies in a manner that was consistent with their beliefs as to the culturally appropriate ways in which to interact with these Europeans (cf. Sabo 1987). As Fray Benito Hernández de Santa Anna noted in 1731, "As each family of the Texas Nation lives separately in its own ranchito. . .they left them [the missionaries] alone, or came and went without settling down. They often come to have the padres cure their deer-skins" (Hackett 1931-1946, vol. 3: para. 421).

The French initiated concerted explorations and trade ventures in Caddoan lands about 1700, with the "expansion of the French frontier towards the valley of the Red River" (Giraud 1974: 333) after the establishment of the Compagnie des Indes in 1712. Louis Juchereau de St. Denis established the post of Fort St. Jean Baptiste aux Natchitoches at the abandoned 1702 Natchitoches village, commencing the trade between the French colonists and the Caddoan peoples in pelts, horses and cattle, salt, and foodstuffs.

The objectives of the French in the Louisiana colony were to develop a mercantilistic trade policy based on the production of exportable goods such as wood, cotton, rice, and indigo, as well as deer pelts, for a profitable sale. The fur trade between Native Americans and the French was one of the first successful aspects of the colonial economy to be developed in Louisiana (Surrey 1916).

The French developed the trade by fostering dependable political and economic relationships between themselves and the Native American groups, as well as stable alliances between various powerful Native American tribes (such as the Wichita and the Comanche). To facilitate these relationships, the French colonial policy was based on the annual supply of goods and presents to the Indians in return for the delivery of products such as pelts, bear oil, horses, and Apache slaves at set negotiated prices (Usner 1987: 172). In the fur trade business, the regulation of market prices by merchant traders was based on the understanding of commercial profit, but also on an accommodation "to Indian insistence that trade be contained within the political sphere of relations" (Usner 1987: 175). Thus, the French offered the Caddoan peoples "fair words and presents," while the Spaniards only "offer fair words" (Hackett 1931-1946, vol. 3: para. 402).

Throughout the eighteenth century, quantities of European trade goods which were made available to the Caddoan peoples as trade payments and annual presents varied significantly from year to year for a number of reasons. Shipping and transportation problems, wars or disputes between the various colonial powers with an interest in the area and the Indian trade, or changes in Indian policies all caused occasional shortages or the lack of trade goods in colonial trade centers such as Natchitoches or New Orleans in French Louisiana. As noted earlier, in Spanish Texas prior to 1762, the colonial Indian policy was not founded on a commercial basis. Trade was permitted only under strict regulations (Bolton 1915: 32-39).

The trade of weapons and ammunition for deer hides and pelts was prohibited in Nueva España at this time, although these items were an essential aspect of the French and British encouragement of the fur trade (Schilz and Worcester 1987; Woods 1980). Grain and livestock shipments between Los Adaes, the Spanish capital of the province of Texas between 1721-1772, and the French post of Natchitoches were apparently a cover for the extensive contraband trading of items from Spanish military and governmental employees with the French and, more importantly in this context, with the Caddoan Indian tribes who lived in the vicinity of these colonial settlements (Bolton 1915: 418; Jackson 1986; Poyo and Hinojosa 1988).

As a result, during the 1751-1759 Spanish-Texas administration of Governor de Barios y Jáurequi, the Spanish trade of merchandise secured at Natchitoches was authorized. Spanish ranchers and farmers used this merchandise in trade exchanges with the Hasinai Caddo tribes for deer hides, horses, and maize, which were eventually conveyed back to Natchitoches as payment (Bolton 1915: 65-66). The active and legal participation of the Spanish colonists with the French in trade with Caddoan peoples closely coincides with the boom in the fur trade of French Louisiana (Surrey 1916), although the legal nature of the trade was short-lived.

Peltry from the Caddoan peoples had already been obtained from the Red River district around Natchitoches in 1716 (Archives Nationales, Colonies Series C-13a, 4: 355-65). By 1725, the contribution of the Red River Caddoan tribes amounted to about 3 percent of the peltry trade in New Orleans (Surrey 1916: 346), approximately 1,000 skins. In 1744, by contrast, 100,000 deerskins were shipped to France, plus buffalo skins (Archives Nationales, Colonies Series C-13a, 28: 35-36). By the 1750s it was reported that there was a French trader living at each of the Caddoan settlements, even those in Spanish Texas. Pichardo noted:

> That in Nachitoos [Natchitoches] there are few inhabitants other than the French soldiers. . . .From Nachitoos to Cadodachos. . .it is about fifty leagues toward the northwest. Between them are French settlements, as there are likewise at the said place of Cadodachos, though these French do not have fixed habitations, but only come and go to sell muskets and other things needed by the Indians, from whom they obtain annually about 100,000 pounds of furs, as well as tallow and the oil of bears, buffaloes, and deer. (Hackett 1931-1946, vol. 3: 417, para. 670)

Between about 1739 and 1756, the yearly contribution of the peltry trade in Louisiana increased 750 percent, from 16,000 to 120,000 *livres* a year (figure 2). During this period the fur trade constituted over 10 percent of the yearly total exports from French Louisiana, then decreased rapidly until Louisiana was ceded to Spain in 1762. It was not the case that the absolute value of deer pelts and hides decreased during that time, but rather that the relative contribution of indigo, tobacco, and other goods to the colonial economy increased much more rapidly over the same period (Surrey 1916). Thus, from the French and Spanish points of view, the peak period in the fur trade appears to have been between ca. 1740-1758 in Louisiana.

The ceding of Louisiana to Spain in 1762, although not completed until 1769, following France's loss to the British in the French and Indian War, led to a reevaluation of Spain's Indian policy concerning trade. The initial reaction of the new Spanish governors of Louisiana was to maintain the French practice of giving annual presents and keeping European traders[2] in each village (Kinnaird 1949: xxii-xxiii). This interim policy was rejected in 1772, however, by the first Viceroy of the Provincias Internas because "he objected to fixed annual gifts to buy peace and wanted presents given only as reward on occasions when Indians had demonstrated their loyalty and devotion to the King" (Bolton 1914, 1: 271). In an effort to maintain some semblance of control of the Indians who were already dependent upon the traders of Louisiana for the acquisition of European trade goods, the Barón de Ripperdá, governor of Texas from 1770-1778, overcame these objections and effected, along with the Louisiana authorities, this new Indian policy more successfully in Texas. The key points of the new Spanish policies in Indian relations in both Louisiana and Texas were:

1. Annual distribution of presents to those tribes considered loyal to the King of Spain.
2. Traders in each village to purchase furs and other items in exchange for supplies. Every village headman or chief was to be provided with a table of prices to ensure that fixed prices could be maintained (Bolton 1914, 1: 66-79).

The types of goods supplied to the Caddo to facilitate economic and political relationships included such items as clothing, muskets and gunflints, copper and brass kettles, powder, lead balls, vermilion, glass beads, metal tools, salt, hawk bells, needles, tobacco, brandy, mirrors, cord, and wire (see Bolton 1914, vol. 1). Similar types of goods were provided in the Spanish-sponsored Barr and

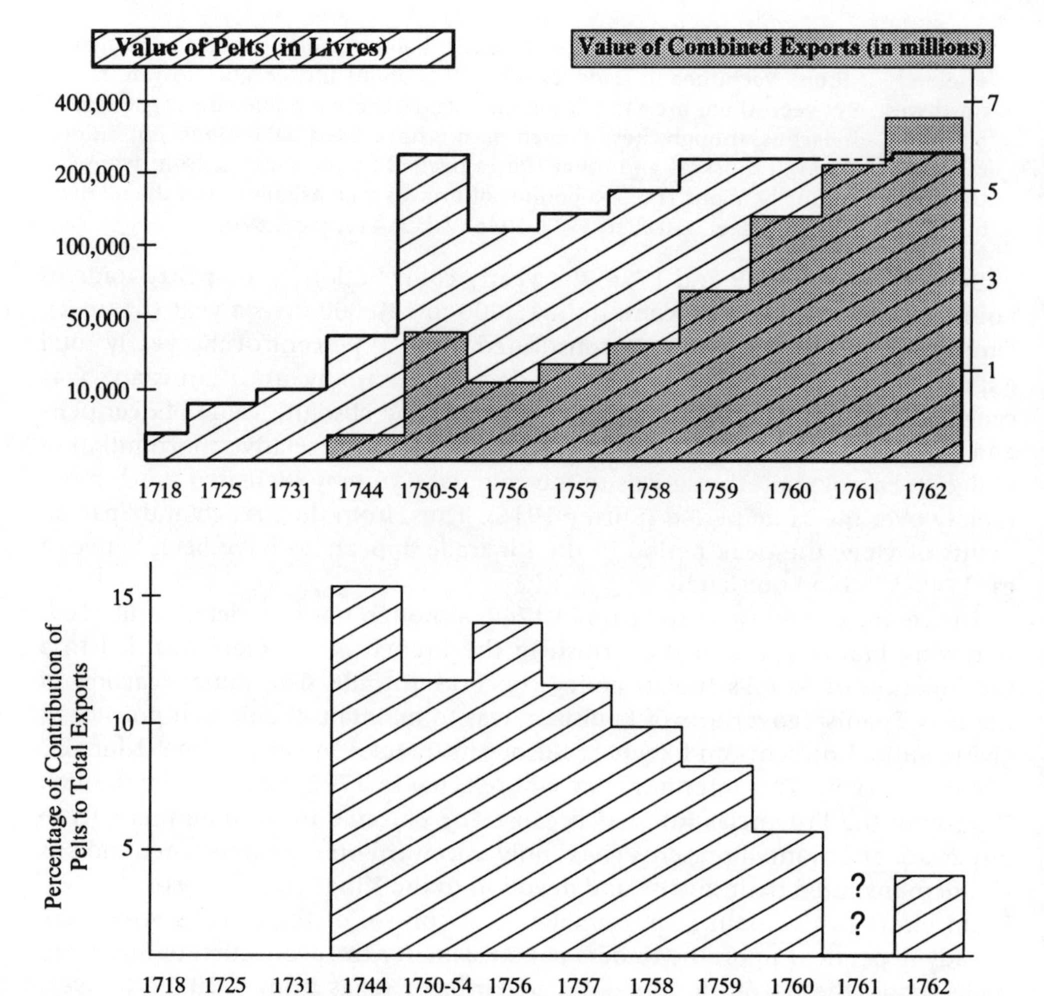

Figure 2. Top: Value of Pelts Compared to Value of Combined Exports for Louisiana, 1718-1762. Bottom: Percentage Contribution of Pelts to Total Louisiana Exports.

Davenport trading house in Nacogdoches and in the American trade factory in Natchitoches (Haggard 1945: 71-72, 75; Letterbook of the Natchitoches-Sulphur Fork Factory, 1809-1821: 22-23). As Flores points out (1985: 30), the most important European trade goods that the Caddoan groups sought to acquire were guns, gunpowder, and lead shot.

For the Native inhabitants of Louisiana, including the various Caddoan groups who traded at Natchitoches and the other trading posts in the colony, the importance of the fur trade continued into the American period (after 1803) and following the establishment of the United States Factory System (Prucha 1962). This is despite the fact that the fur trade represented only about one percent of total U.S. exports (Clayton 1967: 68).[3]

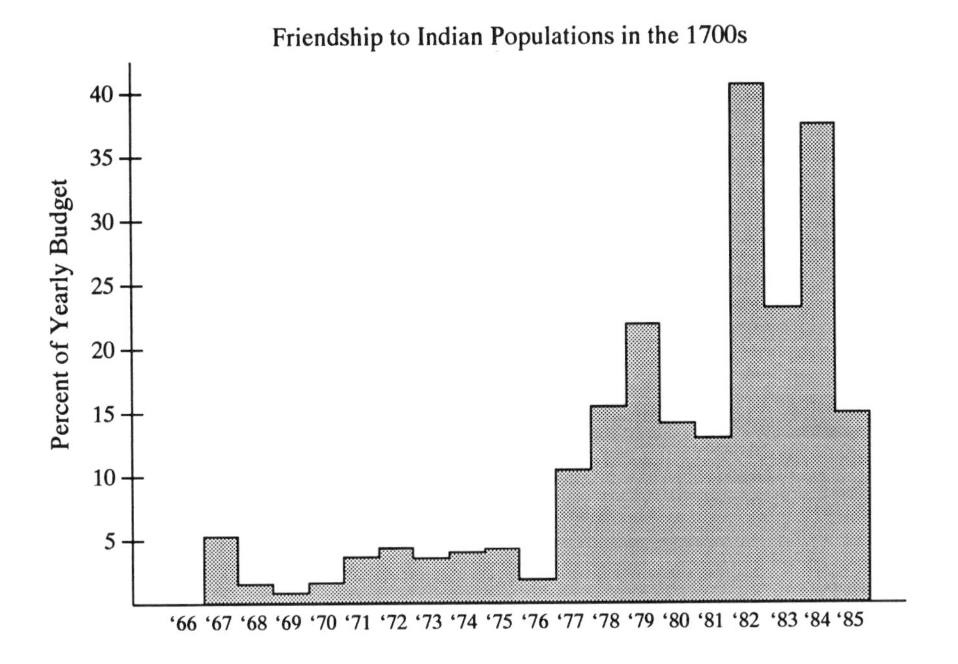

Figure 3. Percentage of Total Expenses of the Province of Louisiana Spent on "Friendship to Indian Populations." (From Archivo General de Indios, Legajos, 1766-1785).

What is significant about these fur trade data, and the availability of trade goods to the different groups, is that they signify that an ever-increasing amount of merchandise was being traded by the French and Spanish colonial governments to the Caddoan peoples during the eighteenth century. Annual presents were distributed in Louisiana even as the cession to Spain took place, with distribution points at Natchitoches, Arkansas Post, New Orleans, and St. Louis. The Kadohadacho and other Caddoan groups living on the Red River received their presents at Natchitoches.

In 1770, approximately 360 *pesos* of goods were distributed to the Kadohadacho; this was probably a typical amount up to 1776, when substantial increases in "Friendship to the Indian populations" occurred (figure 3). The amount of goods necessary to annually supply the Kadohadacho and other Red River Caddoan groups was much higher, perhaps on the order of 7,000 to 10,000 *pesos* per year to stock the Natchitoches post for the Kadohadacho, Natchitoches, and Yatasi needs (Bolton 1914, 1: 132-34, 143-46).

While Caddoan participation in the fur trade probably continued to increase throughout the eighteenth century, their actual contribution to the French and Spanish Louisiana economy continued to decrease relative to the Arkansas (or Quapaw), Osage, and Illinois tribes (cf. Kinnaird 1949: 228). For example, in 1770 Indian presents distributed by the Spanish to the Texas and Louisiana provinces amounted to 3,755 *pesos* (Kinnaird 1949: 148). Only 378 *pesos* (or 10 percent of the

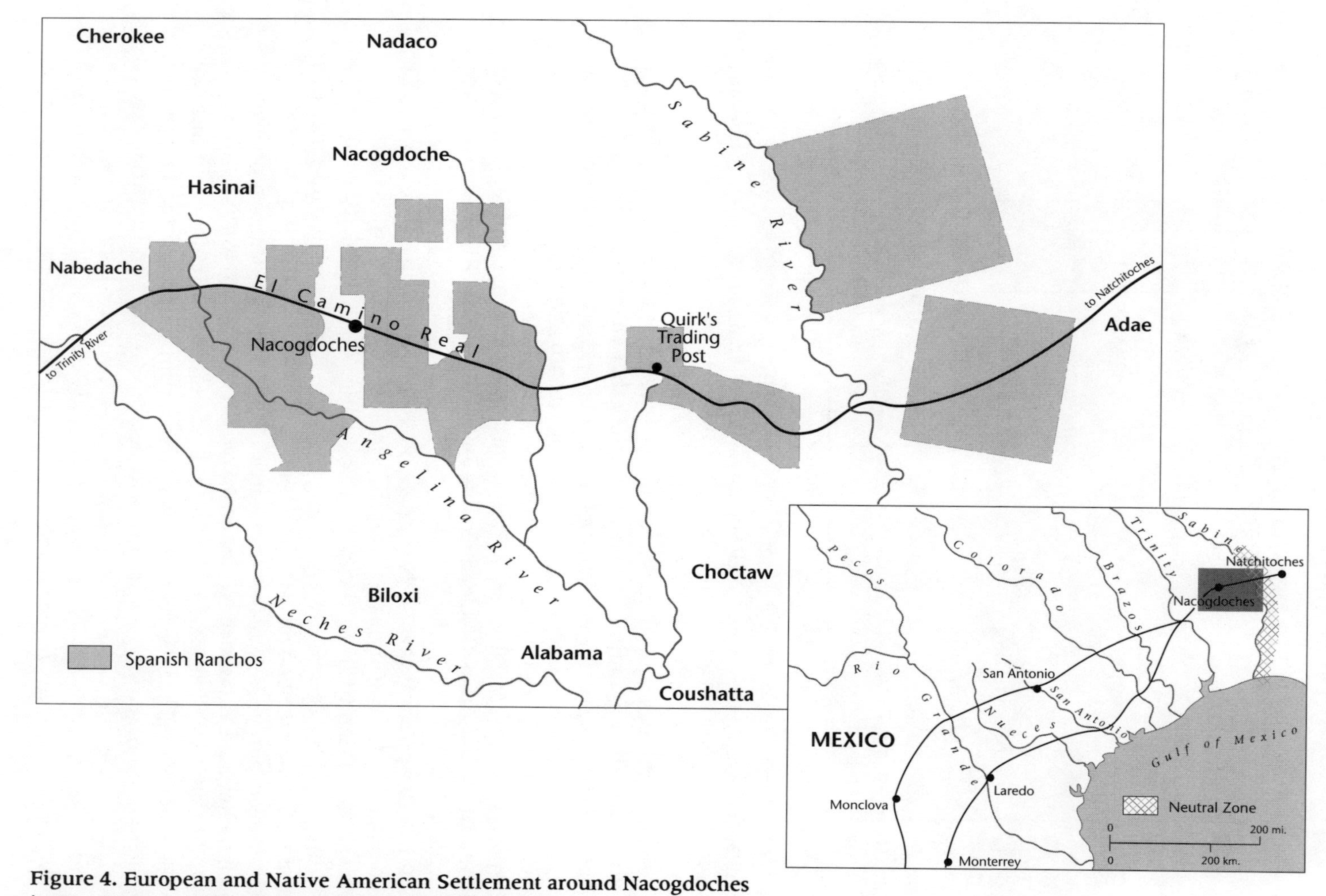

Figure 4. European and Native American Settlement around Nacogdoches in East Texas ca. 1810 (Jackson 1986; Perttula 1993b).

total) were distributed to Caddoan tribes. By comparison, over 33 percent of the presents in that year were distributed to Lower Mississippi Valley tribes, principally the Arkansas (515 *pesos*) and the Tunica (122 *pesos*), and in the province of Illinois 1,600 *pesos* worth of goods were distributed to the Indian tribes.

Following the formal establishment of the Provincias Internas in 1776, annual gifts did begin to increase (see figure 3). Before 1776 annual gifts or "Friendship" to the Indian populations in Louisiana accounted for less than five percent of the total yearly annual expenses. After 1776, however, they accounted for between 10 and 40 percent of the yearly expenses.

In Spanish Texas the colonial administration tried to follow the trade and gift patterns set in Louisiana, as already promised to the Texas Indians by De Mézières in 1779, but they were constrained by the scarcity and cost of trade goods (John 1975: 622). In October 1780, for instance, the supply of trade goods ran out at both Natchitoches and Nacogdoches, the new distribution center in Spanish Texas (see figure 4). Nevertheless, during this period European goods were available to the Caddoan peoples in unprecedented numbers, and it is at this time that European items, particularly guns and ammunition, begin to be strongly represented in aboriginal Caddoan assemblages in the Trans-Mississippi South (Perttula 1993b).

Even as the Spanish began to finally develop a commercially oriented Indian policy in Louisiana and Texas, they faced stiff competition from the English (and later the American) trading houses east of the Mississippi River. The English were able to well supply groups such as the Osage or Pawnee who lived in Spanish Louisiana but who were never consistently favored or considered friendly by Spanish authorities. Furthermore, the English sent trade expeditions along the Texas Gulf Coast and up some of the major streams, maintaining traders among the Caddoan groups in East Texas after 1780 (Pichardo, in Hackett 1931-1946, vol. 2: para. 709). The firm of St. Maxent and Ranson in Pensacola had been appointed commissioners of Indian affairs for Louisiana in 1769, and all goods distributed there were supposed to be purchased only through them. The British, however, had a major controlling interest in the St. Maxent and Ranson firm (Clark 1970), and used the firm to begin the distribution of English trade goods to meet the preferences of the different Indian groups in Texas and Louisiana with which they dealt.

To counteract this, the Barr and Davenport house, headquartered in Nacogdoches between 1798-1812, was fully supported by the Spanish government to maintain the Indian trade in Texas and oppose American commercial relations with the Caddo, Wichita, and Comanche groups in the province (Haggard 1945: 71; Jackson 1986: 451). Governor Manuel Mariá de Salcedo noted this in his report of 8 August 1809:

> The handling of the Indian nations that inhabit this province is also of the greatest importance. . .it would be advantageous for the King. . .or for rich private individuals to establish trading posts or commercial houses to supply the Indians and to

> trade with them better or at least equally in kind and more abundantly than the Anglo-Americans do. Then we would be able to get out of them anything we proposed to do, because the Indians develop and behave like those who trade with them according to the degree of recognized utility, convenience and advantages that are presented to them (Benson 1968: 614).

The volume of trade during this period in Spanish Texas was substantial, although the livestock (cattle and horse) trade by the early 1800s was the backbone of the Barr and Davenport business (cf. Haggard 1945: 73, 75; Jackson 1986: 427). For example, the Caddo and Immigrant Indians (such as the Choctaw, Cherokee, Alabama, and Koasati [Coushatta]) who lived in the vicinity of Nacogdoches (see figure 4), brought more than 40,000 deer skins, 1,500 bear skins, 1,200 otter, and 600 beaver skins to trade in Nacogdoches in one year (Ewers 1969: 47). In 1800, the Barr and Davenport house alone acquired 500 horses in trade with the Indians, merchandise worth about 5,000 *pesos* or $7,225 (cf. Jackson 1986: 472).

THE ARCHAEOLOGICAL RECORD OF THE FUR TRADE

The archaeological record attests to the fact that Caddoan peoples of the Trans-Mississippi South were proficient hunters of deer, bear, and other hide-bearing animals (Story, et al. 1990; Perttula 1990). With the acquisition of the horse in the late seventeenth century, the large game animals on the prairies were also frequently hunted.

Archaeological evidence from the Caddoan Area suggests that the initial Caddoan participation in the fur trade dates from about 1700, at a time when access to European goods (particularly guns) was variable and unreliable. The evidence for the fur trade includes (1) the development of a distinctive lithic tool assemblage for processing hides (see below); (2) group movements into unoccupied hinterland areas or into abandoned river valleys for hunting forays, as well as the relocation and movement of Caddoan groups towards European supply and trade depots established within the Caddoan Area; and (3) the accumulation of trade goods by successful Caddoan traders and hunters, and a larger proportion of Caddoan society, through the trade process.

By 1740-1750, European goods were being distributed by European traders who lived as semi-permanent residents in many Caddoan villages. The continuation of Caddoan participation in the fur trade, even as its relative contribution to the colonial economy was declining, is due primarily to the reason noted previously that the fur trade was well suited to the maintenance of stable trade alliances between the Caddoan peoples and the French colonists.

The economic situation, trade opportunities, and the access to European goods contributed to the acquisition of goods that had considerable economic, social, and military value to the Caddoan peoples. With the increasing availability of French guns and other products, fur trading became one of the more common

Figure 5. Watercolor by Lino Sánchez y Tapia of Coushatta (Koasati) hunters, 1828. From the Collection of Gilcrease Museum, Tulsa.

ways for Caddoan peoples to interact with the Europeans, and also to effect changes in economic, political, and subsistence matters.

Stone projectile points recovered from Caddoan sites indicate the ubiquitous use of the bow and arrow until about 1700, followed by the adoption of the gun by the late seventeenth and early eighteenth centuries (Schilz and Worcester 1987). Solitary stalking and group surround methods were used by the Caddo in the historic period in the capture of deer (Swanton 1942; Griffith 1954). Catastrophic age profiles or mortality curves for white-tailed deer have been documented from the middle eighteenth century Gilbert site faunal assemblage in northeast Texas (Perttula 1990, 2: 56-58). The assemblage is dominated by deer 1.5-4.0 years of age. The more effective utilization of deer as a peltry source involved innovations in hunting techniques and in culling selected age classes, namely the reproductively active middle-age groups as at the Gilbert site. Deer of middle age are mature and have reached their peak in height and weight, as well as pelt condition, and then they gradually decrease in weight with age.

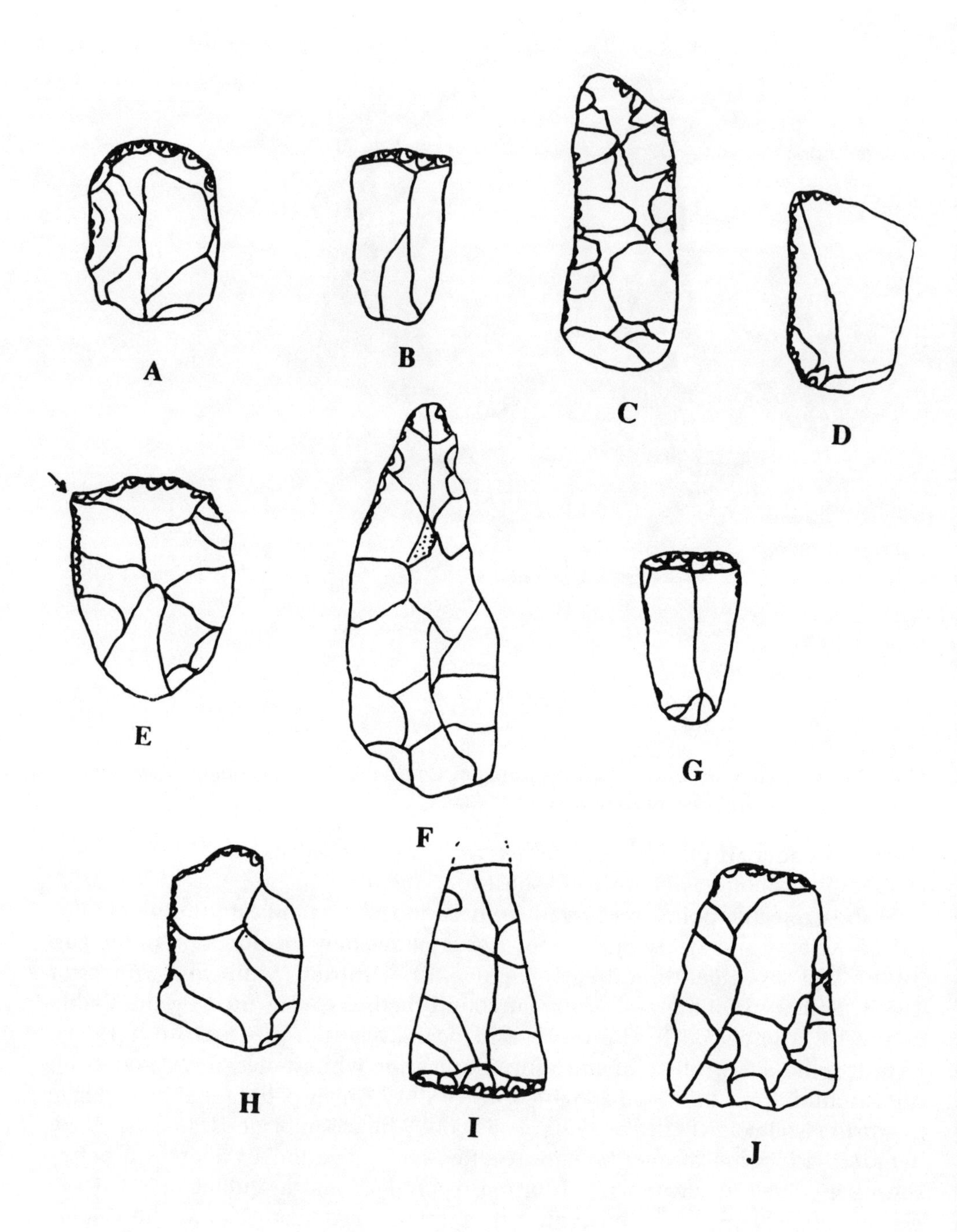

Figure 6. Seventeenth- and Eighteenth-Century Lithic Tools on Aboriginal Sites in the Trans-Mississippi South and the Lower Mississippi Valley.

A,B: Gilbert Site end scraper (Jelks 1967: figure 70a), 1740-1770.
C: Gilbert Site knife (Jelks 1967: Figure 72j), 1740-1770.
D: Womack Site side scraper (Harris et al. 1965: figure 2k), early eighteenth century.
E: Womack Site snub-nose scraper with graver beak (Harris et al. 1965: figure 3a), early eighteenth century.
F: Oliver Site triangular knife (Brain 1988: figure 199ii), ca. 1700.
G: Oliver Site snub-nose end scraper (Brain 1988: figure 199rr), 1700.
H: One Cypress Point Site bifacial cutting tool (Hemmings 1982: figure 48g), ca. 1600-1700.
I: Antioch Site bifacial end scraper (Brown 1985: figure 84f), late seventeenth century.
J: Trinity Site bifacial tool (Brown 1985: figure 115f), early eighteenth century.

The Womack site on the Red River in Lamar County, Texas was occupied ca. 1700-1729 by Caddoan-speaking hunters (Harris, et al. 1965). The archaeological assemblage at the site is dominated by items associated with hunting and hide preparation. This includes stone scrapers (figure 6d-e) and projectile points, as well as iron knives, gun parts, lead shot, and native and French gunflints. Such hunting camps evidence a heavy involvement in the French fur trade (e.g., Gregory 1973: 247) and are also characterized by quantities of other types of trade goods (such as glass beads, copper kettles, and other implements) derived from French payment for the skins. European goods at the Womack site are mainly derived from contact with the French traders operating in the Red River Valley. Similarities between the types of beads at the site and those from Caddoan sites in the Texarkana area suggest that payments and traders originated at the French-controlled Fort de St. Louis established in 1719 (Gilmore 1986; Perttula 1989: 308-12).

Similar archaeological assemblages have been documented from the Lower Mississippi Valley during the historic period among the Tunica and Natchez peoples (Brain 1988; Brown 1985). At sites such as Russell and Oliver, large thumbnail end scrapers, bifacial scrapers, knives and projectile points (see figure 6f-g) dominate the late seventeenth- and early eighteenth-century stone tool assemblages. Late seventeenth- and early eighteenth-century Natchez assemblages from the Natchez Bluffs area (see figure 6i-j) have a similar indigenous lithic technology for the processing of deer skins (Brown 1985: 185). However, when iron and copper implements became available in large quantities, their stone tool technology was not maintained.

Excavations at One Cypress Point in the Felsenthal area of southwest Arkansas have recovered a distinctive hunting camp assemblage, dating from ca. 1600 to 1700, that may also be an early expression of the developing fur trade. No European trade goods or diagnostic aboriginal ceramics were found at the site. Instead the assemblage is composed almost entirely of stone tools and

Figure 7. Watercolor by Lino Sánchez y Tapia of Taovayas (or Tawehash) hunters, 1828. From the Collection of Gilcrease Museum, Tulsa.

Nodena projectile points (Hemmings 1982: 178-85). The most conspicuous class of stone tools present are large flake and bifacial scraping implements (see figure 6h). This type of lithic assemblage had not been previously documented in the region in prehistoric or historic periods, but as noted above has been seen at historic Native American settlements elsewhere in the Lower Mississippi Valley.

Middle to late eighteenth-century archaeological sites in the upper Sabine Basin of northeast Texas appear to be specialized hunting camps of Wichita-Taovayas and Caddoan peoples involved in the fur trade (Gregory 1973: 239-52; Perttula and Skiles 1989). Both the Gilbert (Jelks 1967) and Pearson (Duffield and Jelks 1961) sites have stone tool hunting kits (see figure 6a-c) and quantities of French gunparts and lead balls, as well as a large and varied assortment of European trade materials. In addition to the guns and gun parts, trade goods from the Gilbert site include French clasp knives, axes, wedges, awls, scissors, metal arrowpoints, hawk bells, coins, finger rings, buttons, glass beads, brass kettles, horse trappings, and bottle glass (Jelks 1967: 18-111).

These sites in the Upper Sabine basin, which were occupied from at least 1740 to after 1780, may have been associated with one of several eighteenth-century French "factories" or hunter camps mentioned in archival documents (e.g., Bolton 1915). As described by Gregory:

> French hunters operated from the Natchitoches post on a sort of share cropper basis. Men were outfitted with French firearms, flints, powder and shot, to go to the vicinity of the Wichita to hunt hides. (1973: 243)

Prior to ca. 1730 European trade goods are not common in Caddoan habitation sites or cemeteries, and are generally restricted to goods such as ornamental artifacts and reworked metal tools found primarily as grave goods in mortuary contexts (Perttula 1993a). Guns, axes, knives, powder and shot, and clothing accessories are much more common on trade good inventories after 1740, as discussed above, and as seen in the Caddoan archaeological record. This is a consequence of (1) Caddoan participation in the fur trade; (2) their position as middlemen between Europeans and other Native Americans in the regional trade network; (3) the continued exchange of horses and livestock to the Natchitoches post; and (4) from the acquisition of annual gifts and presents from the Spanish and French colonial governments. The latter was a reflection of political and economic commitments of friendship and alliances between the Caddoan peoples and the Europeans (e.g., Sabo 1987: 42-44).

The trade goods obtained by the Caddoan groups had ceremonial and ideological significance to them. Over time, however, Caddoan perceptions of the exchange process changed significantly, such that the value and importance of the European goods increasingly moved from the ceremonial realm towards the economic and secular realm (Sabo 1987: 38-39).

The individual Caddoan hunter in the fur trade was an important catalyst in this process. He was closely intertwined with matters of political and economic well-being, and with social and power relationships within Caddoan society. Yet, territorial prerogatives shaped by the contest of cultures between the Caddoan peoples, the Europeans, and the other Native American groups in the Trans-Mississippi South also played a large role in the overall nature of the fur and peltry trade as it developed in the eighteenth century.

NOTES

1. Some of the best beaver habitat in the Caddoan Area was along tributaries of the Red River and in the Ouachita Mountains (Flores 1984: 274n.275, 330nn.13, 14).
2. French-speaking traders were preferred by the Caddoan peoples throughout the Historic Period.
3. The Sulphur Fork Factory (1818-1825), at the confluence of the Red River with the Sulphur River in southwest Arkansas, for instance did over $5,000 worth of trade business between 1818 and 1819 with the Native Americans living in the district, including some Red River Caddoan peoples (Magnaghi 1978). Deer pelts comprised about 77 percent of the total revenues in those years, along with beaver, raccoon, otter, and bear skins (Magnaghi 1976). Berlandier (Ewers

1969: 107) pointed out in 1830 that the Kadohadacho cultivated "very little land," followed the migrations of the buffalo herds, and did a "thriving trade in furs" which were exchanged in Natchitoches and other United States government trading houses or factories (see Williams 1964: 552-59).

References

Archivo General de Indios. 1492-1856. Audiencias e Indiferente, Legajos. Seville, Spain.

Archives Nationales, Colonies. 1679-1763. Serie C13a, Correspondence Generale, vols. 1-45. Paris: National Archives.

Benson, N.L. (ed. and trans.). 1968. "A Governor's Report on Texas in 1809." *Southwestern Historical Quarterly* 71: 603-15.

Bolton, H.E. 1914. *Athanase de Mézières and the Louisiana-Texas Frontier, 1768-1780*, 2 vols. Cleveland: Clark Publishing.

______. 1915. *Texas in the Middle Eighteenth Century: Studies in Spanish Colonial History and Administration*. Berkeley: University of California Press.

______. 1917. "The Mission as a Frontier Institution in the Spanish-American Colonies." *American Historical Review* 23: 42-61.

Brain, J.P. 1988. *Tunica Archaeology*. Papers of the Peabody Museum of Archaeology and Ethnology, Harvard University, vol. 78. Cambridge: Harvard University Press.

Brown, I.W. 1985. *Natchez Indian Archaeology: Culture Change and Stability in the Lower Mississippi Valley*. Archaeological Report No. 15. Jackson: Mississippi Department of Archives and History.

Clark, J.G. 1970. *New Orleans, 1718-1812: An Economic History*. Baton Rouge: Louisiana State University Press.

Clayton, J.L. 1967. "The Growth and Economic Significance of the American Fur Trade, 1790-1890." In *Aspects of the Fur Trade: Selected Papers of the 1965 North American Fur Trade Conference*, edited by R.W. Fridley and J.D. Holmquist, 62-72. St. Paul: Minnesota Historical Society.

Duffield, L.F., and E.B. Jelks. 1961. *The Pearson Site: A Historic Indian Site in Iron Bridge Reservoir, Rains County, Texas*. Archaeology Series No. 4. Department of Anthropology, University of Texas, Austin, Texas.

Ewers, J.C. (ed.). 1969. *The Indians of Texas in 1830 by Jean Louis Berlandier*. Washington, D.C.: Smithsonian Institution Press.

Flores, D.L. 1984. *Jefferson and Southwestern Exploration: The Freeman and Custis Accounts of the Red River Expedition of 1806*. Norman: University of Oklahoma Press.

______. 1985. *Journal of an Indian Trader: Anthony Glass and the Texas Frontier, 1790-1810*. College Station: Texas A&M University Press.

Garrett, J.K. 1944. "Letters and Documents: Dr. John Sibley and the Louisiana-Texas Frontier, 1803-1814." *Southwestern Historical Quarterly* 47: 388-91.

Gilmore, K.K. 1986. *French-Indian Interaction at an Early Eighteenth Century Post: The Roseborough Lake Site, Bowie County, Texas*. Contributions in Archaeology, No. 3. North Texas State University, Institute of Applied Sciences, Denton, Texas.

Giraud, M. 1974. *A History of French Louisiana, Volume I, The Reign of Louis XIV, 1698-1715*. Baton Rouge: Louisiana State University Press.

Gregory, H.F. 1973. "Eighteenth Century Caddoan Archaeology: A Study in Models and Interpretation." Ph.D. diss., Southern Methodist University, Dallas.

Griffith, W.J. 1954. *The Hasinai Indians of East Texas as Seen by Europeans, 1687-1772.* Philological and Documentary Studies, vol. 2, no. 3. Middle American Research Institute, Tulane University, New Orleans.

Hackett, C.W. ed. and trans. 1931-1946. *Pichardo's Treatise on the Limits of Louisiana and Texas.* 4 vols. Austin: University of Texas Press.

Haggard, J.V. 1945. "The House of Barr and Davenport." *Southwestern Historical Quarterly* 49: 66-88.

Harris, R.K., I.M. Harris, J.C. Blaine, and J. Blaine. 1965. "A Preliminary Archeological and Documentary Study of the Womack Site, Lamar County, Texas." *Bulletin of the Texas Archeological Society* 36: 287-365.

Hemmings, E.T. 1982. *Human Adaptations in the Grand Marais Lowland.* Research Series No. 17, Arkansas Archeological Survey, Fayetteville.

Jackson, J. 1986. *Los Mesteños: Spanish Ranching in Texas, 1721-1821.* College Station: Texas A&M University Press.

Jelks, E.B. ed. 1967. "The Gilbert Site, A Norteno Focus Site in Northeastern Texas." *Bulletin of the Texas Archeological Society* 37: 1-255.

John, E.A.H. 1975. *Storms Brewed in Other Men's Worlds: The Confrontation of Indians, Spanish, and French in the Southwest, 1540-1795.* College Station: Texas A&M University Press.

Johnson, L., and A.J. McGraw. 1991. "Notes on Mazanet's Coahuilteco Stream Names with Comments on their Linguistic and Historic Value." In *A Texas Legacy: The Old San Antonio Road and the Caminos Reales. A Tricentennial History,* edited by A.J. McGraw, J.W. Clark, and E.A. Robbins, pp. 121-28. Austin: Texas State Department of Highways and Public Transportation, Highway Design Division. Austin.

Kinnaird, L. 1949. *Spain in the Mississippi Valley, 1765-1794.* American Historical Association, Annual Report for the Year 1945, 3 vols. Washington, D.C.

Kinnaird, L., and L.B. Kinnaird. 1980. "Choctaws West of the Mississippi, 1766-1800." *Southwestern Historical Quarterly* 83: 349-70.

Kniffen, F.B., H.F. Gregory, and G.A. Stokes. 1987. *The Historic Indian Tribes of Louisiana: From 1542 to the Present.* Baton Rouge: Louisiana State University Press.

Magnaghi, R.M. 1976. "The Red River Valley North of Natchitoches, 1817-1818." *Louisiana Studies* 15: 286-93.

______. 1978. "Sulphur Fork Factory, 1817-1822." *Arkansas Historical Quarterly* 37: 168-83.

Milanich, J.T. 1990. "The European Entrada into La Florida: An Overview." In *Columbian Consequences, Volume 2. Archaeological and Historical Perspectives on the Spanish Borderlands East,* edited by D.H. Thomas, pp. 3-29. Washington, D.C.: Smithsonian Institution Press.

Natchitoches-Sulphur Fork Factory. 1809-1821. Letterbook, 1809-1821. National Archives and Records Administration, Washington, D.C.

Perttula, T.K. 1989. "Contact and Interaction between Caddoan and European Peoples: The Historic Archaeological and Ethnohistorical Records." Ph.D. diss., University of Washington, Seattle.

______. 1990. "The Development of Agricultural Subsistence, Regional and Diachronic Variability in Caddoan Subsistence, and Implications for the Caddoan Archaeological Record." Ms. on file, Department of Antiquities Protection, Texas Historical Commission. Austin.

______. 1992. *"The Caddo Nation": Archaeological and Ethnohistoric Perspectives.* Austin: University of Texas Press.

______. 1993a. "Kee-oh-na-wah'-wah: The Effects of European Contact on the Caddoan Indians of Texas, Louisiana, Arkansas, and Oklahoma." In *Ethnohistory and*

Archaeology: Approaches to Postcontact Change in the Americas, edited by J. Daniel Rogers and Samuel M. Wilson, pp. 89-109. New York: Plenum Press.

_____. 1993b. Effects of European Contact on Native and Immigrant Indians in Northeast Texas. In *Archeology in the Eastern Planning Region, Texas: A Planning Document* edited by N.A. Kenmotsu and T.K. Perttula, pp. 147-87. Texas Historical Commission, Department of Antiquities Protection, Cultural Resource Management Report 3. Austin.

Perttula, T.K., and B.D. Skiles. 1989. "Another Look at an Eighteenth Century Archaeological Site in Wood County, Texas." *Southwestern Historical Quarterly* 92 (3): 417-35.

Poyo, G.E., and G.M. Hinojosa. 1988. "Spanish Texas and Borderlands Historiography in Transition: Implications for United States History." *The Journal of American History* 75 (2): 393-416.

Prucha, F.P. 1962. *American Indian Policy in the Formative Years: The Indian Trade and Intercourse Acts, 1790-1834.* Lincoln: University of Nebraska Press.

Robbins, E.A. 1991a. "The First Routes into Texas." In *A Texas Legacy: The Old San Antonio Road and the Caminos Reales. A Tricentennial History,* edited by A.J. McGraw, J.W. Clark, and E.A. Robbins, pp. 61-113. Austin: Texas State Department of Highways and Public Transportation, Highway Design Division.

_____. 1991b. "The Natural Setting Encountered: The Scenic Landscape." In *A Texas Legacy: The Old San Antonio Road and the Caminos Reales. A Tricentennial History,* edited by A.J. McGraw, J.W. Clark, and E.A. Robbins, pp. 245-268. Austin: Texas State Department of Highways and Public Transportation, Highway Design Division.

Robertson, J.A. trans. and ed. 1933. *True Relation of the Hardships Suffered by Governor Fernando de Soto and Certain Portuguese Gentlemen During the Discovery of the Province of Florida Now Newly Set Forth by a Gentleman of Elvas.* Publications of the Florida Historical Society, No. 11, Deland, Florida.

Rogers, J.D. In press. "The Caddos." *Handbook of North American Indians, Southeast* vol. 14 Washington, D.C.: Smithsonian Institution Press.

Sabo, G. III. 1987. "Reordering Their World: A Caddoan Ethnohistory." In *Visions and Revisions: Ethnohistoric Perspectives on Southern Cultures,* edited by G. Sabo III and W.M. Schneider, pp. 25-47. Athens: University of Georgia Press.

Schambach, F.F. 1982. "An Outline of Fourche Maline Culture in Southwest Arkansas." In *Arkansas Archeology in Review,* edited by N.L. Trubowitz and M.D. Jeter, pp. 132-97. Research Series No. 15, Arkansas Archeological Survey, Fayetteville.

_____. 1989. "The End of the Trail: The Route of Hernando De Soto's Army Through Southwest Arkansas and East Texas." *The Arkansas Archeologist,* Bulletin 27/28: 9-33.

Schambach, F.F., and A.M. Early. 1983. "Southwest Arkansas." In *A State Plan for the Conservation of Archeological Resources in Arkansas,* edited by H.A. Davis. Research Series No. 21, Arkansas Archeological Survey, Fayetteville.

Schilz, T.F., and D.E. Worcester. 1987. "The Spread of Firearms among the Indian Tribes on the Northern Frontier of New Spain." *The American Indian Quarterly* 11 (1): 1-10.

Sibley, J. 1832. "Historical Sketches of Several Indian Tribes in Louisiana, South of the Arkansas River, and between the Mississippi and River Grande." In *American State Papers, Class II, Indian Affairs,* vol. 1, pp. 721-25. Washington, D.C.: Gales & Seaton.

Smith, F.T. 1991. "The Kadohadacho Indians and the Louisiana-Texas Frontier, 1803-1815." *Southwestern Historical Quarterly* 95: 177-204.

Story, D.A., J.A. Guy, B.A. Burnett, M.D. Freeman, J.C. Rose, D.G. Steele, B.W. Olive, and K.J. Reinhard. 1990. *The Archeology and Bioarcheology of the Gulf Coastal Plain.* Research Series No. 38, Arkansas Archeological Survey, Fayetteville.

Surrey, N.M.M. 1916. *The Commerce of Louisiana during the French Regime, 1699-1763.* Columbia University Studies in History, Economics, and Public Law, Volume 71. New York.

Swanton, J.R. 1942. *Source Material on the History and Ethnology of the Caddo Indians.* Bureau of American Ethnology, Bulletin No. 132. Washington, D.C.

Tanner, H.H. 1974. "The Territory of the Caddo Tribe of Oklahoma." In *Caddo Indians IV,* edited by D. Horr, pp. 9-144. New York: Garland Publishing.

Usner, D.H. 1985. "The Deerskin Trade in French Louisiana." In *Proceedings of the Tenth Meeting of the French Colonial Historical Society, April 12-14, 1984,* edited by P.B. Boucher, pp. 75-93. Boston: University Press of America, Inc.

______. 1987. "The Frontier Exchange Economy of the Lower Mississippi Valley in the 18th Century." *The William and Mary Quarterly* 44: 165-92.

Williams, S. 1964. "The Aboriginal Locations of the Kadohadacho and related Tribes." In *Exploration in Cultural Anthropology,* edited by W. Goodenough, pp. 545-70. New Haven: Yale University Press.

Wilson, S.M., and J.D. Rogers. 1993. "Historical Dynamics in the Contact Era." In *Ethnohistory and Archaeology: Approaches to Postcontact Change in the Americas,* edited by J. Daniel Rogers and Samuel M. Wilson, pp. 3-15. New York: Plenum Press.

Wood, P.H. 1989. "The Changing Population of the Colonial South: An Overview by Race and Religion, 1685-1790." In *Powhatan's Mantle: Indians in the Colonial Southeast,* edited by P.H. Wood, G.A. Waselkov, and M.T. Hatley, pp. 35-103. Lincoln: University of Nebraska Press.

Woods, P.D. 1980. *French-Indian Relations on the Southern Frontier, 1699-1762.* Studies in American History and Culture, no. 18. Ann Arbor: University of Michigan Research Press.

Wyckoff, D.G.1980. "Caddoan Adaptive Strategies in the Arkansas Basin, Eastern Oklahoma." Ph.D. diss., Washington State University, Pullman, WA.

Wyckoff, D.G., and T.G. Baugh. 1980. "Early Historic Hasinai Elites: A Model for the Material Culture of Governing Elites." *Midcontinental Journal of Archaeology* 5: 225-83.

The Flow of European Trade Goods into the Western Great Lakes Region, 1715-1760

Dean L. Anderson

Since the pioneering work of Francis Parkman (1983) and Frederick Jackson Turner (1970) in the late nineteenth century, the North American fur trade has been conceptualized primarily as a Euro-American institution. For the most part, historians have characterized the fur trade as the initial, path-breaking incursion of Euro-American influence into the interior of northeastern North America. Thus, scholarly treatment of the trade has been mainly concerned with the exploits of Euro-American traders and with the role of the trade as the vanguard of Euro-American settlement (Turner 1970) and as the extension of the European economic system into North America (Innis 1970). In this view of the fur trade, Indian peoples have been portrayed as minor characters who played a limited part in the conduct of the trade. Consequently, relatively little attention has been paid to understanding Indian participation in the trade.

Over the past twenty years, however, a different perspective has emerged on the role of Native peoples in the fur trade. A number of studies have disputed the conventional wisdom that Indian peoples were merely passive pawns in the trade who were caught up and swept along in a tide of Euro-American enterprise (Francis and Morantz 1983; Krech 1984; Lohse 1988; Ray 1974; Yerbury 1986). To the contrary, it has been demonstrated that Native peoples were active, and indeed aggressive, participants in the fur trade. No less than their Euro-American counterparts, Indian peoples sought to shape the trade according to their cultural values (B. White 1984; 1986) and to use the trade to serve their best interests. Such studies have emphasized that the fur trade was not organized, controlled, and carried out by Euro-Americans who imposed the trade upon Native peoples. Rather, the trade arose through a process of cultural compromise in which Euro-Americans accommodated Native values and customs at least as much, and perhaps more, than Indian peoples accommodated Euro-American ideas (R. White 1991).

It has become increasingly clear that the fur trade was a cultural partnership and that there is a great deal to be learned about the involvement of Indian peoples in the trade. Toward this end, one of the major trends in current fur trade research is the effort to specifically investigate both the way native peoples contributed to shaping the trade as well as the way they adapted to new conditions produced by the trade (Krech 1984: x).

Indian Peoples and European Trade Goods

The fur trade exchange relationship was a complex one which presented Indian peoples with new social, political, and economic circumstances and opportunities (Peterson and Anfinson 1984). However, the most tangible consequence of the fur trade for Native peoples was the introduction of European manufactured goods. The flow of trade goods into Indian societies was an important part of the impact of the trade upon Native peoples. The adoption of European goods altered Native material culture which, in turn, influenced change in other aspects of Native life.

How did Indian peoples respond to the introduction of European materials? Contrary to the popular perception that Indian peoples were smitten by the irresistible appeal of obviously superior European goods, it has been shown that Native peoples critically evaluated European products and appropriated those that met their needs and interests. Indian peoples were not passive recipients of European goods but aggressive, discriminating consumers (Ray 1980; Krech 1984).

In the active pursuit of European technology, then, what types of goods did Indian peoples seek to obtain and what patterns in Indian acquisition of trade goods can be identified? These may seem like simple questions and it may also seem that they are questions that are already well understood, since there is considerable discussion in the fur trade literature of the types of trade goods acquired by Indian peoples. It is the premise of this study, however, that the flow of European goods into Indian societies is not well understood. While there is a great deal of comment in the literature on the goods traded to Indians, there have been few systematic, quantitative studies of the flow of goods into Indian societies.

This article examines the flow of European goods into the western Great Lakes region (figure 1) during the period from 1715 to 1760. It may be noted that there are several studies which discuss the acquisition of trade goods by Indian peoples during the pre-1760 period in areas to the north of the western Great Lakes region (Ray 1974; 1980; Ray and Freeman 1978; Morantz 1980). In that area, the Hudson's Bay Company was the principal supplier of goods and the vast records of the HBC have served as a valuable source of data on Indian trading habits. By comparison, the flow of goods through the French trade system into the western Great Lakes region during the period prior to 1760 is less well known.

Figure 1. French-period outposts in the western Great Lakes region for which Montreal Merchants' Records data were compiled.

THE MONTREAL MERCHANTS' RECORDS

This paper uses data taken from an extensive collection of documents known as the Montreal Merchants' Records (hereafter referred to as the MMR). The MMR are composed of portions of the business records of several different Montreal merchants. As part of their business, the merchants sold trade goods and supplies to fur traders preparing to travel to posts in the interior. The MMR record the shipment of trade goods to diverse geographic locations during much of the eighteenth century. The documents are, however, an especially important body of data regarding the French-period trade in the western Great Lakes area. Temporally, the documents mainly record the shipment of goods during the period from 1715 to 1760. Further, most of the shipments of goods recorded were to posts in the western Great Lakes region. Importantly, the fact that the documents record the shipment of goods to a number of different posts provides a broad, regional view of the flow of trade goods into the western country.

The merchants' account books contain detailed invoices which list trade goods to be shipped to the posts. In this respect, the MMR are different from Hudson's Bay Company post records that have been used to examine Indian acquisition of trade goods. Hudson's Bay Company post records record the sale of goods by European traders to Indian customers. The MMR, in contrast, record the sale of goods by European merchants to European traders. Although the MMR do not explicitly record the purchase of goods by Indian peoples, it is argued that the MMR still provide a valid, if not precise, record of the goods which Native peoples obtained. It is suggested that although the MMR are not specifically a record of the goods for which Native peoples traded, Indian demand for European goods shaped the contents of the inventories of goods purchased by traders. If we accept that the fur trade was a sophisticated exchange relationship in which both Indian and European participants were knowledgeable about their trading partners, it follows that European traders purchased goods according to their understanding of Indian interests in trade goods. Consequently, it is argued here that the general patterns in trader purchasing of types of goods and quantities of goods recorded in the MMR are a valid reflection of general patterns in Indian trading. This is not to suggest that European traders were always completely accurate in their anticipation of what Indian peoples would purchase. Certainly European traders could not anticipate every change in the needs and desires of their Indian customers. Thus, while the inventories of goods purchased by European traders are not an absolute representation of what Indians ultimately obtained, it is suggested that those inventories are an essentially accurate representation of Indian acquisition of trade goods.

The Fur Trade Invoices

The fur trade invoices in the MMR contain a detailed record of the materials that fur traders purchased from the merchants. The invoices are usually similar in form and include a variety of information. At the head of the invoice, the date of the sale is recorded. Next, a brief statement appears which identifies the purchaser and which usually indicates the post to which the goods were to be taken. The main body of the invoice follows, consisting of an itemized listing of the goods, supplies, and services sold to the trader. While the invoice entries are rather concise, they often describe the items purchased on the basis of type, size, color, material, or place of manufacture. Commonly, the descriptive terms distinguish between items of different price, such as different sizes and styles of knives or different sizes of capotes. Each entry records the quantity of the item purchased and the unit of measure in which it was sold, such as 10 axes, 5 pounds of beads, or 50 ells of cloth. In addition, each invoice entry includes the unit price for the item and the total cost for the quantity purchased. In some invoices, profit margin is added to the itemized charges. All of the price information in the account books is recorded in the French Canadian monetary system of the period, consisting of *livres, sols,* and *deniers* (20 *sols* equal 1 *livre,* 12 *deniers* equal 1 *sol*).

The Outfits

The fur trade invoices in the MMR are scattered throughout the account books and are interspersed among postings for the sale of merchandise to local Montreal citizens. Identifying and organizing those invoices that specifically recorded trade goods presented a problem because of the variability in the invoices. Some fur trade invoices are extremely long and are easily recognizable in the pages of the account books. In these cases, trade goods and supplies were purchased by a trader in one large transaction, resulting in a single invoice that might continue for several pages. In some instances, though, a trader made more than one purchase, perhaps over a period of several days, resulting in two or more invoices. Sometimes a posting for the purchase of just a few items would follow a main invoice, suggesting the addition of goods that were forgotten or added as an afterthought.

Because of the variability in the invoices in the account books, the concept of an "outfit" is used in this study to organize the invoices. As the term is used here, an outfit consists of the trade goods and supplies shipped to a specific location by a trader or partnership of traders within a calendar year, whether the goods are listed in one invoice or in several. In this way, a number of invoices could be consolidated, including those for materials purchased by the trader's *engagés*. This means that a single small invoice was designated as an outfit if it was the only one posted for a specific trader and a specific location during a calendar year. In so doing, the presence of trade goods in a single invoice was the prerequisite for identifying it as an outfit; a lone invoice that was made up entirely of supplies or personal items was not considered an outfit. It is important to point out that the identification of an assemblage of goods as an outfit carries no implications about the size of that group of goods. An outfit may be represented by the purchase of a few items or by the purchase of several thousand *livres* worth of goods.

The Posts

A total of eighty-three outfits shipped to the western Great Lakes region before 1760 were identified in the MMR account books. Thirteen of these outfits were omitted because they lacked certain information, such as prices for goods or the specific destination of the outfit. This left a total of seventy outfits from which data were taken. These outfits represent the shipment of goods to eight different trading posts. The posts, and the number of outfits recorded for each of them, are listed in table 1. The locations of the eight posts are shown in figure 1. The outfits enumerated for each post in table 1 were shipped over the forty-five-year span from 1715 to 1760. Since the total number of outfits for each post is considerably less than forty-five, it is apparent that outfits were not recorded every year for any of the posts. This is because the trader clientele of the merchants fluctuated from year to year. Each year, the merchants did business with different traders who were operating at different posts. Consequently, there is not a continuous, year-by-year record of outfits for any of the posts. Rather, outfits for any given post occur with varying frequency and regularity in the account books.

TABLE 1. NUMBER OF OUTFITS FOR EACH POST, 1715-1760.

Post	Number of Outfits
Detroit	15
Michilimackinac	14
Green Bay	13
Ouiatenon	10
Sioux Post	8
Rainy Lake	6
Nipigon	3
Michipicoten	1

ISOLATING THE TRADE GOODS

The first step in the analysis of the invoice data was to separate the trade goods from the supplies. Although the outfits purchased by the traders were generally composed mainly of goods intended for trade to Indians, they also included a variety of non-trade items. Frequently, various kinds of supplies and equipment for the trip into the interior and for the stay at the post were part of the outfit. For example, canoe gear and the materials needed to repair canoes were commonly listed in the invoices. These included poles to lay in the bottom of the canoe to support cargo, sponge to bail the canoe, and bark, gum, and spruce root to make repairs. On some occasions, even the canoes were purchased through the merchant. Camping gear for the trip was also invoiced, such as bark to construct temporary huts, an axe, a large cooking kettle, and sometimes tents. Provisions such as pork, flour, peas, and biscuit, along with wine and brandy, were also purchased by the trader.

Occasionally items were listed that were purchased by the trader to be given to the *engagés*. These were usually articles of clothing or pieces of cloth but sometimes combs, knives, or even guns were purchased for the *engagés*. In a few of the invoices, some of the non-trade-good materials were specifically identified. Canoe gear and equipment for the trip were listed under the heading "Furnished for the canoes" (Moniere, M849, 8: 358, 409). Provisions were identified as "Food and drink for the engages" (Moniere, M849, 8: 237, 294). And items purchased for the *engagés* were listed as "For the men" or were listed under the names of specific individuals (Moniere, M849, 8: 112-13, 183). In many of the invoices, however, such non-trade items were not explicitly identified.

In addition, a number of items appear in the invoices that may or may not have been intended for trade to Indians. Examples of these include playing cards, drinking glasses, soap, and shoes. Many of these types of items were probably intended for use by Europeans, but at least some of them may have been trade items.

In isolating the trade goods, the invoices were analyzed and each entry in the invoices was designated as either a trade item (for trade to Indians) or as a supply item (for use by Europeans). To make the designations, three criteria were used: (1) archaeological and documentary evidence, (2) the location of the entry in the invoice, and (3) the quantity of the item recorded in the entry. All three criteria do not necessarily apply to each entry, but usually a combination of at least two of the criteria played a part in making a designation.

1. Archaeological and Documentary Evidence

If an item listed in the invoices has been reported to occur on French-period Indian sites, this was considered evidence for designating the item as a trade good. Mainly, evidence used for this purpose came from archaeological sites in the western Great Lakes region including the Lasanen site (Cleland 1971), the Gros Cap Cemetery site (Nern and Cleland 1974), the Bell site (Wittry 1963), the Fletcher site (Mainfort 1979), the Rock Island site (Mason 1986), the Marquette Mission site (Branstner 1984; 1985; 1986; 1987), and the Marina site (Salzer and Birmingham 1981) and the Zimmerman site (Brown 1975), as shown in figure 2. However, other sites were consulted as well, including the Guebert site (Good 1972) in southern Illinois and the Burr's Hill site (Gibson 1980) in Rhode Island. Similarly, if an item listed in the invoices appeared on French-period trade lists in documentary sources, this was also taken as evidence for designating the item as a trade good. In addition to lists of goods specifically for the western Great Lakes region (e.g., WHC 1904), lists for Hudson's Bay Company posts (Ray and Freeman 1978; Heidenreich and Ray 1976) and lists of goods for the Illinois country (Pease and Werner 1934) were also examined.

2. Location of an Entry in the Invoice

The position of an entry in the invoice was often a factor in designating an item as a trade good or as a supply item. If the entry appeared in a list of goods whose purpose was specifically identified, such as those mentioned earlier, the designation was obvious. But there was also a tendency in the invoices, whether the specific purpose of some goods was identified or not, to group supplies and personal items together. The common pattern was for trade goods to be listed first in the invoice and for non-trade materials to follow. Thus, if an entry appeared in the latter part of an invoice surrounded by materials that were apparently supplies, it suggested that the entry in question was also a supply item. By the same token, an entry appearing at the beginning of an invoice was more likely a trade good. The listing of goods by bales and by crates was virtually always done at the very beginning of the invoice. The contents of the bales and crates were heavily dominated by trade goods. If an entry was listed as part of the goods packed in a bale or in a crate, it suggested that the entry was a trade

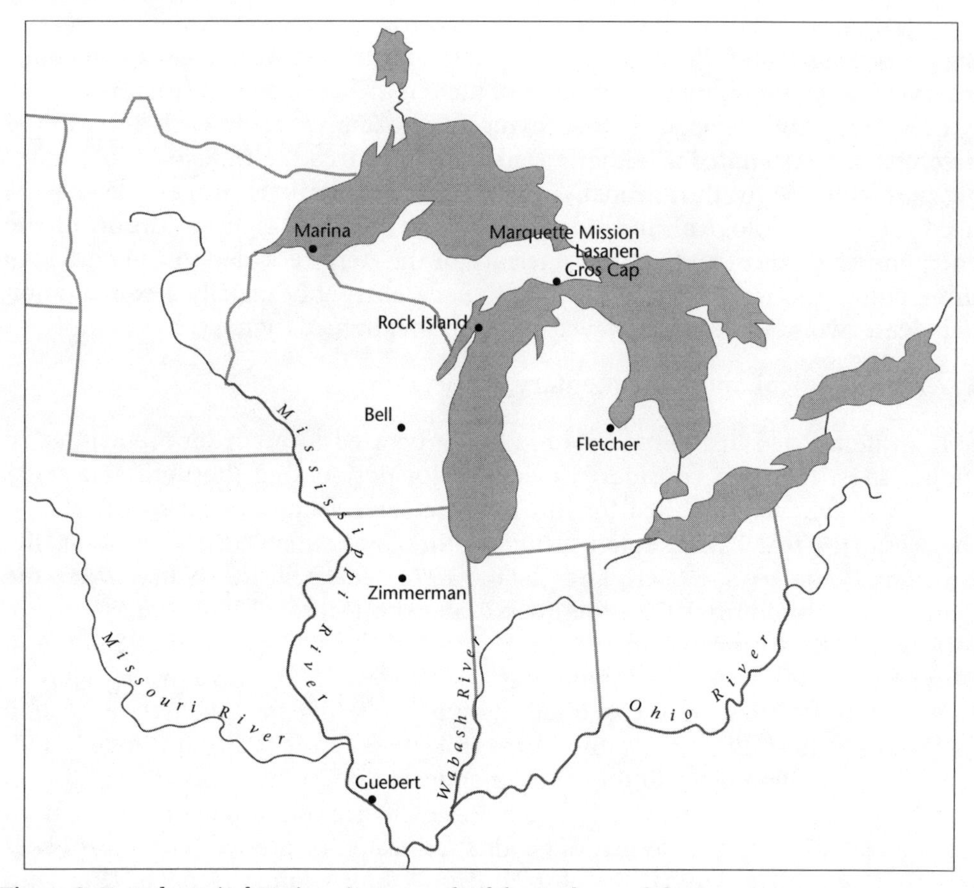

Figure 2. French-period Native sites consulted for trade good data.

good. The inclusion of an item in a bale or crate was not, however, indisputable evidence that it was a trade good. For example, a bale shipped to Green Bay in 1725 contained such probable trade goods as: 42 tomahawks, 300 gunflints, 144 awls, and 9 pounds of glass beads. However, the same bale also contained several items that were probably supplies, namely, one-half-pound of sulphur, one half-pound of alum, two sticks of sealing wax, and 200 flooring nails. Consequently, the presence of an item in a bale or crate was not taken as a definitive indication of its status as a trade good.

3. Quantity of an Item

In some cases, the quantity of an item was also a clue in identifying it as a trade good. As a very general rule, trade goods tended to be purchased in large quantities. Again, this was not a hard and fast guideline. Vermilion, for example, a trade good that was included in most outfits, was often purchased in quantities of one pound or less. The purchase of large amounts of an item, however, especially if it occurred in a number of different outfits, suggests that the item was intended for trade.

Once the trade goods in the invoices had been designated, an inventory of the types of goods shipped to each post during the 1715-1760 period was compiled. Table 2 indicates the number of types of goods in the inventories for each post. The inventories of goods shipped to the posts provide a view of the flow of goods into the western Great Lakes region. Because of the number of types of goods involved, however, it is cumbersome to try and make sense of the flow of goods on the basis of individual types. Instead, an effort was made to clarify Indian interests in trade goods by looking at the flow of goods in terms of activities or purposes represented. Toward this end, the types of goods in the inventories were organized into functional categories.

TABLE 2. NUMBER OF TYPES OF GOODS FOR EACH POST, 1715-1760.

Post	Types of Goods
Green Bay	66
Rainy Lake	66
Michilimackinac	59
Ouiatenon	57
Detroit	56
Sioux Post	54
Nipigon	46
Michipicoten	38

FUNCTIONAL CATEGORIES

The first step in defining functional categories of trade goods was to combine the individual inventories for the eight posts into a single, composite inventory. Then, the duplication of types of goods from different posts was deleted. This produced a comprehensive inventory of the types of goods shipped to the eight posts. This composite inventory consisted of eighty-six types of trade goods. This inventory was then used in defining functional categories. In this way, functional categories could be identified on a regional basis rather than on the basis of individual posts.

In organizing the inventory of types of goods into functional categories, it was assumed that, in use by Indian peoples, the primary functions of trade goods were those intended by the European manufacturers of the goods. Categories were identified with the objective of creating a valid representation of the functional diversity in the inventory. This resulted in the definition of the following thirteen categories: Clothing, Hunting (figure 3), Cooking and Eating (figure 4), Alcohol Use, Tobacco Use, Weapons, Woodworking, Adornment (figure 5), Grooming, Digging/Cultivation, Fishing (figure 3), Maintenance, and Amusements. Table 3 indicates the way the types of goods were grouped in arriving at the identification of these categories.

Figure 3. Hunting category; Fishing category: archaeological examples excavated at Michilimackinac. Clockwise from top: harpoon, spear point, gunflint, gunworm, triggerguard, buttplate, lockplate, cock, fishhook. Courtesy Mackinac State Historic Parks. Photograph by William H. Fritz.

Figure 4. Cooking and Eating category: archaeological examples excavated at Michilimackinac. Clockwise from top: hawkbill clasp knife blade, kettle lug, kettle bail, fork, spoon, case knife, firesteel. Courtesy Mackinac State Historic Parks. Photograph by William H. Fritz.

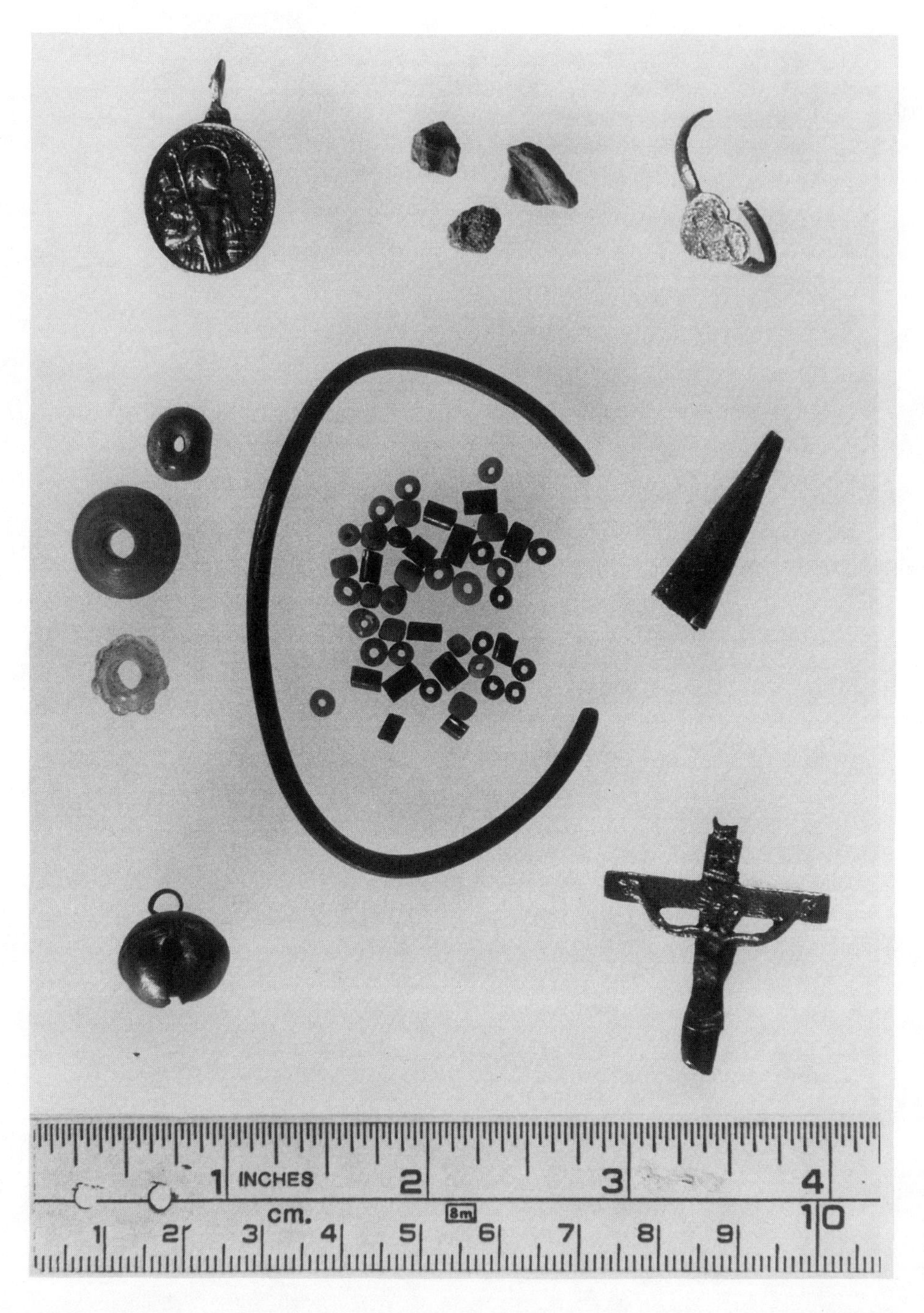

Figure 5. Adornment category: archaeological examples excavated at Michilimackinac. Clockwise from top left: medallion, vermilion, finger ring, tinkling cone, crucifix, hawk bell, necklace beads. Center: C-shaped bracelet, seed beads. Courtesy Mackinac State Historic Parks. Photograph by William H. Fritz.

TABLE 3. TYPES OF GOODS BY FUNCTIONAL CATEGORY.

ADORNMENT	CLOTHING	COOKING	GROOMING	HUNTING	WEAPONS	WOODWORKING
azure	awl	& EATING	brush	dart	bayonet	adze
bead	blanket	firesteel	comb	gun	dagger	ax
bell	breeches	fork	hair puller	gunflint	pistol	
black lead	buckle	kettle	mirror	gunpowder		2
brooch	button	knife		gunsheath	3	
finger ring	cap	ladle	4	gunworm		
glassbead	capote	spoon		ice chisel		
hawkbell	cloth			musketball		
necklace	dress	6		powder horn		
runtee	dress suit			shot		
verdigris	garter			wire		
vermilion	gartering					
	glove			11		
12	gown					
	handkerchief					
	hat					
	laces					
	legging					
	mantelet					
	mitten					
	needle					
	pin					
	scarf					
	scissors					
	shawl					
	shoe	DIGGING	ALCOHOL	FISHING		
AMUSEMENTS	shirt	& CULTIVATION	USE	fishhook	MAINTENANCE	TOBACCO USE
fan	sleeve	hoe	brandy	fishing line	file	pipe
jew's harp	stocking	pickaxe	wine	net	rasp	tobacco
	thimble					
2	thread	2	2	3	2	2
	trim					
	tuque					
	yarn					
	34					

COMPARISON OF THE POSTS

Patterns in the flow of goods into the western Great Lakes region may be sought by comparing the representation of the categories of goods at each of the eight posts. To do this, the individual inventories of goods for each of the posts were organized into the functional categories. Table 4 lists the categories of goods represented at each post. Two questions about the representation of categories at the eight posts were posed. The first question was, are there substantial differences between the posts in terms of which categories are represented at each one? Table 4 indicates that nine of the thirteen categories are represented at all eight posts. Those nine categories are Clothing, Hunting, Cooking and Eating, Tobacco Use, Adornment, Alcohol Use, Grooming, Woodworking, and Digging/Cultivation. At six of the eight posts, at least one category is not represented. There are, however, no more than three unrepresented categories at any post, and that situation occurs only at Michipicoten, for which only one outfit was recorded. In each case, the unrepresented categories are either the Fishing, Maintenance, Amusements, or Weapons categories. The Fishing category is absent at Nipigon, Michipicoten, Detroit, and Michilimackinac. The Maintenance category is absent at Ouiatenon, Michipicoten, and Michilimackinac. The Amusements category is absent at Sioux Post, Nipigon, and Michipicoten. The Weapons category is absent only at Detroit.

The second question posed was, how did the relative emphasis upon different categories of trade goods vary at each of the posts? Addressing this question required that the categories could be measured in some manner. One possibility was to measure the categories in terms of the quantities of goods sold since that information is recorded in the invoice entries. Quantity, however, is not a basis for measurement that is well-suited to making comparisons among types of goods or among functional categories. This is because quantity was measured in numerous different types of units among the trade goods. Many types of goods were measured by count, but others were measured in units of weight, volume, or area. Further, some types of goods were measured in units that are difficult to interpret, such as bundles or masses. This diversity of units of measure makes quantity an unsuitable basis for comparison.

The invoices do, however, record a variable that is common to all types of goods and which is recorded in the same unit of measure. This variable is the cost—or trader expenditure—for the goods. Trader expenditure provides a consistent basis for comparison between the functional categories represented by the inventory of goods at each post. Using the cost information in the invoice entries, trader expenditure can be computed for each type of trade good at each post. Then, trader expenditure for all types of goods within a category can be summed to arrive at total trader expenditure for the category. Expenditure for each category at a given post, then, can be expressed as a percentage of total trader expenditure for all goods for that particular post.

Table 4. Functional Categories in Ranked Order by Percentage of Expenditure.

DETROIT		
1.	CLOTHING	75.58
2.	HUNTING	11.91
3.	ALCOHOL USE	4.83
4.	COOKING & EATING	4.28
5.	ADORNMENT	1.73
6.	GROOMING	.54
7.	TOBACCO USE	.50
8.	WOODWORKING	.46
9.	DIGGING/CULTIVATION	.09
10.	MAINTENANCE	.07
11.	AMUSEMENTS	.02
12.	WEAPONS	———
13.	FISHING	———

MICHIPICOTEN		
1.	CLOTHING	59.82
2.	HUNTING	10.86
3.	ALCOHOL USE	9.02
4.	COOKING & EATING	8.29
5.	WOODWORKING	5.91
6.	TOBACCO USE	3.00
7.	ADORNMENT	1.75
8.	WEAPONS	.57
9.	DIGGING/CULTIVATION	.51
10.	GROOMING	.31
11.	FISHING	———
12.	MAINTENANCE	———
13.	AMUSEMENTS	———

SIOUX POST		
1.	CLOTHING	43.87
2.	HUNTING	25.23
3.	COOKING & EATING	11.73
4.	WOODWORKING	5.17
5.	ADORNMENT	4.69
6.	ALCOHOL USE	4.34
7.	WEAPONS	1.65
8.	TOBACCO USE	1.62
9.	GROOMING	.98
10.	DIGGING/CULTIVATION	.55
11.	FISHING	.07
12.	MAINTENANCE	.04
13.	AMUSEMENTS	———

MICHILIMACKINAC		
1.	CLOTHING	72.04
2.	HUNTING	12.40
3.	ADORNMENT	4.57
4.	COOKING & EATING	3.40
5.	ALCOHOL USE	3.07
6.	TOBACCO USE	2.05
7.	WOODWORKING	1.32
8.	GROOMING	.95
9.	DIGGING/CULTIVATION	.16
10.	WEAPONS	.03
11.	AMUSEMENTS	.01
12.	FISHING	———
13.	MAINTENANCE	———

RAINY LAKE		
1.	CLOTHING	55.28
2.	HUNTING	15.46
3.	ADORNMENT	7.06
4.	ALCOHOL USE	6.92
5.	COOKING & EATING	5.08
6.	WOODWORKING	4.38
7.	TOBACCO USE	3.96
8.	GROOMING	.95
9.	WEAPONS	.44
10.	FISHING	.19
11.	DIGGING/CULTIVATION	.16
12.	MAINTENANCE	.12
13.	AMUSEMENTS	.02

OUIATENON		
1.	CLOTHING	55.04
2.	HUNTING	20.28
3.	COOKING & EATING	7.22
4.	ALCOHOL USE	6.95
5.	ADORNMENT	5.62
6.	WOODWORKING	2.25
7.	GROOMING	1.24
8.	TOBACCO USE	1.20
9.	DIGGING/CULTIVATION	.10
10.	AMUSEMENTS	.08
11.	WEAPONS	.02
12.	FISHING	.01
13.	MAINTENANCE	———

GREEN BAY		
1.	CLOTHING	65.08
2.	HUNTING	18.09
3.	COOKING & EATING	4.59
4.	ALCOHOL USE	4.37
5.	ADORNMENT	2.95
6.	WOODWORKING	2.39
7.	TOBACCO USE	1.61
8.	GROOMING	.87
9.	WEAPONS	.19
10.	DIGGING/CULTIVATION	.07
11.	MAINTENANCE	.06
12.	FISHING	.03
13.	AMUSEMENTS	.01

NIPIGON		
1.	CLOTHING	65.89
2.	HUNTING	13.34
3.	COOKING & EATING	9.28
4.	ALCOHOL USE	3.56
5.	WOODWORKING	3.17
6.	TOBACCO USE	1.64
7.	ADORNMENT	1.53
8.	GROOMING	1.22
9.	DIGGING/CULTIVATION	.24
10.	MAINTENANCE	.08
11.	WEAPONS	.03
12.	FISHING	———
13.	AMUSEMENTS	———

In table 4, the functional categories represented at each post are arranged in ranked order according to the percentage they comprise of total trader expenditure for all goods for the post. Examination of the lists in table 4 indicates that there is considerable consistency among the posts in the ranked order of categories. The Clothing category is ranked number one and the Hunting category is ranked number two at every post. At the bottom end of the rankings, the Maintenance, Fishing, and Amusements categories are three of the last four categories at every post. The remaining eight categories occur in positions three through twelve in the ranked listings, but they do not occur randomly across those positions. Each of the eight categories tends to occur in certain positions and thus to display patterned relationships with the other categories. Table 5 illustrates this by indicating all of the positions in the rankings in which each of the thirteen categories occur.

TABLE 5. RANK POSITIONS IN WHICH EACH CATEGORY OCCURS.

Category	Rank Positions												
Clothing	1												
Hunting		2											
Cooking & Eating			3	4	5								
Alcohol Use			3	4	5	6							
Adornment			3		5		7						
Woodworking				4	5	6	7	8					
Tobacco Use						6	7	8					
Gooming						6	7	8	9	10			
Weapons							7	8	9	10	11	12	
Digging/Cultivation									9	10	11		
Maintenance										10	11	12	13
Fishing										10	11	12	13
Amusements										10	11		13

To gain a summary picture of the flow of goods into the region, trader expenditure for the categories of goods can be determined for the combined inventory of goods for all eight posts. Trader expenditure for each category of goods may be expressed as a percentage of the total expenditure for all goods. Table 6 presents the functional categories of goods in ranked order according to the percentage of expenditure they represent for the combined inventory of goods.

Table 6. Ranked Order of FunctionalCategories For Combined Inventories.

Category	% of Expenditure
1. Clothing	62.85
2. Hunting	17.00
3. Cooking & Eating	5.65
4. Alcohol Use	4.84
5. Adornment	3.73
6. Woodworking	2.71
7. Tobacco Use	1.84
8. Grooming	.75
9. Weapons	.32
10. Digging/Cultivation	.15
11. Maintenance	.06
12. Fishing	.05
13. Amusements	.01

Conclusions

This analysis of the MMR invoice data allows a number of observations to be made about patterns in Indian trading for European goods in the western Great Lakes region during the latter part of the French period. The MMR data suggest the range of functional types of European goods for which Indian peoples traded during this period. The data also suggest that there were marked patterns in the relative emphasis that Native peoples placed upon different functional categories of goods. In addition, the pattern of relative emphasis on trade for different categories of goods was very consistent across the region.

The most striking aspect of the analysis is the indication of a very strong emphasis in the trade upon clothing—both finished clothing and the materials to make clothing. The Clothing category accounts for more than 50 percent of trader expenditure at every post except the Sioux Post, and it accounts for over 60 percent of expenditure for all goods shipped to all eight posts. This is an important observation in light of the common perception that the trade hinged upon firearms and metal implements like kettles and axes. Certainly those goods were important components of the trade. But it is also clear that there was a strong demand for clothing. This demand, in concert with the fact that it was a commodity that would have required virtually constant replenishment, made clothing perhaps the cornerstone commodity of the trade. This pattern has also been demonstrated for British-period trade in the western Great Lakes region (B. White 1987: 170-71).

Figure 6. Native adoption of European textiles. Note sleeves on woman standing at left. ***Ojibwe Women,*** **c. 1856, painted by Eastman Johnson, Courtesy St. Louis County Historical Society, Duluth, Minnesota.**

Figure 7. Native adoption of European textiles. Note sleeves and ribbon used as hair adornment. ***Kay be sen day way We Win,*** **c. 1856, sketched by Eastman Johnson. Courtesy St. Louis County Historical Society, Duluth, Minnesota.**

This importance of cloth and clothing has implications for understanding the part that Native women played in the fur trade. Access to ready-made clothing, bolt cloth, and blankets, along with iron awls, pins, needles, and thread probably reduced the amount of time and labor that women had to invest in the production of clothing. The prominence of clothing and clothing-related materials in the trade suggests that women made considerable input into decisions about the types of goods to be obtained in trade. Further, the savings in time and labor could have been reinvested in the production of clothing in the form of time spent adorning articles of attire with beadwork. Or it could have been invested in endeavors associated with the fur trade, such as the processing of pelts or the production of other trade commodities such as garden produce. If the trade in clothing and textiles reduced the domestic labor requirements for women and allowed them to become more involved in activities related to the trade, it may have had an important impact on women's roles in historical-period Indian societies.

The data also suggest an emphasis on the Hunting category, which ranks second at each post. This reflects an emphasis upon the trade for firearms and the materials necessary for their use. Of course, the prominence of the Hunting category is a result of the decision to categorize firearms as primarily hunting tools rather than as weapons. This is a difficult determination to make, but it was assumed that firearms were probably used more routinely for hunting and were used more sporadically as weapons; thus they were assigned to the Hunting category. With the inclusion of firearms in the Hunting category, it appears that the European technology that was adopted by Indian peoples for subsistence pursuits was mainly materials used in hunting activities. In addition to the firearms complex, these materials included darts (apparently iron projectile points), ice chisels, and wire. Subsistence-related implements are also represented in the Digging/Cultivation category and in the Fishing category. But both of these are relatively minor categories, suggesting that there was not a significant use of European goods in these activities. For some posts, such as Michipicoten, Nipigon, and Rainy Lake, the lack of trade for cultivation implements is not surprising, since these posts were in climatic zones where agriculture was impractical. The data suggest, however, that Native peoples in the western Great Lakes area were not inclined to trade for cultivating tools even in those areas where agriculture was an important part of the subsistence base. A similar situation obtains with regard to the Fishing category. At posts like Ouiatenon or the Sioux Post, one might not expect there to have been a brisk trade in fishing implements. But at the other posts, it would be reasonable to expect an emphasis upon trade for fishing gear given the importance of fishing in the subsistence economy of the western Great Lakes region (Cleland 1982). The fact that the MMR data indicate that neither cultivating implements nor fishing gear were important trade items suggests that Native peoples perceived their traditional technology as perfectly sufficient for their needs and that European versions of those implements did not confer a sufficient advantage to make them a priority in trading.

In addition to the Digging/Cultivation and the Fishing categories, the Maintenance and Amusements categories are also among the lowest-ranked categories. The weak Amusements category indicates that Native peoples had little interest in trading for novelties or trinkets. The poorly represented Maintenance category indicates that Indian peoples were not equipped to repair and resharpen the European goods they acquired in trade. In fact, it could be argued that files and rasps, which comprise the Maintenance category, were not offered as trade items. In analyzing the invoices, files and rasps were designated as trade goods because files appear on lists of goods traded by the Hudson's Bay Company (Ray and Freeman 1978: 92, 130-31; Heidenreich and Ray 1976: 77). However, files and rasps are not common in the MMR invoices and when they do appear, it is not in great numbers, nor does their position in the invoices tend to suggest strongly whether they are trade goods or supplies. But perhaps of more significance is the fact that archaeological evidence for files at French-period Indian sites in the western country is extremely rare. No files or file fragments are reported from the Guebert site (Good 1972), the Lasanen site (Cleland 1971), or the Bell site (Wittry 1963). One file fragment has been recovered from French-period deposits at the Marquette Mission site (Branstner: personal communication). Four triangular file fragments were reported from the Fletcher site, the dating of which spans the end of the French period and the beginning of the British period (Mainfort 1979). A single file fragment is also reported from Rock Island (Mason 1986), but it is unclear whether it was associated with French-period deposits or with later deposits. On the other hand, 37 files were reported by Stone (1974: 298) from excavations at Michilimackinac. He suggests that the specimens date to the period from 1740-1780 and that they were primarily of French use. The archaeological evidence, then, suggests that files were transported to posts during the French period but that they were primarily for European use and were not commonly traded to Indians. In fact, keeping files out of Indians' hands may have been a part of French trading strategy, since it would curtail the opportunity to repair and resharpen implements and thus would promote the replacement of worn and damaged goods.

The Alcohol Use category is, on one hand, among the higher ranking categories, but it is perhaps not as highly ranked as might be expected. The representation of this category in the MMR invoices is difficult to evaluate. It may be that this is a valid picture of the trade in alcohol relative to other important goods such as clothing, firearms, and kettles. The use of alcohol in the trade in the western Great Lakes region had probably not reached its peak by the late French period. On the other hand, if substantial quantities of alcohol were shipped to the western country through channels that pre-empted the recording of it in documents like the merchants' accounting records, the MMR may underrepresent the trade in alcohol.

The MMR data also present an interesting perspective on the materials included in the Adornment category. The trade in articles of adornment has commanded a great deal of attention. Glass beads, in particular, are commonly thought of as the currency of the trade and have been referred to as "the denominator of the trade" (Woodward 1970: 15). This view has resulted in part from archaeological research which has demonstrated that large quantities of glass beads were traded and that other adornment items are common in archaeological deposits as well (e.g., Fitting 1976). The MMR data do not refute the importance of glass beads and other materials in the Adornment category, but they do place the trade in adornment articles in perspective relative to the trade for other types of goods.

In summary, this analysis of data taken from the MMR invoices offers insight into the adoption of European trade goods by Indian peoples in the western Great Lakes region during the last several decades of the French period. Organizing the trade-good data into functional categories allowed the acquisition of goods to be examined in terms of the purposes for which goods were used rather than in terms of individual types of goods. The data suggest that there were definite patterns in the flow of goods into Native societies and that these patterns were quite consistent across the western Great Lakes region. It is clear that Indian peoples traded for a functionally varied group of European goods, but it is also apparent that there was considerable variation in the emphasis placed upon different categories of goods. Most conspicuous in this regard is the indication of a strong demand for clothing and the materials with which to make clothing. While this does not negate the importance of metal implements in the trade, it does temper the perspective that, for Native peoples, the fur trade was an increasingly imperative quest for European metal goods.

References

Branstner, Susan M. 1984. *1983 Archaeological Investigations at the Marquette Mission Site.* Planning Report submitted to the St. Ignace Downtown Development Authority by The Museum, Michigan State University, East Lansing.

_____. 1985. *1984 Archaeological Investigations at the Marquette Mission Site.* Planning Report submitted to the St. Ignace Downtown Development Authority by The Museum, Michigan State University, East Lansing.

_____. 1986. *1985 Archaeological Investigations at the Marquette Mission Site.* Planning Report submitted to the St. Ignace Downtown Development Authority by The Museum, Michigan State University, East Lansing.

_____. 1987. *1986 Archaeological Investigations at the Marquette Mission Site.* Planning Report submitted to the St. Ignace Downtown Development Authority by The Museum, Michigan State University, East Lansing.

Brown, Margaret Kimball. 1975. "The Zimmerman Site: Further Excavations at the Grand Village of Kaskaskia." *Reports of Investigations,* no. 32. Springfield: Illinois State Museum.

Cleland, Charles E., ed. 1971. "The Lasanen Site: An Historic Burial Locality in Mackinac County, Michigan." *Anthropological Series* 1 (1): 1-147. Publications of The Museum, Michigan State University, East Lansing.

Cleland, Charles E. 1982. "The Inland Shore Fishery of the Northern Great Lakes: Its Development and Importance in Prehistory." *American Antiquity* 47 (4): 761-84.

Fitting, James E. 1976. "Patterns of Acculturation at the Straits of Mackinac." In *Cultural Change and Continuity,* edited by Charles E. Cleland. New York: Academic Press.

Francis, Daniel and Toby Morantz. 1983. *Partners in Furs. A History of the Fur Trade in Eastern James Bay 1600-1870.* Kingston and Montreal: McGill-Queen's University Press.

Gibson, Susan G. 1980. "Burr's Hill, A 17th Century Wampanoag Burial Ground in Warren, Rhode Island." In *Studies in Anthropology and Material Culture,* vol. 2. Haffenreffer Museum of Anthroplogy, Brown University, Providence, R.I.

Good, Mary Elizabeth. 1972. "Guebert Site: An 18th Century Historic Kaskaskia Indian Village in Randolph County, Illinois." In *Memoir,* no. 2. St. Louis: Central States Archaeological Societies, Inc.

Heidenreich, Conrad E. and Arthur J. Ray. 1976. *The Early Fur Trades.* Toronto: McClelland and Stewart Ltd.

Innis, Harold A. [1930] 1970. *The Fur Trade in Canada,* rev. ed. Toronto and Buffalo: University of Toronto Press.

Krech, Shepard III, ed. 1984. *The Subarctic Fur Trade: Native Social and Economic Adaptations.* Vancouver: University of British Columbia Press.

Lohse, E. S. 1988. "Trade Goods." In *Handbook of North American Indians: History of Indian-White Relations,* vol. 4, edited by Wilcomb Washburn, 396-403. Washington, D.C.: Smithsonian Institution.

Mainfort, Robert C. Jr. 1979. "Indian Social Dynamics in the Period of European Contact: Fletcher Site Cemetery, Bay County, Michigan." *Anthropological Series* 1 (4): 269-418. Publications of The Museum, Michigan State University, East Lansing.

Mason, Ronald J. 1986. "Rock Island: Historical Indian Archaeology in the Northern Lake Michigan Basin." *MCJA Special Paper No. 6.* Kent, Ohio: Kent State University Press.

Moniere, Alexis. 1712-1768. *Account Books of Eighteenth Century Merchants of Montreal 1712-1806.* Michigan State University Library Microfilm no. 19014 (microfilm of originals housed at the Antiquarian and Numismatic Society of Montreal).

Morantz, Toby. 1980. "The Fur Trade and the Cree of James Bay." In *Old Trails and New Directions, Papers of the Third North American Fur Trade Conference,* edited by Carol Judd and Arthur Ray, 39-58. Toronto: University of Toronto Press.

Nern, Craig F., and Charles E. Cleland. 1974. "The Gros Cap Cemetery Site, St. Ignace, Michigan: A Reconsideration of the Greenlees Collection." In *Michigan Archaeologist* 20 (1): 1-58.

Parkman, Francis. [1865-1892] 1983. *France and England in North America,* 2 vols. New York: The Literary Classics.

Pease, Theodore, and Raymond Werner. 1934. "The French Foundations 1680-1693." French series, vol. 1. In *Collections of the Illinois State Historical Library,* vol. 23. Springfield: Illinois State Historical Library.

Peterson, Jacqueline, and John Anfinson. 1984. "The Indian and the Fur Trade: A Review of Recent Literature." In *Scholars and the Indian Experience,* edited by W.R. Swagerty. Bloomington: Indiana University Press.

Ray, Arthur J. 1974. *Indians in the Fur Trade: Their Role as Trappers, Hunters, and Middlemen in the Lands Southwest of Hudson Bay 1660-1870.* Toronto: University of Toronto Press.

_____. 1980. "Indians as Consumers in the Eighteenth Century." In *Old Trails and New Directions,* Papers of the Third North American Fur Trade Conference, edited by Carol Judd and Arthur Ray, 255-71. Toronto: University of Toronto Press.

Ray, Arthur J., and Donald Freeman. 1978. *'Give Us Good Measure': An Economic Analysis of Relations between the Indians and the Hudson's Bay Company before 1763.* Toronto: University of Toronto Press.

Salzer, Robert J., and Robert A. Birmingham. 1981. *Archaeological Salvage Excavations at the Marina Site (47 As 24) Madeline Island, Wisconsin*. Report submitted to Interagency Archaeological Services, National Park Service, Denver.

Stone, Lyle M. 1974. "Fort Michilimackinac 1715-1781: An Archaeological Perspective on the Revolutionary Frontier." *Anthropological Series* 2: 1-367. Publications of The Museum, Michigan State University, East Lansing.

Turner, Frederick J. [1891] 1970. *The Character and Influence of the Indian Trade in Wisconsin*. New York: Burt Franklin.

WHC. 1904. *Collections of the State Historical Society of Wisconsin*. Madison: State Historical Society of Wisconsin, 16: 400-7.

White, Bruce. 1984. "'Give Us a Little Milk': The Social and Cultural Significance of Gift Giving in the Lake Superior Fur Trade." In *Rendezvous: Selected Papers of the Fourth North American Fur Trade Conference, 1989*, pp. 185-97, edited by Thomas C. Buckley. St. Paul: North American Fur Trade Conference.

_____. 1986. "A Skilled Game of Exchange: Ojibway Fur Trade Protocol." *Minnesota History* 50 (6): 229-40.

_____. 1987. "Montreal Canoes and Their Cargoes." In *Le Castor Fait Tout, Selected Papers of the Fifth North American Fur Trade Conference*, edited by Bruce Trigger, Toby Morantz, and Louise Dechêne, Montreal: The Lake St. Louis Historical Society, 164-92.

White, Richard. 1991. *The Middle Ground: Indians, Empires, and Republics in the Great Lakes Region, 1650-1815*. Cambridge: Cambridge University Press.

Wittry, Warren L. 1963. "The Bell Site, Wn9, An Early Historic Fox Village." *Wisconsin Archaeologist* 44 (1): 1-57.

Woodward, Arthur. 1970. *The Denominators of the Fur Trade: An Anthology of Writings on the Material Culture of the Fur Trade*. Pasadena, Calif.: Socio-Technical Publications.

Yerbury, J. C. 1986. *The Subarctic Indians and the Fur Trade 1680-1860*. Vancouver: University of British Columbia Press.

"No less than 7 different nations": Ethnicity and Culture Contact at Fort George-Buckingham House

Lynda Gullason

This article summarizes archival research undertaken as part of an historical archaeology project on contact and culture change in the early fur trade era in western Canada (Gullason 1990). The purpose of the project was to identify the selective changes in Native material culture and behaviour upon contact with Europeans, using archival and archaeological data from two trading posts in east-central Alberta. But how does one even begin to examine culture contact with "no less than 7 different nations" trading at a post (Morton 1929: 72)? Accordingly, one research objective was to examine ethnic differences in European interaction among visiting tribes at the Fort George-Buckingham House site complex using documentary evidence. A second objective was to understand how these differences would be expressed in the archaeological record of a plantation, or encampment of Native traders, associated with a trading post.

Ethnic differences in European culture transfer are potentially detectable through the study of items brought into trade and European goods acquired. The problem lies in identifying these contact differences through archaeological remains of multiple, short-term, contemporaneous occupations of a single site.

Research Area

The sites selected for this research, Fort George and Buckingham House, are two forts established in east-central Alberta, 200 km east of Edmonton on the northern edge of the aspen parkland (figure 1). They are located on the north side of the North Saskatchewan River, deliberately situated to take advantage of the fur-bearing woods to the north and meat for pemmican production, in the form of bison, to the south. The location of the posts in the Parkland transition zone suggests that the companies were attempting to encourage trade from both Woodland and Plains tribes. Both of these groups made regular use of the Parklands (Ray 1972: 1974). Buckingham House, the Hudson's Bay Company

(HBC) post, lies 300 metres upriver from the North West Company (NWC) post, Fort George and separated by a small ravine. They were both occupied from 1792 to 1800 (figure 2).

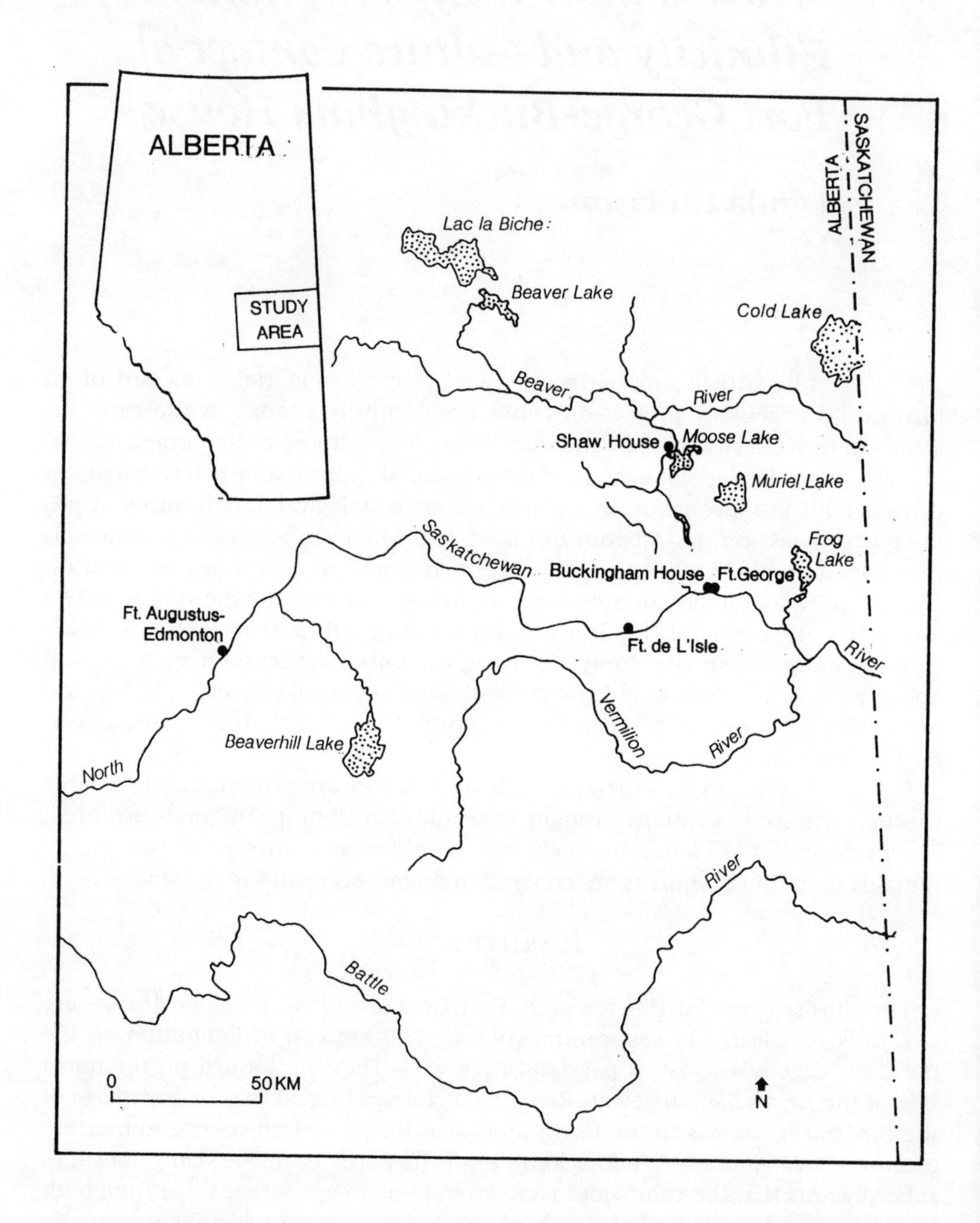

Figure 1. Map of East-Central Alberta Showing Fort George-Buckingham House Site Location.

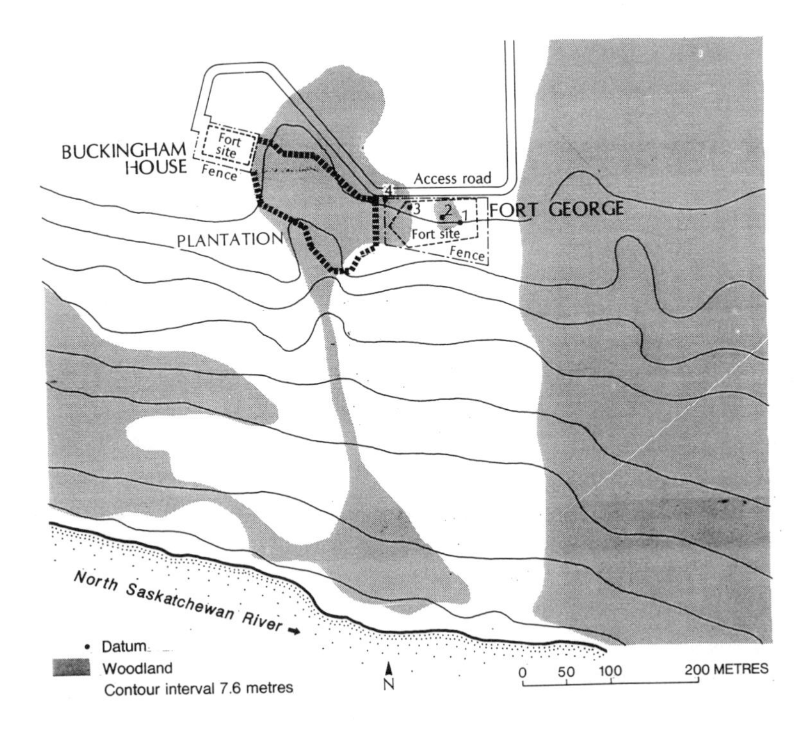

Figure 2. Topographic Map of Fort George-Buckingham House Site Complex (modified from Cornerstone Planning Group Limited, 1983).

The site complex represents a well-documented, brief occupation during the initial period of fur trade contact in the province. The advantages of this data base include the following:

1. The period of occupation is early and relatively short. There is no problem of differentiating among periods of culture contact. There has also been no subsequent re-occupation of the area.
2. Both forts have been previously excavated (Kidd 1970; Losey 1980; Losey, et al. 1978; Losey and Pyszczyk 1979; Nicks 1969; Nicks and Hurlburt 1977). Thus their location and layout have been delineated and comparative collections have been made.
3. Documentary records exist for seven of the eight years of occupation (1792-1800). These accounts (by several different authors) identify, to some extent, the tribes who visited the posts, their number, and their home region, as well as the country goods they brought into trade and the European articles they acquired through gift or purchase. These are the basic categories which frame the following discussion of ethnicity and culture contact.

ARCHIVAL SOURCES AND LIMITATIONS

The archives examined include the daily journals, correspondence, and personal accounts relating to Buckingham House and Fort George. They represent the major source of evidence for tracing culture change through contact despite the drawbacks of variability in the periods covered by the journals and in the amount of detail provided.

The six journals and one personal account of Buckingham House were written by seven different people. Given the variety of authors and writing styles in these documents, it is not surprising that the coverage is uneven. The journals cover a period ranging from six to fourteen months. Only two of them extend through the summer period. Accounts have not survived for the 1795-1796 trading season.

Two drafts exist of the 1796-1797 journal written by Peter Fidler. His rough draft (HBCA B.49/a/27b) includes copious detail, omitted from the sparer, more formal final draft (HBCA B.24/a/4). In the first version, Natives are individually identified and the activities of the competing NWC post are described. In the final copy, the Indian names and the NWC Wactivities are deleted. Additional discrepancies between the two copies exist in terms of dates, details, and quantities.

Typically, the entries may consist of a single line per day, such as: "Men variously employed." References are habitually made to "generic" Indians who came to trade, without disclosing their tribal affiliation or the type of goods exchanged (see, for example, James Gaddy's entries in the 1793-1794 journal).

Unlike the Buckingham House trade, that of Fort George is not described in any surviving complete yearly records. The primary document is Duncan M'Gillivray's personal account of his year at Fort George in 1794-1795 covering the 7-1/2-month trading period of 29 September to 14 May (Morton 1929). We lack the day-to-day detail which was available for Buckingham House. This is compensated by the wealth of information in the form of long accounts describing individual Indians and specific aspects of their lifeways. Nevertheless, the fragmentary nature of the records for both posts and the short period of competition precludes attempts to establish trends in commodities trade over time or to correlate specific commodities with the companies from which they were obtained.

THE PROBLEM

From one perspective, the research area at the Fort George-Buckingham House Plantation seems ideal: a short, early occupation with archival documentation and a comparative data base already excavated. However, the ethnic diversity is a central challenge to any study of culture transfer which uses the archaeological record. The visitors represent a variety of cultural backgrounds and, hence, potentially a variety of responses to the contact situation, which is difficult to differentiate at a single site. In several instances, their ethnic origin is never clearly identified in the literature.

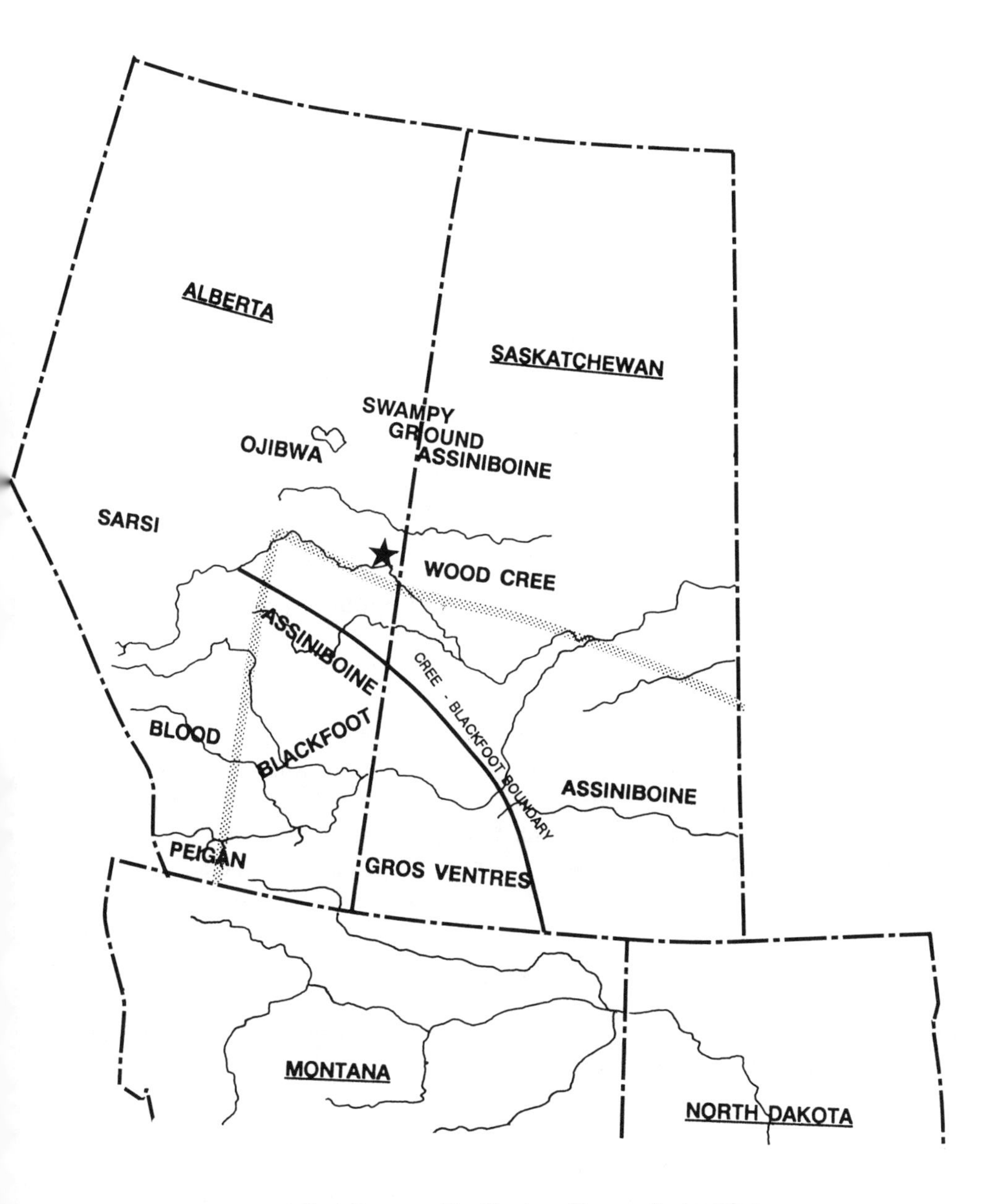

★ Fort George—Buckingham House site location.

Figure 3. Home Regions of Native Visitors Based on M'Gillivray's Account.

To confuse the issue, there is the thorny problem of the emergence of Plains varieties of several Woodland groups during the 1790s (the period of fort occupation), which exhibit real cultural differences from their Woodland progenitors (Andersen 1970: 52-53; Howard 1977: 5; Milloy 1988: 21, 27). References to these tribes of Cree, Ojibwa, and Assiniboine in the journals seldom specify their geographical location. A single term could apply equally to several different groups. The resulting semantic confusion makes attempts to reconstruct ethnohistoric populations and to correlate tribes to ecological zones difficult at best. In addition, although their physical relocation to the Plains may have been completed by the early nineteenth century, universal adoption of a Plains lifestyle by former Woodland groups did not always follow (Howard 1977: 17). Traditional subsistence strategies such as beaver hunting might be undertaken in both the Woodlands and the Grasslands for a number of years, provided relevant environmental conditions prevailed. Finally, there is little scholarly agreement as to what relocations were taking place and when and how they came about. Nevertheless, an attempt has been made to map the home regions of the visiting tribes during the 1790s based on information from NWC factor Duncan M'Gillivray's account (figure 3). It should be noted that these home regions may vary slightly from other published accounts, for this map is based on the testimony of a single source in reference to band members who visited Fort George-Buckingham House; other tribal groups may have been established elsewhere.

Two broad classes, Woodlands and Plains, were used to organize the information on the tribal identity, home territory, and population size of the Native trade partners. A third class of unidentified Indians was used in cases where no evidence of ethnic origin was provided. Inclusion of a band into either of the geographically-based classes was a function of (1) known tribal affiliations, or (2) association with specific geographic areas. Not included in these figures are data concerning Indians employed by the Europeans in various capacities.

Quantifying data about the Indians who came to trade is difficult to assess from the journal evidence. Because exact figures are rarely provided, a numerical ranking system of minimum approximations was developed which was derived from the adjectives employed. For ambiguous references in which quantity was not indicated, such as "Blackfeet came to trade," a minimum number of 2+ was assigned. For groups described as "a few," "some," "several," "a number," "a family," "a band," "a small band," or "a tribe," 3+ is the minimum estimate used, based on references in which group size was described both numerically and alphabetically (see HBCA B.24/a/4, 5 November 1796; HBCA B.49/a/27b, 7 January 1797, for example). A value of 10+ was assigned to "a large band," "a large tribe," or "a great many."

Occasionally, the populations were quantified in terms of the number of lodges or tents. Entries in which both the number of tents and number of individuals are provided suggest that a minimum of 5+ men per tent is a good approximation (HBCA B.24/a/1, 17, 18 January; 20, 22 March 1793). (It is unclear whether women and children routinely accompanied the men.) All tent populations were converted to individuals using this ratio. In cases of discrepancy where the same group is referred to as "2 tents" or "5 able men," the former, larger approximation of 10+ individuals is used.

Clearly, the major drawback of this approach is that it may severely underestimate the number of Indians actually represented by using a single number to represent a variety of quantitative adjectives. "A few" Indians is surely less than "a number" of Indians. However, the variety of authors precludes a more exact numerical ranking of the populations. Some degree of comparability and reproducibility, in terms of population figures and frequency of contact, is assumed if these approximations are used consistently.

VISITING TRIBES

Cree

The Cree were the principal beaver hunters in the area. They occupied the full boreal forest and areas transitional to the prairies primarily north of the Saskatchewan River in Alberta and Saskatchewan. They account for 80 percent of the Woodland visitors to Fort George-Buckingham House.

Sometime in the late eighteenth and early nineteenth centuries, some Parkland Cree bands moved onto the Plains to hunt bison (Milloy 1988: xiv; Smith 1981: 264). There are several theories for this relocation. According to Ray (1972), the Cree were preadapted for this movement because of the seasonal pattern of movement of Plains fauna into and out of the Parkland transition zone. Milloy (1988: 27-29) believes the move may have been linked to several factors: the decline in beaver, the increase in the European demand for provisions, and the relative ease of Plains bison-hunting with the use of horses. Sporadic journal references to Cree using buffalo pounds, accompanying Plains tribes such as the Assiniboine and Blackfoot to the forts with wolf pelts and provisions, and wintering with the Peigans suggest a proto-Plains adaptation was already in place (John Foster, pers. comm. August 1989) (HBCA B.24/a/3, 19 December 1795; PAC MG19 A8, vol. 5, 17 September 1799; Morton 1929: 49, 75). Due to the difficulty in distinguishing these few proto-Plains Cree from the majority of Woodlands Cree other than by the post hoc argument of "identification by association" with other Plains tribes, I have included all Cree under the general term of Woodlands tribes. According to Ray (1974: 99), there were few Plains Cree in 1790 and those "lived close to the forests."

The number of Cree coming to the posts greatly increased during the second and third trading seasons, but by 1795 their number fell. This is the year in which Fort Augustus was built to handle the trade of "the primary beaver hunters" (the Cree, the Assiniboine, and the Sarsi), as the beaver population around Fort George and Buckingham House had declined to the point where beaver hunting was difficult (Morton 1929, 77). However, John McDonald attributes construction of the new fort to an attempt to keep "the many tribes who met there and sometimes quarreled" apart (Masson 1960, 2:22). Milloy (1988: 28) offers an interesting suggestion that builds on McDonald's observation and that of M'Gillivray: the attempt to separate the Cree and Blackfoot was an effort to end the Blackfoot influence on the Cree in order to encourage the Cree to hunt beaver and abandon their growing inclination to follow a Plains lifestyle.

The local Cree bands were the closest equivalent to the homeguard Indians of Hudson Bay (a semi-permanent population of Native employees established at the bayside posts), for they occasionally performed services for the Europeans. Accounts of specific band movements and of individual Cree traders suggest that their contact with the fort employees was often very frequent and the possibility of culture transfer, beyond that available from isolated economic interactions, existed.

Swampy Ground Assiniboine

The Indians generally identified as Assiniboine were another of the more numerous of the fort visitors. They included a variety of bands which are difficult to distinguish as Woodlands- or Plains-adapted people, for the eighteenth-century Assiniboine exhibited an "important diversity in ecological adaptations" (Andersen 1970: 52). Toward the end of the century many of the Parkland Assiniboine were making increasingly greater use of the Plains. One exception seems to be the Swampy Ground Assiniboine from the area of Lac La Biche who David Thompson, in 1799, observed "still continue to prefer their ancient mode of life to living in the Plains where the rest of the tribes are" (Laurie 1957, cited in Andersen 1970: 54).

Ojibwa and Iroquois

Many eastern Woodlands groups, among them the Ojibwa and the Iroquois, followed the fur trade west as hunters, guides, and interpreters. They were encouraged to migrate by the French, who viewed them as replacements for the Cree beaver hunters who were adapting to a Plains lifestyle. During the period of post occupation some Ojibwa relocated to the Plains (Howard 1977: 3). However, references in the local journals to Ojibwa home regions and resources indicate that the visitors were Woodland-adapted Indians living north of the posts, around Lac La Biche and other areas.

Blackfoot

One of the more important of the visiting tribes was the Blackfoot. They were well-represented throughout the entire trading period, for the first post in their territory was not constructed until 1799 (Dickason 1980: 30). The detailed NWC records for 1794-95 demonstrate the Blackfoot's great underrepresentation in other years. Yet their number may be artificially large if the term refers to Indians of the Blackfoot Confederacy, which included Peigan and Blood tribes as well as Blackfoot. This probably happened during the later years, when the records no longer name Peigan and Blood traders. Blackfoot territory stretched from the Rocky Mountains to Saskatchewan and from the Saskatchewan River south to the United States (Jenness 1963: 317).

Peigan, Blood, and Sarsi

The southernmost tribe of the Blackfoot nation, the Peigan, travelled the greatest distance to trade, from the Oldman River area east of the Rocky Mountains. The Blood Indian territory lay intermediate to that of the Peigan to the south and the Sarsi to the north, along the eastern foothills of the Rocky Mountains eastward to the Bow and Red Deer rivers.

The Sarsi were a small Athapascan tribe located in the Plains who were allied with the Blackfoot. According to Alexander Henry the younger(Coues 1897: 532), the Sarsi formerly occupied the north side of the Saskatchewan River, but later dwelt on the south side, south of the Beaver Hills, near the Slaves. They had broken away from the Beaver Indians (a Woodland tribe) "not long before the arrival of the Europeans" and, during the period under discussion, may still have been in transition to a fully Parkland/Plains adaptation (Dickason 1980: 27). Their territory is identified by Jenness (1963: 325) as between the Peace and Red Deer rivers. Their buffalo pounds were situated close enough to the posts that individuals could be sent in regularly for tobacco and ammunition, while the rest of the band arrived after the spring break-up (HBCA B.49/a/27b, 30 January 1797).

Assiniboine

The Assiniboine were also originally a forest-adapted group who became Parkland dwellers several centuries prior to European contact (Andersen 1970: 50). By the eighteenth century, they were hunting buffalo in both the Parkland and the Plains (Ray 1974: 95). All Assiniboine bands were grouped as Plains Indians except for Swampy Ground Assiniboine since, aside from M'Gillivray, the traders do not identify their home regions more specifically.

Gros Ventres

Although mentioned often, especially in reference to their attacks on other forts, the Gros Ventres were the least frequent of the Plains visitors, perhaps because of their quarrelsome nature. A single group appears once in 1798. Known as the Fall or Rapid Indians, in 1772 they lived directly east of the Blackfoot Confederacy, in an area between the branches of the Saskatchewan River (Dickason 1980: 31). By 1781-1782, they began to be pushed south and east to the Missouri River by the Assiniboine and Cree (Dickason 1980: 31; Jenness 1963: 326). They may have occupied an area as far east as Cole's Falls or Nipawa River (Morton 1929: lxvi).

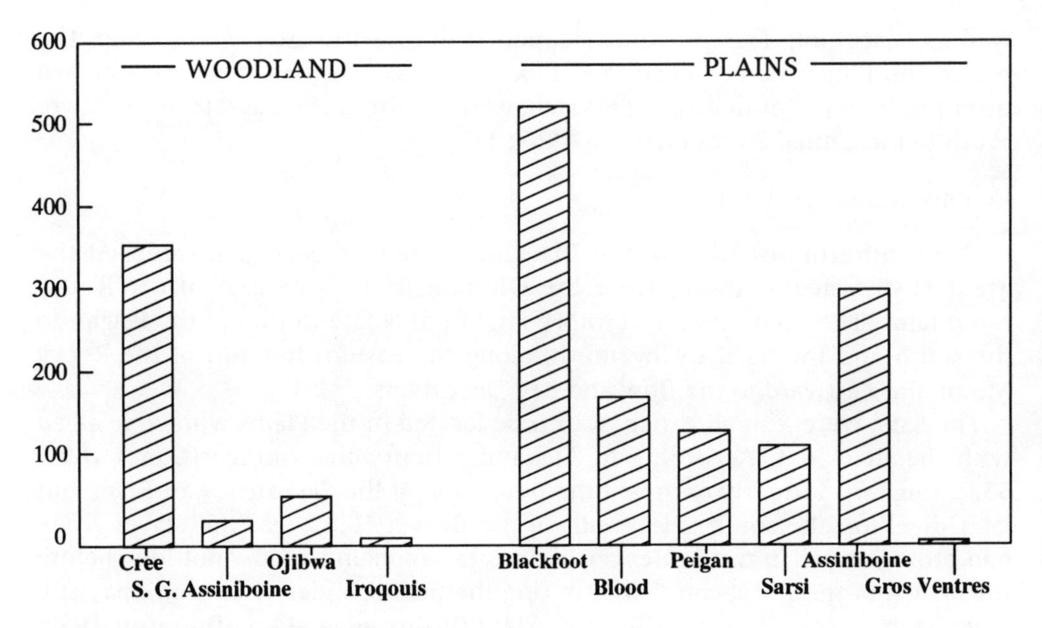

Figure 4. Populations of Visiting Tribes.

While twice as many traders came from the Plains as from the Woodlands, this numerical superiority cannot be equated to a greater dependence on European trade (figure 4). For one thing, these posts were the closest ones to Blackfoot territory, while Woodland Indians had access to other posts. A decrease in Plains trading population is observable after the first three years, perhaps as new posts were constructed closer to their home territory. Secondly, the Plains Indians came for luxuries, according to M'Gillivray; they had a surplus of goods (in the form of provisions) and of time for long-distance travel (Morton 1929: 47-48).

The Cree were the largest group of Woodland traders. Most of the other forest-dwelling Indians, except for the Swampy Ground Assiniboine, were easterners who migrated west with the fur trade. Their presence in the records is characterized by a paucity of detail regarding their number, lifeways, and home region.

Native Commodities

Traditionally, the academic and historic perspective on Native commodities has been a misleading correlation of Woodland Indians with beaver hunting and Plains Indians with bison provisioning. While in some cases the kind and quantity of Native trade goods are broadly indicative of ethnic origin and basic lifeways, in many cases ethnic identity cannot be deduced from the items brought in for exchange.

The aboriginal trade items can be organized into three types: pelts, provisions, and other items such as castoreum and bark (table 1).

Table 1. Native Commodities.

	Pelts									Provisions						Other					
Woodland Tribes	Beaver	Badger	Marten	Otter	Bear	Bison	Wolf	Fox	Skins	Bison	Elk	Moose	Beaver	Geese	Berries	Castoreum	Horses	Bark	Lodges	Canoes	Clothing
Cree	•			•			•	•	•	•				•		•	•	•	•	•	
Swampy Ground Assiniboine	•								•	•											
Ojibwa	•			•					•												
Iroquois	•		•						•												
Indians from Moose Hills									•									•			
Indians from above/within	•								•												
Plains Tribes																					
Blackfoot					•	•	•	•	•	•					•		•				•
Blood	•				•	•	•	•	•	•											
Peigan	•						•	•	•	•							•				•
Sarsi	•						•	•	•	•											
Assiniboine	•	•					•		•	•											
Gros Ventres							•		•	•											
Unidentified Indians	•						•		•	•	•	•	•		•	•		•			

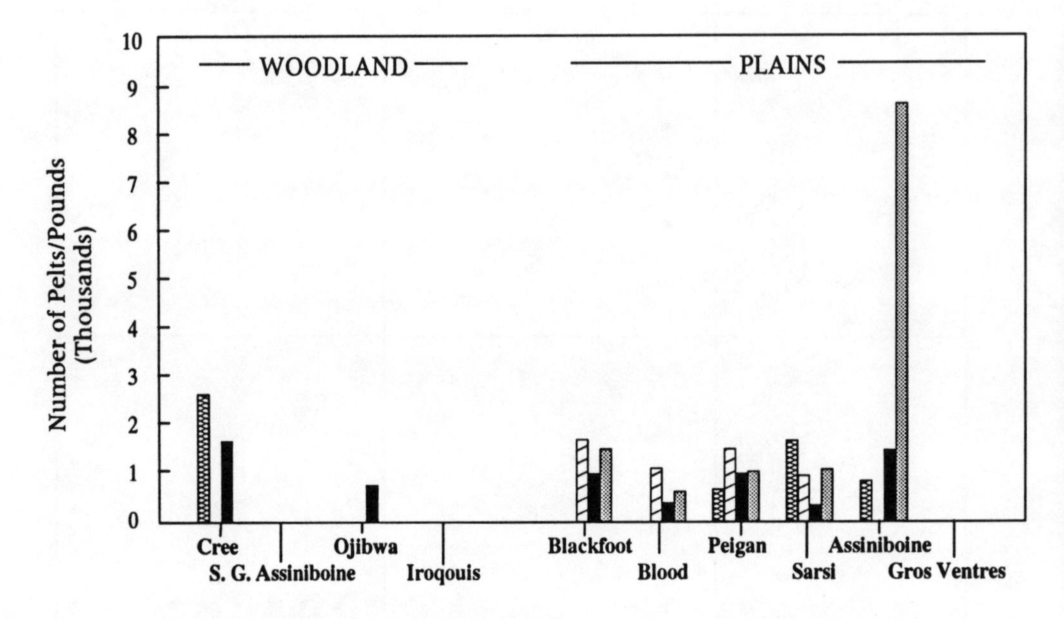

Figure 5. Quantities of Pelts and Provisions Trade.

From the Europeans' standpoint, procuring furs was the most important occupation of their Native trading associates. Those Indians who did not accommodate their wishes were dealt with accordingly: "They are treated with such indifference and contempt, that they resolve to return to their own lands, where they pretend to have been accustomed to receive a better reception" (Morton 1929: 53). References to Native indolence always refer to a relative lack of involvement in trapping activity.

Not unexpectedly, the most common source of pelts was beaver. What is unanticipated is the variety of tribes bringing in beaver (figure 5). In terms of identifiable quantities, the Plains Indians as a group would appear to have been the most significant suppliers during the first two years, although Woodland Indians (especially the Cree) brought in unidentified quantities of trade beaver more often. Of the leading tribes, only the Blackfoot did not appear to deal in this commodity.

Other fur bearing species (such as badger, marten, otter, bison, and bear) were of minor importance; they represented less than 8 percent of the total number of identified pelts traded. The exceptions are the large quantities of wolf and fox skins which were supplied by the Plains groups (figure 5). Their quantity suggests that they were actually two of the more important commodities, yet ones which were rarely mentioned by the clerks in any description of the fur trade. In fact, only slightly fewer wolf and fox were brought in than beaver, and unknown numbers of them were brought in more often. Their significance lies in the fact that they represent one of the few traits for discriminating between Woodland

and Plains Native-European contact. Except for two occasions when Cree (probably Plains Cree) brought in these species, they were supplied entirely by Plains Indians. Among the Blood, Peigan, and Blackfoot tribes there was almost equal representation. The Sarsi supplied about half of what the other tribes did, which may reflect local environmental conditions less suitable for wolf and fox fur production. The Assiniboine, who were major beaver traders, brought in very little wolf and fox. While this appears to suggest a Parkland adaptation involving a retention of Woodland subsistence practises on the part of the Assiniboine, this group was also a major producer of bison provisions.

The most numerous item in the class of trade pelts is unidentified pelts (table 1). Virtually all tribes brought in pelts of some type. While this activity reflects a widespread aboriginal tradition of trapping fur-bearing animals, certainly the scope of the enterprise and the quantity of the product were greatly enhanced with the presence of a European market.

Provisions

In terms of sheer survival, provisions (dried and fresh meat, fat and grease) were the most important items of trade at the posts (figure 5). Not only did the fort personnel require assistance in obtaining food for themselves, but a key reason for the posts' existence was to procure a "portable food" for the voyageurs and for the posts situated along the Athabasca River system, which were far removed from bison herds (Masson 1960: 17).

While a few other food items were occasionally brought in, such as beaver, moose, elk, geese, and berries, provisions consisted almost entirely of bison. Because of this practise, accounts of provisions are assumed to be bison unless otherwise specified. Bison was brought in almost exclusively by the Plains Indians, although it was locally available and indeed was procured by the Europeans and the Native fort hunters they hired. Indians undertook little commercial pemmican production. Far more often, they simply provided the raw ingredients: dried meat and fat.

Other Items

Occasionally, aboriginal traders brought in items that were also of a non-pelt, non-food nature (table 1). These included horses (horse trade was bidirectional, as demand necessitated); birch bark; castoreum; and, especially, news regarding the movements, hunting success, war plans, and changing allegiances of different Native groups, in return for the prospect of reward.

European Commodities

The written records of the European commodities which the Indians received provide the base from which to investigate the archaeological evidence for material culture transfer. To some degree, the journals differentiate among the

Native groups in terms of the type of European articles acquired and between gifts and purchases and necessities and luxuries.

For example, the companies held variable trade policies according to the tribe they were trading with. Rum was "proportioned to the Nation & quality of the Cheif [sic]" (Morton 1929: 30). The Plains Indians were treated with less liberality because their provisions and skins were not rated as highly as the beaver supplies of the other groups. In fact, M'Gillivray notes that the company "Arranged some bad Tobacco for the arrival of the Blackfoot" (Morton 1929: 38).

Problems are, of course, endemic in the data. The most significant one is the absence of detail. Countless entries simply read: "Traded with the Indians and they went away." Rarely is information on the ethnic identity, the population size, the type and quantity of Native goods, and the bartered European items presented concurrently. Therefore, it is not possible to analyze each trade interaction individually. Another problem concerns terms such as "debt" or "credit," which are ambiguous. They could refer to Native goods when, for example, employees were sent out to fetch a band's furs, or they could refer to European products such as when Indians asked for "a little debt" (i.e., an advance of European items). The factors did not keep records of the goods sent out to them from the bayside and the York Factory trade lists do not itemize the goods according to post.

Regrettably, a straightforward division of Plains and Woodland tribes based on the type of European goods they sought is not possible from the little information that is available in the daily records (table 2). Clearly, items which were universal in the trade equation were tobacco and liquor. Tobacco, of course, was already indigenous to eastern North American tribes prior to contact. During the fur trade it was distributed by the Europeans (nearly always in the form of gifts) in twists or pieces or measured off in fathoms, feet, or pounds. Most often, though, quantities were not provided. When identified with specific tribes, it appears to be equally prevalent in nearly all of the larger groups. Tobacco was mentioned more frequently in the first years of trade, perhaps as a device by which to initiate business. Clay pipes were usually imported for the Native trade (Davies 1965: 282), but aboriginal equipment could also have been used.

Liquor was an equally popular trade item which was independent of the recipients' ethnicity. For the Europeans, alcohol represented a superior trade item for two reasons: (1) its ease of transportation and storage (smaller quantities of high or undiluted wines were brought inland and mixed with water in varying strengths according to the tribes in question), and (2) its desirability to the Natives (Morton 1929: lxxiii-lxxiv). The Cree appeared to be the biggest consumers. Liquor was frequently exchanged for beaver on the few occasions it was not given as gifts.

After tobacco and alcohol, sets of clothing or "rigging" were the next most common trade articles identified in the daily accounts, especially in the first three years. However, this type of trade item was mentioned too infrequently to discern temporal patterns in tribal acquisition. Often these outfits were made

Table 2. European Commodities.

Woodland Tribes	Tobacco	Liquor	Guns & Gun Parts	Ammunition	Knives/ Iron Work	Clothing	Decoration Feathers/Vermilion	Horses
Cree	•	•	•	•		•		•
Ojibwa		•	•		•			
Indians from above/within		•						
Plains Tribes								
Blackfoot	•	•		•	•	•	•	
Blood	•	•	•		•	•		
Peigan	•	•				•		
Sarsi	•	•	•	•		•	•	
Assiniboine	•	•	•	•		•		
Gros Ventres	•							

available to band and/or trade chiefs who brought in good trade. According to Morton (1929: 74n), the outfits consisted of a calico coat, other garments, a tall hat, and a flag. M'Gillivray specifically mentions shirts and feather decorations (Morton 1929). "Chiefs whose bands had been indolent and had not hunted and were not able to pay their credits were deprived of their position by withholding these symbols of office" (Morton 1929: 74n). Both Plains tribes and Cree Indians received clothing, although the largest single purchasing group was the Cree. On one occasion, 22 chiefs from a variety of tribes were clothed, an unusually large number according to M'Gillivray (Morton 1929: 75).

The category of guns and ammunition suffers from uneven reporting. The Sarsi were identified as gun consumers, the Cree as the major users of ammunition. Guns were mentioned very infrequently in the trade accounts, yet the factors chronically complained that they were unable to supply guns and therefore lost potential business (HBCA B.24/a/2, 19 January 1794). Except for a single purchase by a Towow (Ottawa?) Indian, the Sarsi were the only consumers identified, and only in the first two seasons of trade. The 18 guns they purchased in 1793 were "more than half of what [the company] had" (HBCA B.24/a/2, 7 December 1793). Gun parts, including gun springs and flints which imply gun use, are identified only in the 1796-1797 report. Ray (1974: 73) has observed a decreased demand for firearms in the eighteenth century which he asserted was not due to supply shortages or price increases. However, while guns were not often mentioned, ammunition—in the form of balls, shot and powder—was a common trade item. In about half the trading situations, ammunition was exchanged in the form of gifts. References to this trade item were sporadic; no mention of ammunition was made at all in 1797-1798. The Cree were the recipients most often identified.

The presence of guns among the Plains people is somewhat surprising given their predilection for traditional methods of subsistence procurement (e.g., using buffalo pounds). However, bison may have been dispatched with guns once in the pound or taken with them while on horseback. More commonly, guns were sought after as prestige items or as weapons of war, rather than as solely subsistence tools.

Some articles were mentioned only a few times. Knives were reportedly traded to Plains Indians on two occasions. Ironwork, which could refer to any number of items (hatchets, knives, awls, etc.), was acquired by the Ojibwa on at least one occasion. "Sundry articles" was an unrevealing term used frequently in the first two seasons, usually in reference to gift items. Finally, general references to presents, supplies, and debts or credits were common. Unfortunately, details on the nature of the items are unavailable, nor is any ethnic pattern of acquisition apparent.

The most popular commodities sought after were as often luxuries as necessities, although such a distinction is surely bounded by ethnocentric prejudice. For example, tobacco, generally considered a non-essential article, could certainly be viewed as necessary to ceremonial practises, while practical articles such as guns were often valued as prestige items. Depending on the tribes who purchased them, the same item could be perceived as either a luxury or as a necessity. Arthur Ray's study of the southwestern Hudson Bay trade (1974: 73-88, 146-156) established contrasting patterns of acquisition for Woodland and Plains/Parkland Indians. He observed that clothing, blankets, guns and ammunition, and metal goods such as chisels and traps were more frequently procured as necessities by Woodland Indians than by Plains or Parkland groups. According to Ray (1974), Plains Indians would have had less need of European technology in their subsistence practises and less opportunity for bringing in firearms to the posts for repair. He also argues for an increasing reliance on cloth or blankets by forest-adapted Indians as animals came to be depleted in their hunting area, while to grassland and Parkland tribes European clothing remained a luxury rather than a necessity because of the continued abundance of big game.

According to the daily accounts, it was the luxury items like rum, tobacco, and chief's clothing and, to a lesser extent, feathers, gartering, and vermilion that were most commonly received, although most of these were often exchanged in the form of gifts, entailing no obligation. In the journal accounts, necessities (for example, items related to subsistence technology, such as guns and ammunition and other iron tools), were less frequently identified. This may be due in part to the use of terms such as "sundry articles" and "iron work" rather than specific names such as "blankets," "hatchets," and so forth.

Trade-Related Activities

In addition to the trade goods data provided in accounts of the actual transactions, the documents also supply information on available European trade goods (although rarely their quantities) through descriptions of trade-related activities of the fort employees (table 3). These include correspondence related to shipping and receiving surplus trade items and the production and repair of trade goods by the blacksmith and the tailor.

Frequent reference is made to the blacksmith repairing trade goods often not mentioned elsewhere. Even more interesting are the accounts of new trade articles being manufactured from other items as well as unpopular trade articles being refashioned into utilitarian items used in the fort. Many times the blacksmith repaired guns previously purchased by Indians, or repaired and cleaned trade guns broken in transit. Other trade items, such as kettles, hatchets, and ice chisels, sometimes required repair, especially after damage caused during shipment. Some trade articles were completely manufactured by the blacksmith: gunworms, firesteels, awl blades, drawing knives, and "small tumblers cups" (although the latter may have been intended for employees). Frequently, trade items were made from worn-out objects. For example, awl blades were made from ill-made beaver hooks and old iron barrel hoops (HBCA B.24/a/1,2, 7 January, 18 November 1793). Worn-out files were the source material for

TABLE 3. ADDITIONAL EUROPEAN COMMODITIES.

Class	Item	Trading Season					
		1792-93	1793-94	1794-95	1796-97	1797-98	1799
Luxury Goods	Tobacco		x	x	343 lb		
	Tobacco boxes						
	-Japanned				15		
	-wooden				6		
	Liquor	2k	28g	10k	8k		
	Kegs		11+				
Guns and Ammunition	Guns	x	4+	x	10		x
	-3.5ft	2			28		
	-4ft	2					
	Pistols*				4		
	Bayonets				100		
	Gunflints	x	200		311		
	Gun Worms				370+		
	Powder				16lb		
					3 meas.		
			3k	1k	2k		
	Ball			1 bag	8 bags		
					420 ball		
	Shot				2 bags		
Tools	Arrow Barks				120		
	Knives			x	273		
	-scalping			144			
	-drawing		x				
	Ice Chisels	7+	x		5		
	Hatchets	x	x	20	24		
	Awl Blades	x	x		531+		
	-of iron hoops		x				
	-of beaver hooks	x					
	Needles**				2		
	Thread*				1		
					2 oz.		
	Firesteels	x	x		175		
							x
	-from files	x					
	Files				18		
	Iron Work				x		
Cooking Items	Pot**				1		
	Kettle	x	x	50 lb	8+		
	Tumblers*				4		
Containers	Wood Box				1		

(continued on next page)

(Table 3—continued)

Class	Item	Trading Season					
		1792-93	1793-94	1794-95	1796-97	1797-98	1799
Personal Ornaments	Bracelets	x					
	Rings				156		
	Beads				13.5 lb		
	Combs				74		
	Paint				2 oz		
Clothing	Blankets			10	24		
	Cloth	x			64.5 yds/x		
	I. Clothing	x	x	x	x		x
	Shirts*				8		
	Hats			x	14+		
	Sashes*				some 8		
	Overcoats			30			
	Sm. Boys' coats	x	x		36+		
	Captains' coats	x	x		7		
	Drawers**				1		
	Gartering			x	36 yds.		
	Silk Handker-chiefs				12		
Transportation	Horse Bells				20		
	Horses			10			
Other	Sundry Article	x	x	x		x	

* perhaps intended for employees only, however the reference to ". . . have sent you nearly all the Trade Goods here. . .as [per] the list enclosed" argues for their inclusion in the table. (3 March 1797, B.49/a/27b).
** the small quantities of these items suggest that they also may have been intended for employees' use.
Key
k = keg
g = gallon
meas. = measure

firesteels (HBCA B.24/a/1,2, 8 March 1793). On two occasions, after Indians had refused poor-quality ice chisels, these items were made into door and gate hinges (HBCA B.24/a/1, 2 January 1793; HBCA B.24/a/2, 22 April 1794).

Information about available European goods also comes from journal entries relating to the HBC tailor's activities (apparently there was no NWC tailor). Peter Fidler's 1796-1797 account is the most detailed in terms of the yardage, color, and price of cloth in made beaver (see, for example, HBCA B.49/a/27b, 31 October 1796). Mentioned as frequently as the blacksmith, the tailor held just as key a position although, unlike that of the blacksmith, material evidence for it would be highly perishable. Clearly, the products of the tailor's endeavours formed a significant portion of the European material culture introduced to the Indians, despite the infrequent identification of clothing in trade transactions. Perhaps, tailor-made clothing was intended primarily for the Indian residents: the Native wives of the employees and their children. However, countless entries detail the tailor's manufacture of Indian clothing, trade chiefs' clothing, children's clothing, or clothing for the Native fort hunter. Few details are provided regarding the type of garment, the ethnic origin of the style, or the "hardware," such as bone or metal decorations or fasteners, which might remain in the archaeological record. The specific garments mentioned are small coats, boys' coats, captains' coats, hats, and a pair of drawers made for trade. They were made from a variety of fabrics (printed linen, cotton, baize, cloth of colours, aurora cloth, red and blue corduroy, and "fine Blue"). Thus it seems likely that the tailor-made clothing for trade was European in design, certainly in raw material and execution.

Other trade-related activities such as drying tobacco and making carrot tobacco, and drying wet cases of knives, hats, and powder, provide further evidence for available trade goods as do accounts of the transportation and distribution of alcohol (HBCA B.24/a/2, 11 November 1793; HBCA B.24/a/4, 15 November 1796; Morton 1929: 33). Liquor was sent out to the posts in a concentrated form known as "high wines" and was subsequently watered down. It was contained and traded in skins and kegs. Several times liquor kegs were cut down to make smaller kegs in which to dispense alcohol to the Indians, and empty kegs were collected for subsequent reuse (HBCA B.24/a/2, 15 April 1794).

As table 3 illustrates, the additional data on available European goods greatly increase the range of European items which might be expected in an associated aboriginal site, such as a plantation. These accounts substantiate the significance of alcohol and tobacco to the trade but also illustrate the high regard that Indian traders had for many of the metal goods offered by the Europeans. Multi-purpose tools such as knives and hatchets replaced aboriginal counterparts, while ice chisels were useful in beaver-trapping; files took the place of abraders for wood- and bone-working, and awls and firesteels were used in place of Native domestic goods. There is an unexpectedly wide range of clothing items given this category's brief mention in the trade negotiations. The journals reveal that incorporation of European-made clothing fashioned from European materials and probably styled according to both European and Native tastes occurred early in the contact period. Research by Anderson (see pages 93-115 of this volume) and White (1987) on the Great Lakes trade corroborates the importance of clothing as a fur trade commodity. Guns and gun parts were more commonly acquired items than one would suspect from the daily accounts of the trade, although whether their use was primarily as an item of prestige or warfare or as a subsistence tool cannot be determined. Finally, records of personal items, such as jewellery and combs, argue for the fur trade as both a source of non-essential goods as well as more utilitarian items. Unfortunately, the items identified in these trade-related activities cannot be specifically related to individual tribes.

Native Dependence on European Goods

Central to the issue of culture transfer is the degree of dependence on European goods which the Indians experienced. Nicks (1969: 24) has observed that many writers, including some actually involved in the trade, argue for a great degree of dependence (however, for an alternate perspective of the contact situation, see Thistle 1986). According to Harmon (1957: 65-66), writing in 1802: "The Indians in this quarter [the Swan River in Manitoba] have been so long accustomed to use European goods, that it would be with difficulty that they could now obtain a livelihood without them." Duncan M'Gillivray felt that the Indian traders were "attached to our commodities. . . the only method of procuring their necessarys [sic] is by a regular and peaceable trade . . . ." (Morton 1929: 64). However, developing a taste for exotic luxuries and requiring foreign goods to sustain existence are two quite different responses to contact, for as the NWC factor writes elsewhere:

> The rest of our commodities are indeed usefull [sic] to the Natives, when they can afford to purchase them, but if they had hitherto lived unacquainted with European productions it would not I beleive [sic] diminish their felicity. (Morton 1929: 48)

Their casual response to the proliferation of European material culture was in part shaped by the competition between the companies, which meant that they could obtain their items quite easily:

> They procure their necessaries at such low prices, that very few skins are then required to satisfy all their wants, and they receive besides very considerable presents. (Morton 1929: 76)

Insights into ethnic differences in dependency on European material culture are limited to M'Gillivray's analysis of Plains Indian trade practises. He credits their offhand response to European contact to their traditional lifeways. According to M'Gillivray, the Plains Indians were "so advantageously situated that they could live very happily independent of our assistance," for they had an abundance of game, which provided food, clothing, and raw materials for producing other items, and highly successful traditional subsistence strategies, which were such that "they stand in no need of ammunition" (Morton 1929: 47). Rather, he claims, it was "*our luxuries* [emphasis added] that attract[ed] them to the Fort and make us so necessary to their happiness" (Morton 1929: 47).

According to M'Gillivray, rum was especially desired by the Plains Indians. Tobacco was another article in great demand, constituting as it did "a principal part of their feasts & Superstitious ceremonies, and in these treaties of peace and councils of War, a few whifs [sic] out of the medicine pipe confirms the articles, that has been mutually agreed upon" (Morton 1929: 47). Even ammunition was a luxury of a sort for these Indians. Its value lay in "the great advantage it gives them over their enemies." It was also used for killing beaver, "but if the Fur Trade had not allured adventurers to this Country there would be no necessity for hunting this animal" (Morton 1929: 47-48). Unfortunately, M'Gillivray's observations regarding the Plains Indians' responses to European contact are not substantiated in the transaction accounts nor in the archaeological record.

DISCUSSION

Ethnic differences in response to contact are difficult to identify at Fort George-Buckingham House. The first problem is identifying who came to trade. Not only was the site complex a locus for many groups, but during the decade of occupation Plains varieties of Woodland groups developed. This situation was complicated by the fact that relocation to the Plains did not necessarily mean adaptation. A simplistic dichotomy of Woodland equals beaver trapping and Plains equals bison provisioning does not accurately reflect the situation here because some of the behaviour (for example, beaver hunting) was universal and all of this behaviour is archaeologically invisible.

To illustrate: although Plains Indians brought in the majority of wolf and fox skins and bison provisions (especially dried meat and fat), thus making these items appear to be good ethnic indicators, these species are not useful archaeologically since their bones rarely became part of the local archaeological record at the fort complex. Due to the policy of preparing skins away from the site complex or even prepackaging the furs in bales, archaeological evidence for hunting fur-bearing animals for trade would be rare at the plantation or Native campsite associated with the forts. For the same reasons of off-site preparation, little evidence for supplying provisions to the Europeans would survive except for bone residue from the less common practise of providing fresh meat. This residue would be indistinguishable from that furnished by the Europeans themselves. The other items brought into trade are of an equally perishable nature.

All of the Native commodities were collected prehistorically, suggesting that traditional activities may have just intensified with European contact. In general, the Plains Indians adapted to the European interests by amplifying their traditional subsistence pattern for the fur trade. Greater quantities of bison, wolf, and fox were procured in exchange for European commodities. However, the Plains Indians also altered their subsistence strategies to include trapping for beaver and the use of European weaponry. One adaptation made by some Woodland bands, perhaps in response to the fur trade, involved their movement onto the Plains and their participation in bison hunting. This lifestyle may have been perceived as an easier means with which to obtain European luxuries, especially given the rapid decline of local beaver shortly after the trading posts opened.

A more effective means of identifying Native ethnic groups archaeologically would logically involve the European goods they acquired. There are two reasons for this. First, variable trade policies for the tribes were established. Second,

M'Gillivray's observations that the Plains Indians could live without European assistance but that they loved the luxuries that the trade provided suggest a difference in dependence on European goods for the Plains and the Woodland Indians (Morton 1929: 47, 48). This is substantiated by Ray's (1974) documentation of the contrasting buying patterns of Woodland and Plains/Parkland Indians in southwestern Hudson Bay. However, the exchange of European commodities is difficult to assess. There is one reality expressed in the daily accounts, of the fur trade as a source of luxury items and gifts, and another reality in the descriptions of related activities which emphasize the importance of metal items and clothing. Neither source is explicitly informative regarding ethnic differences in the degree and direction of culture transfer.

Although characterized by a lack of detail, the daily transaction accounts offer at least a preliminary insight into the aboriginal material adaptation to the European trade. From these, we learn of the premier importance of tobacco and liquor which were frequently received by the Indians as gifts (however, for an alternative ranking from records of the Great Lakes trade see Anderson this volume). According to these records, ammunition, and to a lesser extent clothing, were commonly obtained articles of trade, while guns and "ironwork" were mentioned less frequently. Based on these data, a rather misleading interpretation of the fur trade primarily as a source of luxuries and gifts and secondarily as a source of weapons would result.

The accounts concerning the shipment and local production and repair of items are more informative. They support the importance of liquor and tobacco as commodities while substantiating the significance to the trade of a variety of metal goods, clothing, and firearms as well as personal items, such as jewellery and combs. These accounts illustrate the very limited perspective of the trade which is obtained from the transaction records. Many trade items were never listed in daily trade accounts or in merchant supply lists from Montreal or London. Instead, such items were manufactured or repaired on site, reworked into other trade items, refashioned into utilitarian items for the posts, or shipped to and from other posts as demand dictated. By considering documentary records other than those dealing exclusively with the commercial transactions, a fuller picture of the European contact as equally a source of both luxury and utilitarian items is apparent.

The ethnic diversity of the Native traders was not detectable in the archaeological record of the Native encampment between the two posts. An extensive program of judgmental and probabalistic excavation of a 120 m by 80 m area between the posts yielded little evidence for an historic Native presence in the form of features or artifacts. (For a complete description of the archaeological investigations, which is beyond the scope of this paper, see Gullason 1990.) Instead, a thin, sheet-like scatter of primarily European cultural material characterized the distribution pattern. The archaeological invisibility of the plantation site may be partly explained by cultural site formation processes. The Fort George-Buckingham House Plantation is characterized by multiple brief occupations by various ethnic groups (including Europeans) in which specialized activities were undertaken which left little archaeological residue. The absence of tipi ring and hearth features, together with the small artifact assemblage, make it difficult to differentiate Native occupations from occasional use of the site by the Europeans. Given the short occupation period (1 to 3 days), the social nature of the activities (smoking, drinking, and visiting), which would leave few traces, and the routine cleanup of the area by the Europeans, the lack of evidence for Native use of the site as a trade camp is not completely unexpected.

Excavations of the employees' residences located in and around Fort George were more successful in demonstrating culture transfer, although Native ethnic markers were absent. A Native female presence is well documented at both posts. As "country wives" of the post employees, the strongest archaeological evidence for their identity would be found in the men's quarters. Data from investigations of the dwellings established two important facts: (1) they corroborated the importance of luxury goods such as jewellery, identified in the discussions of the trade activities but not in the transactions themselves (with the recovery of beads, pendants, tinkling cones, crucifixes, earrings, rings, armbands, and brooches), and (2) they underlined the fact of both the retention of a range of aboriginal activities—such as clothing construction (with the finds of bone and metal awls, a bone scraper, and a bone flesher) as well as evidence for the extremely selective use of metal tools to make traditional items (metal file marks were observed on some of the traditional bone tools). Thus, an important consideration in any historical study of culture contact is the archaeological data, because one of the responses to contact is no response at all—*cultural retention,* in other words—and that will only be obvious in the material record.

Considered together, the archaeological and archival data for the Fort George-Buckingham House site complex suggest that both cultural retention and incorporation (the transfer and integration of foreign elements to conform to traditional values) characterized the Native response to the early contact situation. Unfortunately, it was not possible to isolate specific ethnic responses to European contact. Some European items, such as cloth and tools, were generally useful and thus widely appealing. Given the overlap in lifeways of Woodland and Plains peoples during the late eighteenth century, similarities in their patterns of acquisition of European goods is perhaps not unexpected.

ACKNOWLEDGEMENTS

I wish to thank Peter Hawker, Toby Morantz and James Savelle for their thoughtful comments on a version of this paper. The larger research project from which this article is drawn benefitted from the careful supervision provided by Raymond LeBlanc, Clifford Hickey, and Roderick Macleod.

Douglas Babcock, historian for the 1989 Fort George Project, and John Foster kindly shared their knowledge with me. Geoffrey Lester and his team of cartographers were responsible for the fine quality of figures 1 and 2.

Financial support for this research was generously provided by the Boreal Institute for Northern Studies, the Alberta Historical Resources Foundation, the Province of Alberta Scholarship Fund, and by Student Employment and Economic Development (S.E.E.D.) and Student Temporary Employment Programme (S.T.E.P.), federal and provincial hiring programmes, respectively.

References

Andersen, R. R. 1970. "Alberta Stoney (Assiniboin) Origins and Adaptations: A Case for Reappraisal." *Ethnohistory* 17: 49-61.

Coues, E., ed. [1897] 1965. *New Light on the Early History of the Greater Northwest: The Manuscript Journals of Alexander Henry and of David Thompson, 1799-1814,* 2 vols. Minneapolis: Ross and Haines.

Davies, K. G. 1965. *Letters From Hudson Bay 1703-40,* vol.25. London: Hudson's Bay Record Society.

Dickason, O. 1980. "A Historical Reconstruction for the Northwestern Plains." *Prairie Forum* 1: 19-37.

Gullason, Lynda. 1990. "The Fort George-Buckingham House Plantation (1792-1800): Native-European Contact in the Fur Trade Era." Unpublished M.A. thesis, Department of Anthropology, University of Alberta, Edmonton.

Harmon, D. W. 1957. *Sixteen Years in the Indian Country,* edited by W.K. Lamb. Toronto: Macmillan.

Howard, J.H. 1977. *The Plains-Ojibwa or Bungi: Hunters and Warriors of the Northern Plains with Special Reference to the Turtle Mountain Band.* Reprints in Anthropology vol. 7. Lincoln, Neb.: J. & L. Reprint.

Hudson's Bay Company. 1792-1793. (Buckingham House Post Journal) Manuscript B.24/a/1 in Hudson's Bay Company Archives (HBCA). Provincial Archives of Manitoba, Winnipeg, Canada.

———. 1793-1794. (Buckingham House Post Journal) Manuscript B.24/a/2.

———. 1794-1795. (Buckingham House Post Journal) Manuscript B.24/a/3.

———. 1796-1797. (Buckingham House Post Journal) Manuscript B.24/a/4.

———. 1797-1798. (Buckingham House Post Journal) Manuscript B.24/a/5.

———. 1798-1799. (Buckingham House Post Journal) Manuscript B.24/a/6.

Jenness, D. 1963. *The Indians of Canada.* Bulletin of the National Museum of Canada, no. 65, Anthropological Series, no. 15. Ottawa: Queen's Printer.

Kidd, R. S. 1970. *Fort George and the Early Fur Trade in Alberta.* Provincial Museum and Archives of Alberta Publication no. 2. Edmonton: L. S. Wall, Queen's Printer for Alberta.

Losey, T.C. 1980. Fort George Project Interim Report No. 3: Archaeological Investigations, 1979. Archaeological Survey of Alberta, Edmonton.

Losey, T.C., H. Pyszczyk, P. Bobrowsky, L. Chan, and K. Hardie. 1978. Archaeological Investigations: Fort George 1977. Archaeological Survey of Alberta, Edmonton.

Losey, T.C., and H. Pyszczyk. 1979. Archaeological Investigations at Fort George 1978. Archaeological Survey of Alberta, Edmonton.

Masson, L. R., ed. 1960. *Les Bourgeois de la Compagnie du Nord-Ouest: Récits de Voyages, Lettres et Rapports Inédits Relatifs au Nord-Ouest Canadien,* vol 2. 1890. Reprint. New York: Antiquarian Press.

Milloy, J. S. 1988. *The Plains Cree: Trade, Diplomacy and War, 1790 to 1870.* Winnipeg: University of Manitoba Press.

Morton, A. S., ed. 1929. *The Journal of Duncan M'Gillivray of the North West Company at Fort George on the Saskatchewan River, 1794-1795.* Toronto: Hunter-Ross.

National Archives of Canada (NAC). MG 19 A8 vol. 5 David Thompson Journal 1799, 5-28 September. Ottawa.

______. MG 19 A17. Autobiographical Notes—John McDonald of Garth. Ottawa.

Nicks, G. C. 1969. "The Archaeology of Two Hudson's Bay Company Posts: Buckingham House (1792-1800) and Edmonton House III (1810-1813)." Master's thesis, Department of Anthropology, University of Alberta.

Nicks, J., and N. Hurlburt. 1977. The Archaeology of Buckingham House. MS. 630, Historic Sites Service, Edmonton.

Ray, A. 1972. "Indian Adaptation to the Forest-Grassland Boundary of Manitoba and Saskatchewan, 1650-1821: Some Implications for Interregional Migration." *Canadian Geographer* 16: 103-18.

______. 1974. *Indians in the Fur Trade: Their Role as Trappers, Hunters, and Middlemen in the Lands Southwest of Hudson Bay 1660-1870.* Toronto: University of Toronto Press.

Smith, J.G.E. 1981. "Western Woods Cree." In *Subarctic,* edited by June Helm, 256-70. *Handbook of North American Indians,* vol. 6, general editor, William G. Sturtevant, Washington, D.C.: Smithsonian Institution.

Thistle, P. 1986. *Indian-European Trade Relations in the Lower Saskatchewan River Region to 1840.* Winnipeg: University of Manitoba Press.

White, B. 1987. "Montreal Canoes and Their Cargoes." In *Le Castor Fait Tout, Selected Papers of the Fifth North American Fur Trade Conference,* edited by Bruce G. Trigger, Toby Morantz, and Louise Dechêne, 164-92. Montreal: Lake St. Louis Historical Society of Montreal.

Looking at the Ledgers: Sauk and Mesquakie Trade Debts, 1820-1840

Royce Kurtz

The extension of credit to Native Americans was the ruination of the fur-trading companies according to their main offices, but the financial mainspring of the hunt according to the wintering traders; it was an unconscionable lure to an ingenuous savage according to missionaries, but a necessity against starvation according to Native American chiefs and headmen. Wherever the fur trade flourished in North America, barter/credit became a way of life and the accumulating debts became the trade's most controversial issue. Even modern scholars have viewed these cumulative debts as the cause of the decline of independent, self-sufficient Native American communities. Trade debts were the insidious vehicle for foreign state domination.[1]

For all the ink spilled over Indian indebtedness, scholars have neglected the most obvious source in creating their models of barter/credit—the account books recording these transactions. Rather, scholars have relied on the testimony of the traders and government officials, but these descriptions are summary statements that emphasize the problems and tensions of credit relations more than its workaday intricacies. Knowledge of the actual working of credit arrangements leads to a revision of these generally accepted descriptions.

In analyzing the credit arrangements for the Sauk and Mesquakie of Iowa territory (also known as the Sac and Fox), I made use of half a dozen surviving credit ledgers spanning a time period from 1819 to 1841.[2] Three of the ledgers covered a consecutive period—1826, 1827, and 1828, the very height of the trade in furs and hides in Iowa territory. Combined with inventories, daybooks, journals, letters, and government reports, a detailed picture of the 1820s foreign trade relations of the Sauk and Mesquakie emerges, and with data from a later ledger, 1840/41, a glimpse of a disastrously altered world sets these earlier years in stark relief.

The ledgers reveal that at the height of the trade in the 1820s, reasons for acquiring and repaying trade debts were more complex and variable than would be assumed by the testimony of traders, bureaucrats, and chiefs. There was no standardized kit of essential goods passed out to individual hunters in the fall of each year by the trader. Rather, the hunter could exercise a number of economic options regarding credit and even participation in the trade. These credit arrangements south of the Great Lakes changed quickly after the 1820s. The trade switched from one centered on hides to a trade based on proceeds from land sales. When the trade moved away from fur procurement, a whole series of changes followed. The seasonal emphasis on fall credits with a spring repayment disappeared. Credit no longer supplied goods related to the hunt and its ultimate return in furs. With furs no longer the payment, the individual hunter ceased to be the locus for debt responsibility. Credit loosed from its grounding in the hunt and the return in furs evolved quickly into a very different system. I will first describe the functional relations of credit in the 1820s and then point out how these elements changed to create the 1840s credit pattern.

During the first quarter of the nineteenth century, the Sauk and Mesquakie, two closely allied nations, lived in villages scattered along the Mississippi River from Prairie du Chien to the Des Moines River. In the first quarter of the nineteenth century they numbered roughly 4,500 souls, and 1,100 warriors hunted the forests and prairies of Illinois, Iowa, and northern Missouri. The annual hunting cycle began with the major fall deer hunt starting in October. The whole nation left their summer villages to hunt the wooded borders of midwestern rivers and streams. In early spring (March or April), the Sauk and Mesquakie hunters dispersed from their maple sugar camps to hunt muskrat and waterfowl. Finally, small parties left the summer villages in July to hunt deer and buffalo, returning in time for the fall harvest.[3]

When the American Fur Company moved into the Upper Midwest to take over British trading interests after the War of 1812, the Sauk and Mesquakie had already been regular participants in the fur and hide trade for one hundred fifty years, and the system of credit had been operative at least since the early 1750s.[4] George Davenport and Russell Farnham represented the American Fur Company in the 1820s, and it is their ledgers dating from 1826-1828 that provide a detailed snapshot of the Sauk and Mesquakie trade in deer, raccoon, muskrat, and other furs. Through their trading posts at Fort Armstrong, Rock Island, Illinois, and Fort Edwards, near the mouth of the Des Moines River, the two traders served around 800 of the Sauk and Mesquakie hunters. (Several of the more northerly Mesquakie villages took their business to Prairie du Chien, Wisconsin.[5]) While Davenport and Farnham were never without competitors, analysis of trading licenses and correspondence leads me to believe they controlled about three-fourths of an annual trade with the Sauk and Mesquakie, a trade running to $80,000 retail.[6] Each family acquired on the average $75 to $80 in European goods. (Schoolcraft had estimated $96 retail for the Ojibwa trade.[7])

A major shift in trade relations occurred after the Black Hawk War of 1832. The war signalled a disastrous decline in the Sauk and Mesquakie population, which dropped to 2,300 individuals by 1841.[8] They lost their Mississippi River villages in 1832 and were forced into repeated relocations upriver on the Iowa and Des Moines rivers. The land sales which triggered these removals provided a

Figure 1. Small groups of Sauk and Mesquakie left the spring maple sugar camps to hunt muskrats for the trade. The rat spear, five to six feet long, was used while ponds were still frozen. Along with traps, rifles, and powder, the rat spear was part of the hunting supplies given on credit. This drawing by Seth Eastman appeared as Plate 5, opposite page 50 in vol. 2 of Henry Rowe Schoolcraft, *Information Respecting the History, Condition, and Prospects of the Indian Tribes of the United States* (Philadelphia: Lippincott, Grambo, and Co., 1852). Courtesy of the William L. Clements Library, The University of Michigan.

new source of revenue. The U.S. government paid for the land in yearly installments. These payments, known in the contemporary literature as the "annuities," ranged from $27,000 to $57,000 annually between 1833 and 1842.[9]

The credit ledger of J.P. Eddy & Company has survived for the period 1840 to 1841, giving a glimpse of this altered world. J.P. Eddy, unlike Davenport and Farnham, was a small, local trader. Eddy had run a dry goods store in one of the border towns before being licensed to trade in Indian country. He competed with two large firms and numerous border traders. The two large firms were Chouteau and Company, a reorganization of the American Fur Company's western division, and Ewing and Company, a fiercely competitive firm with a reputation for sharp dealings.[10] While the population of the Sauk and Mesquakie plummeted, the purchase of European goods skyrocketed. For the year covered by Eddy's ledger, I have estimated Sauk and Mesquakie purchases at $115,000 or $200 per family.[11] Eddy had about 25 percent of this market.

The four ledger books used in this study are similar in broad outline. The trader recorded each credit under the name of an individual Sauk or Mesquakie and the long list of goods under each name is typical of the Indian trade in the early nineteenth century. There are also two differences between the 1820s ledgers and the 1840 ledger which stand out even on cursory inspection. First,

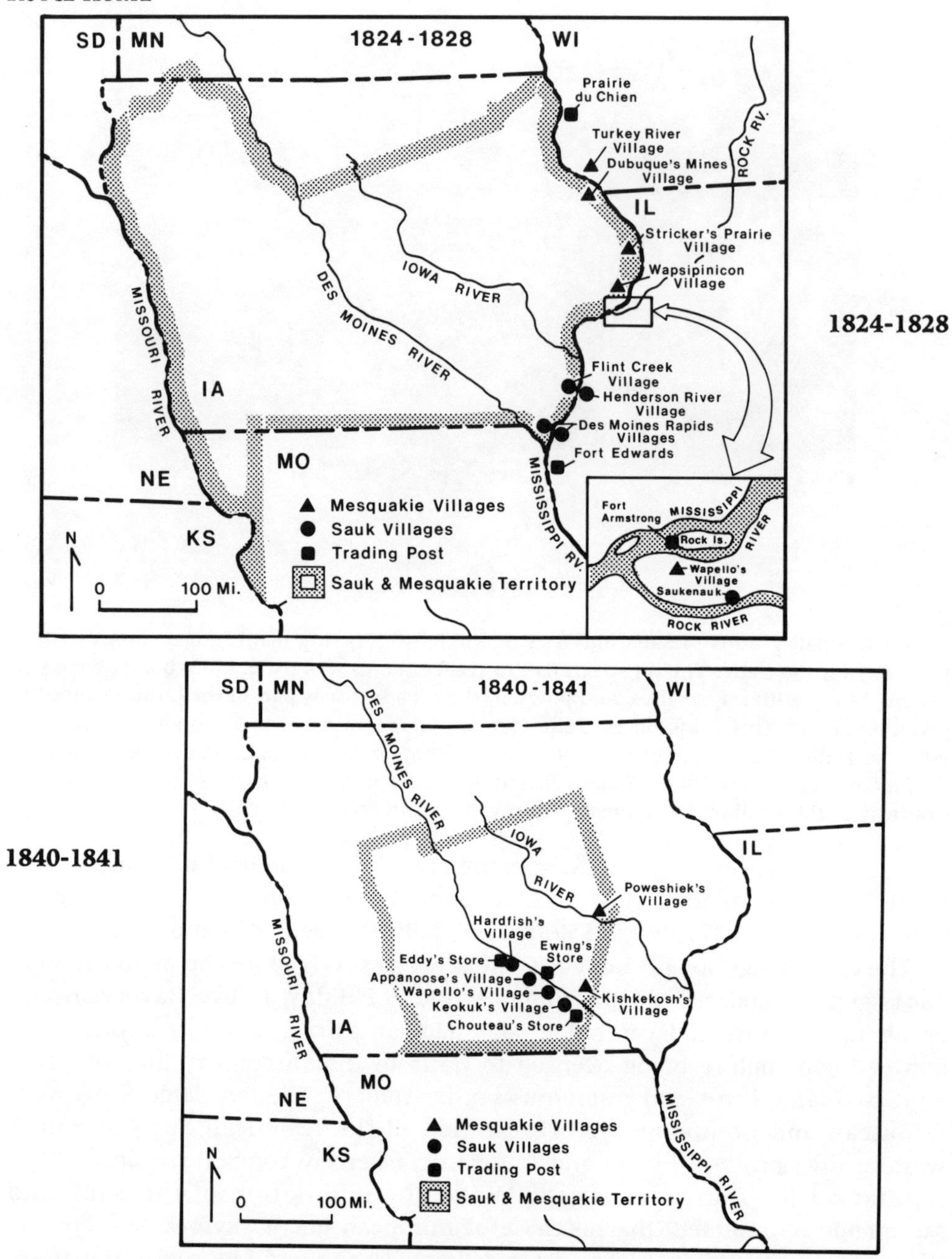

Figure 2. Annuities money recast the whole barter/credit system. Sources: Royce Kurtz, "Economic and Political History of the Sauk and Mesquakie, 1780s-1845" (Ph.D. dissertation, University of Iowa, 1986), 17-37; Helen Hornbeck Tanner, *Atlas of Great Lakes Indian History* (Norman: University of Oklahoma Press, 1987), 140; Charles Royce, *Indian Land Cessions in the United States*, Bureau of American Ethnology Annual Report no. 18, 2 vols. (Washington, D.C.: Bureau of American Ethnology, 1899), 2: 131; maps drawn by Paul Mitchell.

the marginal dates reveal that credit was taken in the fall of the year in the 1820s but was given year-round by 1840. Second, in the 1820s ledgers next to each individual's list of trade goods is a column recording repayment. Here the trader recorded the furs and hides each hunter used to repay his or her debt, or more often the trader simply wrote a short phrase such as "Paid in Skins" or "All Paid" to indicate the completion of a reciprocal business agreement. No such column exists in the 1840 Eddy ledger. This missing column symbolizes significant changes in the Sauk and Mesquakie subsistence economy and their relations with the U.S. government. Money from treaty negotiations, not furs and hides, balanced the ledger.

The number of hunters taking credit, the average credit purchase, and the total amount of credit given are summarized in table 1. In any one year one-third of the Sauk and Mesquakie hunters took credit with Farnham and Davenport in the 1820s. Twelve years later, in 1840, almost all of the heads of households in the Sauk and Mesquakie nations took some credit with Eddy, although his trade was generally with members of the villages of chiefs Hardfish and Kishkekosh. Through all four ledgers there is a great disparity in individual credit, ranging from fifty cents to several hundred dollars; the small credit customers, those in the lower third, took less than 10 percent of the total dollar amount of credit, while the large credit customers, the top one-third, received two-thirds of all the credit given out. While this pattern is constant from 1826 to 1840, the reasons for the disparity change through time.

Table 1. Summary of Debits in Ledgers 1826-1840.

Year	Number of cases	Mean Purchase on credit	Minimum Debit	Maximum Debit	Total
1826	316	$59.38	$1.00	$218.50	$18,764.60
1827	310	$43.45	$1.00	$173.50	$13,470.00
1828	289	$46.67	$1.50	$252.00	$13,487.50
1840	549	$51.47	$0.50	$491.13	$28,257.42[1]

(1) Does not include sums charged to the Sauk and Mesquakie nation as a whole.

Sources: Credit Ledgers, 1826, 1827, and 1828, George Davenport Papers, Augustana College, Rock Island, Illinois; J.P. Eddy and Company, Credit Ledger, 1840-1841, Ottumwa Public Library, Ottumwa, Iowa (photocopy, State Historical Society of Iowa, Iowa City).

The early dynamics of debt creation and relief among the Sauk and Mesquakie can be traced in some detail in the three credit ledgers of the 1820s. Figure 3 outlines the repayment of debts. Debts could be expunged by paying in skins or by returning some of the more expensive, durable merchandise such as rifles, guns, or kettles (at full credit value), but it was the return in furs and hides that made

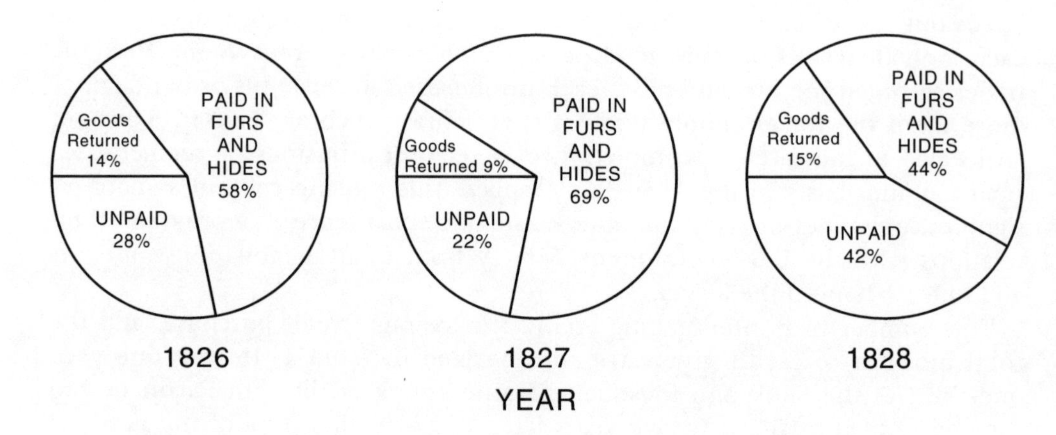

Figure 3. Return on Credit. Sources: Credit Ledgers, 1826, 1827, and 1828, George Davenport Papers, Augustana College, Rock Island, Illinois. Figures drawn by Paul Mitchell.

the trader's profit. In the best scenario a return in skins of 50 percent on credit goods was necessary to break even. In the 1826 ledger there was a skin return of 58 percent, and the company lost money. The summer of 1826 was unusually dry, and game, particularly muskrats, were scarce that winter. The year 1828 was even more disastrous. A war with the Dakota caused the Sauk and Mesquakie to call an abrupt halt to the winter hunt, and its effects are obvious in the ledger.[12]

Between 80 percent and 90 percent of the hunters did make some effort to repay their debts, but the repayment varied depending on whether their debts were relatively large or small. Almost all (97 percent) of the large credit takers paid something on their debts, the amount they paid back varying from 63 percent in a particularly bad year, 1828, to 82 percent in 1827, an average season. Only 60 percent to 78 percent of the small credit takers made an attempt to pay back their debts, but the general strategy for these small debtors was to either pay their debts off completely or forget them entirely; the success of the season was crucial in determining how many of them paid their debts.

The top credit users were disproportionately the regular or repeat users of credit. Regulars took larger credits on the average and paid back at higher rates. They dominated the top third, forming 80 percent to 90 percent of this group, while the bottom third was evenly split between regular and one-time credit users. The one-timers as a group returned 50 percent to 60 percent on their credits, while the regulars returned 60 percent to 80 percent. If fur and hide returns had to be above 50 percent in order to realize a profit, then Davenport and Farnham's business relied on good returns from regulars to keep their business going.

The Sauk and Mesquakie hunters were not credit "maximizers." They did not pay back credit in order to obtain more goods on credit the next year. I compared hunters who had received credits above the mean in 1826 but paid back below the sample mean for that year with a group who did the reverse, that is, received credits below the mean but paid back at a rate higher than the mean percentage return. Those who had large credits and made poor returns tended in the succeeding years to obtain credit above the mean and pay back at rates below average. The second group of hunters did exactly the reverse; they continued to take credits below the mean and pay back at rates slightly higher than the mean. There were also 283 hunters identified as receiving credit only once in the three years from 1826 to 1828. Of these, 210 made a return on credit. Certainly many of these individuals were eligible for future extensions of credit, but they did not exercise the option. While nonpayment of debts surely weighed against future extensions of credit, Sauk and Mesquakie hunters were not behaving as though credit were scarce, competitive, or necessary. They showed no particular desire to work for increased credit purchases over time.

A look at the individual trade goods taken on credit fills out the picture of credit utilization in the 1820s, and the different goods purchased on credit indicate the changes that were taking place in the Sauk and Mesquakie economy in the 1830s and 1840s. Between fifty and one hundred different kinds of trade goods show up with varying frequency in the credit ledgers, ranging from blankets, yardgoods, and shirts through knives, hatchets, and kettles to flints, traps, powder, and rifles. Conspicuously missing from the credit ledgers (but prominent in inventories) were items of personal adornment, such as beads, vermilion, and armbands. Traders were generally unwilling to risk these items on credit. Spirituous liquor is another item not in the ledgers. Descriptions from the 1820s suggest that it entered the trade as a present or as a direct purchase.[13] In the 1840s it was supplied by border traders who exchanged liquor for trade goods which were then traded back to the licensed traders.[14]

Two simple ways to analyze goods taken on credit are to look at the most frequently purchased goods and the goods consuming the most credit (figure 4 and 5). The most popular credit goods in the 1820s were generally hunt-related—lead, flints, powder, and knives—although blankets were common as well as tobacco. The 1840s are strikingly different. The year-round credit business is reflected in the changed mix of goods. Blanket sales dominated the fall credits, while cottons were popular at other times of the year. The appearance of shirts (as well as stockings, breeches, and shoes) is indicative of increased use and reliance on ready-made clothing. Flour was also a benchmark of the rapid deterioration of self-reliance in the Sauk and Mesquakie economy. Including lard, beef, and pork, Eddy furnished over 45,000 pounds of food on credit. Food items were a rarity in the 1820s ledgers as well as in the early inventories. While hunting was still an important pursuit in the 1840s, it was no longer as productive of food or furs. (Chouteau and Company, with better access to eastern and international markets, was the provider of what rifles and guns were necessary for the fall hunt.[15])

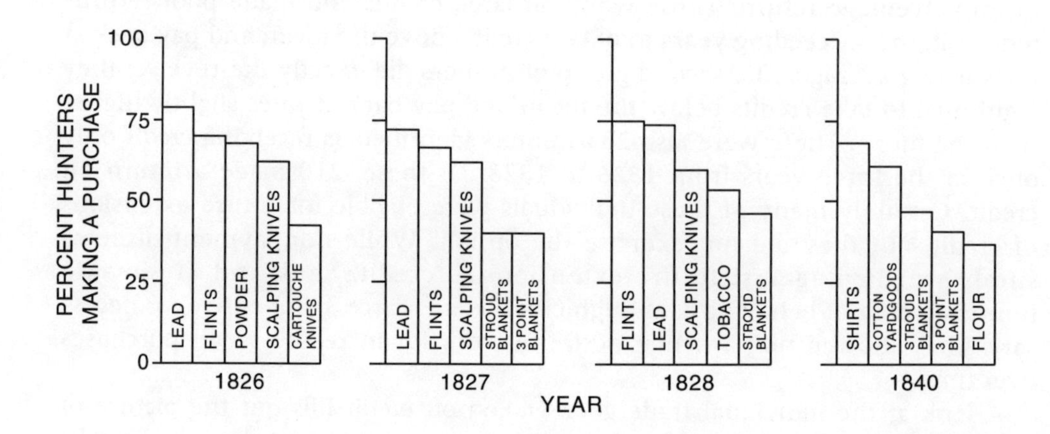

Figure 4. The Five Items Most Frequently Purchased on Credit. Sources: Credit Ledgers, 1826, 1827, and 1828, George Davenport Papers, Augustana College, Rock Island, Illinois. Figure drawn by Paul Mitchell.

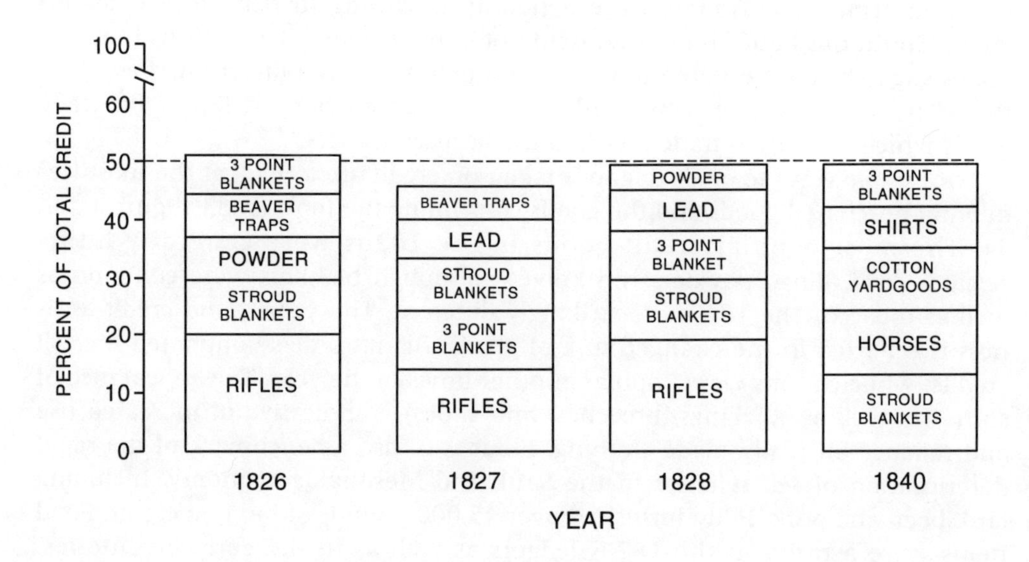

Figure 5. The Five Items Consuming the Largest Percentage of Credit. Sources: Credit Ledgers, 1826, 1827, and 1828, George Davenport Papers, Augustana College, Rock Island, Illinois. Figure drawn by Paul Mitchell.

In the 1820s, two items that were never "frequently" purchased—rifles and beaver traps—accounted for upwards of a quarter of the total credit outlay (see figure 5). Beaver traps at $6.00 to $8.00 apiece were purchased almost exclusively by large credit takers. The chiefs and older men were the beaver hunters. They had the horses and political connections to hunt beyond the boundaries of conventional Sauk and Mesquakie territory, which had long been trapped out of beaver.[16]

Horses rather than hunting equipment were important credit purchases from Eddy in 1840. Horses and horse equipment were products of local, frontier markets. As the frontier moved closer, these markets were more accessible; but also, as the Sauk and Mesquakie moved west, the utility of the horse increased. The ledgers and contemporary literature reflect an increased demand, increased availability, and increased ability to purchase horses. These purchases replace the earlier beaver traps and rifles in being a set of goods that highlight the purchases of the heavy credit users.

The general impression left by writers of the early nineteenth century was that fall credit provided goods essential to the livelihood of the hunter. The 1820s ledgers certainly featured goods essential to the fall hunt, with the preponderance in credit layout for rifles, traps, powder, lead, knives, and blankets. What belies these statements is the fact that many hunters made what may best be described as only token purchases on credit. Certainly a hunter with a credit purchase of 15 flints and a 2-point blanket was not outfitted for the winter hunt. Yet fully one-third of the 1820s credit purchases were of this ilk. The purchases of small credit takers were not even as concentrated on the most essential items of flint, powder, and lead as those of heavier users of credit, who purchased these items more frequently. With increasing credit individuals tended to purchase "essential," small-priced items more frequently as well as the high-priced items responsible for large outlays of credit. For example, small debtors in the 1820s included flints in their credit purchases only about half the time, while large credit takers bought flints over 80 percent of the time.

Two strategies appear to have been operating in the purchase of goods on credit. First, the average hunter probably purchased a mix of goods outright with skins and on credit. Because the items acquired on credit were more expensive than the items purchased outright, surely some hunters operated on a purchase basis, relying on credit for only a few missing items.[17] The goods could be purchased with the proceeds of the summer deer hunt conducted in July and August.

Second, a number of hunters (some of whom were leaders of hunting bands) were making multiple purchases of many items, suggesting that they were supplying others in their hunting band with partial outfits. The combination of outright purchase and the acceptance of goods from another hunter's credit purchases meant that an individual's credit could range widely from a dollar to over $250, with a mean settling around the standard amount for credit purchases of $30.00 to $50.00. A "bare bones hunting kit," which should have been particularly apparent at the lower end of the credit scale, did not exist. Purchases by small credit takers were almost random as hunters added the small and miscellaneous items to their hunting equipages that were missed, used up, or not obtainable through gift or loan from the leader of their hunting group.

The 1820s credit ledgers reflect seasonal preference for different goods, the willingness of the trader to risk certain goods on credit and not others, his desire to curtail credit (which was dependent on surrounding competition), the prospects for the fall hunt, the chances of war, and finally, the differing economic strategies of the hunters themselves. These economic strategies in turn were rooted in the socio-political organization of Sauk and Mesquakie society. The top credit takers were often the leaders of hunting parties and were important individuals in the political councils of the tribe. They were supplying confreres, probably members of their hunting bands, with goods purchased on credit.

While the individual hunter in the heyday of the fur trade was responsible for setting his or her own debts, there are scattered statements indicating that band leaders and councils, in a fashion reminiscent of the more northerly trading chiefs, did intercede between their constituency and the trader. These early instances perhaps provided a model for the credit system as it emerged in the 1830s and 1840s.[18]

The traders were quick to realize that annuity payments from land sales were a valuable source of specie and used the credit system to gain access to these funds. Even the two thousand dollars received annually from the 1804 and 1824 treaties brought an avid response from the traders. Davenport wrote on 27 June 1826, "I have credited the Sack and Fox chiefs good to the amt. of one thousand dollars to be payed in cash as soon as they [have] received [it] from Mr. Forsyth [the Indian agent]."[19] The process of indemnifying tribal funds through purchases made by the chiefs had begun; the chiefs in turn were using treaty funds to cover purchases used as presents to the loyal and needy. By 1835, credit was given on a year-round basis, and the extension of credit for the purpose of creating debts collectible from money provided by treaties was recognized by all parties as a business quite apart from the older, ongoing use of credit in the fur trade.[20] This system evolved to such an extent that by 1840 J.P. Eddy, as a matter of course, kept separate ledger entries entitled "Foxes in General Bill," "Sac and Fox General Bill," and "Wase cam ma quats [Hardfish] Village." This "national debt" composed 16 percent of Eddy's total charges against the Sauk and Mesquakie. In contrast to individual debts, the largest proportion of the national debt was for food, with flour and corn being the largest purchases, although beef and pork were not inconsequential. Powder, lead, and vermilion were also frequently occurring items on the General Bill. All of these goods were readily divisible for easy distribution. The General Bill was used in part for meeting the social and economic obligations of the chiefs and had replaced the presents provided by the U.S. and British in the early 1820s as a source for distribution to the poor, needy, and loyal.[21]

By the mid-1830s, chiefs were also given more access to personal credit, undoubtedly because of their ability to control the payment of debts through treaty negotiations. Caroline Phelps, wife of a fur trader, asked for advice from

Indian Agent Joseph Street on giving credit to several Mesquakies. She had been left with instructions to credit no one but chiefs and was anxious to know if the chiefly claims of the current applicants for credit were indeed true.[22]

The chiefs in any one year did not form a large part of the credit takers—around 6 percent, similar to or a little higher than their frequency in the larger pool of Sauk and Mesquakie hunters.[23] They did receive, on the average, larger amounts of credit than the common hunter (see table 2); they also tended to pay back at higher rates than the average credit taker. There is little reason to believe that chiefs prior to 1830 were accumulating any significant amounts of personal debt or that their use of credit differed markedly from that of other leaders of hunting groups. Even chiefs' names appeared and disappeared from the ledger book. The choice between hunting or war was a particularly tempting one for chiefs building a reputation. Chiefs also travelled extensively and could be gone for several years at a time. The 1820s traders, if they were wooing political favors, were doing so with gifts and other means outside the credit system.

TABLE 2. PERSONAL CREDIT OF CHIEFS.

	1826	1827	1828	1840
Number (chiefs)	18	18	17	14
Mean	$ 99.65	$ 70.58	$ 68.47	$ 147.11
%Return	88%	89%	63%	—
Total debtors	316	310	289	549
Mean	$ 59.38	$ 43.45	$ 46.67	$ 51.47
%Return	72%	78%	58%	—

Sources: See table 1; Royce Kurtz, "Economic and Political History of the Sauk and Mesquakie, 1780s-1845" (Ph.D. dissertation, University of Iowa), 252-259.

Looking at the top few credit takers in each of the four ledgers, only in 1840 do the top positions correspond with the most powerful individuals. While Keokuk and Pashapaho were the two most powerful individuals in the Sauk nation in the 1820s, they were never the first or second heaviest users of credit. Ten years later, when credit was tied to annuity money and annuities were paid to those chiefs who were heads of villages and had the political clout to demand a share, Kishkekosh and Hardfish were at the top of Eddy's credit ledger.

While both defenders and detractors have left descriptions of the credit arrangements between trader and Native American, none hinted at the number of options, strategies, and different patterns of utilization that were found by analyzing the 1820s ledgers. The trade was truly a negotiated business. The traders Davenport and Farnham were never without competition, although they generally controlled three-fourths of the trade. In any one year, only one-third of

Figures 6 and 7. *Keokuk* and the old civil chief, *Pashapaho* (on the right), were two of the most powerful headmen of the large Sauk town of Saukenauk. Prior to the Black Hawk War of 1832, the Sauk council could, and did, make foreign policy independently of the needs and wishes of the traders. Painted by George Catlin. National Museum of American Art, Smithsonian Institution, gift of Mrs. Joseph Harrison, Jr.

Figure 8. Kishkekosh was the leader of a Mesquakie village closely allied with the trader J.P. Eddy. After the Black Hawk War, traders seeking money from annuities and treaties were active and decisive players in Sauk and Mesquakie foreign policy. This painting first appeared in *History of the Indian Tribes of North America*, by Thomas L. McKenney and James Hall (Philadelphia: Daniel Rice and James G. Clark, 1842), vol. 2, following page 48. Courtesy of the William L. Clements Library, The University of Michigan.

the area's hunters took credit with Davenport and Farnham. The rest found credit from other traders, received goods from confreres (who were often band leaders), purchased their goods outright, or simply did not participate in the trade, being involved in war, travel, or other pursuits. The trader, for his part, was more or less eager to give out credit, depending on competition, the mood of the main office, the prospects of the season for game, and the chances of war, but then the credit was only for goods related to hunting, trapping, and camp life. Roughly 40 percent of the trader's goods went out on credit, and the trader needed a return in furs and hides of at least 50 percent to break even.

He relied on his regular customers to turn a profit, and his regular customers were generally the heavier users of credit, although even here the amount paid back was only one of many factors influencing next year's credit. The Sauk and Mesquakie hunters did not pay off their debts in order to obtain larger credits the next year. The socio-political structure of the Sauk and Mesquakie hunting bands also affected credit patterns. Band and group leaders were often heavy credit takers and shared their credit purchases with other hunters. Because of their organizational abilities and their kin networks, they could also pay off their debts.

This viable world had changed radically by 1840. While credit was still given to individuals, the individual was no longer responsible for payment. The money from land sales now covered trade goods debts. The ongoing hide trade was a very small part of the business, and with the loss of valuable hunting grounds to the advancing Anglo-American frontier, the ability of the hunt to sustain either the subsistence economy or the trade faltered. Products from the local frontier, including food, liquor, ready-made clothing, and horses, became popular and expensive items in the trade, symbolizing the rapid collapse of Sauk and Mesquakie economic self-reliance. As the heads of villages controlled the annuities payments, their credit lines were the largest, and they used items purchased on credit to reward the loyal and care for the needy. Credit and payback no longer reflected a range of choices and life-ways based on hunting but symbolized a growing dependence on foreign goods for basic needs. Credit became an issue of national policy for both the Sauk and Mesquakie and the U.S. government; but with the large amounts of hard currency from land sales and with increasing numbers of traders, store owners, and frontier settlers vying for this money, corrupt practices soon infected both commercial and political dealings.

Contemporary chroniclers reported events from their own vantage point, be it Sauk chief, British trader, or American government agent. Speeches, letters, and reports emphasized nagging problems and detailed new happenings, accenting those issues speakers wished their audience to know. The anthropologist and the social historian must see around these discussions of problems and events in recreating the workaday world of Native American and European interaction; ledgers kept by trading companies provide an excellent access to that social and economic world created by traders and hunters. The columned ledger pages allow the historian to analyze thousands of routine meetings between traders and hunters. They reveal that the Sauk and Mesquakie hunters were not as debt ridden as their harried (albeit solvent) merchants would have had us believe. Nor was the average hunter as addicted to trade goods as the council of chiefs and the reports of Indian agents would have suggested. Ledgers also provide insight into topics seldom mentioned in the written record, such as Sauk and Mesquakie attitudes toward credit and the social organization of hunting bands. The Sauk and Mesquakie hunters did not try to increase their access to credit from one year to the next, rather, band leaders were the larger credit takers and shared their goods with fellow hunters. Finally, the comparison of ledgers from different years reveals radical changes in how the Sauk and Mesquakie nations dealt with their traders. Not only did the mix of goods purchased change over time, but there was also a growing rapprochement between political power and access to trade goods. Ledger books with their tattered corners and repetitious columns of script and cipher, of debits and credits, can speak intimately of the conflicts and compromises that created the negotiated world of European traders and Sauk and Mesquakie hunters.

NOTES

1. Harold Hickerson, "Fur Trade Colonialism and the North American Indians," *Journal of Ethnic Studies* 1 (1973): 15-44; Robert F. Murphy and Julian Steward, "Tappers and Trappers: Parallel Processes in Acculturation," *Development and Cultural Change* 4 (1956): 335-55; Francis Jennings, *Empire of Fortune; Crowns, Colonies, and Tribes in the Seven Years War in America* (New York: W.W. Norton, 1988), 50; Daniel H. Usner, *Indians, Settlers, and Slaves in a Frontier Exchange Economy* (Chapel Hill: The University of North Carolina Press, 1992), 261-66, 284; see also discussion of trade dependency in Richard White, *The Middle Ground; Indians, Empires, and Republics in the Great Lakes Region, 1650-1815* (Cambridge: Cambridge University Press, 1991), 476-93.
2. Credit Ledgers, 1819, 1826, 1827, 1828, and 1830, George Davenport Papers, Augustana College, Rock Island, Ill.; J.P. Eddy and Company, Credit Ledger, 1840-1841, Ottumwa Public Library, Ottumwa, Iowa (photocopy, State Historical Society of Iowa, Iowa City, Iowa).
3. For details on population, territory, and subsistence, see Royce Kurtz, "Economic and Political History of the Sauk and Mesquakie, 1780s-1845" (Ph.D. diss., University of Iowa, 1986).
4. Claude Charles Le Roy, Bacqueville de la Potherie, "History of the Savage Peoples Who Are Allies of New France," in *The Indian Tribes of the Upper Mississippi Valley and Region of the Great Lakes,* 2 vols., ed. Emma Helen Blair (Cleveland, Ohio: Arthur H. Clark Co., 1911-1912), 1: 217-319; Paul Marin, "Journal de Marin, fils, 1753-1754," *Rapport des Archives du Quebec* 41(1963), 255; Peter Pond, "The Narrative of Peter Pond," in *Five Fur Traders of the Northwest,* ed. Charles M. Gates (Minneapolis: University of Minnesota Press, 1965), 34, 40.
5. David Lavender, *The Fist in the Wilderness* (Garden City, N.Y.: Doubleday, 1964), 270-71, 338-42; U.S. Congress, Senate, *Message from the President of the United States, in Compliance with a Resolution of the Senate Concerning the Fur Trade, and Inland Trade to Mexico,* 22nd Cong., 1st Sess., S. Doc. 90 (Serial 213), 70.

6. Kurtz, "Economic and Political History," 141-46.
7. U.S. Congress, Senate, *Fur Trade and Inland Trade*, 45.
8. Receipt Rolls, 19 October 1841, Papers of Joseph Montfort Street, 1806-1844, Aldrich Collection, Iowa State Department of Archives and History, Des Moines (microfilm, University of Iowa Library).
9. Sums compiled from ratified treaties, Charles J. Kappler, *Indian Treaties, 1778-1883* (New York: Interland Publishers, 1972).
10. Robert A. Trennert, *Indian Traders on the Middle Border; The House of Ewing, 1827-54* (Lincoln, Neb.: University of Nebraska Press, 1981).
11. Kurtz, "Political and Economic History," 168.
12. Davenport to Crooks, 3 November 1826, Farnham to Bostwick, 28 November 1826, Chouteau-Papin Collection, 1822-1826; Davenport to main office, 23 December 1828, Maffitt Collection, 1827-1834, Missouri Historical Society, St. Louis.
13. Black Hawk, *Ma-Ka-Tai-Me-She-Kia-Kiak, Black Hawk, An Autobiography*, ed. Donald Jackson (Urbana, Ill.: University of Illinois Press, 1955), 101-2.
14. Chambers to Office of Indian Affairs, 24 October 1841, *Letters Received by the Office of Indian Affairs, 1824- 41; Sac and Fox Agency, 1824-1880*, National Archives Microfilm Publications M234, microfilm reel 731 (Washington, D.C., 1956).
15. Pierre Chouteau, Jr., and Co., Invoices Outward, February 1834-October 1839, Vol. Y; Invoice Blotter, 1839-1842, Vol. DD, Missouri Historical Society, St. Louis.
16. Thomas Forsyth, *Thomas Forsyth Papers, 1812-1832*, 9 vols., Draper Manuscript Series T, microfilm reel 53, State Historical Society of Wisconsin, Madison, 4: 168-69, 216, 222.
17. Thomas Anderson, "Narrative of Capt. Thomas G. Anderson," *Wisconsin Historical Collections* 9 (1882): 150; U.S. Congress, Senate, *Fur Trade and Inland Trade*, 72.
18. Black Hawk, *Ma-Ka-Tai-Me-She-Kia-Kiak*, 107; George Hunt, "Old Fort Madison: Some Source Materials," *Iowa Journal of History and Politics* 11 (1913): 520.
19. Davenport to Bostwick, 27 June 1826, Chouteau-Papin Collection.
20. Council held 4 June 1835, *Letters Received: Sac and Fox Agency*, microfilm reel 729; Allen to Jones, 16 June 1844, *Letters Received by the Office of Indians Affairs, 1824-81; Raccoon Agency, 1843-1845*, National Archives, Microfilm Publications M234, microfilm reel 714 (Washington, D.C., 1959).
21. For references to presents made by the U.S. government, see *Forsyth Papers* 3:11, 16, 35, 37, 43; 4:159; for mention of presents received from the British government in Canada, see *Forsyth Papers* 4: 48, 177, 193, 260; 6: 88, 95.
22. Phelps to Street, n.d., Papers of Joseph Montfort Street.
23. Kurtz, "Political and Economic History," 252-59.

"Half-Breed" Rolls and Fur Trade Families in the Great Lakes Region—An Introduction and Bibliography

James L. Hansen

Most of the individuals who worked in the fur trade, as in many occupational fields, are very poorly documented. Because much fur trade activity took place in areas with little or no governmental control, comparatively few records were created, outside the trade itself, that even named the workers. Typically, identifying or quantifying these individuals can be accomplished only by extremely careful comparison of such arid sources as contracts, licenses, accounts, and *engagements*. Therefore, any source providing significant detail on these workers, their families, and connections, should be welcome to researchers. In the course of research on the early settlement of Prairie du Chien, it has been possible to identify a significant body of material that has apparently not come to the attention of historians of the Upper Midwest fur trade—the records relating to payments from the U.S. government to the mixed bloods of the various Midwestern tribes. The records relating to these payments, though widely scattered and often difficult to find, can be an important and useful source of information on many of the individuals involved in the fur trade with those tribes. They are described in detail in the bibliography below.

When the U.S. government entered into treaties with the various Indian tribes, it was concerned mainly with obtaining land and making whatever arrangements were necessary to obtain that land. During the period of major cessions in the Great Lakes-Upper Mississippi region, the tribes also came to expect some sort of settlement for their mixed-blood relations. Because those relations, not being members of the tribe, did not normally benefit from the annuities and other settlements, special provision was made for them. Between 1817 and 1833 that provision was normally for reserves, grants of federal land to specified individuals.[1] Because the reserves system was discovered to be so cumbersome, a system of cash payments was decided upon and was first brought into effect at the Treaty of Chicago in 1833. From 1833 to 1849 the government, when negotiating and drawing up a treaty, normally set aside a sum of money to be divided among the mixed bloods.[2]

Although the exact procedure varied from treaty to treaty, it was customary in the early (reserves) period for the individuals to be identified by name in the

Figure 1. *Prairie du Chien* painted by Seth Eastman. Watercolor, 1846-1848. Courtesy of Minnesota Historical Society, No. 56236.

treaty itself or in a separate council; the list was then forwarded to the federal authorities for action. That action was often very slow in coming. The "half-breed tract" granted to the eastern Sioux in 1830 was not divided and made available for more than twenty-five years, despite continued importunities from the individuals involved. By the time it was available the pressure for white settlement was so strong that, in exchange for relinquishing their claims to the tract, the mixed bloods were granted certificates to obtain federal land elsewhere.

Because they took so long to be settled, the reserves created a sizeable mass of paperwork, correspondence, petitions, claims, depositions, and complaints. Some of this material is found in the general correspondence of the Bureau of Indian Affairs, but much of it appears either in the "reserves" supplement to individual agencies' correspondence, or in the reserves files in the records of the BIA (RG 75) at the National Archives. This material frequently contains considerable biographical and genealogical information on the individuals involved, information that is otherwise not easily come by. Also, because the reserves system involved the granting of land, additional records will often be found in the records of the General Land Office (RG 49) at the National Archives.

The records relating to cash payments are usually not as voluminous as the reserves records nor do they cover as broad a span of time, but they typically relate to larger numbers of individuals and provide a "snapshot" of a mixed-blood community at a particular time. Although details varied from treaty to

Figure 2. Rachel (Lawe) Grignon (1808-1876), daughter of John Lawe of Green Bay and his wife Therese Rankin, daughter of David Rankin and Therese "Neckickoqua," a Chippewa of Lac du Flambeau. Courtesy of State Historical Society of Wisconsin, WHi (X3) 24634.

treaty, the normal prcedure was for a sum of money to be set aside specifically for the mixed bloods. The president appointed a commissioner or commissioners to take testimony and, with the approval of a tribal council, to judge whether particular claims were valid and see that the money was distributed accordingly. The commissioner usually created a roll of the applicants, listing for each the name, age, residence, fraction of blood, and specific tribe claimed, whether the claim was accepted or rejected, and the amount awarded. Some commissioners added further details such as birthplace, name of spouse, parent, or guardian, or the reason for the denial of a claim.

The rolls usually listed applicants in family groups, so they can be of considerable value in sorting out the members of complex families. Also, because the rolls typically listed all applicants, whether successful or not, the range of families covered is often quite broad. Considerable care must be taken, however, when drawing biographical or genealogical conclusions from these records. The qualifications were often quite specific, so rejection did not necessarily mean that the applicants were not mixed bloods of the particular tribe or band involved in that particular treaty; perhaps the family simply resided outside the bounds of the land ceded in the treaty (a common exclusion), or did not meet some other technical qualification.

The information that can be gleaned from these records, even for comparatively significant and well-documented families, can be demonstrated by a brief look at the family of Archibald/John Campbell of Prairie du Chien.[3] Archibald (known generally as John) Campbell traded in the Prairie du Chien area from the late 1780s until his death in a duel at Michilimackinac in 1808. Because of his influence with the Indian tribes in the area and his pro-American sympathies, he was named Indian agent in December 1807. At his death he left two apparently white sons (John and Jeremiah) and five mixed-blood children—three boys (Colin, Duncan, and Scott) and two girls (Nancy and Margaret). Those mixed-blood children all had connections to the fur trade and the mixed-blood records provide much useful detail about them. They help separate Duncan (who died ca. 1840) from his son, Duncan, Jr., and clearly identify Colin with the Colin Campbell active at Fort Pierre with the American Fur Company (and thus separate him from others of the name).[4] The records testify to the continuing family connections and the geographic range of the family—in 1855 Scott Campbell's son, Antoine Joseph, provided the depositions supporting the claims of his uncle Colin (of Fort Pierre) and his aunt Nancy, wife of John Palmer Bourke of the Red River settlement in Canada. Also, they provide evidence that Margaret Campbell had a long-term relationship with Hercules Dousman of Prairie du Chien and had two children by him. In fact, Archibald/John Campbell's sons, John and Jeremiah, are much more difficult to separate and identify in the records precisely because they were not mixed bloods.

These records are not a magical guide—they were created for a specific and limited purpose—but when used in conjunction with the more traditional fur trade records, correspondence and accounts, treaty traders' claims, census, court and land records, they can be a useful addition to the resources available to the researcher.

BIBLIOGRAPHY: UPPER-MIDWEST MIXED-BLOOD ROLLS AND RELATED RECORDS, 1824-1857

The materials described below are only the basic records relating to these mixed-blood treaty settlements. Additional material will often be found in the correspondence of the Bureau of Indian Affairs, both incoming and outgoing for the various agencies, sub-agencies, and superintendencies involved, in petition files of federal and state/territorial legislative bodies, in manuscript collections of individuals involved in the treaties and payments, and in the land and court records of the appropriate jurisdictions. Details of treaty provisions are from volume 2 of *Indian Affairs. Laws and Treaties* by Charles J. Kappler (Washington, D.C., 1904).

Treaty with the Sauk and Fox, 4 August 1824 at Washington, D.C.

Article 1 set aside "the small tract of land lying between the rivers Desmoin and the Mississippi, and the section of the above line between the Mississippi and the Desmoin" for "the use of the half-breeds of the Sock and Fox nation." A list of mixed-blood Sauk and Fox eligible is in the papers of Thomas Forsythe (2T8) in the Draper manuscript collection, State Historical Society of Wisconsin, with copies in the William Clark Papers, Kansas Historical Society. Claims and supporting testimony, ca. 1834, are also in the Clark papers, vol. 36 (roll 6 of the microfilm edition).

Treaty with the Chippewa, 5 August 1826 at Fond du Lac on Lake Superior

A half-breed tract set aside in article 4. A schedule of ca. 90 half-breeds was appended to the treaty (Kappler, 2:272-273). Article 4 was not confirmed by the Senate, so no further files were created.

Treaty with the Chippewa, Ottawa, and Potawatomie, 29 July 1829 at Prairie du Chien

Article 4 granted reserves to 14 named individuals.

Treaty with the Winnebago, 1 August 1829 at Prairie du Chien

Article 5 granted reserves to 41 named individuals. Extensive files related to these reserves, including many petitions and depositions, are in reserves file A, records of the Bureau of Indian Affairs, record group 75, National Archives. Additional records are in "Winnebago Agency Reserves, 1836-1847," "Letters

Received by the Bureau of Indian Affairs" (National Archives Microfilm, M234 roll 947).

Treaty with the Sauk and Fox, several bands of the Sioux, the Omaha, Iowa, Otoe, and Missouri, 15 July 1830 at Prairie du Chien

Article 9 set aside the Lake Pepin half-breed tract. Although the treaty was made in 1830, most of the records relating to the half-breed tract date from the 1850s. Because of repeated delays by the government, despite regular pleas from those interested in the tract, the tide of white settlement had reached the area with the status still unsettled. The mixed bloods were persuaded to relinquish their interest in the tract in exchange for certificates allowing them to enter federal land elsewhere. A commission in 1855 took testimony and prepared a roll of eligible persons. The roll, identifying 642 individuals plus a supplement of 38, lists the name, age, fraction of blood, parent or guardian, and residence of each individual; this is inventory #378, records of the Bureau of Indian Affairs, RG 75, National Archives. A transcript by James L. Hansen was published as "A Roll of Mixed-Blood Sioux, 1855-56" in *Minnesota Genealogical Journal* no. 7 (Nov. 1987): 601-20. The receipt roll is inventory #381, RG 75, National Archives. The testimony upon which the rolls were based is in the Miscellaneous Reserves file, records of the Bureau of Indian Affairs, RG 75, National Archives, along with a wealth of correspondence, depositions, and powers of attorney relating to the claims. Records relating to the individuals and the scrip received and its use are in "Sioux half-breed scrip," inventory #24, "Land Entry Papers at the General Land Office," RG 49, National Archives. Correspondence, petitions and claims from the 1830s into the early 1850s can be found in the correspondence of the various agencies and superintendencies, especially "St. Peter's Agency Reserves, 1839-1849" (M 234 roll 766) and some items misfiled in "Upper Missouri Agency Reserve, 1837-1849" (M 234 roll 888).

Article 10 set aside the Little Nemaha half-breed tract. Its history was similar to that of the Lake Pepin tract. The roll, "List of Half-Breeds and Mixed Blood Indians composed of Omahas, Ioways, Ottoes and Yancton and Santee Sioux entitled under Treaty of July 15, 1830 to Participate in the Benefits of the Half Breed Reservation lying between the Great and Little Nemaha Rivers" is inventory #399, records of the Bureau of Indian Affairs, RG 75, National Archives. The history of the tract is detailed in Tanis C. Thorne's "People of the River: Mixed-Blood Families on the Lower Missouri" (Ph.D. diss. University of California at Los Angeles, 1987), especially chapter 7, "The Great Nemaha Tract," 350-406.

Treaty with the Chippewa, Ottawa, and Potawatomie, 26 September 1833 at Chicago

Article 3 set aside $100,000 "to satisfy sundry individuals," nearly all mixed bloods. An appended "Schedule A" contained the names and "sums payable to individuals in Lieu of reservations" (Kappler, 2: 404-6). Supplementary articles to the treaty, 27 Sept. 1833, in article 2 set aside an additional $10,000 "to satisfy sundry individuals," about 30 more (Kappler, 2: 412).

Treaty with bands of the Ottawa and Chippewa, 28 March 1836 at Washington, D.C.

Article 6 set aside $150,000 for the half-breeds, $10,000 of that sum for poor relief, along with detailed instructions for making the payment. The roll of 4 September 1836, identifying 584 individuals, listing for each the name, age, residence and length of residence, fraction of blood and tribe, the decision of the commissioner, the amount paid and to whom payable, and "remarks" on most is in file #124, "Claim of Charles (or Isaac) Butterfield," "Special Files of the Office of Indian Affairs" (National Archives Microfilm Publication, M574 roll 23).

Treaty with the Menominee, 3 September 1836 at Cedar Point on the Fox River near Green Bay

Article 2 set aside $80,000 for the mixed-bloods. The actual roll, naming more than 500 individuals, listing for each the name, age, residence, length of residence, fraction of Menominee blood, and to whom payable has not been found, but notes of the testimony taken by the commissioner, John W. Edmonds, are in "Journals of Commissions, 1824-1839," RG 75, National Archives. Two excerpts from the roll related to late payments have been identified, one (68 names) in the "Records of the Wisconsin Superintendency, 1836-1848" (M 951, roll 1), the other (12 names) in the 1839 claim of John Garland in "Indian Accounts," records of the General Accounting Office, RG 217, National Archives.

Treaty with the Sauk and Fox, 28 September 1836 in Dubuque County, Wisconsin Territory

Article 4 made provision for seven half-breed children.

Treaty with the Chippewa, 29 July 1837 at St. Peters

Article 3 set aside $100,000 to the half-breeds of the Chippewa nation. Payment was made in 1839. The roll naming 879 claimants, their fraction of Chippewa blood, age, residence, birthplace and the decision of the commissioner is in the claim of Henry R. Schoolcraft, 1840, in the "Indian Accounts," records of the General Accounting Office, RG 217, National Archives. A transcript by James L. Hansen appeared as "A List of the Mixed-Blood Chippewa of Lake Superior, 1839" in *Lost in Canada?; Canadian-American Genealogical Journal* 16 no. 1 (Spring 1991): 27-45.

Treaty with the Sioux, 29 September 1837 at Washington D.C.

The 3rd article set aside "to pay to the relatives and friends of the chiefs and braves, as aforesaid having not less than one quarter of Sioux blood, $110,000." The pay roll, listing for each of 200 individuals the name, age, fraction of Sioux blood (half or quarter), and residence appears in File #200, "Special Files of the Office of Indian Affairs" (M 574, roll 59). A transcript by James L. Hansen appeared as part of "Two Early Lists of Mixed-Blood Sioux" in *Minnesota Genealogical Journal*, no. 6 (Nov. 1986): 523-30.

Treaty with the Winnebago, 1 November 1837 at Washington D.C.

Article 4, part 2, set aside $100,000 "to relatives and friends having at least 1/4 blood." An extensive file of applications, depositions, petitions, and correspondence relating to the claims is in files #161, 186, 190, 197, 206, "Special Files of the Office of Indian Affairs," (M 574 rolls 34, 53, 55, 58), also found in the microfilmed "Territorial Papers of the United States; Wisconsin" (M 236 rolls 41-42). Special File #206 is only in M236.

Treaty with the Chippewa, 4 October 1842 at Lapointe

Article 4 set aside $15,000 to the half-breed relatives, to be paid next year to the Indians as a present to be disposed of as they determine in council. No further records found.

Treaty with the Menominee, 18 October 1848 at Lake Pow-aw-hay-kan-nay, Wis.

Article 4 set aside $40,000 to the mixed bloods of the tribe. The pay roll, "Payment made by Commissioner Thomas Wistar, Jr. to the Mixed Menominee in conformance with the treaty of Oct. 18, 1848" is in file #226, "Special Files of the Office of Indian Affairs" (M574 Roll 65). It identified 759 people, naming the head of the household, age, sex, and number of men, women, and children in the family, the amount of the award, date of the payment, and by whom received.

Treaty with the Chippewa, 30 September 1854 at Lapointe

Article 2, part 7: "Each head of a family or single person over 21 years of age at the present time of the mixed bloods belonging to the Chippewa of Lake Superior shall be entitled to 80 acres of land, to be selected by them under the direction of the president, and which shall be secured to them by patent in the usual form." The most substantial record of the outcome of this provision is a published report, "Issuance of Scrip to Half Breeds or Mixed Bloods Belonging to Chippewa Indians of Lake Superior," House Executive Documents, 42nd Congress, 2nd Session (1871-72), Serial Set #1513.

Article 4: $6000 in agricultural implements, household furniture and cooking utensils to be distributed at the next annuity payment, among the mixed bloods.

Notes

1. Paul W. Gates, "Indian Allotments Preceding the Dawes Act" in *The Frontier Challenge: Responses to the Trans-Mississippi West*, ed. John G. Clark (Lawrence: University Press of Kansas, 1971), 141-70.
2. Francis Paul Prucha, *The Great Father: The United States Government and the American Indians*, vol. 1 (Lincoln: University of Nebraska Press, 1984), 247.
3. There is no detailed account in print of this family or any of its individual members. The most substantial discussion is in John S. Wozniak, *Contact, Negotiation and Conflict: An Ethnohistory of the Eastern Dakota, 1819-1839* (Washington, D.C.: University Press of America, 1978), 118-24. See also *Wisconsin Historical Collections* (Madison: State Historical Society of Wisconsin, 1909), 9: 464-65.
4. Charles Hanson, Jr., "Frederick Laboue and His River," *The Museum of the Fur Trade Quarterly* 27, nos. 1 & 2 (Spring/Summer 1991): 23.

Part III

Becoming a Trader: Origins, Lives, and Survival

The Career of Joseph La France, Coureur de Bois *in the Upper Great Lakes*

Helen Hornbeck Tanner

Of all the categories of people involved in the French fur trade, the most elusive are the *coureurs de bois*. They are always mentioned as the precursors of "real" explorers, whose ventures are documented in written records. Because they settled comfortably in Indian communities, they also receive credit for creating the first generation of *métis* in the Upper Great Lakes region. Known for their skill in evading trade regulations, these men exasperated officials of both France and Great Britain with their ability to carry on illegal commerce.

Though often identified as belonging to a separate class in the fur trade, the individual *coureur de bois* remains a rather obscure figure. The name, which has no satisfactory English translation, has created the impression that he is a person who is just running around in the forest on some unknown pathway. Now, however, adequate information is available concerning the network of canoe routes and trails to Indian villages and hunting grounds so that the activities of *coureurs de bois* can be described with more confidence.

The only *coureur de bois* for whom extensive autobiographical information is available, so far as I know, is Joseph La France, who was taken into custody by the British at York Fort on Hudson Bay in June 1742.[1] Hudson's Bay Company rules forbade harboring French traders, so Joseph La France was sent to England in September on a vessel under the command of Captain George Spurrell, who had long been in the service of the Company.[2] In London, La France came into the care of an antiquarian and literary man, Walter Bowman, who was also a friend of Sir Arthur Dobbs, a politically prominent Irishman. Dobbs was interested in promoting the search of the Northwest Passage and exposing mismanagement of the Hudson's Bay Company. Bowman picked up La France on the recommendation of Captain Christopher Middleton, who had been persuaded by Sir Arthur Dobbs to leave the Hudson's Bay Company and head an expedition to search for the Northwest Passage, an exploratory journey that had begun in 1741. Captain Middleton met La France at York Fort before continuing his own explorations during the summer of 1742 and returning to England.[3]

Bowman supported La France until Dobbs could come to England to conduct a series of interviews with the *coureur de bois*. Dobbs reported that he queried La

France in French, then immediately made an English translation which he discussed with him before writing down the reply. He repeated questions, often waiting a fortnight before asking a question the second time. Using this procedure, he found that La France was consistent in the descriptions of his experiences, and Captain Middleton attested to his good reputation.[4] Hoping to have La France available for a later expedition to Hudson Bay, Dobbs arranged with the Admiralty Department to have La France kept on board a guard ship at Chatham. A few months later, however, in the year 1743, La France died of "fever and ague" at age thirty-six.[5]

The life story of Joseph La France, up to the time he arrived at York Fort, probably parallels the experience of hundreds of other *coureurs de bois* who operated throughout the *pays d'en haut* west of Montreal during the years when French and British rivalry over the fur trade was reaching a climax in the mid-eighteenth century. For this reason, I think his career is worth describing as a basis for a few observations on the significance of these men in an overall view of the fur trade.

Joseph La France was born about 1707 at Michilimackinac, according to his own statements.[6] During that era, the eastern end of the Upper Peninsula of Michigan and, in fact, the entire region of the straits between Lake Huron and Lake Michigan was known as "Michilimackinac." At the time Joseph La France was born, the main trading base in the region was located on the north side of the straits at present day St. Ignace, Michigan. The father of Joseph La France was a French trader from Quebec, his mother a woman of the Ojibwa people called "Saulteurs" who lived in the district around the rapids of the St. Mary's River, near present Sault Ste. Marie.[7] He was only five or six years old when he made his first trip over the hazardous portages of the well-traveled canoe route connecting the straits region with the St. Lawrence River. Following the channel on the north side of Manitoulin Island opening into Georgian Bay, the journey continued up the French River to Lake Nipissing, then down the short Mattawa River, and finally the swifter Ottawa to reach the St. Lawrence Valley. Joseph left the upper country soon after his mother's death, when his father took him to Quebec for six months during the winter to learn French.

Joseph La France spent the rest of his childhood years with his father in the Michilimackinac district. Presumably, he learned the rudiments of trading before he reached the age of fourteen, when his father died. When he was sixteen years old, probably in 1723-1724, Joseph made the trip alone to Montreal and back to sell the furs and peltry that his father had left him. During the next decade, he hunted and traded principally among his mother's people living on the northeast shore of Lake Superior around Michipicoten. He became familiar with the streams on the Canadian shield, the rocky region north of Lake Superior. He located good beaver grounds in the marshes and lakes above the falls of the Pic River and the upper branches of the Magpie and other streams near Michipicoten. Like his Indian kinfolk, he learned the animal and plant resources of the islands on the north side of the lake, particularly three located

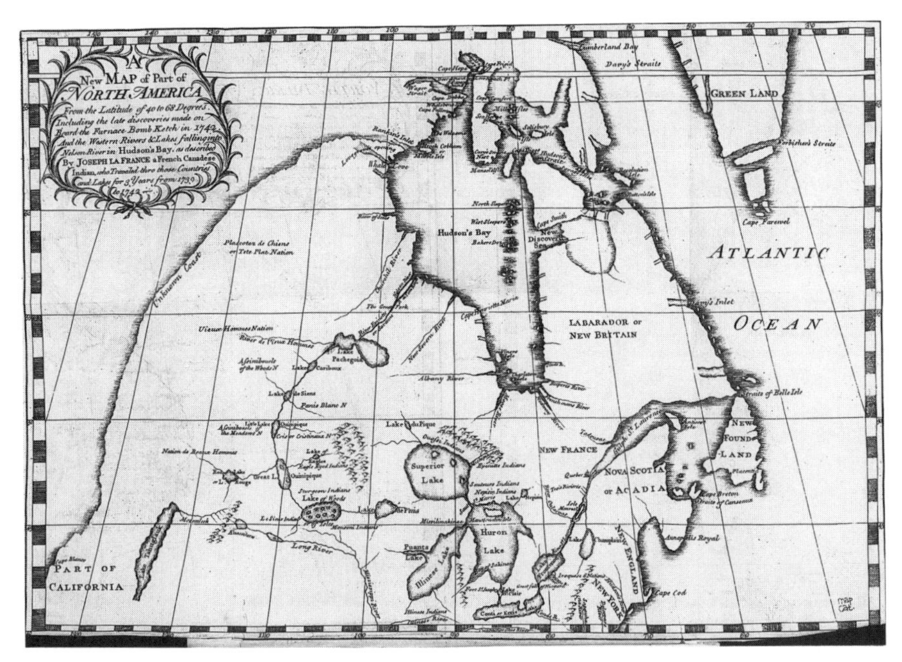

Figure 1. "A New Map of Part of North America," from Arthur Dobbs, *An Account of the Countries Adjoining Hudson's Bay in the North-West Part of North America* (London, 1744). The information attributable to La France is found along the curved water course from Lake of the Woods to the Nelson River, as well as tribal names of Indians north of Lake Superior. Courtesy of Everett D. Graff Collection, The Newberry Library, Chicago, Illinois.

about ten miles offshore. He mastered the survival skills of the people who called themselves "Anishinabeg" but who were identified as "Saulteurs" by the French and "Ojibwa," often corrupted to "Chippewa," by the British.[8]

Joseph La France began his independent career when the fur trade was on the upswing. His father had survived the difficult years between 1698 and 1715 when royal authorities tried to curtail trading in the *pays d'en haut.* The French edict of 1696 closing western posts, including Michilimackinac, forced traders in the upper country to make the long journey to Quebec or Montreal, or trade surreptitiously with the British at Albany, New York, or the Hudson's Bay Company post on James Bay. Only meager supplies of trade goods reached Fort Bourbon, the French post at the mouth of the Nelson River on Hudson Bay, though the French held the location from 1697 to 1714. The western posts were officially closed after too many beaver pelts had accumulated, and prices in European markets plummeted. Nevertheless, the governor general managed to keep supplies flowing to about fifteen Canadian traders at Michilimackinac, which was also the principal base for the *coureurs de bois.*[9]

Following the Treaty of Utrecht in 1713, which occurred while Joseph La France and his father were in Quebec, the market was much improved. At the end of the long period of warfare, merchants discovered that the skins stored for more than a decade were not usable, and consequently there was a sudden

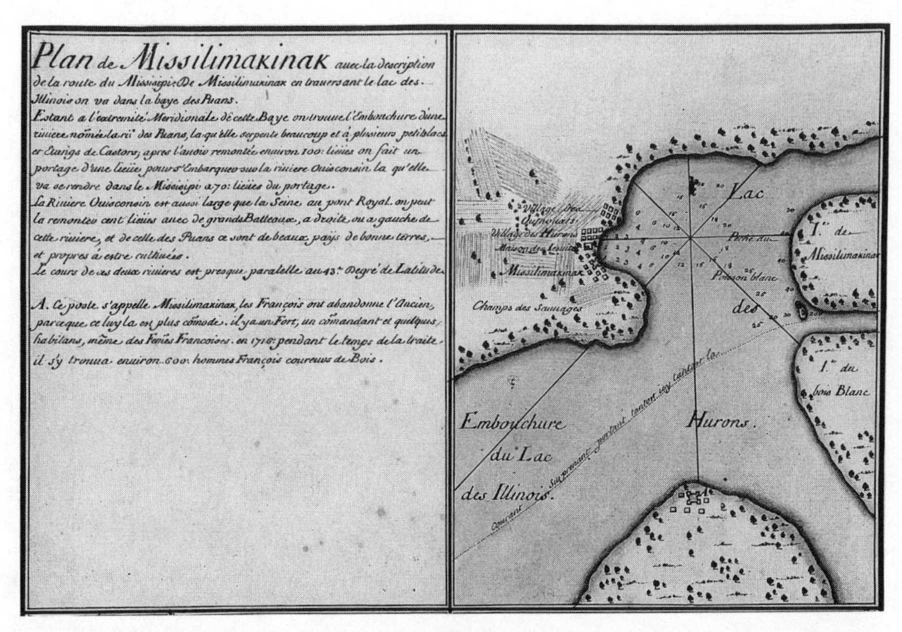

Figure 2. "Plan de Missilimakinak," anonymous manuscript map c. 1717, from the Cartes Marines. The legend notes the Indian villages and Jesuit mission on the north side of the Straits of Mackinac at present-day St. Ignace. The French fort established in 1715 is shown on the south side of the Straits, with the added information that the inhabitants include some French women, and about 600 *coureurs de bois* during the trading season in 1716. Courtesy of Edward E. Ayer Collection, The Newberry Library, Chicago, Illinois.

demand for a large volume of beaver pelts. To promote and regulate the fur trade, military posts were reestablished in the upper Great Lakes and a new licensing system introduced.[10] The first post reestablished in the upper country was Fort Michilimackinac, built in 1715 at a new site on the south side of the straits that had long provided a vital communications channel for the Great Lakes region. As a result, economic prospects were greatly improved in the 1720s, when Joseph La France commenced trading in the hinterland using goods procured at the new fort.[11] His annual round for ten years took him back and forth from Michilimackinac to northern Lake Superior and his local trading base, probably Michipicoten.[12]

In 1734, Joseph La France abandoned his accustomed routine and began exploring new country. This change in career pattern came at the time of the great western expansion of French trade following the explorations of Pierre Gaultier de Varennes de La Vérendrye and the conclusion of warfare with the Fox (or Mesquakie) Indians that involved the entire Great Lakes region.[13] La France set out in the spring on a year-long journey, crossing Wisconsin to the Mississippi River and returning through Illinois and southwestern Michigan.[14] This was a trip he could not have made safely any earlier because the main travel route, the Fox-Wisconsin waterway, had been a war zone for most of the previous twenty years. The Fox Indians living on the lower course of the Fox

River near Green Bay had virtually prevented the French from using the waterway throughout the long period of intermittently violent warfare. Only a few French traders risked their lives to cross the portage.

The French were forced to abandon Fort La Baye, the post at the mouth of the Fox River, in 1728 and did not return until 1731, after a massive military onslaught against the Fox camps on the Wisconsin River, and an expedition against Fox fleeing into Illinois. Several hundred Fox were captured, but some survivors took refuge with the Sauk living at Green Bay. When the French demanded that the Sauk turn over the Fox refugees, the Sauk, along with their Fox guests, first resisted, then fled west of the Mississippi River in 1733.[15] Consequently, Joseph La France traveled in the spring of 1734 through recently and temporarily vacated lands in Wisconsin. At the beginning of his exploratory journey, La France undoubtedly followed the main canoe route from Michilimackinac, skirting the north shore of Lake Michigan to Green Bay. His account includes no details of the trip, but information is available about the country he passed through.

At the southern tip of Green Bay, the French maintained a fortified post, Fort La Baye, the strategic location reoccupied in 1731 to monitor travel along the Fox-Wisconsin waterway connecting Lake Michigan and the Mississippi River. In ascending the Fox River from Green Bay, La France passed by the Winnebago village at the north end of Lake Winnebago; from the lake, the upper Fox River led him to the portage to the Wisconsin River. Along the course of the lower Wisconsin River, he also passed two abandoned Mesquakie villages and the former site of Fort St. Nicholas, a trading post established about 1684 by the former *coureur de bois* Nicolas Perrot at the juncture of the Wisconsin and Mississippi Rivers, later the trade center of Prairie du Chien.[16] In 1738, four years after La France traversed the region, Fort Marin was established on the west bank opposite the mouth of the Wisconsin River. Continuing down the Mississippi River, he passed the mouth of the Rock River, where the Sauk established new headquarters sometime during the same year (1734) that he advanced downriver.[17]

Joseph La France evidently was following a plan, and had gained advance information about the country before he traversed it for the first time. He descended the Mississippi River only to the Missouri before reversing direction to return by way of the Illinois River. He was probably wary about going further south. If he had traveled downstream another day or two beyond the mouth of the Missouri River, he would have come upon the villages of Illinois Indians and the French agricultural communities above Fort de Chartres, the principal French military establishment on the Mississippi River. These settlements at Cahokia, Prairie du Rocher, and Kaskaskia marked the upper limits of Louisiana, governed from New Orleans, with separate trade regulations and export restrictions. He may have turned back to avoid contact with Louisiana provincial authorities. Furthermore, a smallpox epidemic had struck Indians of the lower Mississippi valley, who were still suffering from repercussions of the French warfare undertaken in 1731 to exterminate the Natchez.

The broad course of the Mississippi River, with stretches of high, wooded bluffs, the flat prairie of Iowa, and the veritable sea of grass in central Illinois interrupted only by small groves called "islands"—these sights presented a terrain vastly different from his home country, dominated by the sheer rock faces and jagged headlands of the mountainous country north of Lake Superior. On the northward return route through Illinois and Michigan he passed by two widely separated trading centers. The first was the small settlement on the Illinois River at present-day Peoria, in French documents often called "Pimitoui," where *métis* traders and Indians were regathering following the Fox campaigns of 1730-31 in central Illinois. He then followed the Kankakee branch of the Illinois River, paddling eastward to a point where he could portage to the vicinity of present South Bend, Indiana, and the lower course of the St. Joseph River flowing into Lake Michigan. After reaching this stream, he made his way downriver about a dozen miles to Fort St. Joseph (Niles, Michigan), situated near Potawatomi and Miami Indian communities. The garrison of this important post consisted of only fifteen men but, like the French communities near Fort de Chartres, it was an old location for traders, missionaries, and several families of *habitants*. Since the personnel at Fort St. Joseph traveled seasonally to Michilimackinac, he very likely had friends or acquaintances in the community.

Leaving the fort, he noted the rapid current of the St. Joseph River that carried him swiftly out into Lake Michigan for the final leg of his journey along the sandy beaches on the eastern shore of the lake. As he proceeded northward, he came in sight of several stretches of high dunes. In describing his return route, he mentioned passing "the Bay of L'Our qui Dort, so called from a Heap of Sand upon a Point which resembled a Bear sleeping."[18] This description clearly identifies Sleeping Bear sand dune, which rises precipitously 450 feet from the water's edge in a National Lakeshore area north of present-day Empire, Michigan. The last stretch of this long canoe voyage took him through treacherous waters of the Manitou passage, between the mainland and islands of northern Lake Michigan, a passage with shoals less dangerous for a canoe than a sailing vessel. Finally, he rounded Waugochance point and entered the strong east-flowing currents of the Straits of Mackinac.

La France's experience in the Wisconsin and Illinois country apparently was not sufficiently attractive or lucrative to warrant a second trip. In 1736 he changed direction, heading this time toward Oswego, the British fort on the southeast shore of Lake Ontario built in 1727, particularly to divert trade from the *pays d'en haut* through Iroquois country. Illegal trade with the British in New York was particularly heavy during the period 1735-38.[19] La France appears to have been part of this new trend. His decision to smuggle furs to New York probably also reflected changes in the management of the trade in the Michilimackinac district. Up to 1734, the commandant and officers at military posts entered into active partnerships in fur trade enterprises. Subsequently, they leased trading privileges at some posts for a payment of fees. Leasing arrangements for control of the fur trade at Michipicoten, for a long time the home base for Joseph La France, were made in 1735.[20]

La France tried to travel inconspicuously to Fort Oswego in company with eight Iroquois in two canoes. Proceeding southward along the west side of Lake Huron, they made the risky transit of sixty miles across the mouth of Saginaw Bay, then gained speed on their descent of the St. Clair River to shallow Lake St. Clair before entering the Detroit River. They scheduled their resting points so that they could slip past the French fort at Detroit during the night and reach the relative safety of Lake Erie. At the time Detroit was becoming a substantial community, with the palisaded fort on the river bank and a settlement of about a hundred houses. Narrow ribbon strips of farmland along the river marked the fields of the *habitants*. Beyond the area of French occupation, villages of Potawatomi, Huron (Wendat), and Ottawa on both sides of the river formed part of the larger community.

When La France and his companions arrived at the Niagara River, he paid the Iroquois one hundred beaver pelts to portage his canoes and accumulated harvest of furs around the south side of the falls to Lake Ontario. They carefully avoided Fort Niagara, the French military post in the forest near the river mouth. At Oswego the Iroquois handled the entire trading transaction while Joseph La France hid in the woods at some distance from the fort. He then retraced his route back north.[21]

By 1737, Joseph La France's trading enterprises were clearly profitable. He had the assistance of two Indian slaves, possibly acquired in the Illinois country or through trade with Indians far west of Lake Superior.[22] The Illinois Indians raided villages west of the Mississippi River to bring back captives, whom they sold. In the contemporary French records these slaves are called *Panis* because Pawnee villages were principal targets of the slave raids. Looking to a future as a legitimate trader, La France decided to go to Montreal and try to secure a *congé* or license.

Using three small canoes, he and his two Indians went downriver to Montreal with a considerable cargo of furs in the fall of 1737. In the expectation of receiving a *congé* for the next year, he paid the governor-general one thousand crowns and gave an additional present of a pack of valuable marten skins.[23] In the spring, he was completely dismayed when the governor charged him with selling brandy to Indians, a common practice though officially prohibited. On these grounds, the governor refused to give him a license but retained the gifts, and threatened to arrest him if he tried to regain his money. Under these circumstances, La France left town quickly with whatever goods he could procure in exchange for the balance of his furs and headed for Lake Superior. He spent forty days paddling upstream and crossing the thirty-six portages between Montreal and Lake Nipissing, a trip that had taken only eighteen days going downstream the previous autumn. From Lake Nipissing, two days were required to descend the French River with its three waterfalls, and another two or three days to follow the chain of islands in northern Lake Huron to Fort Michilimackinac.[24]

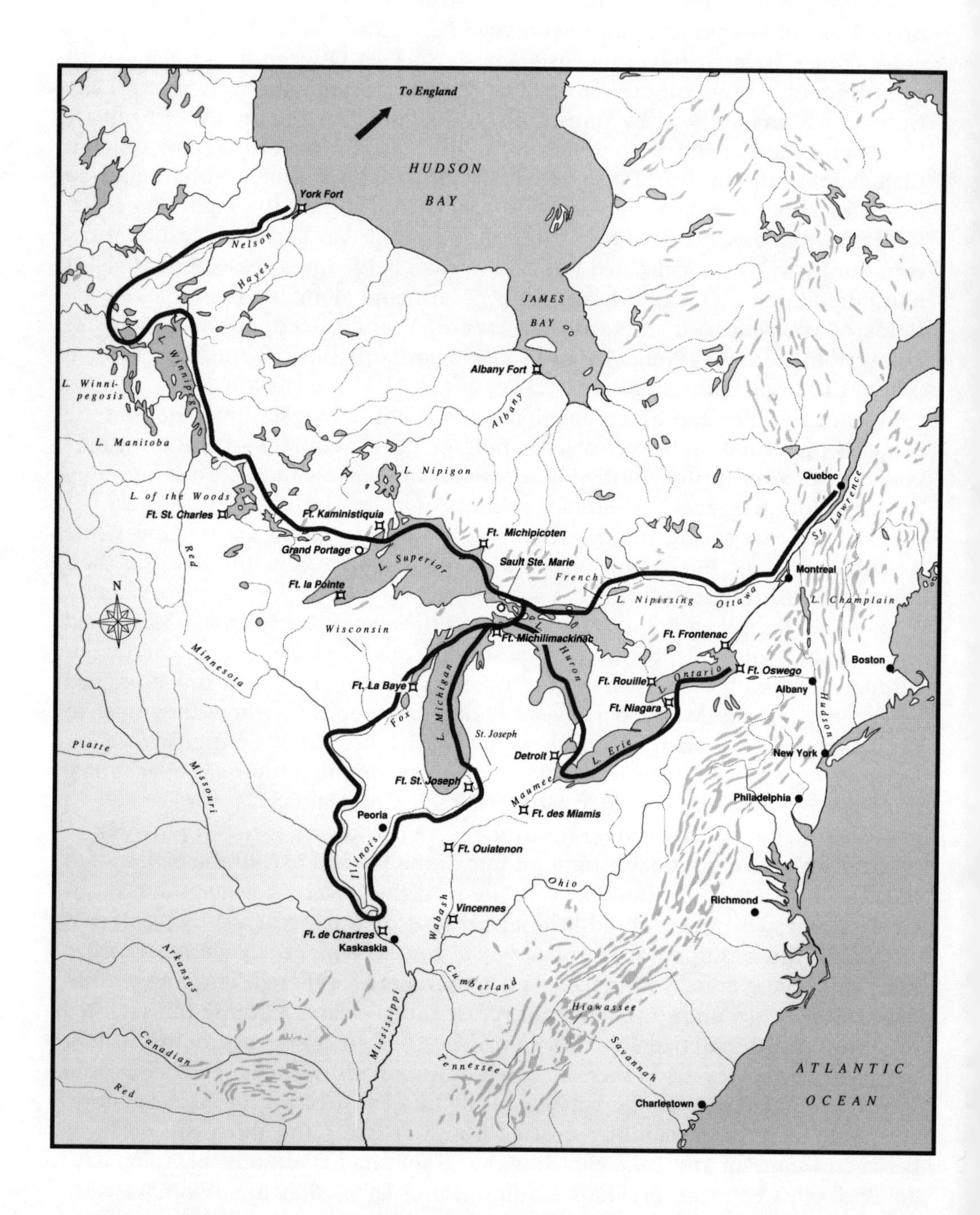

Figure 3. Travels of Joseph La France, *Coureur de Bois*, 1724-1742. Cartography by Tom Willcockson, Newberry Library.

Despite his initial rebuff in Montreal, Joseph La France decided to try to make peace with the governor. According to his statements to Dobbs, at the time that he again left Michilimackinac, probably in 1738, there were only two men with the commandant in the garrison and their chief function was to open and shut the gates. The French trade from Michilimackinac was so reduced that not more than twelve canoes a year left for Montreal, and those licenses were generally given to superannuated officers. La France declared that the decline in French trade was attributable to the success of the English in supplying the Indians with much cheaper and better goods, and the ease of transportation through the lakes to the Niagara district. He also reported that the "avarice and injustice" of the governor of Canada had "disgusted the Natives."[25]

Joseph La France was optimistic when he set out once more for Montreal, still hoping to achieve the status of a legal trader. The second attempt to acquire a *congé* led to complete disaster. Accompanied again by his two Indians, Joseph La France had traveled only as far as a sharp bend on the French River east of Georgian Bay when he met a brigade of nine canoes bringing a contingent of thirty men and supplies to Fort Michilimackinac. The leader of the expedition was the governor's brother-in-law, who seized La France as a runaway along with his slaves, canoes, and furs. Facing imprisonment if taken to Montreal, La France managed to steal away in the night, taking with him only his gun and five charges of powder and ball. He made his way alone through the rugged back country north of Lake Huron for six weeks before he came across some Mississauga Indians, then continued on to Sault Ste. Marie. He was alive, but he had lost his assets and his two Indian assistants.

At this critical point in his life, Joseph La France decided to go to the British post, York Fort on Hudson Bay, with the further hope of reaching France. But first he spent the early part of the winter 1739-40 hunting and living with his Ojibwa relatives in the vicinity of the Michipicoten River. La France explained that the river separated the home country of two different tribes of Sauteurs, the "Epinette Nation" living on the east side and the "Ouassi" on the west.[26] In March of 1740, while the ice was still firm in the bays and river mouths, he started westward on a 350-mile trek around Lake Superior. On the northwestern side, he met Indians who had large chunks of copper ore brought down from the mountains as well as a metal called "lead" (in the Dobbs *Account*) but which possibly was silver, readily available at a tiny island in Thunder Bay.[27]

By early April 1740, La France and some Indian companions had passed the vicinity of Fort Kaministiquia on Thunder Bay and were in ice-free territory on the southwestern side of this "upper lake." From Grand Portage (Minnesota) they crossed the strenuous nine-mile portage to the upper Pigeon River and plodded through marshes and bogs until they reached the head of the Rainy River. Here they stopped to make canoes from the big birches, then paddled westward to Rainy Lake and Lake of the Woods. La France traveled at a leisurely pace, lingering for ten days in late April to fish at the falls, where Indian villages were situated on both banks of the river. He called these people "Monsoni" and "Gens d'Original."[28] He spent more time at an island in Lake of the Woods joining "Monsoni and Sturgeon Indians," gathered for a full month of ceremonies, diplomatic conferences, and general "merriment."

It seems curious that La France made no direct reference to the prior presence of La Vérendrye's men in this area, where they had been active since 1731, according to reports. La France stated that the French never came this way because the portages were too long, an impression probably created by the general knowledge that La Vérendrye's porters refused to tackle the "grand portage" in 1731, forcing him to return with most of his men to Kaministiquia for the winter. His nephew nevertheless forged ahead to establish Fort St. Pierre on Rainy River. Yet La France must have passed the site of Fort St. Pierre, and been close to abandoned Fort St. Charles, established by La Vérendrye in 1732 on a southwest bay of Lake of the Woods in present-day Minnesota. At the time La France passed through this country, the La Vérendryes were not in the area. The elder La Vérendrye was back in Montreal or had returned to Michilimackinac, and a son was in the upper Missouri country. The local Indian people may have tactfully refrained from mentioning that four years earlier, in June 1736, the elder son of La Vérendrye and twenty other Frenchmen had been killed by a large Sioux war party on present-day Massacre Island in Lake of the Woods, just twenty-one miles from Fort St. Charles.[29]

Under questioning from Dobbs, La France described the distribution of the Indian population northwest of Lake Superior. His Monsoni and Sturgeon Indian friends lived "on the north side" of the Lake of the Woods. East of Lake Winnipeg was the country of the Crees or "Christinaux." The Sioux lived southwest of Lake Winnipeg, while the Assiniboins of the Prairies occupied the country directly west of Lake Winnipegosis, with the Assiniboins of the Woods further north. The "Nation of Beaux Hommes," almost certainly the tribe later known as Gros Ventres, lived in the area south of the Assiniboins and north of the Sioux. Southeast of Lake Winnipeg, between the Lake of the Woods and Lake Superior, the "Migechichilinious or Eagle-eyed Indians" occupied the shores of a lake with islands that were a favorite breeding ground for eagles.[30]

Resuming his travels, La France descended the rapids of the Winnipeg River, the outlet of Lake of the Woods, and spent the fall of the year 1740 along the east shore of Lake Winnipeg, wintering among the Cree on the northwest side of the lake. The following year, he crossed westward to the territory beyond Lake Winnipegosis toward the Saskatchewan River and modern The Pas as well as Moose Lake. He was still trading as well as hunting, although he mentions no source of supply. On the other hand, records indicate that La Vérendrye's son Pierre probably set up two new trading posts in the fall of 1741: Fort Dauphin (the first by this name) on the western side of Lake Winnipegosis, as well as the first Fort Bourbon on Cedar Lake. During the period 1739-1741, the elder La Vérendrye spent most of his time in Michilimackinac or Montreal. As La France approached the end of his last season in the bush, he had only thirty cowrie shells and a few hawks bells, a favorite gift of Indian men to their wives. He commented to Dobbs that the Indian people were very fond of pictures or images of any kind, but he had none.

By March 1742, La France joined the Indian people collecting at Cedar Lake for the annual spring trip to York Fort. La France was chosen to be one of the leaders of the flotilla of one hundred canoes. During three days in early April, they made new canoes, then started out with precariously heavy loads. When winds on the lake rose, they carried the canoes and contents across points of land in order to avoid the waves in open water. Frequently they stopped to collect provisions, since the canoes were too small to hold food as well as furs. When they reached the Nelson River in May, the entire brigade slowed the daily pace to enjoy warm weather and trees in full leaf. They knew the season would be much delayed and weather much colder at York Fort. Indeed, they had three inches of snow after arriving at their destination in late June. Here the career of Joseph La France as a *coureur de bois* came to an end at the headquarters for the Hudson's Bay Company in North America, the embattled post that had been one of the points of contention in the imperial struggle between France and Great Britain until it was regained by the British in the Treaty of Utrecht (1713).

The story of Joseph La France provides some insight into the activities of *coureurs de bois* during the first half of the eighteenth century. By the time he reached York Fort in 1742, he had canoed more than 17,000 miles and traveled overland an additional 500 miles, according to rough calculations (see figure 3). Joseph La France was a member of the second generation involved in this freelance branch of the Indian trade. Other *coureurs de bois* preceded him and La Vérendrye's men by more than fifty years. The most prominent of the first wave of law-defying adventurers were Pierre Esprit Radisson and Médart Chouart des Groseilliers, who were among the thirty or so to reach the western country as early as 1656. Radisson spent two years on the Mississippi River followed by another two years around Lake Superior by 1663.[31] He was closely followed by Jean Peré, sent in 1663 to search for the copper mines reported near Lake Superior and on its islands. In the course of a varied career, Peré managed to be arrested both by the British in New York in the 1670s and on Hudson Bay in 1684 before returning to a more conventional business career in France.[32] Following the initial exploration by René-Robert Cavelier, Sieur de La Salle, down the Mississippi River in 1682, his men extended trade contacts northwest to the Assiniboin country.[33]

Up to 1680, French law forbade the activities of the *coureurs de bois*. By that time, there were too many to control or punish. Although they were granted amnesty, with the expectation that they would return and henceforth take turns in receiving official licenses to trade, few changed their habits. Instead, their ranks increased during an expansionist period in French colonial policy. No satisfactory documentary record exists to chronicle the trading pursuits of the contemporaries of Joseph La France and his father. Information is limited because of incomplete records, the interest of the *coureurs de bois* in having their names and locations remain unknown, and the efforts of French authorities to conceal and sometimes connive in illegal trade.[34] Total numbers of *coureurs de bois* may all be open to question but are nevertheless worth citing. Jean-Baptiste Patoulet, a deputy to intendant Jean Talon, estimated in 1672 that there were about 300 or 400 illegal traders at that time. By 1680, according to the intendant Jacques Duchesneau, there were at least 800, a high figure. The growth in the estimated number of traders may reflect the substantial increase in the population of French Canada, which rose from 3,000 in 1665 to 15,000 in 1700. In 1692, Jean Bochart de Champigny observed with regret the inclination of Canadian youth to live in the forest like Indians for two or three years at a time.[35] The men usually operated in groups of about twenty, and seasonally dispersed singly or as partners. A typical example is the eighteen Frenchmen reported wintering at Keweenaw Bay on the south shore of Lake Superior in 1683.[36]

The ingenuity and flexibility of this class of traders were further demonstrated after the French edict of 1696 closing the western posts supplied from the St. Lawrence River. In response, fur traders dispersed from the upper Great Lakes. When French supplies were meager, *coureurs de bois* smuggled furs to the British at Albany Fort on James Bay, as well as to British posts south of the Great Lakes, including Albany, New York. From La Pointe on Chequamegon Bay of Lake Superior, from Lake Nipigon and Michipicoten, the *coureurs de bois* early ventured into the northland. They headed south as well. The French post at Detroit was established in 1701 to intercept furs destined for Albany as well as to exploit the hunting grounds between the Great Lakes and the Ohio River and prevent British traders from advancing westward into the Ohio country. Yet *coureurs de bois* had already made their way from Canada far south of the Great Lakes, even forming part of the first successful French expedition to the Gulf Coast that landed on Biloxi Bay in January 1699.[37]

For a brief period at the turn of the century, *coureurs de bois* diverted a small stream of the trade from the Great Lakes district to the British at Charles Town in Carolina by way of the Mississippi, Ohio, and Tennessee rivers. The pioneer of this interior trade route was Jean Couture, former member of the La Salle expedition down the Mississippi in 1682, who transferred his allegiance to the British about 1693.[38] Late in 1700, four *coureurs de bois* ascended the Tennessee River to the Cherokee towns on the headwaters of the Hiawassee or Little Tennessee rivers east of modern Chattanooga. There they followed the portage of only a league and a half to the Savannah River, giving them access to the Atlantic coast. In February 1701 they negotiated with Governor James Moore at his plantation near Charles Town to open trade for themselves and fifteen friends left behind on the Mississippi River. In 1702 exports of beaver skins from Charles Town were double the number reported for any other year between 1699 and 1715.[39]

Bellefeuille and Sauton, two of the *coureurs de bois* who met Governor Moore in Carolina early in 1701, turned up at Fort Maurepas on Biloxi Bay later that year after retracing their route back to the Tamaroa village on the Mississippi River. At about the same time that they reached Biloxi Bay, Charles Juchereau de Saint-Denis with thirty men was establishing a fort and tannery five miles up the Ohio River from its juncture with the Mississippi. The tannery continued only until his death in 1703. His objective in establishing this outpost of the fledgling Louisiana colony was not only to process buffalo hides and deerskins but to intercept traffic from the Mississippi River to the English colonies by way of the Ohio River. Bellefeuille and Sauton apparently returned to the French trading system, for they were granted townlots when lands were laid out around Fort Louis de Louisiana on the Mobile River in 1702.[40] The growth of the settlement at Mobile Bay (Mississippi), along with the establishment of a post at Natchitoches (Louisiana) on the Red River in 1713 and the founding of New Orleans (Louisiana) in 1718, successfully channeled the southern branch of the French fur trade through ports in the province of Louisiana. During the period of La France's career, the adventurous Canadians also struck out west of the Mississippi, reaching the Apaches far out on the plains beyond the Missouri in 1724, and the Spanish trading post at Santa Fé by 1739.[41]

The first generation of *coureurs de bois* was French, but the later generations, including Joseph La France and his contemporaries, were predominantly *métis*. Although some established bases in remote locations, most of this new social class collected around trading locations that became French military posts after 1715. The principal sites of *métis* trading communities in the upper country, where *coureurs de bois* were active in the seventeenth century, are: St. Ignace (the first site of Fort Michilimackinac), Sault Ste. Marie, Detroit, and Niles (Fort St. Joseph), Michigan; Fort Wayne (Fort des Miamis), Lafayette (Fort Ouiatenon), and Vincennes (Indiana); La Pointe (Madeline Island), Green Bay, and Prairie du Chien (Wisconsin); Kaskaskia, Cahokia, and Peoria (Illinois); and Michipicoten, Lake Nipigon, Thunder Bay, and Winnipeg (Canada).[42] In Canada *métis* became a separate occupational class and carried on an independent trading tradition, but in American territory they more often were absorbed into settler populations or Indian communities. Many residents of Indian reservations carry the French names of old Canadian families, such as Duchesneau, Beaubien, Amiotte, or Pelletier.

The French government's measures to control the fur trade proved threatening to many *coureurs de bois*. For example, Canadian authorities reported in 1715 that around one hundred had "escaped" to join forty-seven other illegal traders in Cahokia, generally considered a safe haven for outlaws from both Canada and Louisiana.[43] Joseph La France did not appear to feel the pressure of government trade regulations until the 1730s, when he began to make forays away from his accustomed trading circuit from Michipicoten to Sault Ste. Marie and Michilimackinac. The last decade of his career came in the twilight of the *coureur de bois* era. He himself realized that his future as a trader depended on his success in securing a license and becoming part of the legal trading enterprises.

The end of Joseph La France's individual life story as a *coureur de bois* was certainly atypical. Furthermore, the whole subject of his family relationships is remarkably blank. This absence of personal data is probably due to the restricted line of questioning pursued by Sir Arthur Dobbs, or his selection of information for public presentation. It is disconcerting to know that Captain George Spurrell, with whom La France returned to England, reported at a parliamentary hearing that La France told him many things during the voyage that contradicted the account presented by Dobbs. Capt. Spurrell believed that La France went to York Fort after he had killed his Indian "consort." He also commented that La France read frequently from his French prayerbook.[44]

Joseph La France in all probability left descendants in the Lake Superior region or further west. A trader identified only by the name La France was one of three Montreal "pedlars" killed during an Indian attack on the Assiniboine River near Portage La Prairie in 1781.[45] The family name also occurs among the *métis* and Indian population on the Turtle Mountain Chippewa reservation in northern North Dakota. Despite the impossibility of reconstructing many aspects of his life, his individual career reveals the characteristic pattern of a *coureur de bois*. He did, indeed, follow many pathways through the woods.

The *coureurs de bois* accumulated information about the price and quality of goods available at different locations served by both French and British traders. They were alert to new opportunities both to acquire and to sell furs. As individuals, they maintained great flexibility in their operations. They took advantage of their ability to remain mobile and live off the land, skills acquired from their Indians friends and relations. An additional 300 to 800 travel itineraries similar to that of Joseph La France, mentally projected on the same map, would create a more realistic impression of the pervasive contacts established by *coureurs de bois* in interior North America. As capital and credit arrangements in the fur trade developed greater complexity, the independent *coureurs de bois* became incorporated in the larger commercial organizations which enjoyed political support. Yet the cumulative decisions of several hundred men like Joseph La France, each a minor figure, combined to form a major element in the overall scope of ventures undertaken during the formative years of the fur trade in North America.[46]

NOTES

1. Arthur Dobbs, *An Account of the Countries Adjoining Hudson's Bay in the North-West Part of America* (London: J. Robinson, 1744), 29-45. This section of Dobbs' publication provides the framework for reconstructing a life story for Joseph La France. Gratien Allaire reports that he has found no satisfactory identification of either Joseph La France or his father among the records for pertinent years. The closest approximation is a hiring contract in 1728 for a "Joseph Daragon *dit* La France," resident of St. Laurent, a community near Montreal. He was hired by Jean Baptiste Charly, a well-known Montreal merchant, for "the north." Although this is the only hiring contract including the designation "La France" for the decade of the 1720s, contracts for others named "Daragon" exist for the 1730s and 1740s. Personal communication, 15 January 1992.
2. Arthur S. Morton, *A History of the Canadian West to 1870-71*, 2d ed. (Toronto and Buffalo: University of Toronto Press, 1973), 225. He was probably sent to

England by the factor, Thomas White, according to Hartwell Bowsfield, "Joseph La France," in *Dictionary of Canadian Biography* (Toronto: University of Toronto Press, 1974), 3: 341-42.

3. Christian Brun, "Dobbs and the Passage," *The Beaver* (Autumn 1958): 27. See also Desmond Clark, *Arthur Dobbs, 1689-1765: Surveyor-General of Ireland, Prospector and Governor of North Carolina* (Chapel Hill: University of North Carolina Press, 1908), 57; and Morton, 209-10.
4. Dobbs later described his procedure on the witness stand, adding that he had destroyed his original "minutes" after publication of his book in 1744. The information obtained from La France, and published by Dobbs, was included as an appendix to the report printed by the House of Commons. See *Report from the Committee Appointed to Inquire into the State and Condition of the Country Adjoining to Hudson's Bay and the Trade Carried on There* (London, 1749). Two copies at the Newberry Library, Chicago, Illinois.
5. Walter Bowman, "The Controversy Concerning the Northwest Passage into the American Ocean Betwixt Arthur Dobbs Esq. and Christopher Middleton sent in the Furnace Bomb-Ketch to make the Discovery in MDCCXII," ms. no. 1744, William L. Clements Library, Ann Arbor, Michigan.
6. Dobbs, 29. The date is established by the statement that La France was 36 in 1743.
7. Ibid., 26.
8. The singular form "Anishinabe" is common among Amerindians who speak Algonquian languages, including those identified by outsiders as Ojibwa, Ottawa, Potawatomi, and Algonquin. The French used the name "Saulteur" for the people they found living at the falls of the St. Marys River, present-day Sault Ste. Marie. Today, a variant form "Saulteaux" is used in western Canada.
9. W. J. Eccles, *The Canadian Frontier, 1534-1760*, rev. ed. (Albuquerque: University of New Mexico Press, 1983), 109, 137.
10. Ibid., 145.
11. Gratien Allaire, "Les engagements pour la traite des fourrures—evaluation de la documentation," *Revue d'histoire de l'Amérique francaise* 34, no. 1 (June 1980): 17.
12. In 1727, Michipicoten became an outpost of the fort at Nipigon, a subsidiary of Ft. Kaministiquia which was designated as the headquarters for *Les postes du nord* established in 1717.
13. Allaire, "Les engagements," 15.
14. Dobbs, 29, reported that La France returned "the way he came," inferring that he returned through Wisconsin. This is an error. It is clear from a later reference to the Sleeping Bear sand dune, a well-known landmark, that he returned along the eastern shore of Lake Michigan.
15. For a brief summary of the Fox warfare, see Helen Hornbeck Tanner, ed., *Atlas of Great Lakes Indian History* (Norman: University of Oklahoma Press, 1987), 42; R. David Edmunds and Joseph L. Peyser, *The Fox Wars: The Mesquakie Challenge to New France* (Norman: University of Oklahoma Press, 1993).
16. The fort was established "a few years before 1687." See "Account of Perrot's Life," Appendix A, Emma Helen Blair, trans. and ed., *The Indian Tribes of the Upper Mississippi Valley and the Region of the Great Lakes*, 2 vols. (Cleveland: Arthur H. Clark, 1911), 2: 253. Fort St. Nicholas was among the western posts vacated in 1697. Nicolas Perrot had been preceded by Jean Nicollet, who reached the western shores of Lake Michigan and Green Bay in 1634. See also Map 6, "The

Iroquois Wars 1641-1701," in Tanner, ed., *Atlas*, 32-33.

17. The site of Fort Marin became Fort Vaudreuil in 1753. For the location of Indian villages and forts for this time period, see Map 9, "The French Era, 1720-1761," in Tanner, *Atlas*, 41-42.
18. Dobbs, 29.
19. Allaire, "Les engagements," 15n.39, citing Maurice Filion, *La pensée et l'action coloniales de Maurepas vis-a-vis du Canada, 1723-1749, L'age d'or de la colonie* (Montreal: Lemeac, 1972), 359-64.
20. Gratien Allaire, "Officers et marchands: les societes de commerce des fourrures, 1715-1760," *Revue d'histoire de l'Amérique francaise* 40, no. 3 (Winter 1987), 424.
21. In 1749, French authorities made a tardy effort to curtail illegal traffic to Oswego by constructing Fort Rouillé at present-day Toronto. This was an important location at the end of a short-cut route from Georgian Bay to Lake Ontario. Toronto was also the launching point for canoes crossing to Oswego. See also Ernest Voorhis, comp., "Historic forts and trading posts of the French regime and of the English fur trading companies," Ottawa, Department of Interior, National Resources and Intelligence Service, 1930.
22. Eccles, 149. At western posts, trade in Indian slaves was carried on, some were sent down to Montreal.
23. Charles de la Boische, Marquis de Beauharnois, served as governor general of New France from 1726 to 1747. He was accused of abusing the sale of fur trade licenses and demanding payments from commanders of the western posts. Although regulations provided for issuing 25 *congés* annually at 250 *livres* each, he sometimes issued as many as 50 for 500 *livres* each. S. Dale Standen, "Charles de la Boische," in *Dictionary of Canadian Biography* (Toronto: University of Toronto Press, 1974), 3: 44, 47.
24. Dobbs, 30-31.
25. Ibid., 31.
26. Ibid., 32.
27. Ibid., No sources of lead are known for the region adjoining northwestern Lake Superior. A likely nearby source for metal is Silver Islet, across from Thunder Bay. Prospectors found pure nuggets of silver there in 1868. More than $3 million worth of silver was taken from shafts made in the rock that rose only 2.5 feet above the surface of the water. See *Canadian Encyclopedia* (Edmonton: Hurtig Publishers, 1985), 3: 1699.
28. "Monsoni" means "moose," while the French term "Gens d'Original" is a direct translation of the Ojibwa self-designation *Anishinabeg* (HHT); Thomas Vennum, Jr., *Wild Rice and the Ojibwa People* (St. Paul: Minnesota Historical Society Press, 1988), 55.
29. Morton, 173-76, 186.
30. Dobbs, 34-35. The Gros Ventre identification is made by Morton, 16.
31. Arthur T. Adams, ed., *The Explorations of Pierre Esprit Radisson* (Minneapolis: Ross and Haines, 1961), iv-vii.
32. Leopold Lamontagne, "Jean Peré," *Dictionary of Canadian Biography* (Toronto: University of Toronto Press, 1966), 1: 636-37.
33. Eccles, 109.
34. Allaire, "Les engagements," 26; Eccles, 110, on reports that associates of *coureurs de bois* covered up for them; 124, Frontenac was careful to write as little as possible about western trade ventures.

35. Eccles, 90, 101, 110, 112, I wish to thank John Jackson for sharing his interesting research on multiple intertwined biographies of many *coureurs de bois*, including the names of several women.
36. Dulhut (Daniel Greysolon), Letter of 12 April 1683, in *The French Regime in Wisconsin, 1634-1717, Collections of the State Historical Society of Wisconsin*, Reuben G. Thwaites, ed. (Madison, 1902), 16: 114.
37. Marcel Giraud, *A History of French Louisiana*. Vol. I. *The Reign of Louis XIV 1698-1715* (Baton Rouge: Louisiana State University Press, 1974), 33-34, 43. The occupying force included 60 Canadians. Fort Maurepas near present-day Biloxi, Mississippi, was completed on 25 April 1699. The site was abandoned in 1701 and a new settlement established 55 miles up the Mobile River in Alabama where Fort Louis de Louisiana was completed in 1702. Canadian voyageurs were granted allotments in the new town.
38. Vernor Crane, "The Tennessee River as the Road to Carolina: The Beginnings of Exploration and Trade," *The Mississippi Valley Historical Review* 3, no. 1 (June 1916): 8-9n.17.
39. Ibid.,13, 16-17n.40.
40. Giraud, 51-52, 43.
41. Martha Royce Blaine, "French Efforts to Reach Santa Fe: Andre Fabry de la Bruyere's Voyage up the Canadian River in 1741-42," *Louisiana History* 20, no. 2 (1979): 134-35.
42. Jacqueline Peterson, "Many roads to Red River: Métis genesis in the Great Lakes region, 1680-1815," in *The New Peoples, Being and Becoming Métis in North America*, Jacqueline Peterson and Jennifer S.H. Brown, eds. (Lincoln: University of Nebraska Press, 1986), 43-45.
43. Ibid., 43.
44. Morton, 225.
45. Ibid., 329, citing information from Alexander Henry the Younger.
46. The author appreciates the suggestions of S. Dale Standen concerning additional French source material, as well as the critique of the editorial committee.

The Cadottes: Five Generations of Fur Traders on Lake Superior

Theresa M. Schenck

Between 1686 and 1840 five generations of the Cadotte family were active in the Lake Superior fur trade. At one time or another they were involved in almost every aspect of this lucrative commerce: as voyageurs, clerks, traders, interpreters, and even as financiers. Some sought to make a fortune, others pursued adventure; many more were born to the fur trade and knew no other life.

Although Mathurin Cadot[1] had made his first voyage to Sault Ste. Marie with Nicolas Perrot and Daumont de Saint-Lusson in 1670 and was probably a *coureur de bois* for many years, it was not until 1686 that he received his first *congé* to trade among the *"sauvages esloignez"*—distant nations.[2] Forming a partnership with several friends, he continued his activities among the Ottawa at least until 1690, when he hired his wife's half-brother to take his place. About to become a father for the first time, he retired to the quiet life of a *habitant* at Bécancour, near Trois Rivières, and later, in Batiscan.

Memories of the fur trade were kept alive in the Cadot family, and in 1717 Mathurin's eldest son, Jean-François, made his only recorded voyage to Michilimackinac. Two other sons, René and Charles, followed, each making several trips here between 1722 and 1733.[3] Upon their return, these young men used their earnings to establish themselves by purchasing cleared land, and were thus able to marry and begin families. Hence the fur trade, while it did not bring great wealth to the voyageurs, brought at least some access to security.

It was not until the third generation that a permanent commitment to this new country was made. Inspired by his grandfather's tales of adventure, as well as by those of his father and his uncles, Jean-Baptiste—the eldest son of Jean-François Cadot—entered the fur trade at the age of 18. On 23 June 1742 he contracted with Jean-Baptiste-Nicolas Roch de Ramezay to go to the post of Nipigon with the first canoes to leave that year. He agreed to hunt, fish—in a word, to do all that was commanded him for a period of three years, during which time he could engage in no private trade. At the completion of his term, on his return to Montreal, he would be paid the sum of 700 *livres*.[4]

But the young Jean-Baptiste did not return to Montreal. For him the family farm in Batiscan held no attraction, even though his father's death in 1743 had

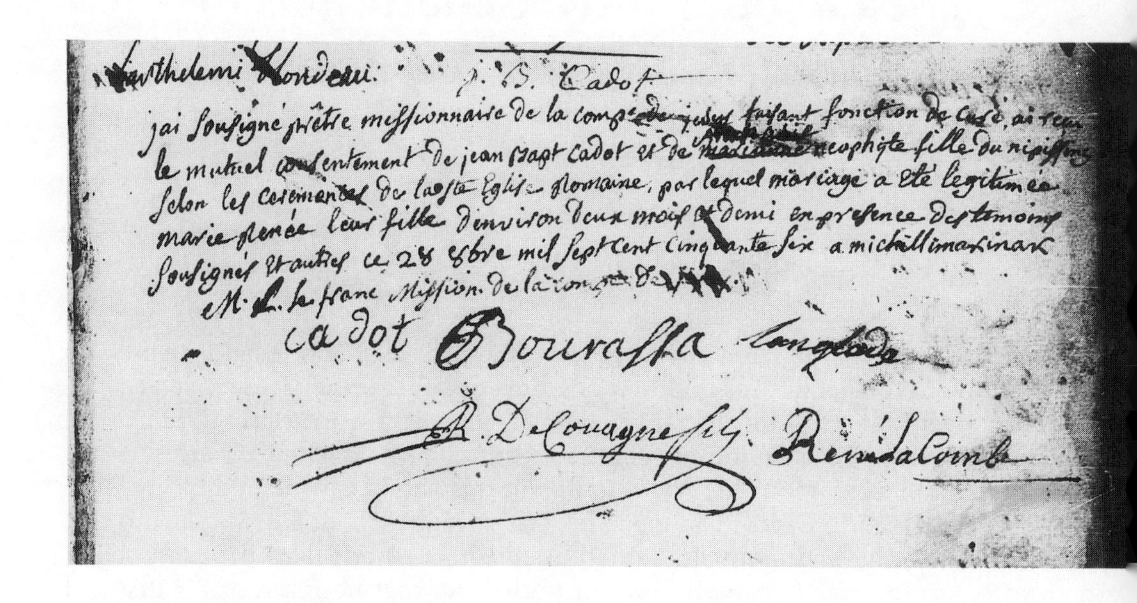
Barthelemi Bondeau   J. B. Cadot
jai Soussigné prêtre missionnaire de la comp. de jesus faisant fonction de curé, ai reçu
le mutuel consentement de jean bapt cadot et de [crossed out] neophyte fille du nipissing
selon les ceremonies de la ste Eglise Romaine, par lequel mariage a été legitimée
marie renée leur fille d'environ deux mois et demi en presence des temoins
soussignés et autres ce 28 8bre mil sept cent cinquante six a michillimakinac
M. L. le franc Mission. de la comp. de J.
cadot Bourassa langlade
R. Decouagne fils. René Lacombe

Figure 1. Record of marriage of Jean-Baptiste Cadot, Ste. Anne's Register. Courtesy of Ste. Anne's Church, Mackinac Island, Michigan.

left him to manage the estate. Here, in the *"pays d'en haut,"*—upper country—he would live out his life and found a new family. By the mid-eighteenth century, Sault Ste. Marie was important not only as the gateway to Lake Superior but also as a summer rendezvous for Indians and voyageurs alike. The French, realizing its strategic value in controlling the fur trade, decided to establish a fort there to intercept Indians bringing their furs to trade with the British. When Louis Legardeur de Repentigny arrived in the fall of 1750 to take charge of this new *seigneury*, he found a Frenchman living there married to a Native woman, and hired them to clear the land and prepare it for planting.[5] The Frenchman, later revealed to be Jean-Baptiste Cadot,[6] stayed on to become interpreter at the fort and an effective mediator with the Indians. The fact that his wife was related to several of the local chiefs, including Madjekewiss, must have helped considerably.

When the British trader Alexander Henry the elder, reached the Sault on 19 May 1762, at the end of the Seven Years War, he found that the French had already left, and "the only family was that of M. Cadotte, the interpreter, whose wife was a Chipeway."[7] Realizing the importance of learning the Native language in order to establish himself in the Indian trade, Henry resolved to spend the winter with the family, where Chippewa was the only language spoken. Later that summer, a small detachment of British soldiers arrived under Lt. John

Jamet. Cadot stayed on as interpreter, and was perhaps effective in averting a catastrophe. The new commanding officer, "unable to believe that his troops would have need to live on fish during the winter," intended to trade liquor to the Indians in return for a regular supply of venison and other food.[8] On the night of 22 December, a fire destroyed all the houses at the fort except Cadot's, and all the soldiers were obliged to return to Fort Michilimackinac, except Lt. Jamet, who had been badly burned. At the end of February, after a winter of ice-fishing, the lieutenant was ready to join his command at Michilimackinac, and Cadot was only too glad to accompany him.

With the departure of the British garrison, Cadot, the illiterate voyageur who could barely sign his name, was once more in charge. It was he who restrained the warriors of the Sault from participating in the Indians' attack on Fort Michilimackinac in 1763. Again the following year he was influential in keeping the Natives from going south to attack Detroit.[9] By 1765 the British were letting him represent them in Indian affairs at the Sault. When Cadot visited Fort Michilimackinac that spring, Captain William Howard sent him back to the Sault with a wampum belt "to shew all the Indians that should come to St. Mary's, to acquaint them of the news of the peace" which had recently been negotiated with the Shawnee and the Delaware.[10] It was hoped that Cadot would influence the Chippewa, too, toward peace.

The Indians were willing to accept the peace, but they also wanted to resume the trade which had been suspended two years earlier after the massacre at the fort. In June 1765 Cadot was back in Michilimackinac with eighty canoes of Indians from Lake Superior. Captain Howard wrote to Sir William Johnson that

> they represented to me the miserable situation they had been in for want of trade, and beged I would send some Trader to them, and asked for Mr. Caddot ... I propose to let Mr. Caddot go to Lapoint in Lake Superior, and to let a few English merchants go to other Places, as Mr. Caddot will be near the Center, am Convinced that all the Indians will remain in our Interest.[11]

Alexander Henry, ever anxious to convey his own importance, put it differently: "The exclusive trade of Lake Superior was given to myself. . . .I took into partnership M. Cadotte."[12]

Jean-Baptiste Cadot remained an important figure in the Lake Superior area for the next twenty years, often serving as ambassador to the Indians on behalf of the British and helping to maintain good relations between the fur traders and the Natives. "A man who was much esteemed by Sir William Johnson," wrote Patrick Sinclair, Lt. Governor of Michilimackinac. "He has great influence with the Indians and is considered by them as a great Village Orator."[13] In one of his last missions on behalf of the British, Cadot accompanied Madjekewiss to Chequamegon Bay in an effort to bring about peace among the warring factions of Chippewa (Ojibwa), Sioux and Fox.[14]

While he was very much involved in Indian affairs, Cadot did not neglect the fur trade, the principal source of his income. He continued his association with

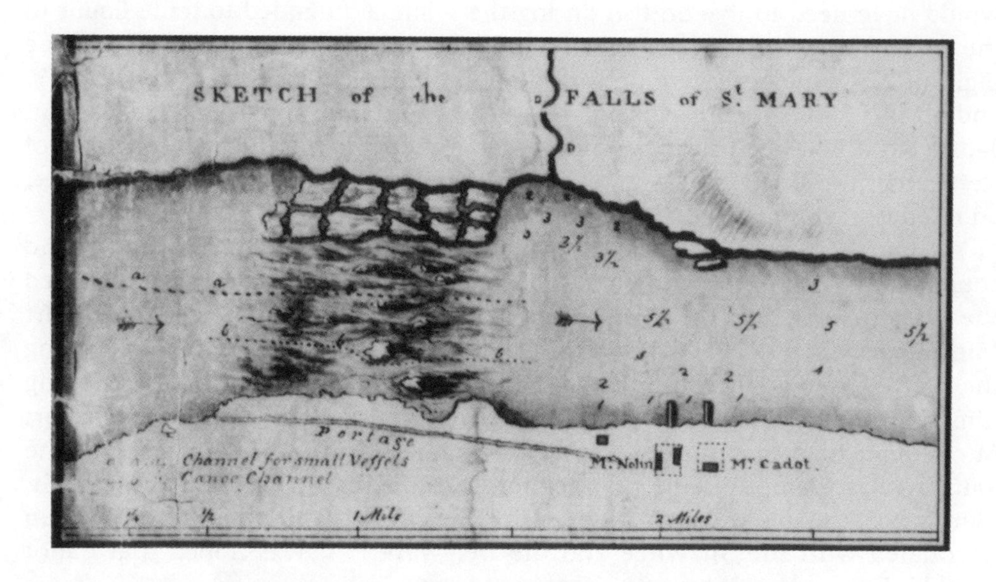

Figure 2. Inset on *Sketch of Lake Huron*, 1788, by Gother Mann, which shows the Cadot post next to that of Jean-Baptiste Nolin. National Archives of Canada, NMC 18557.

Alexander Henry, who often stood security for him in the difficult business of acquiring a license. In 1767, the first year for which we have a record of Cadot's trade, he took out two canoes to Sault Ste. Marie with goods worth £1200.[15] Six years later François Cazeau, his Montreal supplier, was sending him merchandise valued at 9335 *livres*.[16] By then his wife and three surviving children were living in Montreal where he had sent them, in the care of Cazeau, to provide for their education. His records show that he had expanded his trade, acquiring the post at l'Anse, and was now supplying at least one other trader in the area.[17]

In 1775 Cadot accompanied Henry and a group of merchants to Saskatchewan to open up trade with the North. Taking four canoes, he wintered at Fort des Prairies, and returned to the Sault late in the spring of 1776. There he learned that his Native wife had died in Montreal on 18 May, leaving his two sons, Jean-Baptiste, age thirteen, and Michel, age eleven, in the care of their older sister, Marie-Renée, who was then twenty. Soon after, François Cazeau, who had not only supplied Cadot's merchandise and marketed his furs, but also managed the family's affairs in Montreal, was arrested for having sold goods to the Americans during their invasion of Quebec in 1775. It is no wonder that the records are silent on the Cadot enterprise in the year 1776.

Cadot's trade at the Sault had suffered considerably during his absence, and in 1777 he was able to collect furs worth only 593 *livres* to take with him to Montreal.[18] There he made arrangements with Maurice Blondeau to manage

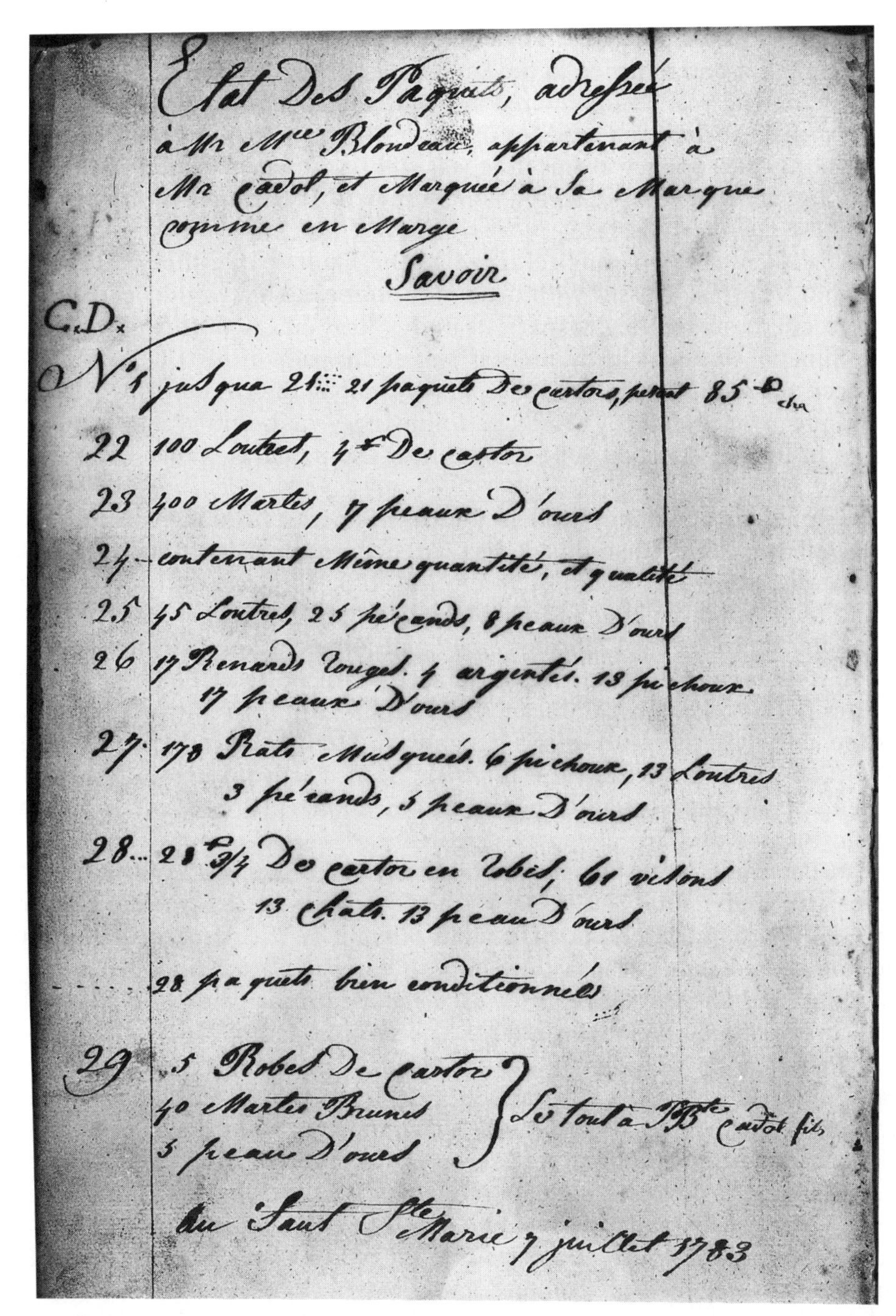

État Des Paquets, adressé
à Mr Mce Blondeau, appartenant à
Mr Cadot, et Marqué à Sa Marque
comme en Marge

Savoir

C.D.

No 1 jusqua 21 ... 21 paquets Des castors, pesant 85

22 100 Loutres, 4 # De castor

23 400 Martes, 7 peaux D'ours

24 contenant Même quantité, et qualité

25 45 Loutres, 25 pécands, 8 peaux D'ours

26 17 Renards rouges. 4 argentés. 18 pichoux.
17 peaux D'ours

27 178 Rats Musqués. 6 pichoux, 13 Loutres
3 pécands, 5 peaux D'ours

28 21 3/4 De castor en robes; 61 vitons
13 Chats. 13 peau D'ours

28 paquets bien conditionnés

29 5 Robes De castor
40 Martes Brunes
5 peau D'ours
} Le tout a Bte Cadot fils

Au Saut Ste Marie 7 juillet 1783

Figure 3. Page from Cadot Ledger showing 28 packs of fur sent in 1783 and the 29th pack belonging to Jean-Baptiste Cadot, Jr. Courtesy of the University of Notre Dame Archives, Notre Dame, Indiana.

his affairs in Montreal while his three children boarded with Blondeau's parents on the rue Nôtre-Dame near their respective schools. Cadot took only one canoe that year and returned to the Sault.

The following year Cadot entered into partnership with Jean-Baptiste Barthe, newly arrived at the Sault, and for the next five years their business prospered. Cadot's only dependency at this time was still l'Anse, managed by L'Étang until 1778, and thereafter by Cazelet. The values of furs traded averaged about 30,000 *livres* per year.[19]

In 1782 Cadot's two sons returned to the Sault, while their sister stayed behind in Montreal to assist with the family business. That winter Jean-Baptiste, Jr., sent out to one of the distant posts in the Fond du Lac district at the head of Lake Superior, brought in by himself one entire pack of furs: beaver, marten, and bear. His proud father listed it separately among the twenty-nine packs sent to Blondeau on 7 July 1783.[20] The following year he put his eldest son in charge of the new post at Folle Avoine near the upper St. Croix River in present-day Wisconsin.

The importance of Cadot's role in the Lake Superior fur trade was recognized by his fellow traders when, on 6 July 1784, he was one of eight men selected to govern Michigan's first Board of Trade.[21] In 1785 fifty-one packs of furs were sent to Montreal, bringing in a total of 36,279 *livres*.[22] This was the peak year of the Cadot fur trade. By 1786 the family had formed a new partnership, Mssrs Cadot et Compagnie. Trade was extensive, with posts at Folle Avoine, Lac Courtes Oreilles, L'Aile au Corbeau, and l'Anse.[23] But fur returns had begun to decline and, with the death of his daughter in Montreal during the summer of 1786, Cadot withdrew from the fur trade. Henceforth his accounts would be turned over to the Société Générale de Michilimackinac, which would also employ his sons.[24]

Jean-Baptiste Cadotte, Jr., meanwhile, was developing his skills as an interpreter and trader. In 1789 he and other members of the Société Générale arranged to occupy different departments of Fond du Lac. Cadotte was assigned Lac Rouge, and thus began a thirteen year career as a fur trader in northern Minnesota and Canada. He returned each summer to the Sault, bringing his furs to Michilimackinac and looking after the needs of his father.

Invited by John Gregory to join the North West Company for three years, Jean-Baptiste, Jr. signed a contract on 2 September 1795 for £3600 annually. Included in the contract was a provision guaranteeing wheat and corn at Detroit prices for his father and his father's second family at Sault Ste. Marie. After only one year, the North West Company offered him another contract for five years, making him a trader and assigning him Red Lake and its dependencies.[25]

Jean-Baptiste continued as a partner in the North West Company until 1803, when he was expelled for conduct found "highly improper and inconsistent with his duty. . . he having indulged himself in drunkeness and riot to the great loss and injury of the said concern."[26] He finished out his days as an interpreter in the Indian Department in Lower Canada.

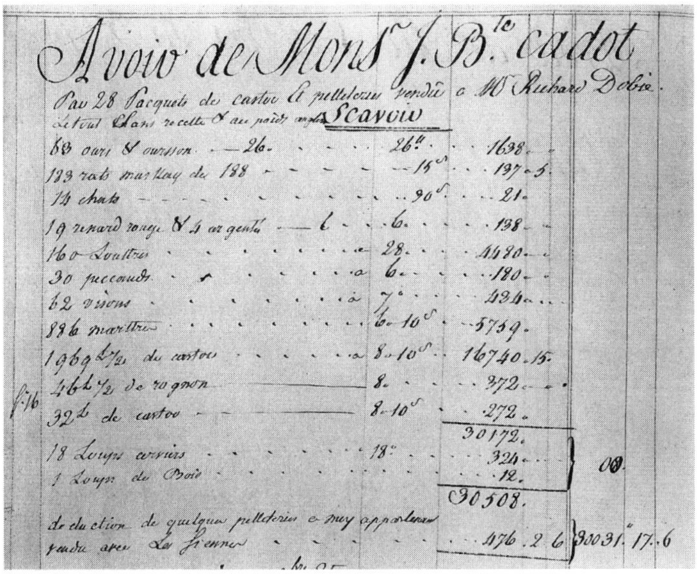

Figure 4. Detail from a page in the Blondeau Account Book showing sale of Cadot fur in 1783. Maurice Blondeau's fur trade account book, plate 91, M13027, Archives, McCord Museum of Canadian History, Montreal.

Like his older brother, Michel Cadotte worked for his father after his return from Montreal in 1782, and later for the Société Générale in the region south of Chequamegon Bay. He eventually settled on Michael's Island, afterwards called Madeline Island in honor of his Ojibwa wife. From his post there he developed an extensive trade extending from Lac du Flambeau to Folle Avoine and all along the upper Chippewa River. In 1799 he was listed as a partner of the North West Company in the South of Lake Superior.[27] Four years later the company offered him a contract for the trade of Point Chequamegon, the Chippewa River, and Lac Courtes Oreilles for a period of three years. According to the terms of the agreement, Cadotte and the North West Company would share equally in profit and loss; Cadotte would purchase all his merchandise from the company at a fixed percentage over Montreal prices, and he would sell his furs to the company at agreed prices. Furthermore, he would not interfere with other traders of the same company, but he would do his best to harm the trade of opposing companies. The contract was renewed for another three years on 5 July 1805, and then assumed by the Michilimackinac Company in 1806 when the North West Company relinquished its trade on the south shore of Lake Superior to the Americans.[28]

In 1807, Cadotte's business suffered irreparable damage when his Lac Courtes Oreilles trading post was burned, with all the winter's furs, during an uprising fomented by the message of the Shawnee Prophet. The value of his destroyed property was later placed at $5000.[29] However, in spite of his loss, Cadotte did

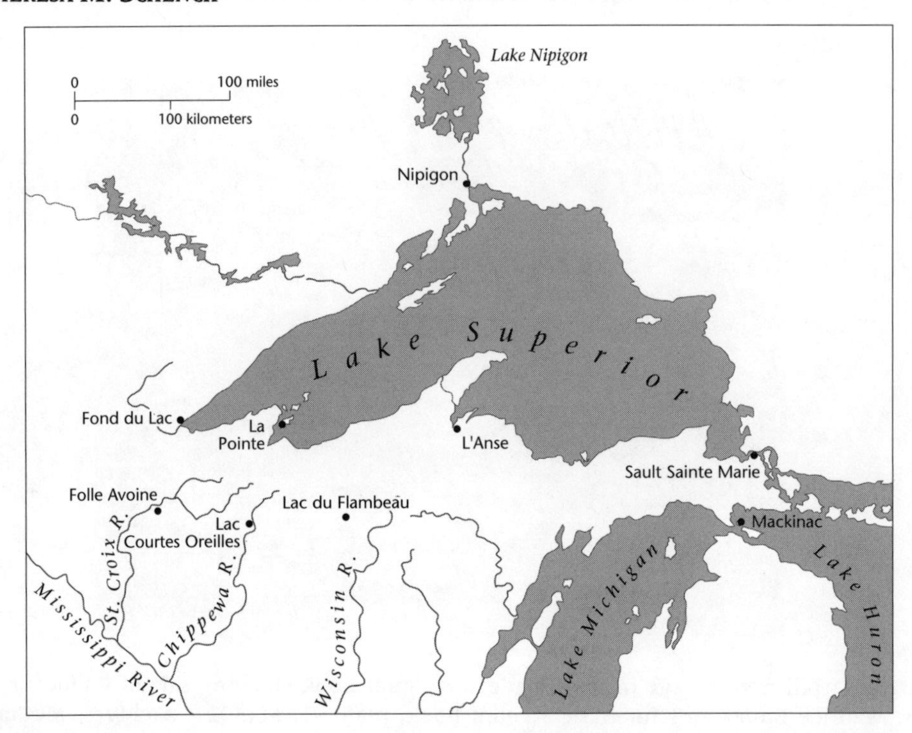

Figure 5. Map of the Lake Superior region showing the location of many of the Cadot fur-trading posts.

not abandon the fur trade. In 1809 he had eight men employed at Lac Courtes Oreilles and La Pointe. The following year he had only four men at Folle Avoine.[30] Fur trade returns had already begun to decline.

In 1811, the Michilimackinac Company and John Jacob Astor agreed to form a new company, the South West Fur Company. Thereafter, and throughout the War of 1812, records are sparse, but it is likely that Cadotte, like most of the Lake Superior traders, continued to send his furs to Canada whenever possible. Astor, meanwhile, was working for passage of a law which would exclude non-citizens from the fur trade within the United States. The law was passed in 1816.

Although Cadotte tried to continue doing business on the Canadian side of the Sault,[31] American traders made it almost impossible for him to collect furs in what had once been his territory. On 2 August 1819 Ramsay Crooks wrote to Cadotte asking him to cooperate with the company traders and not go beyond the places he usually visited.[32] With this warning in mind, Cadotte arrived at the American Fur Company offices in Mackinac the following summer with furs valued at $1151.28.[33] Three weeks later he purchased American citizenship for $5.[34]

In 1821 Cadotte's two sons, Michel, Jr. and Augustin, began to work for the American Fur Company's Lac du Flambeau outfit as interpreters, although their father continued to trade independently from his post at La Pointe. In July 1822 he was able to send only $793.69 in furs to Mackinac, and returned with sundry goods valued at $731.89.[35] The next year he did better, bringing in furs worth $1227.22, mostly muskrat.[36]

In 1822 the Lac du Flambeau outfit was purchased by two brothers from New York, Lyman and Truman Warren,[37] who later married daughters of Michel Cadotte and took over much of his trade. After 1826 the American Fur Company records show that all of Cadotte's trade was carried on within Lyman Warren's outfit, which now included Lac Courtes Oreilles, Lac du Flambeau, and Folle Avoine. By 1827 Warren had taken over the La Pointe post, and was one of the partners of the Lake Superior outfit. Michel Cadotte had effectively retired from the fur trade.

All the sons of Michel Cadotte were active in the fur trade for as long as it lasted at La Pointe. Michel, Jr., Augustin, and Antoine maintained accounts with the American Fur Company in Mackinac at least until 1834, as did some of their Canadian cousins. After this date, as the amount of furs had already declined drastically, the company turned to developing a fishing industry. The Cadottes, all of whom had married Ojibwa women, stayed with their people. They are still there today—at Lac Courtes Oreilles, L'Anse, Red Cliff, Bad River, and Bay Mills—for unlike the white fur traders, they were not there to exploit the Native people, but to share their life.

Notes

1. The spelling "Cadotte" was initiated by the English after 1780 and never used by the first three generations.
2. *Congé* dated 14 June 1686, Archives Nationales du Québec, Montreal.
3. Etude Adhémar, 8 May 1717; Etude David, 4 May 1722; Etude Adhémar, 28 April 1724; Etude Adhémar, 1 May 1724; Etude Adhémar, 28 May 1732; Etude Porlier, 26 May 1733, Archives Nationales du Québec, Montreal.
4. Etude Blanzy, 23 June 1742, Archives Nationales du Québec, Montreal.
5. M. de La Jonquière to Minister of the Colonies, 17 September 1751, MG 1, France, Archives des Colonies, Serie C11A, vol. 95, 104-7. Correspondance Générale, Canada. National Archives of Canada, Ottawa.
6. Testimony of Francis X. Biron, *The United States vs. De Repentigny et al., United States Supreme Court, Transcript of Records* (Washington D.C.: Government Printing Office,1866), 5: 70-71.
7. Alexander Henry, *Travels and Adventures in Canada* (Ann Arbor, MI: University Microfilms, Inc., 1966), 58.
8. Ibid., 63.
9. Ibid., 164-65.
10. William Howard to William Johnson, 17 May 1765, in *Sir William Johnson Papers*, 14 vols. ed., James Sullivan (Albany: State University New York Press, 1921-1965), 11: 739. Hereafter the *Sir William Johnson Papers* cited as *SWJP*.
11. Idem., 24 June 1765, 11: 805.
12. Henry, *Travels and Adventures in Canada*, 193.

13. Patrick Sinclair to Dietrich Brehm, 29 October 1779, Haldimand Papers, *Michigan Pioneer and Historical Collections,* 40 vols. (Lansing, 1874-1929), 10: 530. Hereafter the Michigan Pioneer and Historical Collections cited as *MPHC.*
14. Daniel Robertson to Daniel Claus, 7 September 1783, Haldimand Papers, *MPHC,* 11: 383.
15. Fur Trade Returns 1767, Colonial Office Papers, London, *Canadian Historical Review* 3 (1922): 352.
16. 11 May 1773, Cadotte Account Book, University of Notre Dame Archives, Notre Dame, Ind.
17. 18 July 1773 and 1 August 1773, Cadotte Account Book.
18. 26 September 1777, Blondeau Account Book, McCord Museum, Montreal.
19. Ibid., 1778-1786.
20. 7 July 1783, Cadotte Account Book.
21. Bond Papers, 6 July 1784, *MPHC* 37: 424.
22. 1 September 1785, Cadotte Account Book; 30 September 1785, Blondeau Account Book, McCord Museum, Montreal.
23. Cadotte Account Book, 1785-1786.
24. Cadotte Account Book, 1787.
25. Jean-Baptiste Cadotte Papers, National Archives of Canada, Ottawa.
26. W.S. Wallace, ed., *Documents Relating to the North West Company* (Toronto: The Champlain Society, 1935), 172.
27. "Arrangements of the Proprietors, Clerks, Interpreters, etc. of the North-West Company in the Indian Departments 1799, " in L. R. Masson, *Les Bourgeois de la Compagnie du Nord-Ovest,* 2 vols. (New York: Antiquarian Press, 1960), 1:65.
28. Wallace, *Documents,* 76-78, 224-26.
29. 4 September 1841, Indian Affairs, Records of the La Pointe Sub-Agency, Roll 388, National Archives, Washington, D.C.
30. Notarial Records of the Michilimackinac Company, Abbott Account Book, Bayless Public Library, Sault Ste. Marie.
31. John Johnston Waste Book, 14 July 1817 and 20 September 1821, Henry Rowe Schoolcraft Papers, Reel 68, Library of Congress.
32. Mackinac Letter Book, 8 July 1819 - 30 December 1819, American Fur Company Papers, Minnesota Historical Society.
33. American Fur Company Account Book, 24 July 1820, National Archives of Canada, Reel 1.
34. Ibid., 15 August 1820.
35. Ibid., 18 July 1822.
36. Ibid., 8 July 1823.
37. Ibid., Reel 2, 22 July 1823.

The Fear of Pillaging: Economic Folktales of the Great Lakes Fur Trade

Bruce M. White

Throughout the history of the fur trade in the western Great Lakes, European traders and Native people employed a variety of means to insure the peaceful operation of trade.[1] These methods, which included gift-giving and trade protocol, were designed to prevent the possibility of violence, the pillage or theft of furs or goods by either trader or Native customer. While violence was infrequent in the trade, the fear of pillaging, including both the fear of being pillaged and the fear of the consequences of pillaging someone, was one of the motivating factors for trade gift-giving and protocol. This fear of pillaging was one of the most important themes in the stories that traders and Native people told each other about the fur trade.

In 1880 the retired fur trader, Paul H. Beaulieu, wrote a sketch of the business methods of the fur trade among the Anishinabe or Ojibwa-speaking people in the region south of Lake Superior, in which he and his family had been involved for several generations. Beaulieu concluded the description with a tantalizing statement: "The winter evenings were spent in forming plans of the various and different trips to be made, talking of old Supernatural beliefs, how to manage in the divers situations that a voyageur may be placed &c &c."[2]

Beaulieu is not specific about these "divers situations," nor the form in which advice was shared among fur traders on winter evenings. It is likely, however, that much of the discussion on how to manage in a variety of situations took the form of storytelling, accounts of the way in which other traders managed in particular situations. By telling stories of what people were said to have done in the past, traders laid plans for what they themselves might do when faced with dangerous situations.

This is another way of saying that fur traders in the Great Lakes shared a kind of occupational folklore, one in which they explained and defined their relationships with Native peoples. This folklore survives today in a variety of apparently historical accounts, stories which purport to give truthful descriptions of events that happened to actual fur traders in the past. Recurring motifs in these stories suggest, moreover, that these historical accounts are less important for any factual content than they are as remnants of folktales that fur traders once told each other, stories that reveal a great deal about the nature of Indian-trader economic and social relationships.

One of the more striking of the recurring stories found in historical accounts of the trade has to do with the theme of pillage. The story concerns a fur trader, a group of Native people, a burning firebrand, and a keg of gunpowder. The story survives in at least six different versions, each independent of the other, each with different names, dates, and other details. As is often the case with folktales, each version was told with the understanding that it actually happened either to the person telling the story or to someone known to him. Some folklorists would describe such apparently "true tales" as legends, "belief stories," or "memorates" rather than folktales.[3]

The first known example was recorded in 1751. Jacques Repentigny Legardeur de Saint Pierre, a military officer involved in the fur trade, set out from Lake Superior "in search of the western sea." He described the incident in his journal written for his superiors. He was at Fort la Reine, at Portage la Prairie on the Assiniboine, he said, when it happened. He was sitting quietly in his room when 200 armed Assiniboine entered the fort. Some of them took possession of the guard house.[4]

> I ran to the guard house and demanded from them, through a [Cree man], who was in my service as interpreter, what were their views . . . . My interpreter, who betrayed me, said these Indians had no bad intentions, at the very same time an [Assiniboine] orator, who had been constantly making fine speeches to me, had told the interpreter, that in spite of him, his nation would kill and rob me. I had scarcely made out their intentions, than I forgot it was necessary to take the arms from them. I seized hold of a blazing brand, broke in the door of the powder magazine, knocked down a barrel of powder, over which I passed the brand, telling the Indians in an assured tone, that I expected nothing at their hands, and that in dying I would have the glory of subjecting them to the same fate. No sooner had the Indians seen my lighted brand and my barrel of powder with its head staved in, and heard my interpreter, than they all fled out of the gate of the fort, which they damaged considerably in their hurried flight. I soon gave up my brand, and had nothing more urgent to do than to close the gate of the fort.[5]

The basis of Legardeur's threat and the cause for its believability was the knowledge by all parties concerned of what could happen to a keg of gunpowder when set afire. Few Indian groups around Lake Superior could have been unfamiliar with these effects, at least by the eighteenth century. In fact, the French appear to have occasionally put on demonstrations of the power of gunpowder to groups with whom they sought to establish trade.[6]

Legardeur's description of what he said happened at Fort La Reine sets the tone for many other versions of the story. The trader is not prepared. He is lied to by people whom he thought he could trust. His men abandon him. He thinks all is lost. Then he seizes the only opportunity left to him, threatening assured mutual destruction to save his goods and himself. The Indians believe his threat and are impressed by his courage. Coolly the trader closes the gate of the fort.

The next version of the story dates from the late 1770s. The story was told in a 1791 book credited to a British trader named "J. Long," in an account of the trade north of Lake Superior. Long told how he saved a neighboring trader named Shaw from some "Hudson Bay Indians" who were threatening pillage. Shaw's Canadian employees "fled to the woods." Shaw lived in a house surrounded by "high pickets." As the group of armed men came toward the post they announced that they did not mean to kill Shaw but simply take control of the post and all that was in it. J. Long, who had been given the name "Beaver" by another group of Indians, had an idea:[7]

> A fortunate thought came into my head, which I instantly put into practice: I went into the store, and rolling a barrel of gunpowder into the outer room, knocked out the head. I had scarcely finished it, before the Savages arrived, and advancing to the door, armed with spears and tomahawks, said to each other . . . "you go first." We stood ready to receive them, and gave them to understand we were not afraid of them. One of the band entered the house, and I said to him sternly . . . "Who now among you old women is a brave soldier?" and immediately pointing my pistol cocked to the barrel of gunpowder cried out with great emphasis . . . "We will all die this day." On hearing the words they ran from the door, crying, . . . "The master of Life has given the Beaver great strength and courage."[8]

This story and other sections of Long's narrative have often been accepted as true accounts of the Lake Superior fur trade. Many of the details in his work are corroborated by other sources. However, research by historian Michael Blanar points out that there is no record of a fur trader of that name in the region of Lake Superior at that period. Thus, far from being the autobiographical account it purports to be, Long's narrative may really be a collection of stories, some invented, some obtained from a variety of people knowledgeable about the Great Lakes fur trade. One way or another Long's version of this pillaging story has many similarities to Legardeur's, as well as a few differences.[9]

Although Long stated that he had time to roll a keg of powder from one room to another and knock open its head, he did not have time to grab a burning firebrand. Perhaps there was no fire burning. In any case, the firebrand was not absolutely necessary to bring off this bluff. A loaded gun would do as well. On the other hand, as Long goes on to say, it was necessary to be "cool, firm, and, in the case of emergency, brave, but not rash or hasty."[10] Further, eloquence, strong words or, as Legardeur put it, "a serious tone," appears to have been important so as to make sure that those invading the trading post understood the complete seriousness of the trader.

Other versions of the story were told not by the traders who claimed it happened to them but by others who had heard it. The European-Anishinabe historian William Warren recorded a version of the story, describing an incident that was supposed to have occurred in 1793, though it was not written down until the 1850s, nor was it published until 1885. The incident was said to have occurred on the Red River, when a group of fur traders led by Warren's grandfather, Michel Cadotte, and Cadotte's brother, Jean Baptiste Cadotte, Jr., had gone with a group of Anishinabe to the border country with the Dakota, in order to take advantage of the unexploited game resources. According to Warren, the group went down the Red River in order to travel to Grand Portage on Lake Superior.[11]

William Warren heard this account either from his grandmother Madeleine Cadotte, Michel's wife, or from an elderly fur trader named Charles Bruce, both of whom were there when it happened:

> It is stated that at Prairie Portage after the traders had all again collected in the spring, the Dakotas in large numbers made demonstrations to fall upon and pillage them, and the only manner in which the whites succeeded in intimidating them to forego their designs, was to heap their remaining powder kegs into a pile in the centre of the camp, and threatening to set fire to them the moment the Dakotas attempted to pillage.[12]

Supposedly the Dakota were especially impressed by this kind of bluff by a desperate trader. Louis Provençalle, a trader along the Minnesota River in the early years of the 19th century, was apparently forced to use the same strategy. Henry H. Sibley of the American Fur Company, an employer of Provençalle, said of him:

> He it is of whom it is truly related, that when threatened by a band of wild Dakotas with the pillage of his goods, he seized a firebrand, and holding it within a few inches of an open keg filled with gunpowder, he declared his determination to blow them, with himself, into the air, if they seized upon a single article. It is hardly necessary to mention that his reckless conduct had the desired effect, for he suffered no further annoyance of a like kind.[13]

A contemporary of Provençalle's, the American Fur Company trader William Farnsworth, was recorded to have pursued a similar strategy during his first year among the Menominee, around 1818. The story was published in his obituary in 1860. The author, Morgan L. Martin, stated that Farnsworth had scarcely settled into a "rude log cabin" with his winter's supply of goods and provisions when the head men of the nearby community, fifteen or twenty men in all, paid him a visit to warn him that he must either leave their country or give up his goods. Farnsworth was accompanied only by a single terrified man, who could not be relied upon for assistance "if force alone were to decide the contest."

> In this dilemma, Farnsworth seized a keg of powder, placed it in the centre of the room, and fixed a stump of burning candle in the orifice at the top. He then addressed them in a calm but determined tone of voice, that he knew they were "braves"—that he also was a *brave* of the white men; and if his property and life must be sacrified, they must all suffer the same fate; no truly *brave* man should ever fear death. Nothing further was said, but as the candle had nearly burned out, one after another of the Indians left the house in great haste, and the trader having got rid of his visitors, extinguished the lighted candle.

From then on Farnsworth was said to have traded many years unmolested,

> . . . and his powder plot or scheme, by which the threats of the Indians were counteracted, and which convinced them of his fearless courage, and resolute determination to pursue his vocation, and stay among them as a trader, made a large portion of the tribe his devoted friends.[14]

In each of these stories, the strategy of the trader, who is sometimes said to be a novice, is to try to bluff the Native people with a grand gesture and in some cases with grand words and an appearance of recklessness. What happened if the bluff was called, if the Indians were even more reckless than the one making the threat? One version of the story involves just such a possibility. The incident apparently occurred at Isle à la Crosse on the English River. The author, George Nelson, wrote about it in the 1830s. He heard about it from some French Canadians on the Winnipeg River in 1805, who told of what happened to a trader named Le Sieur in the 1780s.

Le Sieur was a canny trader, said always to be prepared for the worst. He was "brave & resolute," but "haughty & blustering." On this occasion a large group of Indians had gathered outside his house to pillage his goods. Expecting this he had prepared a nine-gallon keg full of ashes or dirt and laid on the surface a couple of inches of powder so that it would resemble a full keg of gunpowder. When the Indians arrived and began to be "very clamorous & unruly," he told them, "Well, since there is no avoiding, let us all die together for I am resolved to perish sooner than have my property plundered from me." He seized a firebrand and walked into his shop.

> The Indians rose, many ran out apprehending the consequence, butt many followed. He uncovered the powder, in a rage told the chief (the Marten was his name) "here—you see this Keg of Powder? if you do not retire I shall blow you all up"! and made a sham push—The Marten tore the brand out of his hand & exclaimed "those old women! it is thus thou woulds't play with men? do thy worst. Blow us up & we'll all go together—" and actually was thrusting the brand in to the Powder, but his friends prevented him saying: "seest thou not how that old woman [Le Sieur?] is afraid—why should we men all perish where is no necessitty for the sake of this *faintheart.*" They mastered him at this time . . . .[One who was there] told me the havock & uproar they made was frightful indeed; they would undoubtedly have been all killed had not a few of the more peaceable ones interfered & protected them, at the hazard of their own lives.[15]

Le Sieur and his men escaped without injury, but not because of their own maneuvres.[16]

Nelson's version suggests the degree to which each folktale in this series contains a bit of the author's own character. Legardeur writes like someone eager to impress his superiors. The cynical J. Long seems eager to show up everyone as a fool but himself. Nelson's story is anti-heroic, displaying Nelson's sense of human vanity and what it leads people to do.

Nelson's version is also the most literary version of these accounts, at least in stylistic terms. Nelson, however, was not the only skillful writer to have given a literary twist to the story. William Joseph Snelling, in his pioneering collection of short stories and sketches *Tales of the Northwest*, provided one of the earliest overtly fictional uses of the story.[17] Snelling spent several years in the Minnesota region in the 1820s, where his father Josiah Snelling was a commandant at Fort Snelling, military post at the confluence of the Minnesota and Mississippi rivers. William Joseph Snelling travelled throughout the region and had direct contact with both fur trader and Indian. For at least one year, Snelling was also a licensed trader among the Dakota.

When Snelling returned to Boston after 1828 to take up the career of journalist and editor, he wrote the book *Tales of the Northwest*, based on his many experiences. Some pieces in this 1830 collection were direct descriptions of the experiences of a variety of well-known frontier figures. Other stories, though containing authentic details of the region, were intended to be fictional. In the story "Pinchon," set in the early 1700s, Snelling claims to be telling the experiences of the French ancestor, five generations before, of a Dakota chief whom Snelling had known at Fort Snelling. The man's ancestor, Antoine Pinchon, described as "one of the first traders who pushed their fortunes among the Dahcotahs," was an unremitting, though audacious, scoundrel. To show his unearthly ability to manipulate people, Snelling has Pinchon, on his first trip from Montreal to the Upper Mississippi, face down an entire Winnebago village, who "swarmed about the boat, and were clamorous for the accustomed tribute, paid by traders on passing the lake, and seemed much disposed to help themselves." The entire action takes place in a birch-bark canoe in the center of Lake Winnebago.

Pinchon sends one of his fellow traders named Joe Le Duc to ask the Winnebagoes what they want. Their reply was that they wanted gunpowder.

> To work he went, and having placed all the powder kegs in the centre of the boat, in the midst of the cases of bullets he told Le Duc to desire them to draw near. They came to him; some producing their powder horns, others their calico shirts, and in short, everything that might contain the nitre. "Now, Le Duc," said Pinchon, raising his voice, "tell them to let their bravest man come forward, and take what he wants. Tell them that he who puts his hand on anything here, does it at his peril." With these words he knocked in the head of one of the kegs, cocked his gun, and buried its muzzle in the powder.

The result, according to Snelling was terror and confusion on the part of the Winnebago. The Indians jumped in the water to swim to shore. "The Indians gained their village with all possible expedition, and no more was seen of them."[18]

It is possible that there are many other versions of this story of powderkeg and pillage, whether apparently fictional or apparently factual. There are, in fact, versions of this story set outside a fur-trade context. Some nineteenth-century accounts of the American Revolutionary War General Israel Putnam tell how he bluffed during a duel with a British officer by threatening to light a barrel of

Figure 1. Stories of wily heroes bluffing opponents by threatening to blow up kegs of gunpowder are not unique to the fur trade. The American Revolutionary war hero General Israel Putnam was said to have bluffed a British officer by threatening to light a barrel of onions disguised as a keg of gunpowder. In this nineteenth-century engraving, Putnam sits in readiness on the barrel, holding his pipe. The British officer makes a "precipitate retreat." Taken from William Cutter, *The Life of Israel Putnam, . . .* (New York: Derby & Jackson, 1859), 363.

onions disguised as a keg of gunpowder.[19] These other versions of the folktale, of course, have their own special meaning, dependent on the context in which they were told. The versions we have examined from the fur trade make it clear that for the fur traders themselves, these recurring incidents had a particular resonance. Whether or not they actually ever occurred, their truthfulness rests in what they may reveal about the situation and state of mind of the fur trader.

This fur-trade preoccupation with the theme of pillaging is understandable. If his merchandise was taken from him without return, it effectively ended the trader's year's work and might destroy his credit with his company. Another apparent example of trade folklore tells of a trader who could not face this prospect. Thomas L. McKenney, in his 1826 trip along the south shore of Lake Superior, noted that there was once a North West Company post there. According to McKenney, who probably heard the story from his fur-trade guides, its clerk was a Frenchman.

> The Indians beset his establishment, and resolved to take away his goods. He being unwilling to survive the odium of being vanquished, or the suspicion of having been accessory to plunder, drew his pistol and shot himself.[20]

The fear of being in such a situation provided the fur trader with a strong motive for telling stories about pillage. Such stories functioned as *cautionary tales*. As the folklorist Jack Santino notes, this kind of story is one of the major forms of occupational folklore. In the case of occupations predominately involving manual labor, such stories often involve accidents and how to prevent them.[21] In the case of the fur trader, whose power in part came from his ability to manipulate people, these cautionary tales involved mistakes of another kind, namely, errors in human relationships that disturbed the balance of trust that was necessary for the long-term functioning of trade.

The trader's power, the respect he had in the community with which he traded, came in part from his merchandise. His power to manipulate people in this community came from his ability to play upon their desire for merchandise. It was the intensity of this desire among his customers for merchandise, paradoxically, that could cause the trader to lose everything. The trader needed to try to prevent the situation from ever arising, by giving away some of his merchandise while retaining enough of it to carry on actual trade of furs for goods. But the trader also needed to be prepared should he be unable to create the proper balance.

The economic constraints that fur traders were under meant that traders themselves felt justified, by their own admission, in pillaging the furs of Indians, if it was necessary to prevent their being taken to opposition traders.[22] However, only a few traders or writers on the fur trade used the word pillage in relation to the behavior of Europeans. So far, however, we have looked at the theme of pillage from the trader's point of view. It is time to consider the point of view of Native people, the people who traders consistently feared would pillage them. Throughout the various versions of the powderkeg/firebrand story, Native people have been merely cardboard figures. Did the people like the Anishinabeg pillage traders? If so, what might have been their motives?

To Pillage or Not to Pillage

The message of these common descriptions of pillaging in fur-trade accounts is not that life was routinely dangerous for traders in the western Great Lakes. In each account the story is described as an extraordinary event. Statistically the pillage rate and the death rate for fur traders in the western Great Lakes was probably not very high between 1650 and 1850, though there may have been times and places that were more dangerous than others.[23]

An examination of some of the journals of traders who dealt with the Anishinabeg west of Lake Superior in the late eighteenth and early nineteenth centuries suggests that pillaging by the Anishinabeg was threatened far more than it was ever practiced. Charles Chaboillez, a trader on the Red River in 1797, reported rumors of several plots to pillage his post. In one case, "In the night an old Woman came to the Door of the Fort & informed us of the Indians intending to make a Trial to Pilladge." Chaboillez gave each of his men a gun and ordered them to discharge one round with only powder.

> They immediately Came to the fort Door & asked what was the Matter. I told them that I was Inform[ed] that the Dogs wanted to bite us, & that I was preparing to receive them. They went to their Tents & were very quiet all Night.[24]

Commenting on incidents like this, Chaboillez's editor, anthropologist Harold Hickerson, argued that

> the threat of pillage was actually the one reasonable weapon of retaliation the Indians possessed in an unequal commercial relationship. The fact that these plots were almost invariably exposed or arrested by the Indians themselves, would indicate either that the Indians were divided among themselves, or that the point of retaliation was the threat and not the practice of pillage.

Clearly, whether or not the trader's customers ever intended to pillage him, the possibility could influence him. As historian Frederic Lane has suggested, violence and its threat has long been a part of European economic history.[26] Rumors of pillage or worse were sometimes spread by competing traders as a means of intimidation.[27] Some instances of pillage were actually initiated by traders as a competitive practice against other traders. For Native people, on the other hand, threatening to pillage could be a valuable bargaining tool, one of a number of strategies at the hands of Native customers for improving the rates of exchange of furs for merchandise and making the trader more generous in gifts, even at times when trade monopolies existed. The threat to pillage may even, as some of the powderkeg/firebrand stories suggest, have been more commonly tried against young inexperienced traders, a quick way of training the novice in generosity.[28] The very possibility of pillage suggests that the relationship between fur trader and Native customer was inherently far more balanced than Hickerson was willing to admit.

To threaten pillage was to remind the trader that he was, comparatively speaking, a wealthy man in a community that respected sharing and generosity more than it did wealth. It also reminded the trader of the inescapable fact that he was vastly outnumbered. This awareness may have improved the behavior of fur traders. It also appears to have influenced the actions of European government officials in the Great Lakes. Far from being controlled militarily by European governments, Native people exerted a great deal of control over their relationships, over what they gave and what they got. Even when they allied themselves militarily to Europeans, they did so on their own terms.

The narrative of Alexander Henry, the elder, on the fur trade of the British period makes this clear. Henry went west from Montreal in 1761 in "a premature attempt to share in the fur-trade of Canada, directly on the conquest of the country."[29] In June 1763, Henry experienced one of the most famous attacks by Anishinabeg and related groups on Europeans, the siege of Fort Michilimackinac. In one sense this attack was a military battle, in which groups that had been allied with the French continued hostilities against the English after the French themselves had surrendered. One Anishinabe leader explained to Henry shortly after his arrival that though the English had conquered the

French, "you have not conquered us." He added, "Your king has never sent us any presents, nor entered into any treaty with us, wherefore he and we are still at war." British traders, though they did not represent their government, were still viewed with suspicion. Thus, the attack on the British garrison was also a pillage in which the goods of British traders were seized.[30]

Subsequently, as Alexander Henry himself described, the British did succeed in making treaties with the Indian groups of the western Great Lakes, in which gifts and pleasant words were exchanged.[31] These treaties, however, were not necessarily binding on any particular group or individual that a fur trader might encounter. At least during initial encounters with particular Native groups, individual traders were strangers. There was always the potential that they could become enemies as much as friends. And enemy was likely to pillage enemy.

In 1765, Alexander Henry arrived at Chequamegon on the south shore of Lake Superior to trade with Anishinabeg who, because of the recent war, had not received any goods for a number of years. He built a trading house, and as was the usual practice advanced goods to the Indians, particularly clothing. When the first group of hunters brought in their furs, Henry experienced "some disorderly behavior; but happily without serious issue." The incident took place when all the men were in his trading house.

> Having crowded into my house, and demanded rum, which I refused them, they talked of indulging themselves in a general pillage, and I found myself abandoned by all my men. Fortunately, I was able to arm myself; and on my threatening to shoot the first who should lay his hands on any thing, the tumult began to subside, and was presently after at an end. . . . Admonished of my danger, I now resolved on burying the liquor which I had; and the Indians, once persuaded that I had none to give them, went and came very peaceably, paying their debts and purchasing goods.[32]

Henry's account of this incident represents another common kind of story about pillaging. Though it includes neither firebrand nor powderkeg, it involves a trader who is threatened by his Indian customers and abandoned by his employees. It has a kind of formulaic quality, telling of the means by which trader outwits Indian, with eloquence if not with gestures.

The Sault Ste. Marie fur trader John Johnston was said to have had a similar encounter with a noted Anishinabe leader along the south shore of Lake Superior in 1793, also early in his career. The man supposedly threatened Johnston's life for refusing him some liquor. Indian agent Henry Schoolcraft, Johnston's son-in-law, described what happened in an 1827 account:

> Mr. Johnston placing his sword and loaded pistols before him, threatened the life of any Indian who should enter his tent in a hostile manner. His men, being Canadians, fled and secreted themselves in the woods. In this perilous situation, while they were in the act of coming to blows, a sudden storm of rain and wind arose, attended with severe claps of thunder. The Indian was appalled. "Englishman," he exclaimed, "put tobacco in the fire! Your God is stronger than mine." "No! replied Mr. J. "put your tobacco in the fire. I have full confidence in *my God*. Is is against *you* that his anger is excited."[33]

In any given situation threats to the trader's goods could arise, especially if his men could not be counted upon. In particular, demand for merchandise in times of scarcity could lead to individual instances of pillage. Other traders had similar experiences during scarce times in the 1760s. According to Benjamin and Joseph Frobisher, when the first British trader ventured west of Lake Superior in 1765, "the Indians of Lake La Pluye [Rainy Lake] having then been long destitute of Goods, stop't and plundered his Canoes, and would not suffer him to proceed further."[34]

Traders were also said to have been plundered at Rainy Lake in 1766 and 1769. Alexander Henry, the elder, on his first voyage west in 1775, said that the residents of the Anishinabe village on Rainy River

> insist . . . on having goods given them on credit, as well as on receiving some presents. The latter they regarded as an established tribute, paid them on account of the ability they possesed, to put a stop to all trade with the interior.

Henry later mentioned that the Anishinabeg who frequented the trading post at Lake of the Woods in earlier times were known to be troublesome, though he himself successfully traded with them for wild rice. Henry noted that "on account of a particular instance of pillage, they have been called *Pilleurs*."[35]

The Ojibwe name "Muk-im-dwa-win-in-wug," men who take by force, as well as the French *Pilleurs* and the English *Pillagers*, has been most frequently applied to the Anishinabe who lived in the area around Leech Lake, Minnesota. An account of how they got this name was recorded by William Warren, who gathered accounts from Anishinabe elders in the 1840s. Warren stated that the incident took place in the summer of 1781, though it is probable that it dates from an earlier period. Henry Schoolcraft and the physician Douglass Houghton, who together visited the region in 1832 on their way to Lake Itasca, both described a similar incident of pillage, said to have taken place in 1767 or 1768. Whenever the original incident may have taken place, Warren's story began with the Anishinabeg of Leech Lake encamped at a small creek which empties into the Crow Wing River about ten miles above its entrance into the Mississippi. As they were preparing to perform their spring Midewiwin religious ceremonies, a canoe arrived from the Lower Mississippi bearing a fur trader and his men.

Not having seen traders for quite some time, the Anishinabeg were pleased to see the man and eager to begin trading. The trader, however, was ill and was not able to begin trading right away. Also, his goods had gotten wet in a recent rain. The trader's men untied the bundles of goods and left them in the sun to dry.

During the Midewiwin it was customary for the Anishinabeg, in the words of Warren, "to display all the finery of which they are possessed." Consequently the people, who had plenty of furs, "offered repeatedly to exchange, but the trader's men refused to enter into a trade till their master was sufficiently recovered to oversee it."

Figure 2. A mixed European-Anishinabe, William Warren is the source for several stories of pillaging, from the point of view of both the Anishinabeg and fur traders. Courtesy of the Minnesota Historical Society.

It was only then that the pillaging began. Warren's informants insisted that there was no concerted plan to pillage the trader. But seeing the goods laid out in front of them, the people began to take what they wanted, saying at first that they would pay the trader when he got well again.

> The young pillagers taking their trophies to the lodges the excitement in the village became general, as each person became determined to possess a share of the trader's remaining bales. The crediting of goods was now changed to actual pillage, and the only anxiety evinced by the Indian men, women, and children, was, who would secure the greatest quantity.

The trader and his men became frightened and quickly embarked to set off down the river. It was said that the trader died soon after.[36]

Other Leech Lake Anishinabeg were not happy with the incident. The following spring a delegation went to Michilimackinac to present goods to the British officials as an apology for their actions. The British commandant accepted the gifts, assuring them of his goodwill and friendship. He strengthened his words "by giving their leader a medal, flag, coat, and a bale of goods." In giving these things he requested that the chief not unfurl the flag nor distribute the goods until he arrived at Leech Lake.

The chief complied with the request until he reached Fond du Lac, where he was tempted to open the bale to display the gifts to his followers. Shortly afterwards he and many others became sick and died. "It proved to be the smallpox," wrote Warren,

> and many of the Anishinabe, believed and it is a common saying to this day, that the white men purposely inflicted it on them by secreting bad medicine in the bale of goods, in punishment for the pillage which the Leech Lake band had committed on one of their traders.[37]

This story of how the Leech Lake Pillagers got their name is a counterpoint to the stories fur traders themselves told about pillaging. It is not about the trader's fear of being pillaged but about Anishinabe fear of pillaging traders. Whoever told Warren the story may have included the ending out of regard for Warren's fur-trader ancestry. On the other hand, it is probable that such treatment of traders was not considered normal or desirable. Most Anishinabe communities were interested in long-term relationships with traders. Pillaging might cut off the flow of merchandise coming into the community, since trade companies would avoid sending traders back again. In fact, the Leech Lake Anishinabeg continued to have a bad reputation among traders for many years. William Johnston, who traded at Leech Lake in 1833 and admired the Anishinabe people there, stated that

> this band is noted for the disrespect and contempt, with which they have always treated the traders; and especially the men in their employ, frequently taking from the dishes of food, while they were in the act of eating.[38]

Warren's story, however, humanizes the people who pillage, in ways that the stories told by traders fail to do. Warren explains how peaceful people in an abnormal situation might have been motivated to pillage a trader. The people were in need of trade goods and were eager to trade, prevented only by the unreadiness of the trader. These Anishinabeg did not steal from a trader they had known before, nor had they yet established any social relations with him. The man was a complete stranger. He was not a trader who followed the usual pattern of those who wintered over with them. No ceremonial expressions of friendship had yet taken place. No gifts were exchanged. No credits were given. Thus, as much as this Anishinabe narrative may have been a warning for the Anishinabeg to refrain from pillaging traders, it was also a cautionary tale told by the Anishinabeg for the benefit of traders who might come to trade in their midst. The story reinforced the need to establish social relationships for economic purposes.

The fate of Jean-Baptiste Corbin's trading post has a similar message. The post that Corbin operated for Michel Cadotte at Lac Courtes Oreilles was pillaged, according to William Warren, in the summer of 1808. The event, which Warren apparently recorded from Corbin himself, occurred at the time the teachings of Tenskwatawa, the Shawnee Prophet, were spreading throughout the Great Lakes. These teachings encouraged Native people to discard European trade goods entirely. According to Warren, many around Lac Courtes Oreilles were impressed by these teachings and called for the destruction of trading posts.[39]

Like many before him, Jean-Baptiste Corbin, who had been in the area for at least four years, had married the daughter of an influential family. In the midst of the excitement about the new doctrines of the Shawnee prophet, Corbin "found occasion to give his wife a severe beating, and to send her away almost naked, from under his roof to her parents['] wigwam." Precisely which aspect of Corbin's behavior was offensive to the people of the village is not clear. It may have been the fact of the beating itself or simply that returning the woman to her parents was considered to be an insult to the family. In any case, word of this action spread among the people of Lac Courtes Oreilles. "The young men leaped into their canoes and paddling over to the trading house, which stood about one mile opposite their village, they broke open the doors and helped themselves to all which the storehouses contained." Warren's account places more emphasis on Corbin's actions than on the advice of the Prophet, since he makes no mention of the people destroying the goods they had taken.[40]

For both trader and Native people, pillage was an important aspect of trade strategy. For the people of Lac Courtes Oreilles, pillage was the result of, if not the punishment for, a breakdown in normal social relationships. Pillage or its threat could be a means of encouraging the trader to be fair and honest, to live by the rules of trade, as well as a remedy if the trader did not live up to his responsibilities. Though an actual pillage of a trader might produce goods in the short run, this might not be in a community's long-term best interest. For the trader, on the other hand, pillage was something often feared but seldom experienced. The fear of being pillaged was the ultimate fear. In order to deal with it they resorted to a variety of strategies. If it ever came about, they believed they knew what to do.

Notes

1. This article is an extension of the author's earlier descriptions of fur-trade gift giving and protocol in "'Give Us a Little Milk': The Social and Cultural Significance of Gift Giving in the Lake Superior Fur Trade," in *Selected Papers of the Fourth North American Fur Trade Conference, 1981*, ed. Thomas Buckley (St. Paul: North American Fur Trade Conference, 1984), 185-197; "A Skilled Game of Exchange: Ojibway Fur Trade Protocol," *Minnesota History* 50 (Summer 1987): 229-40. The author would like to thank all those who have offered comments and suggestions on this paper, in particular Anne Kaplan and Douglas A. Birk.
2. Paul H. Beaulieu, "The Fur Trade by Paul H. Beaulieu, 1880," in *Escorts to White Earth 1868 to 1968, 100 Year Reservation*, Gerald R. Vizenor (Minneapolis: The Four Winds, 1968), 91.
3. See Jan Harold Brunvand, *The Study of American Folklore: An Introduction* (New York: W.W. Norton & Co., Inc., 1968), 78. Stith Thompson gives the name folktale to all forms of prose narrative that "have come to be handed down" and states that the "English language has never derived a satisfactory term" for "true tales." See Stith Thompson, *The Folktale* (1946; reprint, Berkeley: University of California Press, 1977), 4, 8, 235n.2. Gillian Bennett describes some of the problems involved in defining these terms in "'Belief Stories': The Forgotten Genre," *Western Folklore* 48 (October 1989): 289-311. On memorates, see Linda Dégh and Andrew Vázsonyi, "The Memorate and the Proto-Memorate," *Journal of American Folklore* 87 (July-Sept. 1974): 225-39.
4. Public Archives of Canada, *Report on Canadian Archives*, 1886, clvii-clxv. On Legardeur, see *Dictionary of Canadian Biography*, vol. 3 (Toronto: University of Toronto Press, 1974), 374-76.
5. Ibid., clxv.
6. Pierre Radisson, for one, told of the consternation among a group of Dakota whom he sought to assure of the undying friendship of Frenchmen. He and his fellow traders threw gunpowder into a fire as a kind of offering, in the same way that the Dakota did with tobacco. The resulting explosion sent people fleeing from the scene. Similar stories occur in other early accounts. Pierre Radisson, *Voyages of Pierre Esprit Radisson* (1885; reprint, New York: Burt Franklin, 1967), 209. See also Emma H. Blair, ed., *The Indian Tribes of the Upper Mississippi Valley and the Region of the Great Lakes*, vol. 1 (Cleveland: Arthur H. Clark Co., 1911), 163.
7. J. Long, *Voyages and Travels of an Indian Interpreter and Trader* (1791; reprint, Toronto: Coles Publishing Co., 1971), 58-71
8. Ibid., 70.
9. See pages 447-63 of this work, Michael Blanar, "Long's *Voyages and Travels*: Fact and Fiction."
10. Long, *Voyages and Travels*, 71.
11. William Warren, *History of the Ojibway People* (1885; reprint, St. Paul: Minnesota Historical Society, 1984), 279-89.

12. Ibid., 288. The "Mr. Bruce" of Warren's narrative is clearly the same as Charles Gaspard Brousse, the retired fur trader who settled near Stillwater, Minn., in 1838. See Lucile M. Kane, *The Northern Expeditions of Stephen H. Long: The Journals of 1817 and 1823 and Related Documents* (St. Paul: Minnesota Historical Society Press, 1978), 191n.1. On Madeleine Cadotte, see Hamilton Ross, *La Pointe: Village Outpost* (Ann Arbor, Mich.: Edward Brothers, Inc., 1960), 65.
13. Henry H. Sibley, "Reminiscences; Historical and Personal," *Minnesota Historical Society Collections*, vol. 1 (1872; reprint, St. Paul: Minnesota Historical Society, 1902), 382.
14. Morgan L. Martin, "Sketch of William Farnsworth," in *Collections of the State Historical Society of Wisconsin*, vol. 9 (1882; reprint, Madison: State Historical Society of Wisconsin, 1909), 398.
15. George Nelson, "Reminiscences," George Nelson Papers, Toronto Public Library, 68-69.
16. A few years after hearing this story, Nelson himself felt the consequences of an exploding keg of gunpowder near Lake Winnipeg in September 1807. Nelson and some other men were sitting around a fire, telling stories and waiting for the cook to prepare breakfast. A damaged nine-gallon keg of gunpowder stood nearby, someone having forgotten to carry it down to the canoes as had been ordered. Suddenly there was "a terrible noise, a thick smoke, & all quietness an instant after." Someone had set off the powder when getting up to light his pipe. One man who had been ten feet away from the keg was badly burned but survived 39 days. Nelson, who had been 32 to 34 inches away from the keg, but sitting on the ground, with a box in between, survived. However, he was burned all over his body. The skin of both of his hands had peeled off "like an eel." Even after applications of various salves, it was a month before he could hold anything in his hands. See Nelson, "Reminiscences," 78-79.
17. William Joseph Snelling, *Tales of the Northwest*, ed., John T. Flanagan (1936; reprint, Minneapolis: Ross & Haines, Inc., 1971), ix-xv.
18. Ibid., 195-96. Interestingly, Snelling's version of the story may very well have been derived from the same source as that recorded by Sibley. Snelling names Pinchon's first fur-trade employer Louis Provencal, the same name as the trader who was the key figure in Sibley's account. Clearly, Snelling could have met the real Louis Provençalle while at Fort Snelling in the 1820s.
19. On Israel Putnam, see William Cutter, *The Life of Israel Putnam* (New York: Derby & Jackson, [1846] 1859), 363-64; Constance Rourke, *American Humor: A Study of National Character* (1931; reprint, Garden City: Doubleday & Co., Inc., 1953), 99. Two similar versions not involving Putnam are found in American almanacs dated around 1800. See J. Michael Stitt, *A Tale Type and Motif Index of Early U.S. Almanacs* (New York: Greenwood Press, 1991), 191.
20. Thomas L. McKenney, *Sketches of a Tour to the Lakes* (1827; reprint, Minneapolis: Ross & Haines, Inc., 1959), 231.
21. Jack Santino, "Occupational Narrative," in *Working Americans: Contemporary Approaches to Occupational Folklife*, no. 3 (Washington, D.C.: Smithsonian Folklife Studies, 1978), 60.
22. See George Nelson, *Journal, 1803-04*, George Nelson Papers, Toronto Public Library, 7.
23. Richard White states that "violence and interracial murder as a whole were inextricably bound up with commerce," but he cites statistics for only one year, 1684,

when 39 Frenchmen died at the hands of "their Algonquian allies." Richard White, *The Middle Ground: Indians, Empires, and Republics in the Great Lakes Region, 1650-1815* (Cambridge, England: Cambridge University Press, 1991), 75.

24. Harold Hickerson, ed., "Journal of Charles Jean Baptiste Chaboillez, 1797-1798," *Ethnohistory* 6 (1959): 291.
25. Ibid., 315n.98.
26. Frederic Lane, *Profits from Power: Readings in Protection Rent and Violence-Controlling Enterprises* (Albany: State University of New York Press, 1979), 1, 22-36, 50-65.
27. See Thomas G. Anderson, "Narrative of Thomas G. Anderson," *Collections of the State Historical Society of Wisconsin*, vol. 9 (1882; reprint, Madison: State Historical Society of Wisconsin, 1909), 149; François Victoire Malhiot, "4 February1805," *Journal, 1804-05*, McGill University Library, Rare Books and Special Collections.
28. See for example the way in which the threat to pillage intimidated the novice trader Michel Curot into increased generosity, in Michel Curot, *Journal, 1803-04*, Masson Collection, National Archives of Canada, 6.
29. Alexander Henry, *Travels and Adventures in Canada and the Indian Territories* (1809; reprint, New York: Garland Publishing Inc., 1976), v.
30. Ibid., 76-93.
31. Ibid., 165-66; Peter S. Schmalz, *The Ojibway of Southern Ontario* (Toronto: University of Toronto Press, 1991), 76-77.
32. Henry, *Travels and Adventures*, 200.
33. Henry R. Schoolcraft, *The Literary Voyageur or Muzzeniegun*, ed. Philip P. Mason (East Lansing: Michigan State University Press, 1962), 136.
34. W. Stewart Wallace, *Documents Relating to the North West Company*, 70-71 (Toronto: Champlain Society, 1934), 70-71.
35. Henry, *Travels and Adventures*, 242, 245.
36. Warren, *History*, 256-59. The Schoolcraft/Houghton version of the story involves a British trader named Berti who, after trading with the Leech Lake people sought to go south to trade with the Dakota. He was robbed and "overwhelmed by his misfortune," he soon died. See Philip P. Mason, ed. *Schoolcraft's Expedition to Lake Itasca: The Discovery of the Source of the Mississippi* (East Lansing: Michigan State University Press, 1958), 57-58, 101n.58, 71, 210, 301-2.
37. Douglas Houghton, in his version of the story, says that Leech Lake people who went to Mackinac in the spring of 1770 as a delegation were given articles poisoned with smallpox by "the agent of the fur company at Mackinac." See Mason, ed., *Schoolcraft's Expedition*, 301-2. A similar story about the introduction of smallpox among the Odawa is given by Andrew J. Blackbird, *Complete both Early and Late History of the Ottawa and Chippewa Indians of Michigan* (Harbor Springs, Mich.: Babcock and Darling, 1897), 2-3:

    > The Ottawas were greatly reduced from what they were in former times, on account of their mortality with small-pox which they brought from Montreal during the French war with Great Britain. This small-pox was sold to them shut up in a showy tin box, with the strict injunction not to open the box on their way homeward, but only when they should reach their country: and that this box contained something that would do them and their people great good. The superstitious and foolish people really believed there was something in the box supernatural, that would do them great good. Accordingly, after they reached home, they opened the box; but behold there was another tin box inside, smaller. They took it out and opened the second box, and

behold, still there was another box inside of the second box, smaller yet. So they kept on in this way till they came to a very small box, which was not more than an inch long; and when they opened the last one they found nothing but mouldy particles in this last little box. They wondered very much what it was, and a great many closely inspected it to try to find out what it meant. But alas, alas! pretty soon there burst out a strange and terrible sickness among them.

38. William Johnston, "Letters on the Fur Trade 1833," in *Michigan Pioneer and Historical Collections* (Lansing: Michigan Pioneer and Historical Society, 1909), 37:185.
39. Warren, *History*, 321-26.
40. Ibid., 325.

Roots in the Mohawk Valley: Sir William Johnson's Legacy in the North West Company

Heather Devine

Several fur-trade researchers have attempted to identify the factors influencing the rapid rise of the Scottish Nor'Westers to business prominence. A shared ethnic identity, military experience, and the adoption of effective trading practices from the French have all been cited as sources of the effective corporate behaviors demonstrated by the Scottish expatriates who comprised the bulk of the North West Company's directorship. However these factors do not adequately account for the considerable speed and success of the Scots' adaptation to the North American fur trade, particularly in light of their relatively brief residency in British North America as compared to their French and Dutch competitors.

Sylvia Van Kirk,[1] in her examination of research trends within the field of fur-trade history, noted that much of the research revolves around three major themes: the differing organizational and personnel structures of the North West and Hudson's Bay companies; the nature of HBC and NWC interactions with the Indians, particularly concerning intermarriage; and the divergent experiences of mixed-blood children from the Hudson's Bay Company and North West Company traditions. In summarizing the major research studies dealing with these areas of interest, Van Kirk went on to identify those areas of fur trade social history that are poorly understood and require further investigation. The bulk of these topics lie within the study of the organizational and personnel structures of the two companies.

Van Kirk noted, for example, that there are no studies of the social antecedents of the Nor'Westers which might identify or incorporate useful models for understanding the organizational/personnel hierarchy of the company, such as Peter Laslett's patriarchal household model,[2] which was utilized by both Jennifer Brown[3] and John Foster[4] in their studies of the Hudson's Bay Company traditions. She went on to suggest that perhaps the study of the social structure of the Highland Scots clan might serve as a useful model for assessing NWC structures.[5]

A second area for further investigation concerns the concepts of horizontal versus vertical integration as applied to the interpretation of company hierarchical

Figure 1. Sir William Johnson, c. 1772, attributed to Matthew Pratt. Courtesy of the New York State Office of Parks, Recreation and Historic Preservation, Johnson Hall State Historic Site.

structures. Jennifer Brown has argued that the life of the Hudson's Bay employee was based largely on kinship and employment ties forged within the context of the company itself.[6] The North West Company employee, on the other hand, brought his prior personal and familial relationships with him into the company, and these prior associations subsequently influenced the personnel and hierarchical patterns within the company. Van Kirk cautions, however, that the concepts of vertical and horizontal integration require further investigation in order to assess their validity, particularly as applied to the experience of the laboring classes within the two companies.

In the case of the North West Company, further research into the sociocultural influences affecting company partners and employees is essential. The suggestion that the North West Company's socioeconomic structures were influenced by prior personal and family relationships may reflect on the assumption that the clan-based socioeconomic relationships of some Scottish Nor'Westers were maintained after emigration to North America and persisted as an influence over any other sociocultural relationships in which they might subsequently have engaged.[7] Further investigation into the ethnohistorical background of the Scots partners of the North West Company serves to shed new light on these issues.

Two significant events occurred in the forty years prior to the formation of the North West Company in 1779-1784. One was the legislated dismantling of the Highland clan system after the Jacobite defeat at Culloden in 1746 and the subsequent dislocation of clan members. The other was the development of new patronage relationships in Britain and North America.

The layperson might assume that traditional loyalties between clan chieftains and their followers persisted despite the punitive legislation introduced by the British after the violent suppression of the Jacobites in 1746. It might also be assumed that the dismantling of the clan system was an event that was regretted by all the participants involved.[8] A considerable body of scholarly research dealing with eighteenth-century Scottish social history, however, indicates clearly that this was not the case.[9]

Debt-ridden Highland chieftains were more than happy to shed the financial responsibilities of clan leadership, and divested themselves of their patriarchal obligations to their followers with unseemly rapidity. They evicted clansmen from ancestral lands and converted the property to more profitable pastureland, leaving the dispossessed crofters to cope as best they could with the abrupt changes in the social order. Tacksmen, the influential clan members who managed clan property in return for military service, were dismissed abruptly once military tenure was abolished and clansmen were evicted.[10]

As a result of this betrayal by their chiefs, tacksmen and other clansmen aggressively pursued other avenues for social mobility and financial security, setting aside their traditional family loyalties for the opportunity to participate in other, non-clan-based patronage systems established under the auspices of the British government, such as those of the military. The advent of the Seven

Years War with the French (1755-1763) brought several entire Scottish regiments to North America,[11] where their commanding officers exploited the various opportunities for social and economic advancement that existed for ambitious men in colonial cities and frontier settlements.

Another significant step taken by many tacksmen and lesser gentry was emigration as civilians from Scotland to North America. What began as a trickle of Jacobite refugees to the tobacco plantations of Carolina and Virginia after 1746 became a veritable flood of migrants to the thirteen colonies by 1773, where they were quickly integrated into the military and plantation oligarchies which dominated life in the colonial countryside. During the pre-Revolutionary period they acquired many of the values, attitudes, and skills that would enable them to function successfully and profitably in the New World. By shifting their loyalties to landed British proprietors for fixed periods of time, the expatriate Scots who labored as tenants on colonial plantations hoped to recoup their lost fortunes and rebuild their shattered societies.[12]

One particular colonial frontier, the Mohawk Valley in the colony of New York, became the locus of a significant, but largely ignored, influence over the eventual development of the North West Company's personnel and social hierarchies. It was here that Scottish *emigrés* involved themselves in the economic, social, and political networks established by Sir William Johnson, Superintendent of Indian Affairs for British colonial New York between 1755 and 1774.

Sir William Johnson dominated the Indian trade in colonial America by virtue of his administrative role in the Indian Department. He was responsible for ensuring that the Indians remained loyal to British interests. He controlled the issuing of trading licenses and he regulated the trading relationships between Natives and colonial entrepreneurs. During the Seven Years War he commanded local militia companies and Iroquois warriors, and eventually assumed control over British army units during key battles. He had at least two liaisons with Indian women that produced children, and through his marital alliances and professional responsibilities enjoyed considerable personal prestige with, and influence over, the Mohawk Indians.[13]

Of additional interest to fur-trade scholars is the development of Johnson's estate in the Mohawk Valley.[14] Johnson endeavored to administer the property that he acquired in the manner of an Ulster plantation colony.[15] He sponsored the overseas passage of groups of Highland Scots and Irish who subsequently worked as tenants on his estate alongside Palatine Germans, who had emigrated to America some years earlier. He also furthered the interests of individual Scots, former Highlanders of stature and good education who needed a start in the New World.

Johnson's achievement in establishing his wilderness fiefdom in such a brief time was not based solely on access to vast amounts of capital, military, or natural resources. John Guzzardo has argued, rather, that Johnson's success resulted largely from his systematic application of the principles of patronage to the administration of his estates and the maintenance of his interpersonal relationships.[16]

This article investigates Sir William Johnson's patronage relationships with Scottish expatriates prior to the American Revolution, with particular emphasis on how membership in Sir William Johnson's "family" may have contributed to the eventual establishment and operation of the North West Company. In doing so, it addresses at least two areas of concern identified by Van Kirk—those being the need for further investigation into the social and ethnic antecedents of the Nor'Westers, and the application of new models to the interpretation of corporate behaviors within the North West Company.

SIR WILLIAM JOHNSON: A FRONTIER PATRON

Sir William Johnson was born in Smithstown, County Meath, Ireland in 1715, the son of Christopher Johnson and Anne Warren Johnson. The immediate family—comprised of the parents, three sons, and five daughters resided in Smithstown House in the centre of a 200-acre estate, where they lived a comfortable but not wealthy existence as rural gentry.[17]

Most members of the genteel classes actively cultivated professional and personal alliances for their children that would ensure a degree of social mobility and financial security. The Johnsons were no exception, and by 1737 William Johnson's sponsorship career began under the patronage of his maternal uncle, Sir Peter Warren, who wanted William to manage his estate in the Mohawk Valley of New York, known as Warrensbush. Warren was a naval hero who had married into the wealthy and influential De Lancey mercantile family shortly after his arrival in America, and who had since involved himself in a variety of commercial endeavors, including real estate speculation. Having begun the construction of a palatial home in New York, Warren was eager to develop his rural property and derive additional income from the timber and produce it could provide. To that end he instructed his nephew William to recruit a number of families from County Meath and bring them to New York to settle on his Mohawk Valley estate as tenants.[18]

Upon arriving in the New World, Johnson wasted little time in the development of his uncle's property.[19] Within three years Johnson was producing corn, flour, and timber from the Warrensbush estate, which was then shipped down the Mohawk and Hudson rivers to New York, and from there to their final destination in the West Indies. During this period Johnson began to cultivate what would eventually be long-term personal and business relationships with the German, Irish, and Dutch settlers who lived in proximity to the Warren estate, and with officers and soldiers stationed at the Fort Hunter garrison a few miles away.

When William Johnson first settled in the Mohawk Valley, his social standing was more or less equivalent to that of the local community leaders and lesser officers at Fort Hunter. Johnson cemented his regional friendships by learning to speak German, by fraternizing with his neighbors at various community and garrison social functions, and by acting as sponsor to neighbors' children at their baptisms.[20]

Meanwhile Uncle Peter wanted to augment his farm revenue through involvement in the fur trade, which was dominated by colonial merchants of Dutch extraction who conducted business in Albany[21] and at Oswego, a fortified settlement at the mouth of the Oswego River where it flowed into Lake Ontario. Established in 1727 by Governor William Burnet to "bleed off" the Indian trade from the markets in Montreal, Oswego was in a strategic position to offer Native groups English trade goods without a protracted trip west along the shores of Lake Ontario to the French post at Niagara. Oswego served as a base of operations for as many as 300 traders, some of whom handled the summer trade of Indian groups coming to the fort to trade, and some who travelled into the interior and lived *en dérouine* with the Indians. Oswego was manned with a garrison of English soldiers who ensured that the lucrative trade was protected.

Johnson entered the Indian trade at Oswego by sending bateau loads of trade goods to the *en dérouine* traders and accepting their furs in return for eventual shipment to New York, saving the inland traders the time and aggravation of a supply expedition outward. No doubt Johnson recognized that his success in entering the fur trade depended upon his ability to offer superior services to customers, in this case providing delivery of trade goods directly to the marketplace. Johnson also expanded his trading activities to other settlements by dispatching members of his household staff to act as agents on his behalf. Johnson further attracted and maintained both white and Indian clientele by offering quality goods for trade and by offering fair market value for his customers' furs. Soon his reputation for fair dealing resulted in his engagement as a contractor to supply trade goods to merchants working within the Oswego trading house.

Johnson profited at the expense of the ethnic Dutch traders based in Albany, who up to his arrival had enjoyed a virtual monopoly over fur trading in the region. Over time they had apparently grown accustomed to abusing the privileges that this monopoly engendered, evidenced by their rapacious treatment of customers in general and the Natives in particular.[22] Despite the efforts of the Albany merchants to thwart Johnson's increasing popularity amongst their customers, he eventually became the official supplier of the Oswego military garrison as well.[23]

By 1739 Johnson had also managed to buy his own property, a parcel of land across the Mohawk River from his uncle's estate. Johnson had agreed to administer Warren's estate for three years, however, and so he remained on the Warrensbush property, developing markets for agricultural produce, acting as provisioner and supplier for traders, soldiers, and Indians, and as storekeeper for his German, Dutch, and British neighbors.

By 1742 Johnson had increased the number of tenant leases on his uncle's land from 12 to 26 families. Many of these leases were awarded to Palatine German families who had migrated from the Hudson Valley to the Mohawk Valley in previous years. Other leases were given to discharged English soldiers from the garrisons of nearby Fort Hunter and Schenectady. Finally, Johnson's three-year promise to remain on his uncle's property expired, and Johnson moved his family

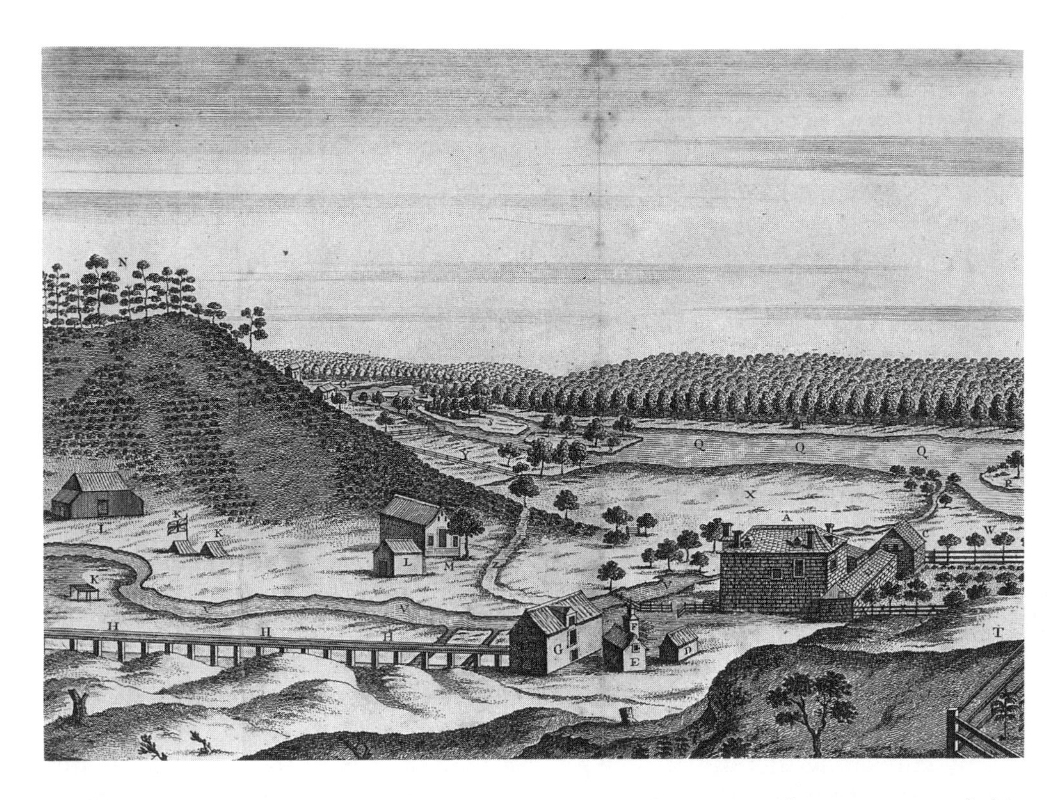

Figure 2. Sir William Johnson's nephew and son-in-law, Guy Johnson, prepared this sketch of the Fort Johnson estate, which was published in the *Royal Magazine,* Vol. I., October 1759, in London (original engraving by Hulett). Credit: The National Archives of Canada Library/C-003442.

and his ever-increasing retinue of household servants and tradespeople to his own estate for good. From here Johnson, now a recognized patron in his own right, administered both his own and his uncle's property from a fortified stone residence variously called "Mount Johnson" or "Johnson Castle."[24]

By 1745 William Johnson had become the most powerful landed proprietor in the colony of New York. From his Mount Johnson residence he controlled a vast trading and agricultural empire. He was a justice of the peace and a local militia commander. His home was the preferred meeting place of the local gentry, of army officers, and of distinguished visitors from Britain and the coastal cities of the colonies.

During his years as fur trader and military commander, Johnson had managed to cultivate and secure the friendship and trust of most of the war chiefs and *sachems,* or councillors, of the Six Nations.[25] Johnson came to enjoy considerable influence among the Mohawk, who named him *Warraghiyagey*—"he who does much business,"—and were later to make him a *sachem* in their central longhouse. His fair dealings in matters of trade had earned Johnson the initial trust of the Mohawks and other Natives, and he strove to solidify these relationships by developing a knowledge and understanding of Mohawk language and culture. By 1747, a scant decade after his arrival in the Mohawk Valley, he had mastered a smattering of Mohawk[26] and could demonstrate culturally appropriate behaviors when required.[27]

The key to developing successful relations with the Iroquois was recognition of the unifying force in the Iroquois Confederacy—the maternal clan structure.[28] Successful use of patronage within the clan structure was based on influencing the clan mothers, whose responsibility it was to designate clan members as sachems to village councils. Together the sachems and clan mothers were instrumental in regulating the behavior of the warriors.

It is debatable whether Sir William Johnson ever possessed an intimate understanding of the workings of the Iroquois clan system. However, Johnson's efforts to understand Mohawk culture, combined with his intuitive understanding of the workings of patronage, enabled him to identify, and exploit successfully, the clan-based patronage networks within the Mohawk community.

Johnson directed his efforts towards winning the trust of the clan leaders by granting a number of favors to gain their approval. He bought lavish gifts of food, clothing, and provisions for the Mohawk women. He arranged to have Mohawk villages protected by his militia in the absence of their warriors. He had stockades constructed and repaired at key Mohawk villages, and permitted Mohawk women and children to stay in his blockhouses for additional security.[29]

By cultivating friendships with a series of related clans, he was able to influence large coalitions of clans within the confederacy and ensure their political and military support of British imperial interests. To ensure that his influence was maintained within the confederacy, he extended patronage to—and through—key individuals, such as the Mohawk sachem "King" Hendrick (a.k.a. Tiyanoga). He also established familial ties with Molly (a.k.a. Konwatsi'tsiaiénne) and her brother Joseph Brant (a.k.a Thayendanegea). These relationships were mutually rewarding. Johnson benefitted from his alliance *à la façon du pays* with Molly Brant, who headed a society of clan matrons,[30] and enjoyed much higher status than her brother. Both Hendrick's and the Brants' association with Johnson, in turn, enhanced their status and facilitated their maintenance of authority within their communities.[31]

Gradually the gifts and the provision of military services created a formidable debt of obligation to Johnson. The increasing dependence of Mohawk associates on Johnson's gifts as a means of securing and maintaining rank within their communities effectively diffused any indigenous political challenge to Johnson's authority that might have emerged.[32] By 1755, Johnson was appointed British Indian Superintendent of the Northern Department. Until his death in 1774, Johnson literally divided his time between his Indian Department responsibilities and his commercial activities as a colonial planter, conducting Indian affairs in the morning and plantation pursuits in the afternoon.[33]

Managing the complex relationships of the colonial frontier was an undertaking which required an intimate and empathetic understanding of diverse Native perspectives. It also demanded a sensitive but shrewd application of diplomacy and tact. Because Johnson could not possibly conduct all of his Indian Department duties on his own, he relied on the services of his hand-picked Indian Department agents to conduct business in the Johnson style.

Johnson was always on the lookout for promising candidates for Indian Department posts and demanded that candidates possess the appropriate skills. Agents were required to master a number of different Indian languages and dialects, and their duties required a mastery of the various skills associated with living in the bush. Military experience was also a valuable commodity. The frontier was a violent place, and the abilities to command soldiers, use weapons, and construct fortifications were necessary skills.

Johnson also demanded that his officers possess the character and personality traits necessary to deal with the disparate individuals on the frontier. These traits—self-discipline, courage, mental toughness, an air of authority combined with the ability to lead, and a certain amount of personal attractiveness (charisma, if you like)—were essential if Indian Department officials were to keep the undisciplined ranks of militiamen and Indian warriors in line.

Johnson first identified promising candidates from within his own family and household circle. Then he looked farther afield for potential employees—from within the community, from neighboring military garrisons, from relatives and friends overseas, and from individuals referred to him by his friends or business acquaintances. These candidates would be assigned some introductory responsibilities based on their kinship to Johnson personally, their race or ethnic origin, their level of education, their religious persuasion, and their demonstrated intellectual and personal aptitude at first meeting. Depending on their ability to perform these tasks, they would be given greater or lesser responsibilities. Although individuals were recruited on the basis of the somewhat arbitrary measures of race, ethnicity, education, and religion, these qualifiers were not limiting factors in terms of one's opportunity to ascend the hierarchy of Johnson's "family."[34]

Johnson and the Scots

It was in the context of frontier patronage, during and after the Seven Years' War, that Johnson became acquainted with the first of a succession of expatriate Scots who would eventually become his clients and later be instrumental in the future development of the North West Company. Scottish *émigrés*, particularly Scottish soldiers, were ideal potential clients for Johnson. Not only were they reasonably well-educated and hardworking, but they were also used to the hardships associated with living in marginal areas. More importantly, however, Scottish *émigrés* were themselves products of a sociopolitical environment where patronage relationships governed most aspects of life.

Johnson's family connections in the military, combined with his business and social connections with the various regiments stationed in the region, resulted in his acquaintance with several Scottish army officers, many of whom were to become his clients. Perhaps the earliest of these was Normand MacLeod, a captain with the 80th British Regiment, who had passed through the Mohawk Valley on his way to a military posting at Oswego (renamed Fort Ontario in 1759). After a pleasant initial meeting with Johnson, the two were to develop a mutually beneficial business and personal relationship. MacLeod performed a variety of services for Johnson, ranging from rather mundane household favors to becoming the Johnson-appointed commissary of Forts Ontario (1765) and Niagara (1767). After the British government abandoned the commissary network following the end of the Seven Years' War, Johnson obtained a 3,000-acre land patent for MacLeod situated between the estates of his son John and his son-in-law Daniel Claus. On this site Normand MacLeod became a planter himself, eventually importing some of his own relations from Scotland to become his tenants in 1772.[35] By 1776 MacLeod had established himself as a trader in Detroit, and in 1783 he became a partner in the firm of Gregory, MacLeod and Co., later absorbed into the North West Company.[36]

Another, even more significant Scottish client of Johnson was Lieutenant Hugh Fraser of the 78th Regiment (the Frasers' Highlanders[37]), who was introduced to Johnson by William Hunter of Newport, Rhode Island in 1763. At that time Fraser approached Johnson about the prospect of settling soldiers mustered out of the British Army at Quebec in 1763. With Fraser's assistance, Johnson was able to attract at least twenty tenant families from among the veterans. Johnson then helped Fraser and his father-in-law, Lieutenant John McTavish (also a member of the Fraser's Highlanders) obtain military bounty lands in northern New York.[38] McTavish and Fraser settled temporarily on the Kingsborough Patent with various family members. One of these kinsmen was John McTavish's son and Hugh Fraser's brother-in-law, Simon McTavish, who worked in Johnson's household as a clerk and who later became the single most powerful influence over the development of the North West Company.

In a letter dated 28 November 1766, William Johnson wrote to his good friend in New York, Goldsbrow Banyar,[39] in regard to the young Simon McTavish:

> If You want a Lad of abt 16 Years, who can write a tollerable good running hand, there is one who lived about 2 Years with me, would be verry willing to Serve You the first Year for his Cloaths Lodging & Diet. His father was Lt. McTavish of ye Highlanders Lt. Fraser now here is his Brother in Law, The Boy Has no Vice as yet that I know & is verry smart, I should be glad to know whether You want such or not.[40]

What is most interesting about this passage is not the fact that Simon McTavish was on the Johnson estate; several sources have already placed Simon McTavish there after his arrival in America.[41] What is intriguing is that little is known about Simon McTavish's activities or whereabouts from the time he went to the Johnson estates to the time he appeared in fur trade documents as a trader at Albany and Detroit.[42] Campbell states that McTavish did his apprenticeship with Johnson, but cites no evidence to support this claim.[43] Also, there appear to

Figure 3. Simon McTavish, North West Company partner and Johnson protégé. Artist unknown. Credit: The National Archives of Canada/C-000164.

be no subsequent references to Simon McTavish in the Johnson Papers. This circumstance is odd when one considers the number of tradespeople, tenants, and minor functionaries who are mentioned repeatedly in the papers. Placing McTavish in the employ of Goldsbrow Banyar as an apprentice, however, might explain why there are no subsequent references to McTavish in the Johnson Papers, and also could explain how and where Simon McTavish acquired much of his business and legal expertise.[44]

There is no doubt, however, that Sir William Johnson would have made a formidable impression on an adolescent boy recently transplanted to the American frontier. Even before coming to America, it is possible that Simon McTavish read about Sir William Johnson's exploits in English and Scottish newspapers which had served to transform Johnson into a larger-than-life folk hero. In 1764, when Simon McTavish first arrived on the estate at age 14, he would have been taken to the hub of Johnson's vast plantation network, Johnson Hall, an impressive two-story mansion tastefully appointed with lavish furnishings and flanked by massive stone blockhouses on the wings of the building.[45]

The mansion itself was a hive of activity, with individuals of diverse race, color, and creed—black slaves, Mohawk Indians, German tradespeople, British army officers and Indian Department officials, Irish relatives[46] and cronies, visiting gentry from the cities—all going about their business in the entourage of Sir William Johnson. Outside the mansion, militia units, comprised of Johnson's tenants and local community members, practised their drills under the watchful eye of Sir William Johnson himself. The regular activities of the Indian Department attracted groups of Indians, who camped on the grounds of the estate. During his stay at Johnson Hall, McTavish would have observed the civil and even preferential treatment accorded to the Natives by Johnson and his non-Native associates, noting that they had free access to the house and surrounding property even though their peaceable incursions would leave these areas in a perpetual state of untidiness.[47] He may have been personally acquainted with both Molly and Joseph Brant, the influential Mohawks so closely associated with Johnson's success in Indian diplomacy. He may also have become acquainted with some of Johnson's mixed-blood children, although Johnson sent most of his children away for formal schooling until a local school was established to serve both tenant and Johnson-family pupils.[48]

While young McTavish would have taken part in most of the daily business, recreational, and social activities during his tenure on the Johnson estate, he would also have noticed that some institutions, such as the local Masonic Lodge, were off-limits to him. He would have observed that those who did attend Masonic meetings were close associates who espoused the causes of Johnson, whether they were Johnson relatives like son-in-law Daniel Claus and nephew Guy Johnson, or military clients like Normand MacLeod and McTavish's own brother-in-law Hugh Fraser.[49]

The Johnson estate would have provided Simon McTavish with an irreplaceable learning opportunity: direct training and experience in the business of fur-

Figure 4. *Colonel Guy Johnson and Karonghyontye (Captain David Hill)*, by Sir Benjamin West, Andrew W. Mellon Collection, © 1993 National Gallery of Art, Washington.

trading, exposure to all of the diverse personalities of the frontier, and extensive involvement in the day-to-day social intercourse necessary to the administration of a complex wilderness enterprise. In retrospect, it is small wonder that certain aspects of Simon McTavish's own life—the rapid development of his vast and successful fur trading concern, his patronage of trusted friends and relatives, his love of opulence, his acquisition of McTavish armorial bearings, and the building of his own mansion in Montreal—mirror so closely the practices of Sir William Johnson.[50]

Normand MacLeod and Simon McTavish were not the only Nor' Westers who experienced Johnson's largesse. James Phyn and Alexander Ellice, two Scottish expatriates who had originally been part of John Duncan's trading company based in Schenectady and Detroit, relied heavily on the patronage of William Johnson in the expansion of their trading business. Phyn and Ellice acted as provisioners of trade goods to military posts in the interior. Sir William Johnson, as Superintendent of the Indian Department, maintained an account with the firm, as he did with another Scottish trader based in Schenectady, Daniel Campbell.[51] Johnson purchased trade goods from these companies which he used for distribution among the Indians as presents for keeping the peace or as payment for land.

Phyn and Ellice benefitted both socially and economically from Johnson's patronage. The Scottish partners were able to establish important personal and professional contacts through their relationship with Johnson.[52] As their fur trading concern prospered, they branched out into other enterprises, such as the construction of a water mill on the Mohawk River for the production of flour, an economic activity inspired by Sir William Johnson's own agricultural activities on the Mohawk River.[53] Phyn and Ellice also engaged personnel in the manner of Sir William Johnson, carefully recruiting promising young men from amongst their relatives or friends to receive practical training as apprentices in their trading establishment.[54]

Prior to William Johnson's death in July of 1774, he arranged for the recruitment of the last of several groups of Scots Highlanders to settle on the large (50,000 acres) tract of Johnson property known as the Kingsborough Patent. Johnson had been seeking new tenants to settle on his Mohawk Valley properties when several Roman Catholic Highland families from Lochaber in Scotland were also looking to seek their fortunes elsewhere. The local parish priest of Lochaber, Father John McKenna, recruited 600 Highlanders from the region. A British naval frigate, the *Pearl*, was chartered to transport the colonists, who included among others some distant Scottish relations of Sir William Johnson.[55]

Johnson's paternal ancestors were originally an Irish branch of the Scottish McDonald clan of Glencoe. It was members of this clan, the Macdonnells, who sought to emigrate to America from Lochaber after their dismissal as tacksmen. The leaders of the Macdonnells included John of Leek, Allan of Collachie, Alexander of Aberchalder, their cousin "Spanish John" of Crowlin,[56] and their brother-in-law Ranald of Ardnabee. They were accompanied by their families and other dependants, among them assorted Camerons, Chisolms, Frasers, McRaes, Macintoshes, McDougalds, and McMillans.[57] They joined other Highland Scots already resident on the Kingsborough Patent. Names common to several North West Company rolls, such as McKay, Taylor, McLeod, Ross, Munro, Grant, and McGillis, appear on the Rent Roll for this period.[58]

The Highlanders arrived in September of 1773 and immediately began to clear their leases and build cabins before winter arrived. For the next two years the Highlanders and other residents of the Johnson estates lived more or less unmolested in the Mohawk Valley until 1775, when the American Revolution intruded into Johnson's fiefdom on the frontier.

Even before Johnson's death, there were rumblings of discontent in the Mohawk Valley. New England freeholders who had recently moved into the area resented both the royalist sympathies of Johnson and his political, social, and economic domination of the entire region. They also distrusted the members of Johnson's immediate and extended "family"—his German, Irish, and Scottish tenants, the functionaries within the Indian Department and the Mohawk Indians. Johnson's associates were disliked not only because they were culturally alien to the New Englanders but because they posed a formidable military threat to the rebel cause.

After Johnson's death in 1774, his estates and titles were inherited by his son, Sir John Johnson. Almost immediately rebel animosity was directed towards him. The regional "Committee of Safety" was quick to take preemptive action against the Johnson community. Under the leadership of General Philip Schuyler, the congressional forces invaded the Johnson estate in 1775, disarming the Highlanders and taking their family heads hostage in return for an oath of neutrality from Sir John Johnson.[59]

Rather than remain to be arrested and imprisoned, Johnson and a party of Highland Scots and Palatine German tenants escaped through the Adirondacks to the St. Regis (Akwesasne) Mohawk village and down the St. Lawrence River to safe haven in Canada. Upon his arrival, Johnson was granted a commission to raise a Loyalist regiment from among his German and Scottish tenants. This regiment, the King's Royal Regiment of New York (K.R.R.N.Y., a.k.a. "The Royal Greens"),[60] carried on the battle for the Mohawk Valley from their northern refuge, launching sporadic raids at different rebel targets over the course of the war.[61] Another Loyalist regiment initiated amongst the Highland *émigrés* of North Carolina, the Royal Highland Emigrants under the leadership of Col. Allen Maclean, recruited additional soldiers from the Johnson estates in the fall of 1775 and travelled northward to eventually assume responsibility for the defense of Quebec.[62]

At the conclusion of the war, the British government settled the discharged soldiers of the Royal Greens, the Royal Highland Emigrants, and their families in the present-day eastern Ontario counties of Lennox, Addington, Stormont, Dundas, and Glengarry on the north shore of the Upper St. Lawrence River, in an area known in Loyalist histories as the Old Eastern District.[63] A community called New Johnstown (now Cornwall, Ontario) in Stormont County became the home of Sir John Johnson and many of his tenant soldiers from the King's Royal Regiment of New York. The remnants of the 84th Regiment, the Royal Highland Emigrants, settled in Glengarry.

The Mohawks of the village of St. Regis, who had given Sir John Johnson and his tenants protection and assistance during their flight from the American colonies, renewed their ties with Johnson and his allies. A member of the McDonnell clan, Father Roderick McDonnell, assumed the role of parish priest to the St. Regis community.[64] Their Mohawk kinsmen from New York, who had so faithfully served Sir William Johnson during his life, and who had fought with the Loyalist militias during the war, also migrated to Canada with other refugees from the Mohawk Valley. In 1784 Joseph Brant, Molly Brant's brother and one of William Johnson's Indian Department employees, settled next to the Grand River and established a community near what is now known as Brantford, Ontario. Molly Brant, William Johnson's country wife and mother of several of his children, settled in a community west of Ft. Cataraqui, now Kingston, Ontario.[65]

Once these settlements were established they recreated the closely-knit society they had left in the Mohawk Valley and resumed the economic pursuits that had sustained and enriched Sir William Johnson and his family—farming and fur trading.

There is some evidence to suggest that the business and social links that Sir William Johnson had established in the Great Lakes region under the auspices of the Indian Department persisted after the American Revolution drove most of the key participants northward to Canada. A nucleus of merchants and traders who had previously participated in the Great Lakes fur trade resumed their trading endeavors but coordinated their business activities through Montreal and Cataraqui instead of Michilimackinac, Detroit, Schenectady, and Albany. Cataraqui's strategic geographical location at the junction of the St. Lawrence River and Lake Ontario made it the hub for transshipping trade goods, furs, and other commodities east and west. Cataraqui merchants such as Richard Cartwright and Joseph Forsyth,[66] who were connected by blood, marriage, or friendship to several Nor'Westers, acted as middlemen between the Montreal merchants and customers further inland. They quickly established partnerships with their Montreal colleagues to outfit ships for the transportation of furs and agricultural products between Cataraqui and Niagara, and soon dominated the movement of goods in the region.[67]

Sir John Johnson, who was appointed to the position of Superintendent-General of Indian Affairs for British North America in 1783 (a position previously held by his father Sir William and his cousin Guy Johnson), continued the same type of patronage relationships with the Montreal- and Cataraqui-based traders that had been in place in colonial New York, maintaining the network of business and personal relationships established under the auspices of his father prior to the Revolution. The persistence of these relationships, and the continued mixing of fur trade business, Indian Department administration, and social activity exemplified by Sir John Johnson's occasional attendance at Beaver Club functions up to his death in 1830, suggests that he did not tinker with the effective patronage "machine" developed by his father.[68]

As former Mohawk Valley residents or relations of refugees from the Mohawk Valley, the Montreal entrepreneurs later looked actively to the communities in the Old Eastern District for relatives and friends whose sons would become their labourers and clerks. There they knew that they would find a labor force admirably suited to the social and hierarchical structure of the wilderness-driven enterprise they created—the North West Company.

Conclusion

While it would be incorrect to overemphasize Sir William Johnson's influence over the eventual founding of the North West Company, it cannot be denied that his economic and political activities in the Mohawk Valley served to instruct and inspire a number of key individuals who were later to involve themselves in the Montreal fur trade. The continued residence of several Scottish expatriates in North America after the Seven Years' War, and their subsequent involvement in the fur trade, is directly attributable to their establishment of patronage connections with the Johnson "family" prior to the American Revolution.

The first of these Scottish clients were the Highland soldiers and their offspring, who found themselves in the Mohawk Valley during and after the Seven Years' War. Sir William Johnson's friendships with the military evolved into sustained patron-client relationships as Scottish companions became Indian Department officers in his service, partners in business, or tenants on his estate. These wartime friendships had a significant long-term effect on the eventual formation of the North West Company. It is debatable whether the expatriate Scots who found their way to North America would have entered the fur trade at all had it not been for their initial exposure to both fur trading and Indian diplomacy under the patronage of Sir William Johnson. Although the Nor'Westers inherited the fur-trade structures of the French regime, the British expatriates who comprised the bulk of the North West Company partners had few official connections with the French-controlled fur trade prior to their relocation to Montreal. Therefore, they had few direct opportunities to acquire the methods of the French, other than those provided through intercourse with ethnic French traders at British posts. They did, however, acquire direct experience with American colonial fur trading under the auspices of Sir William Johnson.

The Scottish entrepreneurs involved in the colonial fur trade of Michilimackinac, Detroit, Schenectady, and Albany, such as Normand MacLeod, Simon McTavish, James Phyn, Alexander Ellice, James McGill, and John Richardson (to name a few), were compelled to operate their fur-trading businesses in accordance with the rules and regulations established by Sir William Johnson. All matters pertaining to transactions with the Indians, particularly those involving the fur trade, were sanctioned by and monitored through the Indian Department. Because the Indian Department was an important corporate client, colonial traders developed close working relationships with Johnson's Indian Department officers. Some of the traders were former Indian Department employees themselves. Indeed, almost any personal or professional affiliation with Johnson's household (particularly one's employment as an Indian Department officer) was in itself an apprenticeship for the fur trade, as the careers of Normand MacLeod and Simon McTavish attest. When these colonial traders relocated in Canada, they maintained their links with the now Canada-based Indian Department, which continued to be administered by Johnson family members and associates.

In short, Scots who participated in Sir William Johnson's Indian Department as officers, or as suppliers and agents with Johnson's fur-trading concerns, gained geographically, culturally, and temporally appropriate experiences which they could adopt and apply to the administration of their own North American enterprises, strategies which were far more accessible and observable than those employed by the French.

Another significant influence that Sir William Johnson had over the future operation of the North West Company was his "planting" of Highland tenants on his properties prior to the American Revolution. His settlement of successive parties of Scottish migrants on his estate, culminating in the arrival of the McDonnell clan on the *Pearl* in 1773, brought the ancestors of several North West Company employees to North America. It also brought them into contact with the German, Dutch, and Irish tenants with whom they would relocate to Upper Canada and, in some cases, marry.[69]

The settlement of William Johnson's estate, therefore, is significant to the fortunes of the North West Company because it brought together a racially, ethnically, and religiously diverse community of tenants who functioned in harmony because Johnson had supplanted their indigenous affiliations and redirected their loyalties towards himself and his family. Johnson's development of tenant militias and his establishment of plantation-based institutions such as churches, schools, businesses, and fraternal organizations served to integrate, assimilate, and indoctrinate his multiethnic clientele. The roles and responsibilities of individuals within these community institutions, particularly the Indian Department, also served to develop and reinforce a social hierarchy within the community itself. The socialization of these tenants in the context of the Johnson plantation community, the transferral of their filial loyalty to Sir John Johnson after William Johnson's death, their forced flight to Canada, and their subsequent settlement as an extended unit in adjacent counties along the upper St. Lawrence River testify to the strength of the patronage bonds that tied the Johnson community together.[70]

It is the community consciousness and consanguineal loyalties fostered on the Johnson estate, embodied in its refugee tenants, which are the true legacy of Sir William Johnson to the North West Company. The members of the Johnson "family" had been nurtured in an environment which provided the North West Company partners with a hardworking, loyal labor pool already accustomed to the informal hierarchy established in the Mohawk Valley and transplanted to Canada. The relatively high incidence of North West Company clerks recruited from the Loyalist settlements on the St. Lawrence, and the persistence of business and personal relationships between the leaders of these communities and the North West Company partners, support the notion that Sir John Johnson and his North West Company compatriates viewed the fur trade, the Indian Department, and the extended communities of tenants and Natives to be components of an organic entity—a sociocultural complex.[71]

Further research into the activities of the North West Company, particularly regarding those questions relating to the recruitment and promotion of staff, the manning of wintering posts in the interior, and the development of business and personal relationships with Natives may benefit from further research into the Mohawk Valley antecedents of the Nor'Westers. Investigation of these and related issues offers fur-trade researchers new and exciting avenues for further study into the organizational and structural hierarchies of the North West Company.

Notes

1. Sylvia Van Kirk, "Fur Trade Social History: Some Recent Trends," in *Old Trails and New Directions: Papers of the Third North American Fur Trade Conference*, ed. Carol M. Judd and J. Arthur Ray (Toronto: University of Toronto Press, 1980), 160-73.
2. Peter Laslett, *The World We Have Lost*, 3d ed. (New York: Charles Scribner's Sons, 1984).
3. Jennifer S.H. Brown, "Company Men and Native Families: Fur Trade Social and Domestic Relations in Canada's Old Northwest" (Ph.D. diss., University of Chicago, 1976).
4. John Foster, "The Country-Born in the Red River Settlement" (Ph.D. diss., University of Alberta, 1972).
5. Van Kirk, "Fur Trade Social History," 162.
6. Jennifer S.H. Brown, "Two Companies in Search of Traders: Personnel and Promotion Patterns in Canada's Early British Fur Trade," *Proceedings of the Second Congress, Canadian Ethnology Society*, 2, no. 28 (1975): 623-43.
7. The assumption that eighteenth-century Scottish expatriates in North America might still demonstrate the values, attitudes, and modes of behavior appropriate to the Scottish Highlands is not unreasonable. Indeed, historian J.M. Bumsted has recently suggested that even the Scots themselves believed this to be true. Bumsted's recent analysis of Lord Selkirk's problems with his North American settlements suggests that some of Selkirk's difficulties were based on his mistaken assumption that expatriate Highlanders, such as Alexander and Miles McDonnell, could adequately manage his settlements because of their Highland heritage. But as Bumsted points out, "Both McDonnells, however, had lived

their lives in North America, and completely failed to achieve any sympathy or empathy with the ordinary Highlander. Their problems were doubtless exacerbated by their mistaken belief that they did understand Highlanders." See J.M. Bumsted, "A Tale of Three Settlements," *The Beaver* 72, no. 3 (June/July 1992): 38-39.

8. An abiding affection for the Highland clan system and the family loyalties it engendered is obvious among North Americans of Scottish ancestry today; Scottish societies, pipe bands, and Highland family organizations that continue to thrive in Canada and, to a lesser degree, the U.S. This nostalgia is also reflected in popular (as opposed to scholarly) fur trade literature which often stresses the influence of clan ties on the Scottish Nor'Westers. For example, Marjorie Campbell comments that most of the Nor'Westers were "Highland Scots, still harbouring the splendid loyalties and bitter enmities of their native glens. . . ." (see Marjorie W. Campbell, *The North West Company* [Vancouver: Douglas & McIntyre, 1983], 1). In her biography of William McGillivray, Campbell states that the Nor'Westers were a "tough, individualistic breed, stubborn and clannish, loyal to their ancient Scottish heritage. . . ." (see Marjorie W. Campbell, *Northwest to the Sea* [Toronto: Clarke, Irwin and Co., 1975], 10). More recent expression of these sentiments can be found in the writing of Peter C. Newman, who suggests in *Caesars of the Wilderness* (Toronto: Viking Books, 1987) that the North West Company partners behaved "as though they were chiefs of a transcontinental clan, claiming all the traditions and especially the loyalties due in such a feudal structure. . . ." Newman goes on to state that it was the extensive family ties of the partners which contributed to the NWC's *esprit de corps* (8).
9. See the following articles from *People and Society in Scotland Volume 1, 1760-1830*, T.M. Devine and Rosalind Mitchison, eds. (Edinburgh: The Economic and Social History Society of Scotland, 1988); Allen I. Macinnes, "Scottish Gaeldom: The First Phase of Clearance," 70-90; Alexander Murdoch and Richard B. Sher, "Literacy and Learned Culture" (127-42); Stana Nenadic, "The Rise of the Urban Middle Class," 109-26. See also H. Grey Graham, *The Social Life of Scotland in the Eighteenth Century*, 5th ed. (London: Adam and Charles Black, 1969); Bruce Lenman, *Integration, Enlightenment and Industrialization: Scotland 1746-1832* (Toronto: University of Toronto Press 1981); T.C. Smout, *A History of the Scottish People 1560-1830* (New York: Charles Scribner's Sons, 1969).
10. Macinnes, "Scottish Gaeldom," 72.
11. Ibid., 82-83; see also Lenman, *Scotland 1746-1832*, 65-66.
12. See Ian Charles Cargill Graham, *Colonists from Scotland: Emigration to North America 1707-1783* (Ithaca: Cornell University Press, 1956), 43, 70-73, 106-9, for a discussion of the factors surrounding the emigration of several Scottish groups to the North American colonies.
13. Numerous biographies of William Johnson have been written over the years. A few rather sensationalized portrayals written after his successful military campaigns on the frontier gave him folk hero status in the colonies, Britain, and Europe. Scholarly treatments of Johnson's life used in the preparation of this paper include Arthur Pound, *Johnson of the Mohawks* (New York: Macmillan, 1930), James Flexner, *Lord of the Mohawks* (Boston: Little, Brown and Co., 1959); Milton W. Hamilton, *Sir William Johnson, Colonial American 1715-1763* (Port Washington, N.Y.: Kennikat Press, 1976). Other biographical sources

include historical articles and Loyalist reminiscences, such as A.H. Young, "Sir William Johnson, Baronet, 1715-1774" in *Papers and Records*, vol. 27 (Toronto: Ontario Historical Society, 1931), 575-62; see also Blanche Macdonell, "Two Great Colonial Magnates: Sir William and Sir John Johnson" in *Annual Transactions—1904 to 1913*, United Empire Loyalists' Association, 6: 69-80.

14. See Jennifer S.H. Brown, *Strangers in Blood: Fur Trade Company Families in Indian Country* (Vancouver: University of British Columbia Press, 1980), 35-44, for her succinct overview of Scottish migration to the Johnson estates, the subsequent migration of Johnson's Scottish tenants to Canada, and her identification of some of the North West Company members originating from this group. This paper endeavors to "flesh out" this overview by exploring the fundamental characteristics of Johnson's application of patronage, and by providing additional information about Johnson's patronage relationships with Scots prior to, and including, the McDonnell migration to the Mohawk Valley in 1773.
15. One of the most thorough examinations of Sir William Johnson's patronage practices is John Guzzardo, "Sir William Johnson's Official Family: Patrons and Clients in an Anglo-American Empire" (Ph.D. diss., Syracuse University, Syracuse, N.Y. , 1975), which argues that Johnson's approaches to the development of his plantation were, in turn, influenced by Tudor and Elizabethan approaches to the settlement of his native Ireland.
16. Ibid.
17. The settings and surroundings of Smithstown House imply "the family of Christopher Johnson belonged to that 'class of small fortune,' the rural gentry." Hamilton, *Sir William Johnson*, 5.
18. Ibid., 6-7.
19. Guzzardo, "Sir William Johnson's Official Family," 38-41.
20. Ibid., 22.
21. Albany was originally Fort Orange, founded by the Dutch in 1624. Despite the British takeover in 1664, Albany remained "essentially a Dutch town until well into the eighteenth century." See Francis Jennings "Dutch and Swedish Indian Policies" in *History of Indian-White Relations—Handbook of North American Indians*, ed. Wilcomb B. Washburn, vol. 4. (Washington, D.C.: Smithsonian Institution, 1988), 19.
22. The Dutch of New Netherland did not have a comprehensive approach to Indian diplomacy. Rather, it was based on the interests of individual communities, which might be hostile or benign. The official policy of the Dutch West India Company was to promote good will with the Indians, though it has been noted that "their people on the scene aimed at exploiting the Indians for personal advantage, frequently without care about arousing the hostility of the despised 'wild men.'" See Jennings, 14.
23. Hamilton, *Sir William Johnson*, 15-22. Guzzardo, "Sir William Johnson's Official Family," 42-46.
24. Guzzardo, "Sir William Johnson's Official Family," 41-42.
25. Ibid., 55.
26. There has been some debate over whether Sir William Johnson could actually speak the Mohawk language, given the regular presence of interpreters at Indian negotiations. Contemporary descriptions of Johnson would appear to support the notion that Johnson had at least some familiarity with Indian languages. See *The Gentleman's Magazine* 25 (1755): 426. To wit: "Being surrounded

with Indians, he [Johnson] speaks several of their languages well and always has some of them with him." See also Yasuhide Kawashima, "Colonial Governmental Agencies," in *Indian White Relations—Handbook of North American Indians*, ed. Wilcomb B. Washburn, vol. 4 (Washington: Smithsonian Institution, 1988), "Although he [Johnson] used interpreters and rarely acted as his own interpreter, he more than once corrected his interpreter's translations" (253).

27. *The Gentleman's Magazine*, noted, "He [Johnson] takes care of their wives and children when they go out on parties, and even wears their dress. . . ." See also Hamilton *Sir William Johnson*, 54, who noted that Johnson demonstrated a personal identification with the Mohawks by wearing their dress and warpaint and by demonstrating appropriate (i.e. Mohawk) behaviors and reactions when in their company (226).
28. See Lewis H. Morgan, *League of the Ho-de-no-sau-nee, Iroquois* (Rochester: Sage and Brother, 1851; reprinted, New Haven, Ct.: Human Relations Area Files, 1954), 74-98. See also William N. Fenton, "Structure, Continuity and Change in the Process of Iroquois Treaty Making," in *The History and Culture of Iroquois Diplomacy*, eds. Francis Jennings, et al. (Syracuse: Syracuse University Press, 1985), 3-36.
29. See *The Gentleman's Magazine* 25 (1755): 426. See also Guzzardo,"Sir William Johnson's Official Family," 247-48.
30. See Donald B. Smith, "Joseph Brant" and "Mary Brant," in *The Canadian Encyclopedia*, vol. 1 (Edmonton: Hurtig Publishers, 1985), 214-15. See also Olive Dickason, *Canada's First Nations* (Toronto: McClelland & Stewart Ltd., 1992), 470-71n.35.
31. See Guzzardo, "Sir William Johnson's Official Family," 249-68.
32. Ibid., 268-70.
33. Ibid., 271. See also Johnson's obituary in the Boston *Post-Boy*, 1 August 1774, 3. To wit: "We hear that Sir William Johnson, Bart., about three hours before his death, finished a negotiation with upwards of two hundred Indians, and dismissed them in perfect peace, after they had given him the strongest assurance of their good dispositions to the English nation. The Indians exhibited, on the occasion of Sir William's death, the most extraordinary shews of distress and sincere affliction that ever were before observed among that people."
34. See Guzzardo, "Sir William Johnson's Official Family," 60-61, 108-10, 125-37.
35. Ibid., 178-80.
36. W. Stewart Wallace, ed., *The Macmillan Dictionary of Canadian Biography*, 3d ed. (Toronto: The Macmillan Company of Canada, 1963), 478-79. It is Wallace who writes ". . . it is probable that he is the Captain Normand MacLeod who was a friend and correspondent of Sir William Johnson . . . ."
37. For additional biographical information on the members of this regiment and their North West Company connections see W.S. Wallace, "Some Notes on Fraser's Highlanders," *Canadian Historical Review* 18 (1937): 131-40.
38. Guzzardo, "Sir William Johnson's Official Family," 180-81. Later, in 1769, Hugh Fraser bought 500 acres of land near Bennington, New York and several of his kinsmen settled there. Simon Fraser, the famous NWC trader and explorer, was born in the Bennington area in 1776 and fled to Canada with his widowed mother after his father died in jail during the American Revolution. Most, if not all, of the Frasers who found their way into the fur trade were the children of

soldiers and officers of the 78th Regiment who had settled on bounty lands in Quebec or New York State after the Seven Years' War. See Duncan Fraser, "Sir John Johnson's Rent Roll of the Kingsborough Patent," *Ontario History* 52, no. 3 (1960): 180-81 for additional discussion of the Fraser-Johnson transaction.

39. Goldsbrow Banyar was an influential civil servant in colonial New York State who held a variety of political postings during the pre-Revolutionary period. In 1746 he was made Deputy Secretary of the Province, Deputy Clerk of the Council, and Deputy Clerk of the Supreme Court. Later he was Registrar of the Court of Chancery, Judge of Probate, and Examiner in the Prerogative Court. In his capacity as Registrar of the Court of Chancery, he would have been responsible for the monitoring of all public records, particularly those to do with land transactions in the province. See also Hamilton, *Sir William Johnson*, 89, 347; Phyllis A. Klein, ed., *Calendar of the Goldsbrow Banyar Land Papers 1728-1868* (unpublished manuscript on file, Manuscript Department, New-York Historical Society, 1979), 1-7.
40. James Sullivan, et al., eds., *The Papers of Sir William Johnson*, 14 vols. (Albany: 1921-1965), 12: 224.
41. Marjorie Wilkins Campbell, in her research on the McGillivray brothers (*Northwest to the Sea: A Biography of William McGillivray* [Toronto: Clark, Irwin and Co. 1975]) was told by family descendants that McTavish had spent his first years on the Johnson estates. Loyalist historians, such as Fraser, ("Sir John Johnson's Rent Roll" 180-89), also establish McTavish's presence there.
42. See Wallace, ed., *Macmillan Dictionary*, 488.
43. Campbell, *Northwest to the Sea*, 10-11.
44. The Goldsbrow Banyar papers are part of the holdings of the New-York Historical Society in New York City. Unfortunately, there are no finding aids to the papers at present (personal correspondence from Richard Frum, Manuscript Dept., New-York Historical Society, 29 August 1990). However, a closer scrutiny of the collected papers may reveal references to Simon McTavish or perhaps correspondence to and from McTavish himself which might serve to place McTavish in the employ of Banyar.
45. Guzzardo, "Sir William Johnson's Official Family," 155-58.
46. One of the many Johnson relatives who joined the household staff was John Dease, Johnson's nephew, who became Sir William's personal physician and an officer in the Indian Department. See Pound, *Johnson of the Mohawks*, 497. Dease's sons would go on to establish active North West Company and Hudson's Bay Company careers. Charles Johnson Warren Dease joined the NWC as a clerk in 1814; John Warren Dease was stationed at Rainy Lake with the NWC ca. 1816; Peter Warren Dease, who was situated in the Mackenzie River District when employed with the NWC, eventually became a chief factor with the Hudson's Bay Company in 1826. At that time he was able to facilitate the entry of yet another brother into the fur trade, Francis Michael Dease, in 1827 (Wallace, ed., *Macmillan Dictionary*, 152-53).
47. See Hamilton, *Sir William Johnson*, 316-17; see also Flexner, *Lord of the Mohawks*, 306-8.
48. See Pound, *Johnson of the Mohawks*, 388-89; Flexner, *Lord of the Mohawks*, 300-2.
49. William Johnson founded St. Patrick's Lodge #4, P.G.L.N.Y., at Jamestown, New York in 1766. Hugh Fraser became a member of this Lodge in 1767. See Fraser, "Sir John Johnson's Rent Roll," 180-81. Sir John Johnson was to become a

prominent Canadian Freemason. Several members of his Loyalist regiment, the King's Royal Regiment of New York, were also Freemasons, and went on to establish some of the earliest Freemasonry Lodges in Canada upon their settlement in the Old Eastern District. See A.J.B. Milborne, P.D.D.G.M.,G.L.Q., *Freemasonry in the Province of Quebec* (Knowlton, P.Q.: Author, 1959), 38-39. See also J. Ross Robertson, *The History of Freemasonry in Canada*, 2 vols. (Toronto: George N. Morang and Co. Ltd, 1900). It is possible that participation in Freemasonry may have had some influence over membership in, and structure of, the fur trade as well, considering the exclusive, highly-structured nature of the business. Both of Simon McTavish's nephews, William and Simon McGillivray, were high-ranking Freemasons, as were many prominent political and military figures in the Montreal area. Indeed, the final meetings of the Beaver Club were held in the Masonic Lodge Hotel in Montreal, built by another prominent Freemason, A.J. Molson. See Milborne, 72-73; Clifford B. Wilson "The Beaver Club," *The Beaver*, March 1937, 64.

50. Even McTavish's initial entry into the fur-trade business is reminiscent of Johnson's approach to gaining a foothold in this highly competitive business. According to R.H. Fleming ("Phyn, Ellice and Company of Schenectady," *Contributions to Canadian Economics*, vol. 4, 1932 [Toronto: 1932], 29), McTavish first entered the fur trade in the New York-Great Lakes area by travelling into the interior via the Hudson River route to contact inland traders. By supplying *en dérouine* traders with trade goods at fair market value—and saving the traders an arduous overland trip in the bargain—McTavish (like Johnson before him) succeeded in "bleeding off" business for himself despite his comparative inexperience in the business. This technique of intercepting fur-trade business by travelling into the interior via bateaux to supply inland traders was later adapted and perfected by the partners of the North West Company, who kept their inland posts well stocked with goods delivered via a laborious, but effective, canoe-based transportation system.
51. A detailed look at the business partnerships that comprised the British fur trade in the Great Lakes region, with particular emphasis on the trade from Detroit and Schenectady, is provided in Fleming's "Phyn, Ellice and Company."
52. James Phyn's wife, for example, was the daughter of Dr. John Constable, a close friend of Sir William Johnson. See Fleming, "Phyn, Ellice and Company," 14.
53. Ibid., 27.
54. The Hon. John Forsyth and Hon. John Richardson, two Scotsmen who later became partners in the North West Company, were related by blood and/or marriage to both Phyn and Ellice, and got their introduction to the North American fur trade through these gentlemen, as did several other individuals. See Fleming, "Phyn, Ellice and Company," 26; Wallace, ed., *Macmillan Dictionary*, 240, 267; Frances G. Halpenny, *Dictionary of Canadian Biography*, vol. 5, 1801-1820 (Toronto: University of Toronto Press, 1983), 517-25, for further biographical information about Forsyth and Richardson.
55. See Ian Charles Cargill Graham, *Colonists from Scotland: Emigration to North America 1707-1783* (Ithaca: Cornell University Press, 1956), 81-85. See also 43, 70-73, and 106-9 for discussion of the factors surrounding the emigration of other Scottish groups to the North American colonies.
56. John Macdonell, a partner in the North West Company ca. 1796, was the eldest son of "Spanish John." Another of Spanish John's sons was Miles Macdonell,

appointed as Governor of Assiniboia by Lord Selkirk in 1811. Alexander Greenfield Macdonell, North West Company partner ca. 1814, was a second cousin of John and Miles. See Wallace, ed., *Macmillan Dictionary*, 442-46.

57. William Perkins Bull, *Macdonell to McGuigan: The History of the Growth of the Roman Catholic Church in Upper Canada* (Toronto: The Perkins Bull Foundation, 1939), Chapter 3. See also E.A. Cruikshank, "The King's Royal Regiment of New York," *Papers and Records-Ontario Historical Society*, vol. 27 (Toronto: Ontario Historical Society, 1931), 193.
58. See Fraser, "Sir John Johnson's Rent Roll," 184-89. See also Wallace, ed., *Macmillan Dictionary of Canadian Biography*, for genealogical notes concerning several of these surnames, which provide ample proof of the Mohawk Valley antecedents of several North West Company families. The Donald McGillis family, for example, had at least two sons who joined the North West Company (Wallace, 453). Another useful source for determining the Mohawk Valley origins of various Scots is the "Proceedings of the Loyalist Commissioners, Montreal 1787," some of whom are included in the *Second Report of the Bureau of Archives*, Alexander Fraser, Provincial Archivist, ed. (L.K. Cameron, 1904). This volume contains a series of Loyalist refugee affidavits which note the American colonial residence of the claimant, their family members, their membership in Loyalist militia regiments, and the amount of property forfeited prior to their flight into Canada. Another historical volume dealing with the Loyalist settlement of the Upper St. Lawrence is Richard A. Preston, ed., *Kingston Before the War of 1812* (Toronto: Champlain Society, 1959).
59. Bull, *Macdonell to McGuigan*, Appendix, p. "C".
60. Alexander Mackenzie, the fur trader and Nor'Wester, spent about two years at Johnson Hall prior to his escape to Canada in 1778. During this period, his father and uncle fought in the King's Royal Regiment of New York. See W.K. Lamb, ed., *The Journals and Letters of Alexander Mackenzie* (Toronto: Macmillan of Canada, 1970), 2-3.
61. There are several descriptions of the breakup of the Johnson plantations, the flight of Sir John Johnson to Canada, and the subsequent formation of the King's Royal Regiment of New York. See also P.H. Bryce, "The Quinte Loyalists of 1784," *Papers and Records-Ontario Historical Society* (Toronto: Ontario Historical Society, 1931), 5-14; Bull, *Macdonell to McGuigan*, chap. 3, pp. 3-4; Cruikshank, "The King's Royal Regiment," 193-323; Alexander Clark Casselman, "The Highland Scotch U.E. Loyalists," *Annual Transactions, Vol. 4, 1901-1902, The United Empire Loyalists' Association* (Toronto: The United Empire Loyalists' Association, 1902), 100-9. See also Robert S. Allen, *The Loyal Americans: The Military Role of the Loyalist Provincial Corps and Their Settlement in British North America 1775-1784* (Ottawa: National Museums of Canada, 1983). For a useful summary of archival military records pertaining to the Loyalist period, see Timothy Dubé, *Tracing Your Loyalist Military Ancestors: Military Organization and Archival Records of the American Revolution* (unpublished monograph, Ottawa, National Museums of Canada, 1990).
62. Bryce, The Quinte Loyalists," 7-8.
63. See Jacob Farrand Pringle, *Lunenburgh, or the Old Eastern District* (Cornwall, Ontario, Author, 1890), for a detailed history of the Loyalist settlement of this area.
64. See P.C.T. White, ed., *Lord Selkirk's Diary 1803-1804* (Toronto: Champlain Society, 1958), 196.

65. Cataraqui was renamed Kingston in 1788.
66. Cartwright, a Mohawk Valley refugee and former secretary to Colonel Butler of the Queen's Rangers, became the Kingston agent for James McGill, a Scotsman who, while not a Nor'Wester, was closely affiliated with the company and enjoyed membership in the Beaver Club. Joseph Forsyth, brother of John Forsyth of Forsyth, Richardson and Company and nephew of both James Phyn and Alexander Ellice, came to Canada in 1784 and eventually became a prominent merchant of Kingston. See Halpenny, ed., *Dictionary of Canadian Biography, 5:* 167-72, 325-27, for information on Cartwright and Forsyth, respectively.
67. The commercial vessel *Simcoe* was registered in 1794 to a partnership comprised of the firms Todd and McGill, and Richardson and Forsyth. Ownership of the boat was later transferred to various owners, Hamilton, Todd, Ellice and Company, Hamilton and Cartwright, and Joseph Forsyth. See Preston, ed., *Kingston Before the War of 1812*, lxv-lxxiv. The rapid success of the Montreal merchants and their Cataraqui partners in the transshipping business alarmed Governor Simcoe, who expressed fear that they would establish a monopoly over the agricultural trade as they had over furs (lxxiv).
68. Sir John Johnson did attend Beaver Club functions from time to time, but he should not be confused with the trader John Johnston of the Sault, who attended regularly, and whose name appears often in the records. See Wilson, "The Beaver Club," 19-24, 64.
69. John Duncan Campbell (1773-1835), the North West Company partner in charge of the English River Department ca. 1803, was born in Scoharie, New York, the son of Loyalists Alexander Campbell and Magdalena Van Sice. A brother, Colin Campbell, entered the service of the North West Company in 1804 as a clerk and finished his fur trade career in 1853 as a Chief Trader with the Hudson's Bay Company (see Wallace, ed., *Macmillan Dictionary*, 108-9). No doubt a closer study of marriage records in Glengarry County would yield additional interethnic unions.
70. See Guzzardo, "Sir William Johnson's Official Family," 344-48.
71. The common bonds uniting the Mohawk Valley Loyalists with the Montreal merchants are amply illustrated by Lord Selkirk's diary entries during his travels from Kingston to Montreal in the winter of 1804. On his journey through the Loyalist townships en route to Montreal, he was hosted by a succession of Mohawk Valley Loyalists with family and business connections to the North West Company, such as Richard Cartwright, Alexander Fisher, Thomas Fraser, Miles McDonnell, Father Roderick McDonnell, and Rev. John Bethune. Selkirk's trip culminated with his sojourn in Montreal, where he was lavishly entertained by "the nabobs of the North West Company" and Sir John Johnson. See White, ed., *Lord Selkirk's Diary*, 184-223.

Faithful Service under Different Flags: A Socioeconomic Profile of the Columbia District, Hudson's Bay Company and the Upper Missouri Outfit, American Fur Company, 1825-1835

William R. Swagerty and Dick A. Wilson

In the late spring of 1825, a peculiar event occurred along the banks of the Bear River in present-day Utah. Twenty-three freemen[1] attached to the Hudson's Bay Company's Snake River Brigade under the command of Peter Skene Ogden absconded with their traps, horses, and furs, most leaving unpaid debts for the company to absorb. Desertion was not a new theme to the HBC. Individuals and small groups of men—both engaged and free—could be expected to walk off the job annually, but this incident was quite different. In a letter to HBC Governor George Simpson, Ogden explained the loss.

> On the 23 [of May 1825] a party of 15 Canadians and Spanjards [sic] headed by one [Etienne] Provost[2] and François [François Sansfaçon][3] an Iroquois Chief who deserted from our party two Years since joined us. . . .Shortly after the arrival of the above party another of 25 to 30 Americans headed by one Gardner [Johnson Gardner, a free trapper active on Bear River since 1824][4] and a Spanjard with 15 of our trappers who had been absent about two days also made their appearance; they encamped within 100 yards of our Camp and hoisted the American Flag, and proclaimed to all that they were in the United States Territories and were all Free indebted or engaged, it was now night and nothing more transpired, the ensuing morning Gardner came to my tent and after a few words of no import he questioned me as follows, do you know in whose country you are? to which I made answer that I did not, as it was not determined between Great Britain and America to whom it belonged. . . .He then left my tent and seeing him go in an Iroquois tent (belonging to John Grey [Ignace Hatchiorauquasha])[5] I followed him. On my entering this villain Gray said, I must now tell you that all the Iroquois as well as myself have long wished for an opportunity to join the Americans, and if we did not the last three Years, it was owing to our bad luck in not meeting them, but now we go, and all you can say or do cannot prevent us. During this conversation Gardner was silent, but on going out he said you have had these Men too long in your Service and have most shamefully imposed on them, treating them as Slaves selling them Goods at high prices and giving them nothing for their Furs, Gray

> then said that it is all true and alluding to the Gentlemen he had been with in the Columbia, they are says he the greatest villains in the World, and if they were here I would shoot them, but as for you Sir you have dealt fair with us all. We have now been five Years in your Service, the longer we remain the more indebted we become, altho' we give 150 Beaver a year, we are now in a free Country and have friends to support us, and go we will, and If every Man in the Camp does not leave you they do not seek their own interest.

Ogden concluded his summation to Governor Simpson, remarking that John Grey "then gave orders to raise Camp and in an instant all the Iroquois were in motion and ready to start; this example was soon followed by others, a scene of confusion now ensued. . : Finding myself with only 20 Trappers left surrounded on all sides by enemies I resolved on returning to the Snake River. . . ."[6]

Six weeks later, on 2 July, William H. Ashley and between fifty and one hundred men (including several HBC deserters) broke camp, thus ending the first organized annual Rocky Mountain rendezvous.[7] On that same day, far to their north at York Factory on Hudson Bay, the HBC Council of chief factors met behind closed doors. Their purpose and strategy had not changed much since the merger with the North West Company in 1821: to assess the status of the trade during the previous twelve months and to reorganize for the coming year's outfit. The "Minutes" of that six-day council leave the impression that Governor Simpson and the twelve chief factors present slept little.[8] Many matters of policy, procedure, and personnel needed action, but no crisis seemed at hand. They had not been apprised of Ogden's losses, whose communique was in transit as the convention disbanded. Nor did they benefit from a firsthand report on the Columbia District by its chief officer, John McLoughlin, unable to attend that year's meeting.

In hindsight, we know that many storms generated from competition and aggressive capitalism to the south of the Bay lurked menacingly on the horizon.[9] But these were not recorded at the meeting, nor were many of the internal problems well known to the Governor and chief factors present, problems such as disaffected personnel like Alexander Ross. Once a brigade leader, he was now eager to retire from the trade at the rank of clerk but was unwilling to keep his vitriolic opinions about ill-management of the Company from influencing others.[10]

The matter of increased pressure and traffic by Americans intent on pursuing to the letter the spirit of the joint occupancy of the Oregon country was not brought up, but from correspondence and journals, we know the Convention of 1818 had not resolved the problem of jurisdiction in the minds of some diplomats and fur barons on both sides. Nor would the 1846 Oregon Treaty boundary fully resolve overlapping political and commercial boundaries. Until 1870, Americans and British citizens would live side by side, cooperating as well as competing on a shared settlement landscape.[11]

The records of the Hudson's Bay Company's 1825 Council minutes provide an outline of the internal structure of the Company's North American operations.

Figure 1. John Grey (Gray) (ca. 1790-ca. 1844), also known by his Iroquoian name Ignace Hatchiorauquasha, entered the western fur trade in 1816 to work for the North West Company. After the 1821 merger, Grey and many other eastern Indians hired on with the HBC as part of the Snake Country Expeditions. Grey emerged as a spokesman for the Iroquois freemen and left the trade in 1836 to settle near present-day Kansas City. In 1841, Grey served as a guide to the DeSmet Party. This sketch was drawn by Father Nicolas Point, S.J. on that trip. Reproduction courtesy of Historical Photograph Collections, Washington State University Libraries, Neg. No. 88-359.

As such, they contain a wealth of detailed information on the places, policies, and people who required the immediate attention of the Council that summer at York Factory. Most of the 147 itemized articles concerned HBC personnel. Many reiterated terms agreed upon in the original Deed Poll of 1821.[12] Conditions of employment, including scale of wages by rank, occupation, and by district were given, as were special provisions for tariffs on goods and furs at posts, transfers of people and accounts, permissions for planned retirements (including that of Ross), and changes or new directions in policies affecting Indians and company personnel.

Article sixty-six of the Minutes listed the appointments of fifteen Columbia River District officers, under the supervision of recently promoted Chief Factor, Dr. John McLoughlin. Of special interest, modifications beyond the previous year's council meeting received individual attention on the final document. These measures, designed for tighter control of personnel and better accounting of goods, furs, and wages, are socioeconomic barometers of the hierarchical structure of the company and its fiscally conservative methods of operation. For example, Article 112 specified:

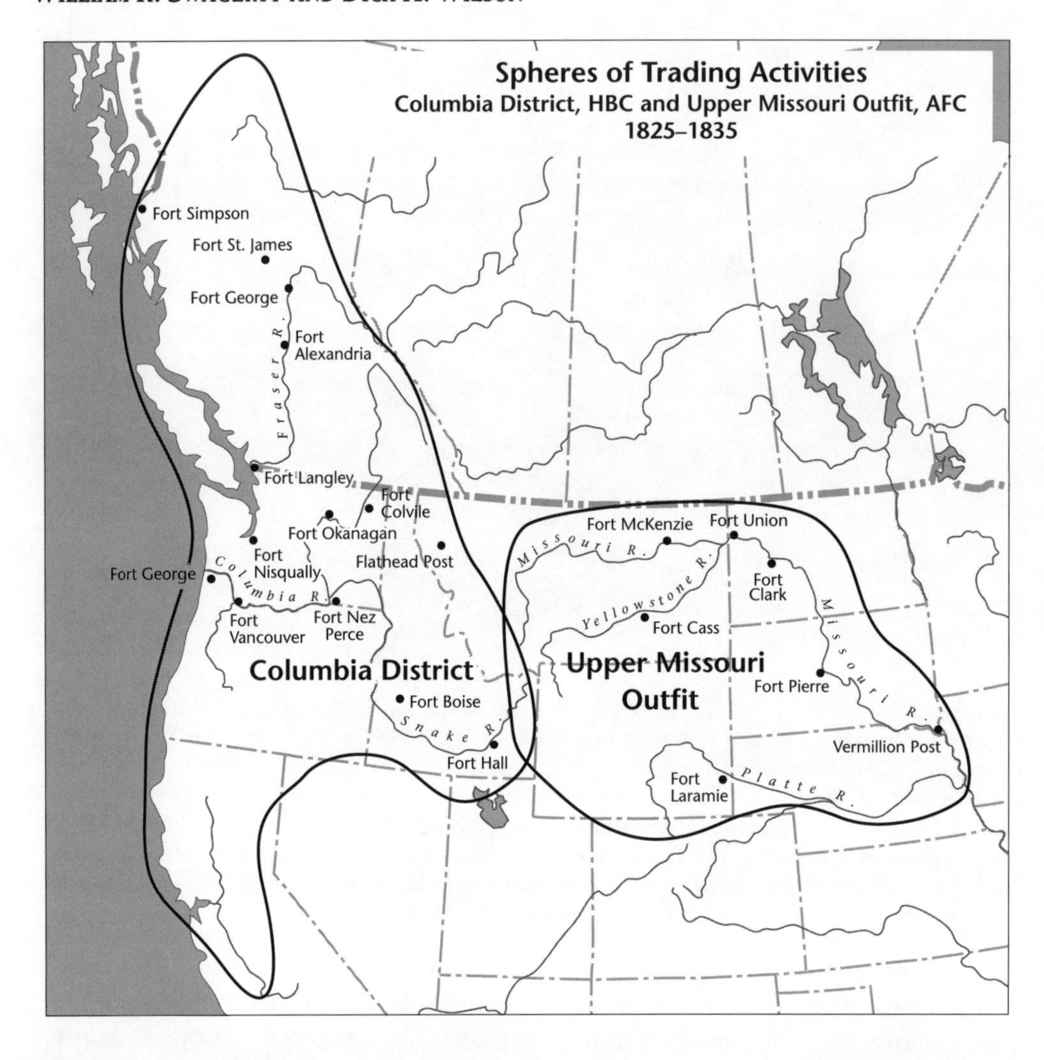

Figure 2. Spheres of Trading Activities.

> That the practice of allowing Servants to Trade Provisions, Leather or other articles be discontinued, and that no barter or traffic of any kind be permitted with either freemen or Indians under penalty of a Fine to be imposed by Council for each offence.[13]

This provision was followed with one stipulating that "no Guide or Interpreter whether at the Factory Depot or inland, be permitted to mess with commissioned Gentlemen or Clerks in charge of Posts. . ." but that the same be given extra rations beyond those issued to the *engagés*.[14] Further on, the minutes specified that "no money transaction, barter, or traffic between Clerks and other Servants be allowed without the special permission of Council."[15] Another article declared, "As an inducement to those Servants now on Canadian terms. . . .That all debts exceeding 1,000 *livres* due by them to the Company be reduced to that sum on condition of their rehiring for 3 years. . . ."[16] One article directly addressed the question of freemen's indebtedness. It required:

> That all Freemen Half breed or Iroquois Trappers having no other means of paying [for] their supplies than with their Hunts be treated on the footing of Indians. . . and that Freemen not coming under that description having Funds in the Companys hands and unable to pay their supplies with Furs, be charged 200 p. Cent on the District Inventory prices and that no money in payment of Furs or other articles be allowed either class without directions from Council.[17]

Given these regulations, and the personal statement of John Grey as reported by Ogden to the Council, one could easily conclude that the Snake Brigade Mutiny of 1825 was bound to occur. Wide cultural chasms separated Indian, Métis, and Anglo worlds in that era. But were their economic worlds as dissimilar as John Grey's complaint and explanation for leaving Ogden suggest? In the aftermath of the affair, John McLoughlin analyzed the economic implications. In a letter to his superiors, he wrote:

> By the desertion of these men the Concern has lost between two and three thousand Skins in furs and their future services, add to this the loss they cause by disabling the Remainder from going to where they intended and finally if the Saskatchewan freemen have determined on abandoning this side of the Mountains we may say the desertion of these men will prevent our getting four thousand Skins annually from that part of the Country.[18]

Loss of allegiance to the company over wages or specific working conditions could be corrected. However, loss of furs, Indian clients, and servants to rival concerns offering not only higher pay for peltries but increased independence in the workplace was vexing to Company officers and was clearly anathema to their tradition. Fortunately for the HBC, the historical record reveals that most servants did not share the Iroquois and Saskatchewan Métis' conviction that total independence or service under a different flag were preferable to the predictable, if restrictive, life under the seal of the HBC, even those assigned to the most remote parts of Rupert's Land along the Pacific slope. Writing in 1845, Commodore Charles Wilkes of the United States Exploring Expedition gave the readers of his official Report the following positive image of the loyalty and perseverance of HBC servants. In direct reference to the men serving under Ogden, he wrote:

> To all appearance, there is seldom to be found a more laborious set of men; nor one so willing, particularly when their remuneration of no more than seventeen pounds sterling a-year, and the fare they receive, are considered. The latter would be considered with us incapable of supporting any human being. It consists of coarse unbolted bread, dried salmon, fat (tallow), and dried peas. I am satisfied that no American would submit to such food: the Canadian and Iroquois Indians use it without murmuring, except to strangers, to whom they complain much of their scanty pay and food. The discipline is strict, and of an arbitrary kind; yet they

> do not find fault with it. . . .Very few of those who embark or join this Company's service, ever leave the part of the country they have been employed in; for after the expiration of five years, they usually enlist for three more. This service of eight years in a life of so much adventure and hazard, attaches them to it, and they generally continue until they become old men; when, being married, and having families by Indian women, they retire, under the auspices of the Company, to some small farm, either on the Red or Columbia rivers.[19]

Wilkes was describing the milieux of typical day laborers, whose wages had not increased since the 1820s. Their counterparts on American soil and elsewhere in Rupert's Land were the *voyageur* and *mangeurs de lard* class, who made up the rank-and-file of the trade for all large companies.[20] The life styles and working conditions of this large aggregate in the work force have received very little serious attention by historians in the twentieth century. One persistent image is that rendered by Hiram M. Chittenden in his influential *The American Fur Trade of the Far West*, published in 1902. It was a grim, unquantified assessment:

> They were bound for a period of five years under the most rigorous engagement, and at wages that made it impossible for them to arrive at the end of their term without being in their employer's debt. As there was no way for them to get passage out of the country while so in debt, they were compelled to remain and keep at work or resort to the dangerous expedient of desertion.[21]

This brings us to an important question that still looms large in the historiography of the fur trade:[22] In the competitive, capitalist environment of North America in the 1820s through the 1840s, was the western fur trade a successful way to make a living and one that carried some economic opportunity for those on the bottom and those on the middle rungs as well as those on the top of the fur trade socioeconomic ladder? Did those voyageurs in the employ of American companies stick it out like their counterparts in the British company?

Contrary to many popular stereotypes of the western trade, we know that the doors of Western economic opportunity were not entirely open on an equal footing to all interested in entrepreneurial ventures large and small. From Washington, D.C. to St. Louis, rules and regulations of a very different nature from those of the HBC Council had been formulated to control the Indian trade of the unorganized territories beyond Missouri. In that creole mecca where Mediterranean social regard for extended family networking merged with Yankee entrepreneurial skills, Superintendent of Indian Affairs William Clark busied himself during the autumn of 1825 redrafting his map of licensed traders permitted to enter Indian country.[23] Unlike the British, who placed responsibility for both trade and diplomacy in the hands of the same power, the American Congress did not trust its wealthy Western citizenry. Instead, the War Department and its bureaus, especially the Office of Indian Affairs, made an effort to control the flow of people, goods, and especially liquor passing from the States into Indian country. Clark and his small staff of Indian agents had an impossible task and were thus bound to rely upon the consciences of the river city's merchant elite and their connections linking the trade from the decision centers in St. Louis, Washington, London, Montreal, and New York with Indian tribes and white fur trade personnel living on Indian hunting grounds of the Plains and in the mountains separating British from American posts and settlements. In both trade spheres, "rules and regulations" were only as good as the company personnel who enforced them and were only effective in the long run where they took into account cultural as well as economic needs, wants, and priorities.

The manner in which the Indian Office handled licensing has not been fully studied, nor have Clark's manuscript maps surfaced, but we know that the U.S. Government concerned itself annually with reassessing the character of traders permitted to traffic in Indian country. Clark's personal attention to the detail of reaffirming locations of each post, as well as its correlation with bands of Indians with whom traders were authorized to exchange goods for skins and furs, indicates this was not the whiskey-laced laissez faire free trade zone often portrayed in the literature.[24]

This study compares economic opportunity and indebtedness among HBC personnel in the Columbia District with a comparable set of data on American-based servants working for the American Fur Company under similar conditions along the Missouri River and its tributaries, drawing from financial ledgers and employee rosters of the Hudson's Bay Company from 1825 to 1835 and equivalent ledgers of the St. Louis-based Western Department of the American Fur Company (AFC), 1826 through 1835. We have chosen these companies because they were the two largest and most influential business concerns active in the Far West at that time. The main questions we pose are these:

1. Who were the servants of both companies, by ethnicity, occupational group, and rank?
2. What was the average wage for each rank?
3. What employment longevity did these company servants have in the trade?
4. What vertical mobility is discernable from the financial ledgers?
5. What do book debits and credits tell us about the validity of stereotypes such as those by Commodore Wilkes on HBC men and by Colonel Chittenden on AFC men, respectively?

Both companies were organized with four tiers of personnel: (1) owners and partners, as well as officers under contract as shareholders or under appointment for set terms at an annual salary; (2) those in positions of mid-level management, including clerks, postmasters, traders, interpreters and, occasionally, guides; (3) the general mass of skilled and unskilled employees; and (4) those individuals not engaged to the companies who supplied goods or services on a non-contractual basis at elastic rates, determined by management or field personnel and determined in some measure by market prices as well as local pressures. This latter category included freemen, independent traders, and consumers. Of the four categories, only that of mid-level management differed significantly between the two companies. Clerks in both companies were considered "gentlemen" and were usually addressed as "Mr." Whereas the American Fur Company often combined responsibilities of clerk/trader with interpreter/trader, the HBC did not. Traders, interpreters, and guides were clearly distinguished from officers and gentlemen at HBC posts, where they worked and lived among others in the "servant" class.[25]

In 1821, after the merger with the North West Company, the reorganized Hudson's Bay Company had around 2,000 employees in northern North America. By 1826, the regular salaried workforce had been cut to fewer than 700 people. This number rose again to 1,140 employees in 1839.[26] Of these, in 1830, the Fort Vancouver ledgers listed 406 employees in the Columbia District, including those men assigned to New Caledonia.[27]

The Western Department of the American Fur Company was formed in 1822, with Bernard Pratte and Company of St. Louis managing field operations and the New York house of J. J. Astor buying merchandise for the trade and selling furs acquired from the interior for a percentage of the total profits.[28] The Upper Missouri Outfit (UMO), formed in 1827, had a paid workforce of 287 in 1830.[29] This represents more than one-half of the 535 employees whose names appear on the St. Louis ledgers from 1831 to 1836.[30]

A comparison of the companies' occupational and wage structures in 1830 reveals some similarities and some differences (tables 1 and 2).[31] If we factor out officers above the rank of clerk, within the Hudson's Bay Company, the following picture emerges: for one year's service, the average pay of apprentices was £11.17.02 or $62.98 at the prevailing exchange rate of £1.0.0 to $5.31, a figure that was fairly constant throughout the nineteenth century.[32] The next rung up the wage ladder was that of common laborers, who earned an average of £17.16.07 ($94.68) in 1830.

TABLE 1. OCCUPATIONAL RANKINGS AND AVERAGE PAY, 1830.

American Fur Company/Upper Missouri Outfit

Rank	Number	Average Pay (dollars)
Interpreter	7	380.33
Clerk & Trader	27	371.94
Trader & Voyageur	1	360.00
Clerk & Interpreter	9	333.33
Patroon	6	284.50
Hunter	2	250.00
Tradesman	5	160.29
Voyageur	233	132.84

Source: Missouri Historical Society, St. Louis.

Table 2. Occupational Rankings and Average Pay, 1830.
Hudson's Bay Company/Columbia District

Rank	Number	Average Pay (pounds)	Average Pay (dollars)
Clerk	16	90.18.10	482.89
Guide & Interpreter	4	45.00.00	238.95
Tradesman	31	30.07.00	161.16
Voyageur/Hunter	236	19.00.02	100.94
Laborer	6	17.16.07	94.68
Apprentice	21	11.17.02	62.98
Ship Master & Mate	9	67.02.02	356.35
Sailor	33	30.12.02	162.54

Source: Hudson's Bay Company Archives, Winnipeg.

Voyageurs, hunters, and "servants" were the jacks-of-all-trades who worked about the forts, tended livestock, farmed, and performed other semi-skilled tasks at the various trade shops. Some had fixed assignments at important posts like Fort Vancouver, while others traveled in hunting or freighting brigades. They earned on average about £19 ($100). Their counterparts with the American Fur Company, usually listed on contracts as "voyageur, chasseur, et hivernant," averaged 32 percent more per man at $132.85. The AFC hired a small, but separate class of hunters, responsible for feeding personnel at the posts and those on expeditions between St. Louis and the Upper Missouri. In 1830, hunters averaged $250.00, slightly less than patroons, the steersmen of Missouri River keelboats.

The patroons of the American company outpaced their British counterparts, the "boutes," whose roles as bowsmen and steersmen in HBC canoes and boats were critical on northern rivers but whose numbers and rate of pay indicate they were easily replaced. AFC patroons averaged $284.50, while a typical Columbia River boute earned £22 ($116.82). Boutes on the Fraser River earned £2 more, owing to winter conditions and hazards of travel.[33] The "Old French" system, inherited from the North West Company, provided all boutes and milieux with annual outfits consisting of one 3-point blanket, one 2-1/2-point blanket, 2 striped cotton shirts, 2 yards of common cloth, and between 6 and 9 pounds of tobacco until 1830, when, as a cost-saving measure, outfits of gear were no longer supplied as part of a contract.[34] Missouri River men, however, continued to receive outfits as incentives for reengagement. In 1832, 119 UMO engagés at the rank of voyageur were issued one 3-point blanket, 1 1/2 yards of blue stroud cloth, 1 handkerchief, 1 checkered shirt, 1 scalping knife, and 3 pounds of tobacco, the sum of which cost the company $7.20 per man.[35]

HBC tradesmen such as blacksmiths, coopers, carpenters, and shipwrights earned around £30 ($161.16), a figure almost identical for the same skilled personnel of the AFC. Some HBC guides and interpreters were paid at this same rate, but the average for this category with the British company was £45 ($238.95). In contrast, interpreters with the AFC commanded an average of $380.33, more than half again as much as HBC men. This disparity can be explained in part because the HBC expected clerks and traders to acquaint themselves with local Native languages. AFC clerks sometimes acquired such skills. Successful AFC traders assigned to specific bands of Indian hunters or small wintering houses far from major forts learned Indian languages out of necessity. However, the AFC did not pay clerks and traders at rates comparable to the HBC, the latter of which gave clerks (on average and across all four "classes" within that rank) £90.18.10 or the equivalent of $482.89. Twenty-seven clerks and traders in the Upper Missouri Outfit in 1830 earned an average of $371.94, or 30 percent less than their British counterparts.[36]

Breakdown of both companies' rosters using surnames as indicators of ethnicity yields the following pattern in 1830. Hudson's Bay Company officers included equal proportions of English and Scots or Scotch-Irish. Anglo-Celtic names make up 79 percent of those at the rank of clerk, but some opportunities existed for French-North Americans, who comprised 21 percent of that group.[37]

Below clerks, Columbia District servants were a mixture of French-Canadians (56 percent), English (20 percent), Hawaiians (12 percent), Scots and Scotch-Irish (7 percent), and Indians (5 percent).[38] The records are unclear how French-North Americans and Native Americans self-identified, but we are able to distinguish Iroquoian names like Laurent Karonhitchego in the District Statements.[39]

The Upper Missouri Outfit was not as ethnically diverse, but the highest echelons of the company were much more open to those of non-Anglo background than the Hudson's Bay Company, which was closed to non-British and non-British-Canadians. All three owners of the Western Department—Pierre Chouteau, Jr. Bernard Pratte, and Bartholomew Berthold—were of French-North American upper class backgrounds, while the three partners in the UMO—Kenneth McKenzie, supreme "Agent," William Laidlaw, bourgeois (officer in charge) at Fort Tecumseh (later Fort Pierre), and Daniel Lamont, the partisan or officer in charge of logistics between St. Louis and the posts—claimed Scotland as a birthplace.[40]

Employees below these officers represented French-North American and Métis families from the St. Lawrence to the Mississippi delta. At the rank of Clerk & Trader, 15 UMO men (62.50 percent of the total) were of French or French-North American ancestry, while five of nine or 56 percent of those at the rank of Clerk & Interpreter were also French. So were all seven interpreters, some of whom had Indian parentage but none of whom are identified in the records as mixed-bloods. Patroons were generally French-North American, but one Spanish-North American by the name of Hernández joined this rank as steersman on a keelboat. Tradesmen were a mix of French and Anglo backgrounds, but those in the rank-and-file of the voyageur class (207 out of 233 men or 88.84 percent) had French surnames.

Figure 3. Kenneth McKenzie (1797-1861), the primary architect of the American Fur Company's Upper Missouri Outfit, left Scotland in 1816 to work for the North West Company. In the wake of the reorganization of the Canadian-based companies, McKenzie immigrated to the United States in 1822 as a partner in the Columbia Fur Company. His active years in association with the American Fur Company began in 1827. After a short and controversial, but highly successful career, McKenzie withdrew from the fur trade in the mid 1830s. Photograph reprinted from Hiram Martin Chittenden, *History of Early Steamboat Navigation on the Missouri River*, 2 vols. (New York: Francis P. Harper, 1903), 2: ii.

The 1830 roster showed no Hawaiians or Iroquois working for the UMO, but an occasional Plains Indian worker appeared in the correspondence or in the financial ledgers during that decade. These were not full-time workers; rather, they provided specific services without contracts. For example, Louis Brulé appears on the 1831-1836 financial ledger with "Indian" written beside his name. During the fall of 1833, he earned $140 for delivering two herds of horses and for other unspecified "special services."[41]

Servants in the UMO included Blacks. Some of the officers brought Black slaves upriver from St. Louis. These individuals are not listed as wage earners, but their contributions toward the economic well-being of the company are noted. For example, in 1833, the company transferred $120.00 in profit to the account of Kenneth McKenzie for the labor of his slave, John Duchouquette.[42] Freedmen of African descent were rare on the Upper Missouri, but they did exist. James Beckwourth was hired to serve as a liaison with the Crow in the early 1830s. A letter from Kenneth McKenzie, dated Fort Union, 21 July 1836, asked the central office in St. Louis to pay "James Beckwith the Sum of three hundred and forty one dollars and seventy five cents for the value received."[43]

What can be said about worker satisfaction with conditions of employment among both groups of salaried servants? Our data indicates three markers on this important question: length of employment, upward mobility, and desertion rates. We tracked all UMO employees known to have been under contract for the year 1829, back to 1827 (the first year of the outfit), and forward to 1848 (the last year a servant from 1829 was still active within the company). The average length of service was 15.0 years for owners and officers; 6.3 years for mid-level management, including clerks and traders; and 2.7 years for servants in the rank-and-file. The mean for all ranks was 3.1 years.[44]

How does this relatively low employment longevity compare with Hudson's Bay Company data? Using biographical files from the HBC Archives for Columbia District servants active between 1825 and 1835, we traced beginning and terminal points of employment. For thirty-four men at all ranks, the average length of service was 23.0 years. The mean for officers (eight men) including Chief Traders such as Peter Ogden, Jr. was 34.6 years; for mid-level management (seven men) including clerks, 21.0 years; and for 19 servants, 18.9 years (figure 4).[45] Compared with the fifteen years of average length of service or activity in the trade for 292 subjects surveyed in LeRoy R. Hafen's *The Mountain Men and the Fur Trade of the Far West*, the AFC average is very low while the HBC average is somewhat higher.[46]

Many variables skew the data for all three samples. Hafen series biographies and HBC biographical files are limited to individuals for whom we have sufficient documentation to reconstruct entire or partial life histories. The AFC and HBC personnel surveyed by Hafen included owners, factors, partners, traders, and clerks. Rank-and-file servants are missing, with the exception of the occasional man who made a name for himself through unusual vertical mobility within the company or as an independent after leaving the employ of the large

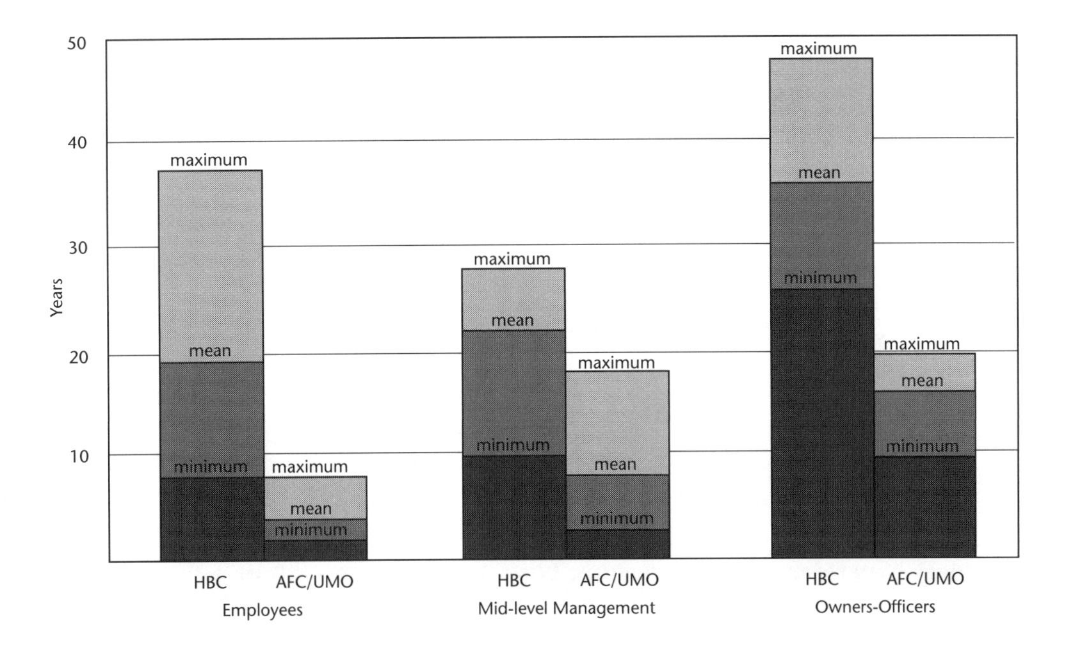

Figure 4. Years of Employment by Class, HBC (1811-1861); AFC/UMO (1826-1848). Source: Hudson's Bay Company Archives, Winnipeg and Missouri Historical Society, St. Louis.

company. Our hunch is that the true years of longevity in the fur trade for all personnel—salaried and independent, literate and illiterate, those at the bottom as well as those at the top—is a figure somewhere between our calculated AFC low of 3.1 years and the Hafen-series sample average of 15 years, a wide bracket.

What do these figures tell us about worker satisfaction? If our samples are indicative of a larger pattern for both companies, does this mean that HBC servants were content with contracts, conditions, and life in the Pacific Northwest, whereas AFC men were not equally satisfied on the Missouri? From this small data base, we cannot draw this conclusion, especially in light of the fact that AFC lower echelon employees made, on average, higher salaries than their HBC counterparts. However, two additional tests shed some light on this question: patterns of vertical mobility and, as a related phenomenon, desertion rates.

For the same small sample groups of 85 UMO men (the 1829 Outfit) and 34 HBC employees, we found that 25 percent of UMO employees and 62 percent of Columbia District personnel improved status either in income or in rank from year one of employment to retirement, termination, or death. In testing the correlation between position improvement at retirement with ethnicity, our sample reveals that, at the end of their careers, 94 percent of AFC servants from voyageurs up through craftsmen had French surnames, whereas only 6 percent were of Anglo extraction. At mid-management levels, French surnames form 66 percent of the rosters upon termination, with Anglos and Scots (including

Scotch-Irish) at approximately 17 percent each. Officers were all Scots, but the true owners of the company back in St. Louis remained predominantly French-North Americans (figure 5).[47]

Among the nineteen HBC retirees at the lower echelons, eight (43 percent) were French-surnamed; four (21 percent) had Scottish surnames; four (21 percent) were Native (mixed-bloods); and one man (5 percent) is specifically identified with each of the following categories: Anglos, Indians, and French-Canadian Métis. Our sample did not include Hawaiians (Kanakas or Sandwich Islanders, as they were known in HBC parlance) but we know that they represented 12 percent of the Columbia District in 1830.

Mid-level management clerks and interpreters with the HBC (earning between £40 and £100) were predominantly Anglos and Scots, with French-North Americans and Métis comprising 14 percent each (1 man each). Officers, including those at the rank of chief trader and above, were 37 percent (3 men) Scot, 25 percent (2 men) Anglo , 25 percent (2 men) Native, and 13 percent (1 man) French-North American (figure 5). What is interesting here is the upward mobility experienced by Native sons, born of unions between Indian women and European officers. The two examples in our sample were Peter Ogden, Jr., who died at the rank of Chief Trader at Fort St. James in 1870 of influenza after 31 years of service; and John Frederick Kennedy, who served 28 years, retiring to Victoria in 1856 at the rank of Chief Trader, having first served as surgeon, then clerk, before promotion in 1847.[48]

Patterns of short-term vertical mobility reveal an upwardly mobile workforce. In the three-year period from 1829 through 1831, 17 percent of the UMO employees gained in pay. During the same period, 28 percent (34 men) of the Columbia District gained. Moreover, during a ten-year period, the typical HBC Columbia District employee improved his pay status 34 percent of the time.

Although wage increases in the AFC were normally small, some employees made significant advances. For instance, Charles Lajeunesse first contracted with the UMO in 1827, earning $110, less than the voyageur's typical $117. There are no contracts extant for him for 1828 or 1829, but he reappears in 1830. By 1831, he earned $150.[49]

Within the HBC, promotion might come slowly or rapidly. Pierre Belleque took five years to progress from middleman to steersman with its £4 per year pay increase.[50] François Annance progressed more rapidly. Entering the Hudson's Bay Company from the North West Company as a £30 interpreter, by 1825 he had been promoted to clerk, with a salary ladder that progressed steadily from £40 to £100.[51]

Ultimately, as has been noted above, 25 percent of the UMO and 62 percent of HBC/ Columbia District employees gained in pay or position. When one considers that the average AFC/UMO employee remained with the company only slightly more than three years, whereas the typical HBC/Columbia District employee remained more than 23 years, one is tempted to conclude that the UMO employee was more upwardly or horizontally mobile than his Columbia

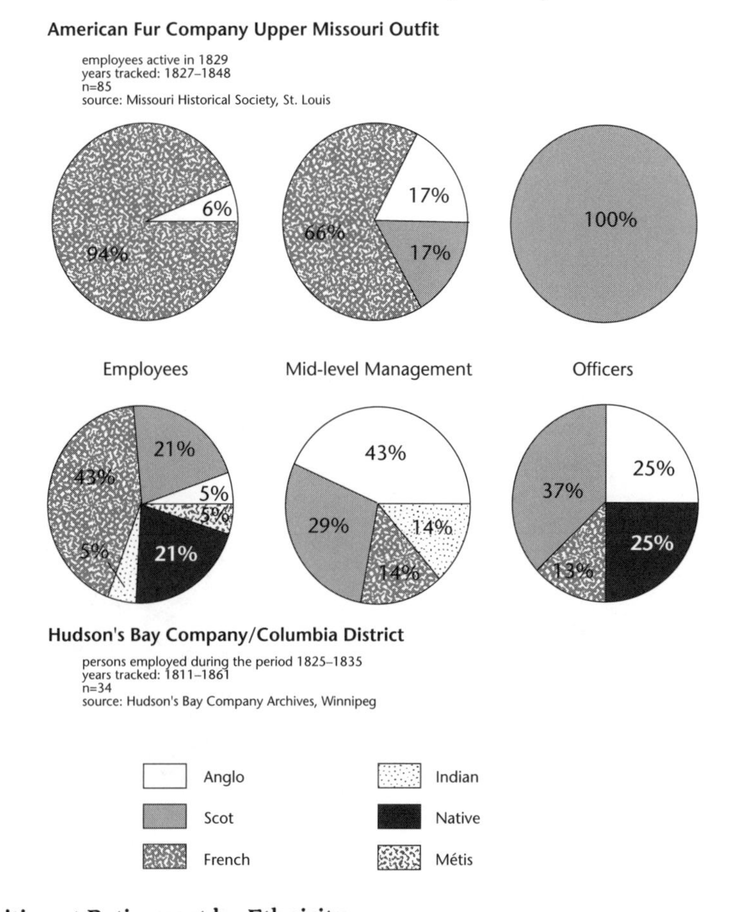

Figure 5. Position at Retirement by Ethnicity.

District counterpart. Stated otherwise, opportunities elsewhere outside of the fur trade entirely, or with other smaller or more loosely organized fur trade concerns, may have been factors drawing servants away from the AFC. An alternative hypothesis is that UMO rank-and-file were dissatisfied with their employer or conditions of employment and they therefore quit at the end of a given contract year; or, alternatively, they walked off the job.

To look further, we tabulated desertion rates of a rather randomly selected sample of 72 HBC Columbia District and 107 UMO employees.[52] In hindsight, the Snake River Brigade Mutiny of 23 freemen in 1825 seems predictable, given the drastic reduction in the permanent salaried workforce after the merger in 1821 and after the raising of the tariff on goods to 200 percent for freemen and Indians in 1825. In the long run, however, desertion did not seem to plague the company. Our sample of men employed between 1825 and 1835 showed only 3 percent of engagés and freemen deserting. On the other hand, the American Fur Company's Upper Missouri Outfit suffered a desertion rate of 12 percent of

Figure 6. Peter Skene Ogden, Jr. (ca. 1821-1870) born to Peter Skene Ogden, Sr. and his Spokane Indian wife, Julie, appears here with his son, Peter Skene Ogden, III, in an undated photograph. Ogden, Jr. entered the trade in 1835 and rose to the rank of Chief Trader in charge of New Caledonia by 1860. Photograph courtesy of British Columbia Archives and Records Service, Cat. No. 4610 A-1922.

all employees on contract between 1831 and 1836. Although no more than 20 men deserted the UMO in the span of twelve contiguous months, those who elected to walk off the job left a long paper trail of debits. The largest single incident of company disloyalty occurred on the night of 24 August 1834 at Fort Pierre. Thirteen *mangeurs de lard* (pork eaters), among them Pierre Bordeau, Etienne Leberge, and Joseph Derosier, stole "a small Mackinaw boat and a skiff" and fled the country. The ledger records that Bordeau, Leberge, and Derosier all returned and were reengaged, only to desert again in October of that same year.[53]

This incident parallels the 1825 Snake Mutiny in that the loss of so many men greatly affected local operations—in this case, at Fort Pierre. Both events must be viewed as extraordinary given the long-term histories of both operations. Nevertheless, if we factor out the deserters of August 1834 from our sample, we still have a UMO desertion rate of 9 percent, three times that of the Columbia District. A desertion rate for the UMO three times higher and a concurrent retention rate seven times lower than the HBC suggests that there were some problems in labor-management relations within the American Fur Company. However, this does not necessarily mean that Hudson's Bay Company Columbia District employees were more satisfied with their employment than those of the American Fur Company Upper Missouri Outfit. More research is necessary on employee levels of satisfaction for both groups.

One point is evident for the two companies: all deserters were in debt at the time they walked away. Joseph Annance, a middleman with the HBC, earned £15 per year, but Annance had accumulated a debt of nearly four years' pay when he escaped HBC service in 1825.[54] By and large, AFC deserters were less in debt than those of the HBC. Louis Gagnier, most in debt in our AFC sample, owed slightly more than two years' pay.[55] The maximum debt in our AFC sample for a non-deserter was roughly one year's pay and that was incurred by Louis Marechal, an employee at the $160-per-year-wage rate.[56]

Deserters aside, employees in both companies were reasonably free of debt. The 1831-1836 ledger of the UMO paints a picture of workers who made net financial gains during the period. Excluding those who died or deserted, roughly two-thirds of the UMO servants made monetary gains. The average annual gain per employee in our sample was $52.29 (figure 7). As one might expect, those at the higher end of the pay scale were able to save more than those at the bottom. For example, clerk and trader Pierre D. Papin tucked away $1,388.50 in one year on a $1500 salary in 1834.[57] When one considers the "savings rate," or that portion of one's income that was saved, the variation between the top and the bottom was small. The average UMO employee saved 18 percent of his income.

HBC employees saved less. Although not generally in debt, the typical milieu had very little to his credit on the company books. Our sample from the Columbia District 1825-1835 Ledger shows milieux ranging from Donald McDonald's £9.14.08 ($48) average annual book savings to Antoine Petit's

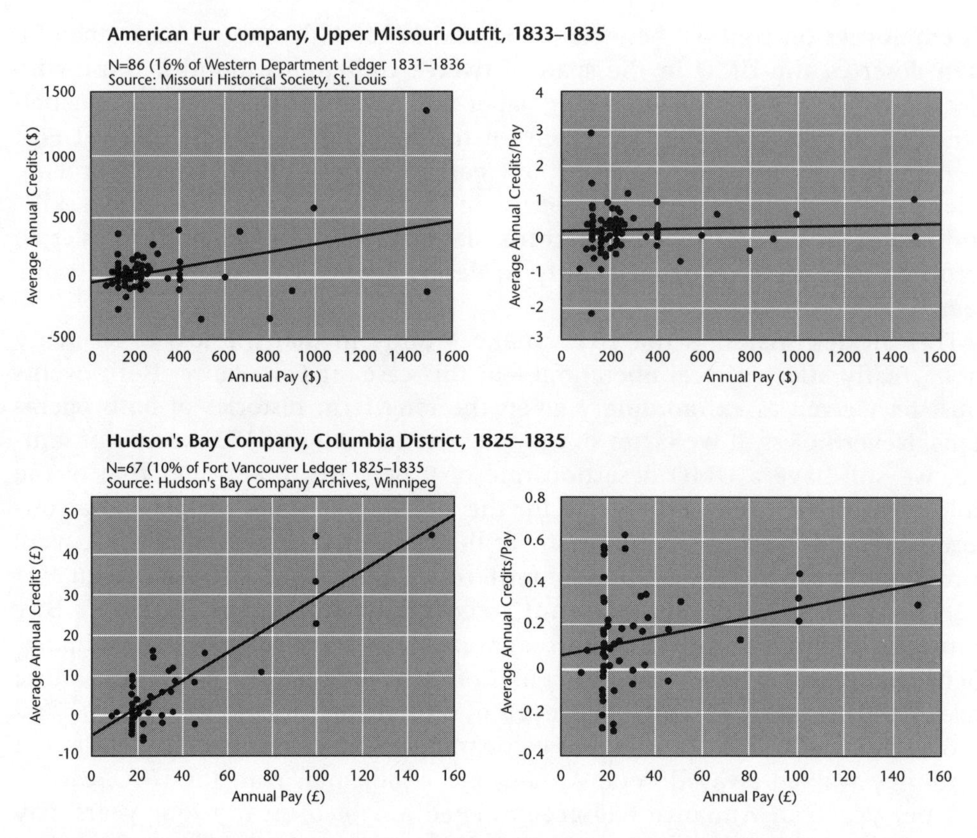

Figure 7. Distribution of Credits on Account, Excluding Deserters and Dead.

£4.13.01 ($21) average annual debt. The average savings for milieux was £1.08.07 ($7) per annum—8 percent of his annual income.[58] If he survived, the HBC freeman fared somewhat better; none were in debt and the most productive, Joseph Gervais, was able to amass £55.09.08 ($292) over six years, averaging £9.14.11 ($56) book credit per year.[59] Overall, the freemen averaged £4.15.02 ($22) annual book savings.

At all ranks (again, excluding deserters), the employees of the Columbia District saved, on average, £4.16.11 ($26) per year (figure 7). Like the American Fur Company, those of the Hudson's Bay Company who earned more saved more. But, unlike the AFC, those of the HBC who earned more saved a greater proportion of their pay. Those at the top of the pay scale (£100/annum) saved nearly 40 percent of their pay. Several factors might influence this disparity. First, as in today's society, those at the bottom of the pay scale had fewer discretionary funds and were therefore less able to save. Post traders and clerks in both companies were often provided with basic as well as some luxury items gratuitously or at cost, thus reducing their out-of-pocket expenses. Yet another explanation would factor in relative cost-of-living. A final explanation, but one beyond the scope of this study, would consider savings as a social ethic. One might expect those on the middle rungs of the occupational-rank ladder to save more than the common laborers; however, the data suggest otherwise.

An anomaly in pay occurs in both the AFC and HBC for those earning just slightly more than the milieu/voyageur. The steersmen of the AFC and the HBC were generally in debt. Our sample showed two-thirds of all AFC patroons were in debt at the annual rate of $22.19, on average. Eighty percent of HBC steersmen were also in the red, at the annual rate of £2.14.05 ($14). Without access to the companies' field day books (unfortunately lost), it is really impossible to explain with certainty why steersmen of both companies carried such large debt. One factor may be that these leadmen in charge of keelboats, canoes and, at times, traplines had to maintain their position by what would be called today "presence." To maintain their presence, they dressed and entertained better than their crews, and that cost additional money. Those with Indian families had many financial obligations beyond their own immediate households. Even among the clerk and trader class, some AFC personnel spent large percentages of their income to supply relatives, friends, and prospective Indian clients with gifts.

What this quantitative assessment has shown is that employment with the two largest companies active in the North American West during the 1820s and 1830s was more similar than dissimilar. Both companies suffered mutinies, but most servants faithfully served, albeit under different flags and for very different lengths of time.

Disparity in pay between the top and the bottom ranks of servants was greater in the HBC than in the UMO. Those in the middle—skilled craftsmen—earned approximately the same. Correlation of pay structure with ethnic composition of the work forces leads us to conclude that the doors of opportunity for advancement were narrower in the HBC than in the American Fur Company. The Columbia District records contain some exceptions, however, especially where those in question (Ogden, Kennedy) were directly related to officers.

More individuals in both groups of employees and across all ranks were in the black than were in the red. The typical AFC employee added $52 on average per year to his account. His Bay Company cohort gained £4.16.11 ($26) per annum. For their time they were savers, although as an aggregate they cannot best be described as expectant capitalists. Contrary to Chittenden's assertion that the American Fur Company induced debt to continue employee servitude and Wilkes' observation that no American would work under such dismal conditions as those he witnessed on the Columbia, our study reveals that economic opportunity existed for all ranks and within both companies. What our statistics cannot demonstrate is why some trade personnel preferred working for these large companies, while others opted for smaller concerns or total independence and still others left the trade altogether. Nor can we explain why, in 1836, John Grey and many other Iroquois trappers backtrailed to the great bend of the Missouri River near Westport to become townsmen, leaving the St. Lawrence and the Columbia to others.[60]

Acknowledgements

For their kind assistance in accessing archival materials used in this study, the authors thank Peter Michel and Martha Clevenger of the Missouri Historical Society; and Judith Beattie, Anne Morton, and Maureen Dolyniuk at the Hudson's Bay Company Archives. They also thank William Hunt of the National Park Service for sharing his compilations of data on the service records of UMO employees.

University of Idaho technical assistance was provided by Dr. Joan West, Professor of French, who has translated many documents at the Missouri Historical Society from the original French into English; and by Lee Cantrell, who assisted with computer statistics and slide imaging. This project was funded, in part, by the Honorable John Calhoun Smith Memorial Fund of the University of Idaho.

Notes

1. *Freemen* is a term used in the western fur trade for those men who participated in organized company activities without salary or contracts. The company expected their allegiance and guaranteed purchase of furs acquired by trapping or trading with Indians. Freemen worked side-by-side regular salaried employees and were generally equal in rank to voyageurs.
2. Etienne Provost was born in Quebec in 1785. He entered the mountain trade as a member of the Chouteau-DeMun party in 1815-17. Thereafter he was active in the trade in Spanish and Mexican territory. By 1824, he was in Green River country and is one of several whites credited with the discovery of Great Salt Lake. Following this incident, he attended the first rendezvous of 1825 and lived another quarter century, dying in St. Louis in 1850. See LeRoy R. Hafen, "Etienne Provost," in *Mountain Men and the Fur Trade of the Far West,* ed. L. R. Hafen, 10 vols. (Glendale: Arthur H. Clark, 1968-1972), 6: 371-85.
3. On the signficance of Iroquois trappers in the West, see John C. Ewers, "Iroquois Indians in the Far West," *Montana, The Magazine of Western History* 13, no. 2 (Spring 1963): 2-10; Theodore J. Karamanski, "The Iroquois and the Fur Trade of the Far West," *The Beaver, Magazine of the North,* Outfit 312, no. 4 (Spring 1982): 4-13.
4. Johnson Gardner may have come up the Missouri with the Ashley-Henry party in 1822 or 1823. He was with a group of free trappers accompanying Captain John Weber in 1824. Gardner was active in the trade until 1833 or 1834, when he was killed by the Arikara. See Aubrey L. Haines, "Johnson Gardner," in *Mountain Men,* Hafen, ed., 2: 157-59.
5. Ignace Hatchiorauquasha (John Grey or John Gray) was with a group of Caughnawagas (Mohawks) who headed west in 1816 to work for the North West Company in the Pacific Northwest. After the merger, Grey and other Iroquois became disaffected freemen and were especially bitter at Alexander Ross, the Snake Brigade leader who totally alienated his Indian freemen. After this incident, Grey joined Gardner and worked as an independent trapper in the Rocky Mountain system. He retired with other Iroquois families to the Kansas

City area in 1836, where he was killed in a fight with a neighbor in 1844. See Merle Wells, "Ignace Hatchiorauquasha (John Grey)," in *Mountain Men*, Hafen, ed., 7: 161-75.

6. P. S. Ogden to the Governor [George Simpson], Chief Factors, and Chief Traders, East Fork, Missouri, 10 July 1825, Hudson's Bay Company Archives, Provincial Archives of Manitoba, Winnipeg; printed in "The Snake Country Expedition Correspondence," ed. Frederick Merk, *Mississippi Valley Historical Review* 21, no.1 (June 1934): 63-75, at 64-67. For Merk's assessment of the importance of this document see his "Snake Country Expedition, 1824-25: An Episode of Fur Trade and Empire," *Mississippi Valley Historical Review* 21, no.1 (June 1934): 49-62. Other references by Ogden and William Kittson to this affair are found in *Peter Skene Ogden's Snake Country Journals, 1824-25 and 1825-26*, eds. E. E. Rich and A. M. Johnson (London: Hudson's Bay Record Society, 1950), 50-53, 234.
7. William H. Ashley, "Diary. . .March 25-June 27, 1825," in *The West of William H. Ashley*, ed. Dale L. Morgan (Denver: The Old West Publishing Company, 1964), 104-29, at 116-17, 129, 283-84nn. Also see Fred R. Gowans, *Rocky Mountain Rendezvous: A History of the Fur Trade Rendezvous 1825-1840* (Provo: Brigham Young University, 1976), 8-16.
8. "Minutes of a Council held at York Factory Northern Department of Ruperts Land this second day of July One thousand eight hundred and Twenty five for the purpose of establishing such Rules and Regulations as may be considered expedient for conducting the business of the said Department and in order to investigate the result of the Trade of last year and determine the Outfits and arrangements of the current year. . . ," in *Minutes of Council, Northern Department of Rupert Land, 1821-31*, R. Harving Fleming, ed., Hudson's Bay Company Series 3 (Toronto: The Champlain Society, 1940), 101-36.
9. We have drawn heavily upon the interpretation of John S. Galbraith, *The Hudson's Bay Company as an Imperial Factor, 1821-1869* (Berkeley: University of California Press, 1957); and upon Frederick Merk, *The Oregon Question* (Cambridge, Mass.: Belknap Press, 1967) in our interpretation here.
10. Alexander Ross's *Adventures of the First Settlers on the Oregon or Columbia River* (London, 1849) and his *The Fur Hunters of the Far West* (London, 1855) provide an overview of why many former North West Company employees found the merger of 1821 dissatisfactory. For an assessment of Ross, see Edgar I. Stewart, "Alexander Ross," in *The Mountain Men*, Hafen, ed., 6: 387-97.
11. Frederick Merk, *The Oregon Question*. Also, Merk, ed., *Fur Trade and Empire: George Simpson's Journal. . .1824-1825* (Cambridge: Harvard University Press and London: Humphrey Milford at Oxford University Press, 1931); and Merk, *Manifest Destiny and Mission in American History: A Reinterpretation* (New York: Alfred A. Knopf, 1963).
12. The original "Deed Poll, March 26, 1821" is printed in *Colin Robertson's Correspondence Book, September 1817 to September 1822*, eds. E. E. Rich and R. Harvey Fleming, Hudson's Bay Record Society Series 2 (Toronto: Champlain Society, 1939), 327-44.
13. "Minutes of Council. . .July, 1825," 115ff., at 127 (see n.8 above).
14. Ibid., Article 113, 127.
15. Ibid., Article 116, 127-28.
16. Ibid., Articles 81-82, 118.

17. Ibid., Article 89, 120.
18. John McLoughlin to the Govr. Deputy Govr. & Committee, Honble. Hudson's Bay Company London, Fort Vancouver 6th Octr. 1825, HBCA, D.4/6, 45-56. Reprinted in *The Letters of John McLoughlin from Fort Vancouver to the Governor and Committee, First Series, 1825-38*, ed. E. E. Rich (Toronto: The Champlain Society, 1941), 9.
19. Charles Wilkes, U.S.N., *The Narrative of the United States Exploring Expedition, during the Years 1838, 1839, 1840, 1841, and 1842*, 5 vols. (Philadelphia: Lea and Blanchard, 1845), 4: 391-92. This statement by Wilkes so impressed one British writer that he quoted it four years later in an influential publication. See R. M. Martin, *The Hudson's Bay Territories and Vancouver's Island with an Exposition of the Chartered Rights, Conduct, and Policy of the Honorable Hudson's Bay Company Corporation* (London: T. and W. Boone, 1849), 61.
20. In Canadian usage, the *mangeurs de lard* ("pork-eaters") handled fur trade transport only as far as Grand Portage or Fort William and then returned, whereas on American soil, the same term was used to designate French-Canadians engaged in Montreal for work in the voyageur class. By 1900, historians such as H. M. Chittenden used the two terms interchangeably for day laborers in the St. Louis-based fur trade.
21. Hiram Martin Chittenden, *The American Fur Trade of the Far West: A History of the Pioneer Trading Posts and Early Fur Companies of the Missouri Valley and the Rocky Mountains and of the Overland Commerce with Santa Fe*, 3 vols. (New York: Francis P. Harper, 1902), 1: 59.
22. This debate was generated by nineteenth-century writers and best explored by William H. Goetzmann, "The Mountain Man as Jacksonian Man," *American Quarterly* 15 (Fall 1963): 402-15. For the view that mountain men did not aspire to advance with their Jacksonian cousins in other occupational areas, see Harvey L. Carter and Marica C. Spencer, "Stereotypes of the Mountain Man," *Western Historical Quarterly* 6 (Jan 1975): 17-32. Also see William R. Swagerty, "Marriage and Settlement Patterns of Rocky Mountain Trappers and Traders," *Western Historical Quarterly* 11 (April 1980): 159-80. Recently, Michael Allen has argued that Goetzmann is right, at least for Mississippi and Ohio rivermen. See Michael Allen, "The Riverman as Jacksonian Man," *Western Historical Quarterly* 21 (August 1990): 305-20.
23. William Clark reports a list of locations designated for carrying on trade with the Indians, Superintendency of Indian Affairs, St. Louis, Decr. 8th 1825, U.S. National Archives, Record Group 75, OIA-LR.
24. On federal policy and the fur trade out of St. Louis, see John E. Sunder, *Joshua Pilcher, Fur Trader and Indian Agent* (Norman: University of Oklahoma Press, 1968); and Sunder, *The Fur Trade on the Upper Missouri, 1840-1865* (Norman: University of Oklahoma Press, 1965). For example, in March 1832 Clark personally wrote the names of 93 men authorized to enter the Upper Missouri country as traders with the American Fur Company. License, U. S. Superintendancy of Ind. Affrs., St. Louis, March 26, 1832, Chouteau Collection, Missouri Historical Society, St. Louis, Box 27 (1832, Jan.-May). James Ronda is currently working on a biography of William Clark during his St. Louis superintendancy years.
25. Philip Goldring has analyzed the labor force of the Northern Department of the Hudson's Bay Company and has distinguished "salaried gentlemen" (clerks and postmasters) from "commissioned gentlemen" (Chief Factors and Chief Traders).

See *Papers on the Labour System of the Hudson's Bay Company, 1821-1900,* vol.1. Parks Canada Manuscript Report 362 (Ottawa: Parks Canada, 1979), 36-37.

26. Glyndwr Williams, "The Hudson's Bay Company and the Fur Trade: 1670-1870," *The Beaver* no. 2 (Autumn 1983): entire issue, at 51.
27. Fort Vancouver Columbia District Statement, 1830, HBCA, Winnipeg, B.223/d/28. The list of 406 employees includes all employees assigned during the outfit year. It does not indicate which employees were "comers and goers." The actual population of the District should be less than 406.
28. Articles of Agreement between AFC and B. Pratte and Co., included with Pierre Chouteau, Jr. to B. Pratte & Co., 21 December 1826, Chouteau Collection, Missouri Historical Society, Box 18 (1825-1826).
29. Persons Employed for the Upper Missouri Outfit for the Year 1830, Chouteau Collection, Box 23 (Jan.-July 1830). This document lists 287 individual names. William Hunt of the National Park Service has tabulated contracts on file in the Chouteau Collection. His research produced 366 names for 1830. The variance might be explained in that not all employees contracting fulfilled their contracts and were thus not included on a payroll ledger.
30. "American Fur Company, Western Department, St. Louis, Retail Store Ledger C, 1831-1836," in *Papers of the St. Louis Fur Trade,* microfilm ed., edited by William R. Swagerty, 23 reels, 2 parts (Bethesda, Md.: University Publications of America, 1991), part 2, reel 5, vol. u.
31. Fort Vancouver District Statements, Outfit 1830, HBCA B.223/d/28.; "Persons Employed for the Upper Missouri Outfit for the Year 1830," Chouteau Collection, Box 23 (Jan.-July 1830).
32. Our figure for exchange rates is derived from B. R. Mitchell, *British Historical Statistics* (Cambridge, Eng.: Cambridge University Press, 1988), 700-3. A British pound sterling in New Orleans banks in 1838 was worth between $5.25 and $5.38. See United States Serial Set No. 318, 4 December 1837, 25th Cong., 2d sess., S. Doc. 457.
33. "Minutes of Council, 2 July, 1828," in *Minutes of Council, Northern Department of Rupert Land, 1821-31,* ed. R. Harvey Fleming, 228.
34. On the system of outfitting servants before and after 1821, see "The Report of George Simpson to the Governor and Committee, 1822, York Factory, 16th July, 1822," in Fleming, ed., *Minutes of Council,* 347.
35. American Fur Company," part 2, reel 5, vol. u: 182.
36. Fort Vancouver Columbia District Statement, Outfit 1830, HBCA B.22/d/28, fos. 2-9; "Persons Employed for the Upper Missouri Outfit for the Year 1830," Chouteau Collection, Missouri Historical Society.
37. To simplify the text of this article, the authors have chosen to use French North American in lieu of French, French-Canadian, French-American, or French-surnamed. A similar pattern was chosen for Scottish, Scot-Irish, and Anglo, all of whom are analyzed as "Anglo," unless they self-identified as "Scottish" or "Irish." Indians and mixed bloods in the employ of the HBC are identified as they appear in Columbia District ledgers. The HBC separated "Indians" from "Natives" in their account books with "Indian" meaning non-mixed, "Native"—mixed bloods, including Métis. In contrast, the AFC did not ethnically identify its employees on its annual rosters. We have therefore used surnames as ethnic markers and acknowledge that many individuals may have self-identified differently than we have them labeled.

38. Fort Vancouver Columbia District Statement, Outfit 1830.
39. Ibid., fo. 2d.
40. For the early organization of the UMO, see Erwin N. Thompson, *Fort Union Trading Post: Fur Trade Empire on the Upper Missouri* (Medora, N.D.: Theodore Roosevelt Nature and History Association, 1986), 1-6. Also see Ray Mattison, "Kenneth McKenzie," and "William Laidlaw" in *Mountain Men*, Hafen, ed., 2: 217-24 and 3: 167-72, respectively. On Lamont's background, see Annie Heloise Abel, ed., *Chardon's Journal at Fort Clark, 1834-1839* (Pierre: Dept. of History, State of South Dakota, 1932), 219.
41. "American Fur Company," part 2, reel 6, vol. w: 6, 47.
42. Ibid., "John Duchouquette," 71.
43. Delmont R. Oswald, "James P. Beckwourth," in *Mountain Men*, Hafen, ed., 6: 37-60, at 48. Kenneth McKenzie to Meessr. Pratte, Chouteau, and Company, St. Louis, July 21, 1836, Fort Union, Chouteau Collection, Box 34, 1837 (Jan-March).
44. Our data set consists of 85 men under contract for Outfit 1829. Data taken from Hunt Compilations, UMO, on file with the authors. We chose this year rather than 1830 because of the smaller sample size.
45. Our HBCA sample of 34 men was chosen from biographical files prepared for researchers in Winnipeg. The sample is not a statistically valid random sampling of Columbia District employees. Rather, it represents men for whom adequate documentation exists to complete collective biographies. The men analyzed from HBCA "Biographical Files" were:
    1. François Noel Annance
    2. Amable Arquoitte
    3. Alexis Aubichon
    4. Pierre Belleque
    5. James Birnie
    6. Laurent Cadotte
    7. Francis Ermatinger
    8. Edward Ermatinger
    9. Charles Dodd
    10. Duncan Finlayson
    11. Dominique Farron
    12. Henry Hanwell, Jr.
    13. Charles Humphreys
    14. John Frederick Kennedy
    15. Louis Labonte
    16. Pierre Lagace
    17. Michel Laframboise
    18. Jean Baptiste Lajoie (Lajois)
    19. Thomas Linklater
    20. John McAulay
    21. William McBean
    22. Annawiskum McDonald
    23. Archibald McDonald
    24. Murdoch McDonald
    25. John McKay
    26. Peter Ogden, Jr.

27. Pierre Pambrun
28. Antoine *dit* Gobin Petit
29. Louis Pichette
30. Joseph Pin
31. Louis Satakarata
32. John Tate
33. Peter Taylor
34. John Work

46. For this average of 15 years, see the discussion in William R. Swagerty, "Marriage and Settlement Patterns of Rocky Mountain Trappers and Traders," *Western Historical Quarterly* 11, no. 2 (April 1980): 159-180 at 163.
47. The exception here is John F.A. Sanford, who married Emilie Chouteau, daughter of Pierre, Jr., in 1832, and who joined Pratte, Chouteau & Company as a partner in 1838. Sanford was born in 1806 of Anglo parents in Virginia. He died in 1857 in New York, following the trial wherein his slave, Dred Scott, brought suit for his freedom. See Janet Lecompte, "John F. A. Sanford," in *Mountain Men*, Hafen, ed., 9: 351-59.
48. "Peter Ogden, Jr.," and "John Frederick Kennedy," Biographical Files, HBCA. On HBC patterns of Native and Métis social mobility, see Jennifer S. H. Brown, *Strangers in Blood: Fur Trade Company Families in Indian Country* (Vancouver: University of British Columbia Press, 1980); and Sylvia Van Kirk, *Many Tender Ties: Women in Fur-Trade Society, 1670-1870* (Winnipeg: Watson & Dwyer, 1980).
49. "Charles Lajeunesse," in Hunt Compilations.
50. "Pierre Belleque," Biographical File, HBCA.
51. Ibid., "François Annance."
52. A 10 percent statistical sample was taken of employees listed in the Fort Vancouver (Columbia District) Ledger 1825-1835, HBCA B.223/d/105a; and a 20 percent sample of the "American Fur Company," part 2, reel 6. The sample size was 72 for the HBC and 107 for the AFC. In evaluating the samples we found that the standard deviation of the AFC sample was much larger than that of the HBC sample. One's confidence in predicting the mean of the actual population from a sample is directly related to the standard deviation of the sample. The sampling error of the AFC statistic was greater than that of the HBC. For instance, in the case of the milieux: from our HBC sample we can estimate the mean credit/debit with 95 percent confidence (within plus or minus £0.14.00 [$3.70 American]). For our AFC sample we can estimate the mean credit/debit with 95 percent confidence (within plus or minus $21.60).
53. "American Fur Company," part 2, reel 6, 82, 86, 90.
54. Fort Vancouver Ledger, 1825-1835, HBCA, B.223/3/105a, 5.
55. "American Fur Company," part 2, reel 6, 1, 95.
56. Ibid., 96.
57. Ibid., 72.
58. Fort Vancouver Ledger, 1825-1835, 12, 283.
59. Ibid., 319.
60. Merle Wells, "Ignace Hatchiorauquasha (John Grey)," in *Mountain Men*, Hafen, ed., 7: 170-75.

Failure on the Columbia: Nathaniel Wyeth's Columbia River Fishing and Trading Company

Bradford R. Cole

Nathaniel Jarvis Wyeth was an important participant in a transitional period of American westward expansion. As a thirty-year-old businessman from Cambridge, Massachusetts, Wyeth in the early 1830s was lured by the West and the potential profits to be made in that part of the country. In 1832 he became a fur trader, making the first of two trips to Oregon. Before entering the fur trade he helped in managing the family-owned Fresh Pond Hotel in Cambridge, and during the winter months, he harvested ice from nearby Cambridge ponds. Wyeth's involvement in the ice business was important to his future. His invention of labor-saving devices in the 1820s earned him the respect of Boston ice merchant Fredric Tudor and an entry into Boston business circles. This entry in the short term, gave him the capital—and the access to capital—that he needed to finance his western enterprises, and in the long term made him a respected New England businessman.[1]

In 1831, the 29-year-old Wyeth turned his energies westward. In June he attended the Boston lectures of the noted Oregon booster Hall J. Kelley. He not only attended Kelley's Boston addresses but enlisted as a captain in Kelley's 1832 Oregon expedition. The two men, however, had different motives for going west. Kelley wanted to be part of what he saw as the American vanguard for settlement in the Oregon country. Wyeth, on the other hand, desired entrepreneurial opportunities. As a result of these differences, Wyeth quickly became disillusioned with Kelley's undertaking when the latter repeatedly delayed his departure date and vacillated on the question of whether women and children should join the company. Due to the uncertainty of Kelley's organization, Wyeth withdrew and formed his own company in 1832.[2] This marked the beginning of a five-year period during which Wyeth attempted to become a power broker in the fur trade. Before he finished, he would outfit two trading expeditions, spend five years exploring the Rocky Mountains, and lose $20,000.[3]

Wyeth's western exploits give him a prominence in the literature of the western fur trade. Ironically, however, this literature recognizes him more for the lasting impact he made upon western settlement, and specifically, for the people whom he brought to Oregon: naturalists, a school teacher, the first Protestant missionaries, and the many men of his company who remained in Oregon and elsewhere as settlers. The construction of Fort Hall in present-day southeastern Idaho, and of Fort William on present-day Sauvie Island in the Willamette River are other notable contributions. Wyeth's presence also aided American claims to the Northwest against the British.

While most authors agree upon Wyeth's accomplishments, confusion and disagreement arise in studying him as a fur trader, and specifically in understanding the causes of his economic failure. These disagreements are aggravated by the shortage of primary sources. Although Wyeth left relatively complete records about his fur trading enterprise, enough gaps occur that some guesswork has been necessary in interpreting his role. Most critical is the lack of source material from his last eighteen months of business, 1835-1837.

An excellent and little-used source that fills this gap is the "Letter Book of Henry Hall."[4] Hall was the oldest partner of Wyeth's Columbia River Fishing and Trading Company and the person for whom Fort Hall was named. Strangely, Hall's "Letter Book," actually a copy book prepared by or for this prominent stockholder, has been used only once in the literature—in an article written by Clement Eaton in 1935, entitled "Nathaniel Wyeth's Oregon Expeditions."[5] Although others have used items from the "Hall Letter Book," they all cite Eaton's article and not the "Letter Book" itself.

The documents contained in the "Letter Book" include the company's articles of incorporation, instructions to principal members of the expedition, directions on how to run trapping parties, reports from Wyeth, and letters from other employees, five of which were written at Fort Hall. Of additional importance is the fact that several of the letters were written after the fall of 1835. No other correspondence from Wyeth or his employees survived from this period.[6] The most important aspect of the "Hall Letter Book" is the description of a rift that grew between Wyeth and second-in-command Joseph Thing about how the trade in the mountains should be conducted. The content of the documents also questions Wyeth's relationship with the Hudson's Bay Company. Overall, the "Letter Book" documents shortcomings in Wyeth's management skills, especially in personnel matters.

Although not a perfect barometer with which to judge Wyeth's activities in the fur trade, his 1832 expedition hints at some of the problems that would come back to haunt his company in 1834. His actions suggest that he thought if he approached the trade with the same tenacity that he put into the ice business, it would be successful. Unfortunately for Wyeth, the business of the Rocky Mountain fur trade was done on a totally different scale than his local ice business. The physical size of the trade was larger, and often the rules of business in the mountains were different than those used in Cambridge.

In both 1832 and 1834, the framework of Wyeth's operation was patterned after John Jacob Astor's Pacific Fur Company of the early 1800s. The main similarity was to establish a link between the east coast of the United States and the

Figure 1. Nathaniel Wyeth, courtesy of the Oregon Historical Society, OrHi 3632.

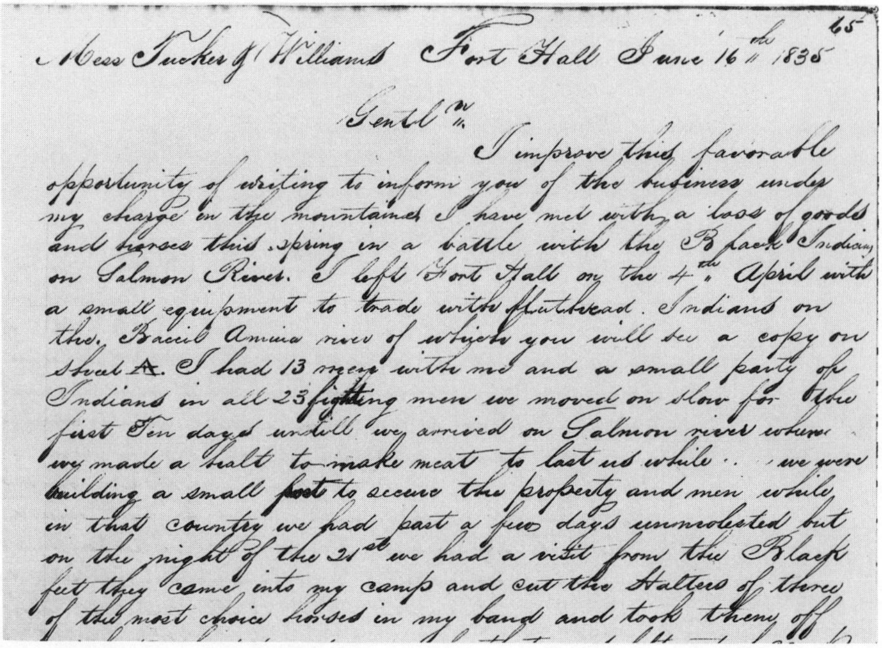
65

Mess Tucker & Williams Fort Hall June 16th 1835

Gentln

I improve this favorable opportunity of writing to inform you of the business under my charge in the mountains I have met with a loss of goods and horses this spring in a battle with the Black Indians on Salmon River. I left Fort Hall on the 4th April with a small equipment to trade with flathead Indians on the Bacus Amira river of which you will see a copy on Sheet A. I had 13 men with me and a small party of Indians in all 23 fighting men we moved on slow for the first Ten days untill we arrived on Salmon river where we made a halt to make meat to last us while we were building a small fort to secure the property and men while in that country we had past a few days unmolested but on the night of the 21st we had a visit from the Black fet they came into my camp and cut the Halters of three of the most choice horses in my band and took them off

Figure 2. Photograph of a page from the "Henry Hall Letter Book." The letter is from Joseph Thing at Fort Hall to Tucker and Williams of Boston, Massachusetts. Courtesy of the Oregon Historical Society, OrHi 85623.

west by means of a sailing vessel. Wyeth thought that if he could bring supplies from the west coast to the Rocky Mountains where the Americans were doing business, he could undercut his American competitors and eventually dominate the Rocky Mountain trade. Unfortunately, he found out that establishing an ocean connection was both difficult and undependable.

His 1832 company consisted wholly of greenhorns who disliked the trip so much that, at the Pierre's Hole rendezvous, they called a group meeting and, over Wyeth's protest, several of the men left to return east, thus leaving the company in shambles.[7] Wyeth was scheduled to meet a trading vessel on the Columbia for more supplies, so with his remaining men he continued. Upon arrival he learned that the vessel he was to meet had been shipwrecked in the South Pacific, putting a final end to his plans.[8] From this point his trip turned into more of an exploratory expedition than a money-making venture. Even this turn of events did not keep Wyeth from scheming on how to approach the fur trade in the future. Out of these schemes came a proposal to John McLoughlin, the Hudson's Bay Company Chief Factor at Fort Vancouver, to enter into a trading agreement and, later in 1833, a proposal to Captain Benjamin Bonneville to make a joint hunt into northern California. Wyeth, during his return trip to the east on 14 August 1833, contracted with Milton Sublette and Thomas Fitzpatrick at the Little Bighorn River to supply their Rocky Mountain Fur Company at the 1834 rendezvous.[9]

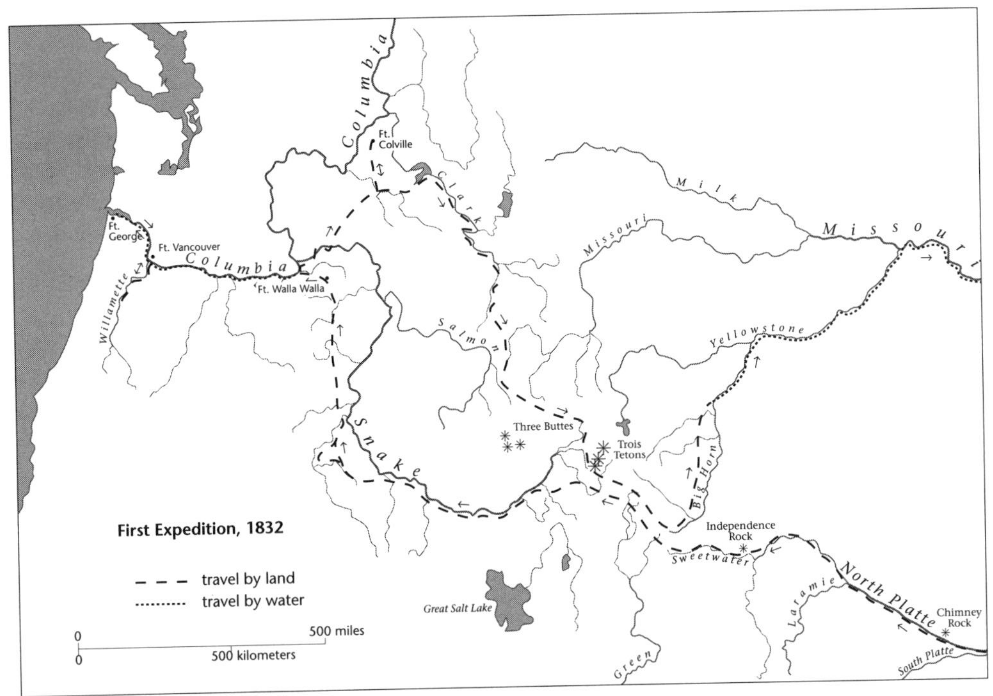

Figure 3. Map of Wyeth's 1832-1833 travels taken from Frederick G. Young's edited volume *The Correspondence and Journals of Captain Nathaniel J. Wyeth 1831-1836* (1899; reprint, New York: Arno Press, 1973), 263.

Wyeth used this contract with the Rocky Mountain Fur Company and his new expertise in the mountainous west as leverage to attract financial backers. Once back in the East, Wyeth attempted to implement a far more grandiose plan than the one he had attempted in 1832. Wyeth had no problems selling his idea to Boston investors, and the Columbia River Fishing and Trading Company was formed in January of 1834. The purpose of the company, as stated in its articles of agreement, was for

> an expedition to be fitted out for the Sandwich Islands Columbia River, & region of the Rocky Mountains for the purpose of carrying on a trade in Fish and Furs in the Islands & River as well as in the Mountains uniting therewith the business of catching & packing salmon. . . .[10]

The company soon purchased the brig *May Dacre* to sail to the Columbia River, hired a second-in-command, Joseph Thing, to help with carrying out the land operation, and began to purchase supplies. Thing was sent to Missouri, where he purchased supplies and hired men for the expedition.[11]

Wyeth planned to travel overland to the rendezvous, where he would trade goods for furs, then continue to the Columbia River, where he would meet a vessel and exchange the furs for trade goods and return to the mountains to repeat the cycle. Unlike Astor, Wyeth did not have the infrastructure of the American Fur Company to rely upon, and probably more telling was his lack of quality

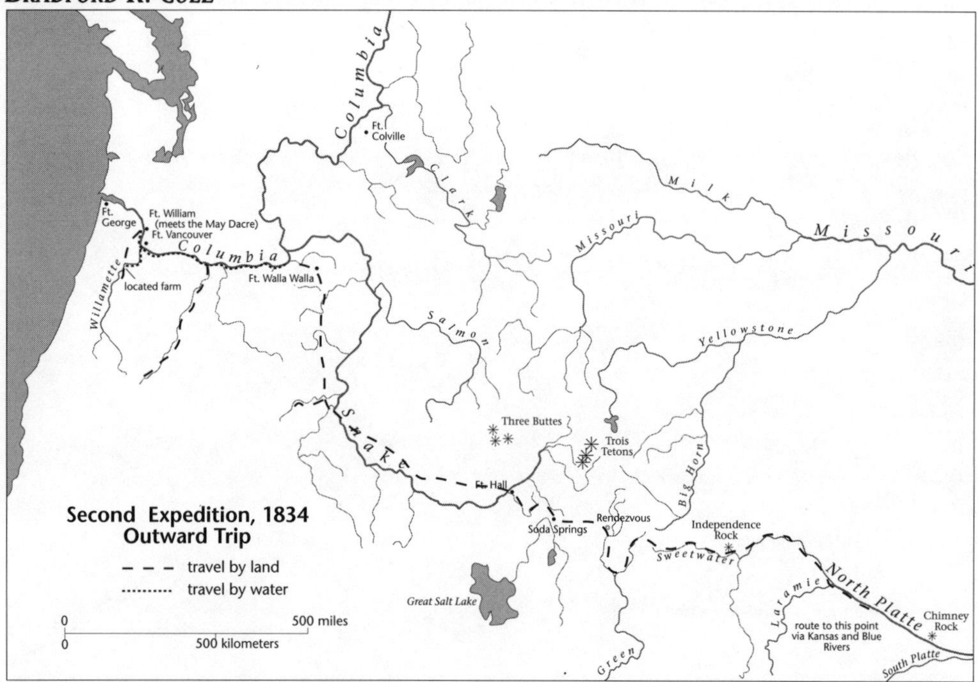

Figure 4. Map of Wyeth's 1834-1836 expedition taken from Frederick G. Young's edited volume *The Correspondence and Journals of Captain Nathaniel J. Wyeth 1831-1836* (1899; reprint, New York: Arno Press, 1973), 264. Wyeth and Thing both made several trips between Fort William and Fort Hall. Wyeth returned to the United States in 1836 by way of Taos and the Arkansas River.

field leaders. A prime example was Wyeth's second-in-command, Joseph Thing, who had never been involved in the fur trade prior to 1834.[12] Thus, when Wyeth left Independence in April of 1834, he was in for a rude awakening.

When Wyeth arrived at the 1834 rendezvous, held on Ham's Fork of the Green River, his initial plan unraveled. As Wyeth traveled west, the Rocky Mountain Fur Company was in the process of being dissolved. He knew, as he left Independence in the spring of 1834, that Robert Campbell and William Sublette were also readying a supply train to the Rocky Mountains. Even with his contract in hand, Wyeth smelled trouble. In May of 1834, William Sublette and Robert Campbell passed Wyeth's caravan in southeast Nebraska. By the time Wyeth arrived at the rendezvous, the former members of the RMFC—using the reason that their company was now defunct—had purchased their goods from former partners Campbell and Sublette.[13]

Because of the broken contract, Wyeth left the 1834 rendezvous and traveled to the confluence of the Snake and Portneuf rivers. His party then moved upstream on the Portneuf and built the trading post named Fort Hall. Wyeth needed the post as a place to merchandise the remainder of his trade goods that the Rocky Mountain Fur Company had refused to buy. Wyeth garrisoned the post with twelve men, placed three trapping parties in the field, and took the remainder of his men and continued on to the mouth of the Columbia River.

After struggling with his business for two more years, Wyeth finally returned home to Cambridge, Massachusetts in 1836, and in 1837 Captain Thing sold Fort Hall to the Hudson's Bay Company.[14] When Wyeth finished his fur-trading venture, he had only a small cargo of furs and some barreled salmon to show for his efforts.

A growing body of western fur-trade literature has attempted to explain why Wyeth failed. With something of an anti-British bias, early writers tended to attribute the collapse of Wyeth's trapping and trading enterprise to cutthroat competition from the Hudson's Bay Company.[15] Although this emphasis was toned down in later studies, the adverse impact of Hudson's Bay tactics has remained a consistent theme. With the increased availability of primary sources, Wyeth's failure has increasingly been attributed to more diverse and complex causes. Explanations that have been advanced include: ineffective coordination of the land and sea operations of the project, inadequate finances, inexperience, and the personnel problems that arose within the company. In addition, some recent scholars attribute Wyeth's failure to the refusal of the Rocky Mountain Fur Company to buy the shipment of goods at the 1834 rendezvous for which they had contracted the previous year.

These interpretations of Wyeth's failure have been derived from primary source materials that have become gradually available by publication or through access to public repositories. The donation of the "Hall Letter Book" to the Oregon Historical Society opens these interpretations to some revision. The unpublished documents contained in the Book fill some of the holes in other source material and shed new light on many misunderstandings that have previously been based upon speculation.

In discussing Wyeth's failure, the repudiation of Wyeth's contract at the 1834 rendezvous and the activities of the Hudson's Bay Company became standard explanations for the failure of Wyeth's company. Although competition by the Hudson's Bay Company definitely added to Wyeth's downfall, too much emphasis has been placed on the broken contract with the Rocky Mountain Fur Company, and not enough on Wyeth's personnel management and the overextension of his abilities.

The actual contract with the Rocky Mountain Fur Company called for Wyeth to supply $3,000 worth of trade goods, for which he would receive $3,500 above the cost, paid in beaver pelts. A $500 penalty fee was specified for a breach of contract. In November of 1833 Wyeth contacted Milton Sublette to inform him that the deal was on. When he arrived at the 1834 rendezvous he brought enough goods to fulfill his contract with the Rocky Mountain Fur Company.[16]

Because William Sublette, a one-time member of the RMFC and a man to whom the previous company members were still indebted, had arrived at the rendezvous before Wyeth, the company instead bought Sublette's goods. They justified their action with the fact that the Rocky Mountain Fur Company had actually been dissolved earlier that summer.[17] When Wyeth arrived and found that his goods were being refused, he became very indignant towards the former Rocky Mountain Fur Company.[18] His reaction was understandable given the circumstances; however, in retrospect, Wyeth did not fare as badly in this situation as has been thought. First, he collected a $500 forfeiture fee from Fitzpatrick, and second, he sold over $800 of goods to William Sublette. In addition, he picked up the help of veteran fur traders Henry Fraeb and Jean Baptiste Gervais, whom he outfitted with $514 worth of goods.[19] So, when Wyeth left the 1834 rendezvous he had recouped $1,300 of the lost contract, and of that amount $500 did not involve the sale of goods. Because of the goods he had on hand at the end of the rendezvous, he was able to proceed up the Portneuf river about nine miles from where it enters the Snake River and build Fort Hall. Wyeth had previously entertained the idea of building a post in this location, but had counted on having to travel first to the Columbia to get supplies from the company's brig.[20] However, the leftover supplies which remained following the refusal of the contract allowed him to build and supply Fort Hall without first making a trip to the Columbia. Thus, the episode of the Rocky Mountain rendezvous was actually a stroke of good fortune.

Although the contract refusal caused logistical troubles for Wyeth, these problems seem insignificant in light of the personnel troubles that Wyeth encountered. Documents in the "Hall Letter Book" suggest that this problem, heretofore lightly touched upon, was much more serious than previously thought. Wyeth's own character seemed to be at the center of many of his employee troubles. Although he was an amiable and well-liked man, he was also a demanding employer. He placed himself in difficult situations, especially with schedules, and then drove everyone to meet those goals. When failure occurred, which it did, he was quick to blame subordinates. The "Henry Hall Letter Book" clearly documents this aspect of Wyeth's character.

After constructing Fort Hall, Wyeth and Thing, along with some of the company employees, journeyed to the mouth of the Columbia River to meet the company's ship. After Wyeth had made arrangements for the brig to sail to the Hawaiian Islands during the winter with a cargo of lumber and to have the crew build a post on the west coast, he sent Thing, with company clerk Abel Baker and twelve Hawaiian laborers, back to Fort Hall. Thing was instructed to build a post on the Big Wood River (Boise River). At some point Thing was to garrison the new post with the men from Fort Hall, leaving the Hawaiians to man Fort Hall. He was then to proceed to Fort Hall to check on operations there and, in the spring of 1835, return to the Columbia to help with the salmon-fishing operation.[21]

In the meantime, Wyeth outlined his business plans for the fall of 1834. First, he planned to leave the lower Columbia River in October and travel to the Nez Percé, among whom it was his purpose to trade and possibly even to build a trading post. He would then travel to the American winter camps near Fort Hall, hoping to drum up business for his new post, and finally arrive at Fort Hall sometime in the winter of 1834-35.[22]

Although this plan seemed ambitious enough, in Wyeth's mind this was barely the beginning. After a quick examination of the Fort Hall operation, he planned to explore the region south of the Great Salt Lake with an eye toward potential trading-post sites. After this excursion he planned to return to Fort Hall, but only long enough to pick up furs and take second-in-command Captain Thing back to the Columbia. The two would then travel to the recently built post on the Big Wood River, finally arriving back at Fort William by 15 May 1835.[23] In Wyeth's scheme, this May arrival was crucial to the company's salmon-fishing operation, because he and Thing represented two of the three supervisors.[24] Overall, this was an ambitious enterprise, dependent upon precise timing and good fortune, neither of which Wyeth's operation had.

A more experienced trader might have allowed himself a more flexible plan, but not Wyeth. For this lack of foresight, he paid dearly. Letters written from Wyeth, Thing, and Baker in 1835 and 1836 explain how the plan unfolded. The letters also described Wyeth's lack of decisive instructions and Thing's free-lancing, behaviors which led to squabbles between the two.[25] The controversy between Wyeth and Thing began in the winter of 1835.

The seeds of discontent were sown shortly after Thing left the Columbia River in the fall of 1835. An uprising of Hawaiian employees who had been sent with Thing thwarted Wyeth's plans. Wyeth heard of the incident and met Thing near Fort Walla Walla where, according to Thing, he gave the second-in-command new verbal instructions. Some of these instructions concerned the management of Fort Hall if the present commander, Robert Evans, was found unsuitable. A letter from Thing indicates that the question was not adequately resolved and became a point of contention between the two in the summer of 1835.[26]

After their Walla Walla meeting, Thing proceeded to Fort Hall as planned. However, instead of building a post on the Big Wood River, he cached some goods in that area. Wyeth, instead of trapping and trading through the Northwest, spent much of the winter of 1834-1835 chasing the runaway Hawaiians.[27]

Thing's party arrived at Fort Hall on 19 December 1834. At the post he found matters in disarray. Abel Baker reported that Robert Evans, whom Wyeth had left in charge of the post,

> partook too freely of the spirituous Liquors and kept a very lo[o]se account of the property entrusted to him, and I found upon examination of his accounts (such as was kept), it impossible to show where the goods had gone or what was done with them and could only content myself, as result of my search to ascertain the goods that were missing, of which no entry were made, and the proceeds of such goods and I have every reason to believe, a considerable proportion of these goods were delivered to the men as called for and no charges made . . . .[28]

By January of 1835, Thing was in a quandary. Thing's primary instructions were to bring the Fort Hall returns to Fort William by the middle of May and then to help with the salmon fishing. However, Thing felt that the problems at

Fort Hall were too great to allow him to leave, and that he should take charge since Evans was unsuitable to command the post. His other main concern was that the men in Wyeth's hire were doing nothing to earn their keep. But when he attempted to discharge most of the trappers from the company's payroll, the men would not be discharged. Thing decided that it would be better to outfit the company trappers on credit than "to lay here idle and let the wages of hired men run away with all of the goods and have no reason to justify the Brig." Thing sent an express message to Wyeth informing him of the change of plans. Wyeth received the news sometime in late April.[29]

Thing's policy spawned an ill-fated trapping and trading expedition to the Flathead country. It also established a peculiar relationship with Thomas McKay of the competing Hudson's Bay Company. Thing, in concert with McKay, outfitted a party to establish a trading post in the Flathead country, most likely somewhere on the Salmon River. This party, however, was routed by Blackfeet Indians in April of 1835.[30]

In June, Thing received word from an unhappy Wyeth that he was to return to the original plan, close the Flathead post (at this point Wyeth did not know the outcome of the Flathead expedition), wind up the spring trapping parties, and return to Fort William by 15 July. Almost everything that Thing did met with Wyeth's disapproval. In a 2 May 1835 letter to Tucker and Williams in Boston, Wyeth commented that "from the time he left me he appears to have paid no attention to the orders that I gave him . . . ." He added that he could not be certain as to the arrangements that Thing had made in the interior but that he feared

> that the Salmon fishing will suffer in consequence of want of whites to direct the exertions of the Islanders that the business in the interior will be so scattered that returns cannot be made of all the collections in season for the vessel that many of the goods will be given on credit to those who will never pay . . . .[31]

Thing outfitted two other trapping parties with Thomas McKay that summer. One of these was pursued by the Blackfeet Indians. Finally, after journeying to the 1835 rendezvous on the Green River, Thing departed for the Columbia on 6 July. He left Robert Evans in charge of the fort and Abel Baker in charge of the store, stating that ". . . the one was a good look out for the other, for they were not the best of friends. . . ."[32]

After seeing the brig *May Dacre* off, Thing and Wyeth returned to Fort Hall in December of 1835. Wyeth was not pleased with the state of affairs at Fort Hall. He seemed most critical about the arrangements that Thing had made for the post the past year. In a letter to Boston dated 16 February 1836, he wrote that Thing's arrangements were "much as I apprehended and all the consequences that I feared have been realised. . . . " The one exception was that the furs from the interior arrived in time to be shipped on the *May Dacre*.[33]

Poor morale at Fort Hall also greeted Wyeth upon his return. Wyeth's chief trapper, Joseph Gale, was hated by the other employees.[34] Other men who worked for Wyeth wanted to be discharged. Among these were clerk Abel Baker and company trapper Osborne Russell. Russell commented that in the future he "determined not to be so green as to bind myself to an arbitrary Rocky Mountain Chieftain to be kicked over hill and dale at his pleasure."[35] Wyeth himself never had confidence in most of the garrison either.

Wyeth left Fort Hall around the first of March, 1836 to return to Fort William and tie up his business interests on the coast so that he would be able to return to Boston. He left Thing in charge of Fort Hall, a move neither man seemed happy about, but it was the only option available. He wrote that Thing was the only one he could trust and ". . . now that he has got a little experience especially as to the results of disobeying orders, I think he may do well. . . ."[36] Thing, however, also desired to return to Boston, although he was willing to spend one more year at Fort Hall as "an accommodation to the company." [37]

In Thing's last letter to the company, he complained of unfair treatment by Wyeth. Wyeth had criticized him for leaving Baker in charge of the store, giving credit to trappers, and for not returning to the West Coast at the appointed time. Not only did Wyeth complain about Thing, he revoked Thing's right to purchase company supplies at a discount rate and told the company's board not to honor Thing's drafts.[38] Thing wrote to the company begging "to be excused . . . for any errors that I have committed in the way of my business and duty they have not been malitious nor wanton they occurred by my trusting to verbal orders and not having the experience necessarry for a trader in this country. . . .[39]

In addition to the serious questions of personnel and management, other internal problems contributed to the demise of the company. One problem was the company's purchase of the brig *May Dacre*, which was to meet Wyeth on the Columbia and engage in salmon fishing. Wyeth would then use the vessel to transport the pelts that he gathered from the mountain trade; at the same time the vessel would bring him fresh supplies. On its way to Oregon, however, the ship was struck by lightning and attacked by Indians near Cape Horn. Because of this mishap, the brig had to be dry-docked for repairs in Valparaiso, Chile and arrived late for the salmon season. This problem has been almost universally factored into Wyeth's failure. But in the "Hall Letter Book" it becomes apparent that the vessel itself was of suspect quality. Captain Lambert wrote to the company after only a month at sea that it was too deep and leaked about the bows, and that the rudder head was split in three places.[40] Even without the devastating injury caused by lightning, the quality of the boat would have hindered the operation. This reflects directly upon the judgment of the company partners.

Finally, the "Hall Letter Book" brings into question the exact relationship between the Hudson's Bay Company and the Columbia River Fishing and Trading Company. Even though Wyeth later contended that the Hudson's Bay Company opposition was the main factor in his business failure, this assertion does not totally square with the facts. Wyeth, since his first trip to Fort Vancouver in 1833, consistently tried to make an arrangement with the Hudson's Bay Company to divide the beaver country.[41] This effort led to a short-lived agreement, drawn up on 27 September 1834, between Wyeth and McLoughlin.[42] Although the agreement was squelched by the HBC management once it heard of the proposal, the agreement—which Thing certainly was privy to—explains the cooperation that occurred between Joseph Thing and Thomas McKay in the winter and spring of 1834-1835.

Thomas McKay, a clerk in the Hudson's Bay Company, was present at the building of Fort Hall and, upon leaving that post, traveled to the Boise River area and built Snake Fort, later called Fort Boise. Most have argued that this was to be the British rival of Fort Hall. Although Fort Boise evolved into the Hudson's Bay Company's competitor to Fort Hall, McKay's original intent is not totally clear.

As mentioned earlier, Thing was to have established a trading post on the Big Wood River but instead cached trading goods in that area. An entry in the Fort Hall journal in March of 1835 indicated that McKay was to raise the cache of goods near the Big Wood River.[43] McKay spent much more time during the winter of 1834-1835 at Fort Hall than he did at his newly established Snake Fort. And one of the men whom McLoughlin sent to winter with McKay in 1834-1835—Finan McDonald—turned up as a member of Thing's Flathead expedition.[44] While it was evident that John McLoughlin was attempting to limit the growth of Wyeth's operation in the Northwest, Wyeth may not have been plagued by the Hudson's Bay Company as much as he insisted, as relations do not appear to have been that strained.

Although Wyeth, in his "Memoir" to Congress faulted the Hudson's Bay Company as the main reason his company failed, the manner in which he dealt with Thomas McKay casts doubt on his statement. Even though the initial Flathead expedition that Thing and McKay jointly outfitted in April of 1835 was done without Wyeth's knowledge, cooperation between McKay and Thing as well as McKay's frequent Fort Hall purchases continued. Therefore, when Wyeth spoke of the HBC men following his men around, it was partly in concert with the Columbia River Fishing and Trading Company.[45]

In light of evidence from the "Hall Letter Book," the activities of Nathaniel Wyeth and the happenings at Fort Hall become more clear in the critical period of the fall and winter of 1834-1835 through 1836, when Wyeth finally left the mountains. The rift between Thing and Wyeth, as well as Thing and Wyeth's disagreement on how to operate the company in the interior, becomes a more important, if not the most important reason for the company's failure. The refusal of the Fitzpatrick and Sublette contract, although a major inconvenience, did not—as historian Bernard DeVoto claims—"smash irretrievably" the company's chances for success.[46] Nor did the competition of the Hudson's Bay Company put Wyeth out of business. Problems with employee management, overextension of human abilities and resources, and lack of foresight in planning were larger factors in Wyeth's failure than has been previously argued.

Notes

1. William Sampson, "Nathaniel Jarvis Wyeth," in *Mountain Men and the Fur Trade,* 10 vols., ed. Leroy Hafen (Glendale, Ca.: Arthur Clark, 1968), 5: 381.
2. Ibid., 5: 383.
3. Nathaniel Wyeth, *The Correspondence and Journals of Captain Nathaniel J. Wyeth, 1831-1836,* ed. F.G. Young (1899; reprint, New York: Arno Press, 1973), 253. All additional citations to Wyeth are to this publication.
4. The Henry Hall Letter Book is located at the Oregon Historical Society Library in Portland, Oregon. It is catalogued as the Fort Hall Copybook, MSS 938-1. Hereafter cited as Hall Letter Book.
5. W. Clement Eaton, "Nathaniel Wyeth's Oregon Expeditions," *Pacific Historical Review* 4 (1935): 101n.
6. Wyeth, 154. In addition, Wyeth's journal entries end in April of 1835. Curiously, the title of the Correspondence and Journals indicates that the book covers the years 1831 through 1836, but in reality the journal and the correspondence end in 1835. The exception to this is one letter in the Appendix written in 1847.
7. Sampson, 387.
8. Ibid., 388.
9. "Copy of Agreement with Sublette & Fitzpatric," Hall Letter Book, 5.
10. "Articles of Agreement," Hall Letter Book, 36. The actual date of the articles of incorporation does not appear on the document, but occurred sometime around 1 January 1834. The date of the incorporation becomes clear because this document stated that Captain James Lambert had already sailed for the Columbia River and Lambert's instructions are dated the 1st of January 1834. Hall Letter Book, 14.
11. Hall Letter Book, "Copy of Captain Thing's Instructions," 18-19; Wyeth, 107-22.
12. Judith Austin, "Joseph Thing," in *Mountain Men and the Fur Trade,* 10 vols., ed. Leroy Hafen (Glendale, Ca.: Arthur Clark, 1972), 9: 365.
13. Sampson, 393; Wyeth, 129, 132.
14. Ibid., 398.
15. Three nineteenth-century historians blamed the Hudson's Bay Company in varying degree. Washington Irving in *The Rocky Mountains* believed the United States failed to support American fur trade interests as effectively as the British government assisted the Hudson's Bay Company, and that this caused the American fur traders to compete at a distinct disadvantage. On the other hand, William H. Gray, writing a *History of Oregon, 1792-1849* in 1870, and Hubert Howe Bancroft, writing in his *History of the Northwest Coast* in 1884, both placed the blame for Wyeth's poor showing squarely on the shoulders of the Hudson's Bay Company. Gray stated that "every possible underhanded and degrading device was practiced, both with the Indians and with his men, to destroy, as much as was possible, the value and profits of his [Wyeth's] trade." William H. Gray, *A History of Oregon, 1792-1849* (1870; reprint, New York: Arno Press, 1973), 41. Hubert Howe Bancroft, *The Northwest Coast,* 2 vols. (San Francisco: A.L. Bancroft and Co., 1884), 2: 595.
16. "Copy of Agreement with Sublette and Fitzpatric," 14 August 1833, Hall Letter Book, 5.
17. Leroy Hafen, *Broken Hand* (Denver: The Old West Publishing Company, 1973), 140-42.

18. Wyeth, 138-39. In addition to Wyeth's own comments, the classic remark from this situation was attributed to Wyeth by Joseph Meek. Meek claimed to overhear Wyeth telling the men of the Rocky Mountain Fur Company, "I will roll a stone into your garden that you will never be able to get out." Frances Fuller Victor, *River of the West* (Oakland, Calif.: Brooks-Sterling, 1974), 164.
19. Henry Fraeb and John Baptiste Gervais were veteran fur traders who had been partners in the Rocky Mountain Fur Company. Both traders show up on the Fort Hall Books in 1834. The company credited Fraeb with $514 worth of goods on 24 June 1834 (Fort Hall Ledger Book no. 1 [Oregon Historical Society], 53), and Gervais' name appeared on 3 October 1834 (Fort Hall Ledger Book no. 1, 43). Both paid off their debts in July of 1835 (Fort Hall Ledger Book, no. 1, 53).
20. There is good evidence that Wyeth had thought about building trading posts in the Rocky Mountains during his first expedition. There is also evidence to suggest that Wyeth had thought of the Fort Hall area as a prime place in which to build such an establishment. Wyeth in 1832 had camped near the confluence of the Portneuf and Snake Rivers. He noted in his journal that the area had a lot of buffalo sign and that the Bannock Indians wintered there (Wyeth, 163). In a November 1833 letter to Tucker and Williams, he commented that if the contracted goods for some reason were not accepted, he would go to a safe place on the Columbia River and leave some men there to trade (Wyeth, 77). Finally, after the goods had been rejected in 1834, he wrote home that he would build a fort on the Lewis River (Snake) about 150 miles west of the rendezvous (Wyeth, 134). Wyeth was most certainly thinking of the area that he had camped at two years previously.
21. Wyeth to Tucker and Williams, 6 October 1834, Hall Letter Book, 45-47.
22. Ibid., 45-47.
23. Ibid.
24. Ibid., Wyeth to Tucker and Williams, 2 May 1835, 63-64.
25. Ibid., Nathaniel Wyeth to Tucker and Williams, 2 May 1835, Hall Letter Book, 63-64; Joseph Thing to Tucker and Williams, July 1836, Hall Letter Book, 73-76.
26. Ibid., Joseph Thing to Tucker and Williams, July 1836, 73-76.
27. Ibid., Nathaniel Wyeth to Tucker and Williams, 2 May 1835, 63-64.
28. Ibid., Abel Baker to Tucker and Williams, 17 June 1835, 68-71.
29. Ibid., Nathaniel Wyeth to Tucker and Williams, 2 May 1835, 63-64.
30. Ibid., Joseph Thing to Tucker and Williams, 2 May 1835, 63-64.
31. Ibid., 64.
32. Ibid., Joseph Thing to Tucker and Williams, July 1836, 74.
33. Ibid., Nathaniel Wyeth to Tucker and Williams, 27 February 1865, 71.
34. Osborne Russell, *Journal of a Trapper*, ed. Aubrey Haines (Portland, Or.: Champoeg Press, 1955), 29.
35. Nathaniel Wyeth to Tucker and Williams, 27 February 1865, Hall Letter Book, 71.
36. Ibid.
37. Ibid., Joseph Thing to Tucker and Williams, July 1836, Hall Letter Book, 73.
38. Joseph Thing's contract stipulated that a penalty of loss of compensation could be enforced due to "wilful disobedience or neglect of duty." Copy of Captain Thing's Instructions, 13 February 1834, Hall Letter Book, 16-17.
39. Ibid., Joseph Thing to Tucker and Williams, July 1836, 76.

40. Ibid., James Lambert to Tucker and Williams, 17 February 1834, 55-56.
41. Wyeth, 77-78.
42. Articles of Agreement between the Hudson's Bay Company and the Columbia River Fishing and Trading Company, Hall Letter Book, 55.
43. Fort Hall Journal, Oregon Historical Society, Portland, 172.
44. Joseph Thing to Tucker and Williams, 16 June 1835, Hall Letter Book, 67; Annie Laurie Bird, *Old Fort Boise* (Parma, Idaho: Old Fort Boise Historical Society, 1971), 32.
45. Mr. Wyeth's Memoir, Appendix 1, 25th Congress, 3d sess., H. Doc. 101 (1839), 20; Joseph Thing to Tucker and Williams, 16 June 1835, Hall Letter Book, 67.
46. Bernard DeVoto, *Across the Wide Missouri* (Boston, Mass.: Houghton Mifflin Co., 1947), 192.

Part IV

The Fur Trade at Mackinac

The Michilimackinac Misfortunes of Commissary Roberts

Peter Marshall

Benjamin Roberts' tour of duty at Michilimackinac as commissary for Indian affairs proved to be brief but, as subsequent events would demonstrate, not mercifully so. He arrived at the Fort on 27 or 28 June 1767 and, after confinement to his quarters, took an involuntary leave early in October.[1] It was a stay plagued by unresolved and protracted consequences, sufficient to bestow upon historians a substantial supply of pleas and petitions. If these serve to rescue Roberts from almost complete obscurity, they also cast light on problems of fur trade regulation in the last years of imperial control.

Had Roberts persisted in the pursuit of a military career, his life and death would most likely have been noted, if at all, as those of an unheralded officer who had served in an undistinguished regiment. Of obscure origins—reference is made only to his mother, a married sister, and an Irish background—he was gazetted ensign in the 46th Regiment of Foot on 23 July 1758 and promoted lieutenant on 12 September 1762. That his commission was not obtained by purchase suggests modest means and subsequently gave rise to difficulties in its disposal.[2] A few more details, chiefly provided by memorials seeking reward for services, survive of his movements. The regiment had served under Loudoun in New York during the winter of 1758-59, and was quartered the following year at Schenectady. By the winter of 1759-60 its ten companies were also to be found at Forts Stanwix, Herkimer, Hendrick, Hunter, and Johnson.[3] It was at this time that Roberts, stationed at Fort Stanwix, having by his own account acquired "some knowledge of Indian languages," had been ordered to assume that responsibility at the post. His abilities gained further recognition with the arrival of General Prideaux to command the British force on the Mohawk: a capacity to lead Indians and knowledge of French kept him in constant employ until 1761 at Niagara, on Lake Ontario and the St. Lawrence. After the surrender of New France his regiment was engaged in the capture of Havana. On its return, he was sent again to Niagara, where he claimed credit for developing and operating the carrying place. In 1766 he became commissary for Indian affairs, allegedly at the urging of General Gage and Sir William Johnson, and assumed his duties at Niagara.[4]

Gage was no more than the official correspondent of a former, very junior, officer. The connection with Johnson proved much more significant, though the link was initially indirect. The prospect of new employment had not been raised by Sir William but by his nephew, Guy Johnson. Still, whatever the immediate attraction of an office that might permit a friendless and poor lieutenant to advance his career and fortune, the outlook remained completely clouded: Roberts would exchange a bleak for a quite uncertain future.

The basic problem to be confronted in the performance of a commissary's duties had been created by the terms of the 1764 "Plan for the Future Management of Indian Affairs." This had proposed the restriction of commerce north of the Ohio to a limited number of posts where it would come under the control of commissaries. Despite Sir William's urging, imperial approval had been withheld. The insuperable obstacle was the cost of administration, a difficulty that only revenue-producing legislation could have overcome. The need to establish some general pattern of regulation remained, however, pressing and apparent to both the superintendent and the commander in chief. By 1766 they had agreed to make appointments, though the powers and financing of the commissaries remained devoid of formal authority. The arrival of these new officials at distant and isolated points would be greeted by military commanders and traders with alarm and suspicion.

Instructions did little to clarify matters. In July 1766 the officer commanding at Niagara was informed by the deputy adjutant general in New York of the terms of appointment:

> The Officers Commanding will be aiding & assisting to them, as far as in their power in carrying on their business & will certify to their Presents & expences incurred, on such occasions. The Comissarys to be furnished with a good room, the interpreters &ca, properly lodged, and all supplied with firing & Provisions, as the rest of the Garrison. . . .[5]

It became rapidly evident that what had been assigned were general divisions of responsibility rather than particular allocations of authority. Only a matter of months after Roberts had taken up his duties, Captain John Brown, the officer commanding at Niagara, was launching a barrage of protests. He cannot have been propitiated by receipt of the superintendent's assurances that the commissary would have the sole direction of trading, could request the post commander's assistance, and in due course would acquire judicial and other powers.[6] The conflict continued. At the year's end, Brown informed Gage that the interpreter would tell him nothing of what Indian arrivals were saying but reported only to the commissary. Gage was moved to comment, "I am surprised as Mr Roberts is an old soldier that he should make any difficulties about it. . . ." But clearly he had. Although these differences amounted to no more than expressions of ill feelings and a proliferation of correspondence, Roberts' record at Niagara should be borne in mind when assessing the part he played in events at Michilimackinac.[7]

Although Gage informed Johnson in April 1767 that only at Niagara had a dispute taken place between a commanding officer and a commissary, correspondence on matters of trade organization had occupied the previous winter. By the close of 1766 five commissaries had been appointed, but a vacancy remained at Michilimackinac, despite Gage's belief, expressed in May of that year, that it was a post much in need of supervision.[8] The gap was not to be filled until late in April 1767 when Roberts, having been replaced at Niagara by Normand MacLeod, left Johnson Hall to take up the duties.[9] In terms of advancing the regulation of the trade, this could be viewed as a crucial development.

The nature, quantity, and extent of trade undertaken from Michilimackinac presented the most substantial challenge to the Plan's essential regulatory element—the restriction and management of commerce at the post—to be found anywhere in the North. In this respect, Roberts had not been given an easy task, even if his assignment had not involved far more than a control of Indian relations: he was to deal not so much with prospects of war as with putting paid to the ambitions of Robert Rogers.

The Major had assumed his command in August 1766, having obtained the appointment while in England, much to the fury and alarm of imperial representatives in America. Rogers' intentions and purpose in securing the post are not the concerns of this paper. What is relevant is that Gage and Johnson, from the moment they received the news, insisted that the superintendent would issue orders and instructions on Indian matters.[10] This was never acceptable to Rogers, who declared that Roberts' arrival "doth not affect me in my Command. . . ." Its terms had been established by the King and included "the Superintendency of Indian affairs."[11] There was more at stake, however, than conflicting interpretations of duties and powers. Rogers' financial activities had long aroused his superiors' suspicion and appeared to be continuing apace at a post where restraints had not been imposed. Gage instructed Johnson that Roberts should "acquaint major Rogers to incurr no more expences, and that you will answer no More Draughts from him. . . ."[12]

More than money was in question. Roberts would later testify that, while at Johnson Hall on his way to Michilimackinac, Sir William had shown him a letter, allegedly written to Rogers by a friend now in the French service. This confirmed a provision of financial rewards if, taking advantage of American protests against imperial policy, he could unite colonists and Indians against the mother country and serve the interest of its old enemy. To watch out for any such attempt was, both Johnson and Gage stressed, a major aspect of Roberts' duties. If necessary, he could apply to the commanding officer for military aid.[13]

On 20 August 1767, less than eight weeks after his arrival at the post, Roberts publicly denounced Rogers and accused him of treason. As he wrote to Captain Spiesmacher, the commanding officer:

> I impeach Robert Rogers Esqr. Commandant of Michilimackinac for holding Secret Correspondence with the Enimies of Great Britain, & forging Conspiracies. I desire

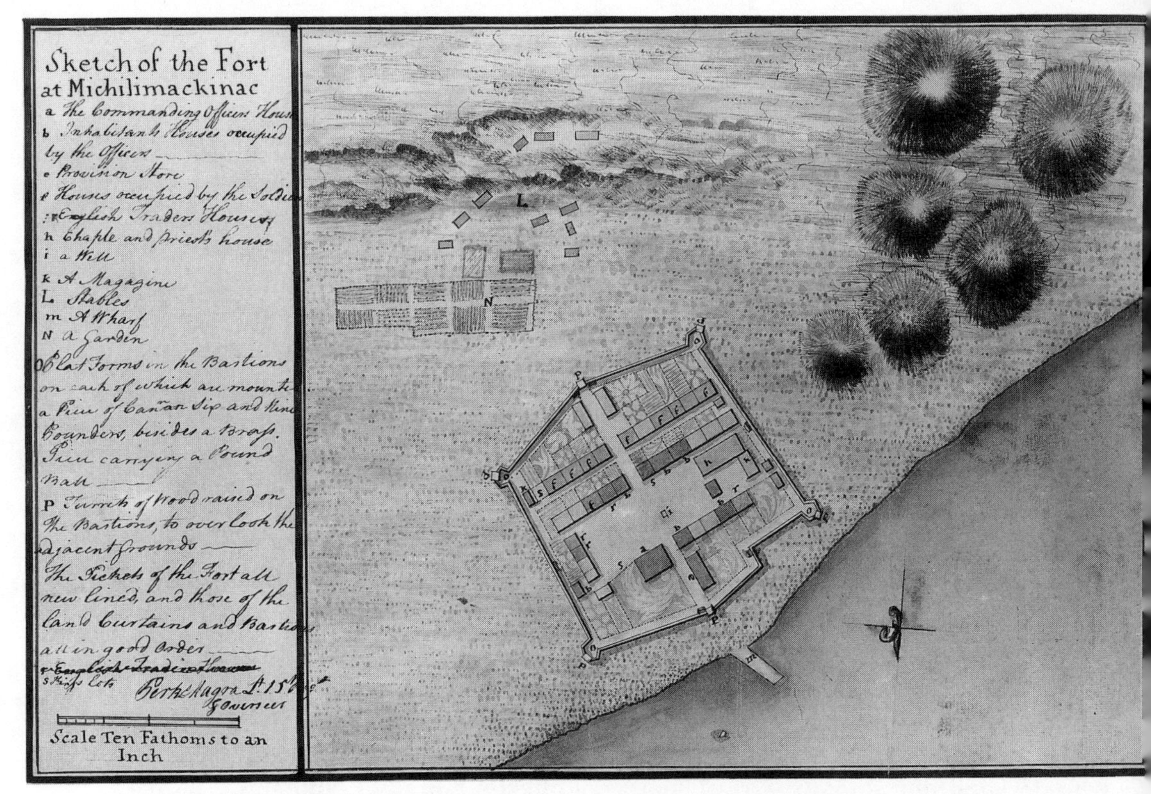

Figure 1. ***Sketch of the Fort at Michilimackinac,*** **drawn by Lieutenant Perkins Magra in 1766. Courtesy of William L. Clements Library, The University of Michigan.**

> you in your Allegiance to Seize his person & papers amongst which you will find Sufficient proof.[14]

It must be noted that the incident giving rise to this charge was not a discovery of imminent treason but, much more prosaically, the disposition of an unauthorized consignment of rum.

Roberts had become alarmed that liquor would reach the Indians at points beyond his control. This concern accorded fully with the role allocated to commissaries under the plan of regulation but grew much more specific through his belief that the distribution was being directed by Rogers. Late on the night of 19 August, rum was removed from the Fort. Roberts believed that this was a prelude to Rogers' joining the Indians in the Spring, a move which he had already urged Captain Spiesmacher to prevent, should it be attempted. The commissary was deeply fearful: "Think on my Situation, my Life, Effects, and Reputation is in danger . . .", with Rogers the main source.[15] When the rum was located on an island near the post, permission was obtained to pay a sergeant and two men to return it. After this had been done, the trouble began. Roberts wished the cargo to be "put into the Kings Store appointed by General Orders of which the Commissary keeps one Key & the Traders another." Rogers replied that only the

Figure 2. Aerial view of the reconstructed Fort at Michilimackinac, 1990. Courtesy of Mackinac State Historic Parks.

commanding officer might say that. From then on, things could, and did, only get worse, ending with Roberts being "lifted up and Carried like a Criminal through the Fort Guarded by Soldiers with fixt bayonets and Cast into his House." The commissary claimed that, as a consequence of this treatment, his authority over the Indians had been subverted and "his military honor as well as his civil character . . . irreparably sullied by such an unheard of Violence. . . ."[16]

Whatever dangers Spiesmacher might have been prepared to confront on joining the British service, he could hardly have anticipated the need to adjudicate, in such a remote location, between two such contrary figures. Embarrassed by the situation, he took refuge in a division of the blame: both "had acted very imprudently." Some sort of reconciliation was brought about: in the commanding officer's presence, apologies were exchanged. Roberts declared that when he had accused Rogers of treason he had nothing more in mind than having been sent to his room like a criminal.[17] It proved to be a superficial and temporary settlement of differences. Exactly a month later, Roberts was again under detention and now threatened with expulsion from the post. Insofar as the bewildered Spiesmacher could get to the bottom of the dispute, it appeared that

Rogers was not prepared to have Roberts undermine his authority "by telling him on the publike Parade, that he did not look on him as his Commanding officer, nor would obey [any?] orders of his, with many other expressions which he aledges is Next [to mu] tiny its Selfs. . . ." Spiesmacher's efforts to smooth matters over failed totally. Rogers was in no mood to forgive his accuser and the post commander could only "have Soom reason to tink by the Many Compleants the lodge agianst on other, their is a personal pique between them."[18]

By the end of September Roberts had regained his liberty but, as far as can be judged from a long and barely coherent letter dispatched to Johnson, little else. Rogers had now added to his crimes by stealing the commissary's clerk. Not only had his former employee written insulting letters but "he has just now openly insulted me attacked me in the Street, held up his fist to me threatned me with a Number of things as if he had it in his power to ruin me. I confined him to the guard. . . ."[19] Soon after this encounter Roberts left for Detroit, perhaps regretful that he did not, as he had predicted, make the journey in irons, but even so hardly departing of his own free will.[20] Effectively, he would not resume his duties as commissary.

This brief tenure of office would engender altogether more persistent consequences. As Roberts made his way back from Detroit, first to Johnson Hall, then to report, though nominally under arrest, to Gage in New York, his account of events was treated with some caution. The superintendent felt that he "might have been more cool" but was anxious that he should return to his post early in the following spring.[21] As far as the commander in chief was concerned, however, Roberts had already rendered his most significant contribution: by early in November, receipt of his letter had served to persuade Gage that a warrant must be issued for Rogers' arrest.[22] The Major's seizure on a charge of High Treason would take place in the first week of December.[23] Consequently, Roberts' task of regulating the Indian trade would be overtaken by that of appearing as witness to the malevolent intentions of the accused traitor.

Vehement public and personal differences obscured a condition common to both men. The motive most generally attributed by his accusers to causing Rogers' defection was a desperate need to secure relief from debt. In this respect, Roberts was no better placed. In March 1766, when Gage was first considering with Johnson who should be named as commissaries, he had remarked that "Lieut. Roberts is in bad Circumstances, and what you propose for him I think the best thing to do. . . ."[24] Thereafter, the most precise and revealing evidence of his movements and activities stems from unsettled accounts and legal actions: by their debts you shall know them.

Roberts did not hurry to return to Michilimackinac, even if the post no longer contained his adversary. He remained in New York, attempting to settle his accounts, until the end of March 1768, and then left for Johnson Hall.[25] His stay there cannot have been particularly brief, since he did not resume his duties until June. Whether he then did more than grace the Fort with his presence seems doubtful. Official correspondence is lacking for a variety of reasons. Imperial regulation of Indian affairs was in process of being abandoned: a board of trade report of 7 March 1768 had recommended that responsibility be returned to the colonies and, in consequence, that the commissaries be discharged. Ministerial approval had been communicated to Gage by June.[26] Before this became known, the fate of the 1764 proposals had grown steadily more uncertain. If Roberts had returned to Michilimackinac sure of indefinite tenure of office, his confidence would have been sadly misplaced. As it was, orders made it clear that priority was to be given not to Indian and trade matters, but to the pursuit of evidence for use against Rogers. Gage had instructed Johnson in April that the commissary was to be called to testify to his original accusation and

> should also endeavor to procure all other Evidence that can in any Shape tend to prove Major Rogers's Designs of Treason by abandoning and Deserting his Post and retiring to the French and Indians, after plundering all the Traders. Also his Intrigues and mismanagement of the Indians, and Disobedience of his orders and Instructions . . .

Writing directly to Roberts a few days later, the commander in chief directed him to assemble proof of his charges and, once their replacements had arrived, to accompany Spiesmacher and two other officers to Montreal, where the court-martial was to be held. Gage did not hesitate to assign responsibility to Roberts' letter of the previous August:

> Great part of the Suspicions that have lighted upon Major Rogers, have took rise therefrom. It behoves you in a very particular manner, to support the Accusation you have made, by Evidence, or corroborating circumstances, that may Amount to a proof. A great Censure must fall upon you, if, after the decisive manner in which you have expressed your Sentiments upon ths Subject, the Accusation against Major Rogers should fall to the ground.[27]

Management of the Indians came a poor second to conviction of Rogers during this brief stay at the Fort.

A single letter, composed to divert, and possibly to enlist on his behalf, a passing acquaintance, casts a contrived light on Roberts' activities. In June 1766 the commissary, newly arrived in office at Niagara, had escorted to the Falls William O'Brien, an Irish actor, and his wife, Lady Susan, daughter of the earl of Ilchester. It supplied a connection he was anxious to maintain and led to the provision of an account calculated to arouse interest. Details of his journey, of the murder of a French trader by Menominee Indians, a description of how the incident had been resolved, and assertions of growing peace and satisfaction deriving from his authority were set against feelings of dissatisfaction: "My employment is so troublesome, laborious & expensive that I am resolved to leave it, if it won't disoblige Sir William, it's shocking to be banished from the World, hourly in danger of having your throat cut." Awaiting the summons to attend Rogers' trial, Roberts concluded by declaring that "he always was a great partizan for the General & Mrs Gage"—perhaps pointedly omitting any reference to his feelings for Sir William Johnson—and lamenting that "I am too poor a fellow to have friends."[28] If this letter sought to prove that this was not so, it failed in its purpose: no answer is to be found.

In August, orders were received for Roberts to journey to Montreal. The case opened on 20 October, with Rogers being accused of planning to desert to the French, plunder the traders and stir up the Indians; corresponding with His Majestey's enemies; and, in accordance with advice from that quarter, disobeying instructions. Roberts was the opening witness for the prosecution. His evidence hardly lived up to Gage's expectations. He admitted that the letter to Rogers from Captain Hopkins, the turncoat serving with the French who was seeking to purchase the Major's support, had been read to him but once by Johnson and that he quoted it from memory. The rest of his evidence recited mistreatment at Rogers' hands and renewed the charge of disloyalty, this time crediting it to Nathaniel Potter, a Michilimackinac companion. Only a deposition, made the previous September, remained of his evidence, for Potter had died at sea on his way home. Much of the next ten days was spent in delineating the series of conflicts and squabbles which had occupied the garrison's time and for the most part involved Roberts. Little light was thus shed on Rogers' guilt. In his closing statement, Rogers paid handsome tribute to his own achievements as commander. His government had won universal applause

> until a Gentleman, I will not say from what View, came to be a Spy over my Conduct, as he himself has been pleased to testify in his Evidence delivered against me. That Gentleman either through prejudice or Inadvertancy, I have but too much reason to think, has with untrue Affidavits made Representations to the Commander in Chief to my Disadvantage, upon which His Excellency has been pleased to treat me as an Enemy to my Country.[29]

Two days later, the court declared Rogers not guilty. Roberts—the individual unmistakably indicated as responsible for the accusations—had failed to carry out the commander in chief's orders. There would be no way back to the army for a commissary about to be relieved of his duties. More than one officer was, effectively, on trial in Montreal.

Despite, or perhaps because of, the court-martial debacle, Roberts showed no anxiety to quit Quebec. What he was doing there, other than fending off a suit commenced against him by a Toronto trader, and claiming that he declined to undertake Indian affairs in the Province, remains unclear.[30] The superintendent was certainly losing patience with him: by March 1769 Roberts was informed, not for the first time but now quite bluntly, that his office had been suppressed and that if he wished to return to Michilimackinac this would have to be undertaken privately.[31] Early in May, Roberts arrived in Montreal from Quebec to find himself in a "disagreeable Situation . . . Surrounded by Enemies & threatned with assassination." On 9 May he had renewed his acquaintance with Rogers, who had overtaken him in the street, demanded satisfaction for his having bribed Potter, and proposed a duel on the spot. Clutching pistols, brandishing a stick, Rogers was reported "pale as death with his teeth Gnashing." Roberts claimed that he had appeared the following morning to answer the challenge but did not meet with his opponent. Both were warned not to persist, but Roberts was convinced that "every body seem prepossessed in his favor. What then can I expect, if any Accident should happen." About to leave for Michilimackinac, not willingly but by press of business, he expressed the hope of arriving at Johnson Hall in July.[32]

A life marked by miscalculation did not change its pattern: Roberts would not reach his destination until the following January. What occupied him meanwhile is debatable. At the end of August he wrote from the Fort, explaining the delay as a result of "having some money due to me, by people not yet come from North West." He found himself acting as the superintendent's representative despite his loss of office: "the Indians will Visit me, beg so hard in your name for rum, & wheedle so much they have had already 10 Eight Gallen Kegs of me. I am sure was I to Attempt to follow trade they would still expect presents so that I am at a loss what way of life to try." He besought a continuation of his allowance since "no person can be a judge of the Expence a man is at, at this place who has no Kings provision but those that try it. . . ." Announcing the belated receipt of two out of six barrels of rum and some rotten tobacco, he lamented that "I am really unlucky." In subsequent statements of his services, Roberts claimed that fear of Indian attacks had led traders and commanding officers to urge him to return "to prevent mischief." His presence, he alleged, had preserved the peace. He would also seek compensation for the seizure of a house he had built there "at a great expence in 1769."[33] Whether these concerns were sufficiently pressing to justify his stay cannot be determined. Normand MacLeod, a fellow commissary, believed that not only business but also female pursuits had occupied his time.[34]

On 6 December 1769 Roberts arrived in Albany to be met by an action taken out against him in the Mayor's court by Henry, Farrell and Abbot, claiming damages for rum seized by the commissary at Michilimackinac in August 1767. Unwilling to be detained there by the suit, Robert succeeded in securing its transfer to New York through the influence of John Weatherhead, Johnson's local man of business, who had arranged matters with the attorney general, John Tabor Kempe.[35] That done, he then made his way up the Mohawk for a belated, and final, visit to the superintendent. This took place in January 1770, and at the end of the month Roberts departed for New York, bearing Johnson's "strongest Recommendation" that Gage should pay the costs of his journey to Michilimackinac. The commander in chief was also urged to extend his protection to Roberts "for doing what was his Duty as Commissary," in consequence of which "he has been already at the Expence & trouble of Several Attendances on Court in consequence of the letigious Action."[36]

Arriving in New York on 6 February, Roberts immediately sought out Gage, informed the city of Johnson's ill-health, and prepared to leave for England.

Payment of accounts had to precede departure, and Roberts was plunged into despair when informed that Gage had ruled that Johnson should have paid them. Shortly before sailing, taking refuge in vague promises of settlement offered by the General's staff, Roberts wound up his American affairs. Writs were issued on his behalf against Henry, Farrell and Abbot, and a power of attorney bestowed upon Weatherhead—a gift the merchant would much regret. This done, he took leave of North America on 12 March 1770.[37]

Roberts had absented himself from a case that would baffle Johnson and Gage, and alarm Weatherhead, for long to come. Although provided with the assistance of the attorney general, Weatherhead found himself unenviably exposed to opponents "resolved to proceed against Mr Roberts with all the Vigour imaginable." No papers had been left from which to prepare a defence, and delay until the commissary returned seemed the only resort. Kempe required papers and proofs that were not available.[38] Although a Chancery injunction secured that autumn a postponement of the trial, all turned on Roberts' presence—a benefit he had never considered bestowing.[39] The case was not heard in the following year, but in October 1772 the claimants, represented by the formidable William Smith, could not longer be denied their day in court. He was thought to have determined to deny that action had been taken or authorised by officers of the Crown, though the fact that the matter had arisen well beyond the limits of New York cast much confusion. Johnson was still disposed to defend, in general, Roberts' behaviour, while remaining particularly sympathetic to Weatherhead's plight.[40] Although in receipt of a subpoena, Johnson did not attend the trial, which took place in late October. No one swore to what instructions had been given to Roberts or could testify to his authority to seize the rum. Gage, who had followed carefully the course of the case, declared, "I really do not know what to do in the affair." The most he could propose was that something might be done if Johnson was prepared to declare that Roberts had acted in accordance with instructions. What this would be, he did not indicate.[41] The court resolved the matter simply on the finding that Roberts had had the rum in his possession and given much of it to the Indians. If it could be shown that this was compatible with his orders, some redress would be possible.[42] Following these suggestions, Weatherhead transmitted a memorial to the commander in chief. Very slowly, compensation was obtained: in April 1773, Gage forwarded to the Treasury Johnson's representation of the injustice suffered by Weatherhead; in August, it was agreed that damages of £171 and costs of £70 should be repaid; in November 1774 Gage finally found time to spare from governing Massachusetts to authorise payment from the army extraordinaries.[43] It had constituted a protracted provision of bail.

These occurrences in his absence did not particularly improve Roberts' prospects. Wherever he went, difficulties accompanied him. Arriving in London on 8 April 1770, he set to work on the task of self-advancement. Carrying letters from Johnson to Lord Hillsborough, the American secretary of state, and enlisting the social and financial aid of John Blackburn, Sir William's London mercantile connection, Roberts exhibited more energy than expertise and more propensity to spend than to persuade. His claims for repayment of outlays fell on deaf ears: he had committed a fatal error for, as Blackburn commented, "He wants Vouchers to authorize His demand."[44] Within a few months financial imprudence and lack of income would raise a general alarm. To this could be added the appearance of a second law-suit, unconnected with the New York case but sharing a common origin in his tenure of office at Michilimackinac.

The originator of the new process was Phineas Atherton, formerly a lieutenant in Rogers' Rangers. According to Roberts, he had arrested him at the post in compliance with Johnson's instructions and at the behest of the sheriff of Albany, from whose gaol he had escaped. Rogers had refused to detain him in 1767, but Spiesmacher had done so in the following year until the debts for which he had been originally confined were paid. Now in London and still, according to Roberts, closely linked to Rogers, Atherton had taken out a writ demanding £4,000 damages for the seizure of four canoes and their merchandise. The case was to come to court in June 1771.[45] Roberts' behavior had not left him well placed to meet this challenge: though Blackburn found him "to be a very honest though imprudent man," others, reporting him "driving in his Charriot & keeping a house & Lady in the Country," predicted, accurately, that he would soon rejoin his old antagonist, this time in gaol.[46]

The hearing was postponed, leading Roberts to declare himself "Shockingly used." When in December 1771 the case came before Lord Mansfield in King's Bench, it was nonsuited. Atherton disappeared, and Roberts' attorney exhausted his funds, forced a surrender of bail, and compelled his imprisonment for debt from March 1772 until at least the summer of 1774.[47] But for Hillsborough's previous provision of a place, as the nominal secretary for Moorish affairs, with a salary of £100 a year kept beyond his creditors' reach, Roberts would not have survived.[48] Johnson, despairing of the recovery of loans, rather sought the transfer of New York land granted Roberts for wartime service. This was not effected in the best of humour. During the last year of his life, Sir William reflected at some length and with conscious restraint on Roberts' stream of accusations: "I am still inclined to attribute his extravagant expressions to the ferment he mentions on his spirits in which his own folly involved him."[49] The commissary had concluded that his best means of escape from King's Bench prison might mark the first and last occasion on which he would be of one mind with Rogers: both seem, in the summer of 1774, to have taken advantage of new bankruptcy developments. Roberts would use his freedom to serve in West Africa during the American war of independence, there to undergo further hardship at the hands of his fellow officers.[50]

Awkward customer as he clearly was, Roberts' worst features became most visible in the setting of Michilimackinac. The introduction to the claustrophobic confines of the remote and isolated post of this former officer, unlikely to accept inferior trading status, there to serve in the company of a figure of greater achievements and ambitions, offered the near certainty of unrestrained conflict.

To add to the degree of risk, those who occupied such positions of authority had more to fear than the prospect of Indian attacks. Greater, more dangerous and persistent enemies had to be confronted. Within the frontier, lawyers and accountants lay in wait: they represented a direct link between Michilimackinac and King's Bench prison.

Acknowledgements

I wish to acknowledge the assistance toward travel costs provided by the British Academy, and the help in research extended by Robert S. Cox, Curator of Manuscripts, William L. Clements Library, Brian Dunnigan, and Ulrike Jordan.

Notes

1. David A. Armour, ed., *Treason? At Michilimackinac*, rev. ed. (Mackinac Island, Mich.: Mackinac Island State Park Commission, 1972), 16; John R. Cuneo, *Robert Rogers of the Rangers* (New York: Oxford University Press, 1959), 220.
2. Roberts to Gage, 24 July 1773, Gage Papers, American Series 118, William L. Clements Library, University of Michigan (hereafter cited as Gage Papers, A.S.); "British Officers Serving in America," *New England Historical and Genealogical Register*, April 1895, 160; Gage to Roberts, 9 June 1766, Gage Papers, A.S. 52.
3. W. Thomas, "Stations of Troops in North America, 1757-1760," *Journal of Society for Army Historical Research* 14 (1935): 235-6.
4. Public Record Office, Kew. Memorial of Benjamin Roberts [30 Nov. 1770], C.O. 5. 114, ff. 175-8.
5. Richard Maitland to O. C. Niagara, 22 July 1766, *The Papers of Sir William Johnson* (Albany, N.Y.: University of the State of New York, 1921-62), 5: 337-8 (hereafter cited as *JP*).
6. William Johnson to John Brown, 31 Oct. 1766. *JP* 5: 404-6.
7. Examples abound. See, for instance, Roberts to Brown, 27 Sept. 1766 and 9 Dec. 1766, Gage Papers A.S. 57, 60; Brown to Roberts, 27 Sept. 1766, Gage Papers A.S. 57; Gage to Brown, 2 Feb. 1767, British Library, Add. MSS 21678, f. 85.
8. Gage to Johnson, 13 Apr. 1767, Shelburne to Johnson, 11 Dec. 1766, 'List of Officers in the Northern Department,' *JP* 5: 535, 448, 444-5; Gage to Johnson, 20 Oct. 1766, 5 May 1766, *JP* 5: 399, 201-2.
9. Johnson to Gage, 18 Apr. 1767, *Documentary History of the State of New York*, vol. 2, ed. E. B. O'Callaghan (Albany: Weed, Parsons, Public Printers, 1849-51), 849.
10. Instructions, Gage to Rogers, 10 Jan. 1766, *Treason? At Michilimackinac*, ed. Armour, 10-11.
11. Rogers to James Tute, 20 July 1767, Rogers' statement at court-martial, 29 October 1768, *Treason? At Michilimackinac*, ed. Armour, 55, 93.
12. Gage to Johnson, 11 May 1767, *JP* 5: 549.
13. Evidence of Roberts, *Treason? At Michilimackinac*, ed. Armour, 16-17.
14. Roberts to Spiesmacher, 20 Aug. 1767, *JP* 5: 629.
15. Ibid., Roberts to Johnson, 12 Aug. 1767, 614; Roberts to Guy Johnson, 20 August 1767, Lyman Copeland Draper and Reuben G. Thwaites, eds. *Collections of the State Historical Society of Wisconsin* 12 (1892): 27-29.

16. Memorial . . . to Spiesmacher, 21 Aug. 1767, *JP* 5: 632-34.
17. Ibid., Spiesmacher to Johnson, 3 Sept. 1767, 652.
18. Ibid., Spiesmacher to Johnson, 22 Sept. 1767, 696-97.
19. Ibid., Roberts to Johnson, 31 Sept. [1 October?] 1767, 710-17.
20. Ibid., Roberts to Spiesmacher, Roberts to Daniel Claus, 21 Sept. 1767, 689-92.
21. Johnson to Gage, 26 Dec. 1767, *Documentary History of New York* 2: 895-96.
22. Gage to Johnson, 9 Nov. 1767, *JP* 12: 377-78.
23. Ibid., Robert Johnston to Johnson, 24 February 1768, 443.
24. Gage to Johnson, 23 March 1766, *JP* 5: 94.
25. Gage to Johnson, 4 April 1768, *JP* 6: 177.
26. Representation of Lords of Trade, 7 Mar. 1768, *Trade and Politics 1767-1769*, eds. C. W. Alvord and C. E. Carter, *Collections* of the Illinois State Historical Library 16 (1921): 183-204; Gage to Hillsborough, 16 June 1768, *JP* 6: 314-21.
27. Gage to Johnson, 25 April 1768, *JP* 6: 208; Gage to Roberts, 2 May 1768, Gage Papers A.S., 76.
28. Roberts to Johnson, 10 June 1766, *JP* 5: 244; Roberts to O'Brien, 19 July 1768, British Library Add. MSS. 51358 f. 13.
29. Roberts' Memorial [30 Nov. 1770] P.R.O. C.O.5. 114, f. 179; *Treason? At Michilimackinac*, ed. Armour, 9-10, 16-23, 94, 98.
30. Roberts to Johnson, 22 Dec. 1768, *JP* 6: 547-48.
31. Ibid., Johnson to Roberts, 24 March 1769, 669.
32. Ibid., Roberts to Johnson, 11 May 1769, 753-6.
33. Roberts to Johnson, 29 Aug. 1769, *JP* 7: 146-7; Memorial, P.R.O. C.O.5. 114. f. 180; Roberts to Gage, 24 July 1773, Gage Papers A.S. 118.
34. MacLeod to Johnson, 27 Jan. 1770, *JP* 12: 773.
35. Memorial, John Weatherhead to Gage, 17 Jan. 1773, *JP* 8: 694-5.
36. Thomas Shipboy to Johnson, 9 Jan. 1770, *JP* 7: 337; Johnson to Gage, 30 Jan. 1770, *JP* 12: 775-6.
37. Roberts to Johnson, 7 Feb., 26 Feb., 5 March 1770, *JP* 7: 374-6, 415-6, 464; Weatherhead to Johnson, 12 March 1770, *JP* 7: 486.
38. Ibid., Weatherhead to Johnson, 24 July 1770, 803-6.
39. Ibid., Weatherhead to Johnson, 29 Nov. 1770, 1014.
40. Johnson to Gage, 14 October 1772, *JP* 8: 616-7.
41. Ibid., Gage to Johnson, 8 Nov. 1772, 634-5.
42. Ibid., Gage to Johnson, 15 Dec. 1772, 660-1.
43. Ibid., Memorial, Weatherhead to Gage, 17 Jan. 1773, 693-6; Gage to John Robinson,, 7 April 1773, Gage Papers, English Series 24; Robinson to Gage, 12 Aug. 1773, Gage Papers, E.S. 24; Gage to Robinson, 15 Nov.1774, Gage Papers, E.S. 17.
44. Roberts to Johnson, 13 April 1770, *JP* 7: 538-40; John Blackburn to Johnson, 4 April 1771, *JP* 8: 59.
45. Roberts to Johnson, 7 June 1771, *JP* 8: 134; Roberts to Gage, 12 July 1773, Gage Papers A.S. 118.
46. Blackburn to Johnson, 3 July 1771, Daniel Claus to Johnson, 3 Aug. 1771, *JP* 8: 173, 211.
47. Roberts to Johnson, 1 Sept. 1771, 3 April 1772, *JP* 8: 244, 439; Roberts to Lord Dartmouth, 21 Dec. 1772, 28 May 1774, Dartmouth Papers, Staffordshire Record Office, Stafford. Atherton was not lost forever. He returned to America when the Revolution broke out, joined the British forces, was captured at

Saratoga, and lived to secure compensation as a Loyalist. P.R.O. A.O. 12/50/327, A.O. 12/109/74.

48. "A Sketch of the Case of Captain Roberts," Hobart Papers, D/MH/War & Colonies/Q/7, Buckinghamshire Record Office, Aylesbury; Blackburn to Johnson, 24 June 1773, *JP* 8: 830-1.
49. Blackburn to Johnson, 20 Jan. 1774, *JP* 8: 1007; Blackburn to Johnson, 24 Aug. 1773, *JP* 8: 870-71.
50. Cuneo, *Robert Rogers*, 254; "A Sketch of the Case of Captain Roberts."

Effects of the American Revolution on Fur-Trade Society at Michilimackinac

Keith R. Widder

Throughout the American Revolution, 1775-1783, the fur-trade society at Michilimackinac and in the western Great Lakes region faced serious challenges. Hence, the formation of a multicultural society centered at the Straits of Mackinac between the 1660s and 1775 seems worthy of a close examination. The fur trade brought together Native North Americans, French missionaries, traders, and soldiers and, after 1760, British merchants and officials in a common interest, namely, the profitable pursuit of the trade. The outbreak of the Revolution, beginning with the American invasion of Canada in late 1775, threatened the continuity of the trade and British hegemony in the region.

Moreover, in order to discover how people at Michilimackinac confronted uncertainties posed by the war, the reactions of the Ottawas, Chippewas, French-Canadians, *métis,* and the British to the presence of George Rogers Clark in the Illinois country in 1778 and 1779 have to be analyzed. Their response drew together, although not always comfortably, the different groups of people not only to resist Clark but also to keep the fur trade functioning. As a result of their successes, the fur-trade society retained its social structure throughout the war. The war effort strengthened interdependence between the Native peoples and the British, a relationship that spelled future trouble for the Native peoples.

Michilimackinac emerged, during the 1670s, as a center for a society that came forth from the fur trade in the region that borders on the western Great Lakes. A large area of this region—which included, at times, most of the future states and provinces of Michigan and Wisconsin, much of Minnesota, and parts of Ontario, Manitoba, Saskatchewan, Indiana, and Illinois—formed the "Michilimackinac sub-region." Native peoples as well as Europeans found Michilimackinac's location at the Straits of Mackinac (Michilimackinac) to be a convenient and strategic stopping place between the forests and streams to the west and Montreal and Quebec to the east. The Straits of Mackinac join Lakes Huron and Michigan, and the entrance to Lake Superior, by way of the St. Marys River, is only fifty miles to the northeast.

French traders and explorers first settled at St. Ignace on the north side of the Straits in the 1660s. By the early 1670s, bands of Huron and Ottawa Indians, driven west by the Iroquois, had migrated to the Straits of Mackinac. Fathers Claude Dablon and Jacques Marquette introduced Roman Catholicism at the Straits when they started their Jesuit mission during the winter of 1670-71. During the 1680s, France expanded its presence in the locality when French soldiers built Fort de Buade.[1]

Before the end of the seventeenth century, Huron, Ottawa, and Chippewa Indians had formed relationships with the French in the Michilimackinac sub-region. With the passage of decades, Indian women and French men created familial ties that not only facilitated much of the fur trade but gave birth to a distinctive society that depended on the trade. Indian men and women exchanged furs, foodstuffs, their knowledge of geography, military service, and their technologies for products of European manufacture, alcohol, the diseases of the intruders, exposure to Roman Catholicism, and involvement in rivalries between France and her enemies, particularly Great Britain.[2]

As the fur-trade society developed, however, Indians and French retained their own identities even as they lived in or near each other's communities. Indian religion, architecture, diet, language, social organization, and government shaped the lives of people living in Indian villages scattered throughout the sub-region. At Michilimackinac and Detroit, Roman Catholicism and French architecture, language, and government were principal influences in the lives of the residents. Pursuit of the fur trade did not require people to surrender either their individual or ethnic identity, but a set of common values and practices grew out of the trade which formed the essence of the fur-trade society.

Kinship ties, religious toleration, diversity of language, the annual cycle, the dependence on trade, and political and military alliances composed the core of the fur-trade society. By the 1760s, intermarriage between French men and Indian women had produced a sizable *métis* population who assumed an intermediary position between their relatives in both Indian and French communities.[3] Despite the objections of the Jesuits, most people living in the Michilimackinac sub-region respected the rights of each other to practice their own religion. The introduction of the French language simply added another tongue to the existing diversity of languages spoken throughout the region. French merchants and Indian hunters and their families worked out mutually acceptable and understandable terms for the exchanges required in the trade. Traders adapted their system for collecting furs to fit into the Indians' annual food cycle by going to their winter hunting grounds

Between 1712 and 1760, French officers negotiated numerous alliances with Ottawa, Chippewa, Potawatomi, and other Indian nations to wage war against enemy tribes, particularly the Fox and Chickasaw, and the English who were hostile to French interests in the region. Wittingly or not, Native peoples were drawn into both the world market and worldwide conflict between France and Britain by traders, soldiers, and missionaries who brought them woven cloth, iron axes, brass kettles, muskets, and the Cross. In North America, the British-

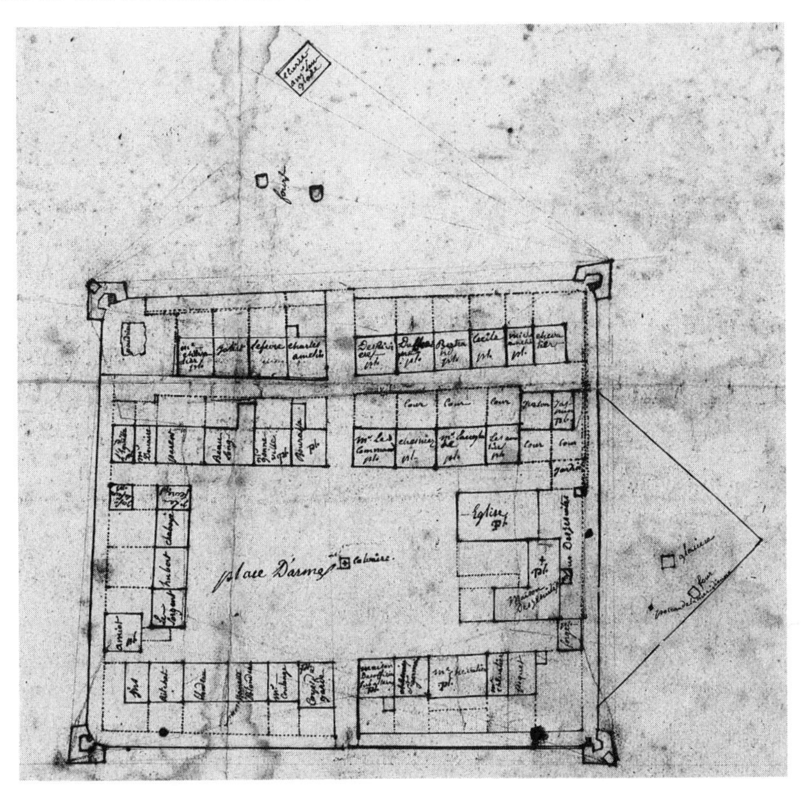

Figure 1. Michel Chartier de Lotbinière produced this plan of Michilimackinac in 1749. French inhabitants retained ownership of most property inside the stockade after the arrival of British traders and soldiers in 1761. Courtesy National Archives of Canada, NMC 12806.

French contest for empire culminated on the Plains of Abraham in 1759, with the subsequent surrender of Canada by France to Britain on 8 September 1760.[4]

The defeat of France did not mean the end of French influence in the Michilimackinac sub-region nor a large-scale out-migration of its French inhabitants, although some French residents did return to Quebec.[5] Rather, most kept on living among their Indian relatives and friends and working in the fur trade itself or in related businesses in Detroit, Michilimackinac, or smaller hamlets scattered throughout the region. French-speaking men and women continued to be vital members of the fur-trade society long after French officials and soldiers left North America.[6]

Indian nations had no intention whatever of leaving the region merely because British officials proclaimed sovereignty over their homeland. Even though many from the western Great Lakes had allied themselves with France during the recent war, Indians did not consider themselves to be a conquered people. In fact, many Indians and their *métis* kin and French-Canadians kept alive a belief that the French king would send an army to liberate them from their British lords.[7] The Indians did demand that British officials and traders respect their social organization, customs and beliefs, and the right to their lands.[8] Indian families, nonetheless, continued to rely upon traders to exchange their goods for furs and food.

The intrusion of British traders and soldiers into the fur-trade society in 1760 threatened to disrupt the social order that had evolved among the French and Indians. British merchants hoped to take control of the fur trade from French-Canadian traders, and the British military intended to force both Indian and French-speaking inhabitants to obey the policies and dictates of London. To complicate matters, British policymakers in New York and London had little knowledge, much less understanding, of the Native peoples living in the region. As a result, General Jeffery Amherst, Commander of British forces in North America, ordered the western commandants to curtail sharply the number of presents and the amount of ammunition they supplied to the Indians.[9] This policy contributed to the Uprising of 1763, when the Chippewa captured Michilimackinac, and the Ottawa and their allies laid siege to Detroit for several months.[10] Reeling from the effects of the Indians' rage, the British in 1764 devised a plan which confined the trade to the western posts. This new policy departed from the French practice whereby traders went among the Indian winter camps, and it resulted in contentious non-compliance.[11] When Indian hunters reacted angrily to the requirement that they travel hundreds of miles to trade their winter catch, Commandants Captain William Howard and Major Robert Rogers allowed some traders to winter away from Michilimackinac, which enraged traders left behind. Discontent caused all groups to seek repeal of unworkable rules.[12] In 1768, the British government put regulation of the Indian trade in the hands of the colonial governments, which enabled the fur trade in the Michilimackinac sub-region to function more as it had in French times.[13]

The fur trade proved to be the common denominator that linked all groups of people residing at Michilimackinac and in the western Great Lakes region before and during the American Revolution. Indian, *métis*, and French-Canadian families depended upon a stable trade in order to make their livings. British and French-Canadian traders, although bitter rivals, had to have peaceful relations between Indian nations throughout the region for their businesses to prosper. If the British government hoped to "govern" the disparate peoples scattered throughout such a large area in an affordable way, it, too, needed a healthy trade in order to maintain peace and instill allegiance to the British crown.[14] The fur trade, however, was much more than a set of economic transactions between buyers and sellers. It encompassed a complex web of social and personal relationships between individuals and groups, giving vitality to fur-trade society.[15] The American Revolution set off convulsions which could have caused chaos. But did it?

In order to understand the vicissitudes generated by the war, it is essential to recognize the importance of Canada's loyalty to Great Britain throughout the conflict. The Americans' failed attempt to conquer Canada in 1775-1776 made it

Figure 2. Arent Schuyler De Peyster from an original painting held by the Burton Historical Collection. Courtesy of the Burton Historical Collection, Detroit Public Library.

possible for the Canadians to keep open the vital Ottawa River fur-trade route to Michilimackinac. The British also kept up a regular traffic on the Great Lakes, although fears of rebel mischief and the British army's demand for provisions frequently interfered with the flow of merchants' goods. Open communication with Montreal enabled the trade to continue throughout the war.[16] This was not the case to the south, where an American presence in the Illinois country and a Spanish presence west of the Mississippi River generated hostility among all groups of people towards the British.[17]

As the war proceeded, American activities caused great concern at Michilimackinac and, particularly in 1776 and 1779, influenced the course of the trade while never completely stopping it. Given the level and extent of the turmoil created by the insurgency, it was remarkable that the primary economic activity of the society centered at Michilimackinac functioned as well as it did. Generally speaking, the people who depended upon Michilimackinac were well-provisioned during the war years in large part because their economic lifeline to Montreal remained open.[18]

Although American rebels never reached Michilimackinac or Detroit during the war, their aspirations and activities brought about fears and anxieties that were foremost in the minds of the people living there. The American expedition against Canada in 1775, the capitulation of General John Burgoyne at Saratoga in 1777, George Rogers Clark's successes in the Illinois country in 1778, Spanish efforts to harass the British from St. Louis, and rebel activities in the Ohio country, among other confrontations, sent shock waves throughout the West and kept the people at Michilimackinac on edge.[19]

Major Arent Schuyler De Peyster, commandant at Michilimackinac, orchestrated responses to resist American threats that brought Indian, French-Canadian, *métis*, and British inhabitants in the Michilimackinac sub-region together. In order to organize against the common danger, British officers had to overcome longstanding tension, suspicion, and even hatred that existed within society at Michilimackinac. Since 1760, British prejudices against both the Indians and the French and the Indians' mistrust of British motives had strained relationships. The belief held by many Indians and *métis* that the French king would send an army to liberate them from British rule further added to the uneasiness that characterized fur-trade society. De Peyster and his successor Lieutenant Governor Patrick Sinclair reasoned that if they employed, whether by conscription or personal choice, *métis* and Indian men in military expeditions or construction projects, they would remain loyal to the British cause.[20] This policy proved effective, but at enormous cost to the British government.[21] An analysis of Michilimackinac's response in 1778 and 1779 to George Rogers Clark in the Illinois country reveals how British policy worked and allowed the fur trade to continue.

Briefly stated, Clark had brought his force of Virginians to Illinois in summer of 1778, gaining control of Kaskaskia, Cahokia, and Vincennes. Local French inhabitants had openly supported him, and most of the Indians living in the

Figure 3. George Rogers Clark from an oil painting by John W. Jarvis. Courtesy Virginia State Library and Archives.

vicinity soon developed sympathies towards Clark. In addition, France had formed an alliance with the rebelling colonies that spring which sustained the hope of both the French-Canadians and Indians that Louis XVI might indeed come to their rescue. For British officers at Detroit and Michilimackinac, Clark's presence portended disaster.[22] They feared he might successfully woo Chippewa, Ottawa, Potawatomi, and other tribes living near them to his cause. Lieutenant Governor Henry Hamilton at Detroit believed that nineteen out of twenty of the French-speaking inhabitants there would support Clark if he advanced upon that settlement.[23] De Peyster had similar anxieties about French loyalty at Michilimackinac. A year after Clark's initial successes, rumors ran rampant throughout the West proclaiming his intentions to send hostile forces against Detroit and Michilimackinac. This state of affairs threatened the very existence of both posts as well as the British presence in the western Great Lakes region and their role in the fur trade.[24]

In May 1779, De Peyster summed up his situation:

> I don't care how soon Mr. Clarke appears provided he comes by Lake Michigan & the Indians prove staunch & above all that the Canadians do not follow the example of their brethren at the Illinois who have joined the Rebels to a man. I am however in hope that their connection at Montreal will be a check upon them.[25]

De Peyster then set about to make sure that his Ottawa and Chippewa allies remained "staunch," and that the French remembered their bread was buttered in Montreal.

The diplomatic and military phase of De Peyster's response brought together Ottawa, Chippewa, *métis*, French, and British men and women to oppose a common enemy. In late 1778, he enlisted interpreters Charles Langlade, Charles Gautier, and Joseph Louis Ainsse to recruit Ottawa and Chippewa men, who had already migrated to their winter camps in southwestern Michigan. These Indians were supposed to join an expedition led by Hamilton at Detroit against the rebels at Vincennes. Although about eighty men had agreed to go, most refused the invitation, saying it was too late in the year and they needed earlier notice before leaving their families.[26] In 1779, De Peyster organized another force—comprised of about twenty British regulars, sixty militia, and 200 Ottawa and Chippewa warriors—under the command of Lieutenant Thomas Bennett, to go to St. Joseph to resist what the British believed was a rebel army led by Godefroy de Linctot.[27] Linctot never appeared, and Bennett found the Potawatomi living near St. Joseph to be hostile to him and loyal to their "former father the French King." The Chippewa and Ottawa, also in a cantankerous mood, accused De Peyster of having "sent them naked from Michilimackinac."[28] The military value of these two operations was minimal, but De Peyster demonstrated that the British actively intended to involve their trading partners and the employees of the trade in the war.

A close look at the Chippewa and Ottawa participation in the expedition directed against Clark reveals that they ultimately cast their lots with the British because that appeared to be in their best interests. Although Ottawa and Chippewa men frequently complained about British parsimony when they were asked to join military contingents, De Peyster provided them with arms and provisions and attempted to feed and clothe their families adequately.[29] At St. Joseph, the Ottawa and Chippewa were tempted by the Potawatomis' expression of hope for the return of the French king's forces, but the French were now allied with the Americans. Anglo colonists living in the East had shown little respect for Indian lands and lives earlier, and there was no evidence that they intended to be more sympathetic now. Of more immediate concern, the Ottawa and Chippewa recognized that neither the Americans nor the French could supply them with trade goods. Quieouigoushkam, an Ottawa leader from nearby L'Arbre Croche, reflecting upon the behavior of his people at St. Joseph, told De Peyster, "We wish not for a French father, we rather have reason to wish for a continuation of the English father who supplies us with all our wants."[30] The Ottawa may not have loved their English neighbors, but only the British commandant and traders could meet their material needs.

Merchants and government officials worked under acute anxiety and tension as they devised a policy that kept the trade going. From the American occupation of Montreal in late 1775 until the end of the war, officers and entrepreneurs listened and watched for signs of rebel activity or influence anywhere in the West. General Guy Carleton, Governor of Quebec, and his successor General Frederick Haldimand both ordered De Peyster and Sinclair to prevent any trader from wintering at Indian hunting camps whose loyalty to the crown was questioned.[31] Furthermore, officials were reluctant to allow traders to go among Indians who may have come under Clark's influence, especially those who lived near the southern and western shores of Lake Michigan, where some Potawatomi had expressed support for the Americans. Nor did the commandant want to have traders working in places where they would be exposed to rebel marauders.[32] Throughout the war the lands bordering on, and extending beyond, Lake Superior remained relatively safe, and the northwest trade continued uninterrupted, although not always at the same level.

Although Clark's presence in Illinois had disruptive implications for the trade in 1779, British officials took measures to allow traders to get merchandise to their Indian customers. This, in turn, contributed to stability throughout the Michilimackinac sub-region.[33] At first, Haldimand delayed the departure of trade canoes from Montreal, but eventually he allowed over sixty to proceed to Michilimackinac. Because they arrived so late in the season, the northwest traders "joined their stock together and made one common interest of the whole" as they took their goods to needy Indian families north and west of Lake Superior.[34] De Peyster convinced many of the other traders to pool their merchandise and form a general store that operated as a single business at Michilimackinac. From among these traders, De Peyster chose the most trustworthy to go to work among Indian winter camps in Wisconsin, along the upper Mississippi River and in lower Michigan.[35]

Figure 4. British soldiers burned the powder magazine at Michilimackinac when they moved the garrison to Mackinac Island in 1781. Archaeologists excavated the site in 1974 and 1975. Courtesy Mackinac State Historic Parks.

British trade policy, combined with diplomatic and military moves at Michilimackinac, kept the fur trade healthy. When confronted with a potentially treacherous enemy, the people of the fur-trade society overcame mistrust and hatred in order to make the trade go and to enable each group to survive. Indian families needed the traders' merchandise; the traders, both French and British, depended upon Indian-produced corn and furs; the British army called upon Indian, *métis*, French, and British males to form the units required to field a fighting force; and French-Canadians and *métis* employed in the trade as voyageurs, clerks, and interpreters knew no other livelihood.[36]

Events of 1778 and 1779 triggered dramatic alterations to the architecture of Michilimackinac. In spring of 1779 rumors suggested that Clark might send a naval force up Lake Michigan from Chicago or Milwaukee to attack the wooden pallisaded settlement.[37] This, coupled with the anti-British sentiments expressed by the Ottawa and Chippewa, bred much anxiety over the security of the post. It had been only sixteen years since the Chippewa, with the complicity of French-Canadians, had captured the fort in 1763, and British officers did not want a repeat of that Chippewa triumph. During 1779, De Peyster employed some troops and French-Canadian and *métis* men to repair the fort's walls, construct stockades around the soldiers' barracks and seal off entry to the powder magazine, tear down two houses that were too close to the outside of the fort, build a banquette, and level off high sand dunes to the west of the fort.[38] It was evident to all that a siege mentality dominated the British consciousness, but De Peyster's works were only the beginning of changes on the local landscape. In October, several days after Patrick Sinclair arrived at Michilimackinac, he determined to move the entire settlement to nearby Mackinac Island.[39]

The personal hardships caused by the disruptive move to the island further bound together the people of this community.[40] Sinclair pressed voyageurs who had paddled canoes to Mackinac from Montreal or the interior to dismantle buildings or construct new ones on the island.[41] This caused consternation for some traders whose canoes were delayed from their normal departure times. Anyone, rich or poor, who lived at Michilimackinac or owned a house there, faced the expensive task of either moving their dwelling to the island or acquiring lumber to build a new one. For a time, at least, the inconveniences created by the move served as a democratizing force, binding everyone together to accomplish the move. Although Sinclair's arrogance caused many disagreeable incidents with his subordinates and civilians, the operation proceeded with dispatch and was completed within two years. Some of the relocation's obvious benefits included a fine natural harbor at the island, the creation of a civilian town outside a military fort, and certainly a more defensible masonry fortification.

At war's end the multiethnic community at Michilimackinac faced the future shaped by events of the previous eight years. Since the Michilimackinac sub-region was not a conquered territory in 1783, the fur-trade society had not

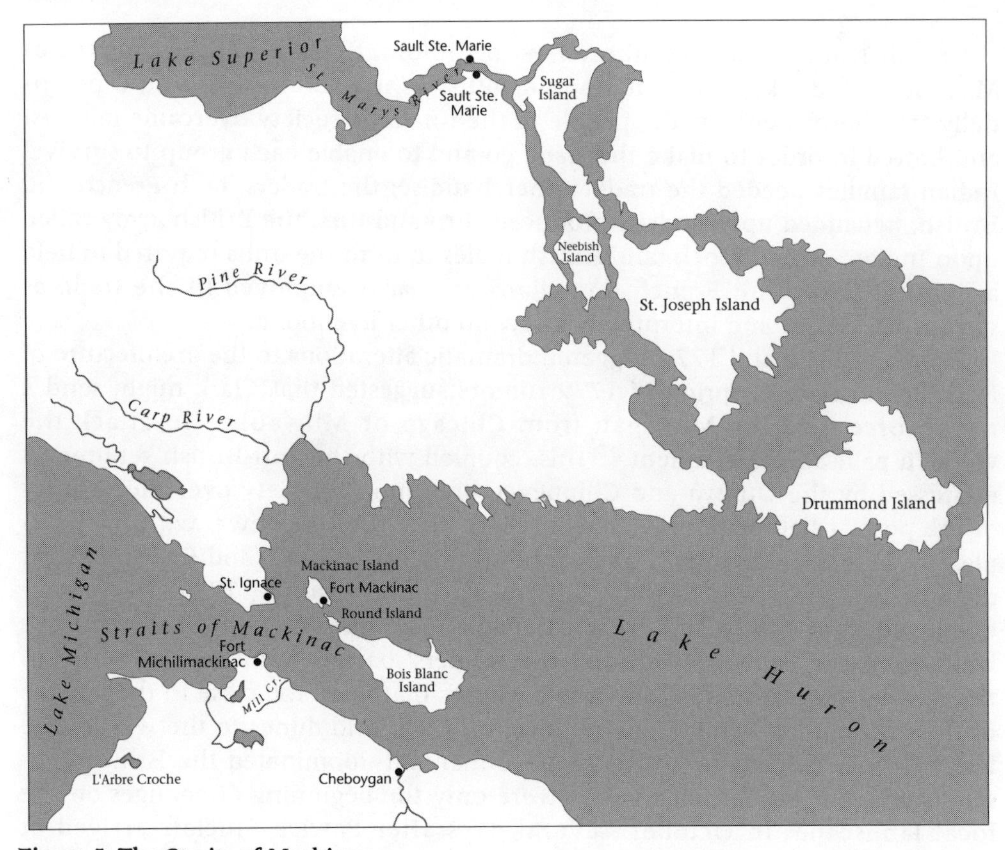

Figure 5. The Straits of Mackinac.

suffered the social decimation that often accompanies military defeat. The war had made it clear to all that France had no intention to reclaim its former position in North America.[42] People at Michilimackinac had pulled together to enable Britain to retain its hold on their homeland. Yet, the positive results of their efforts would only benefit the inhabitants for a few years. At the peace table, British diplomats ceded the territory south of Lakes Huron and Superior, including Michilimackinac, to the United States in the Treaty of Paris of 1783.[43]

Even though Great Britain lost the war, it still controlled the western Great Lakes until 1796, and the inhabitants found themselves more closely tied to Britain than before. The fur trade remained securely in the hands of British entrepreneurs, who continued to expand their financial control of the business. Indian families still sold their furs and corn to many of the same traders who wintered among them a decade before, and French-Canadian and *métis* voyageurs still paddled their canoes between Montreal and Mackinac, and between Mackinac and the interior. The fur-trade society at Mackinac looked to Montreal as the vital center of its economic well-being and connection with European markets and would continue to do so for another thirty years.[44]

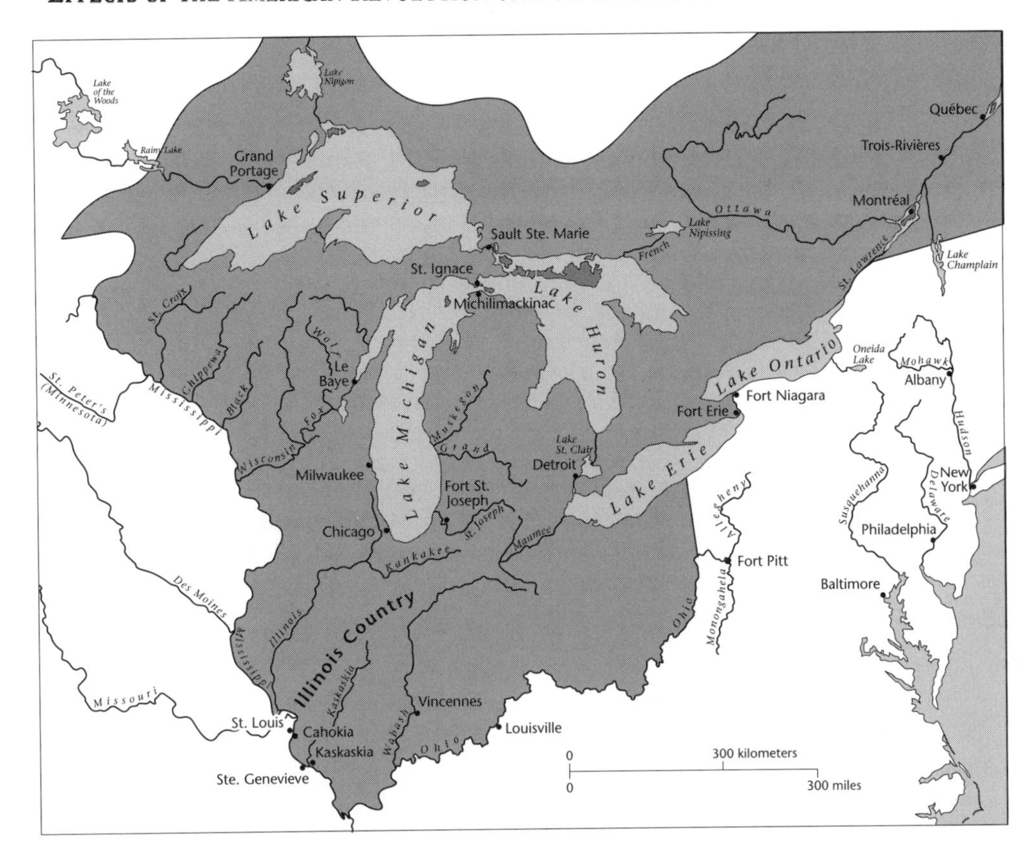

Figure 6. Quebec, 1775.

Ottawas, Chippewas, and the other native groups scattered throughout what would soon become the Northwest Territory now depended upon the British military to help defend them from American soldiers and immigrants. The creation of the new nation unleashed aggressive settlers, who took up residence on Indian lands north of the Ohio River and who would soon cast their covetous eyes on property throughout the Territory. Although Michilimackinac and much of the region to the west did not face large-scale immigration until after 1815, the American government intended to extend its sovereignty over the entire region. In the 1790s, Native peoples discovered that their British protectors were unable or unwilling to defend them in Ohio, and they would be forced to make their own peace with the Americans.[45] At Mackinac, even after American troops and officials replaced the British in 1796, the fur trade continued to dominate society until the 1830s. But by then American law and institutions, not those of the British or French, had been firmly established in the midst of the fur-trade society. The imposition of the ways of the United States upon a society that had evolved as a result of the coming together of Native peoples with, first, French and, later, British men and women was the ultimate effect of the American Revolution at Michilimackinac. But that is another story.

NOTES

1. For discussions of the early development of Michilimackinac and the western Great Lakes region, see Louise Phelps Kellogg, *The French Régime in Wisconsin and the Northwest* (Madison: State Historical Society of Wisconsin, 1925; reprint, 1968); Milo M. Quaife, ed., "The Memoirs of Lamothe Cadillac," in *The Western Country in the 17th Century* (Chicago: The Lakeside Press, 1947): 3-83; Emma Helen Blair, trans. and ed.,"Memoir on the Manners, Customs, and Religion of the Savages of North America; by Nicolas Perrot," and "History of the Savage Peoples who are allies of New France; by Claude Charles Le Roy, Sieur de Bacqueville de la Potherie," in *The Indian Tribes of the Upper Mississippi Valley and Region of the Great Lakes*, 2 vols. (Cleveland: The Arthur H. Clark Co., 1911 and 1912; reprint, 1969); James E. Fitting, "Archaeological Excavations at the Marquette Mission Site, St. Ignace, Michigan, in 1972," *The Michigan Archaeologist* 22, nos. 2-3 (September 1976). Collections of English translations of French-language documents relevant to Michilimackinac appear in W. Vernon Kinietz, *The Indians of the Western Great Lakes, 1615-1760* (Ann Arbor: The University of Michigan Press, 1965); Reuben Gold Thwaites, ed., "The French Regime," *Collections of the State Historical Society of Wisconsin*, 20 vols. [hereafter WHC] (Madison: State Historical Society of Wisconsin, 1903-1911), 16, 17, 18; "The Cadillac Papers," *Michigan Pioneer and Historical Collections*, 40 vols. [hereafter *MPHC*], (Lansing: Michigan Pioneer and Historical Society, 1874-1929), 33, 34; E.B. O'Callaghan, ed., *Documents Relative to the Colonial History of the State of New York*, 10 vols. (Albany: Weed, Parson & Company, 1855, 1858), 9, 10.
2. See Gary Clayton Anderson, *Kinsmen of Another Kind: Dakota-White Relations in the Upper Mississippi Valley, 1650-1862* (Lincoln: University of Nebraska Press, 1984), 1-84; George Irving Quimby, *Indian Culture and European Trade Goods* (Madison: University of Wisconsin Press, 1966); Joseph L. Peyser, "The Fate of the Fox Survivors: A Dark Chapter in the History of the French in the Upper Country, 1726-1737," *Wisconsin Magazine of History* 73, no. 2 (Winter, 1989-1990): 83-110; David A. Armour, "Nissowaquet," *Dictionary of Canadian Biography* [hereafter *DCB*] (Toronto: University of Toronto Press, 1979), 4: 582-83; Paul Trap, "Mouet de Langlade, Charles-Michel," *DCB*, 4: 563-64; W. J. Eccles, *France in America*, rev. ed. (East Lansing: Michigan State University Press, 1990); W. J. Eccles, *The Canadian Frontier: 1534-1760*, rev. ed. (Albuquerque: University of New Mexico Press, 1983).
3. Jacqueline L. Peterson, "The People in Between: Indian-White Marriage and the Genesis of a Métis Society and Culture in the Great Lakes Region, 1680-1830" (Ph.D. diss. University of Illinois-Chicago, 1981); "Many Roads to Red River: Métis Genesis in the Great Lakes Region, 1680-1815," in *The New Peoples: Being and Becoming Métis in North America*, eds. Jacqueline L. Peterson and Jennifer S.H. Brown (Lincoln: University of Nebraska Press, 1985), 37-72.
4. See Richard White, *The Middle Ground: Indians, Empires, and Republics in the Great Lakes Region, 1650-1815* (Cambridge: Cambridge University Press, 1991) for a thorough and original analysis of the growth and development of society in the Great Lakes region. Joseph L. Peyser has translated into English and interpreted previously untranslated French documents in *Letters from New France: The Upper Country 1686-1783* (Urbana: University of Illinois Press, 1992). Both of these works provide keen insights into the formation and the nature of the fur-trade society in the Michilimackinac sub-region.

5. Jill Y. Halchin, *Excavations at Fort Michilimackinac, 1983-1985: House C of the Southeast Row House: The Solomon-Levy-Parant House,* Archaeological Completion Report Series, no. 11 (Mackinac Island: Mackinac Island State Park Commission,1985), 32-41; Elizabeth M. Scott, *French Subsistence at Fort Michilimackinac, 1715-1781: The Clergy and the Traders,* Archaeological Completion Report Series, no. 9 (Mackinac Island: MISPC, 1985).
6. Keith R. Widder, "The Persistence of French-Canadian Ways at Mackinac after 1760," in *Proceedings of the Sixteenth Meeting of the French Colonial Historical Society, Mackinac Island, May 1990,* Patricia Galloway, ed. (Lanham, MD: University Press of America, 1992), 45-56.
7. Gregory Evans Dowd, "The French King Wakes Up in Detroit: 'Pontiac's War' in Rumor and History," *Ethnohistory* 37, no. 3 (Summer 1990): 254-78; Alexander Henry, Deposition taken at Michilimackinac, 22 May 1765, enclosed in William Howard to John Campbell, 2 June 1765 and enclosed in Campbell to Thomas Gage, 30 June 1765, The Papers of Thomas Gage, American Series, William L. Clements Library, University of Michigan, Ann Arbor, Michigan.
8. Donald Campbell to Jeffery Amherst, 22 May 1761, The Papers of Jeffery Amherst, W.O. 34/49: 36-37, Public Record Office, Kew, Richmond, Surrey, England (London: World Microfilms, 1979), reel 40; Henry Balfour's speech to the Indians at Michilimackinac and their answer, 29 September 1761, *The Papers of Sir William Johnson,* 13 vols. (Albany: The University of the State of New York, 1921), 8: 537-45; Proceedings of William Johnson's Indian council held at Detroit in September 1761, Sir William Johnson Minutes, 17 February 1761-17 October 1763, 6: 92-128, Indian Records, rec. grp. 10, ser. 2, microfilm reel C-1222, National Archives of Canada, Ottawa, Ontario; Henry Bouquet to Amherst, 19 May 1763, Papers of Henry Bouquet, ADD MSS 21634: 257-258, British Library, London, England (London: World Microfilms, 1978), reel 2; W. J. Eccles,"Sovereignty Association, 1500-1783," *Canadian Historical Review* 65, no. 4 (December 1984): 475-510.
9. Amherst to D. Campbell, 7 August 1761, Amherst Papers, W.O. 34/49: 286-87; George Croghan to Amherst, 30 April 1763, Bouquet Papers, ADD MSS 21634: 235.
10. For differing interpretations of the Uprising of 1763, see Howard H. Peckham, *Pontiac and the Indian Uprising* (Princeton: Princeton University Press, 1947); Francis Parkman, *The Conspiracy of Pontiac* (New York: Collier Books, 1962); Kerry A. Trask, "In the Name of the Father: Paternalism and the 1763 Indian Uprising at Michilimackinac," *The Old Northwest* 9, no. 1 (Spring, 1983): 3-19; Francis Jennings, *Empire of Fortune: Crown, Colonies & Tribes in the Seven Years War in America* (New York: W. W. Norton & Company, 1988): 438-53.
11. Paul L. Stevens discusses the Plan of 1764 in "His Majesty's Savage Allies: British Policy and the Northern Indians During the Revolutionary War, The Carleton Years, 1774-1778" (Ph.D. diss., State University of New York at Buffalo, 1984), 5-9.
12. William Howard to Eyre Massey, 16 June 1766; Gage to Johnson, 9 June 1766; Memorial from Montreal merchants to Gage, 22 January 1766; George Turnbull to Gage, 19 October 1766, Gage Papers, American Series.
13. Lord Shelburne to Johnson, 20 June 1767, Papers of Lord Shelburne, Clements Library, 53: 331-36; Copy of a minute agreed to by Lord Hillsborough, Major General Harvey and Lord Barrington, 4 April 1768, in Barrington to Gage;

extract from Commissary Roberts Instructions for 1768, 8 April 1768, in Johnson to Gage, 8 April 1768, both in Gage Papers, English Series.

14. Gage to the Earl of Halifax, 21 September 1764; Gage to Hillsborough, 15 May 1768 and 6 May 1772, Gage Papers, English Series.
15. See Elizabeth M. Scott, "'Such Diet as Befitted his Station as Clerk': The Archaeology of Subsistence and Cultural Diversity at Fort Michilimackinac, 1761-1781" (Ph.D. diss., University of Minnesota, Minneapolis, 1991).
16. Consolidated returns of Indian trade licenses, 1777-1790, Canada MSS G, National Archives of Canada; Hilda Neatby, *Quebec: The Revolutionary Age, 1760-1791* (Toronto: McClelland and Stewart, 1966), 142-55; Don Higginbotham, *The War of American Independence: Military Attitudes, Policies, and Practice, 1763-1789* (New York: Macmillan, 1971), 108; Guy Carleton to unaddressed, 22 May 1977, *MPHC*, 9: 348.
17. Arent Schuyler De Peyster to Frederick Haldimand, 15 August 1778, *MPHC*, 9: 368; Richard Macarty to John Askin, 7 June 1778, *MPHC*, 9: 368-69; George Rogers Clark, Clark's Memoir, from W. H. English, *Conquest of the Country Northwest of the Ohio River* (1896; Ann Arbor: University Microfilms, 1966), 457-555.
18. See David A. Armour and Keith R. Widder, *At the Crossroads: Michilimackinac During the American Revolution* (Mackinac Island: MISPC, 1986).
19. De Peyster to Haldimand, 29 March 1779, ADD MSS 21756: 9-10, ADD MSS 21757: 84, Papers of Frederick Haldimand, British Library, also in *MPHC*, 9: 378-79; De Peyster to Haldimand, 2 May 1779, ADD MSS 21756: 10-11, ADD MSS 21757: 92, also in *MPHC*, 9: 379-80; Askin to Richard Dobie, 15 June 1778, in *The John Askin Papers*, ed. Milo M. Quaife (Detroit: Detroit Library Commission, 1928) 1: 131-32.
20. Patrick Sinclair to Dietrich Brehm, 7 October 1779, *MPHC*, 9: 523-27.
21. Francisco Cruzat to Bernardo Galvez, 19 December 1780, *WHC*, 18: 413-15.
22. De Peyster to Haldimand, 31 August 1778, *MPHC*, 9: 369-70; for a discussion of Clark's activities and intentions in Illinois, see George M. Waller, "Target Detroit: Overview of the American Revolution West of the Appalachians," in *The French, The Indians, and George Rogers Clark in the Illinois Country: Proceedings of an Indiana American Revolution Bicentennial Symposium, May 14 and 15, 1976* (Indianapolis: Indiana Historical Society, 1977), 47-66.
23. Henry Hamilton to Haldimand, n.d., *MPHC*, 9: 465.
24. De Peyster to Haldimand, 7 October 1778, *MPHC*, 9: 371-73.
25. Ibid., 13 May 1779, 9: 380-81.
26. De Peyster to Haldimand, 24 October 1778, ADD MSS 21756: 7-8, ADD MSS 21757: 73-74, also in *MPHC*, 9: 374-75; 29 January 1779, ADD MSS 21756: 9, ADD MSS 21757: 80, also in *MPHC*, 9: 377-78.
27. De Peyster to Richard Lernoult, 20 June 1779, *MPHC*, 19: 437; De Peyster to Mason Bolton, 6 July 1779, *MPHC*, 19: 448; De Peyster to Major Nairne, MPHC, 9: 390; "Fourniture fait a differentes personnes-12, 772 livres, 6 Juillet, 1779," Louis Joseph Ainsse Papers, 1673-1874, item no. 68, National Archives of Canada.
28. Thomas Bennett, 9 August 1779, ADD MSS 21757: 188, also in *MPHC*, 9: 392-93.
29. De Peyster to Haldimand, 1 June 1779, *MPHC*, 9: 282-83.
30. Indian Council, 1779, De Peyster, *Miscellanies by an Officer*, 1 (Dumfries, 1813): 15-37.

31. Circular sent to Hamilton, n.d., *MPHC*, 9: 345; Haldimand to De Peyster, 6 May 1779, ADD MSS 21756: 24, ADD MSS 21757: 94, also in MPHC, 9: 357-58.
32. Haldimand to Hamilton, 25 December 1778, *MPHC*, 9: 405-6; see Robert G. Carroon, "Milwaukee and the American Revolution," *Historical Messenger of the Milwaukee County Historical Society* 29, no. 4 (Winter 1973): 118-44.
33. James Bannerman to William Edgar, 22 April 1779, in *Documents Relating to the North West Company*, ed. W. Wallace Stewart (New York: Greenwood Press, 1968): 61; Consolidated returns of Indian trade licenses, 1779.
34. Charles Grant to Haldimand, 24 April 1780, *MPHC*, 19: 511.
35. Articles relative to the establishment of a General Store at Michilimackinac, ADD MSS 21757: 226-29, also in *MPHC*, 10: 305-7.
36. In addition to exchanging trade goods and furs, people in the fur-trade society participated in military expeditions that were organized at Michilimackinac in 1776, 1777, 1778, 1779, 1780, and 1782, and British merchants purchased all of the Indian-grown corn in the region that they could locate. Haldimand to De Peyster, 3 July 1779, *MPHC*, 9: 361-63.
37. De Peyster to Haldimand, 2 May 1779, *MPHC*, 9: 379-80.
38. De Peyster to Brehm, 20 July 1779, *MPHC*, 9: 386-87. See Donald P. Heldman and Roger T. Grange, Jr., *Excavations at Fort Michilimackinac: 1978-1979, The Rue de la Babillarde*, Archaeological Completion Report Series, no. 3 (Mackinac Island: MISPC, 1981), 45-54; Moreau S. Maxwell and Lewis H. Binford, *Excavation at Fort Michilimackinac, Mackinac City, Michigan, 1959 Season* (East Lansing: The Museum, Michigan State University, 1961), 77-79; Heldman, *Excavation at Fort Michilimackinac, 1976: The Southeast and South Southeast Row House*, Archaeological Completion Report Series, no. 1 (Mackinac Island: MISPC, 1977) and *Excavations at Fort Michilimackinac, 1977: House One of the South Southeast Row House*, Archaeological Completion Report Series, no. 2 (Mackinac Island: MISPC, 1978); Heldman and William L. Minnerly, "The Powder Magazine at Fort Michilimackinac: Excavation Report," Reports in Mackinac History and Archaeology, no. 6 (Mackinac Island: MISPC, 1977); Lyle M. Stone, *Fort Michilimackinac, 1715-1781: An Archaeological Perspective on the Revolutionary Frontier* (East Lansing: The Museum, Michigan State University, 1974).
39. Sinclair to Brehm, 7 October 1779, ADD MSS 21757: 262-67, also in *MPHC*, 9: 523-27 and 29 October 1779, ADD MSS 21757: 276-78, also in *MPHC*, 9: 530-33.
40. John Macnamara, et. al., Opinions regarding removal of the fort, 21 June 1780, *MPHC*, 9: 556-57.
41. Sr. Marcotte, et. al., Agreement to furnish corvés to establish the village of Michilimackinac, 24 June 1780, *MPHC*, 10: 405; John Campbell to Robert Mathews, 24 July 1780, *MPHC*, 19: 547; Sinclair to Powell, 6 June 1781, *MPHC*, 19: 638-39; Sinclair to unaddressed, 31 July 1781, ADD MSS 21758: 81, also in *MPHC*, 10: 502-3; Sinclair to Haldimand, 29 April 1782, ADD MSS 21758: 126, also in *MPHC*, 10: 572-73.
42. Eccles, *France in America*, 223-52.
43. Richard Wright to Thomas Williams & Co., 29 May 1783, Thomas Williams Papers, Burton Historical Collection, Detroit Public Library.
44. Two good discussions of Indian policy between 1783 and 1815 are: Reginald Horsman, *Expansion and American Indian Policy, 1783-1812* (East Lansing: Michigan State University Press, 1967) and Colin G. Calloway, *Crown and*

Calumet: British-Indian Relations, 1783-1815 (Norman: University of Oklahoma Press, 1987).

45. Among the works that relate the story of Indian-white conflict in the Old Northwest after 1783 are R. David Edmunds, *Tecumseh and the Quest for Indian Leadership* (Boston: Little, Brown and Company, 1984) and *The Shawnee Prophet* (Lincoln: University of Nebraska Press, 1983); Harvey Lewis Carter, *The Life and Times of Little Turtle: First Sagamore of the Wabash* (Urbana: University of Illinois Press, 1987); Wiley Sword, *President Washington's Indian War: The Struggle for the Old Northwest, 1790-1795* (Norman: University of Oklahoma Press, 1985).

Apprentice Trader: Henry H. Sibley and American Fur at Mackinac

Rhoda R. Gilman

The political power wielded by large fur companies in the northwestern territories of the young American republic and the reciprocal role they played in supporting westward expansion through U.S. acquisition of Indian land are a familiar story. One of the leading chapters in it is the alliance between Lewis Cass, who served as governor of Michigan Territory from 1813 to 1831, and the American Fur Company. The staying power of that alliance and the way in which it was built into the lives of a succeeding generation are illustrated in the careers of younger men like Governor James Duane Doty of Wisconsin and Minnesota's Henry Hastings Sibley.

Sibley, who was elected Minnesota's first delegate to Congress in 1849, and who presided over the state's constitutional convention, became its first governor in 1857, and led its volunteer army against the embattled Dakota Indians in 1862. He had come to the area in 1834 as a representative of the American Fur Company. This fact was not purely fortuitous. His father, Solomon Sibley, had been one of the first American lawyers to take up practice in Detroit and had formed long-time ties as friend, neighbor, and counsel to some of the company's most influential agents. A native of Massachusetts, Solomon Sibley had also served two terms as Congressional delegate from Michigan and was a firm political ally of fellow New Englander Lewis Cass, who ultimately secured Solomon's appointment as chief justice of the territory.[1]

Thus, in 1828, when seventeen-year-old Henry Sibley announced his strong distaste for the legal profession and turned longing eyes toward the remote lake country northwest of Detroit, an apprenticeship in the fur trade was almost inevitable. Like most human stories, however, it seemed far from predestined at the time. Its unfolding gives us at least a distant glimpse of the personal networks, the corporate culture, and the day-to-day operations of the American Fur Company at Mackinac in the early 1830s.

Sibley's first position was not with American Fur, nor was it at Mackinac. Probably through the influence of Henry Rowe Schoolcraft, the Indian agent at Sault Ste. Marie and a friend of the Sibley family, the youth was hired in early summer of 1828 as a clerk in the sutler's store run by Schoolcraft's brother-in-

Figure 1. The earliest known likeness of Henry H. Sibley is this portrait, probably taken in Washington, D.C. in the 1850s during his service as Congressional Delegate from Minnesota Territory. Brady Studios, Washington, D.C., photo courtesy of the Minnesota Historical Society.

law, John Hulbert, at Fort Brady. After several months, the death of Schoolcraft's father-in-law, the trader John Johnston, resulted in moving young Sibley to the Johnston store. He spent the rest of the fall and winter there, working for Susan Johnston, who continued her husband's business.[2]

The change was welcome. Never before away from his parents and the large, warm clan of eight Sibley children, Henry had been bitterly homesick. His strict Calvinist upbringing also produced disgust with much of what he encountered at the fort. "I have seen so much deception practiced here . . . that I hardly know whom to trust," he had written to his brother-in-law and confidant, Charles C. Trowbridge. Life in association with the Johnston-Schoolcraft clan was better. The family included "three educated and lady-like daughters," whose company made him the envy of the unattached officers at the fort. By spring, nevertheless, he was ready to leave the Sault and try his luck at Mackinac.[3]

There, on the 8th of May, 1829, he signed a memorandum of agreement with Robert Stuart, agent of American Fur, under which he was to work as a clerk from 1 June "until the close of business the ensuing fall." Stuart agreed to pay him $40 a month and give him board and lodging. Since Sibley was not needed for the next three weeks, he took the opportunity to make a trip with an old school chum, John Kinzie, who was leaving by ship for Chicago. Kinzie also had worked for Stuart, and it is easy to imagine him briefing Henry on the habits of his formidable new employer.[4]

Without doubt Sibley already had some inkling of Stuart's reputation, for an aura of legend had gathered around the adventurous early life of the tall, rugged Scotsman. In 1810, three years out from Perthshire by way of Montreal, Stuart had become a member of John Jacob Astor's ill-fated expedition to the mouth of the Columbia River. He had sailed around Cape Horn to Oregon and had been the leader of those who trekked back across the Rockies in 1812-13. Enduring awesome hardships, they had been the first band of Americans after Lewis and Clark to cross the continent. Since 1817 Stuart had directed the company's business at Mackinac, second in command only to Ramsay Crooks and Astor himself.[5]

To these well-known facts Kinzie could add stories of Stuart's exacting demands on his employees and his terrible temper—of how he had once nearly brained a defiant voyageur and with quick repentance had stayed by the man's bedside and nursed him until he was out of danger. Kinzie could also tell ruefully of the boisterous, sometimes cruel sense of humor that led Stuart on one occasion to set up a fight between the cocky young clerk and a sour old house-servant. Stuart, Kinzie recalled, had watched through a window and roared with laughter as the youth and the old man threw awkward punches at each other. Yet, just as the Scotsman's rage was matched by equally deep wells of kindness, so his crude practical jokes were offset on occasion by a gorgeous and expressive flow of language and by a perceptive sense of humor.[6]

Since Sibley, like Kinzie, was to be a member of his employer's family, they may also have talked of Betsy Stuart. Motherly and devout, she sometimes interposed to soften her husband's discipline. She had insisted that Kinzie improve his sketchy education by reading aloud and reciting to her in the evenings. Born Elizabeth Sullivan, the daughter of an Irish immigrant in New York City, Betsy had been educated at a well-known seminary operated by Moravian nuns in Bethlehem, Pennsylvania. A few years earlier, Henry Sibley's own mother had attended the same school.[7]

It was Betsy's energetic Christianity that had led the Stuarts to encourage and support the establishment of the mission on Mackinac in 1823, and a school had been opened there for Indian children. Most of those who attended were, in fact, the offspring of traders and Indian women. Through them the mission and its school exerted widespread influence, and in time it sent new offshoots deep into the Upper Lakes country.[8]

Figure 2. Elizabeth and Robert Stuart. Courtesy of Stuart House, Mackinac Island, Michigan.

During the past winter, Sibley learned, a religious revival had swept the island, adding many souls to the small Presbyterian congregation centered around the mission. One of the converts had been crusty Robert Stuart himself. His employees became convinced he had been reborn when they heard him mildly tell a careless voyageur to retrieve a pack of furs that had dropped into the lake. The old Stuart, they agreed, would have knocked the fellow straight in after it.[9]

The summer season of 1829 soon came into full swing, and Mackinac was at its liveliest. But Sibley had little chance to observe it from his clerk's desk. "All the Lake Superior & Fond du Lac traders have arrived," he wrote to Trowbridge in July, "and you may well suppose that I am now much more pressed than ever, in making out Outfits &c. for the interior. . . . Yesterday I rose from bed at 4 o'clock and stopped writing at half past eight in the evening, not having left my desk except to go to my meals, & it is now 4 o'clock in the morning of the 21st."[10]

Sibley expected to return to Detroit in the fall, since American Fur had no immediate openings in sight. But he planned to keep trying. Apparently his own Calvinist background, his training in modesty and propriety, and his hard work had appealed to his boss for, as he confided to Trowbridge, "I think I shall have Mr. Stuart's influence in my favor."[11]

Through the winter of 1829-30, Henry apparently found temporary employment at the Bank of Michigan in Detroit, where his brother-in-law Charles Trowbridge held the post of cashier. There seems little doubt that American Fur had every intention of recruiting young Sibley, but if any additional influence was needed, it appeared in a note to Stuart the following spring from the bank's directors. Of Henry they wrote: "His capacity, we confidently believe, is equal to any task he may undertake, and his zeal and industry in the discharge of his duty commands our warmest commendation." Among the signers was James Abbott, a leading Detroit merchant and brother of Samuel Abbott, one of American Fur's top agents. Trowbridge also signed the letter, and his name was not without influence. He had served for some years as secretary to Governor Cass and had frequently been involved in negotiating Indian treaties.[12]

Apparently Sibley's performance during the summer of 1830 confirmed Stuart's approval, for in September Sibley signed a five-year contract to serve as clerk and storekeeper at Mackinac. The terms were $350 for the first year, $450 for the second, and $550 thereafter, with room, board, and laundry supplied. Clearly Stuart had some special assignments in mind also, for he added: "Should your services be required at any other place than Mackinac, during part of this agreement, you shall *then* receive fifty dollars additional salary."[13]

The next four years may have dampened the young man's hope that he would find adventure in the fur trade. His life at Mackinac held not only hard work but a deepening involvement with religion. Before the end of 1830 he made a public profession of faith and joined the island's Presbyterian congregation, which was guided by the Reverend William M. Ferry who had founded the mission and school.[14]

Stuart's conversion had brought in the rest of the fur company employees (those who were not Catholics) like the members of a highland clan following their chief. A new church was built in 1830, and the congregation was swelled by the town's Anglo-American business community and by officers and men from the fort. After 1833 its members included the Schoolcraft family, for in that year the Indian agency was transferred to Mackinac. Schoolcraft, who had found himself "saved" in 1831, quickly became an elder of the church along with Stuart.[15]

There is no evidence that Sibley's conversion was accompanied by either emotional or intellectual crisis. One sentiment, however, that he expressed frequently and strongly in later years may have reflected his experience on Mackinac. This was a hearty dislike for sectarian rivalries and theological disputes "which, for ages, have been prolific of dissension and intolerance, disgraceful in the eyes of the outside world, and in direct and irrepressible conflict with the teachings of the Prince of Peace."[16]

Figures 3 and 4. The American Fur Company's warehouse (above) and the office and residence of Robert Stuart directly beside it (right), formed the front of a company compound that was the business and financial center of Mackinac Island in the 1830s. Some clerks occupied rooms in the Stuart House. Others lived in a dormitory that stood to the right and behind it. The two buildings, preserved with little alteration, are shown as they look today, facing Market Street. Courtesy Mackinac State Historic Parks, Mackinac Island, Michigan.

Mackinac was an object lesson in the ugliness of intolerance. Spurred on by the spasm of evangelical revivalism that gripped the country in the 1830s, the missionaries sought to save not only the heathen but the Catholics. Nor were they above using their hold over the business and governmental seats of power on the island to advance their cause. French Catholicism had been established at the Straits of Mackinac since 1671, and when challenged, it found eager defenders. The conflict resulted in what one resident recalled as "a religious war," which bitterly divided the small community and in time undermined the mission itself.[17]

Social life for the young storekeeper was limited, but one bright spot was a warm relationship with the Dousman family. Michael Dousman had traded in the northwest country since the 1790s and was a long-time fixture on Mackinac Island, where he had a farm, a sawmill, and other businesses. By the 1830s he was serving as a judge, and it was he who administered the oath when Sibley became a justice of the peace on the island. Dousman's son Hercules, eleven years older than Sibley, was stationed with American Fur's Upper Mississippi Outfit and worked out of Prairie du Chien. He visited Mackinac often, and the acquaintance with Sibley begun during those years ripened in time into a business partnership and lifelong friendship. Meanwhile, the company of Nancy and Kate Dousman helped to replace the camaraderie that Sibley had enjoyed with his own sisters.[18]

As the rangy, six-foot youth matured into a darkly handsome, well-knit man, he no doubt attracted many feminine eyes. Eunice Osmer, a young teacher at the mission, sent several delicately yearning letters to her "beloved brother in Christ" after his departure from Mackinac. But there is no evidence that Sibley ever returned her sentiments.[19]

Work for the company brought Sibley into contact with a broadly colorful collection of traders who had made their livelihoods for varying numbers of years in the fur business. From Mackinac, headquarters of the Northern Department of American Fur, the various districts and dependencies fanned out to the west and south. Most were defined by tribes or bands of Indians rather than strictly by geographic area.

In 1830 the American Fur Company held a nearly complete monopoly in the region. Small-scale individual traders continued in business here and there, but there were no other major suppliers of trade goods. In 1822 Astor had succeeded through concentrated lobbying of Congress in eliminating the competition of the government-operated stores ("factories") which had been created originally to counter the Canadian trade and had persisted in offering Indians an alternative source of supply. In this effort the company had received all-out support from Cass, Doty, Solomon Sibley, and other Michigan politicians.[20]

To the west, American Fur had merged in 1827 with Bernard Pratte & Company of St. Louis. The latter firm, operating as Astor's Western Department, had absorbed an upstart rival on the northern plains known as the Columbia Fur Company and had mounted an aggressive campaign to acquire the trade of the upper Missouri River and the northern Rockies. Thus, from Detroit to the mouth of the Yellowstone and from the banks of the Wabash to the British territory, or more precisely, the southern boundary of Rupert's Lands, the American Fur Company was not only the dominant but almost the only large commercial enterprise.

For the other partners in the trade—the Native American peoples south and west of the Great Lakes—the business that had started more than two hundred years earlier as independent barter between equals had become a crushingly exploitive system. Every small group of Indians had its own trader. In former years, when trade involved travel to some rendezvous, barter had generally been conducted by band leaders. Now it was the business of each individual hunter. The trader advanced on credit ammunition and a meager stock of supplies for the hunter and his family through the winter, to be paid in pelts with the coming of spring. Sometimes he furnished traps, guns, or muskrat spears on loan, with the understanding that these would be turned in at the end of the season and repaired for use again the next year. It was essentially piece work—but piece work in which there was no guaranteed price for the product. For the fiction of independent trade continued, and if the winter's catch, sold at the going price of furs, did not cover the credit received, then a debt was recorded in the trader's book.

The smaller traders were caught in the same system. Most considered themselves independent businessmen, buying their yearly "outfits" from larger

Figure 5. Mackinac Island in the 1830s was a thriving commercial and military center. In this view, believed to have been painted by Hannah White, the U.S. fort can be seen crowning the hill. Offices and warehouses of the American Fur Company, along with other business buildings are near the lakeshore to the left. Courtesy Mackinac State Historic Parks, Mackinac Island, Michigan.

operators on credit. If a series of bad seasons or a slump in the fur market drove the trader out of business, he assigned to his creditor such assets as he had. The principal one was usually his tally of losses in the form of a book of debts owed by his hunters. Passed on from subsidiary traders to the larger companies, these eventually became the basis for claims made against tribes at the treaty table.

Traders' contracts fell into three general classes. There was straight employment, under which the company owned and operated a post through hired clerks; there were joint accounts, by which the larger company advanced capital and the trader worked for a share of the profits; and there was the simple contract for purchase and sale, by which an independent trader with his own capital agreed to buy and sell through a single larger firm. The details of each contract were determined by the particular situation and the bargaining power of the parties involved.

As in the days of the old North West Company, laborers were recruited each year in the St. Lawrence Valley, signing an "engagement" of three to five years. They worked their way to Mackinac, then were parceled out among the various traders, whose contracts with American Fur generally called for the company to supply them with hands as needed.[21]

Sibley was captivated by the voyageurs' flamboyance and zest for life, and he was impressed also by their endurance, their honesty, and their meekness to authority. The memory, no doubt warmed by nostalgia, remained vivid even fifty years later, when he wrote: "It affords me pleasure to bear witness to the fidelity and honesty of the Canadian French voyageurs . . . [which] I found abundant occasion to prove. . . .They were a hardy, cheerful, and courageous race, submitting uncomplainingly to labors and exposures, which no other people could have endured. . . . Notwithstanding . . . the men as a rule, were merry, good natured, and obedient to the orders of their superiors."[22]

Not everyone had seen it that way. James Lockwood, a Prairie du Chien trader of the same period, recalled that the men were "transferable like cattle to any one who wanted them." Their wages were low, their supplies inadequate, and their employers managed to keep them deeply in debt to prevent them from leaving the country. As to honesty, Lockwood pointed out that any goods which disappeared from carelessness or theft were charged in full to the entire crew of the boat. He acknowledged that voyageurs were easily governed—but only by a person with status as their social superior.[23]

Perhaps Henry Sibley's own touch of romantic enthusiasm evoked a matching response in the men under him. In any case, his ability to command the devoted loyalty of a crew of voyageurs became apparent in the summer of 1832. Stuart entrusted him with an urgent request to Governor George B. Porter at Detroit for certain needed trade licenses, and he set out down Lake Huron in an express canoe paddled by nine picked men.[24]

The trip was stormy. After nearly foundering, they lay windbound for three days near Saginaw Bay—long enough for Sibley to discover that his voyageurs were as improvident as they were light-hearted. He found that the supplies for the whole trip had already been eaten. Finally, safe but hungry, they arrived at the first settlement only to learn that a cholera epidemic was raging in Detroit. They pushed on, nevertheless, the men insisting on braving the risk of disease along with their young commander. Half a century later Sibley could still recall with a thrill of pride the fine show they made as they dashed singing down the river, past a wide-eyed crowd on the Detroit wharves, the voyageurs bedecked in their gayest finery, and plumes waving gracefully at the bow and stern of the canoe.

Even then, however, such scenes were an evocation of the past. The days when the great canoe brigades climbed from Montreal through the lakes and over the watersheds to the backbone of the continent were long gone. A stream of goods had once poured through the lakes and fanned out to supply the entire Northwest. Those destined for the Ohio Valley had left the main current at Detroit; goods headed for the Lake Michigan country, the upper Mississippi, and the Missouri went to Mackinac; and those bound for Lake Superior and the country beyond it passed directly through Sault Ste. Marie.

In the 1830s, the returning wave of furs and skins still went eastward via the Great Lakes. This was largely because the coolness of the northern climate retarded losses from spoilage. The channels of supply, however, were shifting rapidly. In the 1820s steamboats began to carry trade goods from St. Louis to Prairie du Chien, bypassing Mackinac. Already the lead mines of northwestern Illinois and southwestern Wisconsin were furnishing the whole Northern Department of American Fur with most of its bullets and bar lead. And in the East, Ohio was becoming the breadbasket of the Great Lakes fur trade.[25]

Pork, flour, corn, and other foodstuffs which in the early years had rarely been carried beyond Mackinac grew increasingly important, not only for supplying the many traders scattered through the country but also for sale to army posts, Indian agencies, missions, and often to the hard-pressed Indians themselves. By 1830 the rich, level valleys of the Scioto and Miami rivers were producing large agricultural surpluses.

Purchasing these supplies was a tedious and time-consuming job, for sellers were small and scattered and travel was slow. Some of it was handled by James Abbott in Detroit, but the company also sent buyers through the Ohio Valley, looking for bargains in items like flour, bacon, lard, cheese, candles, tobacco, and whisky. Winters at Mackinac were slow, and it was probably with an intention of broadening Sibley's experience that the company assigned him to this duty in 1832-33 and again in 1833-34. It proved to be the last stage of his apprenticeship.[26]

Working on horseback out of Cleveland, he spent long weeks criss-crossing rural Ohio and western Pennsylvania, haggling with farmers and small manufacturers and arranging for transportation and storage. These were years of rising prosperity, and in Cleveland itself as well as throughout the Ohio Valley, Sibley could see the stirring of new developments—turnpikes, canals, manufacturing, the increasing use of steam power—and the bursting growth of the country behind the frontier. Statehood for Michigan was on the horizon, and the population of Detroit had more than doubled since 1830.

By contrast the fur trade, even with its veil of remembered glory, could only seem a static and declining business. And without doubt his family and Detroit friends were quick to point this out. Now that he had tasted life in the north for nearly five years, they urged him to turn to something that had more future. Moreover, the American Fur Company itself was undergoing reorganization with the retirement of Astor. Although Sibley's contract had another year to run "if said company so long continue the business," he argued that the reorganized firm was a new company and had no claim on him. This position was given added force by the fact that his mentor and supervisor, Robert Stuart, had been dropped.[27]

In the spring of 1834, secure in two offers of banking positions, one in Detroit and one in Huron, Ohio, Sibley called on Ramsay Crooks, the new president of American Fur. He offered Crooks—"out of respect to him as an old friend of my father and myself"—$1,000 for release from his contract. But clearly Crooks as well as Stuart had been grooming Sibley for a future with the company. He countered with glowing words about Sibley's prospects and an offer that made the young man's mouth water. As partner with Hercules Dousman and Joseph Rolette in a reorganized Upper Mississippi Outfit, he would have independent management of all trade with the Dakota Indians—a territory reaching far out onto the wild plains of the Northwest.[28]

Aided by a little helpful persuasion from Dousman, Sibley convinced himself that with all its uncertainties, a canoe was better than a cashier's cage. August of 1834, therefore, found him headed for Prairie du Chien to confer with his new partners in preparation for taking up his duties at the post of St. Peters, which stood opposite Fort Snelling at the junction of the Mississippi and Minnesota rivers. Back at Mackinac, Ramsay Crooks rubbed his hands and observed to Samuel Abbott that Sibley would "prove I daresay a first rate man for our business."[29]

On the whole the prediction was accurate. Young Sibley quickly established himself as a favorite with the commander and officers at the fort and maintained a polite, if not cordial, relationship with Indian agent Lawrence Taliaferro. Unlike most agents in the region, Taliaferro did not owe his appointment to Lewis Cass, and for fifteen years he had been a thorn in the side of the American Fur Company. Although nothing Sibley could do would change the decline of the fur trade, his network of political connections enabled him to represent the interests of the company effectively with treaty commissioners.

By 1842, which saw both the death of Rolette and the failure of American Fur, Sibley and Hercules Dousman were able to arrange terms with Pierre Chouteau of St. Louis and continue their partnership, which by then was expanding from the fur trade into steamboats, lumber, and land. One final achievement established Sibley's role as a worthy successor to Lewis Cass. With ruthless skill, in 1851 he helped negotiate and lobbied through Congress two treaties that deprived the Dakota Indians of their homeland and opened all of southern Minnesota to white settlement. Unlike Cass, however, he lived to see the bloody results of his work.[30]

Notes

1. Henry H. Sibley has been the subject of numerous sketches, but the only biography of him is Nathaniel West, *The Ancestry, Life and Times of Hon. Henry Hastings Sibley* (St. Paul, Minn.: Pioneer Press Publishing Co., 1889), an adulatory work published with the blessing of the subject and his family. An outline account of his early years is also included in an autobiography which he started to write in 1884 but soon abandoned. See Theodore C. Blegen, ed., *The Unfinished Autobiography of Henry Hastings Sibley* (Minneapolis, Minn.: Voyageur Press, 1932). Henry Sibley's papers (HHSP) are owned by the Minnesota Historical Society, St. Paul, Minn. Solomon Sibley's papers are in the Burton Historical Collection of the Detroit Public Library.
2. Blegen, ed., *Unfinished Autobiography,* 9; Richard G. Bremer, *Indian Agent and Wilderness Scholar: The Life of Henry Rowe Schoolcraft* (Mount Pleasant, Mich.: Central Michigan University, 1987), 102, 105; Henry Rowe Schoolcraft,

"Memoir of John Johnston," *Michigan Pioneer and Historical Collections* (Lansing, Mich.: Michigan Pioneer and Historical Society, 1874-1929), 36: 53-86.
3. Letter from Henry Sibley to Charles Trowbridge, 11 October 1828, in the HHSP; Blegen, ed., *Unfinished Autobiography*, 10.
4. Memorandum of agreement between Henry H. Sibley and Robert Stuart, agent for the American Fur Company, 8 May 1829, in the HHSP; Blegen, ed., *Unfinished Autobiography*, 16. Kinzie's father, also named John, served as U.S. Indian agent at Chicago and had sent his sons to Detroit for schooling. Young John Kinzie later worked for the U.S. Indian Office also.
5. Charles C. Trowbridge, "Sketch of the Life of Hon. Robert Stuart," and Martin Heydenburk, "Incidents in the Life of Robert Stuart," *Michigan Pioneer and Historical Collections* 3: 52-61. See also Donald W. Voelker, "Robert Stuart, A Man Who Meant Business," *Michigan History Magazine*, September/October 1990, 12-19.
6. Gurdon S. Hubbard, *The Autobiography of Gurdon Saltonstall Hubbard* (Chicago: R.R. Donnelley & Sons Co., 1911), 75-80. Stuart's letters are often notable for their expressiveness and humor. A number of them are in the HHSP and many more may be found in the American Fur Company Papers, owned by the New-York Historical Society and in three letter books preserved in the Stuart House at Mackinac Island. The latter, henceforth referred to as Mackinac Letter Books (MLB), include fragments of company correspondence between 1816 and 1830.
7. David Lavender, *The Fist in the Wilderness* (New York: Doubleday, 1964), 135; Mrs. (Elizabeth Fries) Ellet, *Pioneer Women of the West* (New York: Charles Scribner, 1852), 215.
8. Ibid., 316; Martin Heydenburk, "Indian Missions," *Michigan Pioneer and Historical Collections*, 3: 154-58.
9. Edwin O. Wood, *Historic Mackinac*, vol. 1 (New York: Macmillan Co., 1918), 399-407; Charles Trowbridge, *Michigan Pioneer and Historical Collections*, 3: 55.
10. Sibley to Trowbridge, 21 July 1829, HHSP.
11. Ibid.
12. Testimonial letter, 28 April 1830, HHSP; James V. Campbell, "Biographical Sketch of Charles C. Trowbridge," *Michigan Pioneer and Historical Collections*, 6: 478-91.
13. Contract dated 4 September 1830, HHSP.
14. West, *Hon. Henry Hastings Sibley*, 62; Janet White, "William Montague Ferry and the Protestant Mission on Mackinac Island," *Michigan History*, 32: 340-51.
15. Wood, *Historic Mackinac*, 399-407; Bremer, *Indian Agent and Wilderness Scholar*, 109-15.
16. West, *Hon. Henry Hastings Sibley*, 62.
17. Wood, *Historic Mackinac*, 90; Heydenburk, "Life of Robert Stuart, 58; White, "William Montague Ferry," 347; Elizabeth Therese Baird, "Reminiscences of Early Days on Mackinac Island," *Wisconsin Historical Collections*, (Madison, Wis.: State Historical Society of Wisconsin, 1903-1911), 14: 46 (quotation).
18. See Henry H. Sibley, "Memoir of Hercules L. Dousman," *Minnesota Historical Collections*, 3: 192-200; *Michigan Pioneer and Historical Collections*, 36: 416n; Commission as justice of the peace, 29 June 1832, HHSP; Sibley to Nancy and Kate Dousman, 25 March 1833, HHSP.
19. Eunice O. Osmer to Sibley, 12 November 1834, 18 April 1835, HHSP.
20. Lavender, *Fist in the Wilderness*, 319-25.

21. For general information given on the fur trade in the paragraphs here and above, see Lavender, *Fist in the Wilderness*, 377-81; Rhoda R. Gilman, "Last Days of the Upper Mississippi Fur Trade," *Minnesota History* 42: 122-40; Rhoda R. Gilman, "The Fur Trade in the Upper Mississippi Valley, 1630-1850," *Wisconsin Magazine of History*, 58: 2-18.
22. Blegen, ed., *Unfinished Autobiography*, 12, 13.
23. James H. Lockwood, "Early Times and Events in Wisconsin," *Wisconsin Historical Collections*, 2: 110-12.
24. Blegen, ed., *Unfinished Autobiography*, 18-22.
25. The changing patterns of supply and transportation can be clearly seen in a scanning of the MLB.
26. Blegen, ed., *Unfinished Autobiography*, 24.
27. Sibley contract, 4 September 1830, HHSP; Lavender, *Fist in the Wilderness*, 412-14.
28. Blegen, ed., *Unfinished Autobiography*, 25.
29. Crooks to Samuel Abbott, 20 December 1834, American Fur Company Papers.
30. See Gilman, "Last Days of the Upper Mississippi Fur Trade."

Crucifixes and Medallions from Michilimackinac

Charles J. Rinehart

The seventeenth century was a time when Europeans established lasting contacts with American Indians living in the Old Northwest. French Jesuit missionaries were among the earliest Europeans to enter this region. Their objective was to Christianize the Native inhabitants in the beliefs of French Catholicism (Jennings 1975: 101). A tool used to instruct Native Americans was pictures painted by the Jesuit Fathers. Sometimes these paintings were given as presents to converted Natives (Thwaites 1896-1901, 49: 69; 52: 119-21; 53: 203).

Other religious items were also given to American Indians who accepted the Catholic faith. These articles included brass crosses and medals. Frequently the only discriminating characteristic between a Christian and non-Christian Native American was the religious objects that were worn (Thwaites 1896-1901, 50: 173; 60: 137-39; 67: 309).

Recipients of crucifixes and medallions were not solely American Indians. Quite often missionaries handed out such articles to French settlers on New Year's Day (Thwaites 1896-1901, 28: 143; 30: 155; 36: 113). The reasons for this seventeenth-century practice are unclear. However, a possible explanation may be that these people had served the church well in the previous year. Unfortunately, after the 1650s there are no further references to this gift-giving practice, which may mean it was discontinued or became so common that it was no longer noteworthy.

Furthermore, a common practice at Catholic baptisms is to give a person a baptismal name. The name has to be Christian and often is "the name of the saint on whose day one was born" (Attwater 1958: 45). The baptismal name is a reminder that an individual has undergone baptism (*New Catholic Encyclopedia* 1967, 2: 45). Devout Catholics could very well have had items that showed the saint whose name they received.

Since crosses and medals were highly prized (especially by the converted Native Americans), it is possible that such articles were mass-produced and distributed through the fur trade. Yet, specific information on the manufacturing of crucifixes and medallions was not evident in the archaeological or historical material reviewed. On the other hand, other religious items were used by fur traders, for instance, Jesuit rings (Hauser 1982: 60-61) and rosary beads (Halchin 1985: 160-64). Despite a lack of documentary evidence, archaeologists have routinely defined crosses and medals in the category of European trade items (e.g., Quimby 1939: 25-27; Neitzel 1965: 50), yet no one has stated the reasons for such a classification.

Fur trade sources shed no light on whether medallions were used as trade items. However, a couple of references to crucifixes are known. The Michilimackinac trading firm of David McCrae & Co. produced two inventories from 1777 which list "metal crosses" and "metal stone crosses" (Quebec Papers, vol. B., 75: 216-18). While crosses are absent from the other ten years of McCrae lists, such articles at least occasionally were shipped from Montreal. The term "metal crosses" probably applies to the plain, common trade silver crosses. "Metal stone crosses" likely refers to crucifixes that have glass jewel settings (e.g., Brown 1976: 31; Hulse 1977: 168-71: Petersen 1964: 52).

The setting for colonial Michilimackinac was a natural "jewel." The fort was located at the point where Lake Huron and Lake Michigan meet. Michilimackinac was erected in 1715 by the French as a strategic fur trade center (Hauser 1982: 19). The significance of establishing Michilimackinac was recognized by the French military, for it had the largest garrison and the highest-ranking commandant in the Upper Great Lakes (Kellogg 1968: 386). Although French rule ended in 1760 as a result of the Seven Years War with England, the Articles of Capitulation agreed to in Montreal contained provisions that allowed both French and British fur traders to conduct business in the Upper Great Lakes (Stone 1974: 9).

Except when an American Indian attack occurred that temporarily removed the English from Michilimackinac in 1763 (Parkman 1851: 296-98), British control continued until 1781, when a new fortified location (Fort Mackinac on nearby Mackinac Island) was built to defend the Straits of Mackinac (Stone 1974: 11-12). The final British activity at Michilimackinac was to destroy any surviving parts of the fort buildings. While some structures were moved to the new post, all remaining edifices at the old site were intentionally set ablaze by the troops (Heldman and Grange 1981: 52-53).

However, millions of artifacts were left behind at colonial Michilimackinac, including crosses and medals. Comparing crucifixes and medallions yields many similarities and some differences between these artifacts. The material from which nineteen of the crucifixes are constructed is brass, four cruciforms are made of lead, and one is composed of ivory. All but two of the crucifixes bearing any markings are cast. All medallions are made of brass and are also cast. It is unclear if these specific medals and crucifixes were made in North America, in Europe, or both.

Nearly all crucifixes and all medallions unearthed are complete (i.e., not broken). The reason such objects were disposed of was not because they were fragmented. Their locations on the site are due either to loss or to having been

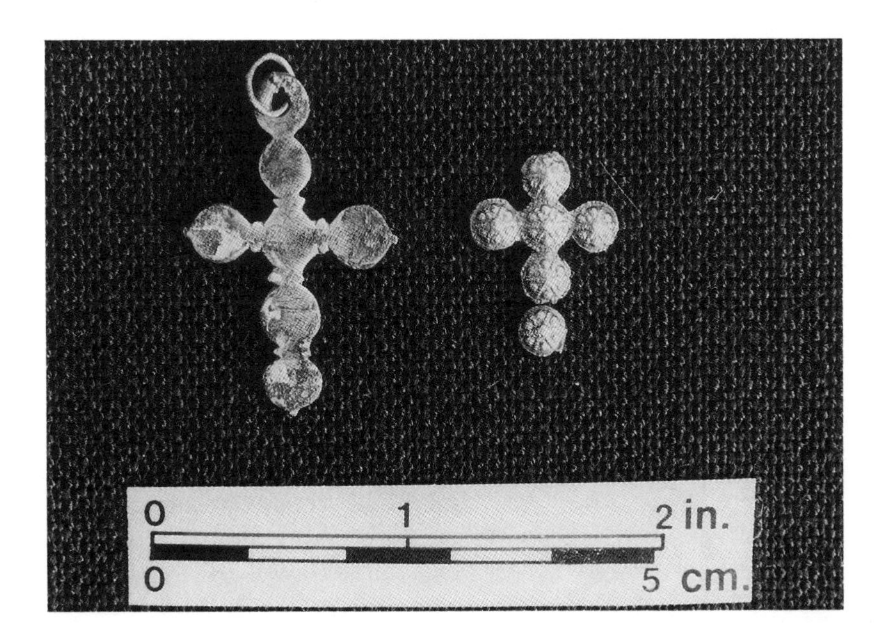

Figure 1. Type 1 Crucifixes. Photograph by Charles J. Rinehart from the collection of Mackinac State Historic Parks.

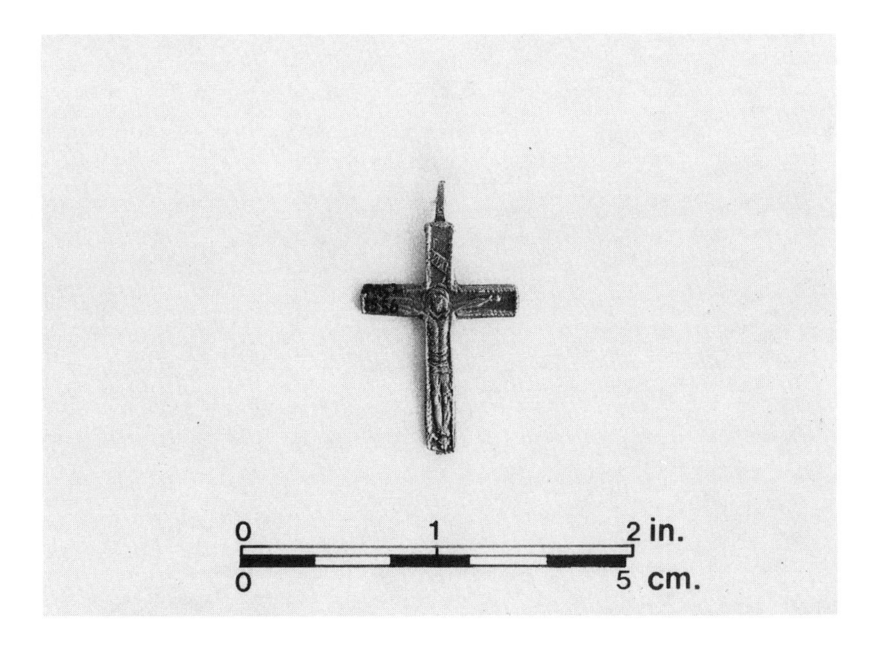

Figure 2. Type 2 Crucifixes. Photograph by Charles J. Rinehart from the collection of Mackinac State Historic Parks.

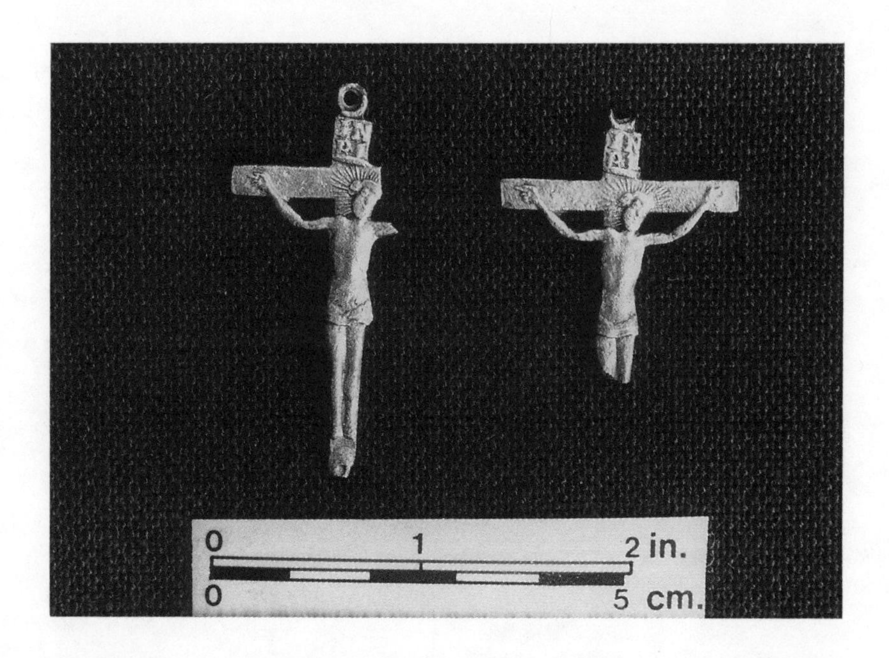

Figure 3. Type 3 Crucifixes. Photograph by Charles J. Rinehart from the collection of Mackinac State Historic Parks.

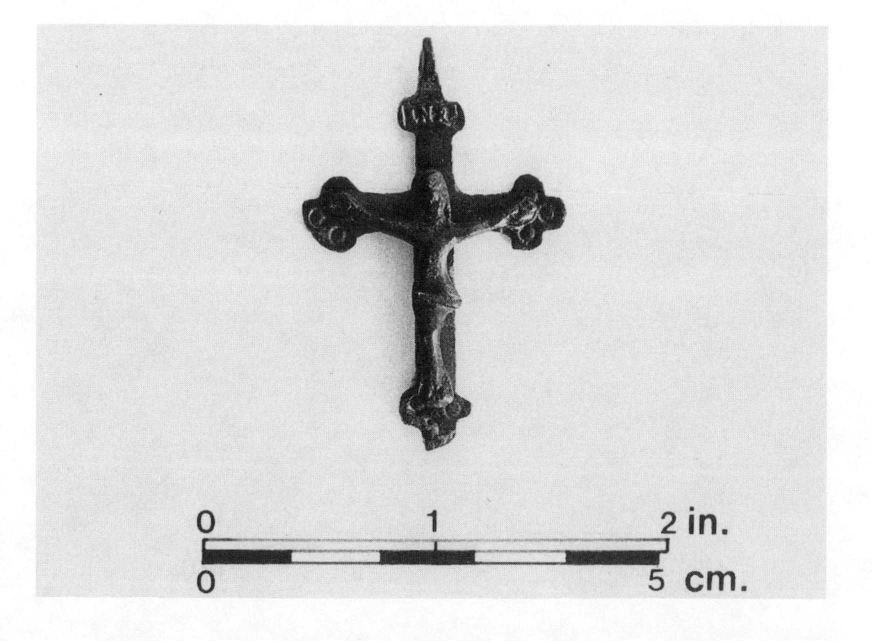

Figure 4. Type 4 Crucifixes. Photograph by Charles J. Rinehart from the collection of Mackinac State Historic Parks.

Figure 5. Type 1 Medallions. Photograph by Charles J. Rinehart from the collection of Mackinac State Historic Parks.

Figure 6. Type 2 Medallions. Photograph by Charles J. Rinehart from the collection of Mackinac State Historic Parks.

consciously tossed away. The number of crosses found is more than twice the number of medals. This may indicate crucifixes are more "common" at Michilimackinac. Noteworthy is that the quantity of medals at the site is less than the amount of coins recovered. The rarity of coins has been noted elsewhere (Heldman 1980: 82).

The physical shape of these "religious" objects is fairly consistent. All but one of the crucifixes are in the shape of a Latin cross. Over three-quarters of the crosses are flat at the end of each arm, yet three crucifixes have round ends to their arms, and two other cruciforms are made up of a series of circular sections. Four varieties of crosses have been defined. Type 1 is composed of brass crosses which do not bear corpora. Type 2 designates straight-edged crosses with raised corpora. Type 3 is recognizable based on the body of Christ forming the lower part of the cross post. The last kind of cross, Type 4, refers to crosses that are irregularly-edged and have a raised corpus (Stone 1974: 117-21; figures 1-4).

The dominant form of medallions is round (Type 1). Over half of the items are of this kind. However, the shape of several medallions is oval. Only four articles are more or less round, yet even these items differ between their widths and lengths. The other form of medals is classified as octagonal (Type 2) (Stone 1974: 121, figures 5-6).

Regardless of function, crucifixes and medallions have specific symbols placed on them. The designs of articles and the symbols present on material items are believed to help indicate function and to illustrate meaning given by people to these objects (Hodder 1982: 9-10). Symbols present on a single side of an artifact are in the same range for both crucifixes and medallions. The normal amount is between two and four insignia on one face. There are several crosses (almost thirty percent) that have five emblems present.

The placement of the symbols on each crucifix and medallion is consistent as well. On the obverse face of most Type 2 crosses, the figure of Christ is contained within the crucifix itself. The letters <u>INRI</u> are above his head, and his head is encircled by light rays. Any other insignia on the front side is located below Christ's feet or beyond his outstreched arms. The reverses are practically the same. A central figure begins at the middle of the cross and extends downward, covering most of the lower arm. One symbol is evident below this key image and on either horizontal arm; also, one or two items are seen above it.

The obverse on most Type 3 crosses has the figure of Christ too, but the body appears to be on top of the crucifix rather than being contained within the cross (giving a three dimentional look to them). As with Type 2 crucifixes, light rays encircle Christ's head and the letters <u>INRI</u> are over his head. Type 1 and Type 4 crosses are not mentioned because they lack the detailed symbols found on Types 2 and 3.

All medallions bear the likeness of at least one saint. When a side shows a saint, generally he or she is placed in the center surrounded by lettering that identifies the saint. When other symbols are present around a saint, they are either held by the saint or are smaller and less prominent. There are two exceptions: one in which the Virgin Mary is portrayed as a child, and one wherein Saint John is carrying the body of Christ. Only one-quarter of the sides do not have a saint represented on them. Three of these faces have the Eucharist, three more illustrate the symbol of the Jesuit order, and the last side depicts the hearts of Jesus and Mary. Also fascinating is that female and male saints are pictured equally on the medallions.

Interestingly, only two symbols—crosses and light rays—are consistently shown on both crucifixes and medallions. Light rays are most frequently present above the heads of venerated people. The cross is highly visible in the overall shape of crucifixes, but it is placed in a secondary position on medallions.

Only two people appear on crucifixes and medallions in any quantity: Jesus Christ and the Virgin Mary. In both cases they are evident on more crosses than medals. The only other person found on a specimen in each category is Saint Anne. She was the patron saint of the fur trade, and her presence *ipso facto* would seem to support the idea that saints represented at the fort had special ties for the inhabitants.

A further indication that saints were important to people at Michilimackinac is two recovered medals bearing "new" saints of the eighteenth century. John Francis Regis and John (of the Cross) were both canonized after Michilimackinac was established (Tylenda 1984: 485-87; Whittlesey 1972: 201-2). Having medallions with such recently named saints would not seem likely if the articles were to be traded to Native Americans.

Overall, there is a greater variety of symbols on medallions than on crucifixes. Thirty-one different emblems can be discerned on medallions compared to twelve on crucifixes. It is important to remember that interpretations given to these insignia are based on the meanings that the European nationals, who produced the items, give to the crucifixes and medallions. Native Americans, who often received these articles, may have given different definitions to the symbols present based on their existing religious and secular beliefs (Emerson 1965: 18, 79).

Cultural definitions are not limited to symbols; they may be found in the way articles are disposed of by people over time. Disposal patterns often become apparent by looking at artifact distributions from a site. Disposal patterns at Michilimackinac provide some interesting information about the location of crosses and medals (figure 7). A cluster may be seen in the northwest quarter of the fort, where 35 percent of all the medallions are situated. Immediately below the cluster is a large section where none occur at all. A large portion of the empty area contains the north-northwest row house and its associated features. If, indeed, individuals had medals bearing saints with whom they identified, it is logical to suggest that strongly religious families would have more of these items in or near their homes. One certainty is that the northwest quarter was the most economically affluent neighborhood at the fort (Heldman and Grange 1981: 22).

Michel Chartier de Lotbinière's 1749 map of colonial Michilimackinac illustrates that land immediately east of the priests' house had restricted access,

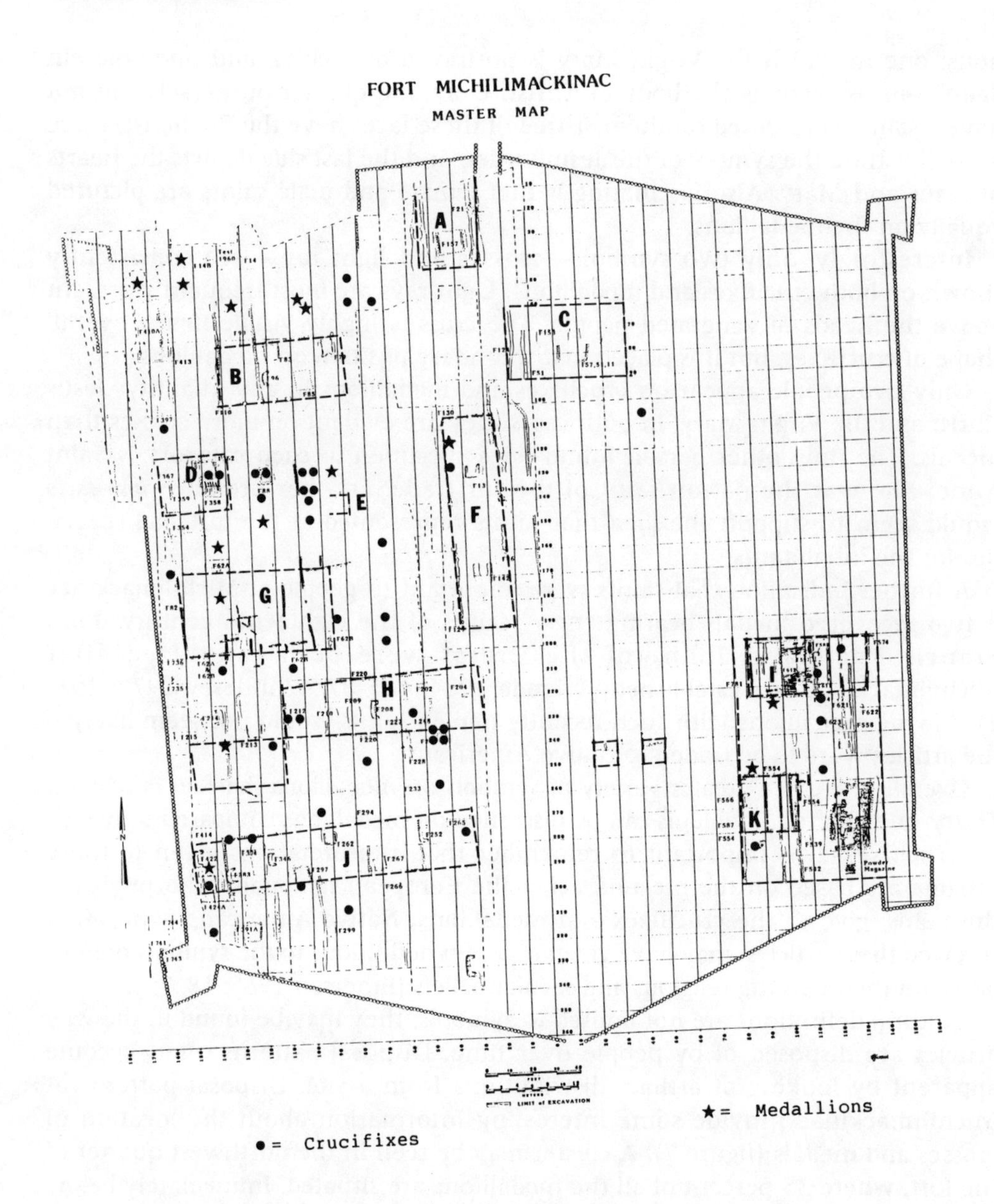

Figure 7. Crucifix and Medallion Distribution. Courtesy of Mackinac State Historic Parks.

Letter Codes

A = British Provisions Storehouse
B = North-Northwest Row House
C = Commanding Officer's House
D = Priest's House
E = Blacksmith Shop
F = British Soldiers Barracks
G = Church
H = Southwest Row House
I = Southeast Row House
J = South-Southwest Row House
K = South-Southeast Row House

presumably for the Jesuits' use only (Gérin-Lajoie 1976: 5). No fence lines were archaeologically uncovered, though fences could have been placed in other features (see Stone 1974: 333). It is within this confined area that the greatest cross and medal concentration, in sheer numbers, is found at the fort. Adding material from inside or adjacent to the Jesuit dwelling and the church, fully 25 percent of the crucifixes and 18 percent of the medallions are positioned in the religious activity area. This suggests that these items served religious purposes, to a degree at least. Also noteworthy is the fact that one cross was retrieved from the forge area north of the priests' house. The area encircling this dwelling could date to the 1715-1730s Delignery's Fort, an earlier settlement which had a strong emphasis on mission work (Heldman, personal communication 14 November 1986).

However, the highest crucifix and medallion concentration inside the fort is immediately outside of the British blacksmith's shop (Stone 1974: 333). The small tract is only 3 percent of the total area at Michilimackinac, but has 17 percent of the combined cross and medal sample. All crosses and medals from around the shop are complete specimens, thus indicating broken articles were not dumped here. A strong case can be made that crosses and medals were made on the site, due to the presence of so many items in such a small space.

An opposing trend may be seen with crucifix and medallion distributions in the vicinity of the church and the southwestern row houses. In this area all medals came from inside structures. Most crosses were located either inside a dwelling or adjacent to a structure, excluding objects placed with burials. In contrast, the north-northwest row house has many articles located far from the building. Differences in disposal practices (and possibly social status and religious beliefs) may be reflected in these differences.

These trends indicate the religious items served, to some extent, a religious purpose. However, since over seventy-five percent of the crucifixes and medallions were retrieved from dwellings, it may be that these objects were trade goods. Support for this claim is the lack of a common fort storage facility for trade goods, thus they are scattered in and near traders' houses (Hauser 1982: 58).

A frequency table was created to determine the number of cases in which a particular artifact type was found with a crucifix or a medallion when excavating a square. The table was devised by using the Statistical Analysis System software, commonly known as SAS (SAS Institute Inc. 1985). An interesting trend is evident: there are no instances where crucifixes and medallions are found in the same square. No other kinds of artifacts have this same absence relationship between them, suggesting that these two kinds of religious objects did not serve the same purpose.

Another interesting point is that over 70 percent of both crosses and medals having a definite cultural identification have come from British deposits. Yet there is evidence that, within the crucifix and medallion classes, certain types appear only in one period. Crucifixes of Type 1 and Type 3 are located just in British zones, while Type 4 is represented solely in French layers. Medallions which are Type 2 specimens come from British levels alone. The totals are small (thirty-seven crosses and ten medals); however, they do hint at possible stylistic changes during the course of Michilimackinac's occupation.

Some changes in design might reflect more than mere shifts in desired motifs; they may reflect a switch in function as well. For example, Type 1 and Type 4 crucifixes found in British layers are more plain than the other types. Trading of crosses would make explicit detail on such articles less necessary, unless desired by the Native Americans. Plain silver crosses dating to British contexts at Fort St. Joseph are one case that tends to affirm this statement (Hulse 1977: 164-69).

During French rule of New France, crucifixes were made mostly of brass, but British hegemony brought a change to silver crosses. Silver items became standard trade goods after ca. 1765 (Quimby 1939: 29). The fact that medallions, unlike crucifixes, did not change to silver is one more indication that they were not trade items. More fascinating, however, is that no silver crosses have been unearthed at Michilimackinac. While merely conjecture, a possible explanation for this absence is that traders who used silver objects lived outside the fort in "the suburbs." This adjacent area has yet to be excavated on any large scale, but may eventually yield such items.

Cultural differences seem apparent too through definite disposal patterning over time. A cluster of crucifixes and medallions just north of the north-northwest row house dates mostly to the British era. But two distinct patterns are noted just below this row house. First, around the priests' house the majority of the items in or adjacent to the dwelling are from French deposits. Second, a distinct change happens in the vicinity of the blacksmith shop; namely, no French specimens were recovered. All objects came from British levels. Religious activity had declined greatly by the British occupation; thus, producing so many articles may have been to use them as trade goods. In sharp contrast, only one cross was located with the French-period forge adjoining the priests' house.

In the vicinity of the church, most crucifixes are from French contexts. Burials with crosses date to this period as well. South of the church, a sharp contrast is evident between the two row houses. The south-southwest row house, and particularly its western half, contains almost exclusively French materials. Conversely, the southwest row house has crucifixes and medallions solely attributed to British levels. Both row houses were occupied throughout the life span of the fort. As mentioned earlier, the pattern of distribution around these buildings is the same. It is possible the "changes" over time may be a reflection of a change in occupants within these house units, and not due to differences in French or British life.

Pattern recognition came to the forefront of historical archaeological research during the late 1970s. As a result, several artifact group models were formulated for inter-site comparisons. Three of these patterns are relevant to the data from Michilimackinac, namely, the Carolina Pattern, the Frontier Pattern (South 1977), and the Early Fur Trade Pattern (Forsman and Gallo 1979) (see appendix A). All artifacts from excavated squares that yielded crucifixes or medallions were grouped into the categories employed in these models.

The Michilimackinac data most clearly parallels the Frontier Pattern. With the Frontier Pattern all artifacts are placed into one of the following groups: Kitchen, Architecture, Furniture, Arms, Clothing, Personal, Pipes, or Activities (South 1977: 145). Any deviations from expected artifact percentage ranges are due to the large amount of goods for the fur trade (see appendix B). Trade activity is reflected throughout the occupation of Michilimackinac, despite a growing emphasis on military activity after 1761.

A difficulty arises with inter- and intra-site comparisons at Michilimackinac. Continuous excavation of the site for over thirty years has been accomplished by assorted field methods. Early field operations made use of shovels, three-inch vertical levels, and screens generally with one-third-inch mesh (Maxwell and Binford 1961: 20). Since the mid 1970s, field-work has employed strictly trowels, two-tenths-of-a-foot vertical levels (which is slightly over two inches), and screening through meshes of one-quarter and one-eighth inch in size; water from a garden hose is used to force soil through the one-eighth-inch window screen (Halchin 1985: 56-57, 66-67). Thus, artifact retrieval rates have been different. Over half of the fort was excavated using the early procedures (Halchin 1985: 56). As a consequence, some artifact groupings are lacking in numbers since those items which were very small fell through the larger-meshed screens. The category most affected is Clothing, since tiny seed beads make up the vast majority of this class (e.g., Heldman and Grange 1981: 210). Despite this problem, however, information about patterned behavior may be gained.

Research at Michilimackinac in the last decade has produced two typologies which are better interpretative guides for analyzing patterned behavior at this location. Heldman and Grange (1981: 209-10) formulated artifact groups that more clearly illustrate the importance of objects used in the fur trade and in everyday life (see appendix C). The names of their artifact categories are: Ceramics, Bottles, Activities, Architecture, Arms, Clothing, Military, Beads, Trade Goods, Kitchen, and Pipes. The eleven artifact groups are then combined into five general fuctional categories: Kitchen, Building, Arms, Trade, and Life.

The Kitchen category is made up of the Ceramic, Bottle, and Kitchen classes. Kitchen items more than quadrupled from French to British contexts for both crucifixes and medallions. Cultural influences may be the reason for this shift. Heldman and Grange (1981: 56) concluded: "The contrast between British and French styles of living at the fort is considerable, as seen in ceramic changes, especially in view of the fact that the late ceramics tend to be fine earthenwares and porcelains." Thus, the social and economic status of British inhabitants was much higher than their French counterparts.

In the second category, Building (or Architecture), crosses increased and medals decreased over the two periods. The reason for this inverse relationship is positively linked at Michilimackinac to where these objects were deposited. Calculations show crucifixes were found in or adjacent to French structures 45 percent of the time and 54 percent for British buildings. Medallions were unearthed from 67 percent French, but only 29 percent British structures.

With the Arms group, crucifixes more than doubled in total for this heading, but the number associated with medals fell slightly. The results in the crucifix class follow previously observed patterns for Arms (Heldman and Grange 1981: 207; Halchin 1985: 178).

The general Trade category is composed of the Trade Goods and Bead classes. The quantity of articles found with crosses was ten times greater in the British than the French layers. On the other hand, medals dropped a fairly substantial degree.

The Life group is made up of the Activities, Clothing, Military, and Pipe classes. The Life heading illustrated a large decline in crosses over time, to one-third less during the British than the French era. Conversely, the medal totals climbed over the same period. Since by definition this category represents much of the "ordinary" day-to-day behavior (Heldman and Grange 1981: 214), the inverse relationship between crucifixes and medallions suggests these articles were utilized in different ways during the French and British occupations.

Another important artifact taxonomy for colonial Michilimackinac is that of Jill Y. Halchin. She has stated that a problem is introduced when including architectural materials for determining behavioral patterns: "Such structural materials made up the building itself and did not serve in a functional role in daily life in quite the same fashion as do less fixed items, such as a bowl or a bale seal" (1985: 113). She contends that true pattern distribution is concealed by building remnants. Halchin (1985: 115-16) has determined twelve artifact categories that more clearly point towards functional use than some of the headings utilized in other artifact studies. These classes are: Activity, Beads, Clothing, Craft, Gun Parts, Kitchen, Jewelry, Military, Pipes, Sewing, Trade, and Shot (see appendix D).

Nearly all of the groups have been covered earlier in this paper. However, two of them require further explanation. One of these groups is Shot. Although not mentioned specifically, it likely was added because it is a single artifact type "with several functions and. . .viewed in conjunction with more than one other group" (Halchin 1985: 114). The second heading is Craft, experimentally included in Halchin's study with the hypothesis that at a frontier settlement inhabitants would have to locally produce many items they needed. The group consists of brass wire and metal scraps/sheets. The belief is that these materials were utilized to make and/or repair trade goods and other base metal objects (Halchin 1985: 167, 169).

One benefit of Halchin's system is that it may clearly show differences in craft production and activities items that would be lost by lumping both groups together. The two categories decreased significantly with respect to crosses and medals during the British occupation. The drop in the Activity category was greatest with medals. On the other hand, crucifixes had a greater decline with the Craft group. The results suggest that craft-related practices were not carried out to make crosses or medals as trade goods. Or possibly the Craft class illustrates items made for other groups, like Activity and Shot. Moreover, as mentioned earlier, crosses and medals were cast. If they were made on site, they would leave few metal scraps compared to the manufacture of other objects (e.g., lead shot, tinkling cones).

In summary, historical documents have provided information about religious activity within Michilimackinac. The earliest known map is Lotbinière's (1749), which details the owners of certain houses and specific activity areas. Later maps and sketches indicate the religious zone was relatively stable over time. Apparent from the results is the fact that religious motivations played a minor role compared to those of the fur trade and military at the fort. Yet, in the beginning, all three spheres were fairly equal in importance. In fact, the Jesuit missionaries were on the scene first at the Straits of Mackinac, prior to the building of Michilimackinac. Through time, though, economic and military concerns came to far outweigh the religious activities.

A few trends become obvious from intra-site archaeological analysis of Michilimackinac that illuminate the differences between crucifixes and medallions. The two artifact group classification systems employed at the site—Heldman-Grange's and Halchin's—both reflect that artifacts associated with fur trade activities increase with crosses and decrease with medals over time. The fur trade grew more prosperous during the British era. The fact that the amount of trade-related goods linked with crucifixes rose seems to indicate that such "religious" items became part of the economic exchange network. The subsequent decrease in medals would seem to prove these objects were not tied to the fur trade; likely they were used and kept in sections of dwellings apart from trade materials and were personal effects.

Future intra-site comparisons at Michilimackinac should use a combination of the Heldman-Grange and Halchin artifact categories. Heldman and Grange provide separate headings for Ceramics and Bottles, which is helpful since some bottles surely were for trade and not domestic use. They also remove Beads and Trade Goods from the more general Clothing group. Both of these classes represent trade activity. Lastly, Heldman and Grange's system, in the creation of their five general groups, illustrates the importance of the fur trade at Michilimackinac.

Halchin's taxonomy has benefits as well. Separating craft-related items from the Activity group more visibly shows how crucial local manufacturing was in the French period. Also, daily life is more easily recognized when the Architecture class is eliminated. The best artifact group analysis would take all of the Heldman and Grange headings, divide some classes further as Halchin did, and remove the Architecture group, such that changes over time of artifacts utilized in certain ways can better be observed.

CONCLUSIONS

There is strong evidence that crucifixes and medallions functioned in different ways at Michilimackinac during the French and British eras. Historical documents point to the initial distribution of crosses and medals in New France by Jesuit missionaries. The earliest French occupation at Michilimackinac shows these articles served religious purposes. Crosses and medals were found only in a few areas, and most were situated in the area of religious activity (i.e., the ecclesiastical properties) at the fort. Also, crucifixes and medallions are overwhelmingly made of brass. In addition, several artifact groups are comparable in order of rank for crosses and medals. Yet the contrasts found in other artifact groups from French levels hint that these two types of items might have been used differently even then.

Clear evidence for multiple and varied uses may be observed with information from the British contexts. Dissimilarities between crucifixes and medallions are illustrated in the areas of deposit, artifact group percentages, and number of different single artifact types (i.e., awls, cuff links, etc.) observed with each artifact category. The results show more pronounced differences than in French layers. The finding which best explains the possible functional difference of the objects, however, is that a cross and a medal have yet to be associated together in the same excavation unit.

The overall results indicate medallions were most likely utilized solely as religious objects at Michilimackinac, by either Jesuit missionaries or Catholic inhabitants. Medals served this purpose throughout occupation of the fort. Crosses apparently underwent a change in function over time, originally having been used in religious activities. During the British period, however, crucifixes seem to have become another commodity in the fur trade.

APPENDIX A:
ARTIFACT GROUP PERCENTAGES FOR THE CAROLINA, FRONTIER, AND EARLY FUR TRADE PATTERNS

	Carolina	Frontier	Early Fur Trade
Kitchen	63.10	27.60	4.64
Architecture	25.50	52.00	6.79
Furniture	0.20	0.20	0.05
Arms	0.50	5.40	4.54
Clothing	3.00	1.70	65.50
Personal	0.20	0.20	8.22
Pipes	5.80	9.10	6.12
Activities	1.70	3.70	4.14

APPENDIX B: SOUTH'S ARTIFACT CATEGORIES

	French Crosses		French Medals	
	#	%	#	%
Kitchen	14	5.26	19	6.69
Architecture	130	48.87	216	76.06
Furniture	0	-	0	-
Arms	8	3.00	6	2.11
Clothing	4	1.50	18	6.34
Personal	1	0.38	1	0.35
Pipe	5	1.88	2	0.70
Activities	104	39.10	22	7.75
Totals	266	99.99	284	100.00

	British Crosses		British Medals	
	#	%	#	%
Kitchen	275	17.78	76	18.63
Architecture	846	54.59	240	58.82
Furniture	1	0.06	1	0.24
Arms	112	7.24	5	1.23
Clothing	162	10.47	31	7.60
Personal	1	0.06	1	0.24
Pipe	66	4.27	33	8.09
Activities	84	5.43	21	5.15
Totals	1547	100.00	408	100.00

APPENDIX C: HELDMAN AND GRANGE'S ARTIFACT GROUPS

	French Crosses		French Medals	
	#	%	#	%
Ceramics	11	4.13	3	1.06
Bottles	2	0.75	6	2.11
Activities	105	39.47	26	9.15
Architecture	130	48.87	216	76.06
Arms	8	3.00	6	2.11
Clothing	2	0.75	1	0.35
Military	1	0.38	1	0.35
Beads	1	0.38	13	4.58
Trade Goods	1	0.38	8	2.82
Kitchen	0	-	2	0.70
Pipes	5	1.88	2	0.70
Totals	266	99.99	284	99.99

CONTINUED ON NEXT PAGE

APPENDIX C: HELDMAN AND GRANGE'S ARTIFACT GROUPS (CONT.)

	French Crosses		French Medals	
	#	%	#	%
KITCHEN	13	4.89	11	3.87
BUILDING	130	48.87	216	76.06
ARMS	8	3.00	6	2.11
TRADE	2	0.75	21	7.39
LIFE	113	42.48	30	10.56
Totals	266	99.99	284	99.99

	British Crosses		British Medals	
	#	%	#	%
Ceramics	174	11.25	54	13.24
Bottles	58	3.75	12	2.94
Activities	86	5.56	20	4.90
Architecture	846	54.69	240	58.82
Arms	112	7.24	5	1.23
Clothing	27	1.74	9	2.20
Military	15	0.97	7	1.72
Beads	80	5.17	8	1.96
Trade Goods	53	3.43	11	2.70
Kitchen	30	1.94	9	2.20
Pipes	66	4.27	33	8.09
Totals	1547	100.01	408	100.00
KITCHEN	262	16.94	75	18.38
BUILDING	846	54.69	240	58.82
ARMS	112	7.24	5	1.23
TRADE	133	8.60	19	4.66
LIFE	194	12.54	69	16.91
Totals	1547	100.01	408	100.00

APPENDIX D: HALCHIN'S ARTIFACT GROUPS

	French Crosses		French Medals	
	#	%	#	%
Activity	14	10.29	17	25.00
Beads	1	0.73	13	19.12
Clothing	2	1.47	1	1.47
Craft	92	67.65	10	14.71
Gun Parts	8	5.88	5	7.35
Kitchen	11	8.09	11	16.18

CONTINUED ON NEXT PAGE

APPENDIX D: HALCHIN'S ARTIFACT GROUPS (CONT.)

	French Crosses		French Medals	
	#	%	#	%
Jewelry	1	0.73	0	-
Military	1	0.73	1	1.47
Pipes	5	3.68	2	2.94
Sewing	0	-	0	-
Trade	1	0.73	7	10.29
Shot	0	-	1	1.47
Totals	136	99.98	68	100.00

	British Crosses		British Medals	
	#	%	#	%
Activity	32	4.56	6	3.57
Beads	80	11.41	8	4.76
Clothing	27	3.85	9	5.36
Craft	33	4.71	11	6.55
Gun Parts	48	6.85	4	2.38
Kitchen	275	39.23	76	45.24
Jewelry	1	0.14	0	-
Military	17	2.43	7	4.17
Pipes	66	9.42	33	19.64
Sewing	14	2.00	2	1.19
Trade	46	6.56	11	6.55
Shot	62	8.84	1	0.60
Totals	701	100.00	168	100.01

REFERENCES

Attwater, Donald, ed. 1958. *A Catholic Dictionary (The Catholic Encyclopedic Dictionary).* New York: The Macmillan Company.

Brown, Margaret Kimball. 1976. *The 1974 Fort de Chartres Excavation Project.* Archaeological Service Report no. 49. Carbondale: University Museum, Southern Illinois University.

Emerson, Ellen Russell. 1965. *Indian Myths or Legends, Traditions, and Symbols of the Aborigines of America: Compared with Those of Other Countries Including Hindostan, Egypt, Persia, Assyria, and China.* Minneapolis: Ross & Haines.

Forsman, Michael R. A., and Joseph G. Gallo. 1979. "The Problem of Archaeological Diversity, Synthesis and Comparison." In *Conference of Historic Site Archaeology Papers,* vol. 13, edited by Stanley South, 238-52. Columbia: South Carolina Institute of Archaeology and Anthropology.

Gérin-Lajoie, Marie. 1976. Fort Michilimackinac in 1749, Lotbinière's Plan and Description. *Mackinac History,* vol. 2, leaflet no. 5, Mackinac Island, Mich.: Mackinac Island State Park Commission.

Halchin, Jill Y. 1985. *Excavations at Fort Michilimackinac, 1983-1985: House C of the Southeast Row House, the Solomon-Levy-Parant House*. Archaeological Completion Report Series, no. 11. Mackinac Island, Mich.: Mackinac Island State Park Commission.

Hauser, Judith Ann. 1982. *Jesuit Rings from Fort Michilimackinac and Other European Contact Sites*. Archaeological Completion Report Series, no. 5. Mackinac Island, Mich.: Mackinac Island State Park Commission.

Heldman, Donald P. 1980. "Coins at Michilimackinac." *Historical Archaeology* 14: 82-107.

Heldman, Donald P., and Roger T. Grange, Jr. 1981. *Excavation at Fort Michilimackinac, 1978-1979: The Rue de la Babillarde*. Archaeological Completion Report Series, no. 3. Mackinac Island, Mich.: Mackinac Island State Park Commission.

Hodder, Ian, ed. 1982. *Symbolic and Structural Archaeology*. Cambridge: Cambridge University Press.

Hulse, Charles A. 1977. "An Archaeological Evaluation of Fort St. Joseph: An Eighteenth Century Military Post and Settlement in Berrien County, Michigan." Master's thesis, Department of Anthropology, Michigan State University, East Lansing, Michigan.

Jennings, Francis. 1975. *The Invasion of America: Indians, Colonialism, and the Cant of Conquest*. New York: W. W. Norton.

Kellogg, Louise Phelps. 1968. *The French Régime in Wisconsin and the Northwest*. New York: Cooper Square.

Maxwell, Moreau S., and Lewis H. Binford. 1961. *Excavation at Fort Michilimackinac, Mackinac City, Michigan: 1959 Season*. Publications of the Museum, Cultural Series, vol. 1, no. 1. East Lansing, Mich.: Michigan State University Museum.

Neitzel, Robert S. 1965. Archaeology of the Fatherland Site: The Grand Village of the Natchez. *Anthropological Papers of the American Museum of Natural History* 51(1): 1-108.

New Catholic Encyclopedia. 1967. Volume 2.Washington, D.C.: The Catholic University of America.

Parkman, Francis, Jr. 1851. *History of the Conspiracy of Pontiac, and the War of the North American Tribes Against the English Colonies after the Conquest of Canada*. Boston: Charles C. Little and James Brown.

Petersen, Eugene T. 1964. *Gentlemen on the Frontier: A Pictorial Record of the Culture of Michilimackinac*. Mackinac Island, Mich.: Mackinac Island State Park Commission.

Quebec Papers. n.d. David McCrae & Co. of Michilimackinac Accounts with William and John Kay of Montreal, 1777-1787. Originals in the Quebec Papers, vol. B, 75: 170-241. Toronto Public Libraries.

Quimby, George I. 1939. European Trade Articles as Chronological Indicators for the Archaeology of the Historic Period in Michigan. *Papers of the Michigan Academy of Science, Arts, and Letters* 24: 25-31.

SAS Institute, Inc. 1985. *SAS Introductory Guide for Personal Computers*. Cary, N.C.: SAS Institute.

South, Stanley. 1977. *Method and Theory in Historical Archaeology*. New York: Academic Press.

Stone, Lyle M. 1974. *Fort Michilimackinac 1715-1781: An Archaeological Perspective on the Revolutionary Frontier*. Publications of the Museum, East Lansing, Mich.: Michigan State University Museum. In cooperation with the Mackinac Island State Park Commission, Mackinac Island, Michigan.

Thwaites, Reuben Gold. 1896-1901. *The Jesuit Relations and Allied Documents*. 73 vols. Cleveland: The Burrows Brothers.

Tylenda, Joseph N., S. J. 1984. *Jesuit Saints and Martyrs: Short Biographies of the Saints, Blessed, Venerables, and Servants of God of the Society of Jesus*. Chicago: Loyola University Press.

Whittlesey, E. S. 1972. *Symbols and Legends in Western Art: A Museum Guide*. New York: Charles Scribner's Sons.

Part V

Archaeology and Material Culture

A Newly-Discovered Trade Gun Type

James R. Duncan

The archaeological record throughout the eastern United States supports a picture of keen competition between Great Britain, France and, to a lesser degree, Spain, for control of the North American fur trade. Distinct small-bore gun barrel fragments, gun parts, and lead shot and bullets from the Plattner site (23SA3) in western Missouri are proof of this competition, and they provide much of the data for research on what appears to be a new and previously unidentified English trade gun type.

It is the purpose of this article to reconstruct and identify small-bore trade guns—guns with bores of .50 caliber (one-half inch) and less—out of a substantial archaeological assemblage of gun parts from several Osage Indian villages in Missouri. In so doing, the discovery of a new trade gun type will be proposed.

The primary site, known as the Plattner site (23SA3) (figure 1), was the Little Osage village on the Missouri River in Saline County, Missouri. Today this site is on the National Register of Historic Places. Several archaeological excavations have been conducted at the Plattner site and at least two more collections have resulted from amateur surface collecting when the site was under cultivation. These collections have been the subject of several monographs (Chapman 1959; Hamilton 1960; Bray 1978).

In 1717 the Little Osage (*Petit Osage*) lived in a village near the historic Missouri Indians and actively engaged in a brisk trade with the French (Chapman 1959: 2; Mathews 1961: 169). By 1723 the French had built Fort d'Orleans near these villages of the Little Osage and the Missouris. Most archaeological materials recovered from the Little Osage village (23SA3) are of European origin, and limited amounts of Native American artifacts indicate that the Little Osage were by this time reliant upon goods of European manufacture (Chapman 1959: 14). Included among these artifacts are bottle glass (Bray 1978), numerous gun parts, lead bullets and shot, and gunflints.

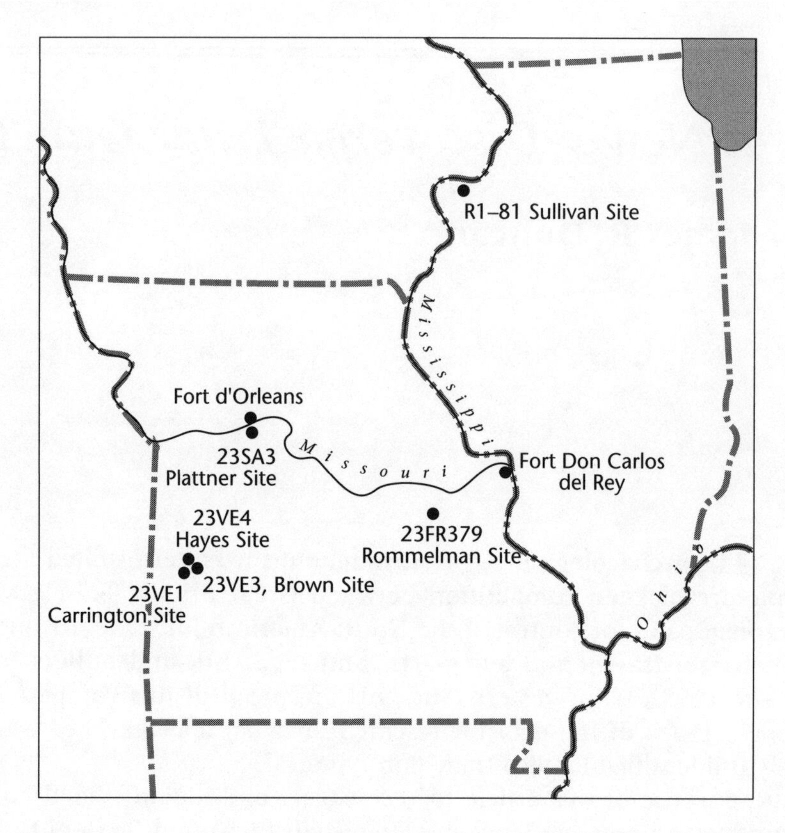

Figure 1. The locations of historic Osage villages and associated archaeological sites in Missouri and Illinois.

BACKGROUND

By 1770 Spanish authorities in Missouri were alarmed because of hostile activities of the Osage, who were using English guns to attack Indians loyal to the Spanish. The Osage had succeeded in driving several groups of these Indians into the area around San Antonio, Texas. The Spanish established Fort Don Carlos del Rey at the mouth of the Missouri River near St. Louis to discourage English traders from ascending the river with their trade goods. Neither the fort nor an associated mission survived very long. A covert action of the Spanish in 1773 resulted in the destruction of the Little Osage and Missouri villages in Saline County and ended the Indian occupation of the Plattner site.

DATA

Of eight (8) measurable gun barrel fragments from Plattner (23SA3), three (3), or 38 percent of the total, are of .50 caliber or less. A check of measurable barrel sections from the archaeological collections from three other historic

Osage sites disclose comparable percentages of small bore barrels: from the Carrington site (23VE1), 35 of 89 (39 percent); from the Brown site (23VE3), 3 of 13 (23 percent); and from the Hayes site (23VE4), 1 of 4 (25 percent) (Hamilton 1960, 81). These figures suggest that small-bore guns were of importance to these Native Americans. One problem with reconstruction of small-bore guns is the absence of complete guns for comparative purposes. To date, none have been recovered by archaeologists, and until recently none were known from private collections.

From the archaeological record it is apparent that several types of trade guns manufactured during the eighteenth century were standardized types specifically intended for the fur trade (Hamilton 1980: 29). At least two French types and one English type are currently recognized and seem to have been manufactured solely for trade with Native North Americans. Other types are also represented in the archaeological record, including military guns and some exclusively for civilian use. Also evident is the presence of "grades" of quality in the finished products. Moreover, the probability of various grades of trade guns is supported by a number of historic accounts which mention "fine guns" and "common guns."

A scatter chart of lead balls, bullets, or shot from 23SA3 shows two major clusters of specific sizes of shot (figure 2). The larger shot cluster ranges from 32 to 26 to the *Livre* (French weight) size, that is, the common French sizes (Hamilton 1980: 130). The other shot cluster falls in the 40 to the *Livre*, or small size shot from .46 to .50 caliber. It is this smaller cluster and the small-bore barrel fragments which have puzzled scholars for many years.

In 1986 George Carroll reported in the *Kentucky Rifle Association Bulletin* on an unusual gun. This gun was found in the Louisville, Kentucky area and its history prior to 1986 is unknown. Presumably the gun was restocked in the 1790s. The furniture, consisting of side plate and trigger guard, are of English manufacture. (For colonial firearm nomenclature, see Hamilton 1976: plates 1, 2, and 3, pages 3 and 5.) The barrel has a bore diameter of .52 caliber, excluding the muzzle which measures .54 caliber. The side plate is identical to a broken section shown in figure 42 of Hamilton's 1960 report on gun parts from the Big Osage village (23VE1) in western Missouri. Hamilton (1980: fig. 56A) also illustrates a complete side plate, identical to the one on the Louisville gun, which Hamilton attributes to collections in the Museum of the Alabama Department of Archives and History. Additionally, Hamilton gives the proveniences of two other fragmentary side plates from Fort Frederica, Georgia, and the Plattner site (23SA3).

The buttplate of the Louisville gun is missing; however, the shape of the finial is preserved in outline in the stock and is of the spiked finial type. Thus, this buttplate is of English manufacture. Similar examples have been found at Plattner (23SA3) and another Osage site (23VE1) in Missouri; at the Sullivan site, R1-81, on the south side of the Rock River south of Rock Island, Illinois; near Montgomery, Alabama; from the Avon Bridge site in New York; from Fort Frederica, St. Simon's Island, Georgia; and from Jamestown, Virginia (figure 3).

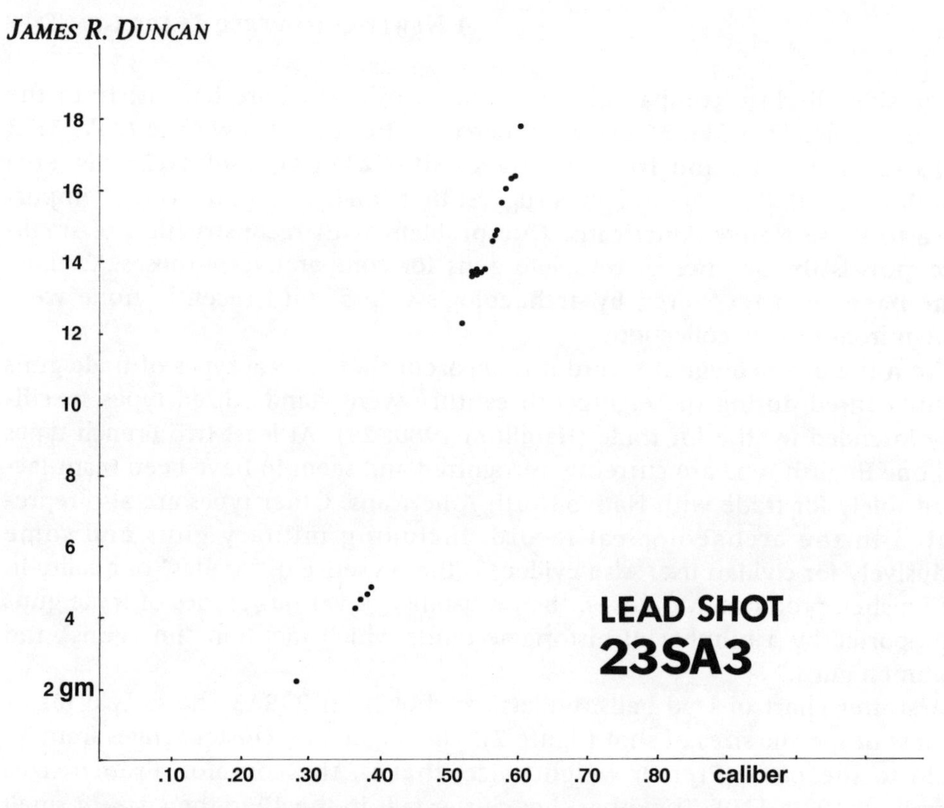

Figure 2. Distribution of bullets or balls from 23SA3, the Plattner Site.

While the photographs of the trigger guard of the Louisville gun are not clear, it appears nonetheless to be of English manufacture, with a three-lobed finial. Examples of the trigger guard have been found in Illinois, on the Sullivan site (R1-81); in Georgia at Fort Frederica; in Alabama at a site near Montgomery (Hamilton 1968: fig. 13); in Michigan at Michilimackinac (Hamilton 1976: fig. 109-1); and possibly in Missouri from the Plattner site (23SA3) (Hamilton 1960: fig. 45).

The lock of the Louisville gun has a flat plate with a flat, bevelled cock and no supporting arm from the pan to the frizzen screw. The barrel has two marks, the London gunmaker's company viewed and proof marks to the left of center near the breech. Recently a colleague contributed photographs of a complete gun similar to the Louisville gun. The photographs show a buttplate with a spiked finial and a trigger guard with an engraved star on the bow; it displays a crudely cast acanthus foliate motif in front of the bow. The side plate is coarsely engraved and is in a rococo foliated design similar in style to the Louisville gun side plate and the side plates from the Plattner site (23SA3) and from Fort Frederica, Georgia.

This gun, named the Arrow Rock gun (figure 4) has a round barrel with a bore of .565 inch or 32 caliber French (Hamilton 1980; 1991). The top of the barrel near the breech is stamped "London," with "Birmingham" viewed and proof marks immediately left of the "London" stamp. Both the barrel and the forestock have been shortened. The lock plate is marked "Ketland & Co" in

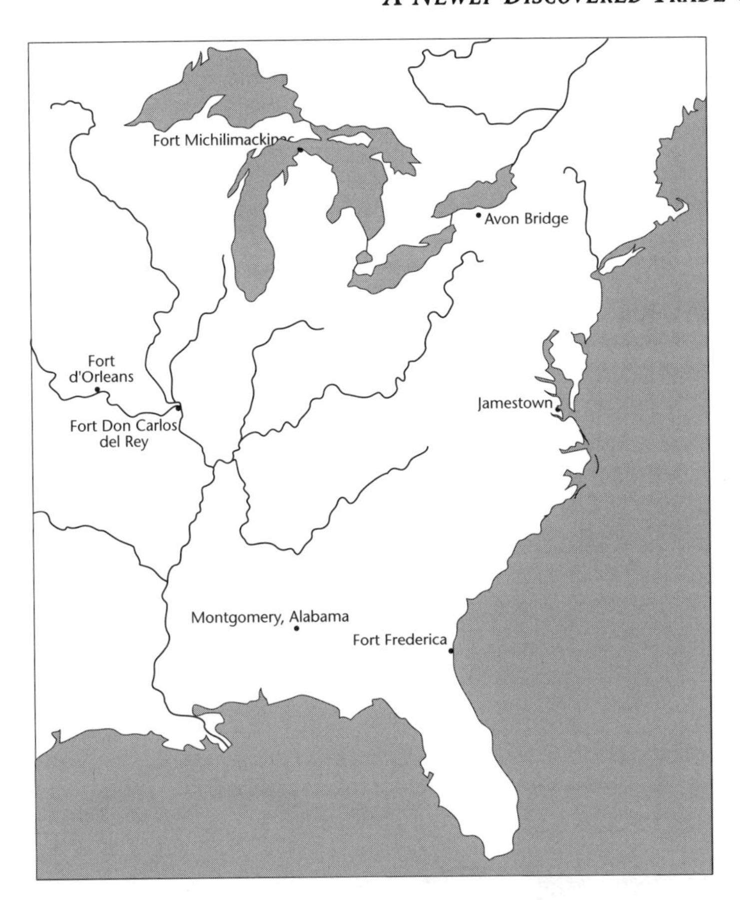

Figure 3. Other archaeological sites referred to in this report; several are associated with English small bore trade guns.

front of the hammer and has "United States" stamped on the tail. The lock plate is flat with a rounded edge and has been converted to percussion. A similar, well-preserved lock plate was found at an antique show in 1989 in Mackinaw City, Michigan. During an NSF-supported field survey of a group of archaeological sites in Missouri, 1989-1991, a six-inch section of barrel, smooth bore with a bore diameter of .490 inch, was found along with some other historic materials at the Rommelman site (23FR379). From the Louisville gun, the Arrow Rock gun, and a closely-related English gun pictured by Hamilton in 1980, it is possible to make the following reconstruction of what may be a hitherto unknown trade gun type.

This small-bore English trade gun (figure 5) has a spiked finial buttplate of brass with outline engraving of the finial and sometimes a rococo design, suggesting foliage in the center of the finial. The brass trigger guard has a three-lobed front finial, suggesting acanthus leaves on better-quality guns, with a small "comma"-shaped trigger loop. The distinctive brass side plate supports two lock bolts and has a rococo design representing foliage. The lock plate is flat and

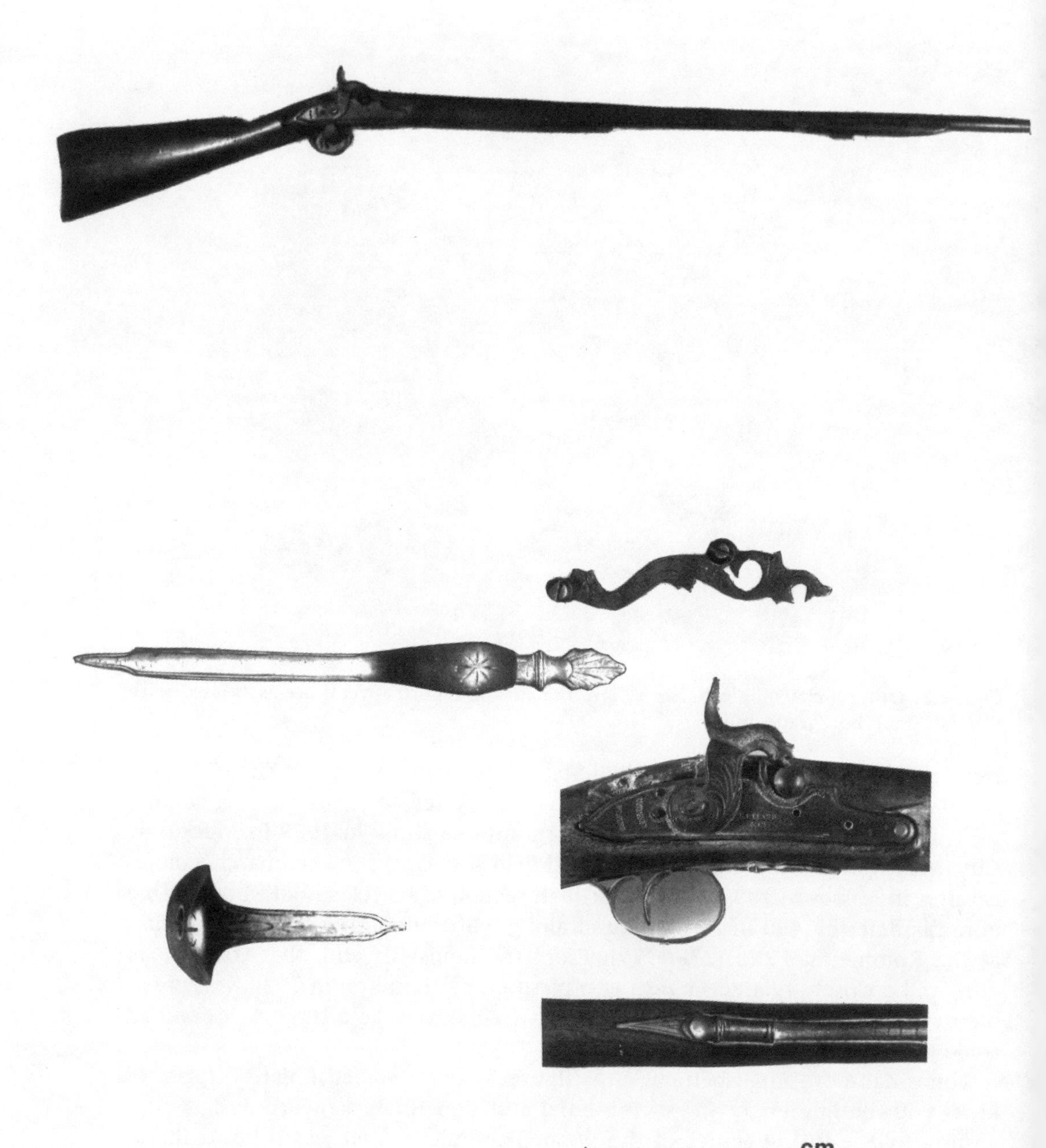

Figure 4. An English trade gun, the Arrow Rock gun, with a bore of .565 inches.

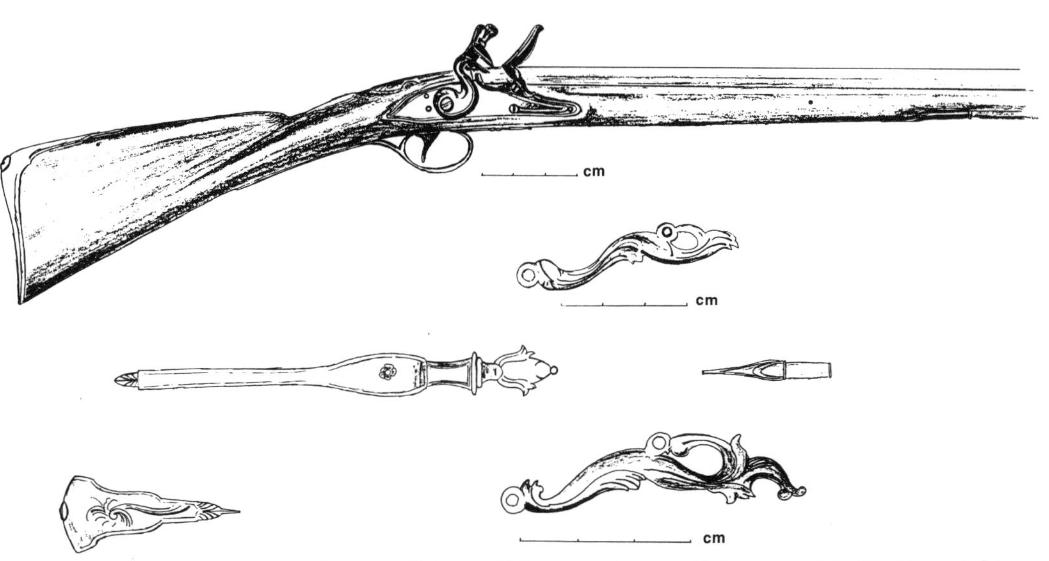

Figure 5. Reconstruction of an English small bore trade gun of the second half of the eighteenth century. Parts of the gun from top to bottom. Top: side view of the entire gun, lock plate center left with trigger and tigger guard beneath; cock attached on left half of lock plate with frizzen and frizzen spring opposing it on the right. Below: side plate; trigger guard; entry pipe; buttplate (top view), side plate. Drawing by James R. Duncan.

the cock is flat. There are no pan or tumbler bridles. The entry pipe has a spiked extension inletted into the forearm and is similar to mid-eighteenth-century English military fusils. The breech is usually one inch wide and octagonally faceted for about one-third of the total barrel length.

While Hamilton stated in 1960 that he thought the French made the small bore guns, he recanted in 1980 and speculated that possibly the Spanish, but more likely the English, created this new trade gun. Recent research seems to support all of Hamilton's speculation. Hanson, in his 1988 article in *The Museum of the Fur Trade Quarterly*, pictures a French gun of .51 caliber with hybrid furniture. Hanson also shows a late seventeenth-century trade gun of Dutch manufacture and gives the caliber range as .50 to .60 (Hamilton 1960). While it is possible that most of the small-bore guns are of English manufacture, the discovery of a complete small bore French trade gun would seem to complicate matters.

A survey of 124 eighteenth-century American guns, as described by Shumway (1980) discloses that 52 percent of guns commonly called Kentucky rifles are smooth bores, and that 20 percent of those have bores of .50 caliber or less. The advantage of a small bore is *economy*. When lead and gun powder were expensive commodities, requiring many hours of trapping and hide preparation in exchange for decent amounts of each, economical small bore guns would have had a widespread appeal. Furthermore, Native American hunters were skillful enough to close in on game and birds, and even dispatch large game animals, with small-bore guns.

With regard to the chronological placement of the newly discovered trade gun, fragments of it found on the Plattner (23SA3) and Big Osage (23VE1) sites in Missouri certainly postdate the French and Indian War. The Osage were allies of the French and did not trade in any quantity with the English until after 1763. But the English trade with the Osage was in full swing at the time the Spanish assumed jurisdiction over the Louisiana Territory. In 1773, after the attack on the Little Osage by Sauk and Fox Indians, who were aided covertly by the Spanish, many survivors had already abandoned Plattner (23SA3) in western Missouri.

Therefore, the English small-bore gun could not have occurred at Plattner in any great numbers after 1773. Fort Frederica, near present-day Brunswick, Georgia, was occupied between 1739 and 1749. These two sites, containing small-bore English gun parts, place the small-bore trade gun in the southeastern United States between about 1739 and 1773. If the small-bore guns were in use about ten years before they were damaged and discarded, then the gun type would have been made no earlier than 1730. The use of rococo decorative motifs is certainly of eighteenth-century origin, and the small-bore trade gun probably survived into the early nineteenth century (Hamilton 1980: 96).

Conclusion

While guns described in this paper exhibit some variation, a sufficient degree of similarity exists to consider them a distinct group or type of trade gun. As early as 1638, the English were manufacturing two varieties of "slight" or light guns for export to North Africa in the saltpeter trade (Stern 1954: 83). These were called Barbary guns and Guiny guns. The Barbary guns were small bore, less than musket bore, and were referred to as a "full Barbary bore." The Guiny guns were of "full pistol bore," with a diameter of .580 inch, the bore of military holster pistols of the period between 1645 and 1660 (Blair 1968: 102). Stern states that the "full Barbary bore" was larger than the Guiny bore (Stern 1954: 84).

References from the first half of the eighteenth century indicate that several types of English trade guns were being sold by Edward Annely, a New York gunsmith, who ran the following advertisement: ". . .a large assortment of guns and pistols, all of Tower [London?] proof; also birding pieces, etc. The right sort of Indian guns with barrels and locks of all sorts." (*New York Gazette*, 1 August 1748; Kauffman, 1952: 67).

Archaeological fragments and complete guns discussed in this paper probably represent examples manufactured between 1730 and 1825. The Louisville and a related gun pictured by Hamilton in 1980 seem to have London proof marks of this period. Moreover, the guns discussed in this paper probably represent a distinct type manufactured in England from 1770 to 1825. The Arrow Rock gun has Birmingham marks used after 1812 (Lindsay 1967: 228). The bores are small, .490 inch to .565 inch, 35 gauge to 23 gauge by Lotbinière's table (Hamilton 1980: 169). These guns were fullstock with an entry pipe with a pointed tail. The side plate is of a common pattern used from 1720 on English pistols, fusils, and fowling pieces. This pattern has a flat brass side plate with two bolt holes. The shape is of an extended "s" with a foliated rococo motif. The earliest known record of this plate is an ornate design from a French pattern book dated to 1657 (Held 1978: 99).

These guns were only a small part of a larger array manufactured to satisfy a dynamic market. Continued archaeological and collections research is needed to further understand this fascinating aspect of the North American fur trade.

REFERENCES

Blair, Claude. 1968. *Pistols of the World*, New York: Viking Press.

Bray, Robert T. 1978. "European Trade Goods from the Utz Site and the Search for Fort Orleans," *The Missouri Archaeologist*, 39 (December): 1-75.

Carroll, George. 1986. "A Smooth Rifle Built from Early Trade Gun Parts," *The Kentucky Rifle Association Bulletin* 13 (1).

Chapman, Carl H. 1959. "The Little Osage and Missouri Indian Village Sites ca. 1727-1777 A.D.," *The Missouri Archaeologist* 13 (1).

Hamilton, T. M., comp. 1960. "Indian Trade Guns," *The Missouri Archaeologist* 22 (December).

______. 1968. *Early Indian Trade Guns. 1625-1775*. Contributions of the Museum of the Great Plains, no. 3: 1-38

______. 1976. *Firearms on the Frontier: Guns at Fort Michilimackinac 1715-1781*. Reports in Mackinac History and Archaeology, Mackinac Island State Park Commission, no. 5.

______. 1980. *Colonial Frontier Guns*. Chadron, Nebraska: The Fur Press.

______. 1985. "The Osage Guns and Gunflints." In *Osage and Missouri Indian Life Cultural Change: 1675-1825*, chp. 6, prt. 4. Final report on National Endowment for the Humanities Research Grant RS-20296, 31 December 1985.

______. 1991. Personal Correspondence, March 1991.

Hanson, Charles E., Jr. 1988. "A Brass Mounted French Trade Gun," *The Museum of the Fur Trade Quarterly* 24 (3): 12-13.

Held, Robert. 1978. *The Age of Firearms*. New York: Bonanza Books.

Lindsay, Merrell. 1967. *One Hundred Great Guns*. New York: Walker and Co.

Kauffman, Henry J. 1952. *Early American Gunsmiths*. New York: Bramhall House.

Mathews, John Joseph. 1961. *The Osage Children of the Middle Waters*, Norman: University of Oklahoma Press.

Peterson, Harold L. 1956. *Arms and Armor in Colonial America 1526-1783*. New York: Bramhall House.

Shumway, George. 1980. *Rifles of Colonial America*, vols. 1 and 2, York, Penn.: G. Shumway, Publisher: 3-655

______. 1988. "Longrifles of Note." *Muzzle Blasts*, 50 (3).

Stern, Walter M. 1954. "Gunmaking in Seventeenth Century London." *Journal of the Arms and Armor Society* 1 (5): 55-100.

When Rivers Were Roads: Deciphering the Role of Canoe Portages in the Western Lake Superior Fur Trade

Douglas A. Birk

When Europeans entered the northern lake-forest regions of North America, they found an intricate network of canoe trails in use by indigenous populations. Carrying places, like land bridges, bypassed obstacles and linked waterways, contributing to the efficiency of what was truly a remarkable inland water transportation system. In regions south and west of the Great Lakes, most of the portage-based canoe trails have now been abandoned in favor of other modes and lanes of transportation. Today archaeologists look upon the old canoe portages, routes, and route systems as past expressions of human adaptation and ingenuity and as vital parts of a natural world that shaped and channeled human behavior. Like historical artifacts, these features and everything about them, from their locations to their names, can be studied to broaden our understanding of former peoples, cultures, and times.

This paper, written from an archaeological perspective, describes some preliminary results of an Institute for Minnesota Archaeology (IMA) study of early water transportation in the area of Minnesota and northern Wisconsin. The study is part of a broader, ongoing IMA research program focused on the investigation of early human geography and cultural landscapes in the western Great Lakes. A goal of the IMA program is to define and explicate human-land and human-water relationships in that region in the period before and during initial white settlement and the development of modern transportation systems. Like most archaeology associated with the North American fur trade, this study has involved a strategy to frame questions, a methodology to derive answers, and the conjoining of written, cartographic, oral, and material evidence to provide a usable database.

Anyone familiar with fur-trade history is aware of the prominent role that geography played in shaping initial European intrusions in North America. Researchers have linked the development and success of the fur trade in the western Great Lakes to everything from climate, transportation, logistics, tribal wisdom, and tribal areas, to the territorial range of animals like the *Castor canadensis* (the beaver) or plants like *Betula papyrifera* (paper birch) (e.g., Ross 1973: ix). Among the variables perhaps most commonly mentioned in this regard are topography, water resources, and drainage patterns (e.g., Innis 1973; Morse 1962; 1969; Wheeler, et al. 1975).

There is little doubt that, in addition to human preferences and capabilities, land- and water-scapes played a major role in influencing the mode, rate, and direction of early westward travel. European colonies set in eastern coastal areas were enveloped by dense forests and devoid of practical roads. Land travel, especially over great distances, was an arduous task. Often the only reasonable means of penetrating inland areas was to ascend rivers (Guillet 1966: 3). With the notable exception of the Hudson River drainage, the existence of long rivers that might facilitate western ingress from the American seaboard settlements was precluded by the Appalachian Highlands (Innis 1973: 10). Mountainous regions like Pennsylvania were dissected by wild, rapid streams which proved a barrier to river traffic (Wallace 1987: 2). In contrast, the French and British found portals for exploration and commerce in the Laurentian outlet and Hudson Bay. Each portal served as a natural extension of the Atlantic Ocean and formed a direct water communication to the ports of Europe, the British Isles, and the Caribbean. The destiny of Canada was thus early linked to water transportation and westward expansion (Morse 1969: 117). To counter those who assert that Canada is a nation "despite her geography," determinists like Harold Innis have argued that "Canada is a nation because of it" (Winks 1973: xv).

Indeed, over half of the fresh-water surface in the world is contained in Canada and the contiguous areas of the United States encompassing the Great Lakes. Arrangement and drainage of these surface waters has formed a vast natural system of inland waterways. Countless lakes and streams, ranging from unnamed "frog ponds" or creeks to celebrated features like Lake Superior or the Mackenzie River, widely interconnect to accommodate the passage of portable, low-displacement watercraft like birch bark canoes (Morse 1969: 27). The peculiarities of climate and geography provided a fairly predictable supply of annual precipitation needed to replenish the system.

Enhancing the utility of these waterways is the nature of the landscape in the continental interior. Despite the far-flung parameters of what might be called the fur trade "canoe country," the land area involved is generally of low relief. The uplands flanking the west side of Hudson Bay, for example, seldom exceed 1,500 feet above sea level. Much of the terrain there is composed of lowlands or is cut by lowland gaps, such as occupied by the Nelson River, and is under 800 feet in height. Similarly, the difference in elevation between the mouth of the St. Lawrence River and the surface of Lake Superior, the highest of the Great Lakes, is only 600 feet. These characteristics made the navigability of northern waterways truly remarkable. Quite literally, the fur traders found it possible to travel to almost any region of the upper Midwest or Canada—from the Atlantic to the Pacific, or from the Arctic Sea to the Gulf of Mexico—by canoe (Morse 1962).

The "bugs" in this system, if such features or conditions can be considered flaws, are the climate (each winter transforms fluid northern waters to rigid ice); the various heights of land, falls, and rapids that interrupt continuous water navigation; and large expanses like the Great Lakes, Lake Winnipeg, and so forth which expose travelers to the dangers of open water or encourage the use of bigger vessels. The Indian fur trade evolved in adaptation to these conditions. In northern trade districts, ice-free periods provided the only real opportunity to move furs and goods between trading posts and supply centers. Winters were more ideally suited for tracking and harvesting animals and served to increase the quality or value of furs. The climate thus provided a rhythm to the trade and, in tandem with the modes and lanes of transportation, shaped travel and logistical strategies like the time and place of the annual *rendezvous* held at Grand Portage or Fort William on the northern rim of Lake Superior (Morse 1969: 27).

It is perhaps unnecessary to say, but should nonetheless be emphasized, that the presence, navigability, and interrelationship of North America's inland waterways were first discovered by Native peoples. Their pioneering work was eased by their development of durable and efficient watercraft like dugouts and bark canoes. Such vessels could be propelled by paddles, allowing paddlers to face the direction of travel and to observe hazards lying in their path (Adney and Chapelle 1964: 3). Long before the Vikings landed at l'Anse aux Meadows or Columbus entered the Caribbean, diverse Indian groups likely understood the small craft use-potential of virtually all interior waterways in North America. At the same time, to surmount or bypass the many serious obstacles found on northern water routes, the Indians had developed an associated system of portages, or "carrying places." So much has been written about portages in the past that it is at first difficult to imagine what remains to be said about such features.

What can be learned from the study of ancient water routes and portages? How did such systems, features, or trails originate, how did they relate to landscapes, and how were they used? Were there recurring "types" of portages and can predictive modeling help to determine their former locations and distribution? What do the placement and orientation of portages reveal about their Native architects, or about those Europeans who later adopted and often modified their use? What are the archaeological potentials of such places? Can certain "rules" or strategies of travel behavior or elements of world view be inferred from portages or water routes? Can the age of canoe travel be inferred from archaeological deposits found at portages or other water-related sites (e.g., Binford 1972: 352-53)? If, as is often claimed, rivers were roads and "roads control all history" (Wallace 1987: 1), is it possible to determine how and to what extent water routes and portages influenced regional cultural developments, human settlement patterns, or historical events in precontact times (or vice versa)? Are there meaningful parallels between the early system of water routes and modern road nets?

Those who wish to use archaeological records to study human settlement or land-use activities in forested areas soon learn that the data needed to discuss spatial or temporal relationships is often lacking or incomplete. In Minnesota, the only kinds of precontact American Indian sites for which there is an adequate knowledge, in terms of their general overall frequencies, distributions, and natural settings, are stone quarries, rock art features, and earthen fortifications and mounds. These sites are generally well known because their surface visibility, even in vegetated areas, has made them easy to find and record.

The only other kind of precontact cultural feature for which wholesale information is currently available in many northern areas is the canoe portage. Data for studying portages comes in various forms and degrees of reliability. The most common sources are place names, maps, explorer accounts, fur trade journals, oral histories, and missionary and land survey records. As demonstrated by many researchers, the study of such evidence can help to identify early travel routes, to describe their basic features in regard to natural settings, and to define their historical development and use (e.g., Black 1968; Morse 1969; Wallace 1987).

I began IMA's portage research by assembling a corpus or file of information on the subject of water travel. To organize information contained in the corpus and to make it useful, I developed a series of base maps which show lakes and streams and canoe routes and portages, and which index the original source materials through bibliographical citations. Because the base maps visually consolidate the known spatial or locational data, they can be used to address research questions that might arise concerning any or all of the travel routes. For example, if a journal reference says that somebody crossed eight portages in going from one named place to another, it is likely that the base maps can be used to identify the actual route taken. From the maps one can also deduce the overall distribution of historic southwestern Ojibway (Ojibwe, Chippewa) canoe routes, infer the probable routes traveled by early white explorers who left limited geographical descriptions, and surmise the routes used by certain tribal groups when they went from their lake-forest homes to hunt on the prairie-forest edge. The study has given me a new appreciation of early human perceptions and use of their natural surroundings and a greater certainty about the importance of water routes as an aspect of the decisionmaking of fur traders in establishing their forts (e.g., Birk 1991: 240-41; Birk and Johnson 1992: 232-33). My work as an archaeologist has allowed me to conduct field investigations in many portage areas, perhaps the best known being offshore excavations at the west end of the Grand Portage done in the 1970s (Wheeler, et al. 1975; Birk and Wheeler 1975; Birk 1975).

The historical documentation on water routes is generally proportional to their actual or rumored use in post-contact times. Major trunk lines, like the "Voyageur's Highway," are obviously well represented in fur trade literature (e.g., Nute 1941; Morse 1969: 75-87). Many lesser or ancillary routes are only known by a line on an old map or a single reference left in a journal. It is the large number of poorly-documented routes that suggests the former vastness of the water transportation systems once used by northern Indians and that truly exposes the very intimate knowledge those peoples had of their natural surroundings. The extent of the system once likely in use in the lake-forest regions around Lake Superior is, in part, suggested by the broad network of water trails and portages yet preserved within the Quetico-Superior Canoe Area and Provincial Park along the International Boundary west of Grand Portage. The Quetico-Superior, together with data in the corpus, provides a model which assists archaeologists in predicting the location of many former canoe routes, portages, and campsites that escaped mention in written and cartographic sources.

Preliminary research suggests that many parts of Minnesota's extant surface waters were essentially unnavigable or were not used on any regular basis for canoe travel by Indian peoples. Of the part of the natural system regularly used, only some lesser percentage of that use is actually documented on historical maps or written records. Finally, the data show that only a limited number of the known Indian canoe routes and portages played any significant role in the transportation of fur traders and fur trade materials.

Canoe routes in themselves were courses of travel that might integrate any number or combination of lakes, streams, wetlands, or portages to get from one place or locale to another. The routes were as varied in length, structure, and use as the landscapes they crossed. Except in areas dominated by the Canadian Shield, most interior water routes in Minnesota and northern Wisconsin traversed glacial landscapes comprised of moraines, till plains, and old glacial lake beds. Lakes and marshes are common in such landscapes, and streams tend to downcut the terrain to expose rocks or to form sand and gravel bars. Abrupt changes in surface elevation are mostly confined to moraines, parts of the northern Shield, stream gorges, and the edges of the Lake Superior basin. Such varied natural conditions, when linked with seasonality, meant that some travel routes enjoyed year-round use while others were favored for only either winter or summer travel.

The rivers in the old Fond du Lac trade district at the head of Lake Superior (Birk 1984: 52-55) are often shallow and sinuated channels, which led trade canoes there to be built in wider and more flat-bottomed forms than seen elsewhere. For example, while a French Montreal canoe might have a length of 33 feet and a 4.5-foot beam (Adney and Chapelle 1964: 152), a much shorter Fond du Lac model could be 5 feet amidships. Because of their great buoyancy, such canoes had a better chance of floating cargoes over the submerged rocks, shoals, and snags common to rivers in northern Minnesota and Wisconsin.

One measure of a waterway's usefulness in canoe transportation is its navigability. For present purposes the term "navigable" might be applied to any lake or stream capable of floating a small canoe, either with or without a cargo. Although a small canoe with even a modest payload can float in just a few inches of water, the depth for safe navigation of larger canoes, especially those hauling quantities of freight, is closer to two feet, the minimum actually prescribed for the operation of most of today's small commercial and pleasure craft (Black 1968: 839).

But navigability is not the only criterion for measuring a stream's usefulness for water transportation. Other factors that come into play are its capacity,

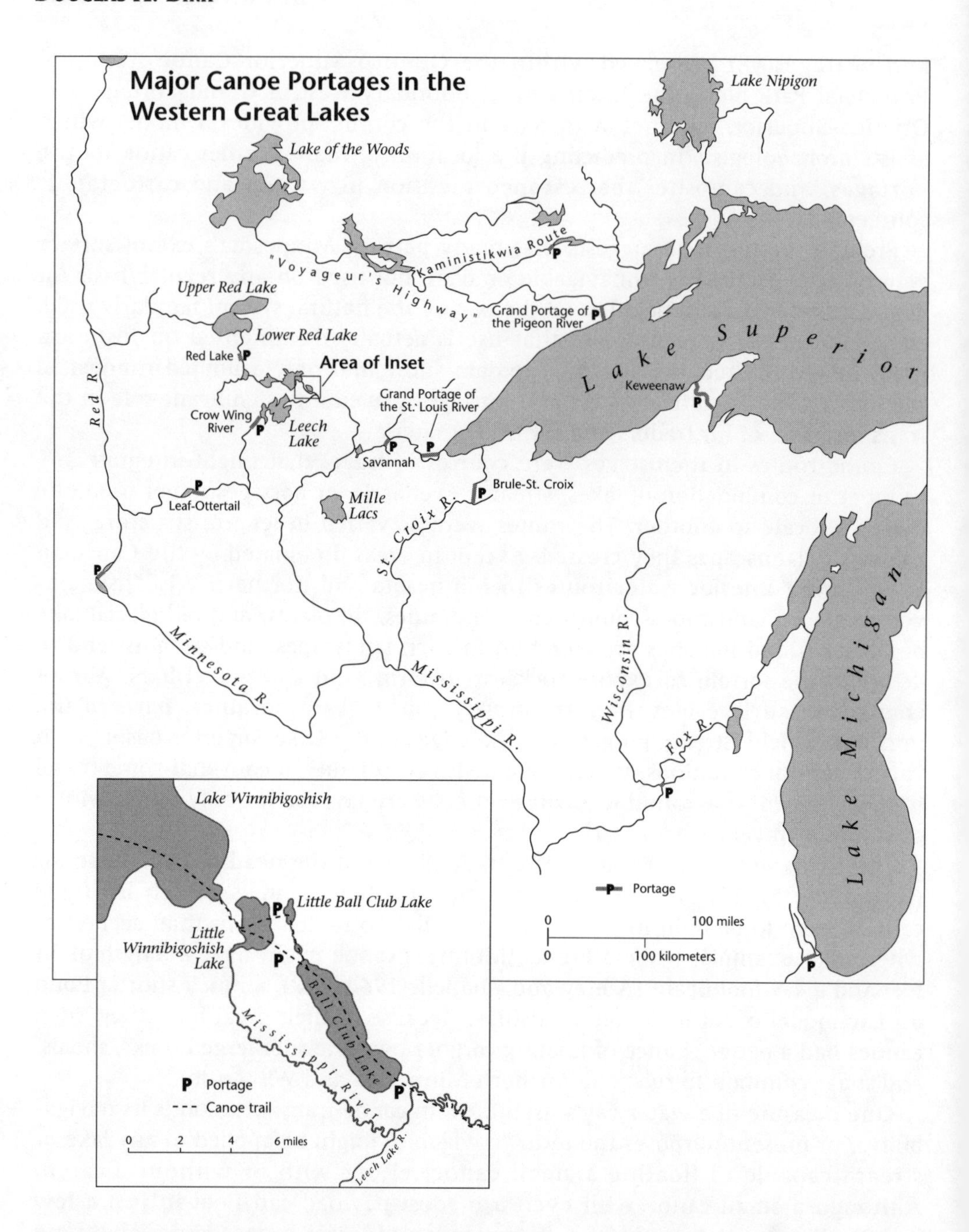

Figure 1. Some of the most celebrated portages in the western Great Lakes include various heights-of-land crossings that interconnected major drainage basins. Lesser-known portage trails were abundant. In the area below Lake Winnibigoshish, where the Mississippi River meanders southward (see inset map), northbound travelers often portaged through the paralleling waters of Ball Club Lake to avoid having to negotiate the current and sinuosity of the Mississippi.

Figure 2. Working a canoe up a rapids on the Ottawa River in the mid-1800s. The number of men shown, their body language, and the focus of their activities, suggest the illustrated canoe was but one of perhaps several traveling in a brigade. There is little question that they are faced with portaging their canoes, equipment, and packaged bales around this ferocious stretch of white water, that Canadian historian and pioneer canoe-route geographer, Eric Morse, believes was the Portage Dufort, now flooded (Morse 1969: 52). Taken from N.P. Willis, *Canadian Scenery*, with illustrations by W.H. Bartlett (London: George Virtue), 2: 44. Courtesy the William L. Clements Library, The University of Michigan.

directness, sinuosity, velocity, and difficulty of travel. A major river like the Mississippi may be followed in a canoe to its source, yet in some places it is so sinuated that traveling upstream against its current can be a lengthy and tedious process. In an area where the Mississippi cuts through an old glacial lake bed in north central Minnesota, one might literally paddle nineteen channel miles to advance ten. To avoid fighting the main channel in such places, northbound travelers might simply take a shorter cross-country route through an interconnection of smaller streams and lakes, or could use several paralleling water options like the Rabbit River or Ball Club Lake. There are, in fact, many examples of parallel water routes in the Minnesota area, any of which might be preferred over another for a number of reasons.

Some water routes were so remote, intricate, obscure, or difficult that they were little penetrated or used by fur traders. Indeed, many Europeans thought the closed forest environment about the head of Lake Superior was a sterile, foreboding, and even claustrophobic place. The Ojibway occupying that region, with their habit of living in scattered enclaves, found protection in the dense foliage and the labyrinthine nature of the surface water system. The same waterways gave them an advantage in warfare in the nineteenth century. If southerly Dakota groups wanted to attack the Ojibway in the Mississippi headwaters, for example, they might first have to paddle canoes upstream against the current for several days and then negotiate narrow tributaries and portages to reach a potential target. Under such circumstances they could arrive at a battleground exhausted, detected, and uncertain of making a clean retreat. The Ojibway, on the other hand, could emerge from the forest in a flotilla of light canoes and, with little effort or fanfare, float downstream and attack the Dakota while still fresh. Then, abandoning their canoes, they could make an all-out dash to return to the security of the northern forests.

Serious water route improvements were rare and seldom enduring (Morse 1969: 31). During the glory days of the North West Company, some canoe routes were improved or maintained by removing fallen trees and beaver dams, trimming limbs and brush to widen stream and trail passages, cutting channels through bogs, or installing catwalks or primitive rock staircases. Some travelers, during droughts, were forced to build dams to ease their passage. In most instances the improvements fell into decay or disrepair when events in the early 1800s disfavored their upkeep. Travelers on some routes after the peak years of Indian commerce lamented their plight in having to follow such neglected trails.

Important components of inland water routes, of course, were the portages, the "carrying places" that might parallel or interconnect waterways, cross islands or points of land on both rivers and lakes, or in some instances, even cross one waterway to get to another. The intended use of each portage is often suggested by its name, location, and physical characteristics. The abundance of records from individual portages has fostered another important aspect of IMA's water transportation study. Information assembled from multiple sources is being used to reconstruct historical profiles or composite views illustrating the features and peculiarities of each portage as seen by different observers at different times. The composite sketches often help to resolve incongruous details about trail length, appearance, or improvements, and are vital to understanding how the use of certain canoe portages or routes varied over the years, between seasons, or among different human groups. A good example of research involving the review of disparate data from a single portage was published in 1977 on the Portage La Loche in Saskatchewan (Kupsch 1977).

Carrying places involved the use of human porters, usually the members of the traveling party but occasionally a crew specifically hired to help advance a canoe party or cargo over an unusually long or rough portage. Such crews might have been voyageurs gathered for a summer rendezvous, or Indians recruited from a nearby camp or village. At key portages, where trails were long and the traffic high, major trade companies sometimes kept canoes at either end to relieve the need for shuttling them across. This practice was documented at Methye Portage, connecting the Churchill and Athabasca watersheds, and the Grand Portages of both the St. Louis and Pigeon rivers in northeastern Minnesota. At the latter trails it was common for traders to substitute smaller interior canoes for the larger models used on Lake Superior. At the Methye and Pigeon River portages the major trade companies also experimented with or used oxen or horses in moving goods over the trails.

To protect its investments and hinder the opposition, the North West Company took other steps to control portage use in the Fond du Lac district. Employees of lesser firms were often harassed or denied "free market" access to buy canoes on Lake Superior. By attempting to control the canoe-building activities of the Lake Superior Ojibway, the North West Company hoped to disallow the sale of smaller Fond du Lac-style canoes to competitors, forcing those with large canoes to carry them over the demanding gateway portages to the Mississippi or St. Croix valleys. Once in the interior, and having suffered the added financial and energy burden and delays attendant to such carries, the competitors were given free rein to buy canoes to more rapidly deplete their stock of merchandise (Birk 1984: 58).

Through repeated use, many portages developed into well-worn paths and acquired names recognizing some person, event, feature, or landscape characteristic important to the trail's use, identity, or overland course. Thus appear such portage names as Savanna, New, Deep, Turtle, Plover, Sioux, Ox, Willow, Prairie, Duck Flutter, Six Poses, and Long Lake. A "Knife Portage" on Minnesota's St. Louis River traversed a protruding incline of outcropped slate rock that was said to cut (like a "knife") into the moccasins and feet of early travelers. At a narrowing of a large island on Lake Vermilion in northern Minnesota was a short trail crossing known simply as the *Onikamisigitchim-nising* or the "Little Portage on a Big Island." The gateway portage at the mouth of the Pigeon River was known as the *Kitchi-Onigaming* or, literally, the "Grand Portage." "Height-of-land" portages usually extended from one major watershed to another. Portage, Wisconsin, for example, is on the height of land separating the Fox River (on the Laurentian drainage) from the Wisconsin River (in the Mississippi basin). Some portages had more than one name, signifying a possible change over time or an inconsistent use by different persons, companies, or cultural groups.

The Ojibway name for portage is *onigum* (Baraga 1966: 197, 330, variably spelled), and in northern Minnesota there is a small reservation community by that name on the narrows of a peninsula on Leech Lake. The place name is a reminder that an *onigum* was made over the narrows to avoid paddling around the peninsula by canoe. Similar *onigums* were sometimes used to cross points of land jutting out into Lake Superior. One short *onigum*, on the north shore of the lake, crossed a long narrow point at the place called "Little Portage Bay." Other short *onigums* crossed Minnesota Point at Duluth harbor and Chequamegon Point at the entrance to Chequamegon Bay. Perhaps the one best known joined with Portage Lake to cross the protruding Keweenaw Peninsula, the "most marked topographical feature" on the south shore (Mason 1958: 176). A like portage also passed over Garden Peninsula, the large point of land projecting from the north shore of Lake Michigan east of the Big Bay de Noc. Such big water portages were used not only as short cuts to decrease trip miles or travel time but also as a means to avoid prolonged or unnecessary exposure to large expanses of open water. Conditions perilous to canoe travelers were frequently encountered on lake crossings, when rounding points of land, or in attempting to pass through confined entrances at the mouths of natural harbors and streams. Fog, high winds, turbulence, currents, reefs, and shoreline or beach characteristics were frequent concerns of big-water travelers.

IMA's corpus also provides clues to other strategies used in canoe travel. Canoemen on the Great Lakes would often journey at night to beat contrary winds, or would hoist a blanket or sail to catch favorable breezes. Similar attempts to economize led to portaging over the narrow necks of land found on large meander loops of the Mississippi River within its headwaters area. The use of meander-loop portages was favored for upstream travel but might be ignored by those moving downstream. To date, no hard evidence has been found to suggest that cargo-laden trade canoes were portaged over the meander-loop carrying places, but such use would be expected on upstream voyages. Such activities would be hard to test archaeologically, because the Mississippi has continued to erode the banks in the old portage locations and, in at least one case, has cut through the neck of land, destroying the portage and cutting off the loop to create an "oxbow" slough.

A similar kind of portage occurred at river junctions. Where navigable streams conjoin, portages might link the two channels somewhere above the confluence, both to make a shorter route and to bypass the often rocky, turbulent, or meandered conditions found in such places. If navigable streams converge at a narrow angle, such as the meeting of the Mississippi and Missouri rivers at St. Louis, a portage trail might appear well above the confluence. Such portages are documented in central Minnesota at the junctions of both the Little Elk and Swan rivers with the Mississippi. Another is seen below the junction of the Yellow and St. Croix rivers in northwestern Wisconsin, where the three-mile "Sioux Portage" cut about thirteen miles from the more lengthy river course.

Portaging was really an improvisational exercise that depended on a range of human and natural variables (Adney and Chapelle 1964: 152). There were, for example, many options for negotiating whitewater. If possible, many canoemen would shoot a rapids going downstream, or make what was called a *demi-chargé* while ascending. A *demi-chargé* meant that the cargo of each canoe was divided and barged upstream through the rapids in two separate loads. Less favorable conditions might prompt a *décharge*, where a canoe would be lined or forced up the rapids with none of its cargo on board (Morse 1969: 5; Wheeler, et al. 1975: 24). Finally, of course, many places required a full portage—the carrying of both vessel and cargo overland.

A variation of *demi-chargé* tactics was used at the place called "Women's Portage" or *Portage de la Femme* on the St. Croix River. The shallow rapids there were often only passable if the women (or others) got out and walked the

Figure 3. A *décharge* at the portage La Petite Faucille on the French River. At this point, where the river turned sharply and dropped over a rocky rapids, up-stream travelers, as shown here, might carry their cargoes over a short portage on the inside bend while the canoes were poled through the white water. Painting by C.R. Forrest. Cat. No. 955.189.6, Courtesy of the Royal Ontario Museum, Toronto, Canada.

portage trail while the men paddled or walked the canoes through. Depending on the depth of the water, the embarking passengers might also be called upon to further lighten the load by carrying some of the cargo. Thus, part of the load was barged while the other part was portaged. "Women's Portages" were also found at either end of the Grand Portage on the St. Louis River southwest of present day Duluth. The one on the downstream end of the Grand Portage was used most often to disembark passengers when traveling upstream.

Portage trails typically ranged in length from a few feet to several miles. The shortest were probably so-called "lift-overs," which might or might not require a cargo displacement to lift a canoe over an obstacle like an *embarrass* or beaver dam. One of the longest portages on record was the 45-mile Montreal River carry on the south shore of Lake Superior. Other portages both celebrated and cursed for their length were the 8-1/2-mile Grand Portage at the Pigeon River and the 12-mile Methye Portage (Morse 1969: 97-98).

Individual portages varied in quality or use over time in response to long-term or seasonal changes associated with climate, vegetation, runoff, fire, insects, or human agencies. Some portages were rendered unnecessary during periods of high runoff when rapids were flooded and the danger of a channel passage was neutralized. A "conditional" portage of this kind, at Little Falls in central Minnesota, was most often used when the Mississippi River was at low stages or at times when the falls was jammed with ice or (in later years) saw logs. A conditional portage might also be made when wild rice glutted a stream channel, making canoe passage impractical (Vennum 1988: 31). High waters, sometimes caused by torrential rains, ice blockages, or beaver dams, could also inundate flood plains, wetlands, isthmuses, and stream meanders, allowing canoers to pass through areas they might not normally be able to enter or negotiate with watercraft. A case is known in central Minnesota where extreme flooding forced river travelers to sleep in their canoes for lack of dry land. Some portages, particularly those paralleling segments of small or shallow rivers, might double or even triple in length when water levels dropped. Lower water levels might also necessitate portaging in places where portages did not normally exist. In one instance fur traders purposely blocked a portage by felling trees across the trail to curtail its use by competitors. More common were trail blockages caused by windfalls.

Long portages (those exceeding about one-half mile in length) were commonly divided by a number of pauses (*posés*) or resting places. The Ojibway name was *pagidjiwanan* (Baraga 1966: 212) or *opuggiddiwanan*, meaning literally "the place of putting down the pack" (Coues 1965, I:136n.48). The interval between pauses varied with "pheric distance," a measure of the time needed to cross that intervening space (Browman 1976: 469). Obviously, in defining such distance, the nature of the terrain came into play. It has been suggested that the average distance between pauses on fairly level and sound terrain was about one-third to one-half mile (Morse 1969: 5; Fritzen 1978: 5) or 600 to 800 yards (Gates 1965: 97n.61). Where marsh, steep or rugged terrain, or other factors increased the time and energy costs of traversing the landscape, the pauses were closer together.

The term *posé* also came to be used as a measure of the distance between resting places and, thus, of the overall length or relative difficulty of portages. That it was considered a valid measure is illustrated by the occurrence of a short portage in northern Wisconsin that was said to be only "one-half pause" long. In contrast, the Montreal River carry on the south shore of Lake Superior involved a whopping 122! A proper idea of the pause-as-distance concept is seen in the comparison of two portages at the west end of Lake Superior. The 8-1/2-mile Grand Portage at the Pigeon River had 16 pauses dividing the trail into 17 segments, each averaging one-half mile in length. The seven-mile Grand Portage on the St. Louis River, which crossed a more demanding terrain, had 19 rest stops, giving it 20 segments with an average length of one-third mile. All pauses, whether covering greater or lesser distances, theoretically required about the same amount of physical exertion.

These data show the demands of different landscapes and can be used by archaeologists to categorize portages or predict where specific portage rests might be located. Knowing the length of portage trails and the number and average distance between pauses is but a first step. What is needed to understand the energy requirements, "danger element," and usefulness of portages is specific information about soils, gradients, drainage, vegetation, orientation, elevation differences between trail heads, and net elevation changes over the length of trails. Rating portages by degree of difficulty, much in the manner that rapids (whitewater areas) are defined, and by their relative efficiency over other options, should further our understanding of route selection and popularity and of the broader impact of geography on human travel, settlement, and land use. The data also prompt other questions, such as, what material remains (artifacts, artifact assemblages, and features) might be expected at pauses? How does the archaeological signature of pauses compare with that of portage termini? On long portages, how might the signature vary from pause to pause and, if it does vary, why? Did pauses used by fur traders differ from those used by tribal peoples in more ancient times? Obviously, to address these issues, it will first be necessary that more archaeologists start recognizing the possible portage function of sites they might now just routinely associate with habitation or subsistence use.

The most favored pauses may have been those on prominent ridges, on islands of dry land (in wetland areas), at intersected streams, or in openings where a breeze might reduce the annoyance of flying insects. Such rest stops occasionally formed loci for overnight camps and, on more heavily-used portages, may have encouraged construction of canoe-rests, shelters, or other improvements. Pauses also served as "temporary depots," as all the packs and equipment were carried forward by some travelers one pause at a time to keep canoe parties together and to increase security (Nute 1941: 54; Gates 1965: 97n.61). Written evidence from the Grand Portage on the St. Louis River hints that pauses were sometimes referred to by number or name, or both. Like the names attached to portages themselves, those of pauses reflected some feature or characteristic of the rest stop. Pause Seven, for example, was also called the "Maple Pause" because of a side trail at that place leading to a sugar bush. Pause Twelve coincided with a marked human interment and was called "The Grave" (Fritzen 1978: 6).

The Ojibway also figured distances over water on a scale relative to the time ("convenience") or physical endurance needed to travel from one place to another. Rest stops, when traveling on water, were called "pipes" from the habit, commonly enjoyed by voyageurs and other canoe travelers, of smoking during the brief interludes of rest (Densmore 1970: 18, 137). Pipes usually lasted from only a few minutes to "perhaps" ten minutes (Nute 1941: 55). Some have guessed that the time interval between pipes ranged from about every half hour or so to every two hours (Gates 1965: 92n.53). Like pauses on land, pipes also became a measure of the distance traveled between stops. Various estimates suggest a pipe might equal from two to over six miles, depending on such things as wind, current, and the speed of the canoe (McKenney 1959: 210; Glover 1962: 202; Morse 1969: 8). Thus it was that a lake 28 miles in length would be referred to as "four pipes" long (Nute 1941: 55), that is, five segments each approximating 5.6 miles. In the Ojibway language, the "pipe," both as a period

Figure 4. In the late 1830s, the French scientist-explorer, Joseph Nicollet, traveled through the headwaters region of the Mississippi making observations and interviewing Native Americans to produce this "Map of the Hydrographical Basin of the Upper Mississippi River." This portion of his famed map shows the relationship of many waterways and portages then utilized by the southwestern Ojibway. Only some of the mainline routes were in regular use by fur traders and other non-Indians. The original of this map is owned by the U.S. Army Corps of Engineers. Courtesy of the William L. Clements Library, The University of Michigan.

of rest (the amount of time it commonly took to smoke a pipe of tobacco) and as a unit for calculating distance, was known as a *ningotopwâgan* (Baraga 1966: 297) or *non'godo'pwagûn* (Densmore 1970: 18).

Places where it was necessary to cross open water in a vessel or where it was necessary to portage across open (treeless) country were commonly called "traverses." Two such crossing places in southern Minnesota were the watery Sand Point traverse near the middle of Lake Pepin, and the upland Traverse des Sioux (formerly the "Crescent") trail cutting across a large bend in the Minnesota River north of Mankato. In the latter case the Traverse first applied to a river crossing or ford used by the Dakota or "Sioux."

Most portage trails were so judiciously located that their position and course cannot be improved even with the use of modern contour maps. Actual pathways did change, however, and were often in a state of perpetual adjustment as segments of trail moved to and fro within the limits of a broader trail corridor to avoid such things as tree falls, washouts, and flooding. The ingenuity of adaptations is shown by the Grand Portage of the Pigeon River, which today incorporates a beaver dam into the trail to bridge a marshy stream. The heads or termini of portages were less apt to change, although they might shift or migrate through extended use or in response to changing cultural or natural conditions. An example of a portage terminus that migrated downstream during its use by French, British, and American travelers is the landing at "Fort Charlotte" on the west end of the Grand Portage at the Pigeon River (e.g., Birk and Wheeler 1975: 798). There are instances where a single portage terminus might furnish access to an intermediate branching trail or serve two or more radiating trails. Many lakes, large and small, also served as "hubs" or intersections for converging portage trails (e.g., Morse 1969: 29-30).

In archaeological terms, sites, artifacts, and artifact scatters related to canoe travel have been found on river bottoms in areas of rapids and falls (e.g., Wheeler, et al. 1975; Lockery 1978) and might be expected along trail corridors, particularly at portage termini and at intermediate pauses and trail junctures. Portage termini commonly served as encampments or villages and, in some places in the Minnesota area, the heads of former portage trails used during Woodland-Mississippian cultural periods are now marked by the presence of one or more earthen "burial" mounds. Mounds might also appear at intermediate trail locations. Victims of fur trade-era mishaps, like voyageurs who drowned in dangerous rapids, were also buried at portages. Occasionally, wooden crosses were erected for the dead whether their bodies were recovered or not (e.g., Harmon 1903: 6; Gates 1965: 71, 84). Some portages enjoyed a spiritual or ritual significance. The explorer David Thompson once saw what he called "a manitou stone" on a northern portage (Glover 1962: 38), and many traders mention frivolous ceremonies sometimes enacted when crossing heights-of-land trails (e.g., Gates 1965: 99). Some portages bypassed water features, like St. Anthony Falls on the Mississippi (at Minneapolis), which were in themselves considered sacred by tribal peoples (Hennepin 1938: 117).

Named portages were often important geographical reference points and, in post-contact times, some were used to define the boundaries of Indian reservations and ceded lands. Other portages, on major fur trade routes or in intertribal contested zones, became portals or gateways that invited political control, confrontation, and warfare. The Grand Portages on the Pigeon and St. Louis rivers, cited earlier as places of petty enforcements by the North West Company, played central roles in negotiations to settle the disputed boundary between Canada and the United States. The reliance of the fur trade on water transportation meant that most trading posts were sited near navigable waters. Portages might be preferred locations for forts or trading depots and such places sometimes grew into communities or urban centers, especially where portages bypassed rapids or falls that were later harnessed as sources of water power. The Minnesota communities of Grand Rapids, Little Falls, and Minneapolis, for example, grew up around portages and early mills on the Mississippi River.

There is little doubt that portages, shore-line sites, canoe routes, and route systems can be studied as artifacts of human adaptation and that each is encoded with information vital to understanding past cultural choices and capabilities. The network of canoe routes and portages blazed by Native North Americans exposes an overall design or determination to provide reasonably safe, direct, expedient, and comfortable transportation. Their development of vessels, routes, and strategies was appropriate to increasing the efficiency of their labors by reducing the energy and time costs associated with water travel. While recreational canoers today enjoy floating down rivers and will often go to great lengths to avoid lifting their canoes from the water, earlier North American Indians apparently thought little of it. Their apparent intention was to generally minimize travel time and not necessarily to maximize the time they spent on water. The legacy of the North American Indians as pathfinders is seen not only in the breadth of their knowledge of northern waterways and landscapes but in the repeated selection of canoe routes and portage locations that could not be readily improved. The northern fur traders, led by Indian guides and Indian example, simply adopted preexisting trade channels, facilities, and strategies in their economic exploitation of the West.

The future of IMA's portage study will be to continue the archival research and field survey of known or suspected portage sites and to condense, interpret, and publish the data from the survey and the corpus. The question now is how much remains to be learned and how far theoretical constructs developed in the Minnesota-Wisconsin area study can be projected to other regions. When I began looking at portages some years ago I was uncertain of where the trail might lead and what, if any, historical contributions could be made. Now, I feel like the real work is only just beginning.

References

Adney, Edwin, and Howard Chapelle. 1964. *The Bark Canoes and Skin Boats of North America.* Washington, D.C.: Smithsonian Institution.

Baraga, Bishop Frederic. 1966. *A Dictionary of the Otchipwe Language, Explained in English.* Reprint. Minneapolis: Ross and Haines.

Binford, Lewis R. 1972. *An Archaeological Perspective.* New York: Seminar Press.

Birk, Douglas A. 1975. "Recent Underwater Recoveries at Fort Charlotte, Grand Portage National Monument, Minnesota." *The International Journal of Nautical Archaeology and Underwater Exploration* 4 (1): 73-84.

______. 1984. "John Sayer and the Fond du Lac Trade: The North West Company in Minnesota and Wisconsin." In *Rendezvous. Selected Papers of the Fourth North American Fur Trade Conference, 1981,* edited by Thomas Buckley, 51-61. St. Paul, Minn.: North American Fur Trade Conference.

______. 1991. "French Presence in Minnesota: The View from Site Mo20 near Little Falls." *French Colonial Archaeology. The Illinois Country and the Western Great Lakes,* edited by John A. Walthall, 237-66. Urbana: University of Illinois Press.

Birk, Douglas A., and Elden Johnson. 1992. "The Mdewakanton Dakota and Initial French Contact." In *Calumet & Fleur-de-Lys. Archaeology of Indian and French Contact in the Midcontinent,* edited by John A. Walthall and Thomas E. Emerson, 203-40. Washington, D.C.: Smithsonian Institution Press.

Birk, Douglas A., and Robert Wheeler. 1975. "Fort Charlotte Underwater Archeology Project." *National Geographic Research Reports 1975.* Washington, D.C.: National Geographic Society, 791-99.

Black, W. 1968. "Navigable Inland Waterways." *Science, History and Hudson Bay,* vol. 2, ed. C. S. Beals. Ottawa: Queen's Printer, 837-69.

Browman, David L. 1976. "Demographic Correlations of the Wari Conquest of Junin." *American Antiquity* 41(4): 465-77.

Coues, Elliott, ed. 1965. *The Expeditions of Zebulon Montgomery Pike,* 2 vols. Reprint. Minneapolis: Ross and Haines.

Densmore, Frances. 1970. *Chippewa Customs.* Minneapolis: Ross and Haines.

Fritzen, John. 1978. *The History of Fond du Lac and Jay Cooke Park.* Duluth, Minn.: St. Louis County Historical Society.

Gates, Charles M. ed. 1965. *Five Fur Traders of the Northwest.* St. Paul: Minnesota Historical Society.

Glover, Richard, ed. 1962. *David Thompson's Narrative, 1784-1812.* Toronto: The Champlain Society.

Guillet, Edwin. 1966. *The Story of Canadian Roads.* Toronto: University of Toronto Press.

Harmon, Daniel W. 1903. *A Journal of Voyages and Travels in the Interior of North America.* New York: A. S. Barnes.

Hennepin, Father Louis. 1938. *Description of Louisiana Newly Discovered to the Southwest of New France by Order of the King,* trans. Marion E. Cross. Minneapolis: University of Minnesota Press.

Innis, Harold. 1973. *The Fur Trade in Canada. An Introduction to Canadian Economic History,* rev. ed. Toronto: University of Toronto Press.

Kupsch, W. 1977. "A Valley View in Verdant Prose: The Clearwater Valley from Portage La Loche." *Musk-Ox* 20: 28-49.

Lockery, Andrew R. 1978. "Fast Water Archaeology in the Winnipeg River, Manitoba, Canada." *The International Journal of Nautical Archaeology and Underwater Exploration,* 7 (4): 321-32.

McKenney, Thomas L. 1959. *Sketches of a Tour to the Lakes, of the Character and Customs of the Chippeway Indians, and of Incidents Connected with The Treaty of Fond du Lac,* reprint. Minneapolis: Ross and Haines.

Mason, Philip, ed. 1958. *Schoolcraft's Expedition to Lake Itasca. The Discovery of the Source of the Mississippi.* East Lansing: Michigan State University Press.

Morse, Eric. 1962. *Canoe Routes of the Voyageurs. The Geography and Logistics of the Canadian Fur Trade.* Reprinted from the Canadian Geographical Journal, May-August, 1961. Toronto: The Quetico Foundation.

_____. 1969. *Fur Trade Canoe Routes of Canada/ Then and Now.* Ottawa: Queen's Printer.

Nute, Grace. 1941. *The Voyageur's Highway. Minnesota's Border Lake Land.* St. Paul: Minnesota Historical Society.

Ross, Eric. 1973. *Beyond the River and the Bay. Some Observations on the State of the Canadian Northwest in 1811 with a View to Providing the Intending Settler with an Intimate Knowledge of That Country.* Toronto: University of Toronto Press.

Vennum, Thomas, Jr. 1988. *Wild Rice and the Ojibway People.* St. Paul: Minnesota Historical Society Press.

Wallace, Paul. 1987. *Indian Paths of Pennsylvania,* 3d printing. Harrisburg: Pennsylvania Historical and Museum Commission.

Wheeler, Robert, et al. 1975. "Voices From the Rapids. An Underwater Search for Fur Trade Artifacts, 1960-73." *Minnesota Historical Archaeology Series,* no. 3. St. Paul: Minnesota Historical Society.

Winks, Robin W. 1973. "Foreword." In *The Fur Trade in Canada. An Introduction to Canadian Economic History,* rev. ed., by Harold Innis. Toronto: University of Toronto Press.

Origins of Fort Union: Archaeology and History

William J. Hunt, Jr.

One of the more famous places in the antebellum American West was Fort Union trading post (figure 1). Located on the Missouri River, immediately above its confluence with the Yellowstone River (figure 2), Fort Union played a significant role in American history. For almost forty years it served as the headquarters of the American Fur Company's Upper Missouri Outfit (UMO), controlling the trade over much of western North Dakota, Montana, and Wyoming. It was also the primary post for the Assiniboin trade and played a prominent role in the Crow, Blackfoot, and Sioux trades. As the center of an American economic empire, it continued to dominate the American fur and bison robe trade until the end of the Civil War.[1]

In addition to its historic economic importance, Fort Union is significant because of the personalities who visited or lived there. Located on the edge of the American frontier, Fort Union offered quite civilized accommodations as a temporary home for such people as Hugh Glass, George Catlin, Prince Maximilian, Edwin Denig, James Kipp, Kenneth McKenzie, Jim Bridger, Father Pierre De Smet, John James Audubon, and General Alfred Sully, to name a few.

In 1867, this old trading post was sold to the U.S. Army and torn down, its building materials used to construct Fort Buford infantry post a few miles away. For almost a century thereafter, the site of Fort Union appeared as little more than a few shallow hummocks and depressions in the prairie grass. Then, in 1965, the site was integrated into the National Park system as Fort Union Trading Post National Historic Site. The National Park Service (NPS) planned to interpret the site through reconstruction and, as a result, a flurry of historical research and archaeological testing followed. Nevertheless, it took another twenty years for Congress to pass a bill mandating the reconstruction of the trading post.

With passage of that measure in 1985, the staff of the NPS-Midwest Archeological Center (MWAC) informed Rocky Mountain Region planners that an important and irreplaceable archaeological resource was about to be

Figure 1. Fort Union, c. 1843 (detail of watercolor by J. Baptiste Moncravie?). Courtesy of the Jesuit Missouri Province Archives, St. Louis, Missouri.

destroyed. After considerable back-and-forth discussion and debate, the NPS directed MWAC to salvage as much information as possible from threatened portions of the site.[2] From 1986 through 1988, MWAC archaeological teams were engaged in extremely large-scale excavations at Fort Union.[3] Excavation was restricted to areas threatened by construction, with the project's highest priority being the recovery of architectural information to aid in reconstruction planning. Despite these restrictions, the project's scope of work included provisions for MWAC's historical archeologists to conduct research on Fort Union's architectural and cultural history.[4] One result of the excavation has been an investigation of a small trading post's remains discovered underneath the larger and later fort the NPS planned to reconstruct.

DOCUMENTARY EVIDENCE

Despite the fact that much information is available relating to Fort Union, many details of its early history remain obscure. Among these ill-defined details are the physical layout and appearance of the original trading post. The understanding of that structural complex is complicated by a massive rebuilding effort initiated in 1832 which replaced every structure on the site by 1835.[5] This is complicated further by the scarcity of historic documents which describe the precursor to the post that Father Pierre De Smet described as "the vastest and finest of the forts that the Fur Company has upon the Missouri."[6] Although the

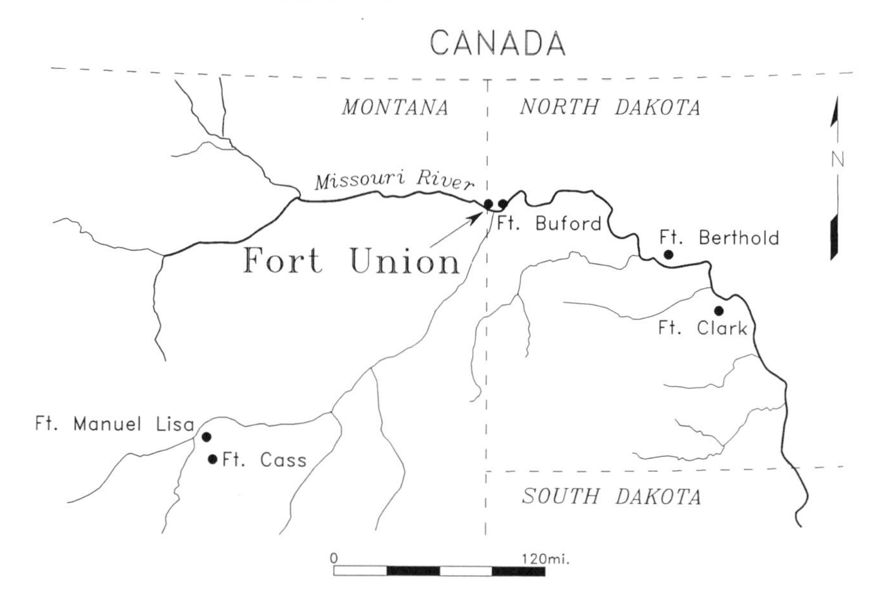

Figure 2. Location of Fort Union. Courtesy of the National Park Service, Midwest Archeological Center, Lincoln, Nebraska.

Fort Union "Letterbooks"[7] contain numerous references to various structures in the post, they may only be used to compile a partial list. Somewhat greater detail is known from documentation left by three individuals who visited the trading post immediately prior to and during the initial stages of building the new Fort Union. These early 1830s visitors were the artist George Catlin, the scientist Prince Maximilian, and Maximilian's artist Karl Bodmer.

George Catlin arrived at the trading post in 1832 to visit the Indians in the Upper Missouri region and document their culture through his paintings. In his *Letters*, Catlin briefly described Fort Union as 300 feet square, having bastions armed with ordnance, eight or ten log-houses and stores, and a spacious ice house.[8] In a painting made during his stay, Fort Union lies dwarfed by the vast expanse of the Dakota landscape.[9] Unfortunately, the perspective is a great distance from Fort Union, so Catlin's painting offers few additional clues to its plan or appearance. The only visible architectural features are the trading post's palisade walls, the northeast and southwest bastions, and a flagpole.

The second and actually best source available for details of Fort Union's structural complex is the journals of a German traveler, Prince Maximilian.[10] A naturalist interested in aboriginal cultures in North America, the prince traveled up the Missouri River, arriving at Fort Union in June of 1833. In his journal, Maximilian sketched a small plan of the fort (figure 3) and concisely described it. He states that the cottonwood palisade was 80-84 of his paces square and 15 to 16 feet high. The front gate was centered in the south palisade and surmounted by a small blockhouse. Near the center of the north palisade was the rear gate, and small blockhouses with pointed roofs sat at the post's southwestern and northeastern corners.

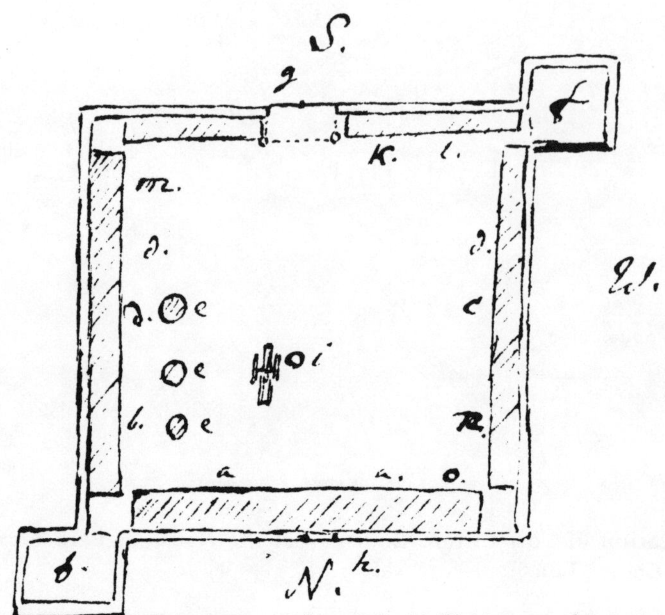

Figure 3. Sketch of Fort Union, 1833. "Prince Maximilian Journal," 2: 143. Courtesy of Joslyn Art Museum, Omaha, Nebraska.

Inside this protective perimeter were five buildings placed directly against the palisade walls. The "mansion" or bourgeois' (superintendent's) house on the north side of the enclosure was one story high, had four glass windows on either side of its front door, and had several apartments in its attic. A building range on the east side contained, from north to south, a store for the whites;[11] two rooms which functioned as apartments for men, stables, fur stocks; and an Indian store. A building shown on the east side of the gate is not labeled or otherwise described, although the structure to the west side of the gate contained a blacksmith shop and a room for visiting Indians. Another building range on the west side of the fort housed, from north to south, the clerks, interpreters and hunters, and the carpenter and tailor, with the last two rooms for other employees. In the courtyard were three Assiniboin tepees inhabited by a few whites and their families, a flagpole, and a cannon.

An 1833 pencil sketch of Fort Union, created by Maximilian's artist, Karl Bodmer, portrays the post at the time of Maximilian's and Bodmer's visit.[12] The perspective is from the hills northeast of the post and, while providing an excellent view of the fort exterior, provides few details of the interior.

Despite the detailed information provided by Maximilian's journal and Bodmer's illustration, there were still a number of issues which remained unclear prior to the MWAC excavations. For example, there was considerable ambiguity regarding the dimensions of the post. Similarly, nothing was known about locations of the post's original structures, their dimensions, or their

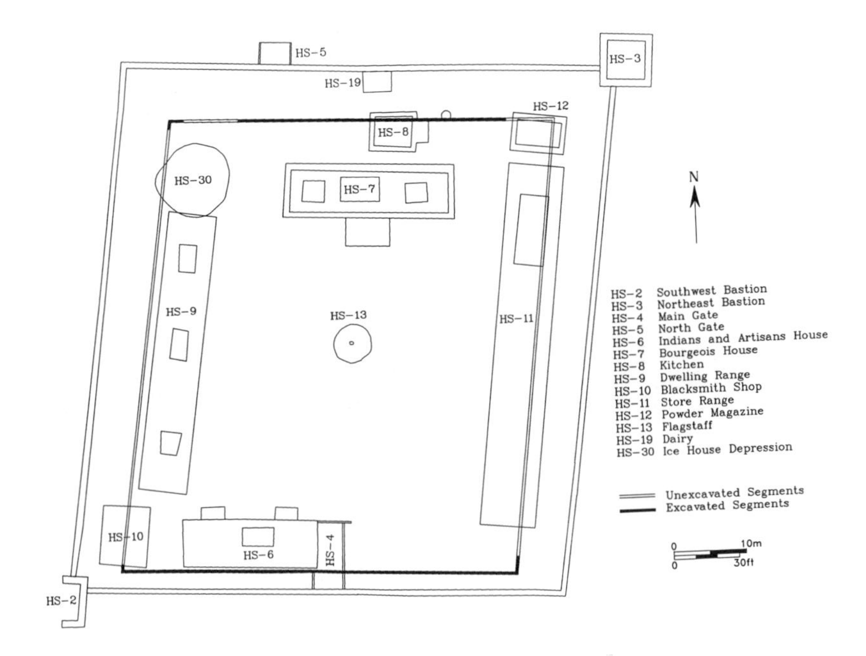

Figure 4. AutoCAD map of 1828-1832 Fort Union palisade elements. Courtesy of the National Park Service, Midwest Archeological Center, Lincoln, Nebraska.

method of construction. For such details, the archaeological record has proved to be our only link to the past.

ARCHAEOLOGICAL EVIDENCE

Excavations at the trading post site in 1986 through 1988 resulted in the recovery of entirely new evidence relating to many of Fort Union's original structures and features. Among the more important of these were details relating to the trading post's palisades, storage facilities, and the bourgeois' or superintendent's house.

The Palisades

One of the more pressing problems facing a trader and his workmen upon arrival at the site chosen for a new fort was protection against attack by Indians and the securing goods and materials against theft. It therefore seems safe to assume that the palisades were among the first structures erected once construction of the new trading post was underway.

Figure 5. Remains of 1828 south palisade pickets. Courtesy of the National Park Service, Midwest Archeological Center, Lincoln, Nebraska.

The Evidence

Elements of Fort Union's original palisades were encountered every year the MWAC crew worked at the site. The north palisade, identified in 1986, was represented by a narrow trench immediately north of the bourgeois house and about 6 m (20 feet) inside the stone foundation of Fort Union's palisade (figure 4). Western and eastern segments of this trench were extensively explored, with the central portion left in place under the kitchen for future researchers. Wood-colored soil stains, or post-molds, were the only evidence of pickets in the eastern segment. In the western segment of the trench, however, bases of vertical timbers were found in place.

The only element of the original trading post within the 1987 excavation area was the northwest corner of the palisade. As in the previous year, this segment was discovered 6 m (20 feet) inside the stone foundations of the second generation palisades.

In 1988, the entire south and west sides of the fort site were opened up. As the western arm of the excavations lay outside the old post's boundaries, nothing could be learned about that portion of the post's palisades or contiguous structures. On the south side, however, excavations revealed the 1828 fort's southwest and southeast palisade corners, south palisade, and main gate. Bases of the wooden pickets were usually well preserved (figure 5). On the basis of this new information, it is possible to determine how palisade pickets were made, identify the construction methods used to erect the palisade itself, and determine precisely the actual size and shape of the original fort.

Archaeological work revealed that whole logs were quite rare in the exposed remnants of the 1828 palisades. Instead, pickets and molds of pickets were usually found to have rough, flat faces, probably a result of splitting large logs into sections with axes or mauls and wedges. Although a few of the log bases were wedge-shaped as a result of trimming with an axe, most were squared as if they had been cut to the proper length with a saw.

The method of construction was also found to vary from one area of the palisade to another, with the north palisade being much less substantial than the south palisade. The picket remnants in the north palisade consisted solely of split planks, each of which was 9 to 10 inches wide and 2 to 3 inches thick. Additional support was afforded by round posts placed at irregular intervals along its interior. These had been set into a trench that was quite narrow and shallow in comparison to its counterpart on the south side of the site.

In contrast, the south palisade was built of 5-to-8-inch-wide pickets which varied in shape. In a few instances, a single row of rectangular "planks," much like those used at the north palisade, were observed. A more common construction technique on this side of the palisade was the use of two rows of pickets, with an inner row of posts alternating with those in an outer row—apparently a means of filling cracks between the pickets as well as strengthening the palisade overall. More commonly, half-round logs were used in the outer row of pickets. The bark was left on the rounded side and the flat side of each picket faced outward. From the outside of the fort, one would not be able to tell the difference between these two picket forms.

The palisades were strengthened against the strong prevailing northwest winds by anchoring the southwest and northwest corners with large square posts set deeply into the ground. No such post was observed at the southeast corner.

Interpretations

Palisade Variations

The question immediately arises as to why Fort Union was constructed in such a seemingly haphazard manner. It has been speculated that the post was constructed by James Kipp, a man who had much experience in building new trading posts for the UMO.[13] If so, the rather unmethodical manner of construction would seem to be out of character. Whether the post was actually built under Kipp's supervision or not, construction variations observed in the archaeological remains of the palisade probably reflect the order in which each palisade section was raised as well as the weather conditions under which that work took place.

Interpretation of the observed construction variations is based upon clues provided by the UMO agent, Kenneth McKenzie.[14] In mid-September 1828,

McKenzie sent a body of men aboard the keelboat *Otter* up the Missouri River to establish a new post at the mouth of the Yellowstone. Its palisades were completed sometime prior to 26 December. The northern location of Fort Union and the late season of its establishment suggest that inclement weather may have influenced Fort Union's construction.

Winter conditions in the Northern Plains often appear quite suddenly and are often earlier in the fall than one might expect. Attesting to the severe weather of the Upper Missouri region is Edwin Denig, a clerk employed at Fort Union in 1833 who lived in the region for twenty-three years, eventually rising to become Fort Union's bourgeois. Among other things, Denig was an excellent observer, preserving through his various writings detailed information on the Native Americans, geography, and climate of the Upper Missouri region. In one of his major works, Denig noted that the Upper Missouri region is characterized by a sudden and often violent transition from summer to winter conditions.[15]

The men aboard the *Otter* ultimately chose a high bank of the Missouri, about three miles upstream from its confluence with the Yellowstone, as the site for Fort Union. At the time of their arrival, sometime around 1 October, the crew was certainly aware of the unpredictable and potentially dangerous situation they were in. Weather was an important consideration, but they would also have been concerned about possible trouble with hostile Indians. Therefore, construction of a strong palisade would have been the first order of the day.

Fort Union's palisades were not completed until sometime in December and it seems certain that winter set in by that time. If so, for weeks after their landing at the site of the new fort, *engagés* and traders probably were faced with an increasingly deteriorating situation: the constant fear of attack; wet, cold weather in which to work; freezing of the river, creating hazardous conditions for transporting logs to the construction site by water; and ground becoming increasingly difficult to dig as it froze to an almost rock-like consistency.

If such conditions prevailed in 1828, it seems reasonable that variations observed in the archaeological remains of the palisade trenches and pickets reflect the sequence in which those trenches were dug and the palisades raised. The south palisade trench is uniformly deep and wide and it seems likely that this may have been one of the first portions raised while the weather was comparatively mild and warm. This conjecture is supported somewhat by the fact that the fur traders may have made a mistake during its excavation, extending the west end of the trench far beyond where the southwest corner of the fort was eventually built.[16] It is unlikely such mistakes would be made if the ground were frozen hard and/or the weather was severely cold.

The shallow, narrow character of the north palisade trench suggests it may have been dug near the end of the palisade construction, perhaps after the ground had frozen. The use of planking for pickets rather than the split and whole logs used in the construction of the south palisade may also be evidence of human stress. Planks could only have been produced with a pit saw and their manufacture. Pickets produced in this way would have required considerably more time and effort to produce than splitting logs or the use of whole logs. Was deteriorating weather preventing new logs from being cut and hauled or floated to the construction site? Were harsh weather and/or threat of attack inducing the traders to speed completion of the palisade by utilizing planking stockpiled for the construction of dwellings and storage buildings? Although it may never be known for certain, the archaeology and historic documents together suggest that this was the case.

Fort Dimensions and Outline

Three of the original trading post's corners had been located by the end of the 1988 field season. The corners and excavated sections of the palisade were then plotted using a computer and AutoCAD drawing software (figure 4).[17] This procedure allowed the fourth corner of the post to be identified (it lay in an area outside the construction/excavation zone) and the size of the post to be electronically measured. The 1828 Fort Union was determined to be about 60 m (198 feet) north-south by 54 m (178 feet) east-west.

The AutoCAD-produced drawing also made clear that the perimeter of the original Fort Union, like the post that followed it, was in the form of a parallelogram rather than a square. This minor alteration allowed the builders to avoid shallow drainages on the east and west sides of the site while utilizing the greatest expanse of flat land at the site and to maximize the size of the fort perimeter. It also enabled the top of the palisade to be kept level without the workers having to cut pickets of various lengths, as would have been the case if the palisade corners had entered the draws. Finally, it avoided drainage problems inside the fort by avoiding sloping ground surfaces at the northwest and southeast corners.[18]

Early Storage Facilities

Second only to the problem of personal protection at the site of a new trading post must have been that of safeguarding food supplies, trade goods, and equipment until formal storage facilities could be established. Archaeological excavations at Fort Union provided some insights into this issue with the discovery of several large storage pits in 1986 and 1988.

The first of these was a large rectangular pit discovered about 4.5 m (15 feet) east of the bourgeois house. Its stratigraphic position at the base of a deep fill sequence implied an early date for this feature. As the pit was excavated, it was found to contain the lower portions of two small barrels similar to those used during the fur trade era to transport and store a variety of goods. As the fill was removed from these containers, a few glass "seed" beads were found just inside their interior rim margins. This particular combination of barrels, beads, and deep stratigraphic position suggested that this was the remains of an underground storage pit which probably dated to the initial construction period of the trading post.

In 1988, a few more early cache pits were found to the west of the main gate, under the lowest of three superimposed buildings. All of these pits were somewhat oval to rectangular-shaped and most were filled with little more than ash and charcoal. Several of the larger pits, however, contained wrought and cut nails, ferrous bucket rims, bear claw pendants, clay pipe fragments, an iron arrow point still attached to its wooden haft, pieces of leather and birch bark, lead spatter, musket balls, a gunflint, a strike-a-light, bone buttons, the wooden handle of a hand auger, a straight pin, a brass finger ring, and the bones of bison, goose, duck, and catfish. Similar in form and stratigraphic position to the pit discovered near the bourgeois house, it is likely that these subfloor pits were used initially to cache trade goods, personal belongings, or foodstuffs. Their contents suggest that, once their storage function had ended, the pits were filled with garbage, particularly refuse from in and around the fireplaces of the original building erected over this location.

One would certainly not expect caching of goods in pits at any trading post if the facility had a store to house them. It seems reasonable to conclude, then, that the pits at Fort Union actually represent elements of the post which existed prior to the construction of the store range and that many more such storage pits must remain intact in unexplored portions of the site.

The Bourgeois House

There are no written documents which relate to the founding of the fort's "mansion." The earliest view of that structure, sketched by Karl Bodmer in 1833, shows only a pitched roof and two small chimneys. It was not until about 1843 that the entire structure was portrayed in a watercolor attributed to Fort Union's clerk Jean Baptiste Moncravie (figure 1). In this view, the house appears quite similar to late eighteenth- and early nineteenth-century French vernacular houses of the St. Louis region. An 1847 sketch by Father Nicolas Point shows little change in the house,[19] but by 1849 or 1850, the structure had been enlarged and modernized in the Greek Revival style. This new facade is illustrated in several pencil sketches and a watercolor made in 1851-52 by Rudolph Kurz, another Fort Union clerk (figure 6). From this time until 1867, when the mansion was torn down with the rest of the post, only minor alterations and additions were made to the structure.

Archaeological Evidence

The various views of the house through its history allow one to identify alterations made in the mansion over time. There is no historic evidence, however, to suggest that the bourgeois house illustrated by Bodmer in 1833 is not the same as that shown in the later views of the structure. Further, no documentary evidence exists which would lead one to believe that this building was not one of the original structures at Fort Union.

The actual origins of the bourgeois house remained unknown until 1986, when several significant features were revealed during excavation of its foundation. As the structure was removed, tell-tale marks of a stonemason's hammer were observed on some of the foundation sandstones. Further, some of the

Figure 6. Bourgeois house, Fort Union, c. 1850-1851, by Rudolph F. Kurz. No. C9-107. Courtesy of the Jesuit Missouri Province Archives, St. Louis, Missouri.

stones at the center and base of the foundation bore fire-reddened and soot-blackened surfaces. The most important information for dating the foundation, however, lay in the clay mortar used to bind the foundation. Within this mortar were a variety of artifacts, including such things as kaolin pipe fragments, buttons, percussion caps, trade beads, lead shot, bottle and window glass fragments, and ceramic shards.

Interpretations

Marks observed on some of the stones in the bourgeois house foundation and the quality of the stonework at the public approaches to the house suggested that a stone mason may have contributed to its construction. Only one stonemason is known to have been employed at Fort Union, a man by the name of Miller whose first name is unknown. He had been brought to Fort Union by the UMO to assist in the construction of the powder magazine (completed in 1833) and the stone bastions. The latter were finished before he left for St. Louis in October 1834.[20] The only Miller identified in employment contracts for the UMO during this time is one Peter Miller, who was engaged in 1831.[21] Thus, if the stone foundation of the bourgeois house was built by this same Peter Miller, it would have to have been sometime between 1831 and October of 1834, which is to say three to six years after Fort Union was founded.

With regard to fire discoloration observed on the inner surfaces of the foundation stones, one may discount the possibility that the marks were created at the time the bourgeois house was dismantled in 1867. If the house were burned at that time, heat-reddened surfaces and soot marks would only have appeared on the exterior, interior, and upper surfaces of the foundation. Rather, it suggests that rock in the foundation may have been recycled from another burned structure, or perhaps from an old fireplace or chimney which had been dismantled.

The only major conflagration known to have occurred at Fort Union was described by Prince Maximilian in his journal.[22] On 3 February 1832, a fire erupted in the dwelling range. High winds quickly transformed the blaze into an inferno which destroyed that building and most of the west palisades before it could be contained. If the stone in the bourgeois house foundation was derived from the dwelling range's foundation or hearths, the mansion would have to have been constructed sometime after February of 1832.

Finally, there is the evidence of artifacts in the clay mortar binding the bourgeois house foundation together. Essentially, clay mortar is little more than mud and it is likely that the mortar was made from dirt obtained at, or very near, the fort. As there is no evidence for prior historic occupations at the Fort Union site, one would not expect mortar made in 1828 to contain historic artifacts. When the foundation was disassembled, however, numerous artifacts were discovered in the foundation's mortar. Their presence in the clay mortar suggested that the mortar was made after the site had been occupied for some time.

One of the more interesting objects recovered from the foundation's mortar was a number of plaster fragments. Many of these had smooth flat faces coated with yellow paint, attributes which imply that the plaster was ultimately derived from another structure's interior walls. Their discovery in 1986 supported the notion that the bourgeois house foundation was actually erected after another structure had been demolished.

Overall, the archaeological evidence implies that the bourgeois house foundation excavated by MWAC in 1986 was not an original foundation on the site. When combined with the documentary evidence, it seems that the bourgeois house's construction probably dates from sometime after the February 1832 fire but before October 1834, when the stonemason left Fort Union. If so, the structure seen in historic views of the fort was actually constructed during the period when the fort was rebuilt between 1833 and 1835.

If the bourgeois house foundation excavated in 1986 represented a second-generation structure, what is the location of the original mansion? Several trenches and posts identified immediately north of the bourgeois house foundation in 1986 may actually represent elements of that structure (figure 7). Their position immediately next to the palisade trench corresponds with Maximilian's 1833 site plan, where the building is illustrated against the central portion of the north palisade. These features would also suggest a building which was somewhat narrower than the later bourgeois house, although its length would have been about the same.[23]

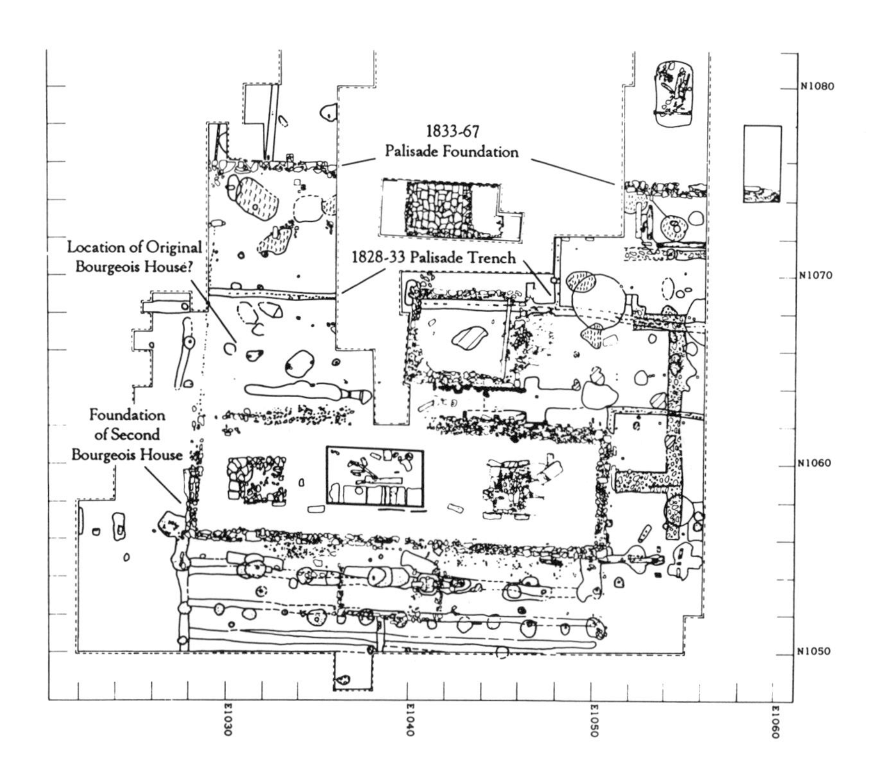

Figure 7. Trench and post hole features which may relate to the c. 1828-1833 mansion. Courtesy of the National Park Service, Midwest Archeological Center, Lincoln, Nebraska.

CONCLUSION

Archaeological excavation at Fort Union has demonstrated a much more complicated site than anyone would have imagined only a few short years ago. Of the more important revelations was the discovery that features of the original Fort Union remain intact at the site, that is, remains of palisades, buildings,[24] and storage/refuse. Data retrieved include methods of palisade construction, the size and shape of the trading post, the sequencing of building construction, and how construction may have been affected by natural and cultural climates of the region. When combined with data for later fort elements, it will be possible to document the physical and organizational alterations and transformations at the site through time as well as identify some of the reasons for these changes.

In short, a great deal has been learned about Fort Union by combining information retrieved in the archaeological investigations with that derived from various primary and secondary documents. Unfortunately, archaeological excavations are destructive, no matter how carefully done. The fieldwork, and the reconstruction which followed, destroyed major portions of the archaeological site. Thus, much of the original fabric of old Fort Union is gone forever.

Nevertheless, it is also true that the NPS has been able to preserve much of Fort Union in a variety of ways. More than half of the site remains intact as a carefully conserved archaeological resource. The remaining portions, excavated in anticipation of the reconstruction, have been conserved at MWAC in the form of an "archaeological library" consisting of thousands of pages of field observations, thousands of photographs and drawings, and literally millions of objects. All records, every object, as well as the undisturbed portions of the site are extremely important because they do much more than simply preserve an element of an old trading post. These can serve as real connections to the past, connections that can actually be seen and touched. The National Park Service will insure that these links to the past will be preserved to enhance the public's understanding of the life and culture of the northern prairie frontier which existed a century and a half ago.

NOTES

1. One of the best sources on the history of Fort Union is Erwin N. Thompson, *Fort Union Trading Post. Historic Structures Report, Part II. Historical Data Section,* National Technical Information Service, doc. PB-203 901 (Washington, D.C.: U.S. Department of Commerce, 1968). This has been reprinted in a somewhat abbreviated version as *Fort Union Trading Post: Fur Trade Empire on the Upper Missouri* (Medora, North Dakota: Theodore Roosevelt Nature and History Association, 1986).
2. Paul R. Huey and William J. Hunt, Jr., "The Great Reconstruction Controversy: A Debate and Discussion," *CRM Bulletin* 13, no. 1 (1990): 1-4.
3. William J. Hunt, Jr. and Lynelle A. Peterson, *Fort Union Trading Post: Archeology and Architecture. The 1986 Excavations* (Lincoln, Neb.: U.S. Department of the Interior, National Park Service, Midwest Archeological Center, 1988); Lynelle A. Peterson and William J. Hunt, Jr., *The 1987 Investigations at Fort Union Trading Post: Archeology and Architecture* (Lincoln, Neb.: U.S. Department of the Interior, National Park Service, Midwest Archeological Center, 1990). A report describing the results of the 1988 field investigations is currently being prepared by Hunt.
4. Douglas D. Scott, Thomas D. Thiessen, and William J. Hunt, Jr., "Scope of Work for 1986 Archeological Investigations at the Fort Union Trading Post National Historic Site in Preparation for Partial Reconstruction" (Lincoln, Neb.: Fort Union Park file, U.S. Department of the Interior, National Park Service, Midwest Archeological Center, 1986).
5. Many of these changes are described by a Fort Union clerk, Charles Larpenteur, in "Original Journal of Charles Larpenteur. Fort Union, 1834-1837" (microfilm), Manuscript Department, Minnesota Historical Society, St. Paul.
6. Hiram M. Chittenden and Alfred T. Richardson, eds., *Life, Letters and Travels of Father Pierre-Jean De Smet, S.J. 1801-1873* (New York: Francis P. Harper, 1905), 244.
7. Chouteau-Moffitt Collection, Missouri Historical Society, St. Louis.

8. George Catlin, *Letters and Notes on the Manners, Customs, and Conditions of the North American Indians* (1844; reprint, New York: Dover Publications, 1973), 14, 22.
9. "Fort Union, Mouth of the Yellowstone River, 2000 Miles Above St. Louis," access. no. 1985.66.388, National Museum of American Art, Smithsonian Institution, Washington, D.C. A small black and white print of this painting appears in Catlin, *Letters and Notes*, Plate 3.
10. Alexander Philip Maximilian, "Diary of a Journey in North America in the Years 1832, 1833 and 1834," original manuscript journals of Prince Alexander Philip Maximilian of Wied-Neuwied, vol. 2, trans. Paul Schach (Omaha, Nebraska: Center for Western Studies, Joslyn Art Museum, nd.).
11. Fort Union's inhabitants were a multiethnic population consisting of Europeans of many nations: Mexicans, French Canadians, Métis, Indians from a variety of northern Plains tribes, and Americans. Prince Maximilian used the term "whites" as an ethnic and racial identifier.
12. "Fort Union at the Mouth of the Yellowstone River," Center for Western Studies, Joslyn Art Museum, Omaha, Nebraska. The sketch has been published in Davis Thomas and Karin Ronnefeldt, eds., *People of the First Man: Life Among the Plains Indians in Their Final Days of Glory* (New York: E.P. Dutton & Co., 1976), 62-63; and Joslyn Art Museum, *Karl Bodmer's America* (Omaha, Neb.: Joslyn Art Museum, Center for Western Studies, 1984), 191.
13. For example, see Ray M. Mattison, "James Kipp," in *The Mountain Men and the Fur Trade of the Far West*, vol. 2, ed. LeRoy R. Hafen (Glendale, Calif.: Arthur H. Clark Co., 1965), 201-5. These assertions appear to be ultimately derived from a remark by Hiram Chittenden to that effect. See Hiram Chittenden, *The American Fur Trade of the Far West* (Lincoln, Neb.: University of Nebraska Press, 1986), 330. This is a republication of a 2-vol., 1935 edition by the Press of the Pioneers, New York which was originally published in 1902 in 3 vols. by Francis P. Harper, New York.
14. Two letters signed by Kenneth McKenzie at the Vermilion River, 2 October 1828, and Fort Tecumseh, 26 December 1828, to Pierre Chouteau, Jr., cited in Chittenden, *American Fur Trade*, 329-30, 932-33.
15. Edwin T. Denig, *Five Indian Tribes of the Upper Missouri* (Norman: University of Oklahoma Press, 1961), 67.

    > No long time intervenes equal to the Indian Summer of the States. A few days is often sufficient to deprive the trees of leaves, freeze up the running streams, and clothe the yet partially green plains with a garment of snow. The winters are variable, mostly very cold, with deep snow. In the severest cold the mercury freezes and the degree cannot be determined in this way. It often remains frozen for several days and for weeks ranging between 30 and 40 degrees below zero. The snow storms in these times are terrible and certain death befalls those who are caught on the plains.

16. This trench actually passed under the stone foundations of the west palisade constructed in 1833. It contained no evidence of pickets in its lower fill. Its upper stratigraphic layers were filled with debris and artifact fragments, suggesting that this feature was used as a garbage pit until it was filled. A couple of pickets in its easterly end, just outside the southwest corner of the 1828 palisade, had been dislodged and snapped off. It looked as if the crews had built the south palisade too far to the west and then attempted to remove the logs after they had been set in place.

17. Bill R. Chada, "AutoCAD and Fort Union Trading Post: The Field Application of a Computer Aided Drafting Program," *CRM Bulletin* 12, no. 1 (1989): 5-6.
18. Problems with drainage became severe and continually troublesome to the occupants of Fort Union when it was expanded in 1833. This was indicated by drainage ditches under the west palisade and several deposits of large amounts of gravel at the northwest and southeast corners.
19. Father Nicolas Point, *Wilderness Kingdom: Indian Life in the Rocky Mountains, 1840-1847*, trans. Joseph P. Donnely (Chicago: Holt, Rinehart, and Winston, 1967), 248.
20. "Miller has finished the bastions and starts today for St. Louis. I offered him $300 he asked for $450 a year. His work is inferior in finish to Pow. Mag. but in other respects I think it is according to contract." A letter signed by Alexander Hamilton, Fort Union, 9 October 1834 to K. McKenzie, "Fort Union Letter Book 1833-1835," Chouteau Collections, Missouri Historical Society, St. Louis.
21. William J. Hunt, Jr., comp., "List of employees of the U.M.O., American Fur Company, 1826-1865." Personal file compiled from information available in the UMO records archived in the Chouteau-Moffitt Collection, Missouri Historical Society, St. Louis.
22. Maximilian, "Diary," 8 October 1833; Thompson, *Historic Structures Report*, 22-23.
23. If these features actually do represent the original mansion, elements of that early structure should have been preserved in unexcavated areas under the kitchen.
24. Other than the bourgeois house, MWAC crews discovered the remains of a structure immediately west of the Fort's south gate. Archaeological data relating to this structure has not been analyzed to date.

Part VI

Into The Twentieth Century

The Hudson's Bay Company in Southwestern Alberta, 1874-1905

Henry C. Klassen

The importance of the British-based Hudson's Bay Company in the economic development of southwestern Alberta between 1874 and 1905 has been insufficiently appreciated. Most historical accounts of the company have briefly noted its inability to compete for market share in the fur trade industry in this region during the 1870s and 1880s with powerful American merchant houses—primarily I.G. Baker & Co. and T.C. Power & Bro. of Fort Benton, Montana. Situated at the head of navigation on the upper Missouri River, both brought capital, fur trade expertise, and entrepreneurial skills into the area as early as 1870 and helped mold the wagon transportation and marketing patterns of the southwestern Alberta country.[1] Arthur J. Ray and Eleanor Jean Stardom have recently provided convincing pictures of the Hudson's Bay Company's role in the fur trade and in retailing in a large part of Canada, including the entire prairie West, in the late nineteenth century.[2] No one, however, has looked closely at why the company reacted hesitantly to the opportunities offered by the fur trade in southwestern Alberta during this period. Moreover, historians have paid little attention to the company's growing strength in the department store business in this region from the early 1890s onwards.

Southwestern Alberta is shaped like a parallelogram, with the Rocky Mountains, the upper Bow River, the Snake Valley and the lower Little Bow River, and the American border marking its four sides. At its greatest extent, southwestern Alberta stretches about 100 miles west to east and about 150 miles north to south. This paper examines the operations of the Hudson's Bay Company in this relatively small region from 1874 to 1905, focusing on two overlapping topics: the difficulties the company faced in competing with Fort Benton merchant houses, and the decisions within the enterprise that led to the expansion of its role in the regional economy. Turn-of-the-century southwestern Alberta needed businesses such as the Hudson's Bay Company, which could learn how to operate efficiently and serve as a symbol of economic well-being, as visible signs of the strength of the region. Not surprisingly, the idea of allowing the company to build a permanent home in the region had numerous supporters. Although the Hudson's Bay Company attracted some criticism from small retailers, there was no crusade against it in southwestern Alberta.

The Hudson's Bay Company had established a presence on the coastline of western Hudson Bay in 1670, and during the next two centuries it had pushed west, northwest, and southwest, probing the rivers including the North Saskatchewan to set up posts among the Native peoples and reaping a large harvest in furs. The Peigan post on the upper Bow River in 1832 became the company's first trading post in southwestern Alberta but was abandoned two years later.[3] Pulling its operations back to the better hunting and trapping grounds along the North Saskatchewan, the company showed no sustained interest in the region until the mid-1870s. Although the enterprise at first had little appreciation for the capital, facilities, and skills needed to become a strong competitor in the buffalo robe and fur trades in southwestern Alberta, it gradually made investments large enough to weave ranchers, farmers, and urban people along with Indians into the fabric of its business. The transformation of the company's fur trading posts into general stores in the mid-1880s, combined with its move to create a network of small, modern department stores in the early 1890s, increased its capacity to compete for market share and profits in the region.

The study of the growth of the Hudson's Bay Company as a modern business enterprise, even on the level of its evolution in a small region, is closely connected to wider trends. Conceptions of modern businesses have varied in recent years, but historian Alfred D. Chandler, Jr. has logically differentiated between traditional and modern enterprises. In his 1977 study of the managerial revolution that began in American business after the mid-nineteenth century, he argued that modern multi-unit firms, unlike traditional single-unit firms which were usually personally owned and managed, relied upon elaborate hierarchies of salaried managers.[4] By itself, a managerial hierarchy did not ensure the continuing growth and transformation of the multi-unit enterprise. It was the managers' decisions that determined the ability of their businesses to compete effectively and grow. The context in which these decision-makers made choices differed considerably from one nation, geographic region, or industry to another; but in order to compete in the marketplace they had to decide how best to improve the coordination of activities between central headquarters and the field, between and within units, and how best to improve the performance of functions such as distribution and finance. While the Hudson's Bay Company had long depended upon a managerial hierarchy, in southwestern Alberta the process of modernization within the enterprise was characterized by gradual advances in the coordination of activities and in the performance of distribution and finance capital as mass marketing techniques were substituted for traditional methods of distribution in anticipation of rising demand for goods.

We can see a development in Hudson's Bay Company marketing and distribution through three stages that reflected the wider evolution of the southwestern Alberta economic and social order. The first stage, between 1874 and 1883, witnessed the operations of a few company fur-trading posts, and especially the one at Calgary, within a developing region controlled by the Blackfoot Indian nation until it signed the Treaty of 1877 with the Canadian government; this region was only sparsely populated by white pioneers, and largely isolated from the outside world.[5] The postmasters carried a limited variety of goods in very small quarters and faced considerable competition. In their transactions with Indians, they at first usually bartered their items for furs and buffalo robes. Similarly, the postmasters sold their goods to nearby white ranchers and farmers, often accepting ranch and farm products in payment. As was the case on other frontiers in North America at the time, cash was in short supply on the southwestern Alberta frontier. Many Indian purchasers, once they received treaty money, paid for some goods in cash. Stock turnover at the posts was nevertheless slow.

The arrival of the Canadian Pacific Railway in Calgary in 1883 opened the way for the second stage of Hudson's Bay Company marketing, which lasted until 1891. In the history of the company's experience in southwestern Alberta, this was the era of the general store. The general store had more square feet and a greater array of merchandise than the trading post but remained relatively small and cramped. With the coming of more white people into the region, the growth of commercial agriculture and the decline of the fur trade, the company's general stores began to rely more on monetary than on barter exchanges. The volume of trade passing through the stores and the speed and efficiency of its movement grew.

The third stage of Hudson's Bay Company marketing saw its adoption of the small department store as its principal mode of reaching its market. The early years of this phase were 1891-1905, in which the enterprise was running four small stores in the region in response to the increasing demand for a wide variety of consumer goods by the buying public. Unquestionably, the company played a significant role in the department store wave that rolled over North American marketing at the turn of the century. The main feature distinguishing the company's stores from large North American department stores such as Marshall Field's in Chicago, Macy's in New York, and Eaton's in Toronto was that they were relatively small in size.[6] Nonetheless, like both large and small department stores elsewhere, the Hudson's Bay Company's department stores in southwestern Alberta occupied modern buildings and pursued the business strategy of seeking profits through volume and low, fixed prices. Besides offering price savings to shoppers, the company's stores provided them with guaranteed products and much choice.

THE BURDENS OF THE FUR-TRADING POSTS

In moving through its first stage in southwestern Alberta, the Hudson's Bay Company encountered serious and persistent problems in its attempt to develop fur-trading posts. Both the company's top executives in London, England and its senior officers in Winnipeg thought that the enterprise could challenge successfully the Fort Benton firms in the region's fur and buffalo robe markets. The

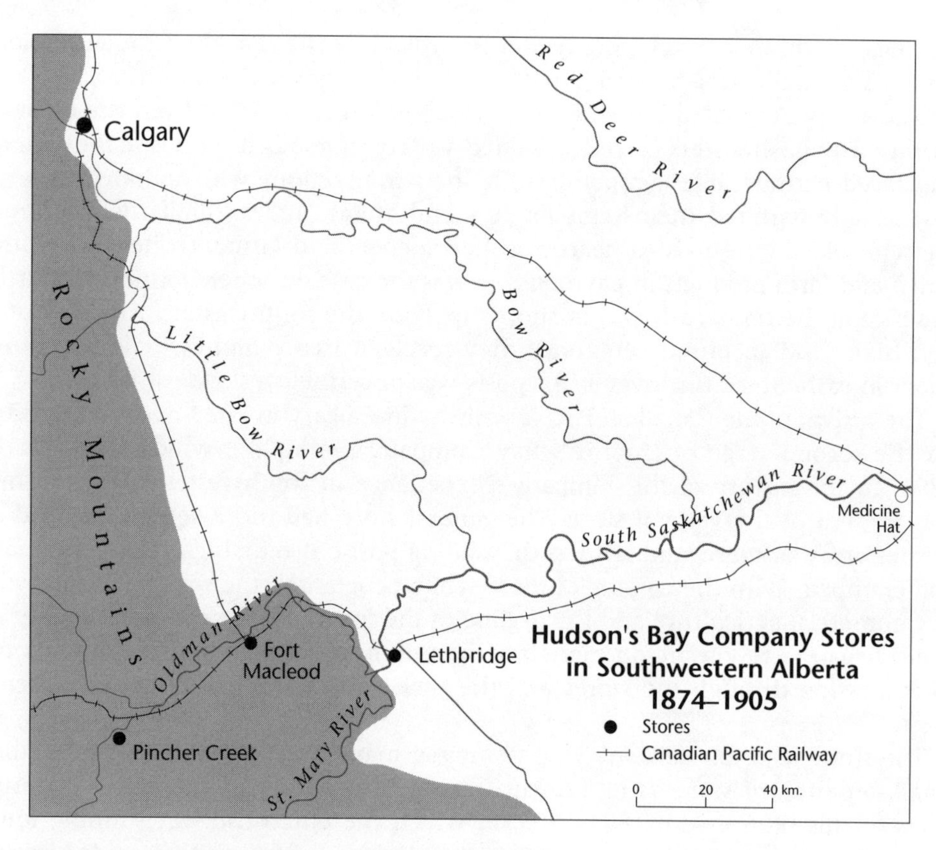

Figure 1. Hudson's Bay Company Stores, 1874-1905.

company's efforts gave it a few gains in market share, but the results were generally disappointing. Moreover, the posts were difficult to maintain in the face of intense competition from the American enterprises.

The Hudson's Bay Company developed its trading facilities partly in reaction to the great success of the Fort Benton firms in southwestern Alberta. Certainly, the concern's small posts were a defensive response to the need to protect its existing and potential opportunities for trade in the rich northern fur districts. This was important because the North was the main source of its income. The company's willingness to move into the southwestern Alberta market helped thwart attempts by its American competitors to establish permanent trading premises in the northern areas. At the same time, the trading facilities of the Hudson's Bay Company in southwestern Alberta became a creative response to the opportunity to make a profit from the trade in furs and buffalo robes.

In 1874 the Hudson's Bay Company began to challenge the Fort Benton merchant houses by opening a trading post at the junction of the Bow and Ghost rivers. That year John Bunn, the post's manager, gathered many buffalo robes. But the limitation of this location quickly asserted itself, for it was too far from the buffalo herds to gain adequate access to the robes the Indian hunters offered

Figure 2. Fur Trading Post, Hudson's Bay Company, Calgary, c. early 1880s. Photo, No. NA 2074-2, courtesy of the Glenbow-Alberta Institute Archives, Calgary, Canada.

in exchange for merchandise. Since there was little incentive to remain, the company soon closed the business down.

Bunn set up a new post at Calgary in 1875 so as to be closer to the autumn grazing grounds of the buffalo. While most of the post's activity focused on buffalo robes, it was also active in the commerce of furs, especially lynx, beaver, and wolf. Yet the Calgary post, because of the stiff competition from American trading firms, was a poor risk for the Hudson's Bay Company, though not a failure. "Our greatest drawback in trade is the want of horses," wrote Bunn.[7] Another critical problem was that he lacked sufficient blankets, clothing, groceries, and repeating rifles. This situation created few earnings for the Hudson's Bay Company. The best profits went to Baker & Co., which carried enough horses, repeating rifles, groceries, blankets, and clothing to meet the Indians' needs, besides offering them competitive prices for their robes and furs and providing them with liberal credit accommodation. Obviously, the finance available to Bunn from the Winnipeg office of the Hudson's Bay Company was not comparable to that of Baker & Co. This often prevented him from adjusting his prices and his credit terms to the needs of the market.

Between 1875 and the early 1880s, the Hudson's Bay Company in southwestern Alberta continued to labour under one difficulty after another. Trade was so poor at the post the company opened in High River in 1875 that it decided to close the business the same year.[8] James Grahame, the company's chief commissioner in Winnipeg, showed little inclination to make large enough investments in the quality and quantity of goods to compete for market share. As a result, the Calgary post had the reputation of offering its customers inferior merchandise, especially flour and blankets, and of often running short of supplies.[9] The inflow of manufactured products from Winnipeg was very irregular, partly because the company's water and land transportation system by way of the North Saskatchewan remained crude.[10] Not surprisingly, its transportation costs for these goods were extremely high. By contrast, the company's Fort Benton rivals paid much less to ship their merchandise into southwestern Alberta by American railroads and their own Missouri River steamboats and prairie wagon trains. Lower transportation costs on the American route likewise gave the Fort Benton firms a competitive edge over the Hudson's Bay Company in shipping furs and robes to the Montreal market.

With such heavy burdens to bear and with so little to show for its efforts at geographical expansion, the Hudson's Bay Company in southwestern Alberta faced bleak prospects. The inadequate financial help from the London and Winnipeg offices added to the difficulties of the enterprise in the region.

WIDENING THE FIELD

By the mid-1880s, however, the Hudson's Bay Company was beginning to widen its field in southwestern Alberta. In doing so, it was moving into its second marketing phase. The process started in 1883, when the coming of a reliable, all-weather transportation and communication infrastructure—the Canadian Pacific Railway, the telegraph and newspaper advertising (the *Macleod Gazette* and the *Calgary Herald*, the region's first newspapers, began in 1882 and 1883, respectively)—set the stage for the building of a modern marketing and distribution enterprise in the region. The revolution in transportation and communication, in addition to bringing lower shipping rates and faster travel, increased and speeded the flow of commercial information across Canada. These changes helped make possible modernization in the Hudson's Bay Company's retailing activities.

The company's investment in more efficient management recruitment also aided modernization. The attitude and standing of the new men assuming management responsibilities in Canada and inspiring change in the enterprise in southwestern Alberta counted heavily. By the mid- and late 1880s, the company enjoyed the advantages of having Joseph Wrigley as the trade commissioner in Winnipeg, James Thomson as the manager of the Calgary general retail store, and E.F. Gigot as the manager of the general retail store in Fort Macleod. A creative approach to the business of marketing guided the conduct of all these men, while a conservative, but sound, point of view was a central dynamic in their handling of the company's financial affairs.

Other important changes which helped transform the Hudson's Bay Company in southwestern Alberta in this period included a new understanding of the need to adjust to the changing economic environment. The years 1879-1883 were mostly ones of transition, in which the buffalo virtually disappeared and the trade in furs declined while the path to the future was formed. Between 1883 and 1891, railway construction, population growth, the coming of commercial agriculture, the rise of small towns, and the appearance of new retail businesses combined to alter the shape of the region. Trying to keep pace with the changing character of the region after 1883 was a challenge which the Hudson's Bay Company accepted.

The company's attempt to keep abreast of this change by rebuilding its business in southwestern Alberta did not, however, lead immediately to complete success. Until 1891 Baker & Co. was consistently more competitive than the Hudson's Bay Company.[11]

Despite the dearth of sales figures for the Hudson's Bay Company's Calgary store between 1883 and 1890, the available evidence suggests that the volume of trade increased erratically. The growth of its business accompanied the growth of Calgary following the arrival of the Canadian Pacific. The Riel Rebellion of 1885 exercised a major influence upon the store's sales.[12] During the rebellion, it delivered a significant volume of ammunition and other supplies to the Canadian militia. The value of the sales for 1884 is unknown, but in 1885 it stood at $47,000. Sales increased to $51,000 in 1886, before dropping to $34,000 in 1887, only to rise again to $38,000 in 1888, during a period when a number of other retail enterprises in the town failed.[13] For the Hudson's Bay Company's Calgary store during the years 1886-1888, the stock-turn averaged 2.5 times while the profit rate on sales averaged 9.5 per cent. Although this performance was not spectacular, the store was now in a better position than it had been before 1883.

Central to the ongoing growth of the Hudson's Bay Company in southwestern Alberta was geographical expansion. In the late 1880s and early 1890s the enterprise made the investments and created the managerial team needed to exploit new markets, especially at Fort Macleod and Pincher Creek.[14] This, coupled with the continuing expansion of regional trade in these years, fueled and sustained the growth of the company's stores in these communities despite opposition from Baker & Co., which had been trading in this section of Alberta since the early 1870s.

To administer its investments at Fort Macleod and Pincher Creek, the Hudson's Bay Company brought in E.F. Gigot from one of its branches in Manitoba to coordinate the activities of its business units in these communities. In 1886 Gigot, from the company's newly opened Fort Macleod general store of which he was the manager, began to build a regionwide distributing organization. Two years later, in 1888, he purchased for the Hudson's Bay Company Schofield & Hyde's general store in Pincher Creek, simultaneously acquiring H.E. Hyde, one of the former owners, to manage it.[15] If the profits at the Fort Macleod and Pincher Creek stores were small, the growth was nevertheless healthy.

From the detailed and reliable reports of Gigot in Fort Macleod and Thomson in Calgary, the Hudson's Bay Company's management at Winnipeg and London could gain an intimate knowledge of the southwestern Alberta market. It was clear that Thomson and Gigot were telling their superiors the truth about the performance of the general stores under their supervision. They also helped build the company in the region into a stable competitor capable of making gradual progress.

This success, however, did not come easily or quickly. Gigot and Thomson had experienced numerous difficulties in developing the general store trade. The major difficulties in this respect were inadequate premises in Calgary, Fort Macleod, and Pincher Creek, growing competition from other retailers, the downswing in the economy in the mid-1880s, and the burdens imposed on ranchers and farmers by the hard winter of 1886-87 and the implications of this problem for the store managers' task of collecting debts. Thomson's and Gigot's clear entrepreneurial instincts, however, helped them adjust to the changing conditions and lead the Hudson's Bay Company in southwestern Alberta in an important new direction—the development of the department store business during its third marketing stage.

THE EMERGENCE OF THE MODERN DEPARTMENT STORES

Although Thomson and Gigot played a major role in moving the Hudson's Bay Company in southwestern Alberta into its third marketing stage, its small, modern department stores in the region did not emerge full-blown from their ideas alone. Elsewhere in the company there were men—especially Wrigley, C.J. Brydges, and C.C. Chipman—who also represented a tradition of innovation. In the 1880s, the need to expand and modernize the company's business in the region was a matter of great concern to Brydges, its land commissioner in Winnipeg.[16] Between 1889 and 1891, Wrigley convinced the reluctant executives at the Hudson's Bay Company in London to make a large enough investment to enter the department store trade in southwestern Alberta.[17] Chipman, who succeeded Wrigley as trade commissioner in Winnipeg in 1891, did much to perpetuate this growing business.

Moreover, outside the Hudson's Bay Company, there were significant examples of department store marketing from which the company could draw. The success of Baker & Co.'s small department store in Calgary was particularly important as a local model for the emergence of the Hudson's Bay Company's department store business. Certainly, the British enterprise looked to Baker & Co. for guidance in the establishment of its own department stores in the region. At the same time, the Hudson's Bay Company also took its cues from British pioneers in department store marketing, such as Whiteley's in London and Jenner's in Edinburgh.[18] Although Jenner's and Whiteley's were much larger and much more oriented toward middle-class shoppers than the company's small department stores in southwestern Alberta, these metropolitan institutions nevertheless offered important precedents for modern department store marketing in the Canadian West.

The growing economic strength and demands of the buying public in southwestern Alberta at the turn of the century facilitated the rise of the company's department stores. Expanding incomes of many urban, ranch, and farm families increased their spending power, which in turn led them to demand much variety as well as high quality in merchandise. Fashion-conscious men and women,

Figure 3. Department Store, Hudson's Bay Company, Fort Macleod, c. 1890s. Photo, No. NA 1087-5, courtesy of the Glenbow-Alberta Institute Archives, Calgary, Canada.

whether in urban or rural communities, created a demand for a comprehensive range of ready-made clothing that reflected the latest styles in dress. Consumption in the high Victorian and Edwardian era in the region was particularly conspicuous in ladies' fashions. As the dietaries of both the middle and working classes improved, there was naturally a greater demand for choice in foods.

These demands and increasing competition for market share encouraged the Hudson's Bay Company to embark on a strategy of growth by making major investments. In the spring of 1891, the enterprise acquired Baker & Co.'s stores and their stock and facilities in Calgary, Fort Macleod, and Lethbridge, thus eliminating its primary competitor in southwestern Alberta and achieving an instant and major gain in market share. In the fall of that year, the British concern opened its own department store in Calgary and sold Baker & Co.'s store in the city to the Imperial Bank of Canada.

The importance of the Hudson's Bay Company's new department store in Calgary had already become evident to Harrison J. Young, one of its officers in Edmonton, in 1890, when the plans to build it were well under way. "It is a standing custom of all opponents of our Company," he wrote to Wrigley, "to state that we are slow and old fashioned and not up to the times. I think the proposed store at Calgary will offer a most *substantial* argument against their assertions."[19]

The company's intention of adopting a modern style of retailing was certainly made explicit in its small Calgary store. It was a two-story, stone building with

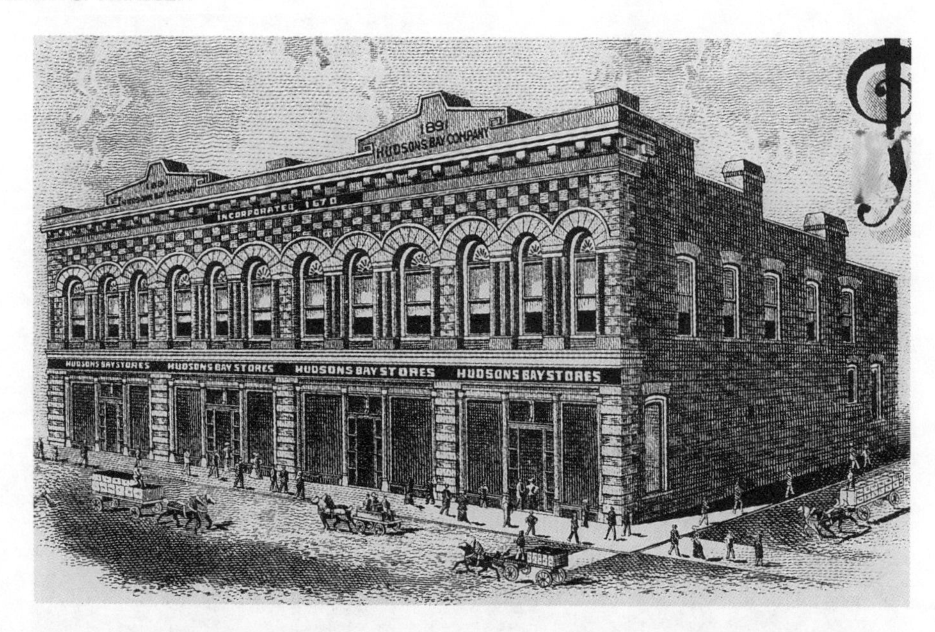

Figure 4. Department Store, Hudson's Bay Company, Calgary, c. 1904. Photo, No. NA 419-1, courtesy of the Glenbow-Alberta Institute Archives, Calgary, Canada.

8,000 square feet of floor space. This enlarged capacity housed separate departments devoted to dry goods, groceries, ladies' clothing, men's clothing, boots and shoes, and dressmaking.[20] The success of the store was such that the company found it necessary to extend the premises in 1895 and then again in 1904. The additional capacity allowed the store to expand its existing lines and open several new departments, including house furnishings, crockery and glassware, and liquor.[21] Equipped with electric lighting and well stocked with a complex variety of goods, all departments offered their customers bright surroundings for their shopping needs.

As time passed, the Hudson's Bay Company's premises elsewhere in southwestern Alberta were no longer adequate, especially when compared to its Calgary store. To overcome this problem, the company built a two-story, stone store in Fort Macleod and a similar one in Lethbridge by the mid-1890s.[22] Simultaneously, it organized these small stores along departmental lines. By the early 1900s, the volume of trade at the company's general store in Pincher Creek was sufficient to warrant its decision to erect a new, two-story, wooden building and transform this outlet into a departmentalized operation as well.[23] Improvements of this kind testify to the company's willingness to invest substantially in modern retailing.

Local managers in Calgary, Lethbridge, Fort Macleod, and Pincher Creek learned, however, that it was not easy to achieve efficiency in the operation of the small department stores. The stock-turn data presented in figure 5 show that managers found it particularly difficult to adjust inventories to consumer demand during the depression in the mid-1890s. In consequence, the stock-turn fell

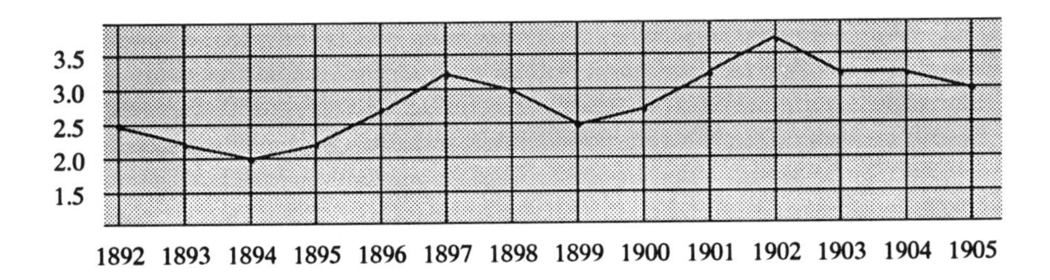

Figure 5. Graph of Average Stock-Turn of the Hudson's Bay Company for Stores at Calgary, Fort Macleod, Lethbridge, and Pincher Creek, 1892-1905. Source: HBCA, D32/4, Abstracts of Balance Sheets, 1892-1905.

significantly from 2.5 times in 1892 to 1.9 in 1894, and then gradually began to improve with the recovery of the economy. Perhaps the improvement also stemmed from the application of increasingly better inventory controls. At any rate, the managers found that, despite some problems in inventory management, their department stores continued to make progress.

A typical small department store in North America at the turn of the century had a stock-turn of between two and three. Thus, as the data in figure 5 illustrate, by the early 1900s the Hudson's Bay Company's stores' rate of turnover in southwestern Alberta showed up very favourably in relation to that of most other small, modern department stores. Certainly the stock-turn figures by this time demonstrate that the store managers were successful in keeping their stocks fresh and clean.

There remains the question of the benefits to the Hudson's Bay Company in southwestern Alberta resulting from its decision to integrate backward into manufacturing.[24] The company produced flour in its flour mill in Winnipeg—prize-winning and profitable flour which won awards at the Winnipeg Industrial Exhibition and at the Paris Exhibition in the early 1900s. In Calgary, Fort Macleod, and Lethbridge, and probably in Pincher Creek as well, the company's stores made dresses and hats for women and girls in their own establishments. Although the enterprise did not go into manufacturing in as big a way as Eaton's department store of Toronto did, it did derive benefit from the production of its own hats, dresses, and flour. These products offered advantages in control of quality and, equally significant, in giving customers the opportunity to identify quality goods with the company's name. But most importantly, they helped make the Hudson's Bay Company a low-priced marketing house. While the enterprise continued to rely on independent suppliers for a large portion of these items, it was able to deliver flour and women's and girls' dresses and hats to its customers in southwestern Alberta fairly cheaply through its own limited manufacturing facilities. In other lines, the company was of course content to leave production completely to large independent manufacturers. These manufacturers could put merchandise on the market at low prices which the company believed

A. Cash Sales (Thousands of Dollars)

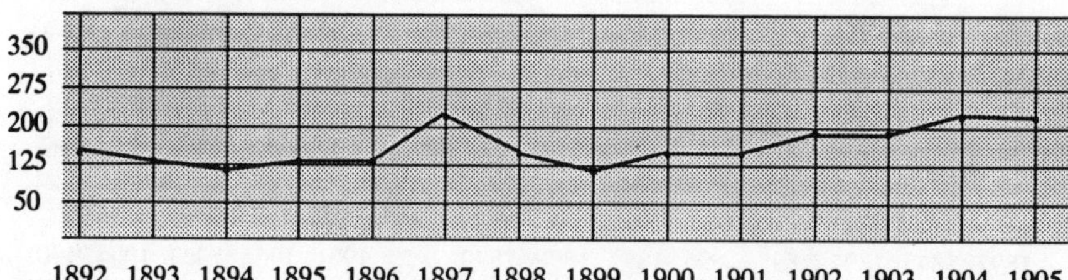

B. Credit Sales (Thousands of Dollars)

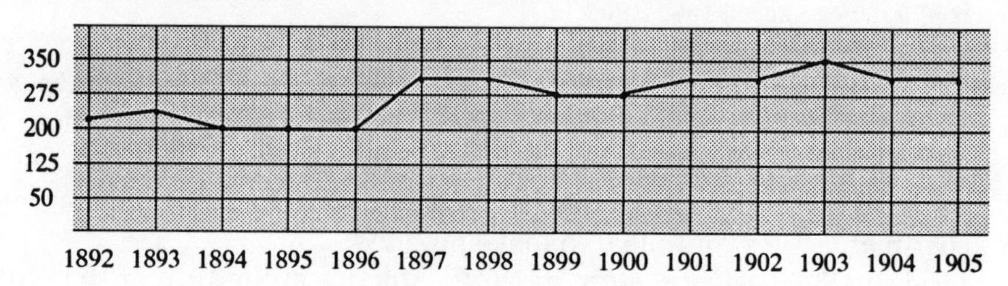

C. Percent of Credit Sales to Total Sales

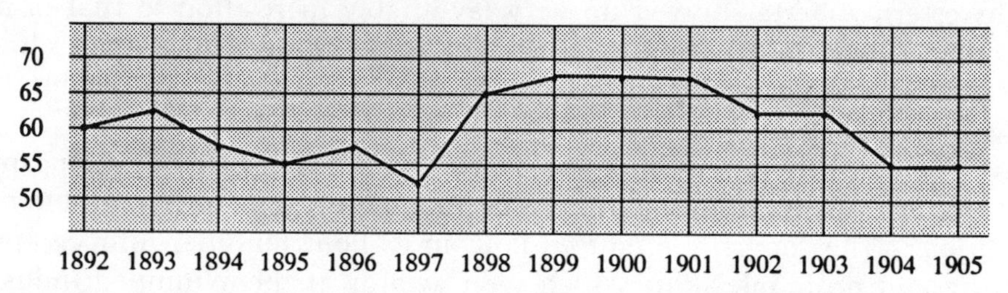

Figure 6. Graph of Cash and Credit Sales of the Hudson's Bay Company for Stores at Calgary, Fort Macleod, Lethbridge, and Pincher Creek, 1892-1905. Source: HBCA, D32/4, Abstracts of Balance Sheets, 1892-1905.

it would not be able to match, though it clearly took advantage of the prices by buying from such producers.

For many consumers the appeal of the Hudson's Bay Company's small department stores lay primarily in their low prices. Each of the company's stores in the region lowered its prices on the assumption that this would give it a competitive advantage over its local rivals. An important part of the price reduction process was the gathering of information about competitors' prices. Generally speaking, the company's stores had the capacity to offer consumers lower prices than most local competitors. Low prices did not, however, necessarily mean an increase in customers for the Hudson's Bay Company. It often also had to provide existing and potential customers with other incentives to buy, including a willingness to be liberal in granting them credit.

A. Net Sales (Thousands of Dollars)

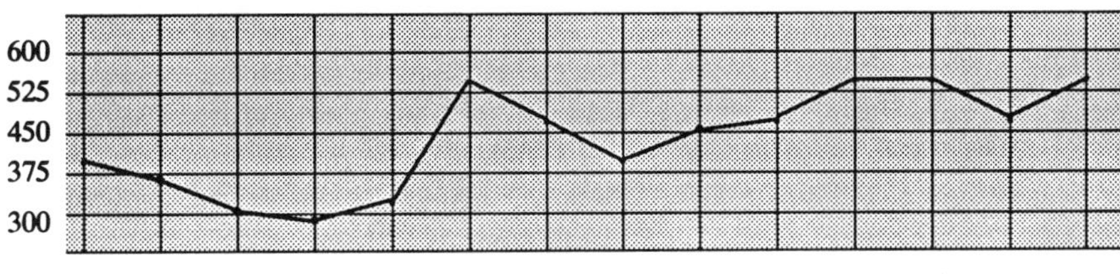

B. Net Profits (Thousands of Dollars)

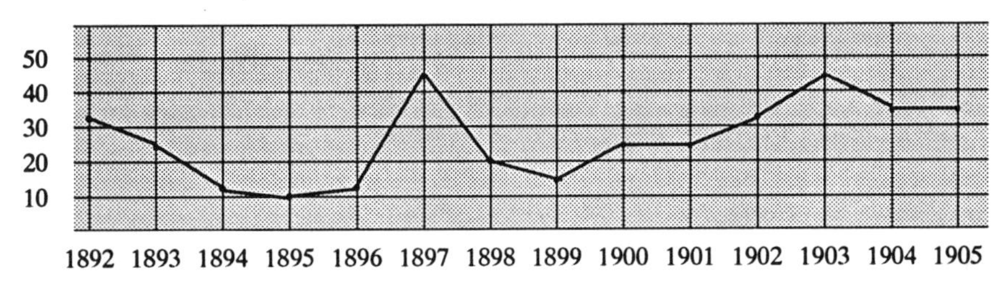

C. Percent of Net Profits to Net Sales

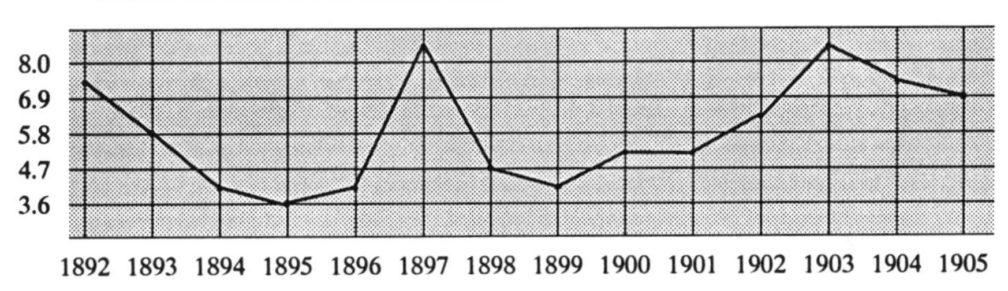

Figure 7. Graph of Net Sales, Net Profits and Profit Rate of the Hudson's Bay Company for stores at Calgary, Fort Macleod, Lethbridge and Pincher Creek, 1892-1905. Source: HBCA, D32/4, Abstracts of Balance Sheets, 1892-1905.

In its attempt to keep customers and attract new ones, the Hudson's Bay Company in southwestern Alberta became quite dependent on credit sales.[25] The enterprise frequently granted short term credit to customers, charging them interest. Between 1892 and 1905, as figure 6 indicates, the company's credit sales ranged from a low of 53.6 percent of its total sales to a high of 64.8 percent. This service to customers, besides involving considerable accounting work for the company, was expensive. There were always problems in providing credit, but the losses from bad debts were generally small. Clearly, the company saw charge customers as a business opportunity. Competition in the credit business was fierce. Rather than risk losing trade with its customers, the company drew upon all its resources to give them generous credit. Overall, this credit strategy helped give the enterprise its competitive edge.

Yet, despite the Hudson's Bay Company's obvious onward march in southwestern Alberta, its growth in terms of total sales and profits at the four stores was uneven, as seen in figure 7. In 1892, in the context of an expanding regional economy, the company generated almost $379 thousand in sales and over $28 thousand in profits. The commercial depression in the mid-1890s was, however, a major inhibiting factor. Between 1893 and 1895, sales dropped from about $378 thousand to about $300 thousand while earnings plunged from about $22 thousand to about $11 thousand. As the economy began to recover in 1896, the Hudson's Bay Company's performance started to improve. With signs of economic strength prevailing during the Klondike gold rush in 1896-1897, the company's sales in southwestern Alberta increased over one and a half times. Profits jumped from about $13 thousand to over $43 thousand. The company's sales volume and earnings sagged in 1898-99. But between 1900 and 1905, its sales grew slowly from about $382 thousand to about $513 thousand and its profits rose gradually from about $18 thousand to about $37 thousand, a reflection of the return to health of the regional and national economies. In figure 7 we see that, whereas a decline in sales volume always caused the percentage of profit to fall, an increase in sales almost always raised the profit rate. It is clear that a large share of an increment in the profit rate could be attributed to an increment in sales.

By 1905, the largest department store business in southwestern Alberta was the Hudson's Bay Company, a fact that emphasizes its considerable stake in the region's retail market. By then the company was fully integrated into the regional economy, played an increasingly important role in applying modern business methods to consumer marketing, and was a significant component of net capital formation in the region. As Chipman's letters indicate, the company continued to improve its performance by setting high staffing and training standards. By 1905, the company had a regional work force of 55 salaried employees, with 29 in Calgary, 12 in Fort Macleod, 7 in Lethbridge, and 7 in Pincher Creek.[26] Its establishments were typical of small, western department stores, such as Baker & Co.'s in Montana and Alberta and Power & Bro.'s in Montana. The Hudson's Bay Company was not without opposition from significant rivals such as T. Lebel & Co.'s small department store in Pincher Creek. Yet in continuing to be progressive and responsive to consumer needs, the company had a key to marketing success in the region.

Conclusion

The history of the Hudson's Bay Company in southwestern Alberta from 1874 to 1905 spans a time period that represents the early years of the continuous investments it made in the region. In this period, the company went through two transformations in this section of Alberta: it grew from a few fur-trading posts into several general stores, and then, at different times after 1890, these outlets became small, modern department stores. As the concern was undergoing these changes, there was evidence that it had not lost its taste for adventure. Ambitious ideas for expansion into new geographical and new product markets gradually became a reality.

Did southwestern Alberta receive a reasonable reward for giving the Hudson's Bay Company a home? The answer to this question is that the region derived considerable benefit from the company's growing presence. Its department stores played an increasingly important role in the evolution of modern capitalism in southwestern Alberta, and in doing so they helped give the region a valuable resource. This resource provided a dynamic for growth that helped make the regional economy more competitive. Although no single business can contribute more than a small part to the total increase in capital formation, the Hudson's Bay Company quickened the pace of economic growth. The last eight and a half decades have brought changes to the company's program, including the closing of its stores in Pincher Creek, Fort Macleod, and Lethbridge. But the company's department store in downtown Calgary, begun a century ago, stands today as the most visible symbol of its long-term and ongoing commitment to retailing in southwestern Alberta.

NOTES

1. See, for example, A.A. den Otter, "The Hudson's Bay Company's Prairie Transportation Problem, 1870-85," in *The Developing West: Essays on Canadian History in Honor of Lewis H. Thomas*, ed. John E. Foster (Edmonton: The University of Alberta Press, 1983), 25-47.
2. Arthur J. Ray, *The Canadian Fur Trade in the Industrial Age* (Toronto: University of Toronto Press, 1990), 329; Eleanor Jean Stardom, "Adapting to Altered Circumstances: Trade Commissioner Joseph Wrigley and the Hudson's Bay Company, 1884-1891" (Master's thesis, University of Manitoba, 1987), 199-247.
3. J.G. Nelson, *The Last Refuge* (Montreal: Harvest House, 1973), 79-81.
4. Alfred D. Chandler, Jr., *The Visible Hand: The Managerial Revolution in American Business* (Cambridge, Mass.: Harvard University Press, 1977), 1-6.
5. Hugh A. Dempsey, *Indian Tribes of Alberta* (Calgary: Glenbow-Alberta Institute, 1979), 14-15.
6. Robert W. Twyman, *History of Marshall Field & Co., 1852-1906* (Philadelphia: University of Pennsylvania Press, 1954); Ralph M. Hower, *History of Macy's of New York, 1858-1919* (Cambridge, Mass.: Harvard University Press, 1943); Joy L. Santink, *Timothy Eaton and the Rise of His Department Store* (Toronto: University of Toronto Press, 1990).
7. John Bunn to Richard Hardisty, 14 December 1875. Richard Hardisty Papers, box 4, Bow River, Glenbow-Alberta Institute Archives.
8. John Bunn to Richard Hardisty, 24 November 1876. Hardisty Papers, box 5, Fort Calgary.
9. Richard Hardisty to James A. Grahame, 18 September 1883. Provincial Archives of Manitoba, Hudson's Bay Company Archives [hereafter HBCA], D20/27, ff. 49-50, Calgary,
10. Den Otter, "The Hudson's Bay Company's Prairie Transportation Problem," 40-41.

11. Henry C. Klassen, "I.G. Baker and Company in Calgary, 1875-1884," *Montana The Magazine of Western History* 35, no. 3 (Summer 1985): 49-50.
12. Richard Hardisty to Joseph Wrigley, 17 April 1885, HBCA, D20/33, ff. 233, Calgary; Richard Hardisty to Joseph Wrigley, May 5, 1885, HBCA, D20/34, ff. 25-26, Calgary. For a discussion of the overall impact of the Rebellion of 1885 on the Hudson's Bay Company, see Stardom, "Adapting to Altered Circumstances," 58-100.
13. James Thomson to Richard Hardisty, 1 May 1889, HBCA, C20/56, ff. 365-68, Calgary.
14. Joseph Wrigley to William Armit, 22 June 1886, HBCA, A12/28, ff.163-64, Winnipeg.
15. E.F. Gigot to Joseph Wrigley, 9 June 1888, HBCA, D20/50, ff. 190-91, Fort Macleod.
16. C.J. Brydges to William Armit, 27 February 1883, HBCA, A12/22, ff. 83-92, Winnipeg.
17. The problems Joseph Wrigley experienced elsewhere in the Hudson's Bay Company, problems which led to his dismissal in 1891, did not prevent him from providing leadership in establishing an impressive department store business in southwestern Alberta.
18. Richard S. Lambert, *The Universal Provider: A Study of William Whiteley and the Rise of the London Department Store* (London: Harrap, 1938); Anthony Slaven, "Charles Jenner," in *Dictionary of Scottish Business Biography 1860-1960: Processing, Distribution, Services*, vol. 2, eds. Anthony Slaven and Sydney Checkland (Aberdeen: Aberdeen University Press, 1990), 370-71.
19. Harrison J. Young to Joseph Wrigley, 22 August 1890, HBCA, D20/62, ff. 211-14, Edmonton.
20. James Thomson to Joseph Wrigley, 5 December 1890, HBCA, D20/57, ff. 298-302, Calgary; *Calgary Herald*, 25 August 1891.
21. C.C. Chipman to William Ware, 15 October 1894, HBCA, A12S. 509/1, ff. 11-12, Winnipeg; *Calgary Herald*, 21 September 1895.
22. *Macleod Gazette*, 22 December 1892; *Lethbridge News*, 27 April 1892.
23. *Rocky Mountain Echo*, 25 August 1903.
24. *Calgary Herald*, 10 August 1901; *Lethbridge News*, 28 October 1891; *Macleod Gazette*, 1 December 1892. There were ups and downs in the Hudson's Bay Company's flour manufacturing industry in various prairie centers during the 1880s and 1890s, but by 1900 its Winnipeg flour mill was performing well.
25. Abstracts of Balance Sheets, 1892-1905, HBCA, D32/4.
26. Ibid.

Creating Corporate Images of the Fur Trade: The Hudson's Bay Company and Public Relations in the 1930s

Peter Geller

The Hudson's Bay Company (HBC) has long held a fascination for those interested in the history of the North American fur trade. Less readily recognized, however, is the HBC's own contribution to the public perception of its image. Given the central role assigned to the fur trade, and to the Hudson's Bay Company in particular, as a factor in North America's historical development in both popular and academic discourse, it is essential to examine the ways in which the officials of the Hudson's Bay Company itself influenced the contours and definitions of this role.[1]

In the course of the 1930s, a decade most often associated with depression and disruption, the HBC consolidated its public relations efforts, employing a variety of strategies and techniques. A study of this material, which included both written texts and a sophisticated use of forms of visual representation, reveals the ways in which the HBC attempted to compose and maintain a company identity that conveyed a strong sense of tradition and continuity as a fur trade enterprise. An exploration of the contours of this representation, centering on the company's magazine *The Beaver*, allows for an analysis of the meanings and interpretations underlying these public presentations of images of the Hudson's Bay Company in the 1930s. The "fur trade" was embraced as a convenient and salient symbol in both words and pictures, serving as a focus for building up a glorious official history and exemplifying the company's "progress" in the present. An integral part of the portrayal of the fur trade involved a preoccupation with defining the Hudson's Bay Company in relationship to Aboriginal people, generating an array of images of these "others." In the course of the 1930s, a number of important changes occurred in the realm of the HBC's approach to public relations; yet throughout the decade, images of fur traders and their Native counterparts remained in the foreground.

Yet the HBC of the twentieth century was a vastly different enterprise than its fur trading predecessor of earlier times. Established by British royal charter in 1670, the company was granted monopoly trading privileges for Rupert's Land, the vast area drained by waters flowing into Hudson Bay (what is now northern Quebec and northern Ontario, all of Manitoba, most of Saskatchewan and

Alberta, and part of the Northwest Territories). The HBC's transfer of control of Rupert's Land to the new Dominion of Canada in 1869 signified the changing nature of the company's political power and economic activities. Under the terms of the Deed of Surrender, the HBC retained title to over seven million acres of land in western Canada, the selling of which formed the basis of an active land department.[2] Beginning in the second decade of the twentieth century, a newly constituted board directed the company's resources towards the building of its retail business.[3] By the outbreak of the war in 1914, fur trading operations ranked behind those of land and retail sales in terms of gross income.[4] Yet despite this increasingly diversified field of operations, governors and officials of the company, both in England and Canada, continued to build on the images of the HBC's fur trading past.

The most sustained attempt at sponsoring a particular set of images, both verbal and visual, is to be found in the Hudson's Bay Company's magazine. *The Beaver*, established in 1920 by the company's Canadian head office in Winnipeg as an in-house journal, quickly impressed itself upon HBC management as a means of promoting morale among a geographically and occupationally diverse staff. Robert Watson, its editor from 1923 to 1933, was actively solicited from within the company, and was considered a desirable candidate because of his fit within the company hierarchy and traditions. Born in Glasgow, Watson moved to Canada in 1908 and joined the HBC as an accountant several years later, following a long line of expatriate Scots, Irish, and English, whose lives in Canada were firmly rooted in their involvement with the Hudson's Bay Company. He was, as one manager phrased it, "one of the Company's own people."[5]

Watson's other main qualification was "his experience in literary work."[6] A contributor to the American *World's Work* and the British *Punch* as well as *The Beaver*, Watson had also published a number of fictional works by the time he became editor in October of 1923.[7] Watson capitalized on his own skills as a writer and encouraged the talents of HBC staff, developing the "Journal of Progress" (as *The Beaver* was subtitled) into a more self-consciously literary publication.

The magazine's format remained relatively unaltered during Watson's tenure as editor, reflecting its continuing primary function as an in-house journal "devoted to the interests of those who serve the Hudson's Bay Company."[8] Within its pages, *The Beaver* of the early 1930s presented a combination of staff news from the stores and departments, biographical profiles, and personal reminiscences of current and former HBC employees. This core of material was accompanied by poetry and fiction, articles on historical subjects and excerpts from documents relating to the HBC, brief inspirational essays on service and loyalty, and the occasional contest or puzzle. Yet, in addition to providing entertainment, amusement, instruction, and news regarding staff activities, *The Beaver* was intended to supply a context in which the reader/employee could locate this information. Underlying the magazine's content, from the amateur poetry to the reporting of staff picnics, was the intention "of acquainting the members of the staff with the Company's glorious history, [and] its present-day vast and varied operations. . . ."[9]

In drawing on the company's history to build up an aura of romance and adventure, Watson (and *The Beaver*) reified the exploits of past Hudson's Bay Company officers and servants as explorers and discoverers. At times, this entailed the retelling or even "rescuing from practical obscurity" the stories of "daring fur traders" and their "exploratory endeavours."[10] The emphasis on the heroism of fur traders, however, also carried over into contemporary accounts, creating a central role for the modern fur trader in the mythology of the company.

A report on the welcome home dinner in honour of General Inspector Hugh Conn, for example, portrayed him as a modern-day adventurer, undergoing "remarkable feats of northern travel. . . in the course of his everyday work." Ignoring the differences of purpose and conditions between Conn's extensive travels and those of his predecessors, this account assured readers that Conn's accomplishments would go down in history and rank with the journeys of the earlier fur traders and explorers.[11] Several issues later an article described Chief Factors C.H. French, the retiring Fur Trade Commissioner, and Ralph Parsons, his successor, as "Two Distinguished Fur Traders," who "will stand shoulder to shoulder with other great men of the Fur Trade when time reveals the full significance of their work in its true perspective."[12] Not surprisingly, the article avoided evaluating the nature or details of their "work," given the boardroom decision to replace the "incompetent" French with Parsons.[13]

This ready (and uncritical) identification of past triumphs with present personalities and their endeavours worked towards the continuing glorification of the HBC enterprise in both the past and present tense. At the same time, the emphasis on continuing tradition tended to highlight the role of Native peoples in company affairs. While Robert Watson's "Gentlemen Adventurers" exclusively celebrated the daring men who came "To blaze the trail, with pride of race;/ Give Canada her rightful place. . . ," *Beaver* contributors were constantly encountering Aboriginal people along the trail.[14] A focus on the fur trade as a site of inspiration and of historical lessons, coupled with the intention of including the writings of members of the Fur Trade Department, led to the inclusion of frequent references to the indigenous peoples who figured so prominently in the activities of the fur trade as labourers, interpreters, technological advisors, companions, producers, and consumers. Yet despite the variety of roles and the diversity of cultural groups and individuals encountered, the articles, poems, and pictorial representations that appeared in *The Beaver* tended to convey an overriding interest in Native people as types.

The tendency of white observers to view Natives "as a separate and single other," as Robert Berkhofer, Jr. commented, was continually reproduced in the contributions that appeared in the HBC's magazine and in its presentation of this material.[15] A full page in the June 1931 issue (figure 1) displayed five photographs, three portraits of Inuit women (one with a child tucked into the back of her parka) and two of Inuit men.[16] The accompanying caption identified the

216 The Beaver JUNE, 1931

Types of Canadian Eskimos

Lower pictures show natives wearing labrets (bone ornaments thrust through sides of lower lip) and snow goggles (Photos by late Chief Factor James L. Cotter, R.H.G. Bonnycastle and Wm. Gibson, Hudson's Bay Company)

Figure 1. *The Beaver*, June 1931, 216. Courtesy *The Beaver*.

photographers as the "late Chief Factor James C. Cotter, R.H.G. Bonnycastle and Wm. Gibson, Hudson's Bay Company," but did not identify the subjects of these portraits, except as "Types of Canadian Eskimos." While these unnamed people were photographed at different times (Cotter's images date to his thirty-odd years of HBC service at various posts on Hudson Bay during the second half of the nineteenth century; Bonnycastle and Gibson were contemporary fur traders), the encompassing title imposes a common identity on five unique portraits. Although an entire page devoted to photography was not a predominant feature during Watson's involvement with *The Beaver*, the Native as a simultaneously anonymous and ideal cultural representation was a common image.[17]

It seems accurate to group the images of Natives or non-whites together as a conceptual category in the minds of *Beaver* editors, contributors, and readers. Both visual images and written texts communicated a way of seeing the Native. Coloured by the conventions of ethnographic discourse, explicated as travel narrative, and appropriated to the HBC version of history-as-progress, white images of Natives exercised a steady appeal. Yet just as the framing of these images varied within the magazine's pages, so too was there a variety of attitudes towards the "Indian" and the "Eskimo."[18]

These depictions tended to be formulated and sustained by viewing indigenous Canadians only in comparison to Euro-Canadian values, as opposed to considering them within their own cultural frameworks.[19] Rarely, however, did *Beaver* articles endorse the view of the "vanishing Indian," or portray Aboriginal people as debauched by the effects of white contact. As the fur trade was still a viable component of the HBC business, the "Indian" remained an integral part of the reality and myth of the corporate repertoire. Since Indians could not disappear, their contacts with whites, and especially fur traders, were consequently portrayed in mutually beneficial terms.

Robert Watson distilled these various attributes of the "Indian" into his essay on "A Company Indian," perpetuating a term that had achieved currency among company historians.[20] He portrayed not only the ideal Indian but also the ideal HBC-Indian relationship. A "Company Indian" was

> an Indian who had proven himself loyal to the Company and to whom the Company had become a kind of father-mother entity, whose word was law. . .and who was considered all powerful and almost infallible.

The image of the "Indian" had a history and popular appeal that found refinement and nuance within *The Beaver*. A "good Indian" who accepted white values and institutions (in the eyes of white observers) became, in Watson's text, a "Company Indian," lauded for his loyalty to the men and aims of the HBC.

A similar process occurred in the depiction of Inuit within *The Beaver*. The elements that constituted the good "Eskimo" became identified with an acceptance of the HBC-Native relationship, envisioned in HBC terms. In a promotion for the company's Fur Trade Department in the September 1930 *Beaver* (figure 2),

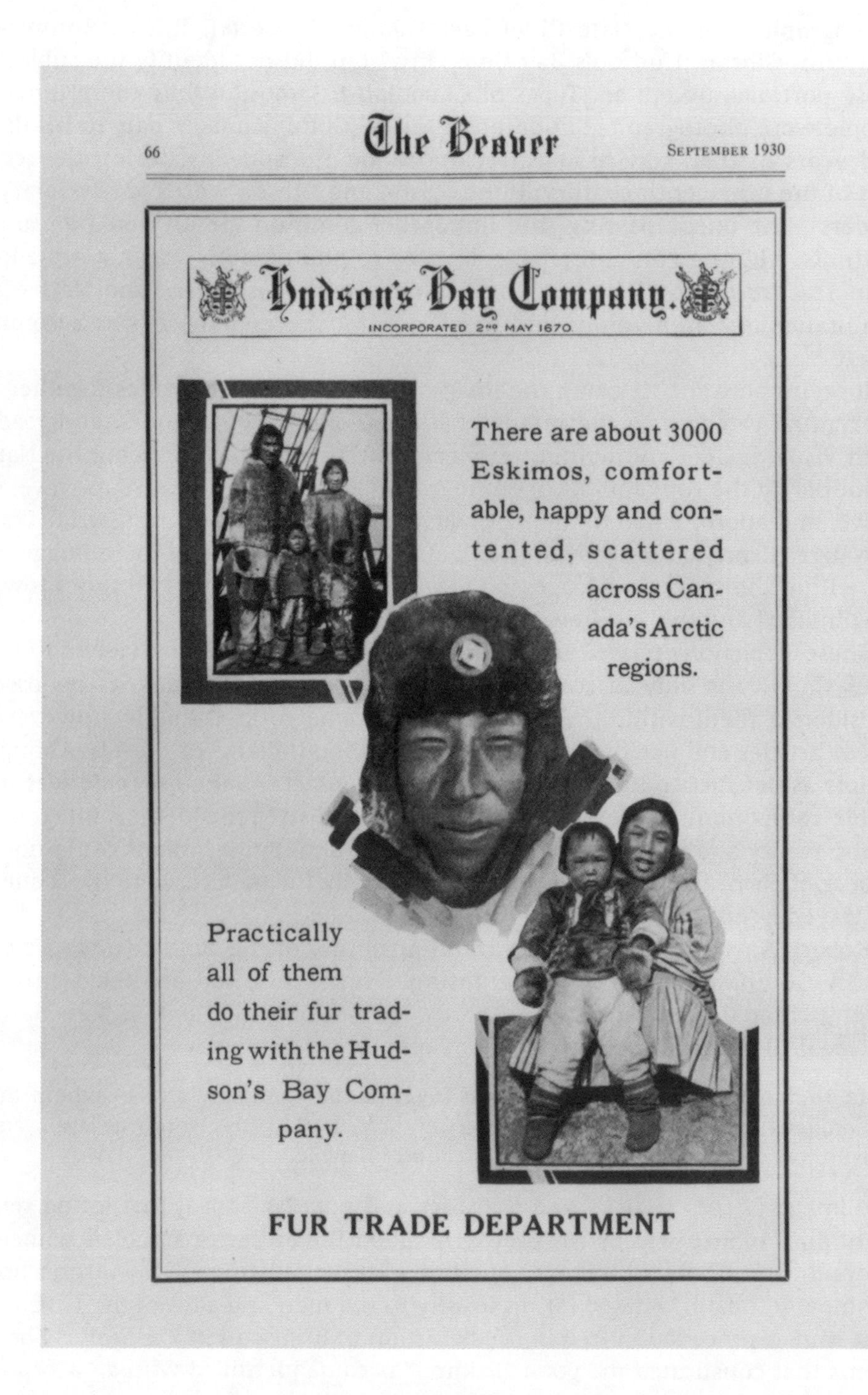
66 The Beaver September 1930

Hudson's Bay Company. The Beaver, September 1930, 66. Courtesy The Beaver.

Figure 2. *The Beaver,* September 1930, 66. Courtesy *The Beaver.*

three unattributed and unidentified photographs stood for "Eskimo," considered within their relationship to the Hudson's Bay Company.[21] A picture of an Inuk man's head, looking out at the viewer, occupied the centre of the page. This image merged with one above of a man, woman, and two children aboard a ship and one below of a woman seated with a child on her knee. The advertisement's text provided a prescription for reading the emotional tone of the subjects photographed:

> There are 3000 Eskimos, comfortable, happy and contented, scattered across Canada's Arctic regions. / Practically all of them do their fur trading with the Hudson's Bay Company.

Taken together with this statement, the slight part in the lips of the central figure seems a happy expression; the group portrait appears as a happy family, despite the ambiguity of their situation. The association between the positive state of "Eskimo" life and involvement with the HBC was reiterated by the layout of the page, the photographs, and their two-sentence moral, unified by their placement within a square black border.

The happy "Eskimo," as a dominant stereotype of northern Natives, achieved a wide distribution within *The Beaver*. While a few observers wrote of them with a measure of revulsion, the *Beaver* reader of the 1930s was left with an overwhelmingly positive image of the "Eskimo."[22] By the late 1920s, the fur trade was more concentrated in the far north than in the early part of the decade, and the HBC continued to exert a northern presence throughout the 1930s.[23] For *The Beaver*, this guaranteed a growing corps of first hand observers of Inuit life.

William (Paddy) Gibson, the company's Inspector for the Western Arctic and frequent contributor to the company magazine until his death in an airplane crash in 1942, wrote of the Netchilingmuit Natives of the Boothia peninsula as "a very interesting and intensely human people." Two years later *The Beaver* published his story "The Seal Hunters," in which he related not the hunters' activities but rather life at the camp while the men were absent. Gibson's story draws a romantic comparison between the Eskimo and the land/nature that was part of their appeal to him: ". . .in this land where the harsh realities of life are unmitigated, the mere joy of living is a keen experience."[24] An article by trader R.H.G. Bonnycastle in the March 1931 *Beaver* offers further insight into the attitudes of HBC fur traders toward the Inuit. In recording his experiences with an Inuit family in "An Igloo Night," he displayed a frank appreciation of Inuit technology: "Scarcely anything civilization produces can compete with these three phenomena [snowhouses, seal oil lamps, and sleds with mud runners] in their own field." Bonnycastle's (like Gibson's) appreciation of Inuit ways was largely a result of reliance on Inuit hospitality and technology, evident in his description of his Igloo night.[25]

These published personal accounts and evaluations of the "Eskimo" offered an optimistic, if romanticized, view of Aboriginal life and culture. Not surprisingly, as *Beaver* articles were channelled through their respective departments, these articles represented not just the personal views of their writers but the policies of the Hudson's Bay Company. In both official correspondence[26] and in their quarterly publication, members of the HBC portrayed the Inuit as ideally suited to the northern fur trade economy. Rebutting the criticisms and challenges of Ottawa-based federal government administrators,[27] company writers dispelled ambiguities with what appeared to be straightforward assertions and illustrations of corporate compassion and Native compliance. *The Beaver*'s promotion of the Fur Trade Department as a beneficial influence on Inuit life must be considered in the light of increasing corporate and government activity in the Canadian north.

In the early 1930s, however, *The Beaver*'s status as a purveyor of HBC propaganda remained uncertain. The Canadian directors, from their base in Winnipeg, began to question the value of a company magazine and Robert Watson's suitability as its editor. Reviewing *The Beaver* in June of 1932, the Canadian board members expressed their continuing dissatisfaction by suspending its publication after the September issue.[28] Recently installed HBC Governor Patrick Ashley Cooper, however, extended *The Beaver*'s lease on life. Echoing the magazine's original purpose, he recommended that a new *Beaver*, with a new editor, be tried for another year, in order to address the important problem of "welding together. . .the present somewhat loose and far-flung organization and creation of a better corporate spirit."[29]

Cooper's instructions to the General Manager of Canadian operations Philip A. Chester to seek an editor with experience in publicity suggested that Watson's "literary" background, while sufficient to secure him the position in 1923, was not an adequate qualification ten years later.[30] Consequently, Chester wrote to a Montreal associate to solicit "a man to edit our *Beaver* magazine, to run the general publicity of our Company's activities, and in connection therewith to study and take full advantage of our long historical background, and to advise and make suggestions in connection with general advertising, etc."[31]

The hiring of Douglas MacKay signalled a shift by HBC management towards a conscious project of company promotion and image-making. MacKay had attended Columbia University's School of Journalism, worked for newspapers in Toronto and New York, and joined the Parliamentary Staff of the Canadian Press Association in 1924. In 1928 he became the publicity manager of Canada Steamship Lines, and then publicity director of the Seigneury Club, Montreal.[32] MacKay's newspaper experience was a common factor among those employed in corporate publicity at this time, reflecting the close relationship between the worlds of public relations and journalism.[33]

MacKay intended *The Beaver* to be a major component of his comprehensive publicity program. While it was still to be a source of inspiration and loyalty within the HBC, it was, more importantly, directed to an outside readership. As MacKay explained, the magazine was intended to "give persons in important positions in the life of this country correct glimpses into the nature of the Company's operations."[34] These readers, targeted because of their positions of economic and political power, were to receive, four times a year, an entertaining and professionally presented information package on the activities and history of the Hudson's Bay Company from the "correct"—that is, company—perspective. By July of 1935, nearly 1500 complimentary issues of *The Beaver* were being distributed to the senior executives of Canadian companies, senior government officials, club reading rooms, and newspaper and magazine editors.[35] The circulation of the journal steadily rose, reaching over 10,000 copies of each quarterly issue before MacKay's death in an airplane accident on 10 January 1938 while on company business.[36]

The Beaver's new appeal, under MacKay's editorial guidance, was to be based on a new look and style. Under Robert Watson's direction, the typical issue was sparsely illustrated with grainy half-tone reproductions of black and white photographs and the occasional line drawing. In addition, the small size and poor quality of reproduction of the illustrations diminished much of their impact. The layout, combined with the technical constraints of the magazine's production, tended to devalue the interest of what were potentially intriguing images of the fur trade.

In *The Beaver* of the early 1930s, then, the power of the visual image to impart meaning and interpretation remained, for the most part, latent. With his focus on the literary, Robert Watson's approach to visual communication was haphazard and ill-defined. Douglas MacKay, on the other hand, fully exploited the possibilities offered by the visual image, and the photograph in particular. With a switch to a larger page size and higher quality paper, the half-tone reproductions of photographs in *The Beaver* were able to more adequately transmit "accurate messages" about the things they pictured.[37] This new, heavily illustrated and slickly produced format announced *The Beaver*'s definition of itself as a magazine for consumption beyond the confines of the company's staff.

In a measure of continuity, however, photographs of the fur trade and by fur traders still graced the pages of the Hudson's Bay Company's publication. As a pictorial magazine, *The Beaver* capitalized on the interest in photography by the company's staff, which provided a steady and inexpensive source of material. This intention was publicized in the June 1933 *Beaver*, with a call for "clear, sharp, action photographs of life and activities in the Company's service."[38] With the intention of improving the quality of submissions, MacKay printed an article on the technical and aesthetic aspects of camera work, "with the Hope of Securing More and Better Photographs from the North," and continued to appeal for "good pictures":

> pictures of men at work, hauling ropes, portaging, gardening, trading, trapping or repairing the roof; pictures of boats in action; pictures of distinguished visitors (with the names from left to right); pictures of intelligent and interesting natives [with no names sought]; pictures of celebrated pilots; action pictures of dog teams. . . .[39]

But a magazine based on the contributions of amateurs could not attain the standard and quality that MacKay wished to achieve. In the June 1937 special "Fur Trade issue" of *The Beaver*, which highlighted staff writings, the cover picture and three photo-features were, significantly, the work of professionals.[40]

Montreal-based Max Sauer, Jr. was the first of many photographers commissioned to take pictures of the fur trade for the magazine.[41] From his vantage point as passenger on the company's annual eastern arctic supply ship the *Nascopie*, in the summer of 1933, Sauer recorded the scenes and people encountered en route. Harvey Basset, of Montreal's Associated Screen News, was aboard the *Nascopie* in 1934 and was flown into the northern Manitoba post of Norway House in January of 1936. That same year, Richard N. Hourde photographed company activities in the western arctic. The work of others, although not specifically commissioned, was also reproduced in the magazine. Margaret Bourke-White, a highly successful American photographer for *Life* and *Fortune*, accompanied Governor General Lord Tweedsmuir's party down the Mackenzie River in 1937. Appearing courtesy of *Life*, Bourke-White's photographs displayed her characteristic preference for shooting from "bizarre angles and in operatic lights."[42]

Although these image-makers brought their own particular vision to their work, *The Beaver*'s layout contextualized their photos, imposing another layer of meaning and interpretation. Winnipeg *Free Press* photographer Nicholas Morant covered the Norway House-Island Lake canoe brigade in northern Manitoba for *The Beaver* in 1936 (figure 3).[43] His images of Natives at work were presented as a commentary on fur trade transportation through the ages. Both a celebration and lament for the "old" ways and a recognition of the new, this photo-essay's captions stressed the continuity and change of Indian labor in the fur trade. Below a photograph picturing an airplane and canoes loading up beside a dock (figure 4), *The Beaver* moralized: "The airplane can do it in a few hours, but the canoe brigade means work for the native while he is not trapping; so the 'outfit' goes by canoe."[44] Irrespective of Morant's intentions, his photographs were framed as an argument supporting the beneficent role of the Hudson's Bay Company and its fur-trading activities.

MacKay's experimentation with layout and graphic design were especially evident in such photo-essays. This new emphasis on the photographic image in *The Beaver* can be seen to reflect a widespread and increasing preoccupation among media producers and the consuming public for different ways of communicating information. In the 1930s, the mass media were becoming increasingly sophisticated in the use of the visual image.[45] In the world of journalism, photo-magazines, using related photographs in sequence to tell a story, were well established in Europe by the end of the 1920s, while in North America the success of *Life* magazine, launched in 1937 and selling a million copies within its first weeks, testified to the enormous popularity of the genre.[46]

Yet if MacKay's efforts substantially altered *The Beaver* in a way that heralded the new age of illustrated magazines in an increasingly visual culture, changes were made within a framework of possibilities that were already present within the journal's pages. As the new editor, MacKay reworked the popular *Beaver* subjects of the fur trade: explorers and adventurers, Natives, and the history and present activities of the HBC. In his last speech, to a convention of HBC wholesale travellers in Vancouver, British Columbia (and posthumously printed in *The Beaver*), MacKay reiterated his basic argument about the Hudson's Bay Company's presence in Canada. Entreating the assembled staff to take the company's history seriously, and to be prepared to defend it if criticized, MacKay provided some guidance: "You will hear men say: 'What did the Hudson's Bay Company ever do to earn that [seven million acres of Western Canadian] land. . .?' [T]he answer is that the... men of the Fur Trade lived and starved and worked for two hundred years maintaining law and order and British justice in the wilderness." He then proceeded to elaborate the company's "peaceful" policies towards Native people and the unique HBC esprit de corps. For MacKay, a proper understanding of the company's history held a practical value, to be impressed upon employee and general public alike. As he concluded his speech, "Never forget that to your customers you are the Hudson's Bay Company."[47]

Accordingly, *The Beaver* cultivated an affinity with the members and image of the fur trade throughout the 1930s. The only Canadian staff news published was that of the Fur Trade Department. And MacKay explained the significance of referring to each volume as an "outfit," a practice dating back to 1926. The fur trade term for a trading year was used because of *The Beaver*'s "close association with. . . the senior branch of the service. . . ."[48]

The June 1937 *Beaver* was, in fact, presented as an "all-fur-trade number," devoted to articles by the company's men in the field. This issue included R.H.G. Bonnycastle's account of the repair of the HBC schooner *Fort James* at Tuktuk in the western arctic; long-time employee J.S.C. Watt's reminiscences of his life as a young clerk for the company in Labrador; soon-to-be assistant fur trade commissioner R.H. Chessire's report on the newly established fur trade training school in Winnipeg; William "Paddy" Gibson's comprehensive history of the last Franklin expedition; and eastern arctic district manager J.W. Anderson's description of the HBC's beaver conservation projects in the James Bay area of Hudson Bay.[49] In their varied styles and subjects, the writings of these active fur traders articulated a positive and progressive vision of the HBC and of their own association with the company. Chessire wrote of the fur trade as poised on "a new era" of improved communications and transportation. Anderson's article, although admitting the risk involved in setting up beaver conservation programs, concluded: "We may or may not succeed, but nevertheless, as many times in the past, the Governor and Company of Adventurers of England trading into Hudson's Bay are again pioneering in the North."[50] In these articles, as in Anderson's use of the pronoun "we," associating himself with the "Company of Adventurers," fur traders were featured as embodying the traditions of the Hudson's Bay Company.

The material presented in the June 1937 *Beaver* exemplified the central role of images of the fur trade in Hudson's Bay Company public relations. Throughout

WITH THE CANOE BRIGADE

A SERIES OF NORTHERN PICTURES BY NICHOLAS MORANT

Despite the advent of the airplane, the canoe is still an important factor in northern transportation. Yet only a few of the old "canoe brigades" still operate, one of these being from Norway House, at the head of Lake Winnipeg, to Island Lake. It is this brigade which is the subject of this series of northern photographs.

Another portage left behind en route from Norway House to Island Lake.

Figure 3. *The Beaver,* September 1936, 31. Courtesy *The Beaver.*

36 THE BEAVER, September 1936

Above: The airplane can do it in a few hours, but the canoe brigade means work for the native while he is not trapping; so the "outfit" goes by canoe.

Figure 4. *The Beaver*, September 1936, 36. Courtesy *The Beaver*.

the 1930s the HBC was portrayed as an agent of "progress," its history one of ever-forward achievement and development. This reification of the fur trade carried along with it not only an interest in the heroic feats of "explorers" and "discoverers" but also a fascination with their modern-day counterparts. Corporate images of the fur trade also entailed the development of another theme: Aboriginal people, as both exotic "others" and familiar friends of the company, were a prevalent feature of the HBC's publicity. In both these incarnations, however, Natives were presented as they appeared to white observers, serving as examples of the company's benevolent influence on "primitive" peoples. In this way, images of "Indian" and "Eskimo" justified the continuation of company policy towards Native people.

Although Douglas MacKay dramatically altered the design and scope of *The Beaver* magazine, its underlying themes and content reflected this continuing preoccupation among company management and staff with the glorification of the fur trade and its perceived traditions. MacKay's addition of an emphasis on visual representation was, however, an enduring mark of his work for the Hudson's Bay Company. Under the brief editorship of Alice MacKay in 1938 and 1939, the magazine remained true to the intentions of her late husband, often memorializing him in the reprints of his speeches and radio broadcasts.[51] *The Beaver* continued to commission professional photographers and to solicit outside writers, while relying on HBC fur trade staff to contribute a sense of authenticity and authority. Alice MacKay added her own distinctive pictorial touches to the magazine, including the use of colour photographs for the cover, but her brief tenure was more marked by a sense of continuity with the previous five years of *The Beaver*'s publication than by substantial change.[52] Clifford P. Wilson, Alice MacKay's successor and *Beaver* editor until 1958, was also greatly influenced by Douglas MacKay's belief in the power of photography as a communications medium.[53] The old fascinations with the heroic male exploits of fur traders and the strange and exotic "other" had successfully merged with the sophisticated techniques and idioms of the world of corporate public relations.

As a twentieth-century business, the directors of the HBC were concerned with fostering an image that contributed to pragmatic initiatives. Building up loyalty within the company and heightening a positive perception of the HBC and its activities to influential individuals outside the company, to customers, and to the general public were the obvious benefits of Hudson's Bay Company propaganda. Throughout the 1930s the company's own magazine, *The Beaver*, constituted a major part of this effort. The writings and photographs within its pages are part of a legacy of popular perceptions and stereotypes that continue to resonate with our own present-day images of the fur trade in North America.

ACKNOWLEDGEMENTS

I wish to acknowledge the support of the Social Sciences and Humanities Research Council of Canada. The staff of the Hudson's Bay Company Archives, Provincial Archives of Manitoba greatly facilitated my research, and the Hudson's Bay Company kindly granted permission to reproduce material from this collection.

NOTES

1. Note that the HBC figures predominantly in the first comprehensive history of the fur trade in the post-1870 period, Arthur J. Ray, *The Canadian Fur Trade in the Industrial Age* (Toronto: University of Toronto Press, 1990). For a glimpse into the lively debate over the domains of fur trade discourse as popular and academic history, see Jennifer S.H. Brown, "Newman's *Company of Adventurers* in Two Solitudes: A Look at Reviews and Responses," *Canadian Historical Review* 67, no. 4 (1986): 562-71 and Peter C. Newman's "Response" in the same issue, 572-78; see also Michael Payne's review, "The Political Sub-text of Fur Trade Historiography" (paper presented at the Canadian Historical Association Meeting, 4 June 1991, Kingston, Ontario).
2. See Shirlee A. Smith, "A Desire to Worry Me Out," *The Beaver*, December-January 1987-88, 4-11.
3. Alex Ross and Anne Morton, "The Hudson's Bay Company and Its Archives," *Business Archives* no. 51 (November 1985): 18-19; David Monod, "Bay Days: The Managerial Revolution and the Hudson's Bay Company Department Stores, 1912-1939," *Historical Papers* (1986), 173-96.
4. Ray, *The Canadian Fur Trade*, 99.
5. British Columbia Stores General Manager H.T. Lockyer to reporting chairman, 10 October 1923, Hudson's Bay Company Archives, Provincial Archives of Manitoba (hereafter HBCA), RG2/3/12; *The Beaver* Office Research Files (Winnipeg, Manitoba), Watson, Robert.
6. Edward FitzGerald (Secretary) to Angus Brabant (Fur Trade Commissioner), 10 August 1923, HBCA, RG2/3/12.
7. "H.B.C. Vernon Accountant Winning Fame as an Author," *The Beaver*, December 1920, 51; "Our New Editor," October 1923, 3.
8. This statement, although appearing on *The Beaver* covers only until June 1926, could serve as an appropriate motto of the magazine throughout Watson's editorship.
9. *The Beaver*, March 1929, 154.
10. R. Watson, "HBC Explorers: Chief Factor Samuel Black," *The Beaver*, June 1928, 10-12; see also, R. Watson, "Chief Trader Alexander Hunter Murray and Fort Youcan," *The Beaver*, June 1929, 211-14.
11. "Welcome to General Inspector Hugh Conn," *The Beaver*, June 1929, 216-17.
12. *The Beaver*, December 1930, 99-101.
13. Ray, *The Canadian Fur Trade*, 173-74.
14. *The Beaver*, November 1923, 71.
15. In *The White Man's Indian: Images of the American Indian from Columbus to the Present* (New York: Vintage Books, 1978), xv; see also Berkhofer, "White

Conceptions of Indians," in *Handbook of North American Indians: History of Indian-White Relations*, vol. 4, ed. Wilcomb E. Washburn (Washington, D.C.: Smithsonian Institution, 1988), 522-47.

16. *The Beaver*, June 1931, 216.
17. See Melissa Banta and Curtis M. Hindley, *From Site to Sight: Anthropology, Photography and the Power of Imagery* (Cambridge: Peabody Museum Press, 1986), 102-4, on the individual photograph standing for the "race" of which it is a part.
18. James Clifford, *The Predicament of Culture: Twentieth Century Ethnography, Literature and Art* (Cambridge and London: Harvard University Press, 1988), especially 21-113, explores the ways in which ethnographers and travellers write about other cultures. For an example of the ethnographic approach in *The Beaver*, see D. Jenness, "Who Are the Eskimos?" September 1931, 267-70; for the travel narrative see Rev. S.M. Stewart, "With the Eskimo of Ungava," September 1929, 253-54; and for the historical approach see December 1927, cover (Kelsey and Indians view the buffalo, painting by C.W. Jefferys) and Robert Watson, "A Company Indian," June 1931, 220-22.
19. See Ronald G. Haycock's assessment of popular magazines available to Canadians from 1900-1970, *The Images of the Indian* (Waterloo: Waterloo Lutheran University, 1971), especially 22; Berkhofer, "White Conceptions of Indians" (526-27), terms this persistent theme in the history of white attitudes toward Native peoples as the "deficiency image."
20. *The Beaver*, June 1931, 220-22. See Sir William Schooling's use of the term in *The Hudson's Bay Company, 1670-1920* (London: Hudson's Bay House, 1920), 45, the HBC's first published official history prepared on the occasion of its two hundred and fiftieth anniversary.
21. *The Beaver*, September 1930, 66.
22. Hugh Brody, *The People's Land: Whites and the Eastern Arctic* (Harmondsworth, England: Penguin Books, 1975 [rpt., 1983]), 75-102, in analyzing the Native-white relationship, discusses the ". . .curious blend of approval and revulsion—approval because he [the Eskimo] had triumphed over nature (thereby achieving the essentially human), but revulsion because he is still part of nature (thereby remaining less than human)." Interestingly, this chapter is introduced by a quote from *The Beaver*, as an example of "White Attitudes to the Eskimo."
23. There were some 250 HBC posts in the arctic and sub-arctic by the mid-1920s. See Morris Zaslow, *The Northward Expansion of Canada, 1914-1967* (Toronto: McClelland and Stewart, 1988), 135-139.
24. "The Victory Relics," *The Beaver*, December 1929, 311-12; December 1931, 347-48.
25. *The Beaver*, March 1931, 163-65. Bonnycastle's northern travels of this period are recounted in Heather Robertson, *A Gentleman Adventurer: The Arctic Diaries of Richard Bonnycastle* (Toronto: Lester and Orpen Dennys, 1984).
26. For example, the correspondence of September 1932 of Ungava District Manager George Watson and Fur Trade Commissioner Ralph Parsons on the beneficial effects of HBC policy on the Inuit (HBCA, RG2/8/902).
27. See Philip Goldring, "Canadian Problems and Foreign Models: O.S. Finnie's Inuit Policy, 1922-1931" (Ottawa: unpublished paper, 1988), on HBC-federal government relations regarding the Inuit, which included outright criticism of HBC activities by the North West Territories and Yukon Branch.
28. Canadian Committee Reviews, Minute 6052, 14 June 1932, HBCA, RG2/10/8.

29. Ibid., Minute 6145, 8 August 1932; see also Brooks, 16 November 1932, A.102/269.
30. Ibid., MacKay personnel file, Memorandum for file, 23 December 1932, RG2/38/71.
31. Ibid., Chester to Charles Vining, of Cockfield Brown Ltd. (Advertising, Merchandising and Commercial Research), 3 October 1932. Chester, although carrying out Cooper's recommendations, was sceptical about this new direction in company policy, reflecting a conservative attitude to business management and a distrust of the new techniques of public relations that had marked the company's approach throughout the previous decade (Ibid., Memorandum for file [undated]).
32. Ibid., Staff Record; Newspaper clipping on MacKay's death [January 1938], E.95/78.
33. On public relations agents and newspaper experience, see Alan R. Raucher, *Public Relations and Business, 1900-1929* (Greenwich, Connecticut: JAI Press, 1979), 84, 94, 112.
34. MacKay to J. Chadwick Brooks (London secretary), 1 August 1933, HBCA, A.102/269.
35. Ibid., MacKay to G. Allan, 3 July 1935, RG2/8/1116.
36. By way of comparison, just over 5,000 copies of each issue were printed at the end of Robert Watson's editorship. Circulation, however, is an underestimate of readership, as magazines have multiple readers. Ibid., RG2/47/1; RG2/47/12; MacKay to Store Managers, 27 September 1935, RG2/8/1116.
37. Estelle Jussim, *Visual Communication and the Graphic Arts: Photographic Technologies in the Nineteenth Century* (New York and London: R.R. Bowker Company, 1974), 21. Jussim breaks the message up into four components: (1) texture gradients; (2) chiaroscuro (variations in light and shade); (3) undulations of both surface and contour; and (4) colour (which, in black and white photographs, is indicated by variation of tone). The graphic changes instituted in *The Beaver* affected all four areas.
38. *The Beaver*, June 1933, 81.
39. C.P. Dettloff, "Comments on Common Errors in Photography," *The Beaver*, December 1934, 40-41; "The HBC Packet," *The Beaver*, September 1934, 5-6.
40. Richard Hourde, cover of *The Beaver*, June 1937, "Three Pictures of Eskimo Life," and "Fifty Years of Steam on the Mackenzie River," June 1937, 18-19 and 42-43; Richard Hourde and Harvey Bassett, "Three Company Posts," June 1937, 40-41.
41. Clifford Wilson to P. Inglis (editor, *Canadian Photography*), 27 August 1954, HBCA, RG2/8/1158.
42. See Max Sauer, Jr., "Four Arctic Photographs," *The Beaver*, March 1934, 15-19; Harvey Bassett, "Norway House," March 1936, 25-29; "From the Western Arctic/ A Series of Pictures taken for *The Beaver* by Richard N. Hourde," December 1936, 29-35; Margaret Bourke-White, "*Life* in the North," December 1937, 12-17; on Bourke-White, see William Stott, *Documentary Expression and Thirties America* (New York: Oxford University Press, 1973), 216-20, 270.
43. "With The Canoe Brigade/ A Series of Northern Pictures by Nicholas Morant," *The Beaver*, September 1936, 31-38.
44. Ibid., 36.
45. See Warren I. Sussman, *Culture as History: The Transformation of American Society in the Twentieth Century* (New York: Pantheon Books, 1984), 160-61; Stott, *Documentary Expression*, 76-77.

46. Stott, *Documentary Expression*, 129; Theodore Peterson, *Magazines in the Twentieth Century* (Urbana: University of Illinois Press, 1956), 311-20.
47. "They Shall Grow Not Old," *The Beaver*, March 1938, 32.
48. *The Beaver*, September 1933, 7.
49. "Salvage by the Midnight Sun," *The Beaver*, September 1933, 12-16; "Labrador Year," 20-29; "Apprentice Training," 33-35; "Sir John Franklin's Last Voyage," 44-75; and "Beaver Sanctuary," 6-11.
50. Ibid., 33; 11.
51. "They Shall Grow Not Old," *The Beaver*, March 1938, 30-32; "Men of the Old Fur Trade," June 1938, 7-9; "More Light on Thomas Simpson," September 1938, 26-31; "In Old Fort Garry Ninety Years Ago," December 1938, 26-28.
52. *The Beaver*, June 1938, cover, drawing of the schooner *Titania* on a background of a burgundy Hudson's Bay Point Blanket; December 1938, cover, flagpole at Pangnirtung, Lorene Squire photographer.
53. See Wilson's introduction to the collection of *Beaver* photographs that he edited, *The New North in Pictures* (Toronto: Ryerson Press, 1946).

Capt. Thierry Mallet: Adventurer, Businessman, Writer

Gwyneth Hoyle

> You men who live in cities. . . .don't you feel at times something tugging at your heart-strings?. . . .Calling and calling in the middle of the night. . .in the flush of dawn when you catch a gleam of sky from your open window?. . . It is the "Call of the Wild". . . .the man who has answered that call will never forget it. . . .A camp pitched here, a meal cooked there. . . The dull roar of the rapid in the distance. The howl of the hunting wolf. The shimmer of the birch leaves. The splash of fish rising. The murmuring of the jack-pines. The Northern lights dancing silently in the sky. Peace and utter freedom![1]

These words in praise of the northern wilderness are taken from the final sketch in *Plain Tales of the North*—fifty vignettes, as spare as line drawings, depicting scenes of life in the North, beyond the railway lines and the limits of civilization. This book, along with *Glimpses of the Barren Lands*, was written by Captain Thierry Mallet, based on his experiences of twenty years of travel in the service of Revillon Frères, the French fur company, as it expanded into the fur trade in Canada and Siberia. The books are treasured by all who love the wilderness. While Mallet was remarkable for his energy, his business skills, and his spirit of adventure, he is remembered today because of his writings.

Thierry Mallet was born in 1884 in Lausanne, Switzerland, into a prominent French banking family. The Mallet family trace their roots back to a family of drapers from Normandy who converted to Protestantism in the sixteenth century and, forced into exile for religious reasons, settled in Geneva, Switzerland.[2] A branch of the family returned to France and founded the bank MM. Mallet Frères et Cie, with its headquarters in Paris on the Rue d'Anjou, not far from the Elysée Palace and the Place de la Concorde. The family members had business connections throughout North Africa and as far away as Argentina and Indo-China, in enterprises as diverse as manufacturing, insurance, mortgages, and mining in addition to banking.[3] Following the family custom, Thierry Mallet was sent to England for his education, to Eton and Oxford. Before he was twenty his education was further enhanced by a trip around the world, acting as private secretary to one of his uncles.[4]

Figure 1. Title page from *Plain Tales of the North*.

A short distance from the Mallet bank, not far from the Place de la Concorde, taking up a whole block of the fashionable Rue de Rivoli, opposite the Tuileries Gardens, stood the offices and fur salons of Revillon Frères. The four Revillon brothers had built a highly successful business on the solid foundation laid by their father early in the nineteenth century, each brother responsible for a different aspect of the business. By the beginning of the twentieth century Revillon Frères had branches on Regent Street in London, on 28th Street in New York City, and a warehouse in Leipzig (the home of the twice-annual European fur auction). The business included the design and manufacture of fashion furs for the retail trade, a wholesale trade in raw furs, and cold storage especially designed for the fur trade.

In charge of the New York business was the grandson and namesake of the founder, Victor Revillon. In 1899 he made a trip north by rail to Edmonton and then on Hudson's Bay Company steamboats down the Mackenzie River, seeing with his own eyes the quality and quantity of furs being loaded aboard the boat at each trading post along the river. He made a persuasive report of his impressions to the family members of the board in Paris, and in 1901 Revillon entered the competition for furs at their source in northern Canada.

Revillon began with six posts along the north shore of the St. Lawrence River in the first year. Adding more each year, by 1905 it had a string of posts around Labrador, Hudson and James bays, and across northern Ontario. Buying out the independent traders Bredin and Cornwall, it reached as far west as the Rocky Mountains.[5] To meet the expense of such an expansion, the closely-knit family company had to take the unprecedented step of raising capital by the sale of stock outside the family.[6]

The initial success of the fur trade in Canada encouraged Revillon Frères to expand to the east as well, into the Persian lamb trade in Turkestan, and north, establishing a branch in Moscow and trading posts in Siberia. By 1908 Revillon's business was worldwide, selling Canadian furs in Moscow and Siberian furs in the Far East.[7] As the proprietors of two established family businesses in the heart of Paris, the Mallet family and the Revillon brothers were well known to each other and good friends.[8] As a banker, Etienne Mallet facilitated Revillon's early dealings in Russia,[9] and it is quite possible that this connection introduced his son, Thierry Mallet, to the North American fur trade.

It is not known exactly where or when Mallet began his employment with Revillon Frères in northern Canada. The unpublished personal diary of a young Revillon employee, Cyril Lech, at Fort Hope in 1908-1909, referred to meeting Mallet in Montreal in early December 1907. Robert Renison, Bishop of Moosonee, in his book of reminiscences, spoke of him as "the Count," and remembered him as a gentleman, a soldier who had served in many parts of the world, an expert engineer, an artist and a disciple of Anatole France. Although Renison's memory was not entirely accurate, he gave a vivid description of entertaining Mallet and the Hudson's Bay Company factor at a Christmas-week dinner in 1907 made uncomfortable by the Scotsman's stoic refusal to speak to his French fur-trade rival. He also described Mallet's winter journey to Fort Albany on which Mallet froze his face and lost his whiskers.[10]

In 1908, having passed his initiation into the fur trade, Mallet was entrusted by the Board of Directors of Revillon in Paris with the management of all of its eastern Canadian posts, with headquarters in Montreal. In that first year, Mallet was everywhere. To improve the transportation system for the posts in Hudson Bay and on the Labrador, he began the year with a visit to Newfoundland to arrange the charter of the 2500-ton ice-breaker *Adventure* as the company's supply ship for the northern posts.[11] While waiting to sail north to inspect those posts around James and Hudson Bay he took the opportunity for an adventure of his own by sailing with the sealing fleet out of Bonavista Bay on the schooner *Neptune* during the month of March. The only written reference to this is a wry story entitled "Sunday" in *Plain Tales of the North*. The Revillon archives contain an album of photographs taken on this expedition which includes pictures of the departure from Pool's Island, scenes of the ice-bound boats being hauled by a long line of seamen, and scenes of the seal hunt. In the photographs, Mallet dressed in seamen's clothing blends easily with the rest of the crew.

In that year of 1908 Mallet inspected all the posts under his management, assessing the buildings, the inventory, the relations with the Indians and the competition, and the abilities and competence of the personnel. His reports were buoyant and optimistic, telling of the completion of the initial building phase of the fur posts and looking toward improved fur collections.[12]

Between his visit to the Bay posts and his fall inspection tour of northern Ontario, Mallet made an exploratory visit to Churchill, Manitoba, with Thévenet, the Revillon manager from Ungava, to assess the fur-trading possibilities of the area and to acquire land there for a company post. Passing themselves off as tourists, they were royally entertained at Norway House by Donald McTavish, the Hudson's Bay Company chief factor of Keewatin district, and later they were given passage by him from Churchill to York Factory by York boat.[13] Discovery of their identity would have jeopardized their movements, since all Indians would have been forbidden to hire with them.

In his memoir *Arctic Trader*, Philip Godsell recalled that Mr. McTavish was quite disarmed by the friendly manner of two men who arrived very unostentatiously, stating that they were mining men, and he gave them all the help he could. "So impressed and friendly did he become that the usually hard-boiled Scotsman had actually opened the books of the York Factory District to display with pride the excellent showing the posts had made under his administration. . . . When Mr. McTavish returned to Norway House and discovered that these two men were *actually* prominent representatives of the Revillon Frères Company who were organizing to challenge the Company's supremacy in the North, his indignation and humiliation knew no bounds."[14] As a junior employee at Norway House, Godsell, by his own account, had suffered the wrath of Donald McTavish on more than one occasion.[15] Godsell was more interested in spinning a good yarn than in historical accuracy, but his story is very similar to the one contained in Mallet's reports.

While the Hudson's Bay Company had vowed to keep Revillon out of the area, Mr. Morrier, the surveyor employed by the government to survey Churchill, and Major Moodie of the Mounted Police were pleased to give assistance to the members of a rival fur-trading company. There was a natural affinity between the French-Canadian, Morrier, and members of a French company. In the case of Major Moodie, Thévenet suspected that the police at Churchill were engaging in fur trading on the side, and this had soured their relations with the Hudson's Bay Company.[16]

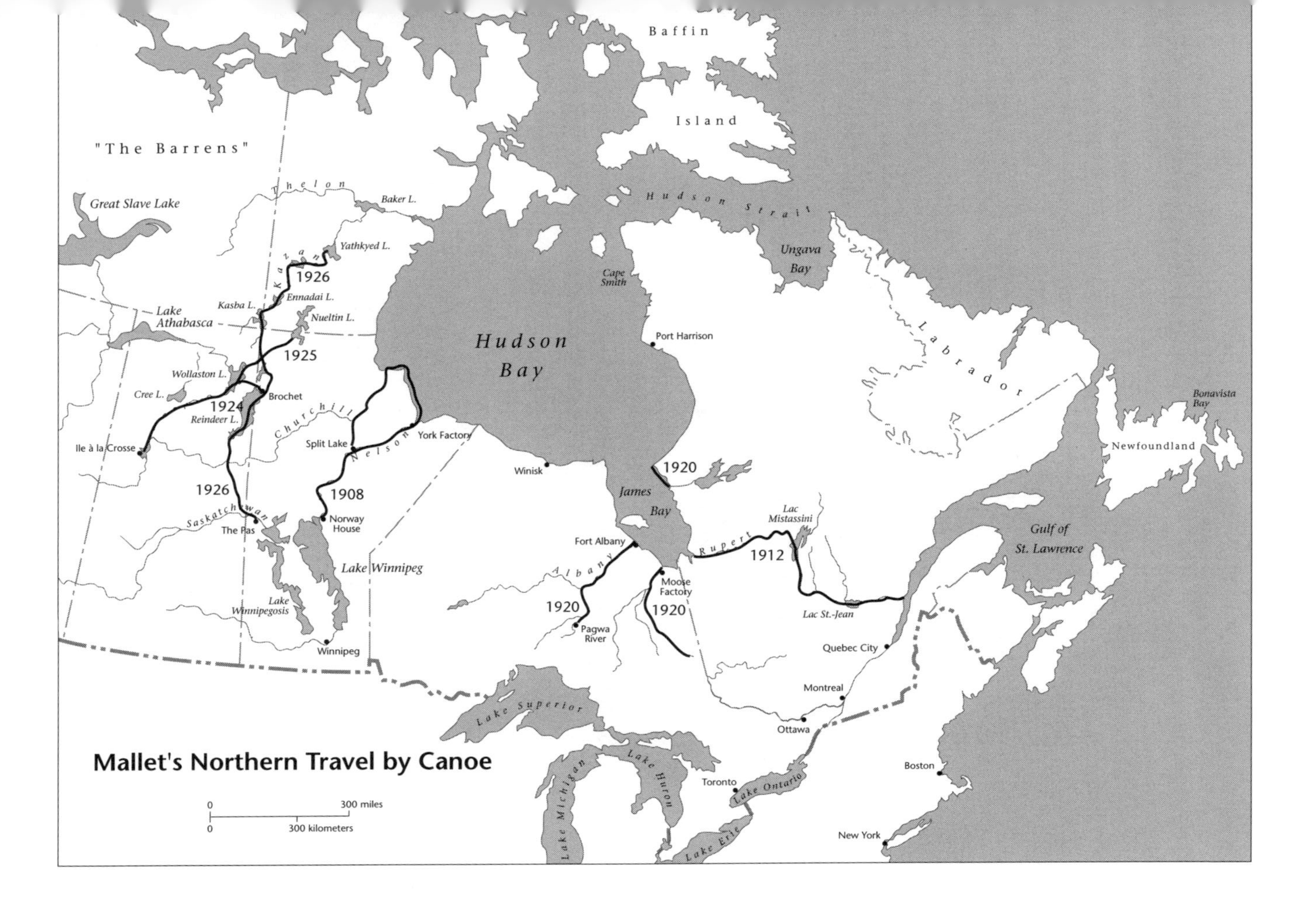

Figure 2. Mallet's Northern Travel by Canoe.

Figure 3. Thierry Mallet on board the *Adventure*, Hudson Bay, c. 1912. National Archives of Canada, Ottawa, Revillon Frères Archives, microfilm reel #F1642, Box 36, by permission of Revillon Archives, Paris.

This may have been Mallet's introduction to canoe travel. His first report to Victor Revillon from Split Lake mentions the portages and rapids on the Nelson River, and that they were "in good health, although already sunburned and dirty!" (translation). His analysis of the potential of Churchill as the site for a trading post and a future port was thorough but pessimistic. Their travel through the rich fur-bearing area, seeing the results obtained by the Hudson's Bay Company, showed them many potential sites for fur-trade posts.[17]

His first year with Revillon's management set the pattern for the future, and travel would be a regular part of Thierry Mallet's life. Although no reports remain, he made an extensive annual inspection tour of the Bay posts each year before World War I, canoeing down to the Bay from the railway line or sailing in through Hudson Strait in the *Adventure*, and at least once he made the trip by poling up the Chamouchaouane River to Lac Mistassini from Lac St. Jean and canoeing out to the coast to investigate the trading potential in the interior of Quebec.[18] The "Call of the Wild" and Mallet's love of adventure were an established part of his psyche.

Very early in his career, Mallet recognized the wastefulness of competition with the Hudson's Bay Company—the higher prices paid to the Indians to attract them to Revillon Frères, the expense of tripping out to the Indian encampments in winter to assure the fur collection. As a member of the central Board of Directors of Revillon, and with his excellent command of English and good connections, he was chosen to negotiate with the Board of the Hudson's Bay Company a proposal for the formation of an international fur-trading company together with the retail houses of Holt Renfrew of Montreal and Sims of Ottawa. The company, to be called the Hudson Bay Fur Trading Company, would end the costly competition for furs between the two major rivals, reduce their expenses, and enable them to control prices in the fur markets of the world. The Hudson's Bay Company flirted with the idea, but communications between the two companies ended abruptly early in 1913 and Mallet felt that he had been lured by the Hudson's Bay Company to disclose Revillon's business arrangements with no intention on their part of coming to an agreement.[19]

With the declaration of war in August 1914, Thierry Mallet immediately returned to France to become a lieutenant in the infantry. Many of Revillon's post managers were ex-officers of the French army and they, too, left for the defence of their homeland as soon as the news of war reached their remote locations.

Of all the horrors of that tragic war, the campaign in which British and French armies fought side by side in the Somme produced the most staggering casualty figures. Thierry Mallet has one story in *Plain Tales of the North* which harkens back to the war. Entitled "Indian Warrior," it is a sketch of his encounter with a dying Cree after a battle in the Somme in the late fall of 1916.

> I knelt beside him and put my water bottle to his lips. Meanwhile I racked my brain for the few words of Cree I still knew. When he had finished drinking I began slowly to tell him, one by one, all the words I remembered. I said in Cree, "lake, fire, bear, moose, tent, axe, canoe". . . .As soon as the Cree warrior heard my first words, he caught hold of my hands with both of his own and held on to them like a drowning man. . .his expression changed little by little. . . . A far away look came into his dying eyes, his features relaxed and a smile hovered on his lips. He had forgotten the battlefield. His thoughts were away, far away, in some part of the Canadian wilderness which he and I knew.[20]

Mallet himself was wounded twice in those battles and decorated several times by both the French and the British.[21]

That war, fought on French soil, was a difficult time for Revillon Frères. While two of the brothers died of natural causes, promising members of the next generation, as well as valued members of the staff, died in battle. The business came to a standstill with one-third of its people called into the army, orders for luxury furs cancelled, and the cold storage building requisitioned by the War Office. The parent company was sustained by its New York and London branches. In addition, the Russian revolution dealt a further blow involving a loss of 10,000,000 francs, as first the Moscow house, then, as the revolution spread, the Siberian branch at Krasnoyarsk, were closed. The personnel escaped with as many furs as they could carry out through Vladivostok.[22]

To Mallet, the war also brought romance. In February of 1917, he was engaged to Martha Allan, the daughter of Sir Montagu Allan, the president of Canada Steamship Lines and a friend from his Montreal days. The engagement was announced in the *London Gazette* as well as Montreal and New York papers.[23] Martha Allan was serving as a volunteer nurse in Paris when she and Mallet renewed their friendship. Their engagement did not survive the war. Martha Allan, a gifted amateur dramatist, never married,[24] and by 1920 Mallet was writing in jaded terms about an employee, head over heels in love with his new wife, who would soon get over it.[25] He himself was married in the 1920s in New York and had one son, Henri-Gerard.[26]

At the end of the war Mallet, promoted to captain and a member of the Legion of Honor, returned to New York as president of Revillon's New York branch and vice-president of U.S. Revillon, Inc. In 1920 he spent three months inspecting the Revillon posts around the Bay, from Winisk to Port Harrison (now Inukjuak). This was his sixth tour of the area, and after an absence of eight years there was much to observe and report. He had gone to the Bay "with the intention of looking around, not mixing myself with any part of Montreal's management. . .of keeping my eyes open and not interfering in anything."[27]

Mallet's visit to the posts as an independent observer with no official duties to perform gave him the time and the freedom to listen to everybody—post managers, clerks, Natives, and clergy. What he heard, combined with what he saw, resulted in a report that provides a bird's eye view of all that was going on in the Bay. Characters and relationships were skillfully drawn, judgments formed, and solutions to problems proposed. The war had shaken world economies to their foundations and the shock waves were only beginning to be felt in the fur trade. Mallet found much to criticise, but he was generous with praise where it was deserved. The mistakes made by the Montreal office and, worse still, their refusal to admit having made mistakes exacerbated the problems of the trading posts. Always Mallet's sympathies lay with the men who lived with the hardship, the isolation, and the uncertainty of the North. Mallet set very high standards for himself, he was fair, just and disciplined, and he was often disappointed when those around him did not measure up. "The truth is that we have no system and no discipline. I loathe a military hierarchy in business, but one must have established responsibility—clear rules and well defined jobs. Without that it is a mess."[28]

Characteristically, Mallet concluded his long tour of the Bay posts with a canoe trip with two Indians, travelling fast and light, upstream on the Albany seven days to English River, and three days on to Pagwa. He had hoped to arrive at the

English River post unannounced, but found that the Montreal office had given due warning of his visit and most signs of carelessness were camouflaged.[29]

Among those travelling north on the *Annie Geele* from Moose to Port Harrison on the 1920 inspection trip was Robert Flaherty, mining prospector, explorer, and about-to-become father of the documentary film. Flaherty, having explored northern Ontario and Quebec with his father's mining engineers and prospectors in his youth, spent the years 1910-1914 searching northern Ungava for iron ore, employed by Sir William MacKenzie, the railway builder. He had wintered in the Nastapoka Islands, on the coast of Baffin Island at Amadjuak, and on the Belcher Islands, which he had mapped, showing for the first time their true extent. In his search for iron ore he had been the first white man to cross Ungava from Great Whale River to Fort Chimo. His six years of living with the Eskimo had given Flaherty a deep appreciation of these people who survived in a land of harsh contrasts and austere beauty. Twice he had made films attempting to depict something of their life, and twice accidents had destroyed these films.[30] "I could not forget the film, I decided to go north again, this time wholly for the purpose of picturing the people I had come to like so well."[31]

By 1920 Flaherty was living modestly in the community of Silvermine, Connecticut, with his wife and three young daughters, writing and seeking a backer who would sponsor his return to the North. At a cocktail party in New York, Flaherty was introduced to Thierry Mallet, and it is easy to imagine these two northern travellers escaping from the encompassing babble to talk of common interests and to compare notes on trips they had both made up and down Hudson Bay. Flaherty had a flawed print of his second film which he arranged to show Mallet in the company of Jean Revillon, and the result was that Revillon Frères agreed to provide Flaherty with the backing and the location, the Revillon post at Port Harrison, to shoot another film of Eskimo life.[32] Flaherty was given total freedom to make the film which had obsessed him since he left the North. In return, Revillon Frères hoped to gain some needed publicity. The result was *Nanook of the North*, the film which has become a classic. It can still be seen occasionally on television, and the caption "Revillon Frères présent," in small print above the title, is the extent of the publicity which the company achieved.

In the 1920s, even though Mallet was based in New York, he continued to make extensive inspection tours, turning his attention to the Prince Albert district in northern Saskatchewan and Manitoba, reaching as far north as Nueltin Lake at the edge of the Barren Lands. He made at least four such trips between 1921 and 1925, each lasting three months. Mallet enjoyed doing the northern part of the circuit with Del Simons, one of the best travellers in Revillon's employ and a thoroughly practical man who had built many of the area post buildings, winter roads, and boats for service on Reindeer Lake.[33] Mallet and Del Simons would make one more trip together in 1926.

As with his trips on the Bay, Mallet's stated intention was to observe, and listen to all complaints and comments but issue no orders and lay no blame, since decisions were to be taken by the Montreal headquarters on the information of the district manager. "The Call of the Wild" dictated the extent of these trips.

Continually cutting expenses and trying to improve efficiency, in each report Mallet looked forward to a general improvement the following year, but low fur returns, mismanagement of Indian debts, forest fires, and increased competition conspired to keep the district from showing profits overall.

In the years before World War I, Revillon Frères appeared to challenge the Hudson's Bay Company position of supremacy in the North American fur trade. Its more than one hundred posts dotted across the country from coast to coast were newer and, deliberately, more attractive than those of its rival. Proud of its handsome buildings in the major world cities, Revillon carried its tradition into the North. Its post managers were better paid, the stock—befitting a modern commercial company—was more varied and up-to-date, and the prices paid to trappers were higher to entice them away from their long-standing loyalty to the Hudson's Bay Company. The journals and memoirs of Hudson's Bay traders ruefully echo these facts.[34] The expense of setting up this huge organization would be recouped when Revillon reaped at least fifty percent of the fur harvest.

After the war the nature of the fur trade changed drastically. White trappers, in the search for quick profit, flooded into areas newly accessible by train and airplane, selling for cash, driving prices up, and depleting the fur stocks.[35] Profits for both the Hudson's Bay Company and Revillon Frères plummetted, but the Hudson's Bay's fall was cushioned by the huge reserves of land granted to it by the Canadian government in 1870 when it gave up its monopoly control of Rupert's Land. Revillon Frères, struggling to recover from the war and the post-war devaluation of the French franc, and needing to raise capital, offered the shares of Revillon Trading Co. stock on the New York exchange in 1926.[36] The Hudson's Bay Company bought 51 percent of the shares, and Mallet's long inspection tours of the North came to an end.

Thierry Mallet was at home in two very different worlds. With his patrician background, he was welcomed in Montreal and New York society and held memberships in two New York clubs, the *Coffee House* and the *Travellers*. At the same time he thrived on hard travel. He could accept without complaint the monotonous diet of salt beef and codfish on the *Annie Geele*, or travel throughout the summer in the North without grumbling about blackflies and mosquitoes. On his travels in the North he was a businessman, taking inventory, assessing personnel, looking at ways to improve the operation, and always concerned about the bottom line. On his return to the city he was haunted by the freedom of the romantic, adventurous life in the wilderness. The travelling businessman wrote detailed reports, factual, sometimes scathing, but always honest. The city-bound adventurer wrote sketches about the North in clean, spare prose that was close to poetry, in which effect took precedence over fact.

On Mallet's inspection tours there were periods of travel to reach a destination, usually by canoe, sometimes by sailing vessel or steamer, when he was freed from the constraints of officialdom and could revel in the pleasures of the

Figure 4. Mallet, on the left, greets Del Simons, Northern Saskatchewan, 1925. National Archives of Canada, Ottawa, Revillon Frères Archives, microfilm reel #F1642, Box 36, by permission of Revillon Archives, Paris.

trail. For example, on the 1920 tour of James Bay when the factor at Fort George was engrossed in post business, Mallet took a five-day trip by canoe with two Indians up the coast of Hudson Bay to Cape Jones (Pte. Louis XIV)—about 60 miles—to shoot ducks. In 1924, in order to arrive at Ile à la Crosse from the north unannounced, he and Del Simons travelled a route no longer used by the Indians, taking 29 days to cross northern Saskatchewan from Brochet via Wollaston Lake and Cree Lake. The following year he repeated that route and continued north with Del Simons to Nueltin Lake and Windy Lake on the edge of the Barrens, where Revillon was trading with the inland Eskimos.

On trips such as these, Mallet absorbed the colour and flavour of the northern bush and the stories that were the natural accompaniment of the campfire. These observations and stories were carried back to New York and stored along with memories of the war and of his early days with Revillon, to be distilled and polished into the fifty sketches that appeared in 1925 as *Plain Tales of the North*. *The Atlantic Monthly* accepted four longer stories which they published in 1927 and 1928. These were reprinted along with three additional stories in *Glimpses of the Barren Lands* in 1930. *The Beaver* printed five of these stories in 1931 and 1932.

The introductions to these books state that "the stories have been gathered and written by Capt. Mallet," and that "each is a true episode of the Far North." This is not to say that each episode was experienced by Mallet himself, even though they are written as first-person accounts for the sake of clarity and impact. The following are two examples of Mallet's use of other peoples' material.

During Flaherty's winter in Port Harrison, the Eskimos persuaded him to make the two-hundred-mile trek north to Cape Smith where female polar bears were reputed to den in numbers. A den would be opened, snow-block by snow-block, the dogs unleashed to circle the opening, and Nanook the hunter would advance armed only with a harpoon to meet the bear which would fight to protect her cubs. The trip would take about a month and the action would create a tremendous scene for the film. Bad weather stretched the trip to two months, poor hunting brought them close to starvation, and to cap their misfortunes, no denning bears could be found. In Flaherty's words:

> At dark the men returned. They saw the tracks of eight bear through various hours of the day, all of them going far out to sea on their hunt for seal. Nanook returned late. How we waited to hear above the din of dogs howling some word of bear caves! But there were many gulps of food and sips of tea before he gave us any news. Saw many, many signs, but no caves. The bear are far out on the ice edge at sea, he thinks. He fears snow is too heavily drifted by recent gales and dens maybe impossible to find.[37]

This description is very different from Mallet's brief tale, "Filming a White Bear on Land":

> The bear was roused out of her lair by a few vigorous pokes of the pole but, instead of showing her head out of the snow and then emerging to give battle, she burst out of her den like a rabbit from its hole. It was a "she" bear all right, but it happened that she had no cubs. In a flash she was through the pack of dogs and away! Before the cameraman could start cranking she was already fifty yards off, racing for the sea with all the huskies after her. We tried to lift the camera, carry it and follow, but it was useless. The bear never stopped for at least a mile.

Flaherty's description has the true ring of one who has lived the experience, but Mallet's story is so vivid that the created picture remains to explain why there is no polar bear (*nanook*) scene in *Nanook of the North.*

In *Glimpses of the Barren Lands* the final story "When the Caribou Failed," is a disturbing description of meeting a starving Eskimo band fishing on a lake at the edge of the Barrens in winter, and of learning of their fate when he returned to the same spot six months later in July. The source of that story can be traced to Mallet's inspection report of the district from Ile à la Crosse to Nueltin Lake in the summer of 1925, as he travelled to Windy Lake where Del Simons had traded the previous winter. "The most harrowing stories were told to me by Mr. Simons—who went this winter, as far as fifty miles from Baker Lake—and by the natives themselves; eight families having waited to see me at Windy Lake last July."[38] Mallet's story is an artistic and polished tale of starvation in the Barrens, haunting and compelling, the bare details etched against the stark beauty of the background.

> It was a beautiful evening, such as one sees so often in the far North during the summer. The horizon was blood red. The canoe, silhouetted in black across the flaming background, glided through waters as still as a mirror and of all the hues of the rainbow. The regular splash of the paddles woke the echoes of the hills behind me, while the scattered drops of water fell back on the surface of the lake, around the canoe, like tongues of fire. . . .For a whole day the four men did not see anything that could make them believe that they were on the right trail. Then, all at once, they began finding things—a fish spear, a telescope, an axe, a snow knife, two pairs of boots. . . they soon guessed what had happened. The weak, straggling band of starving natives had begun there to discard all extra weight. . . .From there on the trail was strewn with every loose article the band had been carrying. It was easy to see that the pace had begun to tell and that the dying natives had decided to throw away everything they had except the rifles. After that, during seven weary days, my man followed the trail by the dead bodies. Generally one alone; sometimes two, side by side; once three, sitting in a group, close to one another behind a rock.[39]

Writing was a natural medium for Mallet, as his inspection reports demonstrated. In 1923 a small book, *Igloo Life*, was published by Revillon Frères, New York, which is attributed to Thierry Mallet, although his name does not appear in it. It presents a simple version of Eskimo life and customs along with a brief history of the Revillon company, illustrated by drawings made from some of Flaherty's photographs. As well, a series of sixty-nine press releases appeared in the *New York Herald Tribune*, *The Evening Sun*, and *The Onlooker* under the heading "The Story of Revillon Furs" to advertise their Fifth Avenue store. The drawings from photographs now in the Revillon archives each headed a succinct, two-paragraph commentary which presented an unusually frank picture of the fur trade. For example, one which carries the picture of the wreck of the *Eldorado*, a Revillon supply ship, bears the comment: "Furs of the North pay a heavy tax to Nature before they arrive at their finished state. Every fur garment at the Revillon showrooms represents risk and hazard to human life as well as to much valuable property."[40] This is an unlikely form of advertising copy, but it tallies with the sentiment expressed in Mallet's story, "A Silver Fox and a Scarf," in *Plain Tales of the North*.

> Some years ago in the Ungava district, two Eskimos, brothers, caught a beautiful Silver Fox late in March. . . .The Eskimo who was breaking the trail ahead of the dogs walked on some thin ice and fell through, team and sleigh following him into the gaping hole. Man and dogs drowned although the other Eskimo made every effort to save them. The lone man who was carrying the Silver Fox in a bag slung on his back kept on and managed to reach the post, covering the last few miles literally on his hands and knees through sheer weakness and exhaustion. . . .The Fox eventually reached our New York house and was sold during the winter. A few months later in a well known restaurant, a lady with a party of friends got up from her table to leave. The waiter picked up and handed to her a Silver Fox scarf which had slipped from her chair and had been lying unnoticed on the floor under the table. It was the Ungava Fox with the little white mark between the eyes.[41]

The concept of the sacrifice and struggle of northern trappers to satisfy the vanity of city women is not unique to Thierry Mallet. Thoughtful Hudson's Bay traders may allude to it, but Erik Munsterhjelme, a Scandinavian trapper, expresses it forcefully in his memoir, *The Wind and the Caribou*.[42] Mallet, with his gift for dramatic understatement, creates a picture which lingers in the mind.

Mallet continued as the president of Revillon Frères, New York, in close association with Jean Revillon, beyond 1935, the year in which the Hudson's Bay Company bought out the Canadian operation completely. The trading posts were amalgamated and the name of Revillon disappeared in the North.

Mallet's next published work, *La Terre Écarlate*, twenty poems written on the island of Madagascar, are in complete contrast to his tales of the North, but the voice is still recognizable: that of the disciplined perfectionist, aloof, observant, and somber, with glints of humour.

After the fall of France, Madagascar was under the control of the Vichy government and vulnerable to occupation by the Japanese for use as a naval base in the Indian Ocean. To prevent this the British mounted a successful invasion of the sensitive northern part of the island early in 1944, overpowered the Vichy forces, and placed the Free French in control, under Gen. Georges Gentilhomme. Capt. Thierry Mallet was sent to Madagascar by the American State Department as deputy consul-general in 1943 until the end of the war.[43]

The twenty poems contained within *La Terre Écarlate*, composed in French, are powerfully evocative of the exotic, tropical island set in the Indian Ocean. The grandeur of the mountains, the majesty of the ocean, the fragrance of a profusion of flowers are set in contrast to tropical decay, destructive storms, and memories of Madagascar's bloody history. The war produces an undercurrent as real as the steady murmur of the distant sea. It is ever-present, from the anguish of the exile for his occupied homeland, to the hope felt when he hears that Paris has been liberated, and the final farewell to Madagascar on 17 May 1945 after victory has been won. Just as he had done in prose in the North, Mallet created a series of vivid word pictures which bring the atmosphere of Madagascar alive for the reader. More than that, he conveyed his own feelings of depression and nostalgia.

Even the depressing atmosphere of Madagascar could not blunt Mallet's energy and his appetite for business. In New York he had been a director of Lancôme Perfume,[44] and during his stay on the island he became a director of two companies, Société des tabacs et oléogineux de Madagascar, and Société de Commerce africain.

After a long absence from the North, Mallet wrote an article for *The Beaver* recalling his final trip in 1926, when he took five months away from his office to attempt to travel from The Pas, Manitoba, down the Kazan River to Baker Lake in the North West Territories. In 1894 J.B. Tyrrell and R.M. Ferguson, working for the Geological Survey of Canada, had followed part of this route to Yathkyed Lake where they turned east to the Hudson Bay coast, and in 1922 a Danish anthropologist, Kaj Birket-Smith, had come up the Kazan from Baker Lake to Yathkyed Lake, but the full route had been neither travelled nor

Figure 5. Thierry Mallet in Europe in the summer of 1939. Courtesy of Col. H.G. Mallet.

mapped.[45] Mallet's crew consisted of Del Simons, his favourite northern traveller, and two Cree Indians, Peter Linklater and Joe Cadotte, using a single nineteen foot canoe with a small outboard motor for the upstream work. At Ennadai Lake they arranged to be guided by Kakoot, an Eskimo whose father had guided Tyrrell. They reached Yathkyed Lake in mid-July to find it solid ice. After waiting three days for a change in the weather, their dwindling food supplies dictated their return up-stream. It would be 1966 before a group of Americans in two canoes travelled the full length of the Kazan River,[46] and in 1968 a group of Canadians were partially blocked by ice and then wind-bound for six days near Yathkyed Lake until rescued by airplane.[47] In 1926 that had not been an option.

Several beautifully crafted stories in *Glimpses of the Barren Lands* are the result of this trip, particularly the title story and "My friend Kakoot." *The Beaver* article, entitled "Exploring the Kazan," and published in 1950, tells the story in more candid terms. The country was "savage and rocky," "its wild beauty is monotonous in the extreme." The "stench of Kakoot's camp was over-powering." After the passage of an immense caribou migration, "the Barren Lands resumed their aspect of utter desolation." Those who travelled with Mallet remembered that he found scouting and tracking the heavy rapids on the Kazan tiresome, and running them, terrifying.[48] By any standard, it was a strenuous and difficult trip. With the publication of this article, the "Call of the Wild" was finally stilled.

With the exception of this final article in *The Beaver*, with its first-person realism, Mallet's writings differ from the memoirs of fur-trade men such as Philip Godsell and J.W.Anderson, and from the books of northern adventurers such as Warburton Pike, David Hanbury, or Robert Flaherty. The writers of those books put themselves in the centre of the narrative. It is their story, and however modest they may be, they cast themselves in a heroic mold, describing extraordinary feats of travel while enduring frigid Arctic weather, the onslaught of insect hordes, and times of starvation and privation. Mallet, on the other hand, picks a scene, a dramatic incident, or a campfire story from his memory-bank, and like someone who has collected pebbles from countless beaches, he rubs and polishes them to a jewel-like perfection. The result is a collection of vignettes which represent the North as much as polished stones represent the earth's crust. The elements of truth are there, the rough edges of reality have been smoothed away.

In his heart, Mallet was a poet. His stories were a poet's distillation of his and others' experiences. *La Terre Écarlate* was a further demonstration of his poetic nature, and of his ability to evoke scenes and moods with a minimum of words.

The audience for which Mallet's writings were originally intended was small and select, unlike the writers mentioned above, who were writing for the general public. *Igloo Life* and *Plain Tales of the North* were published by Revillon Frères for presentation to friends and patrons, a privileged class. When they were so well received, Mallet sent his next stories to *The Atlantic Monthly*, a magazine with high literary standards, rather than to *Outing*, *Scribners*, or *Field and Stream*, the more usual venue for adventure writers.

Mallet's own family background was upper class and artistic; one sister was a very successful author, and the other had been a violin prodigy.[49] Like the fur traders and northern adventurers, he was not a writer by profession but a businessman with a keen sense of observation who took pleasure in creating word-pictures.

Mallet returned to North America after the war, but his marriage had not survived. He returned to Paris and took up his partnership in the family bank, where he continued to work until 1966, despite a debilitating stroke from which he totally recovered. More strokes occurred, and he was brought to a nursing home in Phenix City, Alabama, where he spent his final years near his son, dying in 1969.[50] As a businessman, Mallet strove to make Revillon's venture into the fur trade in Canada a success, endlessly looking for ways to make each trading post efficient, trying to get rid of the debt system of trade, finding innovative ways to transport goods into the North—every improvement that could be thought of was tried. The economic times were wrong, and even the Hudson's Bay Company struggled during some very lean years.

In the service of Revillon Frères, Thierry Mallet logged thousands of miles by canoe on northern lakes and rivers, and by schooner and steamer around the Hudson Bay coastline as a privileged member of the company's executive. In his years of travel he explored some new routes and retraced many familiar ones. This travel was not so much required by Mallet's work as it was demanded by the "Call of the Wild" which had become part of his psyche from his first wilderness experience. In his travels in the North, Mallet was the forerunner of the modern wilderness canoeist. He was a man of position and privilege who annually forsook the civilized comfort of a city home for the hard, spartan life of the trail. However, while he shared the labour of paddle and portage, his companions were hired by himself or his company, not friends or equals.

As a businessman, Mallet's energy and initiative, his understanding of the North, his grasp of technical details, and his keen entrepreneurial sense contributed largely to the success the French company achieved in Canada before 1914. Revillon is now almost forgotten in Canada, and Mallet's adventures have been matched by new generations of canoeists, so it is as a writer that he is now remembered, despite the small body of his published work. *Plain Tales of the North, Glimpses of the Barren Lands,* and *La Terre Écarlate* remain the polished memento of an adventurous, hard-headed romantic.

ACKNOWLEDGEMENTS

I wish to thank Col. Henri Mallet, Columbus, Georgia, for the information he shared with me about his father's life. I also wish to thank Michel Chevalier, Chairman of the Board, Revillon Group, for permitting me to use materials from the Revillon Archives in Paris.

NOTES

1. Thierry Mallet, *Plain Tales of the North* (New York: privately printed for Revillon Frères, 1925), 135.
2. Michèle Therrien, "Relations inter-ethniques et commerce de fourrures: les carnets de voyage du Capitaine Thierry Mallet, Revillon Frères, 1920-1925" *Recherches Amérindiennes au Québec* 16, no. 4 (1986-1987): 35-46.
3. *Who's Who in France, 1963-4* (Paris: Editions Jacque Lafitte, 1964).
4. Conversation with Henri Mallet.
5. Marcel Sexé, *Two Centuries of Fur-Trading, 1723-1923: Romance of the Revillon Family* (Paris: Revillon Frères, 1923), 21-57.

6. Memorandum, 16 February 1904, Revillon Archives [hereafter RA], reel #F1580, National Archives of Canada [hereafter NAC], Ottawa, Canada.
7. Sexé, 101-11.
8. Conversation with Henri Mallet.
9. Note from Etienne Mallet, 26 January 1909, RA, reel #F1615, NAC.
10. Robert J. Renison, *One Day at a Time* (Toronto: Kingswood House, 1957), 56-60. For the sake of the story Renison has combined all the incidents referring to Revillon Frères into one chapter, placing Mallet in charge of Moose River post from the wreck of the *Eldorado* in 1903, and claiming to have entertained Mallet that year at Moose Factory when Bishop Newnham was on furlough in England. In 1903 Mallet was 19 years old and either at Oxford or travelling around the world with his uncle; Bishop Newnham's furlough in England was in 1899 (O.M. Petersen, *Land of Moosoneek* [Toronto: Bryant Press, 1974], 117). Renison was the missionary at Ft. Albany, 1899-1909, and Archdeacon of Moose, 1907-1912 (T.C.B. Boon, *The Anglican Church from the Bay to the Rockies* [Toronto: Ryerson Press, 1962], 144). The Fort Albany post record, 1901-1906, HBCA, B.3/a/205, shows Renison continuously in residence in Fort Albany with frequent trips out to Moose Factory, Attawapiskat, etc. The arrival of Revillon Frères at Fort Albany is faithfully recorded, first as "opposition traders," and then each trader by name. In the years 1905-1906 there appear to be very cordial relations between the two rival posts. Mallet's name does not appear in the Fort Albany post record or in the Moose Factory record, which ends in May 1904, and which contains fewer personal details than the Fort Albany record.
11. Sexé, 71.
12. Letters from Mallet, Ombabika, September 11, 1908 and Montreal, 5 October 1908, RA, reel #F1580, NAC.
13. The York Factory post record, 1903-1909, records the arrival on 6 August 1908 of Chief Factor D.C. McTavish from Churchill with two travellers, Messers.[sic] Tiffany [sic] and Mallet, by the coast boat *Strathcona*. On 9 August Messers. Tiffany [Thévenet] and Mallet left for Norway House, and on 11 August the Split Lake Indians who came with Thévenet and Mallet left for Split Lake. There is no mention of the departure of McTavish, and it is to be assumed that Thévenet and Mallet travelled with him and therefore did not need the Split Lake Indians. Hudson's Bay Company Archives [HBCA], Winnipeg, reel #B239/a/185. Post records for Norway House are not available for 1908.
14. Philip Godsell, *Arctic Trader* (New York: G.P. Putnam's, 1932), 76.
15. Ibid., 38, 50.
16. Report from Thévenet, Montreal, 2 August, 1908, RA, reel #F1580, NAC.
17. Letters from Mallet, Split Lake, 29 June, 1908 and Montreal 2 September 1908, RA, reel #F1580, NAC.
18. Mallet's Diary of James Bay Trip, 1920, RA, reel #F1615, NAC; Mallet. *Plain Tales*, 63.
19. Report 26 December 1912, Letters, December 1912, January, February 1913, RA, reel #F1615, NAC.
20. Mallet, *Plain Tales*, 95.
21. *New York Times*, 17 February 1917, p. 11, col. 4.
22. Sexé, 37-39, 113-15.
23. *London Times*, 15 February 1917, p. 11, col. 2; *Montreal Gazette*, 15 February,1917.

24. *Montreal Gazette*, 2 April 1942, obituary.
25. Mallet's Diary, 1920.
26. *New York Times*, 25 February 1928, p. 9, col. 3.
27. Mallet's Diary, 1920.
28. Ibid.
29. Ibid.
30. Robert Flaherty, *My Eskimo Friends* (Garden City, N.Y.: Doubleday, 1924), 125.
31. Ibid., 133.
32. Arthur Calder-Marshall, *The Innocent Eye* (Baltimore: Penguin, 1970), 78.
33. Mallet's reports on the Prince Albert district, 1923, 1924, 1925, RA, reel #F1615, NAC.
34. Duncan Matheson, 1 January 1905, writing from Ft. Chimo, HBCA, reel A-12/FT.293/1a, and Dudley Copland, from Repulse Bay, 1925, in *Coplalook* (Winnipeg: Watson and Dwyer, 1989), 51, are two examples of this.
35. Arthur J. Ray, *The Canadian Fur Trade in the Industrial Age* (Toronto: University of Toronto Press, 1990), 111.
36. Letter, 10 February 1926, RA, reel #F1615, NAC.
37. Flaherty, 145-65.
38. Mallet's report, 10 September 1925, RA, reel #F1615, NAC.
39. Thierry Mallet, *Glimpses of the Barren Lands*, (New York: privately printed for Revillon Frères, 1930), 136.
40. Album 35, no. 8, Rev. Archives, reel #F1641, NAC.
41. Mallet, *Plain Tales*, 29.
42. Erik Munsterhjelme, *The Wind and the Caribou* (Toronto: Macmillan, 1953), 195.
43. Preface to *La Terre Écarlate* and conversation with Henri Mallet.
44. Conversation with Henri Mallet.
45. John Lentz, "Inuit Ku, Kazan River," *The Beaver*, Outfit #298, 4-11.
46. Ibid.
47. Eric Morse, *Freshwater Saga* (Toronto: University of Toronto Press, 1987), 127-44.
48. R.H. Cockburn, "Distant Summer," *Fram* 1, no. 1 (1984): 101.
49. Conversation with Henri Mallet.
50. Ibid.

WRITINGS OF THIERRY MALLET

From Revillon Archives, which are held in Paris, with microfilm copies at the National Archives of Canada in Ottawa:
Letter from Split Lake, 29 June 1908 - F 1580
Report from Montreal, 2 September 1908 - F 1580
Report from Ombabika, 11 September 1908 - F 1580
Report from Montreal, 5 October 1908 - F 1580
Diary of James Bay trip, June/September 1920 - F 1615
Report of trip to Isle à la Crosse, 1923 - F 1615
Report on Prince Albert Dist., September 1924 - F 1615
Report on Prince Albert Dist.. September 1925 - F 1615
Three reels of microfilmed photographs - F 1640, F 1641, F 1642

PUBLISHED WRITINGS

Igloo Life, Revillon Frères, N.Y., 1923
Plain Tales of the North, Revillon Frères, N.Y., 1925
Glimpses of the Barren Lands, Revillon, N.Y.,l93O
La Terre Écarlate, privately printed, Suisse, 1946
Atlantic Monthly:
  March 1927, "Frozen Diary"
  September 1927, "My Friend Kakoot"
  March 1928, "When the Caribou Failed"
  April 1929, "Furs and Traders"
The Beaver:
  June 1931, "Glimpses of the Barren Lands"
  September 1931, "Caribou"
  December 1931, "Eskimo Grave"
  March 1932, "Battle of the Moose"
  September 1932, "Old, old McF-"
  March 1950, "Exploring the Kazan"

Part VII

Fur Trade Literature and Interpretation: Issues and Problems

Long's Voyages and Travels: *Fact and Fiction*

Michael Blanar

With an impressive "List of Subscribers" containing the names of the most distinguished persons connected with the Hudson's Bay Company and the fur trade, and a four-month advance notice of its impending publication, J. Long's *Voyages and Travels of an Indian Trader and Interpreter . . .* was considered an important document from its very first appearance in February 1791.[1] It was immediately translated into German (Forster 1791; von Zimmermann 1791), and then into French (Billecocq [1794]) and Swedish (Pfeiffer 1798), besides being reviewed and/or having parts reprinted at least fourteen times in the magazines and periodicals of the day. Through the years most critics and readers have accepted it as a very accurate and reliable source of information on North America, on the fur trade in Canada in the latter part of the eighteenth century, and on Indian social customs and language. The two modern editions of the work (Thwaites 1904; Quaife 1911) have merely reinforced that view.

But who was J. Long? Was *Voyages and Travels* indeed a valuable account of the period, the people, and the places mentioned? It is the purpose of this paper to shed light on these questions and to determine the accuracy of some of the information presented. The three major voyages will be examined and, while establishing that Long was certainly in North America, the discrepancies, the inaccuracies, and in some cases, the impossibilities of the account will be discussed. But it is particularly the last years of *Voyages and Travels*, 1785-1788, that will be considered in the light of the documentation uncovered among the legal and administrative documents of Upper and Lower Canada.

The first two expeditions, 1777-1778 and 1778-1779, took Long to the region north of Lake Superior and west of Lake Nipigon known as *"le petit Nord"* [the Little North] and *Lac le Mort*, but he was extremely vague about his movements. Very little had been written about this area; Long's account offered no additional information. However, it was Edward Umfreville's account, *Nipigon to Winnipeg. A Canoe Voyage Through Western Ontario* written eight years later, that provided directions and descriptions "in striking contrast to the elusive narrative of John Long, who traded west of Lake Nipigon . . . ."[2]

VOYAGES AND TRAVELS

OF AN

INDIAN INTERPRETER AND TRADER,

DESCRIBING

The Manners and Customs

OF THE

NORTH AMERICAN INDIANS;

WITH

AN ACCOUNT OF THE POSTS

SITUATED ON

THE RIVER SAINT LAURENCE, LAKE ONTARIO, &c.

TO WHICH IS ADDED,

A VOCABULARY

OF

The Chippeway Language.

Names of Furs and Skins, in English and French.

A LIST OF WORDS

IN THE

IROQUOIS, MOHEGAN, SHAWANEE, AND ESQUIMEAUX TONGUES,

AND A TABLE, SHEWING

The Analogy between the Algonkin and Chippeway Languages.

BY J. LONG.

LONDON:

PRINTED FOR THE AUTHOR; AND SOLD BY ROBSON, BOND-STREET; DEBRETT, PICCADILLY; T. AND J. EGERTON, CHARING-CROSS; WHITE AND SON, FLEET-STREET; SEWELL, CORNHILL; EDWARDS, PALL-MALL; AND MESSRS. TAYLORS, HOLBORN, LONDON; FLETCHER, OXFORD; AND BULL, BATH.

M,DCC,XCI.

Figure 1. Title page of J. Long's *Voyages and Travels,* first published in London in 1791.

These journeys raise other questions: would an inexperienced person, hired as "an interpreter to the north," be given the responsibility of a house and sixteen Canadians? Would he be likely to rescue an experienced trader like Alexander Shaw and then take control of both camps? Would he succeed in fishing and hunting on his first trip to the interior where there is evidence to indicate that others, travelling in the region at that time, spoke of privation in such words as "all the provisions that all the Indians about this part of the country would be able to find would not be Sufficient to last Seven Men a week _____"?[3] Indeed, Long's fellow trader, James Clark, had several men starve at Lake Savan/Poschocoggan Lake in 1777.[4]

An apparent discrepancy in Long's account of this first expedition becomes evident in his record of Jaques Santeron, "in the same employ as myself" (Long, 93). Long related how Santeron took his furs to the Hudson's Bay Company in April 1778; yet there was no record of such a defection *in that year* in any of the company's journals. However, in the following year there was a very clear description of the progress of Germain Maugenest, alias Saint-Terone,[5] who passed through Gloucester House on 10 July 1779 and Henley House on 19 July, finally reaching Albany Fort on 26 July,[6] where Thomas Hutchins, Chief Factor and Governor, received him, his clerk John Coates, seven Canadians, and three Indians in four canoes. They brought with them 1,276 made beaver in seventeen bundles. Commenting on the leader of these new arrivals, Hutchins noted that Maugenest was "a Native of Old France, but many Years a Resident in Montreal where his Wife and Family now are and where he took the Oath of Allegiance to his Majesty on the Reduction of the Place [in 1760] . . ."; he added that Maugenest, "by his Conduct and Behavior appears far above the Rank of what we call Inland Pedlars. . . ."[7]

Long concluded the first excursion into the interior by claiming success—he returned with 140 packs of furs in four canoes, accompanied by sixteen Canadians, one Indian, and his wife. With such a configuration, and aware that "60 B^{r} skins makes a good pack; & evry body knows that all North Canoes carries 25 Packs & 1 Keg of Castor . . ."[8] and that one made beaver weighs 1 3/4 lbs., Long errs: he must not have had enough canoes for such a load; otherwise he had fewer men in each North canoe than was needed to propel it safely, or else he was mistaken in the number of packs he took out. The account of this expedition ended with yet another question about the credibility of J. Long's narrative. And as the journey progressed into the second northern excursion, the vagaries and inaccuracies continued.

Again travelling to the Little North and Lake Schabeechevan, the tale became questionable when matched against other accounts and authorities. In the fall of 1778, Long met some Indians and explained that they "seemed well pleased to find a trader settled among them"(Long, 110), which caused some surprise since there were at least seventeen houses westward of Lake Superior. George Sutherland, in his graphic way, wrote only a year later that "the pedlars are in Every hole and cornor where there are any Indians to be found . . ," adding that

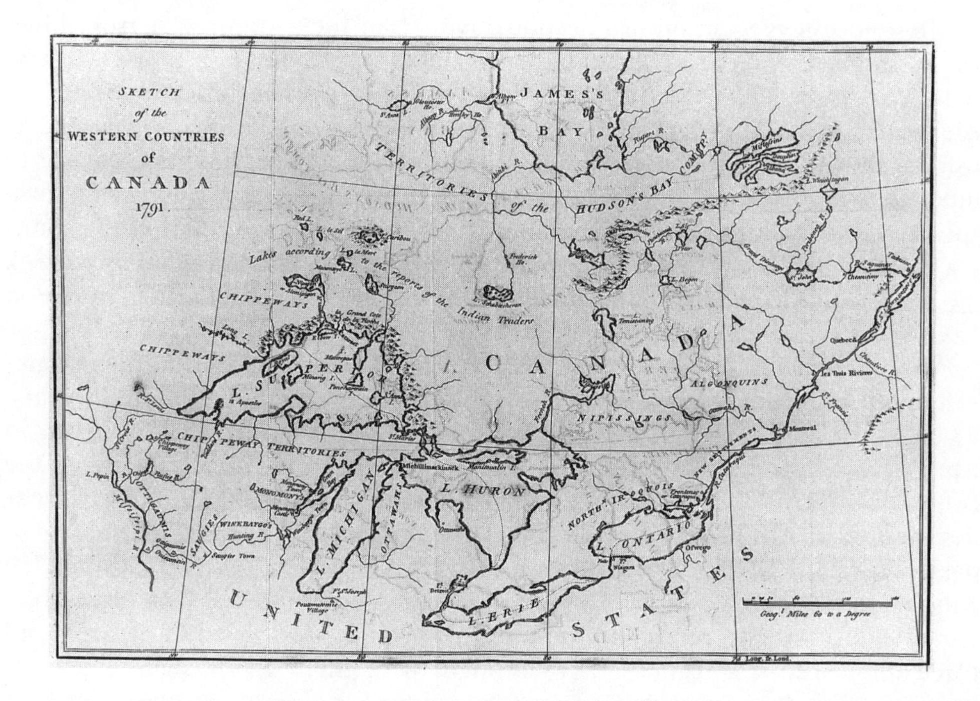

Figure 2. Map centering on area north of the Great Lakes, included in J. Long's original edition of 1791.

the upper country "is poisoned with them [pedlars] . . . for it is impossible for a man to travel 150 miles any course without finding a pedlars house."[9]

In the same vein Long wrote of a visit, in February 1779, by a trader from Fort Albany who was induced to come "from a motive of curiosity to see me, not having heard of any person wintering so far inland before, except the servants belonging to the Hudson's Bay Company"(Long: 125-26). He provided no names, not a shred of other information; nor is this alleged "meeting" to be found recorded in any Company journal to authenticate that visit.

The expedition to Lac St. Jean in 1780-81 once more taxes the reader's credulity. On this journey direction, distance and features of the area are all details that do not bear close scrutiny. Upon leaving Quebec for Tadoussac he visited the village of the Lorette Indians, nine miles from Quebec. What he did not tell the reader was that this was in a direction opposite to where he was headed and that a visit to the Huron habitation necessitated a return to Quebec before "continuing" to Tadoussac. When he reached that place, he gave the impression that "this village" was inhabited by a French clergyman, a Mr. Martin (there is no record of a Catholic priest by that name to have been there at that time), and a brother trader, an Englishman; yet when Long and his "party" attacked the American privateer (Long: 156), he was able to muster "upwards of forty, well armed" men. Where did they all come from? This time of year (the beginning of winter) would have found few, if any, Indians, for it was well known that the Indians only sojourned there at maximum from May to September, according to Mgr. Victor Tremblay.[10] Long's distance of 100 leagues from Tadoussac to Checootimy [Chicoutimi] was in reality 35 leagues by land and even less by water; his "seven days Indian march" to the north-east from Lake Shaboomoochoine (obviously Lake Chamouchouane) was about 280 miles to the east of Lake Abitibi and impossible to cover in such a time because the line cut across the flow of waters, necessitating a number of detours and portages. Long's "salt water" tides were, in the words of Fr. Tremblay, *"une évident blague,"* [obvious nonsense] as the tides and salt water did not reach Checootimy. And the "great many animals"(Long: 158) which he and an Indian trader killed are an exaggeration as there never was much hunting in this region and in 1780 the fur-bearing game (*"le gibier à fourrure"*) had practically disappeared. His claim to have seen "a great many snakes," including a rattlesnake, was completely spurious: *"Le phénomène des serpents en `grand quantité' est absolument invraisemblable* [The phenomenon of snakes in great quantity is absolutely unbelievable]" was Fr. Tremblay's reaction. In all the history of the Saguenay only once has a snake been mentioned, and it was believed that this particular serpent had escaped from a circus which had visited that year.

On this trip Long also claimed to have travelled "farther inland, by near eighty leagues, than any trader had ever been, the only settlement in that part of Canada being at St. Peter's Lake"(Long: 158). However, traders had been dealing with the Indians in this same region for over a hundred years. When Long met a band of Indians on 17 June 1781, he wrote that they were "agreeably surprised . . . and particularly delighted when they heard me speak their own language" at this first meeting (Long: 159). But Indian languages were as diverse and various then as now, and while Long might have had a facility for Native tongues, he would have had difficulty conversing. Where had he learned this language? Mgr. Tremblay's reaction was:

> *Les idiomes étaient tellement différents d'une nation indienne à l'autre, que les missionaires les plus entraînés ne pouvaient comprendre et se faire comprendre qu'après plusiers semaines de séjour* [The idioms or languages were so different from the one Indian nation to the other, that even the best trained missionaries were not able to understand and to make themselves understood except after several weeks of stay among them].

Throughout these journeys Long described himself as a "trader"; however, his name appeared nowhere on the lists of those granted trade licences for the areas mentioned in these three expeditions. These licences were necessary if traders and goods were to engage legally in trade with the Indians, and outposts like those at Michilimackinac and Fort Oswego checked them very carefully. These letters of permission were issued not only for trading in the west, southwest, and northwest, but also for other destinations such as Détroit, Restigouche, "Saguenai," Catarakoui, "La Baye," Illinois, and Sault Ste. Marie. Entered on these licences were the names of the trader, the securities, the interpreter (if

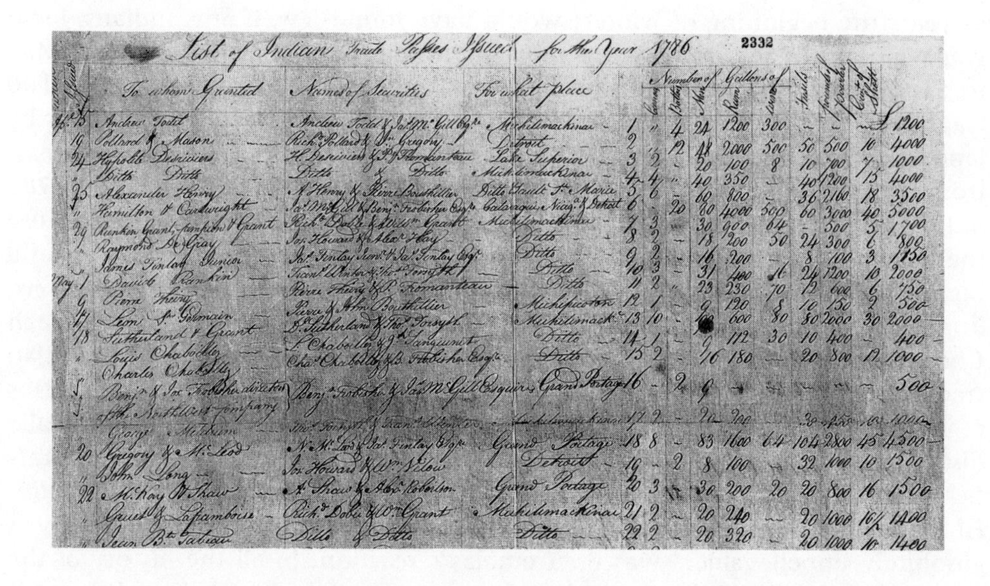

List of Indian Trade Passes Issued for the Year 1786 — 2332

When Issued	To whom Granted	Names of Securities	For what place		Number of Canoes	Number of Batteaux	Number of Men	Gallons of Rum	Gallons of Wine	Fusils	Pounds of Powder	Cwt of Shott	£
Apl. 15	Andrew Todd	Andrew Todd & Jas. McGill Esqrs.	Michilimackinac	1	"	4	24	1200	300	–	–	–	1200
19	Pollard & Mason	Richd. Pollard & Jn. Gregory	Detroit	2		12	48	2000	500	50	500	10	4000
24	Hypolite Desriviers	H. Desriviers & P. Fromanteau	Lake Superior	3	2	–	20	100	8	10	700	7	1000
"	Ditto Ditto	Ditto & Ditto	Michilimackinac	4	4	"	40	350	–	40	1200	15	4000
25	Alexander Henry	A. Henry & Pierre Bouthillier	Ditto Sault Ste. Marie	5	6	–	60	800	–	36	2160	18	3500
"	Hamilton & Cartwright	Jas. McGill & Benjn. Frobisher Esqrs.	Cataraqui, Niaga. & Detroit	6	–	20	80	4000	500	60	3000	40	5000
29	Rankin, Grant, Simpson & Grant	Richd. Dobie & Willm. Grant	Michilimackinac	7	3	–	30	900	64	–	500	5	1700
"	Raymond De Gray	Jos. Howard & Alexr. Hay	Ditto	8	2	–	18	200	50	24	300	6	800
	James Finlay Junior	Jas. Finlay Junr. & Jas. Finlay Esqr.	Ditto	9	2	–	16	200	–	8	100	3	1150
May 1	David Rankin	Vincent Winter & Thos. Forsyth	Ditto	10	3	–	31	400	16	24	1200	10	2000
9	Pierre Theiry	Pierre Theiry & P. Fromanteau	Ditto	11	2	"	23	230	70	12	600	6	750
17	Leon St. Germain	Pierre & Amb. Bouthillier	Michipicoton	12	1	–	9	120	8	10	150	2	500
18	Sutherland & Grant	D. Sutherland & Thos. Forsyth	Michilimackc.	13	10	–	[illegible]	600	80	80	2000	30	2000
"	Louis Chaboillez	L. Chaboillez & J. Sanguinet	Ditto	14	1	–	9	112	30	10	400	–	400
	Charles Chaboillez	Chas. Chaboillez & B. Frobisher Esqr.	~~Ditto~~	15	2	–	16	180	–	20	800	12	1000
5	Benjn. & Jos. Frobisher direction of the NorthWest Company	Benjn. Frobisher & Jas. McGill Esquires	Grand Portage	16	–	2	9	–	–	–	–	–	500
	George Meldrum	Thos. Forsyth & [illegible]	Michilimackinac	17	2	–	20	200	–	30	450	10	1000
20	Gregory & McLeod	N. McLeod & Jas. Finlay Esqrs.	Grand Portage	18	8	–	83	1600	64	104	2800	45	4500
"	John Long	Jos. Howard & Wm. Vilow	Detroit	19	–	2	8	100	–	32	1000	10	1500
22	McKay & Shaw	A. Shaw & Alexr. Robertson	Grand Portage	20	3	–	30	200	20	20	800	16	1500
"	Guest & Laframboise	Richd. Dobie & Wm. Grant	Michilimackinac	21	2	–	20	240	–	20	1000	10½	1400
"	Jean Bte. Tabeau	Ditto & Ditto	Ditto	22	2	–	20	320	–	20	1000	10	1400

Figure 3. Part of the list of trade licences issued for the year 1786. John Long's was granted on May 20. Courtesy of the National Archives of Canada, neg. no. C-139990.

there was one) and the men, as well as the number of canoes, the value of the goods, and the general destination. Among the available records Long's name appeared only once, on licence #19 dated 21 May 1786 to Détroit—a destination he never mentioned—for the 1786-87 season, at a time, which will be shown later, he was otherwise occupied. This licence permitted him to take two batteaux and eight men to Détroit and there to trade 100 gallons of rum, 32 "fusils," 1000 pounds of powder, and 10 hundredweight of "shott."

Many inaccuracies and inconsistencies have been noted, and questions have been raised that, at present, cannot be answered.[12] Long himself noted those from whom he had borrowed, acknowledging them as his sources for some of the information and anecdotes included in his tales of travel—such as Lahontan, Edwards, Carver, Colden, Beatty, and Adair. Other passages came from, as he himself admitted, "the most authentic accounts," or from geographical gazetteers or other such works that were available to him; and as for still others, he wrote, "I have given them as accurately as possible, . . . from my knowledge"(Long: vii). Are the vagueness and unsubstantiated accounts the results of what Quaife conjectured to be when he asked, "Did Long himself prepare the completed narrative in the form in which it was published? Or was his personal narrative turned over to some professional writer to expand to the proportions desired for the forthcoming book?"[13]

Such an example of "borrowing" is evident in two passages from Long's *Voyages and Travels* that concern a Mattaugwessawack Indian by the name of Josepsis. Twice he referred to him and his tribe: once while discussing the

American custom of shooting at officers in the hopes of killing them and setting the opposing army into confusion (Long: 19), and again when he digressed on the subject of ascribing victory in battle to a Supreme Being and the practice of keeping relics of loved ones who have died (Long: 139-40). Long divulged no source for this material. However, the Colonial Office Papers do contain a manuscript copy of "Col. Goldthwaits Talk With a Mat,au,gwe,sauwack Indian who is now among the Penobscot Indians—This talk was in July 1771"; and in the May 1792 issue of *The New London Magazine* there appeared an anonymous two-part article entitled "The talk which passed between a *Mattaugwessawack Indian* and a very curious *Gentleman*, late governor of a Fort in the interior Part of North America (see Appendix, 461-63)."[14]

The manuscript copy consists of 54 questions-and-answers, the questions presumably being posed by Col. Goldthwait, the answers given by an unnamed member of this tribe who comes from "beyond that Lake [Superior] towards the setting of the Sun."[15] The magazine article purported to be a record of a conversation held between an Indian named Josepsis/Josipsis and "a respectable Character," and consists of 79 questions-and-answers, the questions posed by a "Governor of a Fort in North America" and the responses given by an "intelligent Indian." In addition to the questions-and-answers there are parenthetical remarks, explanatory notes, footnotes, *Remarks*, and a closing statement by that "respectable Character" which attests that "I have been acquainted with this Indian several years, and never had any reason to suppose that he had deceived me in the account he gave me"—a kind of assurance or witnessing to the truth of the information contained therein.

Comparing the three versions, one can only conclude that the 1771 Goldthwait conversation must have formed the basis both of Long's 1791 comments on the Mattaugwessawacks and of the 1792 article. Indeed, one might ask if Long were not the author of the anonymous piece, since the use of the name "Josepsis" and the description of the practice of preserving a hand or a foot by salting and drying are found in Long and *The New London Magazine* article but not in the 1771 C.O. manuscript copy.[16] This adds further to the enigma that is Long; since his journal was full of self-aggrandisement, why would he have hidden behind the label of anonymity, or had he merely seen an early manuscript copy of the article and borrowed from it for his own account?

That Long had been in Canada cannot be doubted. He wrote of his arrival in 1768 and of his seven-year apprenticeship, during which he learned something of Indian languages. In 1775, his contractual obligations to his "master" completed, he attained his freedom and immediately volunteered to defend Montreal from Ethan Allen and his Green Mountain Boys. There was a skirmish at Long Point and a Major Carden, Mr. Patterson, and three privates were killed; he himself was wounded in the foot, and Ethan Allen captured and imprisoned (Long: 18-19). These details were corroborated not only by Ethan Allen himself, who had kept a journal of his attack and imprisonment, but also by Guy Carleton's official report.

Allen's *Narrative*, first published in Philadelphia in 1789, confirmed that, when the British engaged the American troops, they had no more "than forty regular troops, together with a mixed multitude, chiefly Canadians, with a number of English who lived in town, and some Indians. . . ." He himself had thirty-one effective men and seven wounded when he surrendered; he was taken to Montreal some two miles away. He also mentioned that a Major Carden (a British officer) had been killed, as well as "an eminent merchant, Patterson, of Montreal."[17]

A complete description from the British point of view is to be found in a report to the Earl of Dartmouth by Guy Carleton, dated Montreal, 25 October 1775. Carleton noted that thirty British regulars had captured thirty-five American men (including five wounded), and that a Major Carden had been killed and Mr. Patterson very seriously wounded.[18] There were *no* other persons listed as killed or wounded.

Long's information was correct. And yet, Long's name appeared nowhere—in no military records, no reports, on no pay sheets, or muster rolls—in fact, in no place where it should have been found had he been engaged as he says he was.

Another example of Long's familiarity with an actual event is the account of his acquaintance with "a Lorette Savage, called Indian John, who had been in the American service all the way, and who waited to receive reward for his fidelity as the Congress were then sitting." John had been in the American service for nine years and in all that time had received as payment but one gun, two blankets, three pieces of gartering, and one hundred paper dollars "which he could not make use of." Long befriended him and decided to help him in his attempts to secure the reimbursement which had been promised him. Long told the readers that he intervened with Congress on behalf of Indian John and was successful in his pleas, and Indian John received his reward (Long: 169-71).

In the *Journal of the United States in Congress Assembled* for 1784-85, the entry for Friday, 18 April 1785 refers to a recommendation from a committee struck to consider the petition of "John Vincent, an Indian of the Huron tribe," —that he be "allowed and paid . . . , the sum of one hundred dollars."[19] And in the Colonial Office Papers are to be found John Vincent's petition and a testimonial by "Coll.º Louis" concerning "John Vancson, Chief, of the Hughrons of Surrett In the Province of Quebec," in which John Vincent's involvement with "Coll.º Allen and Cap.ᵗ Leivingston" at Chambly and Isle aux Noix is described.[20] This testimonial was obviously written to assist John Vincent in his petition.

Long's details were accurate even to the payment of $100 in paper money, and he offered even more bits of information than were contained in the written petition or in the Congress *Journal*—a clear and undeniable indication that he had been privy to more than was known publicly. Though his role in the affair was, according to his writings, rather major, his name as an intervenor, interpreter, or representative appears nowhere.

Thus far what is known is that there are errors—grievous errors in dates, directions and conditions—contained in Long's "journeys" to the interior and

Quebec. Simultaneously, there is evidence that he did indeed exist and did visit this continent, as he included names and events which had not been public knowledge.

The latter part of the narrative, from July 1784 to his final departure in 1787, is a tale not of expeditions, accomplishments, and heroic deeds, but a personal litany of ill-health, poor judgment, and business failure. Unlike the earlier part of the journal where he hid behind a cloak of anonymity, in this section he created a "friend," and it will be clearly demonstrated that the misfortunes that befell his "friend" did, in fact, befall John Long himself.

The consistent use of inaccuracies and scant detail continues.

After a brief sojourn in England (9 November 1783 to mid-July 1784), he returned with goods purchased with borrowed funds for, he wrote, he had "entered into an engagement with a relation . . . "; however, his return to Canada was so late and the trading year so far advanced that he could not proceed to Michilimackinac. He sold his goods at a great loss and remitted to his "relation" in London only "a very small sum in part of payment" (Long: 168).

In February 1785 he went to New York where he met Indian John (Vincent), discussed above; we assume that, because of the contacts he had made, he received credit, purchased goods for trade, and left for "Jenesee Lake" to trade with the Oneidas. His goods were eventually seized, and he returned to Cataraqui on 8 November to find his "friend and correspondent" arrived from England. They remained there until May 1786, at which time they moved to Toniata Creek, near Oswegatche, where Long, impressed with the surrounding country, applied for and received "five hundred acres of land as a loyalist settler" (Long: 175).

There is some confusion here: the usual application by officers was for a grant of 200 acres, and only 100 acres for the non-commissioned ranks. The official documents show that two grants of land had been made to "John Long" in *1789* and not in 1786 as Long claimed. The first was to a "John Long seaman," who had received a total of four lots (three for himself and one for a wife/child) in Nassau District; the second, to a "John Long" (could this be the author?), was one-half of lot #19, consisting of 100 acres (the other half had been granted to a "Conrad Long") in the Township of Richmond, 1st Concession, Charlottenburg.[21]

His "friend" left for Montreal on business, and upon his return they both decamped because, Long noted, "he [his friend] was apprehensive of a seizure for an English debt." They were pursued to Pimitiscotyan where the sheriff seized their goods, removed them to Montreal, and sold them "even to the tent which sheltered us from the weather. . . ." (Long: 175). In fact, Long had gone into debt, and on 3 August 1786 a suit was brought against "Jno. Long, trader in the Upper Country . . . of the new Settlement above Oswegotia" by "Jno. Brookbank, . . . of London Watch Maker."[22] The writ, dated "the City and District of Montreal," commanded the authorities to "attach and hold . . . all such Effects as you find in your District of or belonging unto John Long, . . .to

Keep and Detain" until the suit came to the Court of Common Pleas at Montreal and a decision was reached. This legal action had been taken in order to recover the debt and expenses which amounted to three hundred thirty-three pounds, nine shillings, three pence halfpenny (£333.9.3$^{1}/_{2}$).[23]

And so, when he returned to Oswegatche from Montreal, Long decided to escape with his effects into the woods and thus avoid seizure. Alas, he was not successful. On 20 September 1786 there was a complaint signed by Wm. Powell for the Plaintiff, John Brockbank, and witnessed by Hertell de Mouville, naming "John Long of New Settlements above Oswegatchie Trader" as Defendant. The complaint directed "Honorable the Judges of the Court of Common Pleas" to permit the Plaintiff "to attach and hold" all of John Long's effects, as Brockbank had been informed that the Defendant was "leading an idle and Extravagant life, continually dissipating his property so that the Plaintiff is apprehensive of soon losing his legal recourse [to] the Defendants Effects."[24]

In fact, Long's goods and effects had been seized as witnessed by a document entitled "Common Pleas Montreal John Brookbank vs. John Long—Dated 30th Octr 1786." Under the heading "An account of Articles Taken from Mr. Jno Long of the New Settlements Trader at the suit of Mr. Jno Brookbank of London watchmaker by Titus Simons. 21st Day of Septr 1786" are a series of articles such as "stroud," "Leggons," men's and boys' coats, blankets, and "1 Bear Skin" seized at Cataraqui; there is another list of "Articles sold at Montreal" which includes 1 Boat and Oars, Trunks, 2 "Bottles of Opium," *and* "1 large Tent," and another of articles taken at Lachine. The sum total of articles sold at public vendu (including costs, e.g., "Paid to Sheriff Gray" and "Paid to boatmen for transporting the goods belonging to Mr. Long from Pimitisciouting landing fifty leagues X Cataraqui . . .") was 920 "livers" (*livres)* and 12 Coppers which, the document says , "is equal to £33.3.10." To this was added £6.9.6 belonging to Long and left with Mr. Powell, Attorney, to produce a grand total of £39.13.4, a fraction of the actual value.[25]

Thus, with no goods to trade, Long was destitute, and in this unhappy state he withdrew to the Bay of Quinté to stay with loyalist settlers whom he had befriended. His anguish and suffering must have been very great but the concern of his friends, he wrote, "tended to soften the rigour of distress, and alleviate my sorrows" (Long: 176). He remained with them for ten months, that is, until the spring of the next year—"1786" (in reality, 1787).

Throughout his journal, identifying the correct year is problematical as Long very often dated events one year earlier than the actuality, as in the incident of Jaques Santeron/Germain Maugenest wherein "1778" was in fact 1779, and the news of Admiral La Pérouse's attack, which took place in 1782, not in "1781." In this case Long wrote that it was 1786 when his goods were seized, and then, after a stay of ten months at the "Bay of Kenty," he spoke of "Early in spring, 1786. . . ." (Long: 176). His text had not been particularly well edited.

His attempts to cross into the United States were confounded not only by the lack of a pass but also by the fact that the path to Fort Stanwix had been "entirely obliterated." He returned to Oswego. Noting Long's poor physical condition, the commanding officer suggested that he leave—either return to Montreal or proceed to Niagara; he opted for Montreal where, with the assistance of Lord Dorchester and Lieut. General Hope, he secured employment as interpreter to Sir John Johnson at Carleton Island. This relief, however, was of short duration. Again he returned to the Bay of Quinté and remained with his loyalist friends until the spring of "1787" (1788). Finally he went down to Montreal.

In this state Long must have been driven to distraction, and he was caught stealing. Whether the theft of "sundry articles" was intended to alleviate his hunger and distress or to lighten his debt shall probably never be known. What is known is that item #28 on the schedule for the July 1788 sitting of the General Court of Quarter Sessions of the Peace was the suit of "The King vs. John Long" for Petit Larceny.[26] This date coincides with his narrative—"I . . . arrived at Montreal on the 14th of July" (Long: 177). There are no details concerning what passed at this General Court of Quarter Sessions; what is known, however, is that on Tuesday, 22 July of the "28th year of the Reign of George III" (1788), writs were prepared for Antoine Mandeville, Pierre Valle, Pierre Lanjovin, and Charles Dorion, directing each to deposit a sum of twenty pounds as surety for their appearance at "the next Court of King's Bench . . . to give evidence against John Long." The suit for Petit Larceny must have gone poorly for Long and the charge considered more serious than originally, because the suit was changed to "the King vs. John Long" for Grand Larceny and the four witnesses named above required to appear and "prefer a Bill of Indictment against John Long charged with having stolen sundry articles the property of __________"; no name is entered in the blank. The whole affair was bound over to the higher Court of Kings Bench, which was to meet next in Montreal on the first Monday of September 1788.[27]

It appears that Long decided not to await his trial in September. Rather, he travelled to Quebec City but found no solace in officialdom—Lord Dorchester, his earlier benefactor, refused to see him, and Lieut. General Hope, who had come to his assistance on a previous occasion, had already left for England. He was helped for a while by friends and, in what appears to be a final act of desperation, he had another "friend" forge a pass for him. With it he boarded a ship and sailed off for England "on the 25th of October," thus avoiding further prosecution. It is quite clear that he did not appear at the Court of King's Bench on the first Monday of September, as all references to the indictment and the suit cease abruptly; nor is there any further evidence of action taken against Mandeville, Vallée, Langevin, and Dorion in relation to "The King vs. John Long." His arrival in London at the beginning of December has been noted nowhere—except in his own *Voyages and Travels*.

There is more to the person of J. Long than the biographical note "English traveller; 1768 D.U. [Death Unknown],"[28] although even now he cannot be fully identified. Why is there so little known about him after he returns to

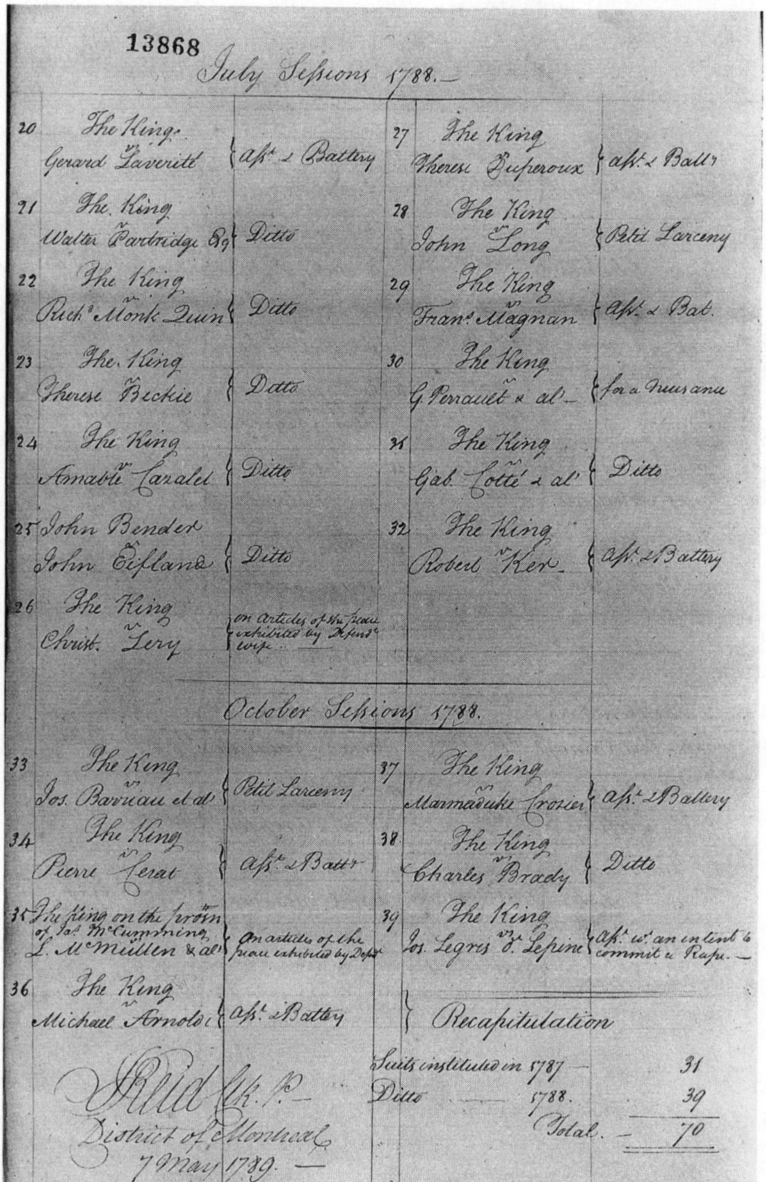

13868

July Sessions 1788.—

20	The King v. Gerard Laverité	Asst & Battery
21	The King v. Walter Partridge Esq	Ditto
22	The King v. Richd Monk Quin	Ditto
23	The King v. Therese Beckie	Ditto
24	The King v. Amable Caralet	Ditto
25	John Bender v. John Eifland	Ditto
26	The King v. Christ. Lery	on Articles of the peace exhibited by Defendt wife
27	The King v. Therese Duperoux	Asst & Batty
28	The King v. John Long	Petit Larceny
29	The King v. Franc. Magnan	Asst & Bat.
30	The King v. G. Perrault & al—	for a Nuisance
31	The King v. Gab. Cotté & al	Ditto
32	The King v. Robert Ker—	Asst & Battery

October Sessions 1788.

33	The King v. Jos. Barriau et al	Petit Larceny
34	The King v. Pierre Lerat	Asst & Battr
35	The King on the prosn of Jas McCumming v. L. McMullen & al	On articles of the peace exhibited by Deft
36	The King v. Michael Arnoldi	Asst & Battery
37	The King v. Marmaduke Crosier	Asst & Battery
38	The King v. Charles Brady	Ditto
39	The King v. Jos. Legris dit Lepine	Asst wt an intent to commit a Rape.—

Recapitulation

Suits instituted in 1787 —	31
Ditto —— 1788.	39
Total. —	70

[illegible] Clk. P.—
District of Montreal
7 May 1789.—

Figure 4. Part of the schedule for the July 1788 sitting of the General Court of Quarter Sessions in Montreal. Item 28 lists John Long as charged with "Petit Larceny." Courtesy of the National Archives of Canada, neg. no. C-139989.

London? No one, not even a single magazine, is able to shed the least ray of light on his identity. Perhaps the reason is that he avoided the limelight so as to evade further prosecution. And that "unflinching directness" and honesty noted by Quaife is put to some question. From the evidence presented it can be safely assumed that Long *was* in North America at the time he claims—the details he presents, and the names and circumstances of too many private events not readily available to the public affirm that he was there; but too many other details are erroneous or so vague as to raise doubts about his presence in those particular places at those particular times. Quaife's conjecture—that the journal probably was so short as to make it unpublishable in that state—may very well be true and the *Voyages and Travels* handed over to an editor who used many of the contemporary travel books as sources from which to give the manuscript publishable bulk, hence the many "digressions."

But he existed. His name appears: on a trading licence to Détroit; on a land grant in Richmond District; on a suit brought against him by John Brockbank; on a "seize-and-attach" order; on writs, one for "Petit Larceny" and another for "Grand Larceny"; and yet he is still unknown. The *Voyages and Travels* raises as many questions as it answers, and like his life is a tale of both fact and fiction.

NOTES

1. J. Long, *Voyages and Travels of an Indian Interpreter and Trader, . . .* (London: for the Author, 1791), 93.
2. R. Douglas, ed., *Nipigon to Winnipeg. A Canoe Voyage Through Western Ontario by Edward Umfreville in 1784. With Extracts from the Writings of Other Early Travellers through the Region* (Ottawa: R. Douglas, 1929), 7.
3. George Sutherland, "A Journal of the most remarkable Transactions and Occurrences Inland with Pedlers from 26th July 1779 to 31st May: 1780," Hudson's Bay Company Archives (hereafter HBCA), B.21/a/1.32.
4. John Best and Thomas Harvey, "Journal OH 25 June 1796-7," HBCA, B.155/a/12.19. See also John Favell, "AR A Journal of the most remarkable Transactions and Occurrences at Henley House from 19th July 1777 to 21st August 1778," HBCA, B.86/a/31. Entry for 5 June 1778.
5. George E. Thorman, "Maugenest," *Dictionary of Canadian Biography*, vol. 4 (Toronto: University of Toronto Press, 1979): 524-25.
6. John Kipling at Gloucester House, HBCA, B.78/a/4; John Favell at Henley House, HBCA, B.86/a/32.
7. Thomas Hutchins at Albany Fort, HBCA, B.3/a/76.
8. John McKay, Osnaburgh House Journal, HBCA, B.155/a/15. Entry for 13 October 1799.
9. Sutherland, "A Journal," 16, 26.
10. Monsignor Victor Tremblay, P.D., archivist and librarian of the Séminaire de Chicoutimi, recognized authority on the history of the Saguenay region in Quebec, and the driving force behind La Société Historique du Saguenay and its organ *Saguenayensia*. The Secréteriat of La Société is located at the Séminaire at

Chicoutimi. Correspondence of Victor Tremblay, 16 August 1963 and 12 September 1963.

11. "Quebec, Lower Canada, Canada East: Applications for Licences, Bonds and Certificates 1763-1867." National Archives of Canada (hereafter NAC), RG4, B28, vol. 115, 2332; microfilm H-1098.
12. For an overview of fur-trading activities in this region, see Victor P. Lytwyn's *The Fur Trade of the Little North: Indians, Pedlars, and Englishmen East of Lake Winnipeg, 1760-1821* (Winnipeg: Rupert's Land Research Centre, University of Winnipeg, 1986); and specifically for Long and the "Incongruities" to be found in the narrative, see pages 11-23.
13. Milo Milton Quaife, ed., *John Long's Voyages and Travels in the Years 1768-1788* (Chicago: The Lakeside Press, R.R. Donnelly & Sons Company, 1922), 20.
14. *The New London Magazine* 8 (May 1792): 224-28, 256-59.
15. Public Record Office (hereafter PRO), London, C.O. 42/87, 207-11.
16. See Appendix, 23.
17. Ethan Allen, *Narrative of the Capture of Ticonderoga, His Captivity, and Treatment of the British,* 5th ed. (Burlington: Goodrich & Nichols, 1849), 12, 15.
18. PRO, C.O. 42/34, 216, 216a, 217a.
19. *Journal of the United States in Congress Assembled: Containing the Proceedings from the First Monday in November 1784.* Published by Order of Congress (Philadelphia: John Dunlap, Printer to the United States Congress Assembled, 1785).
20. NAC (CC 42/8/77), MG23, B3, Folder 1, 137-8, 139-41.
21. "Minutes 1790-1794 Nassau District," NAC, RG1, L4, vol. 5 (microfilm C-14027), 26-7; and "Upper Canada: Land Board Minutes & Records," RG1, L4, vol. 12 (microfilm C-14028), 50-1, 79.
22. "Jno. [John] Brookbank" should be John Brockbank, London watchmaker and clockmaker, member of the Worshipful Company of Clockmakers. John and brother Myles established the shop "Brockbank's," located first in Old Jewry and then at 6 Cowper's-Court, Cornhill. See *G.H. Baillie, Watchmakers and Clockmakers of the World,* 3d ed. (London: N.A.G. Press Ltd., 1963), 40; George Daniels, *Freeman of the Worshipful Company of Clockmakers 1631-1984* (Riversdale: Isle of Man, 1984), 15; C.E. Atkins, comp., *Register of Apprentices of the Worshipful Company of Clockmakers of the City of London From Its Incorporation in 1631 to its Tercentenary in 1931 Compiled from the Records of the Company* (London: Privately Printed for the Company, 1931), 38.
23. "Canada: State Records 1786" (cover and copy of warrant of seizure), NAC, RG4, B17, vol. 12, file 2.
24. Ibid.
25. Ibid., "J. Brookbank vs. John Long: Sale of Defd.^{ts} Effects 21st Septr 1786," Common Pleas Montreal "Documents," 30th October 1786.
26. "Civil and Provincial Secretary, Lower Canada ("S" Series) 1760-1840," NAC, RG4, A1, vol. 42 (microfilm C-3005), 13868.
27. City of Montreal Archives: "At a General Court of Quarter Sessions of the Peace held in and for the district of Montreal on Tuesday the eighth day of July in the Twenty eighth year of the Reign of our Sovereign Lord George the Third" [1788], 78-80, 82.
28. Lawrence B. Phillips, *The Dictionary of Biographical References* (London: Sampson Low, Son and Marston, 1871).

REFERENCES

Billecocq, J.B.L.J., ed., trans., *Voyages and Travels of an Indian Trader and Interpretor. . .* .Paris: Chez Prault l'aîné, 1794.

Forster, Goerg, ed., trans., *Voyages and Travels of an Indian Trader and Interpreter. . .* .Berlin: In der Bossischen Buchhandlung, 1791.

Pfeiffer, Johan, ed., trans., *Voyages and Travels of an Indian Trader and Interpreter. . .* .Stockholm: Tryckt i Rongl. Ordens=Buktryckeriet, 1798.

Quaife, Milo Milton, ed., *Voyages and Travels of an Indian Trader and Interpreter. . .* .The Lakeside Classics. Chicago: The Lakeside Press, R.R. Donnelly & Sons Co., 1911.

Thwaites, Reuben Gold, ed., *Voyages and Travels of an Indian Trader and Interpreter. . .* .Cleveland: Arthur H. Clark Co., 1904.

Zimmerman, E.A.W, ed., trans., *Voyages and Travels of an Indian Trader and Interpreter. . . .* Hamburg: B.G. Hoffman, 1791.

APPENDIX

1791 LONG

". . .the Mattaugwessawacks, whose country lies west-ward of Lake Superior, hold the persons of officers sacred; and Josepsis, one of their tribe, who was taken prisoner, and sold to the Penobscot Indians, says that the Savages they were at war with have adopted the same method."(19)

The C.O. Papers 1771	*The New London Magazine* 1792
Q. Dont the Battle soon become general?	Q. Do not the battle soon become general, and all get into confusion?
A. No the Officers prevent it.	A. No; the officers prevent that.
Q. How can they prevent it?	Q. How can the officers prevent it?
A. The Persons of Officers are sacred. It is immediate Death to any one who aims an Arrow at an Officer, This is the Custom of all those Nations.	A. The persons of officers are sacred on both sides, none dares aim an arrow at an officer or attempt to kill one. This is the custom of our nation.
Q. If Officers are so secure, They needn't have a brave Man for an Officer?	Q. If officers are so secure, what need is there of their being brave men?
A. If he isn't brave he cannot be an Officer.	A. They must be brave, or they cannot be officers.

Q. How then is he appointed?
A. By the People.

Q. How is their appointment?
A. They are chosen by the people. They meet to choose officers, and when one is named, if they like him, they give a great shout.

1791 Long

"The *Mattaugwessawauks*, it is said, do not worship a Supreme Being, and that when success attends them in war, they attribute the merit of the victory to their own valour and skill. But notwithstanding their disbelief of a Master of Life, in some respects, they are not less superstitious than other Savages, for they think that certain places are haunted by evil spirits, whose power they dread, and impressed with these ideas cautiously avoid them. Another proof of their superstition is, if one of their people is killed by accident they preserve a hand or a foot, which they salt, and dry, and keep as a charm to avert calamities; by which it appears, that although they do not acknowledge a dependance on a good spirit, they entertain fears and apprehensions of a bad one; which induces one to hope that such a deviation from the common belief of mankind may never be confirmed, as it would stamp human nature with an odium too horrid to think of." (139-40)

The C.O. Papers 1771

Q. When you return from a great Victory do you giveth to God as the Author of your Sucess?
A. No. We take all the glory of it to ourselves, The People of my Country have no knowledge of God not the least Idea of such a being.

The New London Magazine 1792

Q. When you return from victory, have you any religious ceremony?
A. I do not understand you.
Q. Do you thank God for your victory?
A. No: we take all the honour to ourselves. The people of my country have no knowledge of God. They have not any idea of such a being. When we return from fighting we chew a root that exhilirates the spirits, and we sing and dance.
Q. I have observed that you cross yourself, and use some other signs of worship. What does that mean?
A. I now worship God as this tribe does; (*that is, as the Penobscot Indians do.*) I have been baptised, I am now a christian.

*Remark.*The Penobscot Indians, and the tribes near them profess to be Roman-Catholicks, but they mingle with that religion many of their antient pagan rites, and are full of superstition. When they bury a man of any note they put into his grave with him his bow and arrows, fire arms, and some provisions.—If he was killed by an accident, they preserve his hand or his foot, and first salt it, and then dry it, and make use of it as a charm upon many occasions. It is not at all unusual among the Penobscot Indians, for one to start up and call himself a Santo or sacred person, and pretend that he has a divine mission, which I have thought was encouraged by the French priests. There are certain places which they think are haunted by evil spirits, and always shun those places; nor is the most enlightened Indian I ever met with, free from this superstition.

Q. Dont you Worship the Sun Moon or Stars some animal or something or other?

A. No, We worship nothing, I never heard of Worshiping any thing, till long after I came from my own Country. When we return from Victory we Chew a Root which exhilirates the spirits & makes us sing and dance.

Q. I wish to know whether the Mattaugwessauwack do not worship the sun,moon, or stars; some animal, cows, goats, or something or other?

A. No; we worship nothing. I never heard of worshipping any thing as a God, till long after I came from my own country. It is our fashion to worship our officers.

The HBC's Arctic Expedition 1836-1839: Dease's Field Notes as Compared to Simpson's Narrative[1]

I. S. MacLaren

Seldom in the annals of the literature of exploration does it fall to the second in command to publish the chief narrative account of an expedition, but the Hudson's Bay Company's only nineteenth-century arctic expedition primarily mounted to help discover the Northwest Passage was as uncommon in respect to leadership and to publication as it was in respect to standard company activities. It featured a twenty-eight-year-old who was formally educated at an advanced level, and who was impetuous, gifted, ambitious, vain, physically durable (mentally less so), and ill-fated. This was Thomas Simpson (1808-1840) who as older cousin Governor George Simpson had the acuity to see, needed a bridle, a mentor, a cautionary influence, and a steady hand. These came from Peter Warren Dease (1788-1863), whom the governor made the nominal head of the three seasons' explorations to complete the map of North America's northern coastline.

Dease was a veteran of arctic travel and life; Simpson had never seen the higher latitudes of North America. Together, the two comprised perhaps the consummate arctic explorer. "[N]o expedition fitted out in England, whatever the talents of the officers heading it might be," wrote Sir John Richardson in 1838 to the secretary of the Royal Geographical Society, "could promise greater results than the one now on foot." Richardson found it particularly gratifying "that Mr Dease, (associated with us on Sir John Franklin's [second overland] expedition [1825-1827], and to whose friendly attentions we owed so much,) should be one of the persons to anticipate the attempt of any foreign power to wrest from England the honour of the complete discovery of the arctic coast of America."[2] One of Dease's great supporters, Richardson did, however, infer as well that Simpson, whom he did not know, must have been "eminently gifted with the hardy spirit of enterprise and promptness necessary to form a successful traveller in a country, where the transitory nature of the fine season renders delay for deliberation or the slightest dilatorising destructive to the enterprise." Together, then, the leaders—pretty well co-leaders as the expedition evolved and despite Dease's nominal command—excelled. Thirty years older than the young Scot, Dease managed the expedition consummately, while Simpson champed at the bit to make the discoveries;[3] it is a strong measure of the man's uncommon worth that Dease was able to strike such an uncommon balance for the sake of the expedition's success.

However, the key to success, that fine balance, was not allowed to and does not survive in the published record of the expedition, which takes the forms only of Thomas Simpson's *Narrative of the Discoveries on the North Coast of America* (figure 1), published posthumously in London by Richard Bentley in 1843, and of brother Alexander Simpson's fulsome and indiscreet *Life and Travels of Thomas Simpson, THE Arctic Discoverer* (emphasis added/noted), which Bentley issued two years later, in 1845. It is as if Simpson's failure to recognize that balance was the key (and he the beneficiary of it) influenced even the publication stage of the expedition. Despite the fact that he did not himself live to see this stage realized, his expectations (no, they are grosser: his urges) are clear in his correspondence and draft manuscript: only the exclusive honour of the expedition's new chartings would satisfy him. "Fame I will have but it must be *alone*," he wrote to the governor at the conclusion of the highly successful third season.[4] "My useless senior . . . a perfect supernumerary," he hissed when he would "unbosom [him]self," as he frequently did, "to [his] dear, [his] only brother," and even on occasion to his, he felt, ungenerous older cousin, George himself.[5] The baring of that bosom was not a pretty sight. How such a dither of condemnation must have wounded Dease, retired and fifty-seven years of age in 1845, when the dear brother Alexander published some of Simpson's correspondence. Unable because of financial losses and constraints to enjoy a well-deserved retirement, Dease merited a better fate on several counts. It is the aim of this paper to restore the balance that two publications upset, and to accord Dease the credit he deserves for his intimate involvement in a three-year expedition that is not better known only because it met with nothing but success—no tragedy and no regrettable accidents.[6]

Righting the imbalance involves two things. One is the necessity to assume that Thomas Simpson was indeed the author of the *Narrative of the Discoveries on the North Coast of America*,[7] so that a straightforward comparison may be made between his words and those of Peter Warren Dease, recently found in three notebooks. The other is the acceptance and emphasis of certain previous interpretations. William R. Sampson's entry on him in the *Dictionary of Canadian Biography* exemplifies the support that Dease has occasionally attracted in the historical record.[8] However, that modest support requires substantiation by an examination of new evidence, including Dease's own notebooks (figure 2), which are a fair copy of his incomplete field notes of the expedition. These surfaced about the time of the fifth fur trade conference, and are now being prepared for publication.[9]

First, those field notes clarify right away that Dease was not guilty of the illiteracy with which Simpson rashly and foolishly charged him, and which his brother Alexander effectively brought to public attention in his publication of Thomas' correspondence.[10] Indeed, the notes exhibit a fine writing style, one which several letters from the period, written in less haste and greater ease, also demonstrate. Surely, though, this accomplishment can come as no surprise in a

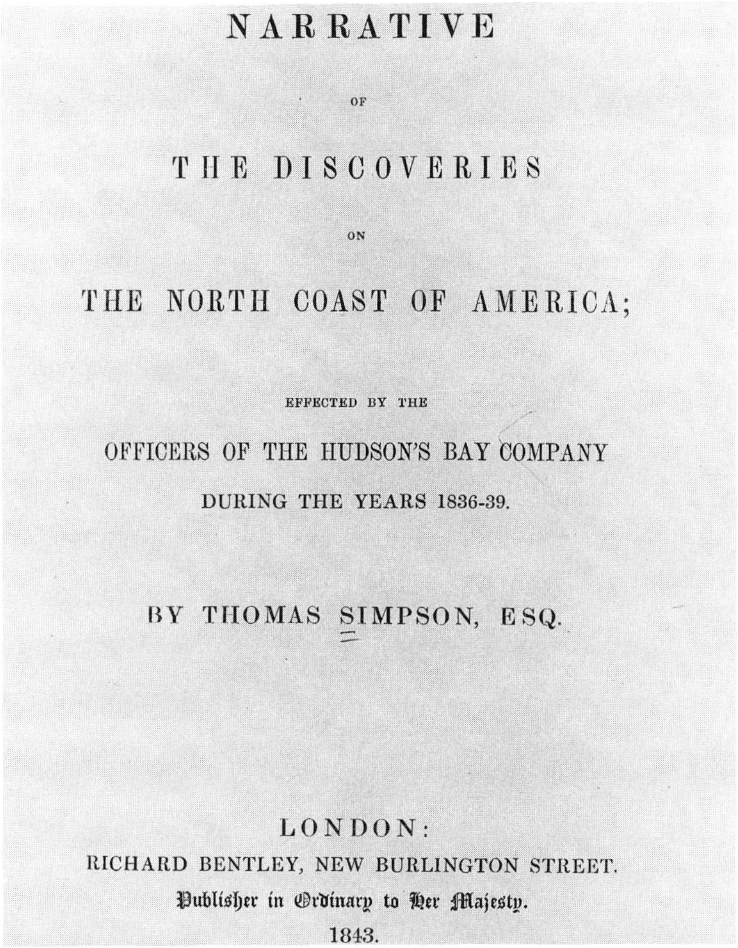

NARRATIVE

OF

THE DISCOVERIES

ON

THE NORTH COAST OF AMERICA;

EFFECTED BY THE

OFFICERS OF THE HUDSON'S BAY COMPANY

DURING THE YEARS 1836-39.

BY THOMAS SIMPSON, ESQ.

LONDON:

RICHARD BENTLEY, NEW BURLINGTON STREET.

Publisher in Ordinary to Her Majesty.

1843.

Figure 1. Title page of the First Edition of Thomas Simpson's posthumously-published *Narrative of the Discoveries on the North Coast of America* (1843). Courtesy Bruce Peel Special Collections Library, University of Alberta, Edmonton.

man who rose to Chief Trader with the Hudson's Bay Company in 1821, to Chief Factor in 1828, and who was the fourth son of a highly educated Irish-born Loyalist, Dr. John Dease (1745-1801), whose five years of study in the field of surgery at the Sorbonne immediately preceded his emigration to the colony of New York in 1771. Deputy Superintendent General of the Western Indians, John Dease moved to Fort Mackinac in 1786, and his wife, Jane French, "possibly a Roman Catholic Caughnawaga Mohawk,"[11] bore their fourth son there in 1788, naming him after the Vice-Admiral and great uncle who took Louisbourg from the French in 1745.

Figure 2. Peter Warren Dease's Field Notes (Fair Copy); these three leather-bound notebooks in a moose-hide pouch were acquired at Lachine, Québec in 1986. Courtesy Mr. Warren Baker.

Peter Warren Dease spent the first eight years of his life on Mackinac Island, benefitting not only from a systematic education given him by a conscientious father, but also from his father's understanding relations with Indians; these manifested themselves most prominently in his successful arrangement among warring nations of the Peace of Michilimackinac in 1787, a success which has earned him the unfortunate sobriquet of "The Paleface Hiawatha."[12] Subsequently, the Dease children's literacy, their education, and their good manners were completed in Montreal, where his father retired in 1796 when Mackinac became an American fort. Soon after, Peter Warren Dease found employ with the North West Company, joining on at the age of thirteen in 1801, the year of his father's death. Having worked in the Athabasca District after the merger in 1821 of the North West and Hudson's Bay companies, he was seconded in 1825 to the second of John Franklin's overland expeditions to the arctic coast and, in his father's footsteps, arranged a peace between the "Red Knives" (Yellowknife, or Copper) and "Slave" (Slavey), which proved vital to the successful supply to Franklin's expedition of local Hare hunters on the western side of Great Bear Lake.[13] Governor Simpson had recommended him to Franklin thus:

> . . . This Gentleman is one of our best voyageurs, of a strong robust habit of body, possessing much firmness of mind joined to a great suavity of manners, and who from his experience in the country, and being inured to the hardships and privations incident thereto, would be a most valuable acquisition to the party in the event of its being unfortunately placed in trying or distressing circumstances; his presence would moreover, give a confidence to the people which that of strangers to the country cannot inspire . . . .[14]

Without all Thomas Simpson's accredited learning, Dease nevertheless blended an extensive knowledge of the North, where the former had never been, with a human decency and breeding, which the Master of Arts from the University of Aberdeen had never learned. No more alike than chalk and cheese, they exhibit their differences most widely in their private correspondences. Enough of the young Scot's has already been quoted above. For his part, Dease wrote modestly about the expedition's achievements, which occurred at the cost of "utmost toil," as he put it so plainly to John Stuart, another old Nor'Wester, who had joined on two years before Dease, who had shot and climbed the Fraser River with Simon Fraser in 1808, and who knew what "utmost toil" meant. When it came to revelling in the applause with which the report of the expedition's first season (1837) was greeted in England, Dease wrote to Stuart as candidly as Simpson wrote to his brother, but Dease's candour differs markedly in tone from Simpson's: "the merit [was] due to Mr T.S. not me, as you know Scientific pursuits are out of my reach therefore do not aspire to undeserved distinction."[15]

Whether officially in a report or confidentially in a letter to an old friend, Dease's references to Simpson are always business-like and proper; nor did he purposely neglect to mention him. For example, Simpson left Dease at Boat Extreme (figure 3), a base camp, on 1 August 1837 in order to reach Point Barrow by foot without the encumbrance of the expedition's boats, which could make their way no farther west through the ocean ice. Dease's field note makes clear not any disappointment over deletion from the party that would complete the charting of the continental coastline west of the Mackenzie Delta but, rather, the simple facts of and need for the decision to send a smaller group forward: "Seeing little prospect along these shores of the Ice clearing to afford us a free passage, we came to the determination to Endeavour to Explore the remainder of the Coast on foot, Consequently 5 men were appointed to accompany Mr T Simpson."[16] But Simpson's *Narrative of the Discoveries* would have you know that *he* imparted to Dease his "desire" to finish the job, and that, after Dease "handsomely consented to remain with the boats," Simpson "selected five" men from among all who "unanimously volunteered to accompany me."[17] Evidently, the opportunity was not lost to introduce into the published account all the tropes

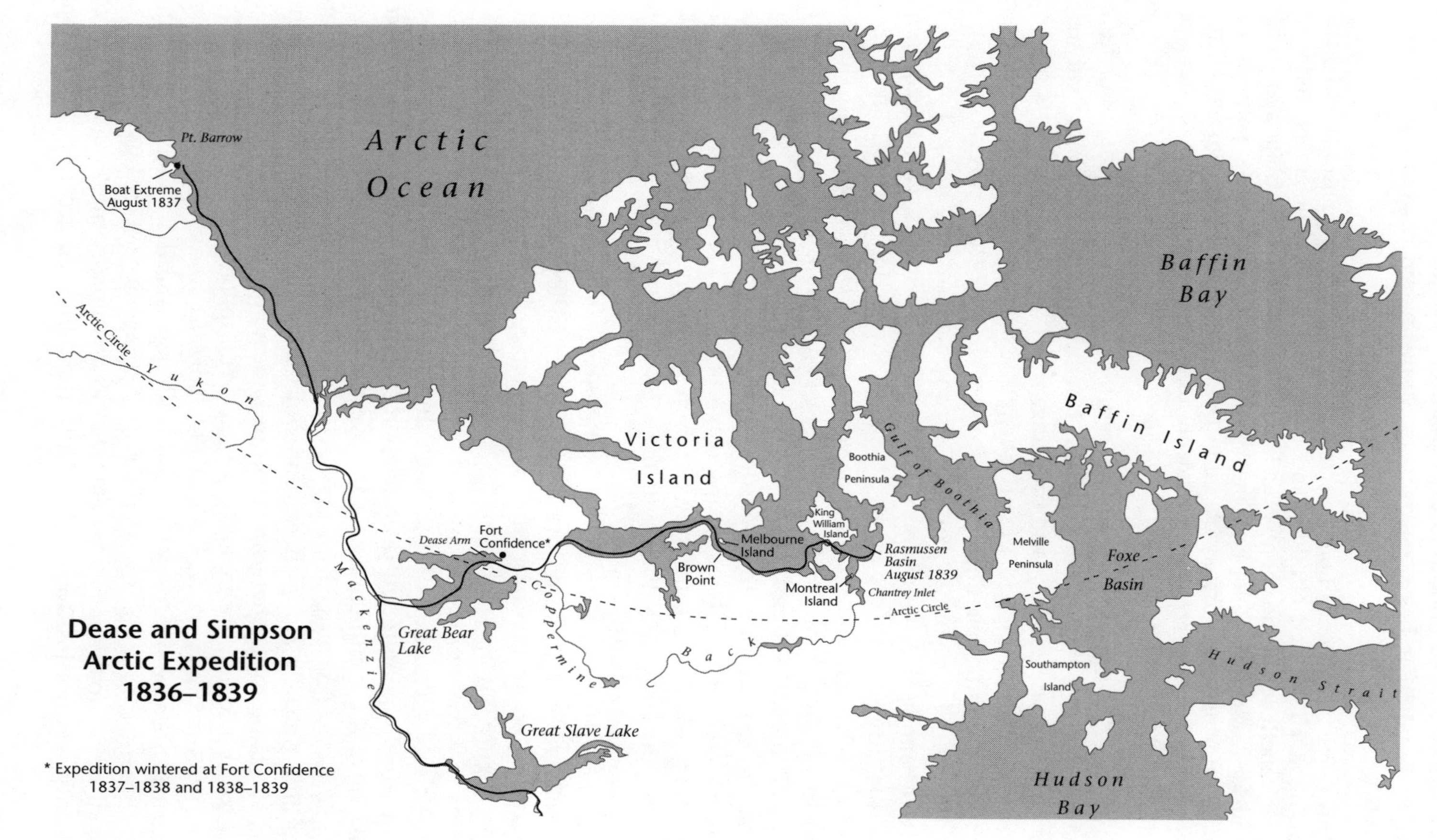
Arctic Ocean
Pt. Barrow
Boat Extreme August 1837
Arctic Circle
Yukon
Baffin Bay
Baffin Island
Victoria Island
Boothia Peninsula
Gulf of Boothia
King William Island
Melbourne Island
Brown Point
Rasmussen Basin August 1839
Montreal Island
Chantrey Inlet
Arctic Circle
Melville Peninsula
Foxe Basin
Southampton Island
Hudson Strait
Hudson Bay
Dease Arm
Fort Confidence*
Mackenzie
Coppermine
Back
Great Bear Lake
Great Slave Lake
Dease and Simpson Arctic Expedition 1836–1839
* Expedition wintered at Fort Confidence 1837–1838 and 1838–1839

Figure 3. Dease and Simpson Arctic Expedition, 1836-1839.

of the intrepid adventurer: the desire; the imagination to settle by oneself on a course of action, then to persuade others of it; the musketeer-like devotion of *all* the men; and the handsome consent of the perfect supernumerary. Meanwhile, Dease's note simply and sincerely bids the advance party farewell on 1 August: "the party are followed by the Good wishes of their remaining friends who are all equally anxious to partake of the labour + toil of their comrades + the satisfaction of completing the Object of the voyage."[18] Whatever disappointment Dease himself might quite naturally have felt cannot be read in these lines, but must be read between them; meanwhile, given that he stays put, it is one thing for him to attest to the unanimity of the men's views, quite another for Simpson to claim such support. Moreover, Dease generously greets with alacrity their return after a successful five-day sojourn; Simpson implies that the men left back at Boat Extreme were "slumbering" throughout his valiant charting. His account bloats into a twenty-three-page rodomontade, in which the extremity of the geographical attainment is mirrored, now that he is on his own, in the encountering of more, and more frequent, extreme conditions: "The day was dark and dismal in the extreme"; "Our route was tortuous in the extreme"; "Here then we encamped, half-congealed by the cold wet fog and wind."[19]

The young fur trader seconded to a survey expedition thus transforms himself into an Odysseus, proceeding undaunted to the ends of the known earth while Penelope slumbers back at the base camp. But there is a wider discrepancy yet: just barely does Simpson manage to allow that the providential appearance of Inuit, complete with a handy borrow-an-oomiak service, renders his chartings quite simple, anything but "tortuous." In his field notes, however, Dease trenchantly registers events as the returning men conveyed them at the time:

> I was rejoiced in hearing that the Object of our voyage had been successfully accomplished by their reaching Point Barrow on the 3rd with the Assistance of an Oomiak procured from a Party of Esqx on the 2nd without which a very deep bay would have caused them great labour if not rendered their departure fruitless.[20]

Why did Simpson suppress such an admission? It may be that he was only vainglorious, and needed the narrative account to retain the image of his having achieved the charting unaided. Alternatively, it may be that, not of mixed blood himself as Dease was, he thought little of the omission because he thought little of the 'savages,' who, the reasoning follows, amount only to agents divinely placed by Providence and, therefore, to be gratefully acknowledged in one's prayers, not in one's book. Were this the case, he would not have been the first explorer to adopt the perspective; a similarly ambitious George Back had done as much in claiming that he alone, not his fellow men and not the Yellowknife Indians, had saved some of the members of the first Franklin expedition from death by starvation.[21]

Certainly, if no more than conventionally, Simpson tends to undervalue or to ignore the role played in his success by Natives. Together with his well-known self-righteous and surely censorious remark to his cousin George—"to the extravagant and profligate habits of half-breed families I have an insuperable aversion"[22]—this tendency may be seen to amount to a prejudice, one which he held against Dease and most of the men with whom he was exploring. But that it arises out of his own confused sense of guilt at having fathered children out of wedlock and quite likely of mixed blood, is another consideration that must also be brought to bear on any consideration of his narrative oversight where Natives are concerned.[23]

That Simpson undervalues and often ignores both observations made by Dease in his field notes and Dease's contributions to the success of the explorations also suggests more than a literary convention at work in his *Narrative*. This last area of inquiry calls for a discussion of the record of the later discoveries made by the expedition in the boats *Castor* and *Pollux* during the summer of 1839. The previous summer's efforts to travel along the coast eastward from the mouth of the Coppermine River had met with little success, and after a second restless winter spent at Fort Confidence (figure 3), on the Dease Arm of Great Bear Lake, the men set out in June 1839 for a final struggle with the unpredictable shoreline ice of the coast.

The pattern of undervaluing and ignoring Dease was detected in Simpson's narrative even before it became a book. In February 1843, Sir Edward Sabine[24] wrote to Sir John Richardson after reading the narrative at the request of Sir John Henry Pelly, London governor of the Hudson's Bay Company, whose baronetcy was conferred in 1840 as a direct result of Dease and Simpson's discoveries.[25] Sabine asked Richardson to "read the proof: it is about 250 pages Ms" (whether Richardson did or not is unknown). He did so because, although he "found it indeed requiring very little alteration;—unusually little," he was disturbed by the fact that Simpson

> by no means puts his companion prominent: indeed he speaks of himself at all times so manifestly as the director of all proceedings, as to have struck me, tho' wholly unacquainted with the matter previously, as somewhat objectionable. Of this, you can form a better judgment than I can, as the two individuals are quite unknown to me, even by character. I see no reason why occasional passages from Mr. Deases [sic] journal may not be introduced in notes, adding to the store of information, and doing justice to all parties, but I should prefer to be guided by your opinion in this respect.[26]

It is possible that the retiring Dease preferred no further exposure than the book gave him, but Sabine was correct to surmise that incorporating portions of Dease's field notes would have added to the store of information provided by Simpson. Moreover, there were precedents, in both of Franklin's narratives, among others, for recording the events occurring on simultaneous detachments of the same expedition.[27] To revert momentarily to the westward chartings of the first summer (1837), Dease's field notes would have added information to the book's account of the separation on 1 August at Boat Extreme, when Simpson continued with five men to Point Barrow. During his five days of what

Figure 4. Ooligbuck (Hullibuck). George Back c. 1826. Ink over graphite on paper, 14.7 x 24.0 cm. National Archives of Canada, C-093039.

Simpson's book had dismissed as "slumbering," Dease's first extended contact with Inuit, on 5 August, permitted him to begin his Inuktitut vocabulary, which occupies more than thirty pages of his first notebook.[28] The world would have benefitted from having it, but Simpson, who nowhere mentions asking to consult Dease's field notes—why would he, if he thought him illiterate?—had nothing other to write than that "our savage companions," whom he encountered on his detachment and who provided the oomiak, "repeated to me a number of their words, most of which correspond with those given in the journal of Sir Edward Parry's second voyage, or vary only in the termination; but a few are entirely different."[29] Here, indeed, Simpson's dismissal of Dease's information exceeds personal considerations, preventing as it does the communication of knowledge which, after all, marked the chief purpose of the expedition in the minds of the English public.[30]

The case is similar for the explorations during the third season (1839), when the men travelled eastward as far as Chantrey Inlet (figure 3), which George Back, coming down what today is the Back River, named in 1834, and what today is known as Rasmussen Basin. Simpson's published narrative is seasoned with observations of Inuit camps, but only Dease pinpoints them and regularly states whether or not they bore signs of recent use. Apparently only a tangential and, despite the oomiak's providential appearance in 1837, extraneous curiosity, the Inuit receive little of Simpson's narrative attention. Moreover, he totalises his observations, leaping from the specific to the general. For example, in reporting two men's encounter of sixteen tents of Inuit near the mouth of the Coppermine

River in June 1839 the Scot, who was not present, only complains that "our dull interpreter," Ooligbuck, (figure 4), who had been in the region with Richardson's detachment of Franklin's second expedition in 1826," could add nothing to our own surmises regarding their mode of life, and the extent of their peregrinations." Certainly, an entirely different response to his abilities as a hunter and a diplomat were offered by Franklin and Richardson, who found him valuable and, occasionally, indispensable;[31] Dease's field notes portray him with similar respect. Simpson, however, concludes obnoxiously and without warrant, "[w]e had, in fact, accurately guessed the whole circle of their little lives."[32] Neither patronizing nor hastily conclusive, Dease keeps his counsel in his field notes, reporting only what the hunters had seen.

Both men were bound to write the Hudson's Bay Company's committee a detailed report of their discoveries, but while Dease evidently did not consider the possibility of a public audience for his field notes, it appears that Simpson could not imagine *not* having one for his journal. There was all the more reason, then, for Simpson, if only out of a sense of responsibility to the public, to incorporate information from Dease's notes. Apparently, however, like the fame he craved, his book would be his alone. But other information that he might have incorporated includes a regular daily record of which men hunted what animals successfully, both on the outward and on the return leg of the voyages. Dease's reader thereby gains a cumulative index of when in the season animals were seen, and when the men had food to eat. As well, one gains a healthy respect for the "utmost toil" being exacted from the men—all of which, by being ignored, is implicitly discounted by the Master of Arts from the University of Aberdeen: "As for our deer and seal hunts, and other exploits of 'venerie,' I shall pass them over entirely, as they were now become mere matters of course, while our whole thoughts were bent upon subjects of far higher interest."[33]

One wonders, however, how much differently the historical record might read had Dease's field notes been incorporated into the expedition's published account; for, less than two years after the book's appearance, Franklin's last and fatal voyage set out for the Arctic. Surely Simpson's *Narrative* was taken along, and surely any detailed accounts of "exploits of 'venerie'" would have leant a providential assistance to the sailors who shaped their desperate course to the mainland, across Simpson Strait, after abandoning their ships *Erebus* and *Terror* in the spring of 1848.[34] Detailed sightings of Inuit camps might also have both inspired the men to abandon ship sooner and helped them to some rescue, they whose whole thoughts were then bent upon subjects of far higher interest than new chartings.

There is the possibility, however, that such details, even had they been incorporated into Simpson's *Narrative*, would not have been unquestioningly credited by practical readers. The reason is Simpson's habit of exaggeration, in contrast to which Dease's modesty, however less literary, shines steadfastly. One example from many may suffice for the present. On 11 August 1839, near Brown Point, on the mainland opposite Melbourne Island (figure 3), Simpson's book states that the expedition had finally reached an

> outlet only three miles wide, to the much desired eastern sea. That glorious sight was first beheld by myself from the top of one of the high limestone islands, and I had the satisfaction of announcing it to some of the men, who, incited by curiosity, followed me thither. The joyful news was soon conveyed to Mr. Dease, who was with the boats at the end of the island, about half a mile off; . . .[35]

This marks a hasty ejaculation of jubilation, typical of Simpson. One must revert to Dease's field notes to gain a measured observation which, in fact, although it was written before the explorations proved as much, is accurate as to the gradual, not any sudden, opening of a route to Chantrey Inlet: "many channels are seen from the summit of the Hill running Eastward, and open sea beyond which leads us to think that a Strait is leading direct to Fish River of C[aptain] Back."[36] Simpson is in fact wrong, or, put another way, he is several degrees of longitude premature of being right. The older leader knows better than to grow excited; events proved that a great deal—"the utmost"—toil yet lay between the party's position on 11 August and its arrival on 16 August at Montreal Island (figure 3), named by Back as his farthest northwest in 1834.

George Sinclair, who had voyaged with Back in 1833-1835, had been at the old encampment on Montreal Island while hunting on 15 August, but only Dease credits him with the rediscovery;[37] meanwhile, in the book's account of the next day's events, Simpson's use of the passive voice avoids the attribution of any credit: "The weather becoming moderate on the 16th, we directed our course, with flags flying, to the Montreal Island, which had been distinguished from the main shore."[38] Distinguished by whom? Simpson does not say. Finding the old encampment there, Sinclair and James McKay, another veteran of the Back River expedition, open an old cache of food, by then rotten. It is a momentous point of connection in the history of arctic exploration. Dease celebrates it narratively by remembering that "we had good reason to offer up our prayers and Thanksgivings to the Almighty Disposer of all Events for his merciful protection of + granting us all life health + Spirits to endeavour as far as our power to meet the views of our Honorable patrons to this Exp[editio]n."[39] For his part, Simpson writes that they took possession of a few "minor articles" from the cache "as memorials of our having breakfasted on the identical spot where the tent of our gallant, though less successful, precursor stood that very day five years before."[40] His blinding ambition permits him to establish the chronological link and coincidence only for the purpose of the advantage over Back that he claims by it, an advantage that is claimed not altogether accurately.

In its attempt to restore the balance between two successful but temperamentally very different explorers, this comparison of one man's published and another man's unpublished narratives has only touched on the many differences and contrasts to be found between the two chief accounts of the Hudson's Bay Company's principal effort to discover the Northwest Passage in the nineteenth century. Meanwhile, it is hoped that the need has been established for an edition of the field notes of Peter Warren Dease, a distinguished, Mackinac-born, arctic explorer.

Notes

1. I wish to acknowledge with gratitude the generous contributions to this research that have been made by Warren Baker, Harry Duckworth, and R. Robert Mutrie.
2. Sir John Richardson to Captain John Washington, R.N., 21 April 1838, Correspondence Files, Royal Geographical Society, London; qtd. by kind permission of the archivist.
3. This view is essentially the one offered by John Gellner in his "Introduction" to the modern edition of Alexander Simpson, *The Life and Travels of Thomas Simpson the Arctic Discoverer* (London: Richard Bentley, 1845; Toronto: Baxter, 1963), vii. All references to this title will depend on the different pagination of the modern edition.
4. Thomas Simpson to George Simpson, 25 October 1839, *The Life and Travels of Thomas Simpson*, 180.
5. Thomas Simpson to Alexander Simpson, 18 September 1838, Thomas Simpson to George Simpson, 25 October 1839, and Thomas Simpson to Alexander Simpson, n.d., *The Life and Travels of Thomas Simpson*, 159, 180, 44.
6. As to Dease's later financial troubles, see Peter Warren Dease, "Memorial and Petition to the Governor, Deputy Governor and Committee of the Honorable the Hudson's Bay Company," 12 January 1861, HBCA A.10/49, with typed copy in Dease Search File; qtd. by kind permission of the archivist.
7. Because other published narratives of exploration and travel are being found to evince much revision by ghost writers and editors, both of style and of attitude on the part of the persona towards Native peoples (see MacLaren, "'I came to rite thare portraits': Paul Kane's Journal of his Western Travels, 1846-1848," *The American Art Journal* 21, no. 2 [Spring 1989]: 6-88; "Samuel Hearne's Accounts of the Massacre at Bloody Fall, 17 July 1771," *Ariel: A Review of International English Literature* 22, no. 1 [Jan. 1991]: 25-51; and "Exploration/Travel Literature and the Evolution of the Author," *International Journal of Canadian Studies/Revue internationale d'études canadiennes* no. 5 [Spring/Printemps 1992]: 39-68), it is necessary to point out the high degree of probability that Simpson, despite his death within a year of the expedition's conclusion, wrote his entire narrative on his own. Several factors suggest as much. He had received a thorough formal education in the advanced Scottish system, and had won the highest prize for "literary merit" at the University of Aberdeen (*The Life and Travels of Thomas Simpson*, 11). He came to British North America to serve as secretary and amanuensis to his cousin. He confidently judged, if mean-spiritedly, the style and presentation of the very capable author George Back in the latter's *Narrative of the Arctic Land Expedition* (Thomas Simpson to George Simpson, 31 May 1837, *The Life and Travels of Thomas Simpson*, 114). It appears that during the seven weeks that he spent at Fort Simpson at the conclusion of the discoveries on the arctic coast, he completed "his Narrative of the Expedition" (*The Life and Travels of Thomas Simpson*, 175), and although a suspiciously long time elapsed before the narra-

tive's posthumous publication, no one else is mentioned in the book contract that Sir John Henry Pelly signed for the Hudson's Bay Company "on the part of the [deceased] author" with the publisher Richard Bentley ("Memorandum of Agreement, 7 June 1843," Agreement Memorandum Books, 55: 177; Richard Bentley Papers, British Library; qtd. by kind permission of the Higher Executive Officer, Department of Manuscripts, British Library). For his part, Sir Edward Sabine, who accompanied William Edward Parry to the Arctic in 1818 and 1819-1820, wrote to Sir John Richardson in 1843 to say that he had altered the journal very little: "At Sir H. Pelly's request I have undertaken to edit Mr. Simpson's narrative—it is prepared by himself, (Simpson), so as to be in his opinion quite ready for the press; and I found it indeed requiring very little alteration;—unusually little—and thus much I have done . . . It appears to me remarkably well done" (Sir Edward Sabine to Sir John Richardson, 9 February 1843, MS 1503/26/2 Richardson-Voss Collection, Scott Polar Research Institute, Cambridge; qtd. by kind permission of Anthony Voss). One cannot absolutely rule out the possibility that Sabine's reference to "Simpson" is to Alexander, the executor, and not to Thomas. Given Alexander's work on *The Life and Travels of Thomas Simpson*, he may have been unable to resist the temptation to step up the journal's characterization of his brother or to omit passages, but Thomas' superior education suggests that Alexander would have had little to offer his brother's own literary ability, much less his overweening ambition.

8. Sampson's is a model biographical sketch, well researched and written, *Dictionary of Canadian Biography*, gen. eds. George W. Brown, David M. Hayne, and Francess G. Halpenny (Toronto and Buffalo: University of Toronto Press, 1976), 9: 196-99. The *Dictionary of Canadian Biography* (hereafter *DCB*) contains no entry for Thomas Simpson, apparently because it was thought that his career was fully covered in the sketch for the *Dictionary of National Biography*, rather than because of any oversight.
9. Dease's notes, in the possession of Mr. Warren Baker of Montréal, are contained in three, leather-bound notebooks that fit into a moose-hide pouch with three ties. Notebook A commences at Norway House on 20 July 1836, and runs to Fort Chipewyan on 4 October 1836 (Simpson was not a part of this portion of the expedition's route). As well, it contains an Inuktitut vocabulary, as described below. Notebook B begins when the expedition leaves the mouth of Mackenzie River on 14 July 1837, covers the western charting of the continental coast, and continues to 9 March 1838, during the expedition's first winter at Fort Confidence. This notebook does not have writing on every page, but it is difficult to know if Dease left off writing, or if a notebook is missing. At any rate, there is a lacuna of 462 days between the last entry in Notebook B and the first in Notebook C, which extends from 15 June 1839, when the expedition set off from Fort Confidence for its third season of chartings, to 14 October 1839, when it arrived at Fort Simpson. It may be that Dease's eyesight hindered him too much to permit writing for a time; he speaks of this painless debility in his letter to John Stuart of 18 December 1838 (see note 15, below).
10. "Mr. Dease and I live together on the happiest footing; his old wife, a little grandchild, and a strapping wench, a daughter of his brother Charles, joining our mess. Dease is a worthy, indolent, illiterate soul, and moves just as I give the impulse" (Thomas Simpson to Alexander Simpson, 29 January 1838, *The Life and Travels of Thomas Simpson*, 142).

11. William R. Sampson, *DCB*, 9: 196.
12. R. Robert Mutrie, "Captain Doctor John Dease," in *Loyalist Vignettes and Sketches*, ed. Arthur Bousfield and Garry Toffoli, co-ord. R. Robert Mutrie (Toronto: Governor Simcoe Branch of the United Empire Loyalists Association, 1984), 72-73; and Clayton W. McCall, "The Peace of Michilimackinac," *Michigan History Magazine* 28, no. 3 (July/September 1944): 367-83. McCall argues for the sobriquet on page 382.
13. Peter Warren Dease to George Simpson, 30 March 1825, collection of Mr. Warren Baker, Montréal; qtd. by kind permission of the owner.
14. George Simpson to Capt. John Franklin, 10 July 1825, HBCA D.4/5, fo.48d, qtd. by kind permission of the archivist.
15. Peter Warren Dease to John Stuart, 18 December 1838, private collection, Toronto, qtd. by kind permission of the owner.
16. Dease, "Field Notes," Monday, 31 July 1837, Notebook B, 10.
17. Thomas Simpson, *Narrative of the Discoveries on the North Coast of America; effected by the Officers of the Hudson's Bay Company during the Years 1836-39* (London: Richard Bentley, 1843; Toronto: Canadiana House, 1970), 141-42. All subsequent references will depend on the modern edition, the pagination of which matches that of the first edition.
18. Dease, "Field Notes," Tuesday, 1 August 1837, Notebook B, 10.
19. Simpson, *Narrative of the Discoveries*, 143, 144, 145.
20. Dease, "Field Notes," Sunday, 6 August 1837, Notebook B, 13.
21. See MacLaren, "Commentary," in *Arctic Artist: The Journal and Paintings of George Back Midshipman with Franklin 1819-1822*, ed. C. Stuart Houston (Kingston & Montréal, Buffalo, London: McGill-Queen's University Press, forthcoming). Both Back's journal and his poem, "Recollections of our unfortunate Voyage," make the claim. On this matter generally, Mary Louise Pratt makes the trenchant point that Native labourers/assistants/agents make only spectral appearances in narratives of travel and exploration; they are the ghosts of such texts, in which the *disponibilité* (availability for exploitation) of their persons and their lands is simply assumed. See Mary Louise Pratt, *Imperial Eyes: Travel Writing and Transculturation* (London and New York: Routledge, 1992), 52.
22. Thomas Simpson to George Simpson, 25 October 1839, *The Life and Travels of Thomas Simpson*, 180.
23. In 1853, Henry Budd (1812-1875) became the first Native minister ordained by the Church of England. A decade earlier, on 8 June 1843, he wrote from The Pas to Donald Ross, Chief Factor at Norway House: "Inclosed with this you will find a list of Articles for the children of the late Mr Thos. Simpson which you will be pleased to send by any opportunity most convenient. I have according to the size of the two Boys calculated upon what quantity they require for each one a suit and what I know they absolutely require to make them comfortable, as well as look descent [sic]. The two Boys are getting on pretty well particularly the eldest [sic], he reads and spells most any book, and has commenced in writing on a slate[;] the youngest [sic] reads and spells in little books taken out of the Scriptures, he's quite averse to learning him, more fond of his play than his books . . ." (Charles Napier Bell Collection, MG19 A30, National Archives of Canada). It is not certain from this positive identification what the ages of the two children were in 1843; but, based on Budd's description of their learning and clothing needs, it is not out of the question to surmise that Simpson engen-

dered them before 1836 or during the Dease and Simpson explorations. Given Simpson's whereabouts during these years, it is almost certain that the boy's mother/mothers was/were not white. Of further intrigue is the certainty that the boys were both several years old when their father died on 15 June 1840, apparently over a dispute having racial overtones.

24. See note 7, above.
25. Lord John Russell to John Henry Pelly, 3 July 1840, HBCA A.13/2 fos.165-66d; John Henry Pelly to Peter Warren Dease, 5 June 1840, copy of original copy, John Henry Pelly Search File, HBCA, qtd. by kind permission of Sir John A. Pelly, Bt.
26. Sir Edward Sabine to Sir John Richardson, 9 February 1843 (see note 7, above). The absence of any notes in Simpson's book suggests that in the four months between Sabine's letter to Richardson and Pelly's signing of the book contract with Richard Bentley (note 7, above), the relative silence accorded by the manuscript to both the figure of Dease and Dease's particular interests underwent no significant alteration.
27. See Capt. John Franklin, *Narrative of a Journey to the Shores of the Polar Sea, in the Years 1819, 20, 21, and 22* (London: John Murray, 1823), 269-86, 449-61, 477-90; Capt. John Franklin, *Narrative of a Second Expedition to the Shores of the Polar Sea, in the Years 1825, 1826, and 1827 . . . Including an Account of the Progress of a Detachment to the Eastward, by John Richardson, M.D., F.R.S., F.L.S., &c. Surgeon and Naturalist to the Expedition* (London: John Murray, 1828), 187-283.
28. Dease, "Field Notes," Notebook A, 16-49.
29. Simpson, *Narrative of the Discoveries*, 165.
30. There is, for example, Sir John Richardson's remark to the secretary of the Royal Geographical Society: "The public spirit of the Hudson's Bay Company deserves the highest commendations[;] they have evinced singular judgment in taking up the business just where government had dropped it—their conduct is the more creditable as it is disinterested, the coast line yielding no furs but white fox skins which will not pay for their transport" (Sir John Richardson to Capt. John Washington, R.N., 21 April 1838, see note 2, above).
31. See, for example, Richardson's account in Franklin, *Narrative of a Second Expedition* (see note 27, above), 224-25.
32. Simpson, *Narrative of the Discoveries*, 353.
33. Ibid., 358.
34. David C. Woodman, *Unravelling the Franklin Mystery: Inuit Testimony* (Montréal & Kingston, Buffalo, London: McGill-Queen's University Press, 1991), provides a new interpretation of the routes followed by Franklin's men before and after the abandonment of the ships.
35. Simpson, *Narrative of the Discoveries*, 366.
36. Dease, "Field Notes," Saturday, 9 August 1839, Notebook C, 26.
37. Dease, "Field Notes," Thursday, 15 August 1839, Notebook C, 29.
38. Simpson, *Narrative of the Discoveries*, 370.
39. Dease, "Field Notes," Friday, 16 August 1839, Notebook C, 30-31.
40. Simpson, *Narrative of the Discoveries*, 371.

Fur Trade Social History and the Public Historian: Some Other Recent Trends

Michael Payne

It is now over fifteen years since the Third North American Fur Trade Conference was held in Winnipeg. The papers presented at that conference had a profound impact on fur trade historiography in their own right, but they also reflected equally significant changes in scholarly research on fur trade subjects which had been taking form over the previous decade. One paper in particular, Sylvia Van Kirk's "Fur Trade Social History: Some Recent Trends," specifically set out to review four relatively recent and very influential doctoral dissertations which together promised to establish what was essentially a new field of fur trade studies: fur trade social history.[1]

Sylvia Van Kirk's paper, however, did more than simply posit the existence of a new school of fur trade studies. In addition to summarizing the main "findings arising from these new works," she went on to suggest a series of topics and questions which these dissertations seemed to suggest would warrant further investigation.[2] The purpose of this paper is not to offer a tedious and second hand précis of the doctoral dissertations of John Foster, Frits Pannekoek, Jennifer Brown, and Sylvia Van Kirk. All are well-known to anyone working in fur trade research, and in varying degrees each has become more or less canonical. Certainly few scholars would have the temerity to ignore completely women or Native groups any more, and the belief that the fur trade needs to be understood as a social as well as a commercial system is now axiomatic. What is less clear, however, is how prophetic Sylvia Van Kirk's article was when it came to outlining where fur trade social history might go over the next decade based upon the issues raised in these dissertations.

In academic circles in Canada, the cynical response might be that fur trade social history has never really gone anywhere, despite the high hopes raised in Winnipeg. Although by no means a perfect reflection of academic interest or activity, a survey of the *Canadian Historical Review's* regular bibliography of "Recent Publications Relating to Canada" makes it clear that the overwhelming majority of these publications concern post-Confederation topics, and very few address the fur trade in any period. Similarly, the Canadian Historical Association's *Register of Dissertations* between 1980 and 1990 contains no more than a handful of doctoral or master's level theses either completed or in progress—let alone abandoned—in the area of fur trade studies.[3] Instead most ongoing scholarly interest in the fur trade has concentrated on relations between Aboriginal peoples and Euro-Canadians as well as on the fur trade as a factor in cultural change and adaptation among native groups. While fur trade social history shares an interest in these matters, they are not its primary focus. According to Van Kirk's analysis—given that the fur trade was a "socio-cultural complex" of some sort—fur trade social history would elaborate the norms and values of that society along with "the differing organizational and personnel structures [of fur trade companies]; the nature of Hudson's Bay and North West Company interaction with the Indians, particularly intermarriage between traders and Indian women; and the different experience of the mixed-blood children of the Hudson's Bay Company tradition and those of the North-West Company tradition."[4]

Thus, although the main protagonists in the definition of fur trade social history have remained active and productive, very few new voices have been raised within the university community.[5] It is perhaps for this reason that at a recent symposium on the future direction of research in fur trade and Native history Arthur Ray commented that, while the writing of the social history of the fur trade is still much discussed, it is less frequently attempted.[6]

Unlike the university community, however, federal and provincial heritage agencies in Canada have taken to fur trade social history like the proverbial ducks to water. For a variety of reasons social history meshed neatly with perceived site development and interpretation needs at fur trade historic sites. As a result, the bulk of new research on fur trade history, and especially fur trade social history, being done in Canada is the product of historians working either directly or on contract for organizations like the Canadian Parks Service or its provincial counterparts.[7]

As C.J. Taylor has noted, many of Canada's historic sites were actually identified prior to 1950, but very few sites were graced with more than a commemorative plaque.[8] In most cases if buildings, or better yet ruins, remained on these sites, some minimal effort was made to prevent further deterioration, but only because such extant remains were seen as adding to the picturesque quality of the site and thus to its historical interest. It was not until the 1960s that the "era of the big project" dawned, and first the Canadian Parks Service and then some provincial and municipal bodies began to get into the full-scale restoration and reconstruction of historic sites.[9]

So long as these agencies primarily concerned themselves with commemoration programs there was no particular need for a research bias in favor of social history. Indeed plaques, cairns, and monuments lent themselves more to biographies of politicians and captains of industry or accounts of battles or marking the locations of significant public buildings than to discussions of changes in social relations or demography. However, as heritage agencies became more and more involved in the preservation of historic buildings and sites and in their

Figure 1. At Dunvegan in Northern Alberta an effort has been made to ensure that research and interpretation recognize the role of Aboriginal peoples in the fur trade. Courtesy of Historic Sites and Archives, Alberta Community Development.

restoration and reconstruction, straightforward textual interpretation of their historical significance seemed increasingly inadequate.

It is conceivable that one might stop and read a roadside sign with 150 words of text commemorating a notable portage or the life and times of an explorer, but a fully restored or reconstructed fur trade post demands something more elaborate in terms of interpretative programming. As a result, the use of docents or either uniformed or costumed guides spread rapidly, and it was then just a short step to the development of first-person animation or "living history" programs in which guides pretended to be actual historical personages associated with the site.[10] Placed on location, if you will, surrounded by period furnishings, and often dressed in period costume, animators and guides inevitably talk about the building they work in, the tools and techniques they use, and why they are dressed in buckskin. As Jay Anderson has commented, the message of these sites is as much a sense of "the *texture* of life in the past" or what "it actually *felt* like to live" in Fort William or Plimouth, as any specific factual material.[11] And in order to achieve the sort of pervasive historical immersion site visitors require to get a sense of "the texture of life," a particular type of social history research is required.

Although site interpreters and operations staff might find this hard to credit, much—probably most—of the work done by the historians and archaeologists employed by heritage agencies is driven either directly by specific information requests from sites or indirectly by anticipated programming needs. This in turn has had some unanticipated consequences. For example, historical archaeology now exists almost exclusively within museum and historic sites services. Some archaeologists feel it has become too subservient to site development and interpretation needs, and it has been criticized as a field of scholarly endeavor for becoming too preoccupied with unearthing artifacts for display and conducting digs for no deeper purpose than to confirm the size and location of buildings.[12] Public historians have also been subjected to similar criticism in reviews of their work by academics who not infrequently muse on the idiocy of devoting public funds to studies of the table service in merchant households in seventeenth-century Louisbourg or some other such purported evidence of rampant antiquarianism. The fact remains, however, that unless sites aspire to no more than being approximately accurate with no glaring anachronisms on exhibit, table service and other such seemingly picayune details do matter and must be researched.

Unfortunately, all too often public historians researching these important details of everyday life have made getting the "facts" right their sole historiographical impulse, and this alone does not produce social history. Where social history and a kind of simple-minded reverence for authenticity part company is in the ends to which a willingness to take material culture seriously are put: as Fernand Braudel has observed, "The ways people eat, dress, or lodge [themselves], are never a matter of indifference."[13] For this reason it is worth considering the kind of work done in the name of social history for fur trade sites and its relationship in turn with broader historiographical currents within the field of social history.

Recent historical research on fur trade sites may be roughly divided into three categories of studies. The first is the kind of specific issue-oriented research which so often appalls other historians. This work is usually intended to assist restoration architects, display designers, and others who require accurate and detailed information on the type of wainscoting used in a mess hall, or the package markings on gun cases, or the number of marten pelts in a typical bale.[14] Obviously a lot of this work is remarkable only as evidence of the diligence of the researchers and their mastery of arcane information sources. While few would argue that an inventory of the suppliers of trade goods to the Hudson's Bay Company between 1820 and 1875, the goods they supplied, and their business addresses is exciting historiographically, such a study has clear practical uses and should not be dismissed too cavalierly.[15] Moreover, land-use and structural histories can do more than outline what building was built where and why mess kitchens were usually built as separate structures so long as there is a willingness to consider the broader implications of the material presented. For example, beneath the detailed narrative of when buildings were erected, repaired, and then torn down, Bruce Donaldson's land-use and structural histories of York Factory reveal a great deal about fur trade social history.

The gradual abandonment of any pretext of defense in the design and layout of post buildings speaks volumes about the changing balance of military and economic power in the fur trade—not only between fur trade companies and their trading partners but also between companies and the colonial empires for which they acted as surrogates. Similarly, changes and adaptations in construction techniques and building design speak of a slow and incremental cultural adjustment to new environmental and social conditions: quite similar, in fact, to the parallel adjustments in marriage and family patterns described by Jennifer Brown and Sylvia Van Kirk.[16]

Worthy as many of these studies are of closer consideration by readers with more than an interest in suppliers of gun flints, they do not, however, represent more than a fraction of the research done on fur trade sites with implications for social history. Most of these works fall into two additional categories of study: broad thematic or narrative studies used to place sites in a general contextual framework, and site-specific studies.[17]

Perhaps the best recent example of the former is a series of studies conducted by Philip Goldring for the Canadian Parks Service on the labor system of the Hudson's Bay Company in the nineteenth century.[18] Goldring's research project was intended to provide a background framework for the interpretation of a number of fur trade sites and was based upon a survey of Hudson's Bay Company employment records at ten-year intervals between 1830-1831 and 1880-1881. It was not, however, intended to be comprehensive. Its focus was on permanent year-round employees hired on contract to work in the Northern Department of the Hudson's Bay Company. As a result, part-time or seasonal employees, not to mention fur trappers themselves who were never considered formal employees of the company—and those who worked in other departments like the Southern and Columbia districts appeared only in passing. Its intent was both revisionist and "quasi-experimental" in that quantifiable employment records would be used to test the validity of a series of theories and conjectures that had been advanced in previous works on fur trade social and economic history.[19]

Goldring's findings were indeed both explicitly and implicitly revisionist in many cases. Among other insights his quantitative analysis of company employment practices made it clear that George Simpson's correspondence must be used very carefully as evidence of anything other than George Simpson's opinion. Certainly on personnel policy and issues, about which Simpson wrote extensively, his theory and company practice were often quite different. For example, Goldring's figures make it hard to support a case for any systematic prejudice against mixed-blood employees, despite Simpson's derogatory comments about them as a group and despite the fact that many mixed-blood employees clearly experienced prejudicial treatment in their own lives. Instead Goldring found that patronage and perhaps even ability were as important in the career prospects of mixed-blood officers as their racial background.[20] In the case of tradesmen and laborers,

Figure 2. As this photograph of Dunvegan indicates, interpretation often concentrates on the techniques or processes of work. Courtesy of Historic Sites and Archives, Alberta Community Development.

> Mixed-bloods very rarely worked for lower wages than imported whites, they achieved such privileges as shorter contracts and more frequent promotions than Scots, and as local casual labourers they earned far more, on a daily calculation, than was paid to imported workers. By the mid-1860s almost every white employee was working—or had once worked—under the supervision of a higher-ranking, better-paid "Native" of the country.[21]

Goldring was not, however, simply an apologist for the Hudson's Bay Company. He argued that the policy of "dispersed recruitment," or hiring in a variety of markets, was clearly adopted as part of a campaign to keep wages down and to limit the potential power of employee "cabals."[22] The company was also not quite the benign and paternalistic employer it claimed to be and was prepared to invoke contract provisions when they favored corporate ends and traditional moral notions of a fair day's work for a fair day's pay when these suited better.[23]

Interestingly, Carol Judd, who was associated with some of the early phases of this work, used essentially the same data to argue a quite different case. She found that over the nineteenth century, opportunities for Native employees of all types—officers and men, Métis, and Indians—declined within the Hudson's Bay Company's service.[24] In addition to reminding us that "facts" rarely speak for themselves, or at least that they rarely speak with a single voice, the debate over employment statistics raises important questions about what some have termed the "social construction of reality."[25] Goldring's work presents a pretty convincing case for the substantial "Nativization" of the fur trade in terms of personnel over the course of the nineteenth century, although this occurred at different rates and in different proportions at different posts and in different districts.[26] Nevertheless, a large number of contemporaneous observers, including many actual participants in the fur trade, detected almost exactly the opposite pattern. As Chief Factor James Sutherland put it, referring to his son's possible employment with the Hudson's Bay Company:

> I could get him in the Cos service, but half-breeds as they are called has[sic] no chance there nor are they respected whatever their abilities may be, by a parcel of upstart Scotchmen, who now hold the power and control in the concern.[27]

Statistics alone cannot resolve this apparent paradox, and given its obvious importance in any interpretation of everyday life in the fur trade, it has become a major theme in other research on fur trade historic sites.

For all of its virtues, however, as both a pioneering work in the use of quantitative methods for fur trade history[28] and as revisionist history, Goldring's study of Hudson's Bay Company recruitment patterns and employment policies has probably had less impact on actual site interpretation than it has on academic research. The reasons for this are both practical and historiographical. It is, of course, almost impossible to present the kind of content found in Philip Goldring's studies using first- or third-person animation—no one is likely to recite a table outlining the deployment of boatbuilders or carpenters in the Northern Department in 1850-1851. Such problems are not, however, completely intractable and could be surmounted were it not for the fact that the history of specific fur trade sites does not always reflect general historical trends very well. Although the Hudson's Bay Company may have set overall trade, transport, and personnel policy, the degree to which any individual post followed these patterns is problematic. Moreover, not all fur trade posts that have been developed as historic sites were either owned by the Hudson's Bay Company or operated in the nineteenth century. For this reason it is extremely difficult to justify broad thematic studies to skeptical senior managers, and in many respects Philip Goldring's work stands in splendid isolation. Certainly in the current climate of fiscal restraint, few agencies are likely to commit the financial or staff resources needed to complete other studies of equivalent complexity. Instead, both the Canadian Parks Service and provincial agencies have tended to concentrate on regional studies of the fur trade and specific post histories over the last decade.[29]

The range and profusion of these studies[30] preclude anything more than a brief discussion of some representative examples of the genre and a consideration of some of their implications for fur trade social history.

One of the peculiarities of historic sites research is that no site is likely to be selected for development because of the quality of the documentation available on it. Sometimes good archival and other primary and secondary sources exist, but there is no assurance that this will be so. The situation of the site researcher

Figure 3. As this photograph from the early 1970s indicates, interpretation programmes often depict women in stereotypical roles. More recent site histories suggest women's work was not just domestic at fur-trade posts. Courtesy of Lower Fort Garry National Historic Site.

interested in writing social history often stands in sharp contrast to that of the academic historian. The latter usually begins any proposed research project with some sort of bibliographical and archival search to see if the available documentation is sufficient to construct a case and justify continuing the study. Site historians rarely have this luxury, as anyone who has ever had to work on Lower Fort Garry knows.

Lower Fort Garry is one of the most visited "fur trade" sites in Canada: as many as 100,000 people per year.[31] It also has an elaborate first-person animation program, a variety of restored and partially reconstructed buildings, and virtually no surviving records from the 1850s, the period interpreted at the site. There are no post journals, just a handful of account books, and a somewhat larger collection of letters from post residents—which unfortunately rarely discuss post operations or events. Balancing the paucity of site-specific records is the fact that Lower Fort Garry was located in the Red River Settlement, one of the most studied and best documented communities in nineteenth century

North America. Thus, site researchers are faced with a form of poverty in the midst of plenty.

Rather sensibly, most have adopted one of two approaches. One of these, dubbed a "comparative" approach by Gregory Thomas,[32] is not really comparative so much as an attempt, *faute de mieux,* to find comparable material from other posts. Although one might argue in the near total absence of direct evidence, that the warehousemen at Lower Fort Garry were as likely to follow their own procedures as those used at York Factory, it is probably better to depict work activities which actually occurred elsewhere in the fur trade rather than simply to invent plausible-seeming ones.

Nonetheless, Thomas's work on Lower Fort Garry represents an attempt to move beyond the somewhat stultifying constraints of structural history and furnishing studies. While dutifully recording the size, shape, and apparent uses of rooms and buildings and the kinds of objects which probably were found within them, Thomas tries to give some sense of the work and, to a lesser extent, the personal lives of Lower Fort Garry's residents. Thomas's bakehouse study is a case in point. He devotes considerable space to a discussion of the baking process and the position of the men described as bakers in the Hudson's Bay Company's service.[33] Unfortunately, he stops short of the detailed consideration of the role that part-time and seasonal work for the company played in the household economies of Red River's settlers, a topic that would have placed his study in a more regional or community context.

This regional or community context represents the sub-text of much of the other work done for the Canadian Parks Service ostensibly for Lower Fort Garry and its other site in the area, the St. Andrew's Rectory. Both Carol Judd's study of Red River society and Bob Coutts's work on the settlement surrounding the rectory and the lower fort suggest a broader interpretative program that would explore Red River as more than just a fur trade center.[34] Indeed, Carol Judd has argued in another work that models of fur trade social relations based on Red River evidence have dubious value for other posts given the fact that Red River was not dominated by the fur trade or the Hudson's Bay Company in the same way as posts like Moose Factory were.[35]

The result of this work is in some respects better social history, or at least history without the obvious problems of evidence inherent in a "comparative" approach, but also brings some loss of interpretative focus on the site. The strong sense of place and time Jay Anderson identifies as the chief virtue of "living history" is dissipated at Lower Fort Garry, where interpretation is too easily driven by a desire to exploit all the possible resources of the site. The highly popular but anachronistic program at the blacksmith's shop is a case in point. Not only was no blacksmith stationed at Lower Fort Garry in the 1840s or 1850s, but most of the work depicted at the site is a kind of generic "olde tyme" smithy work. Still, the fact that a later blacksmith shop exists on the site is too tempting a resource to ignore simply in the name of authenticity. In similar fashion, should the periodic proposals to develop a historical farm at the site be acted upon, the result

Figures 4 and 5. Interpretive programmes often try to depict leisure activities as well as work, giving visitors a sense of the site as a real human community. Courtesy of Lower Fort Garry National Historic Site.

may well be a kind of pre-pioneer pioneer village, even further removed from any grounding in the actual site-specific records available for the post.[36]

The problems posed by a weak documentary base when developing any interpretation or animation program which emphasizes everyday life or the social history of the fur trade are by no means limited to Lower Fort Garry. Although some posts and some periods of the fur trade are remarkably well-documented, others are not. For example, comparatively few North West Company records survive, making research on sites like Fort William or Grand Portage much more difficult than research on Prince of Wales' Fort or York Factory. Without new grist for the analytical mill, much of the research done on such sites cannot possibly consist of anything much more ambitious than the repackaging of insights gleaned from other secondary works.[37] The example of Lower Fort Garry does, however, suggest that in an ideal world a decision to pursue first-person animation should follow a careful analysis of whether the research resources—as opposed to just the extant buildings and other physical resources—available for the site will support such an approach to interpretation.

Obviously, then, not only will programming be stronger at sites where historical documentation is more complete, so too is it easier for researchers to make a contribution to fur trade social history when working on these sites. There are a number of such sites, and the work conducted on Moose Factory by Carol Judd, on Fort Langley by Jamie Morton, and on Rocky Mountain House by David Smyth represent only a few of the better examples of these kinds of site-specific studies. Carol Judd's work on Moose Factory, which has appeared in a variety of internal government reports and several published articles or presentations to scholarly conferences, exhibits some of the potential of this genre of social history. For example, by concentrating on Moose Factory as opposed to general company records, Carol Judd has been able to trace some of the experiences of part-time and seasonal employees of the post, a vital category of employee not really covered in Philip Goldring's studies of the permanent workforce. Judd found that most of these people, who included both men and women, were either Homeguard Cree or of mixed descent and that they set down deep and lasting roots in the post community. Although she does not actually trace the genealogical evidence of family persistence in the area, she describes a traditional way of life that included occasional day or seasonal labor and the provisioning of the post along with hunting, fishing, and trapping and which may be dated back to about 1730.[38] In fact, evidence from other posts lends support to this view of post life, and suggests that the post palisades were a highly permeable boundary.[39] In addition, by focusing on a small and manageable sample of people it is possible to construct or perhaps reconstruct relatively detailed personal and family histories. The advantages of this for first-person animation and indeed for most other varieties of interpretative programming is obvious, but there are also some historiographical benefits as well. Individual biographies and family histories can give flesh and substance to the broad analytical categories used in studies like those of Philip Goldring.[40] This kind of micro rather than macro approach also enables researchers to address the apparent contradictions noted earlier between widely-held perceptions of bias in the hiring and promotion practices of the Hudson's Bay Company and what seems to be the evidence of overall employment statistics. This is, of course, just another version of the endless conundrum facing social historians of finding ways to present historical experience as "embodied in real people and in a real context."[41]

Unfortunately, although Moose Factory would be a good candidate for the kind of intensive site development and elaborate first-person animation programming pursued with mixed success at sites like Lower Fort Garry, its relatively remote location makes such a turn of events unlikely. This is even more true for York Factory, which is blessed in every respect except for location with truly remarkable potential for first-person interpretation. Very few eighteenth- or nineteenth-century communities in Canada are blessed with an equivalent density of documentation detailing everyday life. Even some of the most mundane aspects of the work routine and the personal lives of residents at York Factory are recoverable. For example, post records inform us that while ewers and basins were available in the post sale shop in 1838 for anyone interested in such refinements, most at York preferred to use buckets and pails for their ablutions, and judging by other accounts a fair number preferred to avoid such activities altogether.[42] We have reasonable assurance that the Hargraves and their friends were devotees of whist and, no less amazing, we know many of the titles of the books they and other residents read in their leisure hours.[43] We could even refurnish a residence for the Hargraves down to the color scheme of their chests of drawers and the shape of the pins that held back their curtains.[44] This wealth of evidence on life at York Factory imposes its own constraints on interpretation. It is hard to know what themes or aspects of post life should be emphasized when virtually all could be researched and described. Should interpretation concentrate on work or social relations at York, knowing that York was a rather different community from Churchill or Oxford House? Or should interpretation emphasize recreation and leisure patterns at York, given that we know so little about such matters at other posts?

The sheer volume of research sources and the fact that many of these sources have a strong material culture bias raise some interesting historiographical problems for social historians that have nothing to do with whether they are employed by heritage agencies or universities. Social history has always had practitioners who concerned themselves with what has been characterized as "manners, customs, everyday life," but this aspect of social history is viewed with some suspicion within other branches of the discipline.[45]

There seem to be two reasons for this. First, it has always been a catch-all for a lot of superficial and ill-conceived research that aspires to nothing more than producing compendia of facts.[46] Second, this branch of social history seems to be irretrievably linked to G. M. Trevelyan's supposed definition of social history as a kind of residuum: "the history of a people with the politics left out." Obviously the idea of apolitical social history is ludicrous and so, by extension, the study of "manners, customs, and everyday life" is at best trivial. Unfortunately, Trevelyan did not really suggest that social history was apolitical; instead, he actually argued for a reversal of the tradition of writing political history without reference to the social environment, proposing social history as a link between economic and political history, since economics shape social conditions and social conditions shape politics. As he put it : "Without social history, economic history is barren and political history is unintelligible."[47] This view is much closer to the goal of "total history" espoused by Ladourie and others of the *Annales* school of history than Trevelyan's critics admit. And like the *Annales* approach to social history, the study of "manners, customs and everyday life" does not need to concentrate on events or the explanation of change. Ideally it can seek a balance between structure and event and between understanding the persistence of custom and methods of production and recognizing that change can and does occur at different rates according to different patterns in different aspects of social life. Fur trade social history, as written by public historians for heritage agencies, could and should set itself similar goals.

The study, then, of the "manners, customs, and everyday life" of fur trade posts may stem from the logic of interpretation programs and techniques which in turn are based upon an ever-increasing emphasis on preservation rather than commemoration policies, but this does not have to mean that the resulting research need be apolitical or ahistorical. Indeed, given that heritage agencies show no sign of losing interest in "social" history at the fur trade and other sites they maintain, the challenge to public historians and other researchers is to ensure that their work reflects a clear historiographical problematic.[48] A simple desire to ensure authenticity and an interest in material culture is not enough to justify describing one's research as social history. Moreover, a continued emphasis on "manners, customs and everyday life"—or, as Braudel has put it, "demography, food, costume, lodging"[49]—means the writing of a kind of social history that complements, rather than directly builds upon, the kind of fur trade social history Sylvia Van Kirk envisaged in 1978.

It does, however, offer some challenge to one of the basic presumptions of fur trade social history. Site-specific and regional studies have indicated just how difficult it is to define or even to describe an overarching "fur trade society." The original proponents of the fur trade as a "socio-cultural complex" always understood that it was not monolithic. As Sylvia Van Kirk remarked, "It is misleading to think of them [fur traders] as a single group; within the fur trade, the Hudson's Bay Company and North West Company were two distinct entities with differing social policies and practices."[50] In similar fashion, distinctions based on time period, ethnicity, gender and, to a lesser extent, class were also advanced. However, close examination of individual sites and fur trade regions suggest an even more bewildering variety of fur trade experience. Post communities also differed in significant ways from region to region and by type. For example, provisioning posts had different social structures and work patterns than posts where trade predominated, and outposts were very different places from district headquarters.[51] The more closely we look at the fur trade the more fur trade "society" recedes into a proliferation of increasingly limited "limited identities."[52] At best this society was highly complex, highly segmented, and extremely difficult to describe or define, and at worst it may not have existed at all according to many standard sociological or anthropological definitions of "society."[53]

NOTES

1. Sylvia Van Kirk, "Fur Trade Social History: Some Recent Trends" in *Old Trails and New Directions: Papers of the Third North American Fur Trade Conference*, eds. Arthur J. Ray and Carol Judd (Toronto: University of Toronto Press, 1978), 160-73. The dissertations in question are John Elgin Foster, "The Country-born in the Red River Settlement: 1820-1850" (Ph.D. diss., University of Alberta, 1973); Frits Pannekoek, "The Churches and the Social Structure in the Red River Area, 1818-70" (Ph.D. diss., Queen's University, 1973); Jennifer S. H. Brown, "Company Men and Native Families: Fur Trade Social and Domestic Relations in Canada's Old Northwest" (Ph.D. diss., University of Chicago, 1976); and Sylvia Van Kirk, "The Role of Women in the Fur Trade Society of the Canadian West, 1700-1850" (Ph.D. diss., University of London,1975).
2. Van Kirk, "Fur Trade Social History," 160.
3. To some extent this neglect of fur trade history is more apparent than real. Many interdisciplinary studies fall through the cracks of these bibliographical listings, and there seems to be a growing interest in the fur trade outside of Canada, especially among American scholars. Nevertheless, the attention of Canadian historians now seems to be largely focussed on the post-Confederation period, and when they do address fur trade topics, few specifically set out to discuss social history.
4. Van Kirk, "Fur Trade Social History," 161.
5. Although often cited, the Foster, Brown, Pannekoek, and Van Kirk dissertations have rarely been the subject of explicit critique among new scholars attracted to the field of fur trade social history since 1978. Brian Gallagher's thesis and article represent rare exceptions to this observation. See Brian Gallagher, "The Whig Interpretation of the History of Red River" (Master's thesis, University of British Columbia, 1986), and "A Re-Examination of Race, Class and Society in Red River," *Native Studies Review* 4, nos.1 and 2 (1988): 25-65. Gallagher takes Van Kirk and Pannekoek to task over their treatment of social tensions in Red River, but other historians are increasingly skeptical about the applicability of experiences in Red River to the broader fur trade. See for example, Jacqueline Peterson and Jennifer S. H. Brown, eds., *The New Peoples: Being and Becoming Métis in North America* (Winnipeg: University of Manitoba Press, 1985), 3-15.
6. See Michael B. Payne, "Summary Report Fur Trade and Native History Workshop," *Rupert's Land Research Centre Newsletter* 7, no.1 (Spring 1991): 17.
7. One might compare the paucity of fur trade studies listed in the *Canadian Historical Review* or the *Register of Dissertations* with the number of such studies listed in Frits Pannekoek's list of publications by heritage agencies in Western Canada, "A Selected Western Canada Historical Resources Bibliography to 1985," *Prairie Forum* 15, no. 2 (Fall 1990): 329-74. Nor has the volume of these studies noticeably abated since 1985.

8. Taylor's list of the historic sites commemorated in Canada up to 1950 offers an intriguing glimpse of what people thought was important in our history up to that time. For example, 74 events, persons, or locations were designated in Western Canada, of which, about 37 were primarily fur trade or closely related sites commemorating explorers, trade routes, or the "saving" of the bison. Included within this list of sites are the various posts at Winnipeg and Edmonton, Fort Langley, Lower Fort Garry (though the plaque there commemorated the signing of Treaty Number 1), Prince of Wales' Fort, Cumberland, Jasper and Rocky Mountain Houses, and Forts Fork and Chipewyan. In short, these early sites include almost all of the Canadian Parks Service's most developed fur trade sites, along with a number that have also received attention from provincial heritage agencies and municipal bodies. See C.J. Taylor, "Appendix VII," in "National Historic Parks and Sites, 1880-1951: The Biography of a Federal Cultural Program" (Ph.D diss., Carleton University, 1986), 260-70.

   In his 1985 study of fur trade material culture, Robert Wheeler included a short appendix entitled "Fur Trade Site-Seeing." This list outlines some 128 fur trade sites in the United States and Canada which have been commemorated in some tangible fashion by the U.S. National Parks Service, the Canadian Parks Service, or state or provincial heritage agencies. The 87 sites found in Canada constitute a major proportion of the most highly developed and visited historic sites in Canada (Robert Wheeler, *A Toast to the Fur Trade: A Picture History on Its Material Culture* [n.p.: Wheeler Productions, 1985], 99-101).
9. See C.J. Taylor, "Historic Sites," *Canadian Encyclopedia*, vol. 2 (Edmonton: Hurtig, 1985), 816 and C.J. Taylor, *Negotiating the Past: The Making of Canada's National Historic Sites and Parks* (Montreal and Kingston: McGill-Queen's University Press, 1990).
10. This is not really the time to review the development of animation or interpretation programming at historic sites. Suffice it to say that Canada was relatively late into the field, and most Canadian sites had the advantage of building on decades of experience in Europe and the United States when establishing their programs. According to Jay Anderson, one of the hallmarks of Canadian animation programs is a heavy emphasis on accurate and detailed recreations of "realistic cultural environments." See Jay Anderson, *Time Machines: The World of Living History* (Nashville: The American Association for State and Local History, 1984), 62. Anderson also provides a handy summary of the development of living history interpretation in this volume. It is clear that this movement has always had a strong folk and material culture orientation that lends itself to a certain variety of social history.
11. Ibid., 187. Anderson argues that the usefulness and purpose of living history are found in "felt-truth"; ibid., 191, a combination of thought and feeling that might be characterized as empathy. It should be noted, however, that most sites still try to package a great deal of straight factual information within their "felt-truth."
12. See, for example, David V. Burley's comments in Payne, "Summary Report," 13-14. Obviously not all historical archaeology aspires to do so little, and as Burley points out, many aspects of the fur trade cannot be studied without an archaeological component.
13. Fernand Braudel, *Civilization and Capitalism 15th-18th Century: Volume I, The Structures of Everyday Life: The Limits of the Possible* (New York: Harper and Row, 1981), 27-9.

14. The scope and intent of this sort of historical research are very similar to the kind of historical archaeology David Burley has categorized as "mission-oriented" archaeology. The peril in both fields is that the desire to answer specific factual questions can make practitioners oblivious to the broader implications of their work. See Payne, "Summary Report," 14.
15. See Lester Ross, *An Illustrated Directory of the British Commercial Suppliers Who Provided Manufactures, Products and Provisions Shipped to the Hudson's Bay Company Columbia Department, 1821-52*, Lynne Sussman, *A Directory of the British Commercial Suppliers Who Provided Goods and Services to York Factory and Red River, 1821-53*, and Andre Lafleche, *A List of Suppliers of Goods and Services to the Hudson's Bay Company, 1820-75* (Ottawa: Canadian Parks Service, 1979), Manuscript Report Series no.381, 3 vols. These studies are mentioned as representative of a type and not because their premise or execution is in any way faulty.
16. See Bruce F. Donaldson, *York Factory: A Land-Use History* (Ottawa: Canadian Parks Service, 1981), Manuscript Report Series no.444; Bruce F. Donaldson, *The York Factory "Depot" Warehouse: A Structural and Use History, 1830-1981*, Microfiche Rep. Ser. no. 5 (Ottawa: Canadian Parks Service, 1982).
17. Public historians are no less prone to the conflicting historiographical impulses of the general versus the specific than any other group of historians, and they too wrestle with the balance between theory and empiricism. It is not surprising, then, that their work sometimes emphasizes the typical and sometimes the unusual or distinctive. Ideally, as historians, we should not set a higher value on either impulse but recognize them as different modes of analysis. Stephen J. Gould offers a rather interesting discussion of the social and intellectual consequences of establishing hierarchies of knowledge based on method alone (see Stephen J. Gould, *Wonderful Life: The Burgess Shale and the Nature of History* [New York: W.W. Norton, 1989], 277-91).
18. Philip Goldring, *Papers on the Labour System of the Hudson's Bay Company, 1821-1900*, vols. 1-3, Manuscript Rep. Ser. nos. 362, 412, 299 (Ottawa: Canadian Parks Service, 1979).
19. Ibid., 2: ix-xi.
20. Philip Goldring, "Governor Simpson's Officers: Elite Recruitment in a British Overseas Enterprise, 1834-1870," *Prairie Forum* 10, no. 2 (Autumn 1985): 251-81.
21. Goldring, *Papers*, 3: 202.
22. Ibid., 3: 9-25.
23. Ibid., 3: 5-8.
24. This case is made most strongly in Carol M. Judd, "Native Labour and Social Stratification in the Hudson's Bay Company's Northern Department, 1770-1870," *Canadian Review of Sociology and Anthropology* 17, no.4 (1980): 305-14.
25. See, for example, Peter L. Berger and Thomas Luckmann, *The Social Construction of Reality: A Treatise in the Sociology of Knowledge* (Garden City, New York: Doubleday Anchor, 1967). This is an issue with which social historians have long wrestled in an attempt to avoid the reification of concepts like class and the crudities of simplistic structuralism. For one version of this debate see E.P. Thompson, *The Making of the English Working Class* (London: Pelican Books, 1975), esp. 9-11.
26. This point is made by Goldring, *Papers*, 3: 194-95, and in a number of other works including Michael Payne, *The Most Respectable Place in the Territory:*

Everyday Life in Hudson's Bay Company Service York Factory, 1788 to 1870 (Ottawa: Canadian Parks Service, 1989), 34-49.

27. Glenbow Archives, Sutherland Correspondance, James to John Sutherland, 10 August 1840. Quoted in Frits Pannekoek, *A Snug Little Flock: The Social Origins of the Riel Resistance 1869-70* (Winnipeg: Watson and Dwyer, 1991), 29. As Foster, Brown, Pannekoek, and Van Kirk all indicate, Sutherland's opinion was by no means simply idiosyncratic. Without wishing to engage in anachronistic argument, the situation does seem roughly analogous to current debates over affirmative action hiring programs. Study after study indicates that middle class males, as a group, continue to find it easier to secure high-paying, high prestige jobs than women or other disadvantaged groups, but there is also a widely held perception that reverse bias has made it almost impossible for qualified men to find employment in many fields.
28. Philip Goldring is by no means the only historian to recognize the potential of Hudson's Bay Company Archives records for quantitative history. This has been a regular theme in the work of Arthur Ray in particular, and few other aspects of pre-Confederation Canadian history have received such close attention from the "clio-metricians."
29. The need for a better understanding of geographical and corporate variations in fur trade operations has been recognized for some time. Adrian Tanner made this point with some force in "The End of Fur Trade History," *Queen's Quarterly* 90, no. 1 (Spring 1983): 176-91. One of the ironies of fur trade history is that it developed paradigms like Innis's notion of "staples" and broad historical overviews like those of A.S. Morton and E.E. Rich before there was all that much literature to synthesize. It began, if you will, with a sweeping panorama and not with a series of miniatures.
30. Some idea of the number and range of these studies can be gleaned from a recent listing of the research publications and reports generated as part of the development of two sites in Alberta: Fort George/Buckingham House and Dunvegan. These comprise at least 22 titles—and the list is still growing, covering topics as diverse as historical archaeology and furnishing studies for a clerk's residence and an Oblate mission (Payne, "Summary Report," 22-23).
31. In fact very little trade ever took place at Lower Fort Garry. It was initially built as an administrative center, and later took on some agricultural and warehousing responsibilities. As a center of commerce it really serviced the local—largely farming—population of St. Andrew's.
32. Gregory Thomas, *Lower Fort Garry Warehouse Building: Structural and Use History* Manuscript Rept. Ser. no. 204 (Ottawa: Canadian Parks Service, 1977); *The Men's House, Lower Fort Garry, Its Furnishings and Place within the Hudson's Bay Company Post Environment*, Manuscript Rept. Ser. no. 246 (Ottawa: Canadian Parks Service, 1978); and *North West Bastion Bakehouse, Lower Fort Garry: A Structural and Furnishing Study*, Manuscript Rept. Ser. no. 297 (Ottawa: Canadian Parks Service, 1979).
33. Thomas, *Bakehouse*, 58-69.
34. Carol Livermcre [Judd], *Lower Fort Garry, The Fur Trade and the Settlement at Red River*, Manuscript Rept. Ser. no. 202 (Ottawa: Canadian Parks Service, 1976), and Robert Coutts, *St. Andrew's Parish 1829-1929, and the Church Missionary Society in Red River*, Microfiche Rept. Ser. #361 (Ottawa: Canadian Parks Service, 1986). Robert Coutts has also looked more specifically at agricultural practices in the

settlement in "The Role of Agriculture in an English Speaking Halfbreed Economy: The Case of St. Andrew's, Red River," *Native Studies Review* 4, nos. 1-2 (1988): 67-94.

35. Carol Judd, "Moose Factory was not Red River: A Comparison of Mixed Blood Experiences," unpublished ms. on file with Ontario Ministry of Culture and Recreation, 1983.
36. These kinds of proposals raise interesting questions about relationships between research, interpretation, and site-visitation figures. Not only would a living history farm open up new interpretative possibilities, albeit by further diminishing any supposed connection of the site to the fur trade, but it would provide a shot in the arm to declining visitation figures—especially given the fact that one of the most common criticisms of the site from the public is that there is nothing new to see or do there. The fact that the entire enterprise would be justified by the original and overblown rationale for accepting the fort as a *national* historic site—that it was a major "transhipment depot and industrial-agriculture supply centre for the Rupert's Land fur trade"—adds a certain ironic touch to all the research on Lower Fort Garry done by Parks historians which generally is skeptical of these very claims.
37. No organization is exempt from this, and none should be singled out for particular criticism. It is simply a problem of the availability of evidence and the fact that most historic sites are chosen for reasons that have nothing to do with whether or not there is enough research material to support the interpretive programming they will require.
38. See Carol Judd, "Mixed Bloods of Moose Factory, 1730-1981: A Socio-Economic Study," *American Indian Culture and Research Journal* 6, no. 2 (1982): 65-88 and "Housing the Homeguard at Moose Factory 1730-1982," *The Canadian Journal of Native Studies* 3, no.1 (1983): 23-37.
39. My own work on Churchill, Manitoba suggests some strong parallels existed among post communities around the bayside. See Michael Payne, "Fort Churchill, 1821-1900: An Outpost Community in the Fur Trade," *Manitoba History* no. 20 (Autumn 1990): 2-15.
40. Goldring makes essentially the same point himself and, in an effort to move beyond a purely abstract consideration of the labor market, he examines the careers of five Scottish employees of the Hudson's Bay Company in detail. Goldring, *Papers,* 3: 76-85.
41. Thompson, *English Working Class,* 9.
42. Payne, *Respectable Place,* 101-2, 130, 186.
43. Ibid., 69-79.
44. Ibid., 129.
45. See, for example, E. J. Hobsbawm, "From Social History to the History of Society" in *Historical Studies Today,* eds. Felix Gilbert and Stephen R. Graubard (New York: W.W. Norton, 1972), 2.
46. Of course, were we to reject all branches of history in which such dubious works appear, there would be very few areas left to research. The value of any branch of scholarly discourse should not be determined by the worst examples of the genre.

    Tony Judt has discussed this feature of modern social history at some length. He suggests that some of the blame should be attached to the *Annales* school of social history with its emphasis on structure and relative disinterest in events.

Judt concedes a certain "panache" in the work of Fernand Braudel, but criticizes Braudel's less-able disciples for "a glut of articles about minute or marginal matters: the 'history of footwear' or the 'image of the cooked in pre-modern mentalities'." See Tony Judt, "A Clown in Regal Purple: Social History and the Historians," *History Workshop: A Journal of Socialist Historians* 7 (Spring 1979): 85.

47. G. M. Trevelyan, *Illustrated English Social History*, vol. 1 (London: Longmans, Green and Co., 1949), xi. Trevelyan did emphasize the importance to studying everyday life, but with a view to considering "the human as well as the economic relation of different classes to one another, the character of family and household life, the conditions of labour and leisure, the attitude of man to nature. . .and the ever-changing forms [of] religion, literature and music, architecture, learning and thought." Trevelyan was clearly a political conservative, but his definition of social history seems a lot closer to E.P. Thompson and Eric Hobsbawn than the latter let on.
48. As in so many other aspects of the practise of social history, Fernand Braudel has some useful observations on the role of theory and models in writing social history with a material culture slant. Braudel cites Werner Sombart's dictum: "No theory, no history," and suggests that social history cannot ignore this truism, but that sometimes an overall view or model "against which events can be interpreted" is more practical than general theory. Material life is marked by slow incremental development and periodic setbacks and thus lacks the neatness of pattern and coherence of chronology that support general theory. Nonetheless, it is not random or inexplicable, and social historians have a responsiblity to "bring out resemblances, similarities, recurring features," not to mention particularities, unusual behaviours, and the like. See Fernand Braudel, *Capitalism and Material Life 1400-1800* (Glasgow: Fontana, 1977), xi-xv.
49. Braudel, *Civilization and Capitalism*, 27-29.
50. Van Kirk, *Many Tender Ties*, 3.
51. Some of these issues are explored in greater detail in Payne, "Fort Churchill," 2-12.
52. To borrow a phrase from J.M.S. Careless, "'Limited Identities' in Canada," *Canadian Historical Review* 50 (March 1889): 1-10.
53. Although sociology is still usually defined as the study of "society," and most texts begin with some general definition of what is meant by the term, social scientists are increasingly doubtful about the analytical utility of the term. One recent reference work suggests that "society is one of those concepts that appear to mean everything and nothing" (Adam Kuper and Jessica Kuper, eds., *The Social Science Encyclopedia* [London: Routledge & Kegan Paul, 1985] s.v. "Society," 794-95). In such circumstances Hobsbawm's ideal of social history as the history of society seems increasingly unattainable, and not just for fur trade historians.

About the Authors and Editors

Dean L. Anderson is the historical archaeologist at the Bureau of Michigan History. A recent recipient of a Ph.D. in Anthropology from Michigan State University, his main research interests are the archaeology and ethnohistory of the historical period in the Great Lakes region. His recent work focuses on the interaction between Native peoples and Europeans revealed in the documentary and archaeological records for the French-period fur trade.

Dennis M. Au served as Project Director of the Sixth North American Fur Trade Conference beginning with the call for papers in 1989 until the publication of *The Fur Trade Revisited*. Au holds an M.A.. in History Museum Studies from the State University of New York's Cooperstown Graduate Programs. He has organized a successful series of international symposia on the War of 1812. Au also has published on the fur trade in the lower Great Lakes and French-Canadian folklife in the American Midwest.

Douglas A. Birk is a Senior Research Archaeologist with the Institute for Minnesota Archaeology. His research interests focus on the development and interrelationship of human and natural environments in the western Great Lakes. He has done extensive work on various aspects of the fur trade, including field investigations at Fort Charlotte, Sayer's Post, Fort St. Charles, and a 1750s French colonial outpost (Site 21Mo20) on the Mississippi River in central Minnesota.

Dr. Michael Blanar is professor of English at Brandon University, Brandon, Manitoba, Canada, specializing in eighteenth-century travel literature. He is completing work on a new edition of John Long's *Voyages and Travels of an Indian Interpreter and Trader*, and is preparing a book of pre-1800 views of England by both Euro-Canadian and Aboriginal travellers.

Jennifer S. H. Brown is professor of history at the University of Winnipeg, Manitoba, Canada and holds a Ph.D. in anthropology from the University of Chicago. Her books include *Strangers in Blood: Fur Trade Company Families in Indian Country* and *The New Peoples: Being and Becoming Métis in North America* (co-edited with Jacqueline Peterson). She has also published widely on fur trade and mission history and on subarctic Ojibwa and Cree history and culture.

Bradford R. Cole is Keeper of Manuscripts in the Department of Special Collections, Merrill Library, Utah State University. He has also worked as an archaeologist, historian, and as a ranger for the National Park Service. Cole's interest include Fort Hall and the fur trade of the intermountain region, Western fur trade bibliography, and historic and archaeological site surveys.

Heather Devine is an independent cultural heritage consultant. She holds an advanced degree in secondary education (Educational Media) and is currently a doctoral student in history at the University of Alberta. She has published and presented numerous articles on curriculum development in archaeology, Native history, and heritage interpretation. Her current research interests include Metis and fur trade ethnohistory, cultural resource management, and archival studies.

Harry W. Duckworth is professor of chemistry at the University of Manitoba. Inspired by the presence in his home city, Winnipeg, of the Hudson's Bay Company Archives (the single most important source of material on the Canadian fur trade), he has researched and written several articles on this subject.

James R. Duncan, in addition to being a professional archaeologist and educator, is a renowned gunsmith specializing in the replication and restoration of historic firearms. He has published on the fur trade, trapping, pioneer skills, Native American culture, and historic guns. He lives in St. Louis, Missouri with his wife, Carol, also a professional archaeologist.

W. J. Eccles, Professor Emeritus of history at the University of Toronto, received his Ph.D. from McGill University after pursuing his graduate studies at the Sorbonne. His books and articles on New France earned him several fellowships and awards, as well as appointments as visiting professor. He was awarded the Tyrrell Medal by the Royal Society of Canada in 1979 and the Ll.D., in honoris causa by the University of Genoa in 1992.

Peter Geller is currently finishing his doctorate in history at Carleton University, Ottawa. He wrote his Master's thesis at the University of Winnipeg on Hudson's Bay Company public relations and images of the fur trade, 1920-1945. Geller's interests lie in the area of Canadian cultural history, with a focus on visual representation, especially as it relates to views and attitudes of the Canadian North.

Rhoda R. Gilman retired in 1992 after 34 years with the Minnesota Historical Society. During that time she served as editor of various publications, head of the education division, and senior research fellow. She has written numerous articles and books on the history of the fur trade and Minnesota. Presently she is at work on a biography of Henry H. Sibley.

Lynda Gullason's paper grew out of her University of Alberta Master's thesis on culture contact which dealt with issues of gender and of site formation processes as well as ethnic response to contact. While pursuing her Ph.D. at McGill University, she continues to study the non-universal nature of contact and has completed fieldwork in Frobisher Bay, Baffin Island, N.W.T. on sixteenth-century and nineteenth-century Inuit-European interaction.

James L. Hansen is a reference librarian and genealogical specialist at the library of the State Historical Society of Wisconsin. He has lectured widely and written numerous articles on French-Canadian settlers in seventeenth-century New York and in the Upper Mississippi Valley. His current research concentrates on the settlement and early history of Prairie du Chien, Wisconsin.

Donald P. Heldman received his Ph.D. in anthropological archaeology from the Institute of Archaeology, University of London, England, for research on Postclassic cultures on the extreme northern Mesoamerican frontier in San Luis Potosi, Mexico. He has authored numerous articles and books, and is presently Director of Archaeology for the Mackinac Island State Park Commission, where he is engaged in archaeological research on French and British colonial sites at the Straits of Mackinac.

Gwyneth Hoyle recently retired as College Librarian, Peter Robinson College at Trent University in Peterborough, Ontario. She is now a research associate with the graduate program of the University's Frost Centre of Canadian Heritage and Development Studies. Hoyle is currently preparing for publication an extensive annotated record of one hundred years of travel, mainly by canoe, on Canada's northern rivers.

William J. Hunt, Jr. is currently the Archeologist at the National Park Service-Midwest Archeological Center, Lincoln, Nebraska. He holds a Ph.D. in Historical Archaeology from the University of Pennsylvania's American Civilization Program. He is interested in the fur trade and cultural history of the Northern Plains and Rocky Mountain regions of North America and has published extensively on excavations at Fort Union.

Henry C. Klassen is associate professor of history at the University of Calgary. His interests include social and economic and social development of the Canadian prairie provinces in the late nineteenth and early twentieth centuries. Klassen has published extensively on these topics.

Royce Kurtz is the bibliographer for the social sciences and assistant professor of anthropology at the University of Mississippi. He has worked as an ethnohistorian on archaeological surveys and coauthored *Subarctic Athabaskan Bibliography* and contributed to the *Ethnographic Bibliography of North America*. His publications also include works on Sauk and Mesquakie lead mining and forest resource utilization.

Lily McAuley, of Swampy Cree and Scottish ancestry, is the personal embodiment of the fur trade. Until she went to school at age eight she spoke only Swampy Cree. Her parents reared her in what she describes as the "circle," the seasonal cycle of a trapper's existence. The fur trade has always been a part of her life on the shores of Hudson Bay and in northern Saskatchewan. Recently retired, McAuley worked for over eleven seasons as interpreter, guide, and visitor activities officer for the Canadian Parks Service at Churchill and York Factory, Manitoba.

I.S. MacLaren teaches Canadian Studies and English at the University of Alberta. His interests include the writing and painting of explorers and travelers of the eighteenth- and nineteenth-century Arctic and West, and travel literature generally.

Peter Marshall is Emeritus Professor of American History and Institutions, University of Manchester, England. He holds degrees from both Oxford and Yale. He taught at the University of California, Berkeley and at McGill University. Marshall has published numerous articles on British imperial policy on the eve of the American Revolution, with particular reference to western expansion.

Michael Payne is currently Head of the Research and Publications program of the Historic Sites and Archives Service, Alberta Community Development. He is a graduate of Queen's University, the University of Manitoba, and Carleton University. He has worked on contract and as a staff historian for several heritage agencies in Canada, and has written on the history of Forts Churchill and Dunvegan, Lower Fort Garry, and York Factory.

Timothy K. Perttula is the Assistant Director for Antiquities Review for the Department of Antiquities Protection at the Texas Historical Commission. He edits the *Bulletin of the Texas Archaeological Society* and *Journal of Northeast Texas Archaeology*. The University of Texas published his revised dissertation *"The Caddo Nation": Archaeological and Ethnohistoric Perspectives* in 1992.

Kathleen Pickering is in the doctoral program of the anthropology department in the University of Wisconsin-Madison. She has a J.D. from New York University Law School. Pickering became familiar with the Lakota Sioux culture while working for the Dakota Plains Legal Services from 1987-1989.

Charles J. Rinehart is employed as a staff archaeologist with the South Carolina Department of Transportation. His paper is an expansion of his Master's thesis at the University of South Carolina. Rinehart's interest in the fur trade stems from working on the archaeological excavations at Fort Michilimackinac from 1982-1990.

Theresa M. Schenck is a doctoral candidate in anthropology at Rutgers University, and a former teacher of high school French and Spanish. A member of the

Blackfeet Tribe, Schenck also acknowledges her Ojibwa heritage, and continues to research and publish on Indian and Métis families of the Lake Superior region.

William R. Swagerty is associate professor of history at the University of Idaho. He has spoken and published widely on the topics of Indian-European relations and the early history of Native people and trappers of the West and of the Spanish borderlands.

Helen Hornbeck Tanner is a research associate at the Newberry Library in Chicago. Following early research and publication on the Florida borderlands, she turned to the Great Lakes region, conducting historical investigations for litigation of Indian land claims and fishing rights on behalf of the Ojibwa, Ottawa, Potawatomi, Shawnee, Wyandot, Miami, Sisseton and Wahpeton Sioux, Teton Sioux, and the Caddo Tribe of Oklahoma. She is editor of the *Atlas of Great Lakes Indian History* (1987).

Bruce M. White holds a Masters degree in history from McGill University and a Ph.D. in anthropology from the University of Minnesota. He has conducted extensive research on the fur trade and written numerous articles pertaining to social and economic relationships between people who participated in the trade. White lives in St. Paul where he previously worked as an editor for the Minnesota Historical Society.

Keith R. Widder is Curator of History for Mackinac State Historic Parks. His research focuses on the history of the western Great Lakes region during the eighteenth and nineteenth centuries. He is particularly interested in relationships between Native peoples and Europeans, the significance of the settlements at the Straits of Mackinac, and the cartography of the region.

Thomas Wien is assistant professor at the University of Montreal. He has a Ph.D. in history from McGill University. He has published in both French and English and is working on the economics of the fur trade and *canadien* agriculture and society in the eighteenth century.

Dick A. Wilson is an industrial engineer and retired US Coast Guard Commander. He is currently a graduate student at the University of Idaho specializing in early western history.

Index

A

G

H

K

L

Q

R

S

T

U

V

W

Y

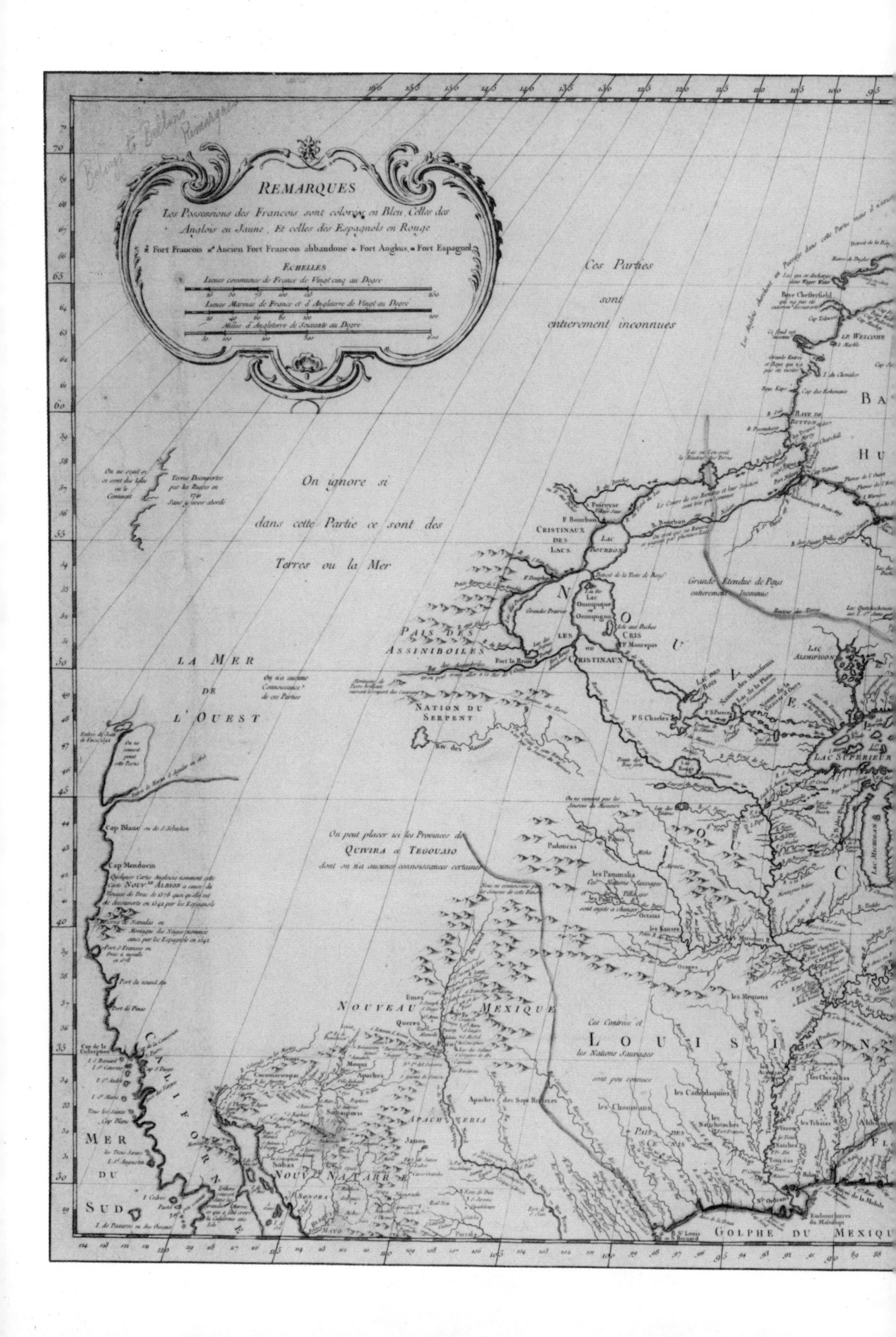
REMARQUES
Les Possessions des Francois sont colorées en Bleu, Celles des Anglois en Jaune, Et celles des Espagnols en Rouge
Fort Francois
Ancien Fort Francois abbandone
Fort Anglois
Fort Espagnol
ECHELLES
Lieues communes de France de Vingt cinq au Degre
Lieues Marines de France et d'Angleterre de Vingt au Degre
Milles d'Angleterre de Soixante au Degre
Ces Parties sont entierement inconnues
On ignore si dans cette Partie ce sont des Terres ou la Mer
LA MER DE L'OUEST
Cap Blanc ou de S. Sebastien
Cap Mendocin
MER DU SUD
Baye Chesterfield
LE WELCOME
BAYE DE BUTTON
CRISTINAUX DES LACS
LAC BOURBON
Grande Etendue de Pays entierement Inconnue
PAIS DES ASSINIBOILES
NATION DU SERPENT
LAC SUPERIEUR
On peut placer ici les Provinces de QUIVIRA et TEGOUAIO dont on n'a aucunes connoissances certaines
Padoucas
les Kansés
Osages
NOUVEAU MEXIQUE
Ces Contrées et les Nations Sauvages sont peu connues
les Cadodaquios
les Choumans
les Natchitoches
APACHERIA
Moqui
Apaches
Janos
SONORA
GOLPHE DU MEXIQU